Human Relations

Mel E. Schnake
Valdosta State College

Merrill Publishing Company
Columbus   Toronto   London   Melbourne

Cover Photo: Myrleen Ferguson

Published by Merrill Publishing Company
Columbus, Ohio 43216

This book was set in Garamond.

Administrative Editor: Linda Sullivan
Developmental Editor: Jennie Owen-Cole
Production Editor: Linda H. Bayma
Art Coordinator: Lorraine Woost
Cover Designer: Russ Maselli
Text Designer: Anne Daly
Photo Editor: Gail Meese

Copyright © 1990 by Merrill Publishing Company. All rights reserved. No part of this book may be reproduced in any form, electronic or mechanical, including photocopy, recording, or any information storage and retrieval system, without permission in writing from the publisher. "Merrill Publishing Company" and "Merrill" are registered trademarks of Merrill Publishing Company.

Library of Congress Catalog Card Number: 89-62909
International Standard Book Number: 0-675-20783-5
Printed in the United States of America
1 2 3 4 5 6 7 8 9—94 93 92 91 90

Photo Credits: All photos copyrighted by individuals or companies listed. Billy E. Barnes, p. 349; *Columbus Dispatch,* p. 67; Haworth, Inc., p. 181; Honda of America, p. 42; McDonald's Corporation, p. 479; Mercedes-Benz, p. 253; Merrill Publishing, pp. 5, 55, 139, 304, 347, 413, 436; Tom Brunk/Merrill, p. 91; Jo Hall/Merrill, p. 220; Larry Hamill/Merrill, pp. 34, 238; Nationwide Insurance, pp. 152, 480; Allen Zak, pp. 18, 284, 306, 372, 398, 453, 464.

Preface

While the field of human relations is not new, its importance to organizations continues to increase. Even with the many exciting new technological developments which make work easier and more efficient, good human relations within the organization remains critical to achieving organizational objectives. For example, computer and communications technology have made it possible to "automate" many offices. Workers may no longer handle mounds of paper, but rather transmit information via personal computers and electronic message systems. However, such improvements in technology cannot be implemented effectively without consideration of the human element. Individuals who have different perceptions, needs, values, and beliefs must still work together on the new technology in order to perform tasks and accomplish organizational objectives. Managers must not only implement the new technology, but help employees adapt to their new work environments. Thus, the study of human relations will continue to increase in importance as we approach the twenty-first century.

This textbook is designed to meet two primary objectives. The first is to present the latest and most up-to-date information available from the behavioral sciences. Several theories which are presented in many introductory management and organizational science textbooks are examined in greater detail in this book. The latest research available is reviewed in order to update what has been learned about these theories in the last few years. The second objective of this book is to describe the implications of these theories for practicing managers and employees. Recognizing that everyone who reads this book may not become a manager, each chapter also includes the practical implications of theories for nonmanagerial employees. After all, good human relations is achieved by managers and employees working together to accomplish the organization's goals.

ORGANIZATION

The book is organized into four parts. Part One sets the stage for an in-depth examination of individual, group, and organization-wide topics. Chapter 1 provides an introduction to the study of human relations. The history of the human relations field is traced and the importance of the behavioral sciences is established. Current and future issues of human relations, such as the changing workforce and changing economy, are also examined. Chapter 2 focuses on the nature of employment. Individual and organizational expectations are examined along with the reasons people work. Motivating properties of tasks are identified as are several methods for making work more motivating and satisfying. Chapter 3 covers the process of staffing the organization. Fair employment legislation and selection of employees are primary topics in this chapter.

Part Two examines individual relationships in organizations. Individual differences in perception, beliefs, values, attitudes, personality, and ability are considered in Chapter 4. Chapters 5 through 11 cover individual motivation, interpersonal communication, appraising and rewarding performance, disciplining and counseling employees, managing stress, managing your career, and decision making and creativity.

Part Three examines group relationships. Chapter 12 describes the development and characteristics of groups, as well as a consideration of why people often behave differently in groups than when they are alone. Chapter 13 covers leadership and team building. Managing conflict between individuals and groups is discussed in Chapter 14.

Part Four looks at the overall organization. Organizational politics is examined in Chapter 15. All organizations are at least to some degree political. Managers and employees must be aware of the politics in their organization and ways to avoid career-damaging political mistakes. Chapter 16 focuses on the importance of organizational culture and its influence upon individual behavior. Organizational culture is the "shadowlike" force which molds the behavior of all organizational members. Chapter 17 covers managing change in organizations. With today's rapidly changing world, change is a fact of organizational life. Managers must be aware of more than the technical aspects of introducing change. They must also consider how employees will react to the change and be able to overcome any potential resistance to the change. Chapter 18 describes human relations in unionized organizations. Finally, human relations in international organizations is examined in Chapter 19. One of the characteristics of today's economy is that domestic markets are being replaced by international markets. More and more organizations are being affected by international trade and competition. We are rapidly moving toward an international economy where employees and managers from a variety of national cultures must work together.

FEATURES

Several features make *Human Relations* a very "reader-interactive" text.

- Prologue. Each chapter begins with a Prologue which sets the stage for the material to be presented in the chapter. The Prologue describes a situation in an organization which requires managerial action.

PREFACE

- Return to the Prologue. Later in the chapter, a Return to the Prologue box discusses another aspect of the case or ways the situation might be handled.
- "Real-World" Examples. Many "real-world" companies are used throughout the text to help illustrate theories and concepts. These are companies which have been in the news and will be recognized by many students.
- Human Relations in Action Box. Each box provides an in-depth example of how a theory or concept worked (or didn't work) in a "real-world" organization.
- What Do You Think? Box. Each of these boxes presents the reader with a question which extends the theory or concept under discussion. In some, a short example from a real-world organization is provided and the reader is asked to decide what should be done next. Answers to the What Do You Think? boxes are provided in Notes at the end of each chapter.
- Developing Your Human Relations Skills Box. Each chapter ends with a box that summarizes the material presented in the chapter and suggests how this material can be translated into practice. Each box presents practical suggestions for practicing managers and nonmanagerial employees alike.
- Other Features. Each chapter contains a chapter summary, list of key terms, discussion questions, an in-class experiential activity, and a case. Selected terms are defined in a glossary at the end of the book.

SUPPLEMENTARY MATERIALS

Two supplements are available—an instructor's manual and a set of transparency masters. The instructor's manual contains these features:

- Summaries of two timely articles from such publications as *Business Week, Fortune, Psychology Today,* and the *Wall Street Journal* for each chapter. The articles relate to and extend the material presented in the chapter by focusing on a real-world company's experience or an unusual application of a theory or concept. These may be assigned to students or used as lecture supplements.
- Answers to discussion questions.
- Suggestions for using the in-class experiential activities.
- Teaching notes for the chapter-end cases.
- A test bank with multiple-choice, true-false, and matching questions.

A set of transparency masters has been prepared to enhance your lecture presentations. The transparency masters contain text illustrations as well as figures not found in the text. Each new illustration is accompanied by a teaching note.

ACKNOWLEDGMENTS

A number of people have assisted in the preparation of this book. I would like to express my sincere appreciation to several people at Merrill Publishing Company who were extremely helpful: Jennie Cole, Jim Kilgore, and Julie Higgins.

PREFACE

Several colleagues reviewed the manuscript, either in whole or in part, and provided helpful comments and suggestions. Among them were

Stephen C. Branz	Triton College
George Burstein	California State University—Los Angeles
John P. Callahan	Florida Institute of Technology
Maxine Gross Christenson	Aims Community College
Annabelle Cromwell	Red Rocks Community College
Robert Freudenthal	Moraine Valley Community College
Jane Whitney Gibson	Nova University
Larry B. Hill	San Jacinto College
Carl Jenks	Purdue University—Calumet
Harriet A. Kandelman	Sangamon State University
Bob Kegel	Cypress College
James A. Lee	Ohio University
Morris James Nead	Vincennes University
Edward J. O'Brien	Embry-Riddle Aeronautical University
Bill Searle	Asnuntuck Community College
Mary Ellen Stepanich	Purdue University
Paul J. Wolff II	University of Maryland and Dundalk Community College
Teresa Yohon	Hutchinson Community College

Finally, I want to express my appreciation to my wife Kathy, and our children, Joe, Beth, Susie, and Ben. Without their patience and support, this book would not have been possible.

Contents

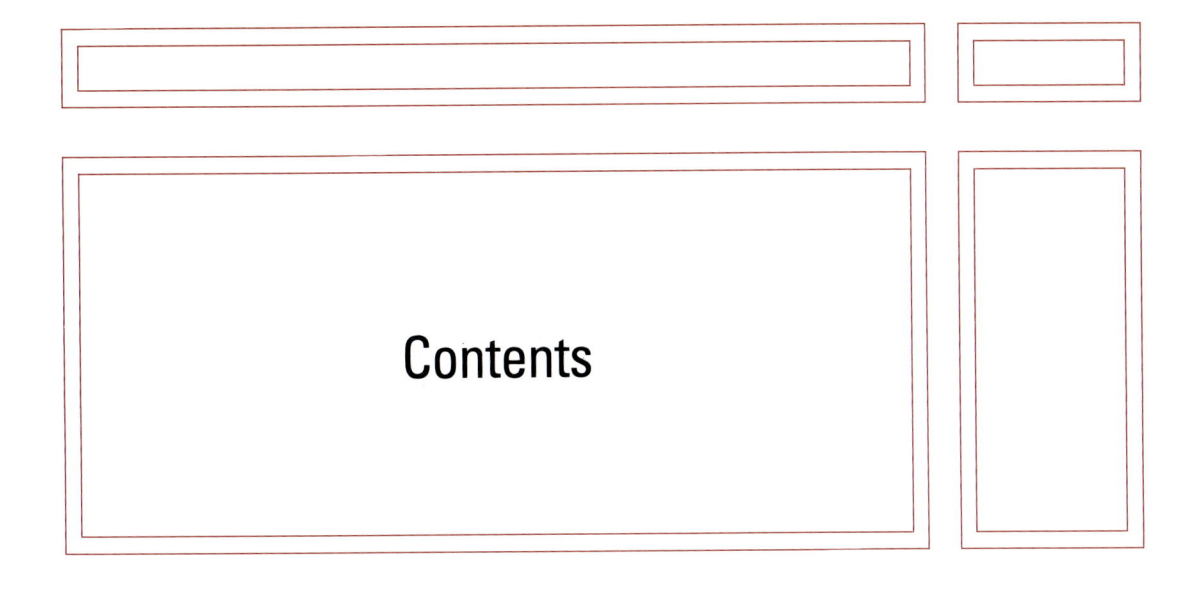

PART ONE
Human Relations in Organizations   1

CHAPTER ONE
Human Relations in Organizations   3

Human Relations   4
Development of the Human Relations Field   8
Human Relations in Organizations of the Future   15

CHAPTER TWO
The Nature of Employment   25

The Nature of Employment   26
Organizational and Individual Expectations   32
The Socialization Process   35
Satisfaction and Productivity   36
Quality of Work Life   38

CHAPTER THREE
Staffing the Organization   51

Human Relations and Staffing   52
Employment-Related Law   52

CONTENTS

The Staffing Process   66
Orientation   73
Termination   74

PART TWO
Individual Relationships   87

CHAPTER FOUR
Individual Differences   89

Differences at Work   90
Perception   90
Perception and Human Relations   97
Values and Attitudes   99
Personality   105
Ability   110

CHAPTER FIVE
Motivating Employees   119

Satisfaction of Needs   121
Categories of Needs   122

CHAPTER SIX
Interpersonal Communication: Getting Your Message Across   145

Communication in Organizations   146
Managers and Communication   148
Interpersonal Communication   148
Perception   149
Nonverbal Communication   152
Feedback   156
Listening   157
Manager-Employee Communications   158
Electronic Communication   162

CHAPTER SEVEN
Appraising and Rewarding Performance — 169

Performance Appraisal and Reward Administration   170
Performance Appraisals   170
Rewarding Employees   183

CHAPTER EIGHT
Disciplining and Counseling Employees — 199

Employee Problems and Human Relations   200
Need for Discipline and Counseling   200
Absenteeism and Turnover   207
Absenteeism   209
Turnover   212
Disciplining Employees and Counseling   214

CHAPTER NINE
Managing Organizational Stress — 227

Stress in the Workplace   228
What Is Stress?   229
Outcomes of Stress   230
Stressors   234
Managing Work-Related Stress   240

CHAPTER TEN
Managing Your Career — 251

Importance of Career Management   252
Career Management   255
Career Planning   255
Organizational Career Development   268

CHAPTER ELEVEN
Decision Making and Creativity — 277

Decision Making in Organizations   278
The Decision-Making Process   278

CONTENTS

Individual Versus Group Decision Making   283
Creativity   287

PART THREE
Group Relationships   301

CHAPTER TWELVE
Relationships Within Groups   303
Groups in Organizations   304
Why Employees Join Groups   308
Process of Group Development   312
Group Structure   313
Making Groups Effective   324

CHAPTER THIRTEEN
Leadership and Team Building   331
Leaders and Leadership   332
Leader Behaviors and Situational Variables   338
Leadership and Teamwork   346

CHAPTER FOURTEEN
Managing Conflict Between Individuals and Groups   357
What Is Organizational Conflict?   358
The Conflict Process   359
Types of Conflict   361
Sources of Conflict   362
Reactions to Conflict   364
Intergroup Conflict   366
Outcomes of Conflict   368
Managing Conflict   371

PART FOUR
Organizational Relationships   383

CHAPTER FIFTEEN
Managing Organizational Politics   385

Organizational Politics 386
What Is Organizational Politics? 387
Conditions Which Give Rise to Organizational Politics 390
Types of Political Behaviors 394
Managing Organizational Politics 397
Should You Engage in Organizational Politics? 399

CHAPTER SIXTEEN
Organizational Culture: Making Sense of Your Surroundings   407

Organizational Culture 408
How Culture Forms 409
How Employees Learn Culture 411
Levels of Organizational Culture 415
Strength of a Culture 416
Culture and Human Relations 417
Managing Organizational Culture 421

CHAPTER SEVENTEEN
Managing Organizational Change   429

Organizational Environments and Organizational Change 430
Types of Change 432
Organizational Change and Organizational Culture 439
Process of Planned Change 439
Employee Resistance to Change 440
Managing Resistance to Change 443

CHAPTER EIGHTEEN
Human Relations in Unionized Organizations   451

Labor Unions and Human Relations 452
How Do Organizations Become Unionized? 455

CONTENTS

Labor Law 457
Managing Under a Labor Agreement 460
The Decertification Process 466
Remaining Union-Free 467
Labor-Management Cooperation 468

CHAPTER NINETEEN
Human Relations in International Organizations 477

The Internationalization of Business 478
Business Problems Due to Lack of Cultural Understanding 480
Culture 481
Japanese Versus American Management 493
Japanese Management Techniques in U.S. Organizations 496

GLOSSARY 505

INDEX 519

Human Relations

PART ONE

Human Relations in Organizations

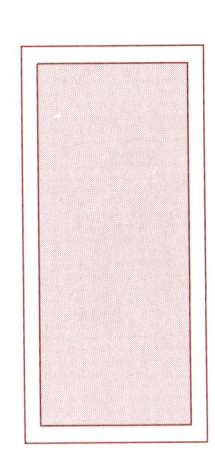

CHAPTER ONE

Human Relations in Organizations

PROLOGUE

Bonnie was excited about her promotion to Manager, Clerical Services. After eleven years with Alto Manufacturing, she had finally earned a managerial position. She had spent four years in the Accounts Payable & Receivable Department as an accounting clerk and five years in Transportation as transportation secretary. Her last two years with the company were spent as assistant to the manager of the Data Processing Department. When Mike Darden interviewed her for the position he had mentioned that interpersonal relations within Clerical Services were at an all-time low. There was a great deal of conflict over job assignments. In addition, the department had recently been "computerized" with personal computers replacing typewriters. Employees seemed upset by the change and departmental productivity had declined substantially. Work that previously took three days might now take two weeks.

    Mike had also said something about the previous manager, Barb Spencer. Apparently, Barb was a no-nonsense type of manager who ran a very tight ship. She closely monitored the performance of her employees and was not at all reluctant to let them know when their performance was not up to par. When Barb retired, her assistant, Tom Burns, functioned as interim manager for six months while Mike searched for a permanent replacement. Tom was the type of manager who gave employees a great deal of freedom. According to Mike, this was part of the problem. "Tom is too easy on those people. The jobs in Clerical Services are so routine that you simply have to stay on employees all the time to ensure that they perform adequately. Tom just lets them do what they want. You must regain control of that department." While Bonnie clearly recognized there were a number of problems in Clerical Services, she felt uncomfortable with Mike's assessment of the situation, and with his suggestion that she needed to "show those employees who's boss." She began wondering if accepting this job had been a mistake.

LEARNING OBJECTIVES

After successful completion of this chapter, you should be able to

- Define human relations,
- Define behavioral sciences,
- Understand the contribution of the behavioral sciences to the field of human relations,
- Explain the differences between common-sense theories and scientific theories,
- Discuss the development of the field of human relations,
- Describe how the movement of the U.S. economy base from manufacturing to service is changing the nature of jobs in the work force, and
- Identify several major trends that are exerting pressure on organizations to change.

HUMAN RELATIONS

Define human relations.

Organizations are extremely important parts of our lives. Most people spend more of their waking hours in their employing organizations than they do in their own homes! Organizations educate us, protect our health and safety, govern us, and provide us with goods and services. It is hard to imagine a world without organizations. While we sometimes complain about red tape and bureaucracy, organizations accomplish many things that we would be unable to accomplish on our own. For example, organizations have put an astronaut on the moon, found cures for many diseases, and fought world wars.

One extremely important aspect of organizational life is that people work together to accomplish organizational goals. Organizations could not accomplish the things they do without individuals working cooperatively toward common goals. It is, of course, important that managers understand such things as manufacturing technology, marketing research, financial ratios, net profit, and market share. However, managers must also understand human behavior. They must understand how to create work environments where individual employees will be motivated to work to their potential and cooperate with other employees in accomplishing organizational goals. This understanding is the topic of this book. **Human relations** is defined as the study of human behavior with the goal of understanding how to design work settings so that employees perform up to their potential, cooperate with other employees, and satisfy their own individual needs and goals.

Human relations implies a concern for the welfare of the employee. However, human relations is not limited to being nice to people; concern for productivity should receive equal emphasis, since both are critical concerns of effective managers. Thus, human relations involves managing employees so that both the organization's and the employee's goals are achieved. The primary goals of human relations are identified in Exhibit 1.1.

Behavioral Sciences

Define behavioral sciences.

The field of human relations draws heavily on the **behavioral sciences** such as psychology, sociology, organizational behavior, and management. These disci-

CHAPTER ONE: Human Relations in Organizations   5

One important aspect of organizational life is people working together to accomplish organizational goals.

plines are all separate, but related, fields of study. Psychology focuses on understanding individual behavior; sociology focuses on understanding group behavior. Organizational behavior centers on understanding the behavior of individuals and groups in organizations, and management is concerned with all aspects of directing organizations and employees.

Understand the contribution of the behavioral sciences to the field of human relations.

Exhibit 1.1
Primary goals of human relations

Employee welfare
Employee productivity
Organizational goal accomplishment
Individual goal accomplishment
Employee job satisfaction
Quality of work life

Before examining behavioral science, we must address the issue of common sense versus theory. Students argue that many of the theories in the behavioral sciences are nothing more than common sense. While observation and common sense are important, they sometimes engender incorrect decisions. Behavioral science theories go beyond the common sense approach, and are often able to assist managers in making important decisions. The accompanying What Do You Think? box gives you a chance to examine your own views on the theory versus common sense issue.

WHAT DO YOU THINK?

Indicate whether you think each of the following statements is true or false by placing a T or F in the blank next to each statement. You may want to give this quiz to several friends or coworkers.

_____ 1. If you pay individuals for doing something they already enjoy, they will come to like this task even more.

_____ 2. Women are more conforming and open to influence than men.

_____ 3. Unpleasant environmental conditions (e.g., crowding, loud noise, high temperatures) produce immediate reductions in performance of many tasks.

_____ 4. In bargaining with others, it is usually best to start with a moderate offer—one fairly close to the desired final agreement.

_____ 5. Directive, authoritative leaders are generally best in attaining high levels of productivity from their subordinates.

_____ 6. In most cases, individuals' behavior is consistent with their attitudes about various issues.

_____ 7. Top executives are usually extremely competitive, hard-driving types.

_____ 8. Most persons are much more concerned with the size of their own salary than with the salary of others.

_____ 9. Direct, face-to-face communication usually enhances cooperation between individuals.

_____ 10. Most persons prefer challenging jobs with a great deal of freedom and autonomy.[1]

Answers to this quiz appear at the end of the chapter.

Explain the differences between common-sense theories and scientific theories.

Theory versus Common Sense

The topics studied in the behavioral sciences (e.g., motivation, conflict, interpersonal communication, leadership—and therefore, human relations) appear to be just common sense. We learn about the behavior of others by simple observation. If you observe that a number of employees are absent after receiving a reprimand from their supervisor, you may develop a **common-sense theory** that reprimands and punishments of employees are ineffective. We have all developed a number of common-sense theories based on our experiences, but our own experiences tend to be quite limited. However, the behavioral sciences go much further. Theories developed by behavioral scientists are typically based on a number of studies that surveyed large numbers of employees in many different organizations. Such theories are based upon scientific research which is generally more accurate than our everyday observations. Scientific research isolates the variables of interest to the researcher, so that any conclusions drawn as a result of the research are based only on these variables.

For instance, to study the effects of reprimands on the absenteeism rates of employees, researchers might examine two identical work groups. Reprimands are given to employees in one work group (the "experimental group") but not the other (the "control group"). If absenteeism of the experimental group increases, while that of the control group remains constant, it can be deduced that the reprimands, and not something else, caused the increase in absenteeism. Such conclusions are warranted only to the extent that the researchers "controlled for" the effects of other variables. In this study, assume that males tend to have higher absenteeism rates than females and the experimental group was all males while the control group was all females. Then, the higher absenteeism rates of the experimental group could be due to the fact that they are all male rather than to the fact that they received reprimands. This can be easily "controlled for" by studying two all-male or all-female work groups, or work groups with the same proportions of males and females.

The point is that common-sense theories do not often take such things into account; they are not controlled for the effects of other variables. Therefore, when we develop a theory about the cause of what appears to be a consistent pattern of behavior we are sometimes wrong. Possibly, the observation was based on an unusual situation not likely to occur again. Or, the observation focused on a group of people who are somehow unusual (highly skilled or unskilled) and who are not likely to perform together again.

A widely held common-sense theory is that managers can increase employee productivity by increasing employee job satisfaction. Behavioral science research has shown that the relationship between job performance and job satisfaction is not simple, and managers are not generally able to increase job performance by increasing job satisfaction levels of employees. Thus, if you held this common-sense theory, you might waste time, effort, and resources trying to increase employees' job performance. It is important that managers have a good knowledge of behavioral science research and how it might be applied in organizational work settings. The field of human relations functions primarily to take findings and theories from behavioral science research and to suggest how to apply them in organizational work settings.

Focus of the Chapter

With this brief introduction to human relations as a background, this chapter will examine both the past and the future of human relations. First, the development of human relations as a field of study will be examined, focusing on three of the most important early research studies and/or theories which helped shape the human relations field. Then, an examination of the future of human relations will identify several trends that are changing organizations and jobs—and, therefore, changing how managers deal with employees.

DEVELOPMENT OF THE HUMAN RELATIONS FIELD

Discuss the development of the field of human relations.

Following the Industrial Revolution, managers were concerned about how they might increase output or productivity. Their attempts to do so focused primarily on how the work was performed (e.g., time and motion studies). Jobs were divided into their smallest components, then analyzed to determine the best way to perform them.[2] Tools and equipment were studied and modified so that employees could use them to achieve maximum productivity. Little thought was given to the workers themselves. It was assumed that workers were motivated solely by economic incentives. Some consideration was given to physical working conditions, but primarily only to create conditions in which employees could achieve maximum productivity. The predominant view of workers at this time seemed to be that they were to do exactly what they were told to receive their pay.

The Hawthorne Studies

The research efforts most often credited with founding the human relations movement and the field of human relations are the **Hawthorne Studies**—a series of studies conducted at the Western Electric Plant in Cicero, Illinois.[3]

The Hawthorne Studies began as an experiment to determine the set of physical working conditions that would facilitate high levels of employee productivity. Various working conditions such as temperature, illumination (brightness of light), length and number of rest breaks, and length of lunch periods were changed and the levels of output recorded. The goal of the research was to find the ideal set of physical working conditions for maximum employee output.

The researchers were surprised at their own findings. In one stage of the study, researchers varied the illumination in a workroom, hoping to find the ideal level of lighting. Beginning with the level of light that existed before the experiment, they gradually increased the brightness of the light. As they expected, when the lighting got brighter, employee output increased. At some point they expected employee output to begin to decline, because the light would be too bright. The point of highest output would be the point at which the lighting would be set in the future. However, as they continued to increase the brightness of the light, employee output continued to increase. When it appeared that employee output would continue to increase indefinitely, the researchers went back to the original levels of lighting and began decreasing the brightness. To their surprise, employee output continued to increase! Comparisons of the expected results with the actual results of this experiment are charted in Exhibit 1.2. How would you interpret the results of this experiment? What do the findings mean?

Exhibit 1.2
Expected and actual results of illumination experiments

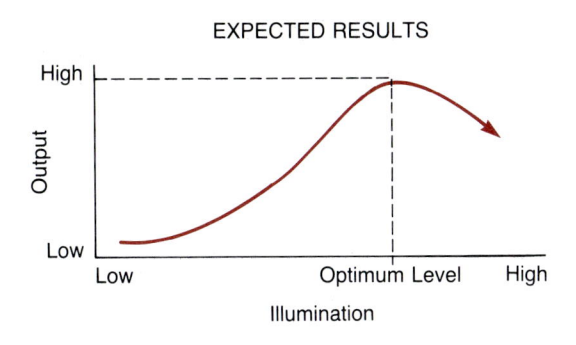

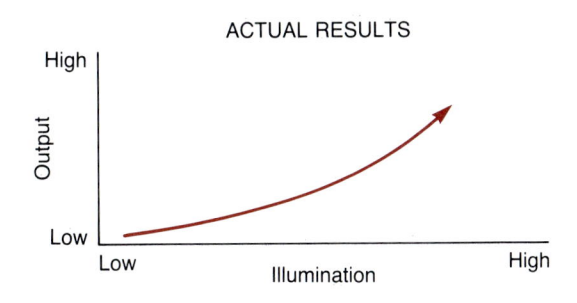

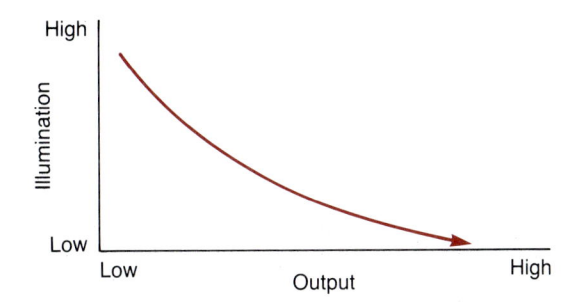

EXPECTED RESULTS

ACTUAL RESULTS

The Discovery of the Importance of Social Needs

The researchers could not explain these results until they began to look beyond the effects of the physical working environment. Talking with employees, the researchers found that more than just the physical working conditions had changed during the experiment. Employees in the lighting experiment had been taken from their normal work assignments and temporarily assigned to work in an experimental room arranged to resemble their normal working conditions. Researchers served as "supervisors" for these employees during the experiment. Employees suggested that the researchers treated them much better than their former supervisor. In the normal work setting, employees were not allowed to socialize during working hours. However, in the experimental workroom, employees were free to socialize with one another during the day. One of the major findings of the Hawthorne Studies was that employees are not motivated solely by economic incentives. Employees also have important **social needs** (e.g., friendship, interaction with others, recognition) which they attempt to satisfy on the job. Thus, managers may be able to motivate employees by providing opportunities for the satisfaction of these social needs.

The Discovery of the Informal Organization
In another segment of the Hawthorne Studies, researchers observed small groups of employees in the bank wiring room. They noticed employees tending to cluster together informally in ways unrelated to the formal structure of the organization. For example, one group consisted of production employees and a supervisor while another group comprised two types of production employees. More importantly, these groups had developed their own rules of behavior, some of which conflicted with organizational rules. In one case, the **informal groups** had developed their own standards of production which were lower than those established by the organization. Individual employees appeared to value membership in these groups and adhered to the informal group's rules of behavior as a condition of membership. Thus, a second major finding of the Hawthorne Studies was the recognition that informal social groups develop within the formal organization. There is much more to organizations than simply the formal structure, where employees report to managers. Employees are also members of several informal groups which do not appear on the organizational chart, but have direct impact on the effectiveness of the formal organization. Furthermore, these informal groups are an important influence on employee behavior.

While the Hawthorne Studies were a series of scientific studies, two other important writings which helped to forge the field of human relations were not. McGregor's **Theory X and Theory Y** comparison and Argyris's **Maturity–Immaturity Continuum** were not scientific research studies, but rather conceptual or theoretical models. Although not based on research data, they both had a significant impact on the field of human relations. They also stimulated many behavioral scientists to engage in research to test the ideas contained in each theory.

Theory X and Theory Y
The Theory X and Theory Y comparison was developed by Douglas McGregor to describe two ways in which managers typically view employees.[4] Managers who hold a Theory X view of employees believe that people basically dislike work and will try to avoid it. These managers also believe that people have little ambition, do not like responsibility, and prefer to be told exactly what to do. These beliefs about the nature of employees influence how managers treat their own employees. Theory X managers believe that employees must be closely controlled to get them to perform adequately. These managers tend to rely on economic incentives to motivate employees—not only providing eco-

nomic rewards for good performance, but also withholding such rewards to coerce employees to perform adequately. Further, Theory X managers generally do not allow employees much freedom in performing their jobs nor do they encourage employees to participate in decision making.

In contrast, Theory Y managers assume that for most people, work is as natural as play. Theory Y managers also believe that most employees are capable of self-control and self-motivation, if they are committed to organizational objectives. In other words, close control and threats of punishment are not necessary to get employees to perform adequately. Further, managers who hold Theory Y views believe employees do not avoid responsibility and often seek additional responsibility. Because of these beliefs, Theory Y managers tend to permit substantial freedom to employees to perform their jobs as they believe best. They also encourage employees to participate in making important decisions that affect their jobs. And, Theory Y managers do not rely solely on economic rewards and threats of punishment to motivate employees.

Comparison of Theory X and Theory Y Assumptions

Assumptions of Theory X and Theory Y are compared in Exhibit 1.3. While it may appear that Theory Y views of employees are superior to Theory X, in fairness, it should be pointed out that at least over the short run, there may be some employees who actually prefer, and perform better under, Theory X managers. It is a mistake to assume that an individual employee prefers one type of treatment to the other, without getting to know that employee. However, over the long term a good case can be made that Theory Y views are

---

Exhibit 1.3
Assumptions of Theory X — Theory Y

Theory X Assumptions

- Most people dislike work and will attempt to avoid it.
- Most people have little ambition and actually prefer to be told exactly what to do.
- Most people do not want to assume responsibility.
- To get employees to perform adequately, they must be closely controlled, and threatened with withdrawal of rewards.

Theory Y Assumptions

- Work is as natural as play for most people.
- Employees who are committed to organizational objectives are capable of self-control and self-motivation.
- Most employees are not only willing to accept responsibility, but also will actually seek additional responsibility.
- Close control and threats of punishment may lower employee motivation and performance rather than increase it.

superior. Employees who prefer Theory X managers may have developed expectations of such treatment from their experiences in work organizations. That is, after years of being managed in a Theory X manner, they not only expect it, but also may even become comfortable with it. If a Theory Y manager were to assume responsibility for this work group, employees might become uncomfortable with assuming responsibility and making decisions on their own. However, since employees learned to expect Theory X treatment, it is reasonable that they can learn to be comfortable with a Theory Y managerial style. Therefore, even though employees seem to respond better to a Theory X management style over the short term, managers may be able to improve conditions for employees and increase productivity over the long term by slowly exposing these employees to Theory Y treatment.

How would you characterize Mike and Barb, the managers in the Prologue? What about Tom, the previous manager of Accounts Receivable and Payable? What should Bonnie do now?

RETURN TO THE PROLOGUE

The manager described in the Prologue which opened this chapter is facing a choice between Theory X and Theory Y treatment of employees. Her boss, Mike, and the person she replaced, Barb, both seem to have Theory X views of employees. It is also apparent that employees in the Clerical Services Department are used to Theory X treatment, but their current behavior suggests that they may not be comfortable with it. Since Bonnie expressed some concern over her boss's views of employees, it may be that she holds Theory Y views of employees. Nevertheless, she will need to be careful about displaying a management style substantially different from the style with which employees are familiar. Bonnie should gradually increase the Theory Y treatment of her employees so that they have time to adjust to her management style. Do you think Bonnie will be comfortable working for Mike? Why or why not?

Argyris' Maturity–Immaturity Continuum

Chris Argyris was interested in the match between organizational work settings and individual personality. He suggested that an individual's personality goes through seven major changes as he matures.[5] These are presented in Exhibit 1.4 in the form of a continuum from immature personality to mature personality.

Individuals with immature personalities are passive and dependent on others. They have developed few abilities, none in depth. They tend to have shallow interests and a short-term time perspective. They perceive themselves as subordinate or inferior to others and have little self-awareness. In contrast, individuals with mature personalities are active and independent, and have developed many abilities, a few in depth. They have also developed several deep, strong interests and a relatively long time perspective. They perceive themselves to be equal to most other people, and superior to some. Finally, they have a good sense of self-awareness.

Exhibit 1.4
Argyris' Maturity–Immaturity Continuum

Immature Personality	Mature Personality
Passive ←	→ Active
Dependent ←	→ Independent
Few abilities ←	→ Many abilities
Shallow interests ←	→ Deep interests
Short-term time perspective ←	→ Long-term time perspective
Subordinate to others ←	→ Equal to and/or superior to
Little self-awareness ←	→ Self-awareness

Personality-Organization Fit

According to Argyris, many organizations seem better suited to immature personalities than to mature personalities.[6] Many organizational/managerial practices and activities seem to encourage employees to be immature. For example, managers who closely control employees and do not allow them to exert any influence on their own jobs or participate in important job-related decisions are encouraging employee behavior consistent with an immature personality. Similarly, jobs consistent with immature personalities are well-defined and highly structured to let employees perform their work mechanically. Further, organizational performance evaluation and reward systems that emphasize the withholding of rewards for failing to perform successfully are patterned for individuals with immature personalities. Finally, jobs which are divided into small components so that employees perform highly specialized and repetitive tasks are consistent with immature personalities.

Argyris' description of the managerial practices most suited for immature personalities appears similar to McGregor's description of Theory X views of employees. Similarly, Theory Y views of employees seem to be associated with Argyris's description of managerial practices that are most suited for, and tend to produce, mature personalities. Are you familiar with any organizations that you believe are best suited for either mature or immature personalities? What exactly does this organization do that encourages maturity or immaturity?

Organizational and Managerial Practices

Theory X organizational and managerial practices may be appropriate (at least in the short term) for employees who have immature personalities. However, when these practices are used with employees who have mature personalities, problems may develop; employees may well fight back and try to change the organization by joining a union. Worse, good employees may leave the organization, either temporarily through absenteeism or permanently through turnover. Employees could also leave the organization psychologically by becoming less involved in the organization, and over time becoming apathetic, and indifferent.[7] However, over the long term, employees with immature personalities who are exposed to Theory Y management practices may grow and develop into mature personalities.

Benefits of Developing Mature Personalities

When employees with mature personalities are exposed to organizational and management practices consistent with their personalities, both employees and the organization benefit. Employees respond with high motivation and self-control; they tend to use initiative and creativity in solving work-related problems. They also become willing to do more than just the minimal amount required. Managers who hold a Theory Y view of employees are more likely to create this type of work environment. An example of an organization which operates in a manner consistent with mature personalities is described in the accompanying Human Relations in Action box.

HUMAN RELATIONS IN ACTION

Everybody is the Boss

Two things are immediately noticed by visitors to the W.L. Gore cable plant near Newark, Delaware. First, employees seem to be highly motivated; everyone seems to work with great intensity and enthusiasm. Second, no one appears to be in charge. Employees are on their own to perform their tasks as they think best.

The founder of the company, Wilbert L. Gore, was a chemist at Du Pont before starting his own business, manufacturing Gore-tex fabrics used in outdoor clothing such as jogging suits (and spacesuits). Gore, who dislikes the "boss-employee" relationships, calls his employees "associates." Associates own about 10 percent of the company through an Associate Stock Ownership Plan. The company contributes 15 percent of each associate's annual pay to this plan. Some of the most senior associates have accumulated as much as $100,000 worth of Gore stock.

The atmosphere at Gore is informal and family-like. Associates are encouraged to learn as much as they can about the company's operations and to assume as much resposibility and leadership as they wish. As a result, close supervision of associates is not necessary. Managers, who are referred to as "area leaders," do not give orders to employees. According to one area leader, "People work harder in this type of atmosphere than when somebody stands over them with a club." One employee who took a $3-per-hour cut in pay to come to Gore said, "We manage ourselves here. If you waste time, you're only wasting your own money."

Source: Hoerr, J. A company where everybody is the boss. *Business Week,* April 15, 1985, p. 98.

EFFECT OF EARLY HUMAN RELATIONS RESEARCH ON MANAGEMENT PRACTICE

Early studies and theories led managers and researchers to look at employees differently. It quickly became clear that to effectively manage employees, managers had to be concerned with more than just physical working conditions and economic incentives. Many employees want more out of their jobs than to just earn a living. They want challenging, interesting, and meaningful work; responsibility; autonomy; safe and healthy working conditions; fair and equitable treatment by superiors; respect from peers and superiors; and social interaction. These needs have always been important in organizational work settings. However, they may become even more important as organizations, jobs, the work force, and employees themselves continue to change.

HUMAN RELATIONS IN ORGANIZATIONS OF THE FUTURE

The U.S. economy has been undergoing substantial change. This has led to many changes in the nature of organizations and in the nature and types of jobs available. Further, several demographic trends are resulting in changes in employees available in the work force. Finally, legislative and social shifts are resulting in changes in the employment relationship between employees and organizations. All of these changes are adding to the complexity and the difficulty of managing organizations and employees. In addition, as a result of these modifications it is becoming increasingly important that managers develop good human relations skills.

Changing Economy

For a number of years, since the Industrial Revolution, the U.S. economy has been a manufacturing-based economy (e.g., steel, paper, aluminum, automobiles, chemicals). American factories could produce products quicker, more effectively, and cheaper than factories in other countries. Within the last few years, however, the manufacturing segment of the economy has been declining. Companies in other countries have begun to compete effectively with American manufacturers, and in some cases (e.g., automobiles, electronics) have captured a large segment of the American market. One important outcome of this increased foreign competition has been the loss of manufacturing jobs. As foreign competitors take market share away from American manufacturers, demand for American products declines, meaning American manufacturers require fewer employees. Thus, one important trend which will continue to affect U.S. businesses is the increasing "internationalization" of business. Manufacturers can no longer be concerned only with American markets; they must look at the **global economy**, because a substantial amount of trade now takes place across international boundaries, not just within countries.

The U.S. economy is now **service-based** (e.g., financial, health care, entertainment, food service) and a greater proportion of jobs, especially new jobs, exist in these service industries. The Bureau of Labor Statistics estimates that by 1995, 74.3 percent of U.S. jobs will be in the service sector.[8] Between now and the year 2000, approximately five million new jobs will be created; nine out of ten of these jobs will be in service industries.[9] The trend has begun; even during times where national unemployment rates were relatively high, companies in the service industry (e.g., fast-food restaurants, convenience

Describe how the movement of the U.S. economy base from manufacturing to service is changing the nature of jobs in the work force.

stores, grocery stores, department stores, hotels, and temporary-help agencies) faced labor shortages.[10]

Several factors account for these labor shortages in the service sector of our economy. First, the supply of 16- to 24-year-old workers is shrinking. With couples having fewer children, higher divorce rates, individuals delaying marriage or opting for a career instead of marriage, there will continue to be a shortage of these entry-level workers. In addition, many of these entry-level service industry jobs pay the minimum wage and are not attractive to many potential employees. Further, as pointed out earlier, the number of jobs in the service industry continues to increase, which compounds the problem. Finally, new immigration laws which make it illegal for employers to knowingly hire illegal aliens have reduced the pool of workers.[11]

Changing Jobs

The change to a service-based economy is also affecting the nature of jobs. Previously, the predominant American worker was the blue-collar worker in a manufacturing firm. Now the white-collar service worker dominates. Whereas the major products of the blue-collar worker were automobiles, steel, paper, and so on, the major product of today's **white-collar worker** is information. The tremendous advances in computer and communications technology have made information almost instantly available to increasing numbers of people. Using satellite television technology, organizations can now link offices and plants from different parts of the world for a teleconference.

Changing Labor Force

The labor shortage mentioned earlier may extend beyond the low-paying segment of the service industry. The Bureau of Labor Statistics has estimated that between now and the year 2000, the demand for workers in a number of occupations will increase substantially due to the creation of new jobs. Among these occupations are retail salesperson, waiter/waitress, nurse, janitor, general manager, cashier, truck driver, office clerk, food counter worker, paralegal, medical assistant, physical therapist, data processing equipment repair, home health aide, systems analyst, medical records technician, employment interviewer, and computer programmer.[12]

Part-Time and Temporary Employees

Increasing use of part-time and temporary employees is one attempt to deal with labor shortages and also to hold down labor costs. Part-time workers, who work less than forty hours a week, do not receive the same fringe benefits as regular full-time employees.

Approximately 13 percent of the work force (12 million people) are part-time workers. While many of these workers prefer part-time work, approximately 5.5 percent are involuntary part-time workers who are seeking full-time jobs.[13] Another more pessimistic estimate is that the number of involuntary **part-time employees** has increased to around 17 percent of the work force.

Adding voluntary part-time workers to this figure produces an estimate that 25 percent of the work force (approximately 25 million people) are part-time workers.[14]

Temporary workers differ from part-time workers in that they usually work forty hours a week, but only for short periods of employment (e.g., during the Christmas rush or other seasonal periods of heavy work load). The widespread use of temporary help has led to the development of a temporary help industry in the U.S. Employment in this industry increased 800 percent between 1963 and 1979. During this same period of time, the number of temporary help placement agencies increased by 330 percent.[15] The jobs of temporary employees are no longer limited to secretaries and factory workers, but now also include engineers, nurses, accountants, and computer programmers.

Part-time and temporary workers provide several advantages to employers. They typically earn less than full-time employees, receive few costly fringe benefits, and can be laid off or terminated much easier than full-time or permanent employees—who may be protected by a labor union or the courts from arbitrary dismissal. Thus, part-time and temporary employees are often used as a buffer for a core of full-time employees. Organizations can promise permanent employees job security and protect them against layoffs by using part-timers and/or temporaries.

Part-time and temporary employees are hired during periods of heavy work load and terminated during slow periods. Voluntary part-time employees accept this sporadic employment because they may not be able to hold down full-time jobs due to other responsibilities (e.g., school, family). However, involuntary part-time and/or temporary workers often feel frustrated at not being able to find full-time, permanent employment.[16] This frustration can be compounded by the feeling that they are only partially accepted by their employing organization. Referred to as "disposable employees" and "**contingent workers**," they receive lower pay than permanent employees and get few fringe benefits. Employees may get trapped in such jobs. Managers must have strong human relations skills to deal with contingent workers and also to integrate contingent workers into the workforce of full-time, permanent employees.

Participation Rate of Women in the Workforce

One of the most important changes to the work force is the increasing participation rate of women. In 1984, over half (53.6 percent) of all adult women worked outside the home. By 1990 sixty percent of all adult women will be in the workforce.[17] Further, these women are choosing careers that were generally not open to their mothers (e.g., construction worker, physician, lawyer, astronaut, police officer, fire fighter). A related trend is the increasing number of men who are entering traditionally female occupations, such as registered nurse and child-care worker. Strong human relations skills are needed to integrate these **nontraditional employees** into work groups.

Identify several major trends that are exerting pressure on organizations to change.

Aging U.S. Population

Another trend that is beginning to affect the work force is the aging of the American worker, due to longer life expectancies, the aging of the post-World

Increasing numbers of women are entering nontraditional occupations.

War II "baby boom" babies, and the raising (or elimination in some cases) of the mandatory retirement age. Probably the major reason for the aging work force is the aging of the population in general. In 1975, there were about 22 million people between the ages of 35 and 45. This segment of the population is expected to increase to about 40 million by 1995. During this same period, the number of people between the ages of 16 and 24 is expected to decline from around 34,500 to 28,500.[18] As mentioned earlier, this decline will create a shortage of younger employees for entry-level positions and an oversupply of middle-aged and older employees for middle- and upper-level management positions.

Higher Educational Levels

The general population is becoming better educated. From 1950 to 1983, the average number of years of education in the U.S. increased from 9.3 to 12.6. The population is also better informed due to the almost immediate availability of information and news that communications technology has provided. Higher educational levels plus increased awareness of current events (such as what is happening in other work organizations) is likely to cause employees to have higher expectations of their jobs and employing organizations. Individuals who have developed skills, abilities, and knowledge tend to prefer jobs which permit them to use the full range of their attributes. Thus, it is increasingly important for managers to ensure that skilled employees are assigned to jobs that are interesting and challenging.

Changing Attitudes

Some research evidence suggests that employees' attitudes toward their jobs, managers, and organizations are changing. One survey, taken between 1950 and 1977 of 175,000 employees in 159 companies, shows that employee attitudes toward work have become more negative or pessimistic. During the time span of this survey, managers tended to be more positive about their jobs, supervisors, and organization, while many clerical and hourly employees' attitudes deteriorated.[19] Exhibit 1.5 lists factors about which employee attitudes have deteriorated.

All of the factors listed in Exhibit 1.5 relate to human relations. The change in some of these attitudes was substantial over the time span of the survey. To illustrate, the percentage of clerical employees who responded either "very good" or "good" when rating their company on its fairness in dealing with employees declined from about 65 percent in 1950 to only about 15 percent by 1977. All of the attitudes in Exhibit 1.5 are under the control of managers;

Exhibit 1.5
Issues about which employee attitudes have deteriorated

1. The work itself
2. Opportunity for advancement
3. Respect shown to employees as individuals
4. Management's willingness to listen to employee problems and complaints
5. Management's success in doing something about employee problems and complaints
6. Management's fairness in dealing with employees

Source: Based upon Cooper, M.R., Morgan, B.S., Foley, P.M. & Kaplan, L.B. Changing employee values: Deepening discontent? *Harvard Business Review,* January-February 1979, 57, 117–125.

> **DEVELOPING YOUR HUMAN RELATIONS SKILLS**
>
> At the end of each of the chapters in the book, a box entitled "Developing Your Human Relations Skills" summarizes and extends the information presented in the chapter. It also provides practical suggestions for you in your role as both a manager responsible for directing the work of employees, and as an individual employee responsible for performing an assigned task.
>
> The information presented in this chapter has several important implications for you in your role as a manager.
>
> 1. Be wary of common sense theories. These theories can be valuable if you make sure your observations are representative of employee behavior and not based upon some unusual circumstances. Recognize that scientific theories, developed by behavioral scientists, take into account any deviations from the norm, and therefore can provide objective insight into how to manage employees.
> 2. Keep in mind the contributions of early human relations research; the findings of these studies are no less true today. Many employees have strong social needs which they attempt to satisfy on the job. As a manager, you may be able to improve human relations by increasing opportunities for employees to satisfy these needs. Informal work groups arise in all organizations. Work with these groups to achieve organizational goals, rather than attempting to ignore or eliminate them. Recognize that many employees, over the long term, prefer to be treated in a manner consistent with a mature personality. Similar to a Theory Y view of employees, this treatment involves providing increased responsibility and autonomy to employees.

perhaps they are so busy dealing with the external environment of their organizations, they neglect human relations issues. Whatever the reason, it is clear that managers must give increased attention to these issues, to prevent further deterioration in employee attitudes—and begin to improve them.

SUMMARY

Human relations is defined as the study of human behavior. One of its primary goals is understanding how to design work settings so that employees perform to their potential, cooperate with other employees, and satisfy their own individual needs and goals. Both productivity and employee welfare are important concerns of human relations. The human relations field draws heavily from the behavioral sciences—particularly psychology, sociology, and organizational behavior.

The beginning of the human relations field is often traced to the Hawthorne Studies. Two of the major findings of these studies were: (1) employees are not motivated solely by economic factors, but also have important social needs which they attempt to satisfy on the job, and (2) employees form informal groups that exert a strong influence on their behavior. Another early human relations axiom is McGregor's Theory X and Theory Y, which describes assumptions managers have about em-

3. Recognize that today's better educated, better informed employees want more from their jobs than a pay check. Many employees have strong needs for growth and development. They want challenging and interesting work that makes a meaningful contribution to the organization and/or society, and they want some control over their job.
4. The many changes that are occurring in society, the labor force, and in organizations suggest that managers must learn to be flexible and adapt to change quickly. Managers of today's complex organizations must deal with many different types of employees with varying needs and interests. They must also respond quickly to unforeseen opportunities or problems that present themselves from time to time.

The information presented in this chapter also has several important implications for you in your role as an employee.

1. Just as managers develop common-sense theories about employees, employees develop common-sense theories about their managers. Before relying on these theories to make important decisions which might affect your career, be sure you have "controlled for" other variables.
2. Get to know yourself. Are you currently a mature or immature personality? Do you prefer Theory X or Theory Y treatment? Are you satisfied with the answers to these questions? If not, consider what steps you can take to change the situation. If your manager is open and approachable, schedule a conference to discuss these issues. Before accepting a promotion or transfer, or taking a new job, consider whether you will be able to perform up to your capabilities in the new working environment.

ployees. Theory X assumptions are that employees do not like to work and therefore must be closely controlled and even coerced to perform. Theory Y assumptions are that employees enjoy work, want additional responsibility and autonomy, and therefore can be encouraged to use self-control and self-motivation. Still another important early theory is Argyris' Maturity–Immaturity Continuum. Argyris argued that organizational policies and management practices often encourage employees to be immature (similar to Theory X assumptions). Routine specialized work, close control and supervision, and discouraging employee participation and initiative encourage employees to be passive, dependent, and subordinate. Fortunately, managers can learn to encourage employees to develop more mature personalities.

The U.S. economy base has changed from manufacturing to service. A greater proportion of jobs is now in the service industry, so the nature of work is changing. Blue-collar manufacturing jobs are declining, while white-collar jobs in the service sector are increasing. The primary product of American workers has become *information*, rather than automobiles, steel, or other durable goods.

Other notable differences that are affecting organizations include the aging of the U.S. work force; the shortage of young, entry-level employees; the increased participation of women in the labor force; increased educational level of the population; and changes in attitudes about work and organizations. These changes make it even more important for managers to develop good human relations skills.

KEY TERMS

human relations
behavioral sciences
common-sense
   theories
Hawthorne Studies
social needs
informal groups
Theory X and
   Theory Y
Maturity–Immaturity
   Continuum

service-based economy
global economy
white-collar workers
contingent workers
part-time employees
temporary employees
nontraditional
   employees

DISCUSSION QUESTIONS

1. In the chapter, human relations was described as much more than simply being nice to employees. What are the goals of human relations?
2. Is human relations more than just "common sense"? Why or why not?
3. What are the primary goals of human relations? What do you think should be added to this list?
4. Briefly describe the Hawthorne Studies. What were their major findings?
5. What are the Theory X assumptions about people? What are the Theory Y assumptions about people?
6. How do a manager's assumptions about employees' nature (e.g., Theory X or Theory Y) affect that manager's treatment of employees?
7. Describe characteristics of both a mature and an immature personality.
8. How do organizations actually encourage employees to develop immature personalities?
9. What can managers do to encourage employees to develop mature personalities?
10. How is the U.S. economy changing? What effect is this having on the nature of jobs?
11. What are the advantages and disadvantages, to organizations and the employees themselves, of using part-time and/or temporary employees?
12. How are employee attitudes toward work changing?

EXERCISE 1.1

Assessing Your Assumptions about Employees

This exercise is an opportunity for you to assess the assumptions that you hold about employees in general. Using the following scale, indicate the extent to which you agree or disagree with each of the following statements. Remember, respond to each statement in terms of how you really feel, not what you think the textbook or instructor says is correct.

Strongly Disagree	Disagree	Can't Decide	Agree	Strongly Agree
1	2	3	4	5

____ 1. It's just human nature to get out of work if possible.

____ 2. Most employees need to be watched relatively closely to ensure that they perform up to standard.

____ 3. Most people don't enjoy working—they work just to make a living.

____ 4. Most employees actually prefer to be told exactly what to do.

____ 5. Employees don't care about organizational objectives, as long as they get their pay check at the end of the week.

____ 6. Involving employees in important decisions is usually a waste of time.

____ 7. If you're too soft on your employees, they will take advantage of you.

____ 8. Managers should never admit mistakes to employees, because employees will lose respect for them.

____ 9. If employees are allowed to determine their own goals and performance standards, they will set them as low as possible.

____ 10. Managers should always retain final decision-making authority, even when employees are permitted to provide inputs.

Total Points _____

Scoring

41–50 points: Strong Theory X beliefs
31–40 points: Moderate Theory X beliefs
21–30 points: Mixture of Theory X and Theory Y beliefs
11–20 points: Moderate Theory Y beliefs
5–10 points: Strong Theory Y beliefs

CASE 1.1

Women at Work

Integrating women into the work setting is one of the human relations challenges that managers face. Increasing numbers of women are entering the work force and entering nontraditional occupations; in fact, women have taken two-thirds of the jobs created in the last ten years.[1] On the surface, this may sound as if women have been given substantially greater opportunities to pursue careers. However, several other facts are pertinent. First, on average, women earn only about 64 percent of the average pay earned by men. There is a trend toward equality, but the gap seems to be narrowing very slowly. Projections for the year 2000 are for women to earn about 74 percent of the average salary for men. One reason for women's lower pay is that they are taking many of the newly created jobs in the lower-paying service industry, many of which are nonunion. In addition, even with all of the protective legislation that has been enacted, discrimination against women can still be found. Such discrimination can result in low wages, small raises, and few opportunities for advancement into higher paying jobs.

Some progress is being made. In 1972 only 20 percent of management and administrative jobs were held by women. By 1987, this figure had increased to 37 percent.[2] However, more progress is needed, particularly since two-thirds of the 15 million individuals entering the work force between 1985 and 1995 will be women.[3]

Unfortunately, women still face many invisible barriers to advancement. While male managers may honestly believe that one's sex should not be considered in employment decisions, they may still be uncomfortable working with, or for, a female manager. According to Linda Jones, president of Women in Management, a professional group of 250 executives in New York, "Male CEOs accept women as professionals, but they're not ready to accept them as true peers. When a top slot opens, it's not part of the thought process to give it to a woman."[4]

QUESTIONS

1. List several *specific* problems which women face in organizational work settings.
2. What can managers/organizations do to improve human relations in a work group or department with equal numbers of male and female employees?

REFERENCES FOR CASE 1.1

[1] Penner, K. & Mervosh, E. Women at work. *Business Week,* January 28, 1985, 80–85.
[2] Baum, L. Corporate women. *Business Week,* June 22, 1987, 72–78.
[3] Brophy, B. & Linnon, N. Why women execs stop before the top. *U.S. News & World Report,* December 29, 1986, 72–73.
[4] Bernstein, A. Business starts tailoring itself to suit working women. *Business Week,* October 6, 1986, 50–54.

REFERENCES

[1] Baron, R.A. *Behavior in organizations: Understanding and managing the human side of work.* Boston: Allyn & Bacon, Inc., 1983, p. 10.

[2] Taylor, F.W. *The principles of scientific management.* New York: Harper & Brothers Publishers, 1911.

[3] Mayo, E. *The human problems of an industrial civilization.* New York: Macmillan, 1933.

[4] McGregor, D. *The human side of enterprise.* New York: McGraw-Hill, 1969.

[5] Argyris, C. *Personality and organization: The conflict between the system and the individual.* New York: Harper & Row, 1969.

[6] Argyris, C. *Integrating the individual and the organization.* New York: Wiley, 1964.

[7] Argyris, C. Personality vs. organization. *Organizational Dynamics,* 1974, *3,* 2–17.

[8] Nulty, P. The economy of the 1990s: How managers will manage. *Fortune,* February 2, 1987, 47–50.

[9] Brody, M. The 1990s. *Fortune,* February 2, 1987, 22–24.

[10] Bernstein, A., Anderson, R.W. & Zellner, W. Help wanted: America faces an era of worker scarcity that may last to the year 2000. *Business Week,* August 10, 1987, 48–53; Brannigan, M. Help wanted: A shortage of youths brings wide changes to the labor market. *Wall Street Journal,* September 2, 1986, pp. 1 and 13.

[11] Ibid.

[12] Ibid.

[13] Wise, D.C., Bernstein, A. & Cuneo, A.Z. Part-time workers: Rising numbers, rising discord. *Business Week,* April 1, 1985, 62–63.

[14] Nasar, S. Jobs go begging at the bottom. *Fortune,* March 17, 1986, 33–37.

[15] Pollock, M.A. & Bernstein, A. The disposable employee is becoming a fact of corporate life. *Business Week,* December 15, 1986, 52–56.

[16] Focus: The temporary help industry. *Personnel Administrator,* 1986, *31*(1), p. 60.

[17] Rubin, D.K. Fifth annual salary survey: Who makes what, where? *Working Woman,* 1984, *9,* 59–63.

[18] Fullerton, H.N. The 1995 labor force: A first look. *Monthly Labor Review,* December 1980, p. 14.

[19] Cooper, M.R., Morgan, B.S., Foley, P.M. & Kaplan, L.B. Changing employee values: Deepening discontent? *Harvard Business Review,* January-February 1979, *57,* 117–125.

WHAT DO YOU THINK? NOTE

Answers to all questions are false, according to the author of the quiz. Each statement represents a common-sense theory that has not been supported by scientific research. In many cases, researchers have found situations in which exactly the opposite of the statement occurs. For example, with regard to statement 1, researchers have found that paying people to engage in tasks they find challenging and interesting actually reduces their enjoyment of these tasks. The point of the quiz is that common-sense theories are often wrong. They are not subject to the same scientific control and rigor as theories developed by behavioral scientists.

Source: Baron, R.A. *Behavior in organizations: Understanding and managing the human side of work.* Boston: Allyn & Bacon, Inc., 1983, p. 10.

CHAPTER TWO

The Nature of Employment

PROLOGUE

Joe couldn't understand what was troubling Tom. Nine months ago, Joe had hired Tom as assistant manager of Accounts Receivable. Joe had been trying to fill that position for the previous three months. When he saw Tom's resume, he knew he wanted him in the job. Tom had a graduate business degree and similar work experience with a competitor.

Joe had gone all out to get Tom. He had told him that the organization was an excellent place to work, that it valued its employees, and rewarded performance. When Tom asked about opportunities for increased responsibility, challenging assignments, and advancement, Joe had responded that the only limits were how hard Tom was willing to work. Tom said that "this sounds like the kind of place I've been looking for" and agreed to take the job.

Now, nine months later, Tom appears to have little enthusiasm for his job and his performance has begun to slip. Yesterday, Joe had overheard Tom complaining that he could finish his work by 10:00 each morning and then have nothing to do for the rest of the day. He also said that he had begun looking for another job. Joe was surprised, since Tom was the highest paid employee in the department. He wondered what he could do to keep Tom from leaving.

LEARNING OBJECTIVES

After successful completion of this chapter, you should be able to

- Discuss several common functions of work,
- Explain the psychological employment contract,
- Describe organizational and individual expectations,
- Explain the socialization and individualization processes,
- Identify and describe the motivating properties of tasks,

25

- Describe the relationship between job satisfaction and job performance,
- Identify several common characteristics of quality of work life (QWL),
- Describe methods of improving quality of work life for employees.

THE NATURE OF EMPLOYMENT

Why do people work? The answer to this question depends on whom you ask. Different individuals are motivated to work for different reasons. It is clear that for most people, work is more than just a way to earn a living (i.e., economic support). A study of male workers conducted during the 1950s found that 20 percent of these men would stop working if they had enough money to live comfortably without working.[1] A similar study conducted approximately 20 years later found a 39 percent increase in the number of men who would stop working if "they were to get enough money to live as comfortably as they would like for the rest of their life."[2] However, even though there was a significant increase in the number of men who would stop working, 72.2 percent (794 out of 1,099 men surveyed) indicated that they would continue working even if they did not have to do so. Thus, while the results of this later study may be interpreted as a decline in the meaning and/or value of work or the Protestant work ethic, the erosion is apparently relatively slow. While there may be cause for concern, organizations appear to have time to reverse this trend before it becomes much worse.

A number of common reasons why people work, called *functions of work*, can be identified. However, it should be recognized that all of these will not be important to all individuals. As you read the discussion of these functions, carefully consider which ones are important to you. Before reading further, stop for a moment and try to identify the reasons you work (or will work in the near future), other than for income. Which needs do you hope to satisfy through working?

Functions of Work

Discuss several common functions of work.

The primary **functions of work** are economic, social, status, identity, and growth.[3] An analysis of these functions will help determine why work is important to individuals. One way to view the functions of work is in terms of the needs that work satisfies for the individual. Individuals accept employment as a way to satisfy important needs; work is important to individuals to the extent it is able to satisfy their important needs.

Economic Function

The most obvious function of work, the economic function, is active when individuals exchange time and effort for income that allows them to buy goods and services. This income determines their standard of living. This economic function is probably the first thing that comes to mind for most people when asked "Why do you work?" However, further consideration of this question reveals several other less obvious reasons.

Social Function

Work also provides opportunities to meet and interact with others; some of our strongest friendships are developed at work. Perhaps you have heard the story of the janitor who won several million dollars in the state lottery. When asked about his plans, he replied that he would buy a new house and a new car and take a couple of weeks off from work. It was surprising to many people that a multimillionaire would continue to work as a janitor. However, if many of his important social relationships were developed with coworkers, he may be afraid of losing them if he quit his job.

Status

Work sometimes serves as a source of status. Individuals may attain status in the community, among friends and relatives and in their employing organization by the type of work they do or by their occupation. Certain occupations are perceived to have higher status than others. Exhibit 2.1 presents a ranking of various occupations. In addition, certain jobs are perceived to have higher status than others within the organization. For example, managers typically have higher status within the organization than nonmanagers. Top-level managers would typically have higher status than first-line supervisors. Even some organizations have more prestige than others (e.g., IBM, GM, the State Department). Which organizations in your geographic area are "high status?" Why are they given that status?

Identity

For some individuals, work is an important source of identity. When these people think about themselves, they think in terms of their jobs. For example, a person might see herself primarily as a professor of management rather than as a wife or daughter. Thus, work can help provide some clue as to who you are. When you meet people for the first time, one of the first questions they ask is "What do you do for a living?" Your occupation helps others form opinions about you and decide how to interact with you.

Growth

If you are fortunate enough to find a job that challenges your skills and abilities, work may provide an important source of growth and development. That is, the job may continually challenge you to stretch your innate abilities and even develop new ones. For some types of people, this is an extremely important function of work. Others, however, may not have a strong need to grow and develop. Do you prefer a job which provides a continuous challenge and test of your abilities, or a job which is relatively easy for you to perform and offers no surprises?

Motivating Properties of Tasks

For individuals who have a strong need for growth and development, it is important that they be assigned to tasks which are themselves motivating. Several motivating properties of tasks have been identified.[4]

Identify and describe the motivating properties of tasks.

Exhibit 2.1
Ranking of selected occupations by prestige

Occupation	Prestige
Parking-lot attendant	8.0
Janitor	12.5
Garbage collector	16.3
Babysitter	18.3
Short-order cook	21.5
Waitress/Waiter	22.1
Coal miner	24.0
Delivery-truck driver	26.9
Assembly-line worker	28.3
Cotton farmer	32.4
Cashier	35.6
Truck driver	40.1
Beautician	42.1
Post office clerk	42.3
Key punch operator	44.6
Typist	44.9
Auto mechanic	44.9
Telephone operator	46.2
Florist	49.7
Bookkeeper	50.0
Office secretary	51.3
Stenographer	52.6
Carpenter	53.5
Assembly-line supervisor in a manufacturing plant	53.8

Autonomy. In general, tasks or jobs which allow employees to use their own discretion and judgment in deciding how the work is to be done are more motivating than jobs where employees are not allowed to make these types of decisions. This **autonomy** allows employees to have a certain amount of control or "ownership" of their jobs. To the extent that you are able to make important decisions which affect your job, you will perceive that you "own" or control your job.

Skill Variety. Tasks which require employees to use a **variety of skills** tend to be more motivating than tasks on which employees perform the same activity over and over again. Most college students develop a number of skills during their education. Would you prefer a job that allowed you to use all or most of these, or one that required you to use the same skill over and over again?

Exhibit 2.1 *(continued)*

Occupation	Prestige
Dental assistant	54.8
Practical nurse	56.4
Car dealer	57.1
Police officer	58.3
Plumber	58.7
Private secretary	60.9
Electrician	62.5
Insurance agent	62.5
Hotel manager	64.1
Grade school teacher	65.4
Office manager	68.3
High school teacher	70.2
Accountant	71.2
Registered nurse	75.0
Chiropractor	75.3
Electrical engineer	79.5
Advertising executive	80.8
Stock broker	81.7
Architect	88.8
Lawyer	90.1
College professor	90.1
Mayor	92.2
Physician	95.8

*Prestige scores ranged from 0 (low) to 100 (high).
Source: Adapted from Bose, C. E. & Rossi, P. H. Gender and jobs: Prestige standings of occupations as affected by gender. *American Sociological Review,* 1983, *48,* 327–328.

Task Identity. The degree to which an employee's task leads to an identifiable portion of the completed work is **task identity**. For example, a person who attaches cords to electric mixers on an assembly line all day has a job very low in task identity. On the other hand, a person who builds electric mixers from start to finish has a job very high in task identity. This person can identify with "making mixers." It is relatively easy to think of yourself as a "mixer maker." It is something in which you can take pride. It is not easy to think of yourself as a "cord attacher." Thus, the first person may have a difficult time identifying with "attaching electric cords." Attaching cords is not a meaningful portion of the entire work process.

Task Significance. Another important property of tasks which makes them motivating to employees is **task significance**—the degree to which an individual's task performance is important to other people, either inside or outside of the organization. For example, if another department depends on you to compile certain information for them each month from which they prepare monthly summary reports, you may experience task significance. Your compilation of the information is important to employees in the other department. How well they perform their assigned tasks depends on how well you perform your tasks. Task significance is also present when your work is important to others outside the organization or to society in general. For example, mechanics who inspect and service aircraft between flights know that the safety of large numbers of people depends upon how well they perform their tasks. Similarly, doctors and scientists engaged in medical research are performing tasks which are important to society.

Task Feedback. Finally, the degree to which completion of tasks provides clear feedback about quality and quantity of performance affects the motivating potential of tasks. Generally, employees receive **task feedback** when they see the results of their efforts. This type of feedback, coming from the task itself, can be as important as verbal feedback from superiors.

The Human Relations in Action box on page 31 describes one method of providing feedback that often decreases employees' motivation. This electronic monitoring method is *not* what is meant by task feedback. Often by considering what *doesn't* work, we can gain a better understanding of what *does* work.

A simple example may help illustrate the importance of task feedback. Professional basketball star Larry Bird of the Boston Celtics is known for his accuracy in shooting from three-point range (beyond 30 feet). Before each game, Bird practiced his shot for about an hour. If he missed a shot, he would make a slight correction in how he held or released the ball, then shoot again. If the correction resulted in his making a basket, he received immediate task feedback—his efforts were successful. As pointed out earlier, this prompt feedback is likely to result in stronger perceptions of responsibility for outcomes. Now imagine what would happen if a curtain were lowered on the basketball court and raised after each shot so that Bird could no longer see the basket. He could continue practicing his shot, since the curtain was not raised to hide the basket until after he released the ball. However, he would no longer receive task feedback. Even if an experienced coach stood behind the curtain and described what happened to each of Bird's shots (providing verbal feedback), it is doubtful if Larry would continue practicing under these conditions. Task feedback provides not only information about the success of one's efforts but also motivations for greater effort. In the workplace, employees can see how they are performing *as they are performing*, they can determine *for themselves* any corrections which are necessary, and then *see the results* of their efforts.

Motivating Work

Skill variety, task identity, and task significance cause employees to perceive that their work is *meaningful*. That is, they perceive that they are performing work which is important, challenging, interesting, and complete (as opposed to simplified or broken down into smaller, specialized activities). Autonomy

HUMAN RELATIONS IN ACTION

The Boss That Never Blinks

It was pointed out in Chapter 1 that one effect of the change from a manufacturing-based economy to a service-based economy is that the jobs of many U.S. workers are also changing. The tremendous advances in computer technology in the last few years now make it extremely likely that all clerical and managerial jobs will involve the use of a computer or computer terminal. In 1986 it was estimated that approximately 13 million American workers used computers in their jobs. It was also estimated that around one third of these workers are being monitored electronically through the very computers on which they work! Another estimate counts 10 to 15 million computer terminals now in use. Projections are that there could be as many as 60 to 70 million terminals by the end of the 1990s. Since the implementation of computer technology is still on the increase, the numbers of employees whose job performance is monitored electronically is likely to increase over the next few years.

One example of electronic monitoring of work performance occurs in the airline industry. Airline reservation computers continuously monitor how long it takes reservation clerks to handle each customer, how long the clerk is idle between customers, and how long the clerk spends at lunch and on break. One large insurance company developed a computer program which continuously monitored the performance of clerks in the group claims processing department. An average time for entering a claim into the computer terminal was developed and used as a goal for all clerks. Each employee's performance was compared to this standard and the amount of time each employee's performance was either above or below this standard continuously flashed in the upper right corner of each clerk's computer screen.

Many employees react negatively to electronic monitoring of their performance. Some employees feel it is an invasion of their privacy and are concerned that organizations may go even further in monitoring employee behavior. Many employees also experience pressure or stress from being monitored every second they are on the job. It should be pointed out that not all employees react negatively to electronic monitoring of their performance. Employees who are extremely high performers often welcome the monitoring and feedback because it documents their high performance levels.

Source: Koepp, S. The boss that never blinks. *Time*, July 28, 1986, pp. 46–47.

---

results in employees feeling they are responsible for the outcomes of their efforts. The more autonomy they have, the more control they exert over their work, and therefore, the more they will feel they had an impact upon outcomes. When the outcomes are particularly good or successful, employees can take credit for them. As a result, employees feel a certain "ownership" of their jobs as opposed to feeling distant and detached. Finally, task feedback enables employees to become aware of how successful their efforts have been. As employees are trying to improve their performance, they can determine for themselves what corrections need to be made to continue to improve. Continued improvement then provides additional feelings of responsibility for outcomes as employees see that their efforts have been successful.

All five of the functions of work may be important to some people, while others may attach importance to only a few, or perhaps only one. The selection of functions important to an individual depends upon personality, expectations, needs, values, age, sex, marital status, beliefs, and attitudes.

PART ONE: Human Relations in Organizations

> **WHAT DO YOU THINK?**
>
> Which of the functions of work are most important to you? Which of the motivating properties of tasks do you view as essential to any job you might take? Are there any that are unimportant to you? Compare the answers to these questions with the job or career you have chosen for yourself. Is there a good match? What are the chances that your chosen career will provide opportunities for you to satisfy the needs that you have identified as important to you?

ORGANIZATIONAL AND INDIVIDUAL EXPECTATIONS

Describe organizational and individual expectations.

It was pointed out earlier that the primary reason people join organizations is to satisfy important needs. Thus, as people are considering joining an organization, they develop **individual expectations** of what they believe the organization will be able to provide to allow them to satisfy these important needs. These expectations may cover any or all of the functions of work or any aspect of employment—from monetary rewards and fringe benefits to social opportunities, participation in decision making, challenge, and responsibility. Indi-

Exhibit 2.2
Individual and organizational expectations

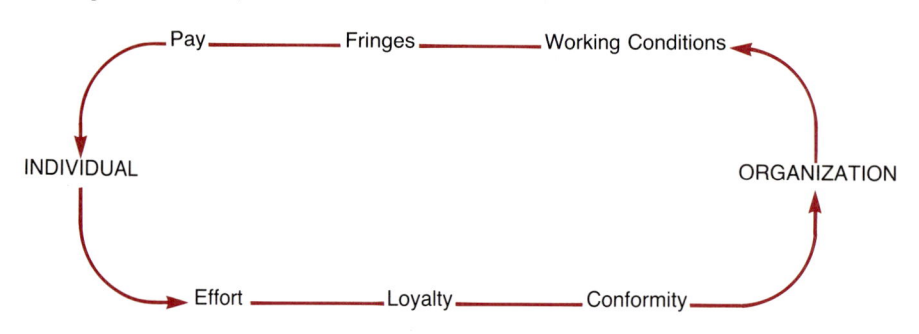

Pay ——— Fringes ——— Working Conditions

INDIVIDUAL   ORGANIZATION

Effort ——— Loyalty ——— Conformity

Individual and Organizational Expectations of What Each Will Receive

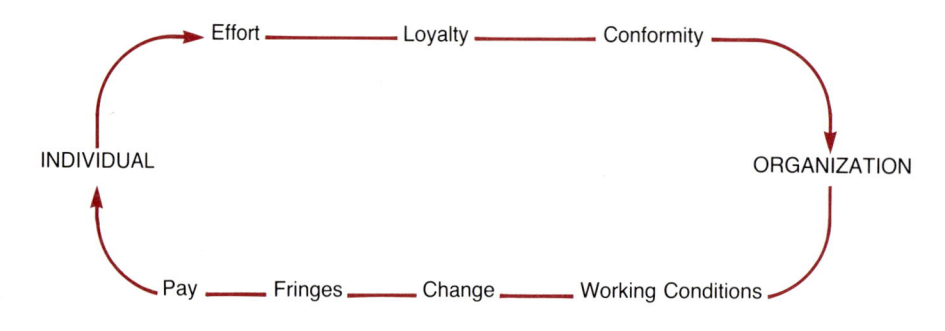

Effort ——— Loyalty ——— Conformity

INDIVIDUAL   ORGANIZATION

Pay ——— Fringes ——— Change ——— Working Conditions

Individual and Organizational Expectations of What Each
Will Have to Provide

viduals may also develop expectations about the effort and loyalty they believe they will need to give to the organization to get the rewards they desire.

At the same time individuals are developing expectations of the organization, the organization is developing expectations of the individuals. **Organizational expectations** include level of effort and performance; loyalty and commitment to the organization; adherence to organizational rules, policies, and procedures; appropriate dress and behavior; punctuality; overtime; conformance; and submission to management authority. Exhibit 2.2 illustrates this process of blending individual and organizational expectations. Do you think that any of these (or others you might identify) organizational expectations of employees are unreasonable or unfair? Which ones? Why?

Psychological Employment Contract

The matching of these two sets of expectations results in a **psychological employment contract**. A psychological contract is not a formal, written document. It is simply the set of both individual expectations of the organization and organizational expectations of the individual. Unfortunately, many of these expectations of both parties go unstated. The result is that the parties are often unaware of some of the other's expectations. In this situation, problems can develop.

Discuss the psychological employment contract.

In the Prologue, Joe painted a very rosy picture of the organization for Tom. As a result, Tom developed certain expectations in terms of what the organization would provide him if he accepted employment. Based on what he was told, Tom certainly expected challenging assignments, a great deal of responsibility, high rewards, and fast promotions. As it turned out, some of these expectations may have been unrealistic; the organization was simply unable or unwilling to provide them. Once it was clear to Tom that many of his expectations were not going to be met, he became unhappy with his employment and began considering a change of jobs. His psychological employment contract had not been fulfilled.

RETURN TO THE PROLOGUE

Unmet Expectations

Edgar Schien suggests that the high turnover rate of college graduates in business can be traced to unmet expectations.[5] Schien traced the employment of the 1962, 1963, and 1964 business graduates of the Massachusetts Institute of Technology and found that by 1968, 50% of the 1964 graduates had changed jobs, 67% of the 1963 graduates had changed jobs, and 73% of the 1962 graduates had changed jobs at least once. Part of the problem, Schien suggests, is that business graduates leave school thinking like top-level managers. They expect to have challenging, responsible assignments, participate in important decisions, have their organization interested in finding better ways of doing things, and have opportunities to learn, grow, and develop. What graduates often find is that their first jobs are not particularly challenging and that other employees are completely satisfied with the status quo. Organizations often are not interested in newcomers' ideas for changing things for the better. Further, graduates often find that the organization makes much greater demands for loyalty and conformity than they expected. Obviously, the organization's expectations of employee loyalty and conformity were different from the individual's, and the individual's expectations of challenging, responsible work assignments differed from the organization's. There must be a substantial degree of overlap of organizational and individual expectations or the employment relationship will be terminated by one or both parties. In the Prologue to this chapter, the organization was unaware that Tom's expectations were not met, so it was Tom who was considering terminating the employment relationship.

Realistic Job Preview

One approach that has been suggested to increase the overlap of organizational and individual expectations is the **realistic job preview**,[6] which provides job applicants with accurate information about the job and the company. Instead of trying to "sell" the organization to the applicant, the interviewer provides realistic information. Thus, the expectations formed by the applicant are likely to be more in line with what the organization is willing and able to offer. Provided with both positive and negative information about the job and the organization, the applicant is able to make a more informed decision regarding employment. This doesn't mean that the interviewer should try to discuss every single negative aspect of the job and the organization, but the discussion should provide a very accurate picture of both to the applicant.

Critics of the realistic job preview argue that it will prevent the organization from recruiting and hiring highly qualified applicants. Research findings do not support this argument, even though realistic job previews have been

Realistic job previews provide applicants with accurate information about the job and the organization.

found to lower initial job expectations. In fact, because of the more practical expectations developed by applicants who are hired, realistic job previews have resulted in lower turnover rates during the initial employment period.[7]

It follows that realistic job previews should be considered good management practice. Since they don't lessen the organization's ability to attract highly qualified applicants, there is little basis for arguing against their use. While an occasional applicant may decline a job offer, over the long run the very high turnover rate during the initial employment period should decline. Further, it seems only fair that applicants be provided with accurate information about the job and the organization. If this isn't done, the new employee may not stay with the organization after the true nature of the job becomes apparent. Finally, it is less costly to the organization if individuals make negative decisions about employment with the organization *before* they are hired rather than after they accept employment. In the early 1980s, the cost of turnover for a nonmanagerial employee was estimated to be between $3,000 and $4,000.[8]

THE SOCIALIZATION PROCESS

While the individual comes to the job with some expectations, others are developed on the job. **Socialization** is the continual process of modifying the set of "entry" expectations based on experience with the organization. Especially during the first few months of employment (the initial employment period), the organization tries to mold the new employee into the type of employee they expect. This socialization may occur in a variety of ways. Some may occur during new employee orientation programs where the employee learns some of the rules, policies, and expectations of the organization. Socialization may also occur as a result of the new employee interacting with other employees who have already been socialized. The new employee learns which behaviors and attitudes are acceptable by watching these other employees receive rewards for acceptable behaviors or punishments for unacceptable behaviors. This process of learning by observing others is called vicarious (indirect) learning. Organizations sometimes purposely assign new employees to work with an experienced employee who displays the kinds of behavior the organization desires so that the new employee learns appropriate behaviors vicariously (i.e., by watching others).

Explain the socialization and individualization processes.

Individualization

At the same time the organization is trying to socialize new employees, the new employee is trying to change the organization so that it better meets their expectations. This process is **individualization**.[9] New employees often make suggestions or prepare plans to submit to their manager. The suggestions and plans often are intended to change the organization in ways to make it more in line with the employee's expectations. Thus, pressure is being exerted on the organization by individuals and on individuals by the organization at the same time. The organization is trying to mold individuals into the type of employee that it desires; the individual is trying to mold the organization into an acceptable work environment. The result is that both are changed to some degree. This constant pressure from both parties continually modifies the psychological employment contract as long as the employment relationship continues.

SATISFACTION AND PRODUCTIVITY

This dynamic psychological contract will certainly affect individual levels of job satisfaction, motivation, productivity, and, ultimately, turnover decisions. For some employees, the gap between their set of expectations and the organization's may be so large that the only decision is to leave the organization (turnover). For others, the gap might not be so large that they consider leaving, but their job satisfaction may be adversely affected. This in turn may create problems in employee motivation, attendance, and productivity.

Job Satisfaction

By definition, **job satisfaction** is the feeling an individual has about the job, after evaluating the job and its working conditions.[10] In other words, job satisfaction is an attitude which reflects an individual's likes and dislikes regarding work experience.

Underlying the concept of overall job satisfaction are a number of separate and important types of job satisfaction. Two employees may have the same level of overall job satisfaction, but will differ substantially on some of the separate dimensions. In other words, they may be satisfied or dissatisfied for much different reasons. To make improvements, employees must examine several dimensions of job satisfaction—including *extrinsic satisfaction, intrinsic satisfaction,* and *social satisfaction.*

Extrinsic Job Satisfaction

Extrinsic job satisfaction includes pay, physical working conditions, management style, promotions, and fringe benefits. Employees are dependent on others (e.g., managers) for the satisfaction of extrinsic needs.

Intrinsic Job Satisfaction

Intrinsic job satisfaction derives from challenging and interesting work assignments, personal freedom to plan and organize one's own work, and participation in making important decisions which affect one's work. As discussed earlier, one important way to increase intrinsic job satisfaction is through the motivating properties of tasks. Managers cannot provide intrinsic job satisfaction *directly,* but they can increase opportunities for employees to experience that satisfaction. By allowing employees to exert more control over their jobs and work environment, soliciting employee participation in major decisions which affect their jobs, and by assigning meaningful and challenging tasks, managers encourage intrinsic job satisfaction.

Social Satisfaction

Employees' acceptance of the social aspects of their work experience leads to **social satisfaction**. Work is a major source of social satisfaction for many people, since it offers the opportunity to develop close friendships and interact with others on the job.

Employees are likely to differ in the degree to which each of these types of job satisfaction is important to them. It is also possible that all three types of job satisfaction are equally important to some employees. The point is, managers must get to know their employees well enough to know which type of job satisfaction is most important to each one. Managers who fail to do this are not likely to be able to motivate their employees effectively or improve employees' quality of work life through increased job satisfaction.

Which of the three dimensions of job satisfaction is most important to you? Are any more important than others? Do you expect that this choice will remain the same throughout your work career? Why or why not?

Job Satisfaction and Job Performance

Managers' interest in job satisfaction is understandable. However, there is a common misperception concerning the relationship between job satisfaction and job performance. Many people assume that job satisfaction causes job performance; that is, that "happy workers are productive workers." But, after over 35 years of research, behavioral scientists have been unable to uncover such a relationship. Thousands of studies consistently report a weak, positive relationship between these two variables. The current belief is that the relationship is too complex to be understood by examining these two variables alone. Rather, a number of other variables, including level of rewards, method of allocating rewards, and the nature of the task must also be considered.[11]

Describe the relationship between job satisfaction and job performance.

While job satisfaction may not exhibit a strong relationship to job performance, it has been shown to be directly related to several other important work outcomes such as absenteeism, turnover, accident rate, and grievance rates.[12] Satisfied employees are absent and turn over (quit their jobs) less frequently, have fewer accidents and file fewer grievances than dissatisfied employees.[13] Further, job satisfaction has been shown to be related to "**good citizen**" **behaviors**, such as coming to work on time, keeping the work area clean and orderly, and helping other employees.[14] Thus, even though managers may not be able to improve employees' job performance by taking steps to increase their job satisfaction, these other outcomes provide adequate reason for managers to be concerned with job satisfaction. As will be shown later, job satisfaction is an important result of quality of work life programs.

Job Satisfaction of American Workers

Given the importance of job satisfaction to human relations in organizational work settings, there is, unfortunately, evidence that job satisfaction levels of American workers may be declining. Gallup polls conducted in 1955 and again in 1980 show significant differences in worker responses to the question "Do you enjoy your work so much that you have a hard time putting it aside?" In 1955, 52 percent said yes. However, in 1980, only 34 percent replied positively. Another question was, "Generally speaking, which do you enjoy more—the hours you are on your job or the hours you are not on your job?" In 1955, 40 percent said they enjoyed hours on the job most. In contrast, only 24 percent of those responding to the 1980 survey picked the job hours.[15] One approach designed to reverse this trend, *quality of work life* programs, has been widely implemented.

QUALITY OF WORK LIFE

Quality of work life (QWL) is not a single technique, or even a single group of techniques. Rather, it is every technique designed to improve the "quality of the human experience in the workplace."[16] A more comprehensive definition of QWL has been developed by the American Center for the Quality of Working Life.[17]

> Quality of work life improvements are defined as any activity which takes place at every level of an organization which seeks greater organizational effectiveness through the enhancement of human dignity and growth. . . .a process through which the stockholders in the organization—management, union(s), and employees—learn how to work together better. . . to determine for themselves what actions, changes and improvements are desirable and workable in order to achieve the twin and simultaneous goals of an improved quality of life at work for all members of the organization and greater effectiveness for both the company and the union(s).

While QWL programs vary from organization to organization, there are a number of relatively common components.[18]

Identify several common characteristics of quality of work life (QWL).

1. Adequate and fair compensation. Employees must be compensated for their contributions to the organization. While it is difficult to determine what is *adequate compensation,* employees must feel their pay is appropriate for the demands placed upon them by their assigned tasks. Adequate compensation is related to the economic function of work discussed earlier in the chapter. Adequate compensation, for most people, is enough to support a standard of living with which they are satisfied. For employees to perceive that their compensation is fair, it must be tied to performance levels; all employees at a specific level of performance must receive the same level of pay. *Fair* compensation does not mean *equal* compensation. It means that compensation is strongly related to level of job performance.
2. Safe and healthy working conditions. Employees should not be exposed to unsafe or unhealthy working conditions. Safety rules should specify safe equipment, particularly protective gear and clothing, for employees exposed to pollutants, chemicals, and noise. While there are laws which provide minimum health and safety standards for working conditions, many QWL programs reach far beyond these minimal standards.
3. Opportunities to use and develop skills and abilities. Quality of work life improves to the extent that employees are given opportunities to use all of their skills and abilities, and to develop new skills and abilities. Many QWL programs will include some form of job enrichment that redesigns jobs to give employees these opportunities. Job enrichment programs involve building into jobs the motivational properties of tasks discussed earlier.
4. Opportunities for growth and development. Employees are likely to experience a higher quality of work life when their organization provides them

opportunities for growth and development. One important aspect of this dimension of QWL is the presence of career opportunities. Employees' QWL is closely related to the number of opportunities for advancement within their organization.

5. Social integration in the organization. Many people have relatively strong needs to be accepted and to belong. Further, work organizations are often the primary means of satisfying these important social needs. Individuals who believe they are not accepted by their work team or department are likely to feel isolated and alone. This element of QWL has become more important in recent years as increasing numbers of men and women have begun to enter nontraditional occupations; that is, occupations that have historically been considered predominantly male or female occupations. For example, increasing numbers of males are becoming registered nurses—an occupation previously considered exclusively female. In addition, increasing numbers of women are entering previously male-dominated occupations such as firefighter, police officer, and construction worker. As workers enter a nontraditional occupation, at least initially, they may not be readily accepted by coworkers. In fact, many nontraditional employees have experienced isolation in their new jobs. QWL programs can be designed to integrate these employees into their work groups and the organization.

6. Employee rights. Many of these rights, personal privacy, free speech, and due process, are not protected by law, but they are becoming more widely recognized by progressive organizations. Further, some states are enacting legislation designed to protect **employee rights**. *Privacy rights* involve the right to have personnel records kept confidential and not released to third parties without the written consent of the employee. *Free speech* refers to the right to disagree with managers and organizational policies without fear of reprisal. *Due process* in organizational work settings has a meaning similar to due process in the legal system. It involves the opportunity for employees to bring problems and complaints to the attention of managers (e.g., a grievance system or open-door policy). Due process more commonly refers to employee rights during discipline and termination. In this regard, due process involves an employee's right to be informed of organizational rules and policies as well as specific forms of discipline associated with violations of each rule or policy, the right to be informed that there is a problem, and the right to be given adequate assistance and time to correct the problem before being terminated.

Some states have enacted laws guaranteeing—and more and more organizations are voluntarily giving—employees the right to view their personnel file and insert statements of explanation regarding any information they believe is incorrect or misleading. Further, the old "termination-at-will" doctrine which gave employers the right to fire employees for no reason or even for a bad or immoral reason has been replaced by the "termination-for-just-cause" doctrine. According to this newer doctrine, employees must be given due process in work organizations just as they must be given due process in the legal system. Terminating employees without a good, job-related reason is becoming increasingly difficult for employers.

7. Balance of work and nonwork. It is widely recognized that work and nonwork experiences are difficult to separate. Problems or stress at work can affect employees' nonwork life, just as problems at home can affect employees' work life. Employees' quality of work life is enhanced to the extent that their employing organizations are sensitive to the need for balance between work and nonwork activities. For example, QWL is enhanced by organizations which do not make heavy travel demands on their employees, but make sure that they have adequate time to spend with their families.

One recent development which may be considered an attempt to improve QWL evolved with the tremendous advances in computer and communications technology. As the Human Relations in Action box on this page illustrates, computer technology is allowing many employees to work at home. While telecommuting is not suitable for all jobs, it does provide many advantages to employees who are able to participate.[19] It may, for example, provide employees the opportunity to achieve the best balance between work and nonwork.

It is also important to point out that just as telecommuting is not appropriate for all types of jobs, it is also not appropriate for all types of employees. One of the often-mentioned advantages of telecommuting is that it

HUMAN RELATIONS IN ACTION

The Changing Nature of Employment: Telecommuting

For many employees, the nature of employment is changing. While the reasons these employees work are not likely to change, the nature of their jobs and their work environment may be substantially different in the near future.

Employees in many companies are now telecommuting. They work in the comfort of their own home and transmit their work electronically via personal computer over the telephone lines to the office. There are substantial benefits to both the employee and the organization. The major advantage to the organization is the savings in office or building space. Organizations can expand without costly additions to their building by allowing employees to work at home. Organizations may also be able to keep valuable, hard-to-replace employees on the payroll by allowing them the flexibility of working at home.

The primary advantage to employees is flexibility and comfort. Instead of rushing to be at the office by 8:30 A.M., telecommuters can get the kids off to school and watch the end of the "Today" show while having an extra cup of coffee before starting work. And, they can begin work without shaving, applying makeup, or even changing out of their pajamas!

The experiences of organizations that have tried telecommuting suggest that productivity decreases temporarily after an employee begins working at home, but then increases to new high levels. Besides, when the blizzard hits this winter, the office won't have to shut down.

Of course, not all types of employees or jobs are appropriate for telecommuting. Employees must be self-starters, requiring very little supervision, and capable of resisting the many distractions (e.g., television, gardening, swimming pool) which might be present at home. In addition, the employee's job must not be highly interdependent with other jobs or require interaction with other employees or customers.

Source: Atkinson, W. Home/work. *Personnel Journal*, 1985, *64*, 105–109.

eliminates the commute to work, and solves related transportation and parking problems. However, some employees might find the drive to and from work relaxing. They may use the drive home as a time to clear their minds of the pressures and problems of work before seeing their families. Therefore, it is important that organizations considering telecommuting make it a voluntary program. It can result in tremendous benefits to employees who willingly participate, but it may cause problems for employees who prefer more traditional work environments.[20]

8. Meaningful, socially responsible work. It is important to a large number of employees that the organizations they work for are socially responsible. That is, these organizations are not polluting the environment, not marketing hazardous or worthless products or services, maintaining fair and equitable employment practices, and so on. QWL is enhanced to the extent that employees perceive their organizations to be not only socially responsible in the sense that they are doing no damage to the environment or to society, but also to the extent that they are active members of society, trying to make improvements in their communities.

QWL programs are implemented by organizations not only to improve satisfaction and human relations, but also to improve productivity and organizational effectiveness. Exhibit 2.3 shows how QWL programs affect productivity in four ways.[21] Since many programs increase employee participation in decision making, there are likely to be increases in communications and coordi-

Exhibit 2.3
Quality of work life and productivity

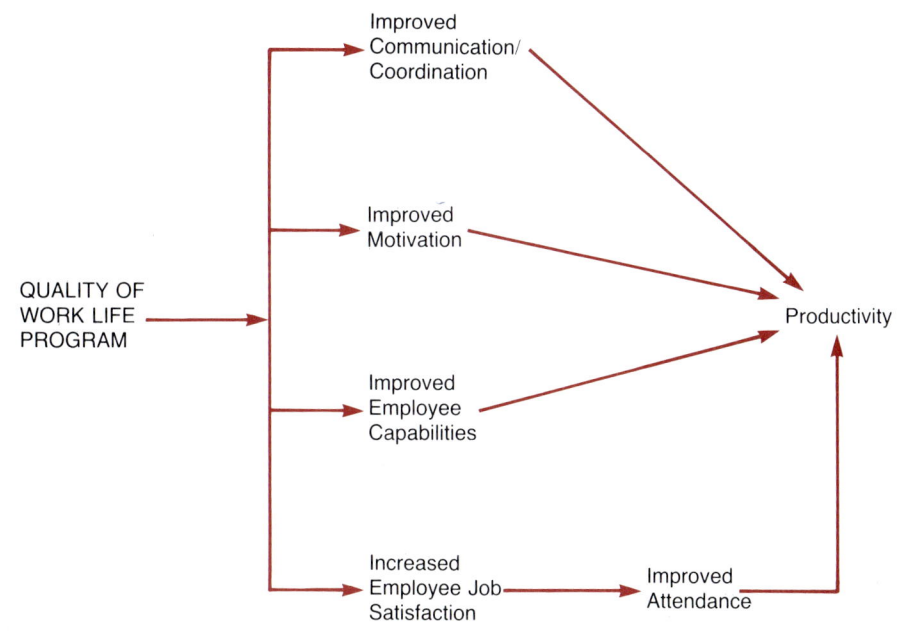

Source: Adapted from Lawler, E. E. & Ledford, G. E. Productivity and the quality of work life. *National Productivity Review,* Winter 1981–82, *2,* 23–36.

nation as well as employee motivation. Further, QWL programs which include job enrichment will result in increased motivation for many employees. Additionally, increased participation and involvement may result in improved capabilities as employees develop. Finally, QWL programs generally result in increased employee job satisfaction, which is strongly related to attendance behavior as well as to **"good citizen" behavior**. These factors also positively influence productivity.

Quality Circles (QCs)

Describe methods of improving quality of work life for employees.

One popular program often associated with QWL is the **quality circle (QC)**. "A quality circle is a small group of employees doing similar work who voluntarily meet regularly to discuss quality problems, analyze the causes of the problems, recommend solutions for management's consideration, and where possible, take action themselves."[22] The departmental supervisor typically serves as QC leader. It has been estimated that over 90 percent of the Fortune 500 companies have implemented quality circle programs.[23]

One feature common to both QWL and QC programs is increased employee participation. Coupled with increased opportunities for interaction, this participation generally produces higher employee job satisfaction levels. And, a number of additional potential benefits of QCs have been identified, some of which appear in Exhibit 2.4. QCs often improve cooperation, teamwork, and communications as employees meet regularly to discuss work-related problems. In those situations where the nature of the work does not permit inter-

Quality Circles (QCs) result in increased employee participation.

> **Exhibit 2.4**
> Potential benefits of quality circles
>
> - increased understanding of job requirements
> - increased and/or improved communication between employees and managers
> - improved cooperation and coordination between work teams
> - improved cooperation and coordination within work teams
> - development of teamwork
> - opportunity to bring problems out into the open for resolution
> - opportunity for employees to participate in making important decisions and to become more involved in the organization
> - increased productivity
> - decreased absenteeism and turnover
> - employee growth and development

Source: Based on Gregerman, I. B. Introduction to quality circles: An approach to participative problem-solving. *Industrial Management,* September–October 1979, *21*(5), 21–26; Marks, M. L., Mirvis, P. H., Hackett, E. J. & Grady, J. F. Employee participation in a quality circle program: Impact on quality of work life, productivity, and absenteeism. *Journal of Applied Psychology,* 1986, *71*(1), 61–69.

action on the job, QCs provide an opportunity for employees and supervisors to communicate. Even where there are no communication barriers, employees and supervisors may be reluctant to discuss problems. Without some incentive or encouragement from some source, discussions may be avoided or put off indefinitely. QC meetings provide opportunities for employees and supervisors to communicate with one another about work-related problems, requirements, and expectations. Increased understanding of job requirements, and of one another, are frequently the result. QC meetings also provide a forum to bring problems out into the open for resolution. Without such an opportunity, small problems may be ignored and allowed to develop into serious problems.

However, QCs are not the answer to every problem managers face and they are not always successful—especially where organizations give only lip service to QCs and where QC recommendations are not really implemented. Would you volunteer to serve on a Quality Circle? Why or why not?

Quality of Work Life and the Nature of Work

Chapter 1 pointed out that the nature of the U.S. economy and the nature of jobs have changed and will continue to change, due primarily to the decline of manufacturing, the rise of the service industry, and the remarkable advances in computer and communications technology. These advances are enabling employees to become better educated and better informed—so they have higher expectations of their jobs and organizations. It follows that issues involving quality of work life are likely to increase in importance.

DEVELOPING YOUR HUMAN RELATIONS SKILLS

The implications of the information presented in this chapter produce guidelines for you in your role as a manager.

1. Recognize that people work for a variety of reasons—not just economic ones. It is a mistake to rely too heavily on economic rewards and incentives, while ignoring the social, status, identity, and growth functions of work. For some employees, the noneconomic reasons for working may be more important than the economic reasons.
2. Give employees realistic expectations about what the organization is like and will be able and willing to provide in terms of rewards. Human relations within the organization is likely to suffer if employees learn that the expectations they formed during the hiring process were unrealistic. It is also a good idea to openly discuss the organization's expectations with employees. Open discussion of both the organization's and the employee's sets of expectations will produce a more accurate psychological employment contract. This contract, in turn, lays a foundation for good human relations within the organization.
3. Recognize that many employees have relatively strong growth needs. For these employees, it is important to increase, to the extent possible, the motivating properties of tasks. For these employees to be motivated and satisfied with their employment, they must perceive that their work is meaningful, that they "own" the job, and that feedback on the success of their efforts is forthcoming.
4. Understand the relationship between job satisfaction and job performance. Don't assume that you will be able to increase performance by increasing employee job satisfaction. It may be possible, but in many cases, it will not. It is more likely that you will be able to solve attendance problems by increasing employee job satisfaction. It is also likely that employee "good citizen" behavior will strengthen with increased job satisfaction. However, job satisfaction is not necessarily a root of good human relations. Recall that *human relations* was defined in Chapter 1 as the study of human behavior with the goal of understanding how to design work settings so that employees perform up to their potential, cooperate with other employees, and satisfy their

SUMMARY

Ask several people why they work and you will probably get several different answers. Work means different things to different people. However, five functions of work—economic, social, status, identity, and growth—have been identified. Some people will consider all five to be important while others will focus on only a few or even a single function of work.

Motivating, challenging work is important to individuals who have strong growth needs. Motivating properties of tasks include

- autonomy, the extent to which employees are allowed to use their own initiative and discretion on their jobs
- skill variety, the degree to which the task requires the employee to use a number of different skills and abilities

own individual needs and goals. Simply providing additional rewards or improving the work setting will not accomplish all of these goals. Job satisfaction of employees is important, but it is only a small part of good human relations.

The information presented in this chapter also has some important guidelines for you in your role as an employee.

1. One of the most important guidelines has to do with the psychological employment contract. Many employment relationships fail due to unrealistic or vague expectations on the part of either the individual or the organization. On the one hand, you should attempt to form as realistic expectations of the organization as possible. This means you must not rely on only one or two sources of information, but gather information from a variety of sources, both within and outside the organization, to form accurate perceptions. If the organization provides realistic job previews, this task is much easier. On the other hand, you must provide the organization with your set of expectations of it. Many problems which surface after employees accept jobs do so because expectations were simply assumed or left unstated. You should know exactly what the organization expects of you in the new job, just as the organization should know exactly what you expect of it. Inaccurate psychological employment contracts often lead to one or both parties terminating the employment relationship.

2. If you have strong growth needs which are not being fulfilled, let your manager know about it. Sometimes it is difficult for managers to know which needs are most important to employees. Don't present it as a major problem, or approach the manager with "I've got important needs which aren't being satisfied around here!" Rather, in the course of conversation, simply mention that you would really like some additional assignments or special projects that would help you learn more about the organization or some specific activity. You might say, "I'd really like to work on the Downer project. I think it would give me an excellent opportunity to learn more about the organization as well as polish my skills in marketing research."

- task identity, the degree to which the employee performs a substantial, meaningful portion of work
- task significance, the degree to which the employee's work is important to others
- task feedback, the degree to which completion of the task provides information concerning the quality and quantity of the individual's task performance.

As individuals consider accepting employment with an organization, they are forming expectations about what rewards the organization will provide to them. They are also forming expectations of what they will have to provide to the organization (e.g., effort, loyalty) in exchange for these rewards. At the same time, the organization is forming expectations about the levels of effort, loyalty and conformity available from the individual. In addition, the organization forms expectations concerning the types and levels of various rewards that it will have to provide to the individual. The product of these two sets of expectations is the psychological employment contract. Without substantial overlap or agreement between these two sets of expectations, one or both parties will consider terminating the employment relationship. One way of increasing the degree of overlap between expectations is the realistic job preview. Once individuals accept employment, the organization begins trying to mold that person into the type of employee desired by the organization. This process is called **socialization**. At the same time, many new employees begin trying to change the organization into the ideal working environment. This process is **individualization**. These two concurrent processes continually modify the psychological employment contract.

Job satisfaction is related to several important work outcomes, such as absenteeism, turnover, grievance rates, and accident rates. It has also been shown to be related to employees' "good citizen" behavior, such as keeping the work area clean. It is difficult, however, to find a strong relationship between job satisfaction and job performance.

Job satisfaction is an important outcome of quality of work life (QWL) programs. QWL is defined as any effort designed to improve the quality of human experience in the workplace. Its programs have eight common features (1) adequate and fair compensation, (2) safe and healthy working conditions, (3) opportunities to use skills and abilities, (4) opportunities to grow and develop, (5) social integration in the organization, (6) employee rights, (7) balance of work and family, and (8) a socially responsible organization.

One popular QWL program is the quality circle (QC)—a group of employees, usually from the same department or division, who voluntarily meet on a regular basis to identify and solve work-related problems. The focus of QC's is more on quality than quantity.

KEY TERMS

functions of work
autonomy
skill variety
task identity
task significance
task feedback
individual expectations
organizational expectations
psychological employment contract
realistic job preview
socialization
individualization
job satisfaction
extrinsic satisfaction
intrinsic satisfaction
social satisfaction
"good citizen" behaviors
quality of work life (QWL)
employee rights
quality circles (QCs)

DISCUSSION QUESTIONS

1. Identify and describe the functions of work. Why aren't all of these important to all people?
2. What should managers do for employees who have strong growth needs?
3. Identify and describe the motivating properties of tasks.
4. What types of expectations of organizations do individuals develop when considering employment opportunities?
5. What is a psychological employment contract? Why is this concept important?
6. What is meant by a realistic job preview? What are the potential advantages of such a process?
7. Briefly describe the socialization and individualization processes.
8. Define job satisfaction and the three dimensions of job satisfaction.
9. Why is job satisfaction important from the organization's perspective?
10. What is quality of work life? What are common features of QWL programs?
11. How does QWL affect productivity and/or organizational effectiveness?
12. What are quality circles? How are they related to QWL?

EXERCISE 2.1

Measuring Job Satisfaction

Using the job satisfaction questionnaire below, interview at least three people who hold full-time jobs. Record their scores to the questionnaire statements and compute the various satisfaction scores indicated below. In addition, record the type of work each person performs. In class you will be able to compare your scores with your classmates to see if there is a pattern among various types of occupations.

1 = Highly Dissatisfied
2 = Slightly Dissatisfied
3 = Neither Satisfied nor Dissatisfied

4 = Slightly Satisfied
5 = Highly Satisfied

In general, how satisfied are you with:

1. your pay _____
2. your fringe benefits _____
3. the people with whom you work _____
4. the amount of freedom you have on your job _____
5. the way you are treated by your coworkers _____
6. the way you are treated by your supervisor _____
7. the amount of challenge and interesting activities provided by your work _____
8. the amount of support provided by your supervisor _____

Scoring

Satisfaction with pay and fringe benefits—Add the scores for statements 1 and 2. _____

Satisfaction with coworkers—Add the scores for statements 3 and 5. _____

Satisfaction with supervision—Add the scores for statements 6 and 8. _____

Satisfaction with the work itself—Add the scores for statements 4 and 7. _____

Overall satisfaction—Add the scores for all eight statements _____

Type of work or occupation of respondent _____

EXERCISE 2.2

Analyzing the Motivational Properties of Tasks

Pick a job with which you are familiar or one where you may observe an employee working for a period of time. Using a grading scale, rate the job on the presence of the five motivating properties of tasks.

1	2	3	4	5
VERY LITTLE		A MODERATE AMOUNT		VERY MUCH

1. Autonomy _____   4. Task significance _____
2. Task identity _____   5. Task feedback _____
3. Skill variety _____

You may want to coordinate this activity with others in your class so that more than one person rates the same job to compare ratings of that job; or to ensure that a variety of jobs are rated to compare different types of jobs.

CASE 2.1

Enriching Jobs in OPS

Sam had received a promotion to Manager, Order Processing Services Department six months ago. Since then he had busied himself learning the operations and tasks of the department. By the end of his sixth month, he was confident that he fully understood the work and the people within the department. One thing that bothered Sam was the relatively high level of turnover and absenteeism (and obviously low morale) in the department. He decided that his first major action as manager should be to correct these situations.

STK Enterprises is a large retailer of farm supply products. The company handles everything from agricultural chemicals and fertilizer to clothing and machinery. Since the company does not manufacture any of its own products, everything is purchased from other suppliers. STK operates retail outlets in nearly every county throughout Illinois, Iowa, Wisconsin, Missouri, Indiana, and Nebraska. Customers place their orders through STK retail stores; the stores then forward the orders to the Order Processing Services Department at STK headquarters in St. Louis. STK minimizes warehouse costs by shipping many customer orders from the supplier/manufacturer directly to the STK retail store.

Order Processing Services (OPS) is a department of approximately seventy-five clerical employees and eight supervisors. Its primary responsibility is taking orders from customers, placing these orders with suppliers, billing customers for their orders, handling order status requests, and approving supplier invoices for payment. All employees perform similar work. Work is divided along product lines—all agricultural fertilizer and chemical orders are placed with one work group, all machinery orders with another work group, and so on. A typical order is handled in a standard series of actions.

An employee in OPS receives a telephone call from one of the retail stores, placing an order for, say, 4 truck tires. The clerk takes the order and enters the retail store's ID number, the product number for the tires, and the order quantity in the computer. If there is only one supplier for tires, the computer automatically selects this supplier ID number and an order is printed. If there are several suppliers for these particular tires, the clerk must select a supplier by entering the supplier ID number. A multi-ply order form is then printed and returned to the clerk, who tears down the order, places one copy in the mail to the retail store, one copy to the supplier, and files two copies. When the supplier receives the order, the tires are shipped to the retail store which then sells them to the customer. When the supplier bills STK for the tires, an invoice is sent to the OPS department and the clerk who placed the order checks the invoice against the file copy of the order to ensure that the proper tires were shipped, the prices and finance terms are correct, and so on. If the invoice is correct, it is stamped and approved for payment. The order is then sent to the Accounts Receivable/Payable Department, which issues a check to the supplier.

If a retail store does not receive an order on time or has a problem with the order, the supervisor of the OPS work group who handled the order is contacted for assistance. One of the biggest complaints of OPS supervisors is that they frequently have to deal with irate retail store managers. However, it is not uncommon for a supervisor to be out of the department, in which case one of the clerical employees must accept the call. A frequently told OPS story is about the day a clerk received an order for six units of Item # 69473—five-gallon drums of weed killer. However, the clerk entered Item # 67493 by mistake. The store received six $10,000 grain storage buildings! The retail store manager called OPS and one of the supervisors got a "real chewing out."

One of the most frequent complaints of OPS clerical employees concerns the wide swings in work load. As an agricultural supply company, STK's sales closely follow the farming season. For example, 90 percent of all fertilizer and chemical orders are placed within a three-month period in the early spring. The result is that employees in this department work several hours of overtime nearly every day during the spring. However, during winter months they don't have enough work to keep themselves busy all day. Another complaint addresses the fatigue, backstrain, and eyestrain associated with sitting in front of computer terminals all day long. As one employee put it, "I'm just another piece of equipment—a link between the phone and the computer. The phone rings, I answer it, take the information, and feed it into the computer. One of these days someone will invent a piece of electronic equipment to do what I do and I'll be out of a job."

QUESTIONS

1. How would you recommend enriching these OPS jobs, making them more challenging and meaningful to the employees?
2. Can all five of the motivating properties of tasks described in the chapter be increased in these OPS clerical jobs? If not, which ones cannot be increased and why?

REFERENCES

[1] Morse, N.C. & Weiss, R.S. The function and meaning of work and the job. *American Sociological Review*, 1955, *20*, 191–198.

[2] Vecchio, R.P. The function and meaning of work and the job: Morse and Weiss (1955) revisited. *Academy of Management Journal*, 1980, *23*, 361–367.

[3] Steers, R.M. *Introduction to organizational behavior*. Second edition. Glenview, IL: Scott, Foresman and Company, 1984.

[4] Hackman, J.R. & Oldham, G. *Work redesign*. Reading, MA: Addison-Wesley, 1980.

[5] Schein, E.H. The first job dilemma: An appraisal of why college graduates change jobs and what can be done about it. *Psychology Today,* 1968, 26–37.

[6] Wanous, J.P. Tell it like it is at realistic job previews. *Personnel,* July-August 1975, 50–60.

[7] Wanous, J.P. Effects of a realistic job preview on job acceptance, job attitudes, and job survival. *Journal of Applied Psychology,* 1973, *58,* 327–332.

[8] Dalton, D.R. & Todor, W.D. Turnover: A lucrative hard dollar phenomenon. *Academy of Management Review,* 1982, *7,* 212–218.

[9] Schein, E.H. Organizational socialization and the profession of management. *Industrial Management Review,* 1968, *9,* 1–16.

[10] Locke, E.A. The nature and causes of job satisfaction. In Dunnette, M.D. (Ed.) *Handbook of industrial and organizational psychology.* Chicago: Rand McNally, 1976, 1297–1349.

[11] Organ, D.W. A reappraisal and reinterpretation of the satisfaction-causes-performance hypothesis. *Academy of Management Review,* 1977, *2,* 46–53; Schwab, D.P. & Cummings, L.L. Theories of performance and satisfaction: A review. *Industrial Relations,* 1970, *9,* 408–430; Iaffaldano, M.T. & Muchinsky, P.M. Job satisfaction and job performance: A meta-analysis. *Psychological Bulletin,* 1985, *97,* 251–273.

[12] Petty, M.M., McGee, G.W., & Cavender, J.W. A meta-analysis of the relationship between individual job satisfaction and individual performance. *Academy of Management Review,* 1984, *9,* 712–721.

[13] Staw, B.M. Organizational behavior: A review and reformulation of the field's outcome variables. *Annual Review of Psychology,* 1984, *35,* 627–666.

[14] Bateman, T.S. & Organ, D.W. Job satisfaction and the good soldier: The relationship between affect and employee "citizenship." *Academy of Management Journal,* 1983, *26,* 587–595.

[15] The last of the happy workers. *Psychology Today,* 1982, *16,* 17–18.

[16] Walton, R.E. Quality of working life: What is it? *Sloan Management Review,* 1973, *15*(1), 11–21.

[17] Ozley, L.M. & Ball, J.S. Quality of work life: Initiating successful efforts in labor-management organizations. *Personnel Administrator,* May 1982, *27,* p. 27.

[18] Walton, R.E. Quality of working life: What is it? *Sloan Management Review,* 1973, *15*(1), 11–21.

[19] Eder, P.F. Telecommuters: The stay-at-home workforce of the future. *The Futurist,* June 1983, *17,* 30–32.

[20] Salomon, I. & Salomon, M. Telecommuting: The employee's perspective. *Technological Forecasting and Social Change,* 1984, *25,* 15–28.

[21] Lawler, E.E. & Ledford, G.E. Productivity and the quality of work life. *National Productivity Review,* Winter 1981–1982, *2,* 23–36.

[22] Jenkins, K.M. & Shimada, J. Quality circles in the service sector. *Supervisory Management,* August 1981, *26,* p. 4.

[23] Lawler, E.E. & Mohrman, S.A. Quality circles after the fad. *Harvard Business Review,* January-February 1985, *63,* 65–71.

[24] Gregerman, I.B. Introduction to quality circles: An approach to participative problem-solving. *Industrial Management,* September-October 1979, *21*(5), 21–26.

WHAT DO YOU THINK? NOTE

There are no incorrect answers to this question. It may be easier to begin by identifying the motivating properties of tasks which you view as unimportant. Then focus on those which you view as essential. Carefully consider your chosen career or job. What will that job provide in terms of the motivating properties you identified as essential to you? If you are not familiar with an occupation or job, you might interview someone in that occupation. Ask them to complete the short questionnaire in Exercise 2.2, and compare their ratings of their job with the motivating properties of tasks that you identified as most important to you. How do your expectations match up to the properties of the job?

CHAPTER THREE

Staffing the Organization

PROLOGUE

Doug picked up the phone to call the personnel department. One of his employees had just resigned to take a higher-paying job with a competitor across town. Doug needed to schedule some interviews right away. He had to fill the position quickly since the company's busy season was rapidly approaching, and he couldn't afford to have that position open when the heavy work load hit. Besides, it would take at least two weeks to orient the replacement and bring him up to speed.

Personnel had several resumes on file and would be able to schedule three interviews per day next week. "I hate to interview job applicants," Doug thought as he hung up the phone. "They're nervous, I'm nervous. And I'm never quite sure what I should ask them."

LEARNING OBJECTIVES

After successful completion of this chapter, you should be able to

- Understand the importance of the staffing process to human relations within organizations,
- Discuss the major employment-related laws that impact staffing decisions,
- Conduct an effective employment interview,
- Discuss several potential problems that commonly arise during the employment interview,
- Understand the importance of orientation programs for new employees,
- Identify important topics these orientation programs should cover, and
- Explain how managers can legally and effectively terminate employees without damaging human relations within the organization.

PART ONE: Human Relations in Organizations

HUMAN RELATIONS AND STAFFING

Understand the importance of the staffing process to human relations within organizations.

This chapter will provide information on the **staffing** process which, for the purposes of this discussion, includes **recruitment, interviewing, selection, orientation**, and **termination**. The information should help managers like Doug become more comfortable and more effective in performing these staffing activities.

The five elements of the staffing process are among the most important activities in which managers engage.[1] They can have a dramatic effect on human relations. New employees are impressionable. They are very receptive to information regarding their new job, the organization, and their manager. Opinions or beliefs formed during the first few weeks on the job may be long-lasting. Thus, not only is it important to carefully select competent new employees from the job applicants, but also it is critical to help these new employees quickly become adjusted to the organization. What happens during the selection and orientation process has long-lasting effects upon human relations within the organization.

Contributing to the difficulties faced in employee staffing are several levels of governmental oversight in the form of employee-related legislation. These laws, primarily designed to ensure equality of employment, are critical in the staffing process.

EMPLOYMENT-RELATED LAW

There are three basic categories of equal-employment laws with which managers and employees must be familiar: federal laws, **common law**, and state and municipal laws. Managers must be informed about these laws so that their staffing activities are in compliance with the provisions of these laws. Further, compliance with these laws generally contributes to good human relations. Employees must be familiar with employment-related laws so they can be sure to obtain their rights under the law. Since most state and municipal laws are based on federal law, the discussion will begin with and emphasize federal law. Common law is frequently overlooked, but several areas of common law can have important implications for managers' selection decisions. Finally, some aspects of state and municipal law will be compared with federal law.

Federal Employment-Related Law

Discuss the major employment-related laws that impact staffing decisions.

Several important federal laws passed since 1960 have important implications for managers making employment decisions. It is imperative to understand the provisions of these laws to avoid exposing your organization to charges of discrimination against, or unfair treatment of, protected groups of employees.

Civil Rights Act of 1964, Title VII

This federal law prohibits discrimination in employment on the basis of an individual's race, color, religion, sex, or national origin. The intent of this legislation is to make these factors irrelevant in employment decisions. In other words, employment decisions must be based entirely upon qualifications and job performance.

This Act also established an enforcement agency, the Equal Employment Opportunity Commission (EEOC). However, this agency had no enforcement power until the Equal Employment Act of 1972 amended Title VII giving the EEOC the power to take employers to court. The Act covers private employers engaged in interstate commerce who have a minimum of 15 employees, as well as federal, state, and municipal governments.

In 1978, Title VII was again amended by the Pregnancy Discrimination Act, which prohibits discrimination in employment on the basis of pregnancy. This law requires employers to treat pregnancy as an illness with respect to time off and other personnel matters. Employees cannot be terminated or refused employment because of pregnancy.

Sexual Discrimination–Sexual Harassment. **Sexual harassment** is not specifically prohibited by the Civil Rights Act of 1964, however, the United States Supreme Court has ruled that it is to be considered a form of prohibited sexual discrimination. This ruling makes sexual harassment, in effect, discrimination on the basis of sex, and mandates coverage under Title VII.

Organizations must develop a clear policy against sexual harassment. Further, given the number of such claims that are reported, and assuming that many more go unreported, organizations must deal with this problem directly. Surveys indicate that somewhere between 42 and 88 percent of all working women have been victims of sexual harassment on the job.[2]

There are two forms of prohibited sexual harassment. The first is requiring sexual favors as a condition of employment; the second is creating a "hostile environment"–subjecting employees to unwelcome sexual advances and/or physical or verbal contact to the extent that the workplace becomes unpleasant for them.[3] While perhaps more common among women, sexual harassment is not limited to female employees. Studies show that approximately 15 percent of working men have experienced sexual harassment on the job.[4]

An effective sexual harassment policy includes several factors. First, sexual harassment should be clearly defined, with examples of prohibited activities provided. To minimize legal liability, organizations must have a formal policy which states in very strong language that sexual harassment will not be tolerated.[5] The confidentiality of victims must be guaranteed. A formal investigation and hearing process should be clearly outlined, so that employees know exactly how to proceed if they become victims of sexual harassment. Finally, specific punishments must be published for employees found guilty of sexual harassment.

The rights of the accused should also be protected. Names of accused employees must be kept strictly confidential throughout the investigation and hearing. These employees should be provided their rights to due process— which includes progressive discipline. It may be desirable to include a formal process of appeal to a higher authority within the organization before severe penalties, such as termination, are imposed.

Equal Pay Act of 1963

This act prohibits employers from paying employees of one sex at different rates for performing substantially similar work. Further, if such a pay inequity is found, the employer cannot reduce the higher wages to eliminate the inequity. To put it simply, the Act prohibits discrimination in pay on the basis of sex. It does not require that the jobs in question be identical, only "substantially equal." And, it does not prohibit differences in pay altogether. However, any pay inequities must be due to differences in skill, effort, responsibility, working conditions, seniority, merit, quantity of production, quality of production, or any factor other than sex.[6] The Act is also administered by the EEOC.

Age Discrimination in Employment Act of 1967

This Act prohibits discrimination in employment on the basis of age for persons between 40 and 70 years of age. Specifically, employers may not refuse to hire or cannot terminate an individual because of age. Also administered by the EEOC, this Act seeks to make age irrelevant in employment decisions unless age is a "bona fide occupational qualification" (BFOQ) to perform the job successfully. There are few jobs where age is critical to job performance. An example might be an actor playing the part of a young child. Obviously, someone between the ages of 40 and 70 would have difficulty performing this job. However, for most jobs in most organizations, age is not a bona fide occupational qualification. It should be noted that BFOQs may be used with respect to any of the other protected groups as well (for example, hiring a female to play the role of a mother in a play).

Vocational Rehabilitation Act of 1973

The Act requires employers having contracts of at least $2,500 with the federal government to take affirmative action to employ the handicapped. Affirmative action means that employers will actively seek out qualified handicapped individuals for employment. A handicapped person is anyone who has a physical or mental disability, has a history of such a disability even though not presently suffering from it, or is considered as having such a disability.[7] In order to be covered by the Act, a handicapped person must be capable of performing the job, "with reasonable accommodation." Employers are required to make reasonable modifications to equipment, furniture, or the way the work is performed to make it possible for handicapped individuals to successfully perform the job.[8] For example, if a person in a wheelchair applied for a secretarial job and was not hired because he couldn't fit his wheelchair under the desk, he would most likely be covered by the Act. A minor modification, such as putting blocks of wood under the legs of the desk, might make it possible for the handicapped person to perform the job. This Act is administered by the Department of Labor's Office of Federal Contract Compliance Programs (OFCCP).

AIDS. The Supreme Court has ruled that a person with a contagious disease may be considered handicapped and therefore covered under the Vocational Rehabilitation Act. Further, AIDS is specifically defined as a protected handicap

Employers must make reasonable modifications to equipment, furniture, or the way the work is performed so that handicapped individuals can perform the job.

in several states such as California, New York, Illinois, Florida, Washington, and Wisconsin.[9] This ruling protects persons with AIDS against discrimination in employment under the provisions of the Act.

Two primary considerations bear on whether an employee with AIDS can continue working. First, the risk posed to other employees. According to health officials, in most work settings there is very little chance of the AIDS virus being transmitted. The second issue is the employee's ability to perform the work. If the employee can adequately perform assigned duties, it is unlikely that the organization could legally terminate that person's employment.[10] To put it simply, "the criteria used to determine whether or not a person with AIDS is physically qualified to perform a specific job should be identical to those used in determining whether or not any handicapped individual is qualified."[11]

Another issue to be addressed is the fear likely to be felt by employees who find they are working alongside a person with AIDS. To some extent, this fear is understandable; according to the National Center for Disease Control, the number of AIDS cases doubles every 12 to 15 months, and there will be 250,000 AIDS patients by 1991.

Organizations must comply with federal employment law which prohibits firing AIDS sufferers who continue to perform adequately on their assigned tasks, and as long as they pose no threat to other employees. At the same time, however, organizations must overcome any fear and anxiety on the part of other employees. Left unchecked, this fear may grow into hysteria which may affect their job performance. Two primary methods of handling this problem are a formal AIDS policy, and information.

The formal policy should consist of several components. Since many employees do not have a good understanding of the disease, the policy statement must first clearly define and describe AIDS. This definition should include a description of how the virus is and is not spread. It must be emphasized that AIDS is not spread by casual contact which occurs on most jobs, nor by eating in common lunchrooms, breathing the same air, and so on. The policy should then describe the federal law which prohibits discrimination against the handicapped, and state clearly that the organization does not discriminate against individuals with AIDS, as long as they pose no hazard to themselves or others.[12] Thus, a good AIDS policy not only clearly addresses how the organization intends to treat employees who contract the AIDS disease, but also provides substantial information about the disease for other employees.

Vietnam-Era Veteran's Readjustment Act of 1974

This Act requires government contractors (having contracts of at least $10,000) and federal agencies to take affirmative action to hire Vietnam-Era Veterans. Thus, employers must actively recruit qualified Vietnam-Era veterans for vacant positions. This Act is administered by the OFCCP.

Occupational Safety and Health Act of 1970

The purpose of this Act is "to assure so far as possible every working man and woman in the Nation safe and healthful working conditions and to preserve our human resource."[13] The Act applies to businesses affecting interstate commerce. The phrase "affecting interstate commerce" is interpreted very broadly so that it covers virtually all businesses in the United States and its territories. The Act also created an administrative agency, the Occupational Safety and Health Administration (OSHA). OSHA has the authority to set standards, conduct inspections, and enforce the provisions of the Act through citations and penalties.

Section 5(a) of the Act states

"Each employer
(1) shall furnish to each of his employees employment and a place of employment which are free from recognized hazards that are causing or are likely to cause death or serious physical harm to his employees;
(2) shall comply with occupational safety and health standards promulgated under the Act."[14]

Further, the Act prohibits employers from retaliating against employees who refuse to perform an assigned job they believe is unsafe, if they are unable to notify OSHA before they are scheduled to perform.

Immigration Reform and Control Act of 1986

This law requires employers to verify a job applicant's employment eligibility. Prior to the passage of this law an employer was permitted to hire an illegal alien. This law makes it illegal to hire an alien who is not eligible to obtain employment in the United States. The Immigration and Naturalization Service, which enforces the law, has a verification form which must be filled out by an employer for each new employee, certifying that the applicant is eligible to work in the U.S. Applicants are currently required to provide documents such as passports, resident alien cards, certificates of U.S. citizenship, Social Security cards, driver's licenses, or birth certificates to prove that they are legally eligible to work in this country.[15]

Common Law

Much attention has been focused on the federal employment-related laws. These might be called statutory law, since they were established by legislation (statute). Another body of law, frequently overlooked by employers, is common law. Common law is not created by legislation, but consists of the set of decisions (opinions) made by judges in actual court cases. These decisions are part of a permanent record that is used to guide other judges in deciding similar cases. Managers must be aware of three distinct areas of common law: (1) employer liability for employee misconduct, (2) **wrongful discharge**, and (3) **defamation**.[16]

Employer Liability for Employee Misconduct

This area of common law covers accidental or deliberate harm caused by an employee to other persons. Two separate doctrines, **respondeat superior** and **negligent hiring and retention**, determine the extent of employer liability.[17]

Respondeat superior covers situations where an employee injures another person during normal work hours. For example, if an employee at the checkout counter of a grocery store dropped a case of soft drinks on a customer's foot, the employer may be held liable for paying for the damages. The employee action must occur at a work location, during normal work hours, and the action must be associated with the employee's normal work activities.[18]

Negligent hiring and retention, a relatively new development, has important implications for employers. A major difference between this doctrine and respondeat superior is that under the doctrine of negligent hiring and retention, the harmful act does not have to occur at a work location, during normal work hours, and does not have to be associated with the employer's normal work activities.[19] The basic idea here is that employers may be held responsible for not exercising proper care in hiring and supervising an employee whose misconduct harms another person. In one instance, a Missouri Court of Appeals ruled that the parents of a secretary had the right to sue the company after their daughter was assaulted and killed by a fellow employee. The employee had served three years in a Missouri prison on a rape and robbery conviction before being hired by the company. The court agreed with the parents' claim that the company should have known that this employee was likely to harm others if not carefully supervised.[20]

To avoid liability under these two doctrines, employers must prove to the court that they engage in careful screening of applicants and responsible supervision of employees to protect the safety and welfare of other employees and the public.

Wrongful Discharge

For many years, employers operated under what has been referred to as the **"employment at will" doctrine**, which permitted employers to fire employees for a good reason, for no reason, or even for a bad reason. This doctrine has been changing over the last 20 years because of court decisions under common law. The trend has been more and more toward what might be called a "termination for good reason" doctrine, under which employers must have a good, job-related reason for terminating employees. During the 1970s, state courts began hearing cases where employees claimed they were fired for no good reason. Employees win approximately 70 percent of these cases that go before a jury, and the average jury award in wrongful discharge cases has been $500,000.[21] Several different types of cases have been tried, including implied contract, violation of public policy, and managerial malpractice.[22]

Courts have found that statements made by managers and statements in employee handbooks are **implied contracts**. For example, if a manager tells an applicant during the employment interview that job security is one important benefit offered by the organization, the courts might interpret this statement as a promise of continued employment. If this employee were later terminated, the courts may require that he be reinstated. Managers must understand that their statements may be viewed by the courts as implied contracts. Managers may unknowingly commit the organization to a long-term relationship with an ineffective employee.

Wrongful discharge can be the result of *managerial malpractice,* should an employee be discharged for actions such as filing a worker's compensation claim, or refusing to perform an unethical or illegal act. Malpractice could also be charged if employees are discharged to avoid paying their pension benefits. And, managerial malpractice is evident when terminated employees have not been provided accurate performance evaluations or were not warned when their jobs were in jeopardy.

Wrongful discharge cases also arise when employees are terminated for reasons that are contrary to public policy. Perhaps the best known of these

---

> ## HUMAN RELATIONS IN ACTION
>
> ### "Name, Rank, and Serial Number"
>
> How many old war movies have you watched where the hero has been captured by the enemy and bravely tells his captors that he will tell them only his name, rank, and serial number? More and more, this is about all you can expect employers to tell you about their previous employees because of potential liability for damages due to employee claims of defamation.
>
> In *Carney vs. Memorial Hospital,* a former employee charged defamation because the hospital stated that he had been discharged "for cause." The hospital argued that it could not have defamed the employee with such a neutral statement as "for cause." The employee claimed that the phrase "for cause" implied that he was incompetent, which makes it more difficult for him to find replacement employment. The New York Court of Appeals agreed and ruled that the employee was entitled to a trial.
>
> In *Lewis vs. Equitable Life,* the employer had a policy of not discussing former employees with prospective employers. The employer discharged four employees for "gross insubordination" and made them aware of the reason for their discharge. However, the employer did not disclose the reasons for discharge to other persons or organizations. The Minnesota Court of Appeals found that when these employees sought new jobs they would certainly be asked by prospective employers the reason they left their previous employer. The Court stated that this gave the employee two choices: he or she could lie about the reasons for dismissal or make the prospective employer aware of the previous employer's reasons for discharge. Since the court felt that the claim of gross insubordination was unsubstantiated, the result was that when one of these employees was asked for the reason he or she was discharged from previous employment and told the truth, the previous employer defamed this employee! These employees received a substantial compensatory and punitive damage award.
>
> Source: Dube, L.E., Jr. Employment references and the law. *Personnel Journal,* 1986, 65, 87–91.

---

cases involves the "whistleblower"—the employee who makes public an organization's illegal or unethical practices.

Defamation

Most of us are familiar with libel (defamation by a written statement) and slander (defamation by an oral statement). Both can cause mental or psychological harm. They typically damage a person's reputation or cause others to avoid doing business with (or hiring) the individual. These concepts have become important in the area of employee selection decisions; in particular, defamation is related to employment references. If an employer provides a negative reference on an employee, the employee may seek damages in court for defamation. Specifically, a manager may be held liable for making a derogatory statement about an employee or former employee that is known to be false or which cannot be verified. Managers may also be liable if they make known derogatory information about employees or former employees to third parties who have no right to such information.[23]

This area of common law varies from state to state. Some states, recognizing that employers need to exchange information about their former employees, provide employers with "qualified" or "conditional" privilege. This privilege offers employers some protection against lawsuits regarding the information they provide about former employees, as long as this information is provided in good faith. If a manager supplied questionable or false information about a former employee with the intent to hurt this employee, the employer would lose protection under qualified or conditional privilege.

This employee reference area can be difficult for managers. Information which managers truly believe to be accurate, but for which there is no proof "beyond a reasonable doubt," may be troublesome. If employees question this type of information, employers may be found liable. Even organizations which try to avoid these problems by offering "no information" may be in trouble; a court found in favor of an employee who charged defamation because his previous employer stated that he had "suddenly resigned."[24] The court stated that the phrase "suddenly resigned" implied resignation under suspicious conditions. Thus, the employee's ability to find subsequent employment in other organizations may have been damaged. As a result of these types of court cases, many employers are now providing only minimal information about their previous employees—date of hire, positions held, final pay rate, and date of separation.

This discussion of defamation has two important implications for managers. First, they must be aware of the possibility of causing their organization to be held liable because of information about a previous employee provided as part of a routine background check by another organization. Managers should never provide any "hearsay," unsubstantiated, or non-job-related information about previous employees. The second implication concerns the quality of information received as part of a background check conducted on a prospective employee. Employers are increasingly reluctant to provide information concerning previous employees; this reluctance makes it advisable to cultivate other sources of information about job applicants.

State and Municipal Laws

While many state and municipal laws simply echo federal laws, in some cases there are important differences. Whenever there is a difference between federal law and state or municipal law, federal law takes precedence—except when the state or municipal law is more stringent or extends protection to groups not covered by federal law. Thus, state and municipal equal employment law can extend, but cannot reduce or eliminate, the provisions of federal law. Managers should recognize that state laws may be more rigorous than federal law. Organizations have run into legal problems when they were in compliance with federal law, but were violating a state law of which they were unaware.

Implications of Equal-Employment Legislation

Coverage of equal-employment legislation is important for two basic reasons. First, managers must be sure their employment decisions are in compliance with federal, state, and municipal laws. Second, and equally important, managers' compliance with these laws can produce positive employee relations. Think about what these laws require. They state that certain factors should be irrelevant in employment decisions—that employment decisions should be

HUMAN RELATIONS IN ACTION

The Other Side of "Name, Rank, and Serial Number"

In 1983, Courtney I. Saunders was hired by the City of New York as an assistant deputy commissioner in the Human Resources Administration. His qualifications included degrees from Amherst College and Columbia University School of Law, and experience as a partner in a Washington law firm. His starting salary was $63,150.

Soon after Saunders was hired, a coworker who had graduated from Columbia University, became suspicious and began checking. He found that C. I. Saunders was really Isaac J. Coleman. Mr. Coleman was a high school dropout who had been arrested 14 times in 7 states! By the time Coleman was jailed, it had cost the city around $10,000 in salary and other expenses. It could have been worse.

This situation is an example of a potentially growing problem. How could something like this have happened, especially in the Human Resources Administration of a major city? There are two primary reasons. One, already discussed in the chapter and in the previous Human Relations in Action box, is the potential liability of employers because of defamatory statements made about previous employees during background checks. As a result, previous employers are extremely reluctant to provide other organizations with anything but "name, rank, and serial number." A second reason has to do with the efforts of employers to hold down costs. Many employers simply cannot afford to conduct expensive, time-consuming background checks of all job applicants. As a result, it is becoming more and more difficult to detect false information that is collected during the selection process.

Some employers are reversing this trend, however. They believe that money spent checking the qualifications of prospective employees is well spent. For example, New York City now requires job applicants to fill out a 20-page questionnaire on their background. The applicant must also have the completed form notarized, which makes providing false information a crime of perjury. McGraw-Hill requires new employees to sign a statement giving it permission to verify university degrees. Other companies are requiring more than one interview as a means of detecting false information.

However, there is a catch to these increased attempts to detect false information provided by job applicants. If an organization engages in too many of these activities, or is too persistent in trying to detect false information, employees may feel they aren't trusted. This attitude can translate into employee discontent and deteriorating human relations within the organization. There is a fine line that organizations must walk between detecting false information provided by prospective employees and maintaining positive human relations.

Source: The boom in digging into a job applicant's past. *Business Week,* June 11, 1984, 68E, 68H.

---

based on job-related qualifications and job-related performance. There are very few situations where an employer can argue that sex, age, race, color, religion, national origin, or handicap influence an individual's ability to successfully perform a job. In other words, there are very few situations where these factors are bona fide occupational qualifications. When a manager ignores the irrelevant factors, and makes decisions based on objective qualifications and job performance, employees will feel they are being equitably treated. These employees will be committed to accomplishing the goals of an organization which deals with them fairly and objectively.

Exhibit 3.1
Pre-employment inquiry guide

Subject	Permissible Inquiries	Inquiries to be Avoided
1. Name	"Have you worked for this company under a different name?" Is any additional information relative to change of name or nickname necessary to enable a check of your work and educational record? If yes, explain.	Inquiries about name which would indicate applicant's lineage, ancestry, national origin, or descent.
2. Marital and family status	Whether applicant can meet specified work schedules or has activities, commitments or responsibilities that may hinder the meeting of work attendance requirements. Inquiries as to a duration of stay on job or anticipated absences which are made to males and females alike.	Any inquiry indicating whether an applicant is married, single, divorced, or engaged, etc. Number and age of children. Information on child-care arrangements. Any questions concerning pregnancy. Any such questions which directly or indirectly result in limitation of job opportunities.
3. Age	Requiring proof of age in the form of a work permit or a certificate of age—if a minor. Requiring proof of age by birth certificate after being hired. Inquiry as to whether or not the applicant meets the minimum age requirements as set by law and requirement that upon hire proof of age must be submitted in the form of a birth certificate or other forms of proof of age. If age is a legal requirement, "if hired, can you furnish proof of age?," or statement that hire is subject to verification of age. Inquiry as to whether or not an applicant is younger than the employer's regular retirement age.	Requirement that applicant state age or date of birth. Requirement that applicant produce proof of age in the form of a birth certificate or baptismal record. The Age Discrimination in Employment Act of 1967 forbids discrimination against persons between the ages of 40 and 70.
4. Handicaps	For employers subject to the provisions of the Rehabilitation Act of 1973, applicants may be "invited" to indicate how and to what extent they are handicapped. The employer must indicate to applicants that: (1) compliance with the invitation is voluntary; (2) the information is being sought only to remedy discrimination or provide opportunities for the handicapped; (3) the information will be kept confidential; and (4) refusing to	Any employer must be prepared to prove that any physical and mental requirements for a job are due to "business necessity" and the safe performance of the job. Except in cases where undue hardship can be proven, employers must make "reasonable accommodation" for the physical and mental limitations of an employee or applicant. "Reasonable accommodation" includes alteration of duties, alteration of work schedule, alteration of physi-

Exhibit 3.1 *(continued)*

Subject	Permissible Inquiries	Inquiries to be Avoided
	provide the information will not result in adverse treatment. All applicants can be asked if they are able to carry out all necessary job assignments and perform them in a safe manner.	cal setting, and provision of aids. The Rehabilitation Act of 1973 forbids employers from asking job applicants general questions about whether they are handicapped or asking them about the nature and severity of their handicaps.
5. Sex	Inquiry or restriction of employment is permissible only where a bona fide occupational qualification exists. (This BFOQ exception is interpreted very narrowly by the courts and the EEOC). The burden of proof rests on the employer to prove that the BFOQ does exist and that *all* members of the affected class are incapable of performing the job. Sex of applicant may be requested (preferably not on the employment application) for affirmative action purposes but may not be used as an employment criterion.	Sex of applicant. Any other inquiry which would indicate sex. Sex is not a BFOQ because a job involves physical labor (such as heavy lifting) beyond the capacity of *some* women nor can employment be restricted because the job is traditionally labeled "men's work" or "women's work." Applicant's sex cannot be used as a factor for determining whether or not an applicant will be satisfied in a particular job. Questions about an applicant's height or weight, unless demonstrably necessary as requirements for the job.
6. Race or color	General distinguishing physical characteristics such as scars, etc., to be used for identification purposes. Race may be requested (preferably not on the employment application) for affirmative action purposes but may not be used as an employment criterion.	Applicant's race. Color of applicant's skin, eyes, hair, etc., or other questions directly or indirectly indicating race or color.
7. Address or duration of residence	Applicant's address. Inquiry into length of stay at current and previous addresses. "How long a resident of this state or city?"	Specific inquiry into foreign address which would indicate national origin. Names and relationship of persons with whom applicant resides. Whether applicant owns or rents home.
8. Birthplace	"Can you after employment submit a birth certificate or other proof of U.S. citizenship?"	Birthplace of applicant. Birthplace of applicant's parents, spouse, or other relatives. Requirement that applicant submit a birth certificate before employment. Any other inquiry into national origin.
9. Religion	An applicant may be advised concerning normal hours and days of work required by the job to avoid possible conflict with religious or other personal conviction. How-	Applicant's religious denomination or affiliation, church, parish, pastor, or religious holidays observed. Any inquiry to indicate or identify religious denomination or customs.

Exhibit 3.1 *(continued)*
Pre-employment inquiry guide

Subject	Permissible Inquiries	Inquiries to be Avoided
	ever, except in cases where undue hardship can be proven, employers and unions must make "reasonable accommodation" for religious practices of an employee or prospective employee. "Reasonable accommodation" may include voluntary substitutes, flexible scheduling, lateral transfer, change of job assignments, or the use of an alternative to payment of union dues.	Applicants may not be told that employees are required to work on religious holidays which are observed as days of complete prayer by members of their specific faith.
10. Military record	Type of education and experience in service as it relates to a particular job.	Type of discharge.
11. Photograph	May be required for identification after hiring.	Requirement that applicant affix a photograph to his application. Request that applicant, at his option, submit photograph. Requirement of photograph after interview but before hiring.
12. Citizenship	"Are you a citizen of the United States?" "Do you intend to remain permanently in the U.S.?" "If not a citizen, are you prevented from becoming lawfully employed because of visa or immigration status?" Statement that, if hired, applicant may be required to submit proof of citizenship.	"Of what country are you a citizen?" Whether applicant or his parents or spouse are naturalized or native-born U.S. citizens. Date when applicant or parents acquired U.S. citizenship. Requirement that applicant produce his naturalization papers. Whether applicant's parents or spouse are citizens of the U.S.
13. Ancestry or national origin	Languages applicant reads, speaks, or writes fluently. (If another language is necessary to perform the job.)	Inquiries into applicant's lineage, ancestry, national origin, descent, birthplace, or native language. National origin of applicant's parent or spouse.
14. Education	Applicant's academic, vocational, or professional education; school attended. Inquiry into language skills such as reading, speaking, and writing foreign languages.	Any inquiry asking specifically the nationality, racial or religious affiliation of a school. Inquiry as to how foreign language ability was acquired.
15. Experience	Applicant's work experience, including names and addresses of previous employers, dates of employment, reasons for leaving, salary history. Other countries visited.	

Exhibit 3.1 *(continued)*

Subject	Permissible Inquiries	Inquiries to be Avoided
16. Conviction, arrest, and court record	Inquiry into actual *convictions* which relate reasonably to fitness to perform a particular job. (A conviction is a court ruling where the party is found guilty as charged. An arrest is merely the apprehending or detaining of the person to answer the alleged crime).	Any inquiry relating to arrests. Any inquiry into or request for a person's arrest, court, or conviction record if not *substantially related* to functions and responsibilities of the particular job in question.
17. Relatives	Names of applicant's relatives already employed by this company. Names and addresses of parents or guardian (if applicant is a minor).	Name or address of any relative of adult applicant.
18. Notice in case of emergency	Name and address of persons to be notified in case of accident or emergency.	Name and address of *relatives* to be notified in case of accident or emergency.
19. Organizations	Inquiry into any organizations of which applicant is a member, providing the name or character of the organizations does not reveal the race, religion, color, or ancestry of the membership. "List all professional organizations to which you belong. What offices do you hold?"	"List all organizations, clubs, societies, and lodges to which you belong." The names of organizations to which the applicant belongs if such information would indicate through character or name the race, religion, color, or ancestry of the membership.
20. References	"By whom were you referred for a position here?" Names of persons willing to provide references for applicant.	Requiring the submission of a religious reference. Requesting reference from applicant's pastor.
21. Credit rating	None.	Any questions concerning credit rating, charge accounts, etc. Ownership of car.
22. Miscellaneous	Notice to applicants that any misstatements or omissions of material facts in the application may be cause for dismissal.	Any inquiry should be avoided which, although not specifically listed among the above, is designed to elicit information concerning race, color, ancestry, age, sex, religion, handicap, or arrest and court record unless based upon a bona fide occupational qualification.

Source: Koen, C. M., Jr. 1980. The pre-employment inquiry guide. Reprinted with the permission of *Personnel Journal, 59,* 825–829.

THE STAFFING PROCESS

This overview of legislation affecting employment decisions provides the necessary background for a consideration of staffing decisions. As you have read, this legislation exerts a strong influence on the staffing process. Legislation has an impact on what types of information can be requested on job application forms, in background checks with previous employers, and during employment interviews. Law influences virtually every other employment-related decision managers might be called upon to make. It guides decisions concerning which employees are selected to enter advanced training programs; reward decisions; promotion decisions; and transfer, demotion, and termination decisions. Knowledge of these laws can prevent requesting or using prohibited information when making employment-related decisions. Exhibit 3.1 presents a list of questions that can and cannot be asked during the selection process.

The staffing process was described earlier as comprising the activities of recruitment, interviewing, selection, orientation, and termination. Exhibit 3.2 expands and illustrates the staffing process.

Recruitment

The selection process typically begins with recruitment, which ensures that the organization has adequate numbers of qualified job applicants available at all times. In practice, recruitment can be divided into two categories, **internal** and **external**. Individual managers are routinely involved in internal recruitment, but only peripherally in external recruitment. Recruitment outside the company is the primary responsibility of the personnel or human resource departments. Both types of recruitment impact human relations within an organization.

Internal Recruitment

Many organizations have a "promote from within" policy. When positions become available, the organization would prefer to fill them with current employees rather than external job applicants. There are several potential advantages to emphasizing internal recruitment.[25]

Current employees have less to learn about the organization and how the work is performed. Thus, promoting a current employee to fill an open posi-

Exhibit 3.2
The staffing process

RECRUITMENT	SELECTION	ORIENTATION	TERMINATION
Internal	Application Blanks	Organizational	Resignation
Job Posting	Resumes	Departmental	Layoff
Career Paths	Background Checks		Retirement
	Interviewing		Discharge
External			

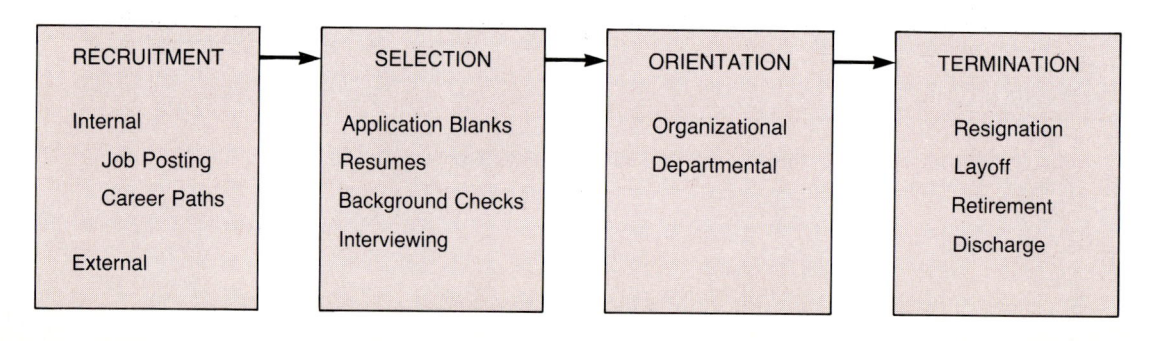

CHAPTER THREE: Staffing the Organization

Newspaper advertising is an effective external recruiting technique for many different types of jobs.

tion will generally result in that person performing at acceptable levels much sooner than someone hired from the outside. And, since the current employee already knows the organization, the probability for this person to be successful on the job is higher than for someone from the outside (assuming both are equally qualified). The current employee knows what the organization expects from its employees and what it provides in terms of rewards. Further, it costs less to recruit current employees to fill positions than to recruit externally. Assuming the organization has an external recruiting procedure in place for entry-level positions, it makes sense to move people up within the organization and recruit externally to refill entry-level positions.

Promoting qualified employees from within shows concern for employees and their careers. This concern encourages employees to be more highly committed to accomplishing the organization's goals and better satisfied with their employment.

Conversely, several potential disadvantages of emphasizing internal recruitment are significant. Since only entry-level employees are hired from the outside, few new ideas and perspectives are brought into the organization. In addition, current employees who are promoted to positions of greater responsibility may need additional training for these new jobs. Further, a promote-from-within policy may create conflict among employees who are in competition for a promotion. Finally, a current employee may not be the most highly qualified person for the job.

Implementation. Schneider and Schmitt identify two primary methods—**job posting** and **career paths**—of implementing internal recruitment.[26] Probably the most frequently used, job posting involves posting open positions on a bulletin board. The information posted typically includes a description of the duties and responsibilities associated with the job, as well as any necessary qualifications. Current employees who are interested in the position and are qualified for it are invited to submit their names for consideration.

Internal recruitment can keep an employee on a career path—a series of jobs or positions through which an individual is likely to progress within the organization. When organizations develop career paths for entry-level positions, they are saying to new employees, "these are the positions you are likely to hold as you progress in your career with us." Employees know that the organization is interested in encouraging their development and progress. Exhibit 3.3 shows a career path in a corporate marketing division.

External Recruitment

In those firms with a promote-from-within policy, recruiting applicants from the outside (external recruitment) typically occurs only for entry-level positions or positions for which no current employees are qualified. However, some firms choose to actively recruit externally for most positions. These firms believe that internal recruitment tends to maintain the status quo. In other words, there are potential advantages to bringing in "new blood" from time to time. New employees often have fresh, and sometimes better, ideas which can improve organizational performance. An in-depth discussion of external recruitment is beyond the scope of this book, since most individual managers are not heavily involved in this process. However, managers do become involved once the personnel department has developed a pool of qualified applicants. They review application blanks, resumes, background checks and any other available sources of information that will help predict the applicant's potential for successful job performance. In addition, the manager in whose department the opening exists will typically conduct the employment interviews.

Exhibit 3.3
Career paths within a marketing division

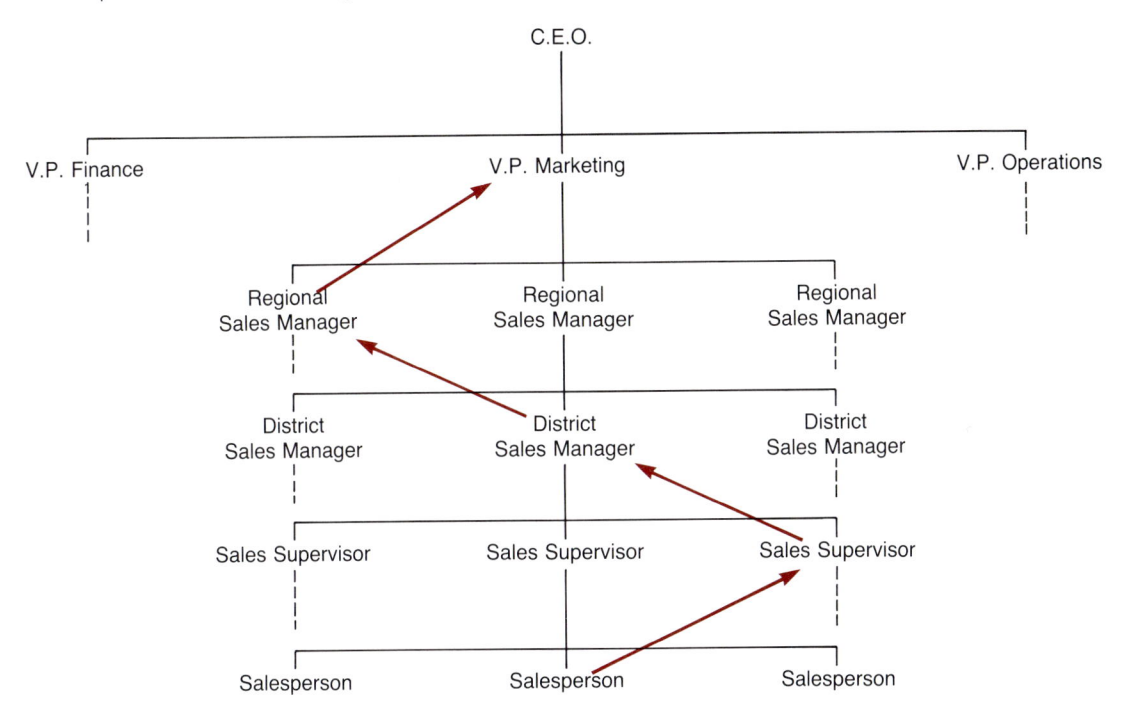

```
                              C.E.O.
                                |
        ┌───────────────────────┼───────────────────────┐
    V.P. Finance            V.P. Marketing          V.P. Operations
                                |
              ┌─────────────────┼─────────────────┐
          Regional           Regional           Regional
        Sales Manager      Sales Manager      Sales Manager
              |                  |                  |
              ┌─────────────────┼─────────────────┐
          District            District           District
        Sales Manager      Sales Manager      Sales Manager
              |                  |                  |
              ┌─────────────────┼─────────────────┐
         Sales Supervisor   Sales Supervisor   Sales Supervisor
              |                  |                  |
              ┌─────────────────┼─────────────────┐
          Salesperson        Salesperson        Salesperson
```

Sources of Selection Information

The primary sources of selection information are application blanks, resumes, background checks, and interviews. The purpose of each of these selection devices is to collect job-related information for use in making the selection decision. One employment-related law discussed earlier requires that any information requested of job applicants be job-related. In other words, the information must be limited to that necessary for the manager to make an informed decision about the applicant's ability to perform the job.

Application Blanks, Background Checks, and Resumes

Application blanks usually ask for general personal information; training, education, and experience; and work-related references. It cannot be stressed too heavily that any information requested must be job related.

Background checks were discussed earlier, pointing out that many employers are reluctant to provide prospective employers with information on previous employees because of potential legal difficulties. As a result, it may be difficult to obtain anything more than minimal information about job applicants from previous employers.

Resumes are quite similar to application blanks. Most job applicants include the same basic categories of information on their resumes as on application blanks. Managers should, however, review an applicant's resume carefully for information not provided by other selection devices.

RETURN TO THE PROLOGUE

In the Prologue, Doug was not looking forward to the selection task facing him. He obviously did not enjoy interviewing job applicants, making selection decisions, or orienting new employees. However, since these activities are the first activities in which new employees are involved, they can substantially affect human relations. Managers like Doug must realize the importance of employee selection and view it not as an unpleasant task to get completed as quickly as possible, but rather as an opportunity to set the tone of future human relations within the department or work group.

Interviews

Interviews are widely accepted by both employers and job applicants. It is difficult to imagine an employer offering a job to an applicant without an interview; it is equally difficult to imagine an applicant accepting a job without being interviewed.

The interview should be viewed as an exchange of information. Unfortunately, managers sometimes conduct interviews as if the only purpose was to collect information from the applicant. It is obviously important to collect information during an interview, but it is equally important to provide information to the applicant concerning the job, the organization, the working conditions, and so on.

Selection decisions are made by two separate parties—the organization and the individual. Both need adequate information about the other, to make decisions that will be acceptable to both parties. Remember the discussion of the psychological employment contract in the previous chapter. This understanding is largely established during the interview and selection process. The information that applicants receive during this process will strongly influence the expectations of the organization that they develop.

The purpose of an interview is the same as that of any other selection device—to collect job-related information about the applicant. Interviews are subject to the same employment-related laws as any other selection device. Below are suggestions for how to conduct an interview that is in compliance with the law.

1. Develop a set of job requirements. This task can be accomplished by means of a job analysis, which is an objective examination of the work, specific duties, and responsibilities. A job analysis typically results in a **job description**, which is a written document that specifies the job title, primary duties, and employee responsibilities. A **job analysis** may also produce **job specifications**, which is a written statement of the minimum qualifications, training, education, and experience necessary for an individual to be able to successfully perform the job.
2. Develop a set of questions based on the results of the job analysis (job description and job specifications).
3. Ask all job applicants the same set of questions.

Types of Interviews. Asking the same standard questions of all job applicants is known as a **structured interview**. In its extreme form, an interviewer would simply read the questions from a prepared interview checklist, and would not ask any other questions. The advantage of this interview form is that it increases the likelihood that the interview will be in compliance with the law. In other words, it decreases the chances that an interviewer may unintentionally ask for information prohibited by one of the state, federal, or municipal laws. The disadvantage of the structured interview is its rigidity. An interviewer might ask an applicant one of the prepared questions and receive a rather strange response, or one that appears to be evasive. In the purely structured interview, the interviewer would not be able to pursue this question further.

The type of interview at the other end of the continuum is the **unstructured interview**. This form of interview does not use a predetermined list of questions. Rather, the interviewer is free to pursue any line of questioning that seems appropriate. The goal is to simply keep the applicant talking, offering information about his qualifications. The disadvantage of this form of interview is its extreme flexibility. The absence of a standard set of questions may lead an inexperienced interviewer to waste time asking for information that is not particularly relevant, while neglecting more important areas. In addition, the possibility of asking for information that is not job-related increases the risk of violating the law.

The most common form of interview is probably the **semistructured interview**, which combines the structured and unstructured forms. The semistructured interview is predominantly (80 to 90 percent) structured. This approach ensures that important questions are asked and any question that might be considered an unfair preemployment inquiry is not asked. The minor portion of the interview that is unstructured provides the interviewer the opportunity to probe into any answers that seem interesting or evasive during the interview.

Conducting the Interview. Having a carefully prepared set of questions will not ensure an effective interview. Much of the effectiveness of the interview depends on the manner in which it is conducted. There are several things which interviewers can do to increase the effectiveness of their interviews.

Conduct an effective employment interview.

1. Preparation. Poor preparation will almost certainly produce an ineffective interview. Good preparation basically involves reviewing all of the selection information (e.g., from resumes, background checks, application blanks) which has been collected prior to the interview. Interviewers should never ask applicants for information that has already been provided (perhaps as many as two or three times). To preclude any doubt about the job requirements or necessary qualifications, the job description and job specifications should be carefully reviewed.
2. Put the applicant at ease. Interviewers should devote the first few minutes of the interview to making the applicant comfortable. Remember, if applicants are uncomfortable or nervous, they may become defensive and less willing to provide information openly. Therefore, a few minutes devoted to

"small talk" about sports, travel to the interview, current events, or the weather may pay great dividends later when the applicant openly talks about his qualifications and background.
3. Ask for job-related information only. This point cannot be overemphasized. Earlier, Exhibit 3.1 presented examples of questions that can and cannot be asked of job applicants.
4. Give the applicant adequate time to ask questions. Applicants should be allowed time to get all of their questions about the job and the organization answered. The applicant also has a very important selection decision to make. He also needs to collect information during the interview in order to make this decision.
5. End the interview positively. Interviews are often rather stressful for applicants. A few minutes of "social time" at the end of the interview may help them relax and feel better about their experience, even if they are not selected for the job. In addition, applicants should be told exactly what will happen next—when a decision is likely to be made, when they can expect to be contacted, and by whom.

Have you ever experienced a particularly bad or good interview, either as a job applicant or interviewer? What exactly made this interview particularly good or particularly bad? As a result of this experience, what advice would you give to managers who must conduct interviews?

> Discuss several potential problems that commonly arise during the employment interview.

Providing Information to Applicants. As mentioned previously, the interview should be viewed as a two-way communication—a process of exchanging, rather than just collecting information. Selection decisions may turn out to be mistakes because the applicant was not provided with enough factual information to make a good decision. As a result, an applicant is placed in a job for which he does not qualify, or the applicant finds that the job isn't at all what was expected. Selection can be a very costly process. Turnover during the initial weeks of employment is a sign of trouble with the organization's selection process. One way to ensure that applicants do have enough good information for their decisions is to conduct realistic job previews, which were discussed in the previous chapter.

Realistic job previews typically occur during the interview. Too often, interviewers paint an extremely "rosy" picture for applicants. They try to sell the applicant on the job and the organization. As a result, applicants may develop unrealistically high expectations of what the organization will provide in terms of rewards and work assignments. When these unrealistic expectations are not met, the new employee may seek other employment, and the selection process must begin again. It is better, in the long run, to risk losing a good applicant during the interview than after he accepts employment. It is less costly to the organization both financially and in terms of its effect upon human relations. Employees with unmet expectations are dissatisfied with their jobs. This dissatisfaction can spread and affect the morale of other employees. Providing realistic information to applicants tells them that the organization is open and honest and trusts its applicants and employees to make their own decisions.

> **WHAT DO YOU THINK?**
>
> The preceding paragraphs have presented several suggestions for managers as they plan and conduct selection interviews. What about the other side of the coin? What should job applicants do before and during selection interviews? How can they best sell themselves to the interviewer? What are some common mistakes that can easily be avoided with a little planning and practice? Given the importance placed on the selection interview in most organizations, job applicants should prepare carefully before each interview.
>
> Develop your own ideas, then turn to the end of the chapter for several attributes that the president of a Los Angeles-based executive search firm looks for in each job applicant.

This openness sets the stage for a positive human relations climate if the applicant joins the organization. The new employee comes into the organization with realistic expectations. This attitude results in generally higher levels of job satisfaction, and lower levels of absenteeism and turnover.[27]

ORIENTATION

Once employees accept employment with the organization, the hiring process moves into another extremely important staffing procedure—orientation of new employees. Orientation is the process of telling new employees about the organization and their job, to help them adjust to the organization and become productive as soon as possible. Orientation can be divided into two categories.[28]

Understand the importance of orientation programs for new employees.

Organizational orientation presents information about the overall organization, its history, its products and activities, its top managers, its personnel policies (such as compensation methods, fringe benefits, health and safety), its physical facilities, and its policies or rules. This orientation is the primary responsibility of the personnel department in most organizations.

Departmental orientation covers job-specific information such as job duties, performance expectations, work rules, rest periods, work hours, a tour of the work station, and introductions to coworkers.

Identify important topics these orientation programs should cover.

An effective orientation program may result in fewer mistakes, higher productivity, higher job satisfaction, lower absenteeism and turnover, and a good human relations climate. While new employees need a great deal of information to adjust to their new surroundings, they should not be overloaded with details. People can receive and digest only a limited amount of information at a time; the orientation program should be scheduled accordingly. Several orientation sessions may be held over the course of several weeks, instead of providing all of the information in a single, long session. It is also a good idea to conduct a follow-up session with new employees to learn if they have retained and understand important information. This session gives new employees a chance to ask about any problems or questions that have arisen that weren't covered in the orientation material. It also provides them the opportunity to clarify any material that they did not understand.

TERMINATION

Explain how managers can legally and effectively terminate employees without damaging human relations within the organizations.

There are four types of termination; resignation, retirement, layoff, and discharge. Resignation, retirement, and even layoff typically do not present the problems that follow discharge. Resignation and retirement are generally voluntary and initiated by the employee. While layoff usually is not a voluntary termination, many employees are at least somewhat understanding when economic necessity makes it necessary to reduce the work force. Discharge, on the other hand, is not so readily accepted by employees.

Managers need to be concerned with these various forms of employment termination for two basic reasons. First, there are the potential legal liabilities associated with wrongful discharge. As mentioned previously, discharged employees are more frequently challenging their discharges in court, and can win, unless the discharge has been carefully planned and executed. Second, but just as important, discharging an employee will often have an impact on the employees who remain. The human relations climate of the entire work group or department can be negatively affected because of an emotional, poorly handled discharge or because of the attention given to a discharge that is challenged in court. On the other hand, a well-managed discharge may actually improve the climate within the work group. If the remaining employees view the discharge as legitimate and necessary, and the discharge is performed in an objective, impersonal manner, remaining employees may react positively.[29]

There are two critical requirements for managers to effectively discharge employees: there must be valid reasons for the discharge, and managers must conduct the discharge interview in a proper manner.

Several categories of misconduct for which employees can be discharged appear in Exhibit 3.4. However, even though an employee engages in one of these forms of misconduct, providing a legitimate reason for discharge, there

---

Exhibit 3.4
Valid reasons for discharging employees

1. Absence without leave
2. Nonperformance of job duties
3. Disobedience of orders
4. Breaches of discipline
5. Disrupting relations with coworkers
6. Lying and falsification
7. Theft
8. Disloyalty and corruption
9. Damage to property or goodwill
10. Disreputable conduct outside the company

Source: Compiled from Avins, A. *Penalties for misconduct on the job.* Dobbs Ferry, New York: Oceana Publications, 1972.

Exhibit 3.5
Guidelines for employee discharge

1. Discharge interviews must be conducted in a private setting.
2. Discharges should not be conducted on a holiday, birthday, or anniversary unless company or employee safety is at stake.
3. Dismissals should not occur on Friday afternoons. This gives the discharged employee the entire weekend to become upset. Discharges should occur early in the week so the employee has a chance to seek other employment immediately.
4. Double-check the frequency with which you counseled, warned, and evaluated the employee. Be sure you have recorded and documented each instance. Include dates and times and take clear notes immediately after each incident. Ask the employee to sign a statement acknowledging that he heard the message.
5. Do not allow poor performers to drag on. Failure to terminate the marginal employee sanctions ineffectiveness and gives the person false hopes.
6. Were the job performance expectations and importance of compliance with company proceudres clarified when the employee was hired?
7. In making the decision to discharge, did you use only firsthand observed evidence?
8. Plan the interview, including the opening, the middle, and the closing.
9. Recognize your own experience or lack thereof. If you are unsure, ask for expert help.
10. Your personal goal in the discharge process is to remain calm, regardless of what the other person does.
11. Identify specific actions and behaviors that necessitated the discharge. Honesty will be respected; placating will not.
12. Encourage discharged employees to talk to you. Let them know you want them to understand the action and feel they deserve straightforward treatment.
13. Assess whether the person you are discharging can endanger you or your organization through reprisal. If you do not trust the employee to leave peacefully, request security support. You must also be aware when the employee has access to sensitive documents and equipment and can endanger or destroy them.
14. Anticipate as many reactions to discharge as possible, remembering who the terminee is. Prepare yourself for loud outbursts, arguments, silence, tears, and disbelief.
15. Never discharge anyone on the phone or with a pink slip in the pay envelope.
16. Treat the person who is losing the job with dignity, even though they may not be able to reciprocate.
17. Avoid talking about how miserable you feel during the interview; this will be perceived as hypocrisy.
18. Do not offer the person advice on how to handle the discharge.
19. Keep the interview short. Long drawn-out discharge interviews prolong the agony and pain for both parties. Avoid telling empathetic stories or quoting from personal experience.
20. Carefully evaluate the advisability of discharging the employee. Have you carefully explored all other alternatives?

Source: Michal-Johnson, P. *Saying good-bye: A manager's guide to employee dismissal.* Glenview, Illinois: Scott, Foresman and Company, 1985, 30–32.

> ### DEVELOPING YOUR HUMAN RELATIONS SKILLS
>
> The information presented in this chapter has significant implications for both managers and employees. As a manager, you should carefully consider the following suggestions.
>
> 1. In all aspects of staffing, collect and retain only job-related information. This not only ensures compliance with the law, it is good practice from two perspectives: making effective staffing decisions, and contributing to good human relations.
> 2. Use many sources of selection information. Do not rely too heavily on just one source such as a resume, application blank or interview. Each of these has its own set of weaknesses and chances for error. Using several sources increases the chances of obtaining accurate information about applicants, since several of these sources may collect similar information.
> 3. Provide only documented job-related information to outside organizations on current and previous employees. Many organizations follow a policy of providing only dates of service of previous employees to outside organizations. This restriction minimizes the chances of being charged with defamation.
> 4. Don't oversell the job and the organization to job applicants. Provide a realistic picture of both, including the good and the bad. Try to give applicants enough accurate information to make an informed decision about working in the organization. In the long run, it is better to lose applicants at this stage before investing money in their training and development than to lose them after they learn the job and/or organization is not what they expected.
> 5. Provide orientation to new employees. Even if your organization does not have a formal orientation program for new employees, develop one on your own for your department. Provide employees with information concerning the organization, the department, and the job to help ensure their success and adjustment to their new surroundings.
> 6. When termination is necessary, follow the progressive discipline process. Be sure that employees have been informed of the specific problem and given time and assistance in correcting their behavior. Be sure also that every step of this process is documented, preferably with a statement (signed by the employee) that he was informed of the problem and offered assistance.

must be *documentation*. Because of the wrongful discharge cases, not only must it be documented that the employee has engaged in some form of misconduct, but also that the employee was counseled and given adequate time to correct the behavior. Most courts look to see if the manager followed a *progressive discipline* program.

Progressive discipline involves the sequential administration of increasingly severe discipline or punishment to an employee who continues to violate rules or engage in misconduct even after being warned. This entire process should be documented. Each time an employee engages in misconduct and is

From your perspective as an employee, the information presented in this chapter also included several suggestions for successful human relations.

1. When seeking a new job, spend sufficient time researching the organization, industry, competitors, products/services, and so on. The degree to which you appear knowledgeable about the organization during the interview may be taken as a surrogate measure of your interest in the job. If the organization had great success or developed a new product that will help cure a terrible disease, you had better know about it when you walk into the room for an interview!
2. Practice interviewing. One of the best ways to rehearse is to engage in mock interviews, perhaps with other students or friends who are about to interview also, and videotape the performances. Among the most educational experiences most of us can have is actually watching ourselves in a particular activity. You may find that you have certain mannerisms or ways of speaking that are annoying or inappropriate for a job interview setting. Sometimes the only way for you to really understand how you will look to a potential employer is to see yourself on tape. This self-appraisal is highly recommended, even for persons who have interviewing experience.
3. Prepare for commonly asked questions. Typical interview questions include "What are you looking for in a job?"; "Why did you apply for a job with us?"; "Describe your ideal job."; "Where do you hope to be in five years? In ten years?"; "We have talked with many applicants. Why should we hire you?". If you are prepared for these and other similar questions, and can handle them easily, your interview will go smoothly. If you aren't prepared and have difficulty answering such questions, you may become upset and have difficulty with other parts of the interview.
4. Ask questions. Being prepared for an interview also means being prepared to ask questions to show your interest in a job with the organization. You should ask questions about the goals and future direction of the organization, as well as about the nature of the job. You should not ask about salary, promotions, or other rewards. These are questions that can be asked once you have been offered the job.

warned, it should be in writing and the employee should be asked to sign a statement acknowledging that he understands what is wrong and what the next step is likely to be.

Conducting the Discharge Interview

From the outset, it should be recognized that a discharge interview is likely to be a very emotional experience for the employee. It requires careful preparation and planning to discharge an employee in such a manner that the employee's dignity remains intact, relations with remaining coworkers are not damaged, and the discharge (if challenged) is not overturned by the courts. Several managers' guidelines for terminating employees are presented in Exhibit 3.5. The importance of planning for the discharge interview cannot be overemphasized; following the guidelines in the table will help prepare for most situations. However, the possibility exists for something unexpected to occur. In this event, the manager should remain calm, not argue with the employee, keep the interview on track, and end it on schedule.

SUMMARY

Managers must be aware of a number of federal, state, and municipal employment-related laws, as well as several areas of common law which impact staffing decisions. The most prominent of the federal laws are Title VII of the Civil Rights Act of 1964, the Equal Pay Act of 1963, the Age Discrimination in Employment Act of 1967, the Vocational Rehabilitation Act of 1973, the Vietnam-Era Veteran's Readjustment Act of 1974, the Occupational Safety and Health Act of 1970, and the Immigration Reform and Control Act of 1986. The intent of this legislation is to make factors such as age, sex, national origin, color, religion, race, marital status, and physical or mental handicap irrelevant in employment decisions. Important areas of common law are: (1) employer liability for employee misconduct (which includes respondeat superior and negligent hiring and retention); (2) wrongful discharge; and (3) defamation.

The staffing process consists of several activities; recruitment, interviewing, selection, orientation, and termination. Managers must weigh the advantages and disadvantages of two forms of recruitment. Internal recruitment may increase employee morale; external recruitment may bring people with new ideas into the organization. Disadvantages of internal recruitment include a lack of new ideas and perspectives, potential conflict among employees who are being considered for a promotion, the need for additional training for current employees who receive promotions, and the possibility that the best person for the job may not be a current employee of the organization.

While application blanks, background checks, and resumes are all methods of collecting selection information, the interview is probably the most widely accepted method. Interviewing job applicants should be seen as a two-way exchange of information. Realistic job previews provide applicants with accurate information (both positive and negative) about the job and the organization. The recommended form of interview is the semistructured interview—a combination of the unstructured and structured forms.

There are two categories of orientation—organizational and departmental. The organizational approach provides new employees with general information about the organization—such as history, structure, top-level managers, fringe benefits, and compensation methods. Departmental orientation covers job-specific information such as job duties, performance expectations, work rules, and work hours.

Employee termination can come about in one of four ways: resignation, retirement, layoff, and discharge. Resignation, retirement and layoff do not present the potential for problems associated with discharge. Employees are discharged for ineffective performance or misconduct. However, discharges must be planned and executed very carefully, to avoid having the discharge challenged in court and ultimately damaging relations with the remaining employees.

KEY TERMS

staffing
recruitment
interviewing
selection
orientation
termination
common law
sexual harassment
wrongful discharge
defamation
respondeat superior
negligent hiring and retention
"employment at will" doctrine
implied contract
internal recruitment
external recruitment
job posting
career path
job description
job analysis
job specifications
structured interview
unstructured interview
semistructured interview

DISCUSSION QUESTIONS

1. What specific activities make up the selection process?
2. What specifically is prohibited by Title VII of the Civil Rights Act of 1964?
3. Identify what is prohibited or required by the Age Discrimination in Employment Act of 1967 and the Equal Pay Act of 1963.
4. Explain how common law might affect employment-related decisions.
5. Explain *respondeat superior*.
6. What limitations are there, if any, to a manager's ability to fire an employee?
7. How could an employee charge defamation by a previous employer?
8. Summarize the implications for managers of federal employment-related legislation, executive orders, state/municipal law, and common law.
9. What advantages are there to internal recruitment?
10. Explain how internal recruitment might be implemented.
11. Are there any advantages to external recruitment?
12. Assume that you could only choose one of the following to use in reaching a decision about a job applicant: application blank, resume, interview, background check. Which would you choose and why?
13. Do you agree that interviews should be seen as two-way communications? Why or why not?
14. Define job analysis, job description, and job specifications. How are they related to the selection process?
15. Explain the advantages and disadvantages of the three forms of interviews.
16. Assume you are responsible for conducting a short training session for newly hired supervisors. You are to give them some guidelines for conducting employment interviews. What would you tell them?
17. What are the two types of new employee orientation? What should be covered in each?
18. For what reasons can employees generally be terminated?
19. What is progressive discipline?
20. You are responsible for conducting a training session for newly hired supervisors on how to discharge employees. What would you tell them?
21. What are the components of an effective AIDS policy?

EXERCISE 3.1

The Application Blank

Examine the application form for XYZ Corporation. Identify and describe (1) any unlawful or unfair pre-employment inquiries contained in this application form and (2) the reason why you think each of these inquiries is unfair.

APPLICATION FOR EMPLOYMENT

XYZ CORPORATION

YOUR APPLICATION WILL BE CONSIDERED CURRENT FOR ONLY 90 DAYS FROM THE DATE COMPLETED. AFTER 90 DAYS, YOU MUST RENEW IT.

ANSWER ALL QUESTIONS COMPLETELY
PLEASE PRINT IN INK OR TYPE.

NAME LAST FIRST MIDDLE OR MAIDEN	DATE OF APPLICATION	FOR WHAT TYPE OF POSITION ARE YOU APPLYING?
ADDRESS: NO. OR RT. STREET OR BOX	HOME PHONE NUMBER	
CITY STATE ZIP	BUSINESS PHONE NUMBER	HOW DID YOU HAPPEN TO APPLY TO XYZ?
DO YOU ☐ OWN HOME ☐ RENT ☐ OTHER	SOCIAL SECURITY NUMBER	

DATE OF BIRTH HEIGHT FT. INCHES	☐ SINGLE ☐ WIDOWED, WHEN?	NO. OF DEPENDENT CHILDREN	THEIR AGES
WEIGHT DATE AVAILABLE LBS.	☐ ENGAGED ☐ SEPARATED, WHEN?	RELATIONSHIP OF OTHER DEPENDENTS	
WILL TRANSPORTATION TO WORK BE A PROBLEM? ☐ YES ☐ NO	☐ MARRIED, WHEN? ☐ DIVORCED, WHEN?	DO ALL DEPENDENTS LIVE WITH YOU ☐ YES ☐ NO	

	NAME	ADDRESS	AGE	WHERE EMPLOYED
SPOUSE				
FATHER				
MOTHER				
BROTHER				
BROTHER				
SISTER				
SISTER				

NAMES OF RELATIVES AND FRIENDS WORKING WITH XYZ
(1)   (2)   (3)   (4)

DO YOU HAVE ANY PHYSICAL DEFECTS OR DISABILITIES? ☐ YES ☐ NO	NATURE		
HAVE YOU EVER SUFFERED ANY INJURIES AT WORK? ☐ YES ☐ NO	WHEN	NATURE OF INJURY	
HAVE YOU EVER BEEN TREATED FOR MENTAL ILLNESS? ☐ YES ☐ NO	WHEN	NATURE OF ILLNESS	
HAVE YOU EVER BEEN CONVICTED OF A CRIME? ☐ YES ☐ NO	WHEN	TYPE OF OFFENSE	GIVE ALL RELEVANT DETAILS
HAVE YOU EVER SERVED IN THE U.S. ARMED FORCES? ☐ YES ☐ NO	DATES OF ACTIVE DUTY	BRANCH OF THE SERVICE	
DO YOU HAVE ANY MILITARY RESERVE OR OBLIGATIONS? ☐ YES ☐ NO	IF YES, WHAT? ☐ READY ☐ STAND BY ☐ RETIRED	UNIT AND BRANCH	

Source: Schnake, M. E. *Principles of Supervision.* Dubuque, IA: Wm. C. Brown Publishers, 1987, pp. 42–43.

(a) Name of Company (b) Address (c) Phone Number	DATES EMPLOYED		POSITION OR TITLE DESCRIBE YOUR DUTIES	IMMEDIATE SUPERVISOR	WAGES OR SALARY	REASON FOR LEAVING
	Month	Year				
A)	From			NAME	START	
B)						
	To			TITLE	LAST	
C)						
A)	From			NAME	START	
B)						
	To			TITLE	LAST	
C)						
A)	From			NAME	START	
B)						
	To			TITLE	LAST	
C)						

HAVE YOU EVER BEEN EMPLOYED BY THIS COMPANY? ☐ YES ☐ NO IF YES, WHEN? FROM ___ TO ___ REASON FOR LEAVING

REFERENCES: LIST THREE PERSONS NOT RELATED TO YOU WHO HAVE KNOWLEDGE OF YOUR QUALIFICATIONS AND FITNESS FOR THE POSITION FOR WHICH YOU ARE APPLYING. DO NOT LIST REPEAT NAMES OF SUPERVISORS LISTED UNDER WORK HISTORY.

NAME	ADDRESS

If relevant to the type of work for which you are applying, indicate any special skills you may have:

Typing speed (WPM) _____ Calculator ☐

Dictaphone ☐ Other _____

Can You Drive A Standard Shift Automobile
YES ☐   NO ☐

EDUCATION	NAME AND ADDRESS	ATTENDED		Did You Graduate?	TYPE OF DEGREE	COURSE OF STUDY
		From	To			
Grammar						
High School						
College						
Other						

XYZ, INC. IS AN EQUAL OPPORTUNITY EMPLOYER FEDERAL LAW PROHIBITS DISCRIMINATION IN EMPLOYMENT PRACTICES BECAUSE OF AGE, RACE, COLOR, RELIGION, SEX OR NATIONAL ORIGIN. FACTS RELATING TO YOUR AGE, RACE, COLOR, RELIGION, SEX, OR NATIONAL ORIGIN ARE NOT CONSIDERED IN DETERMINING YOUR QUALIFICATIONS FOR EMPLOYMENT. I UNDERSTAND THAT ANY FALSE OR MISLEADING INFORMATION OR OMISSIONS IN THIS APPLICATION SHALL BE SUFFICIENT CAUSE FOR REJECTION OR IMMEDIATE DISMISSAL. I AUTHORIZE YOU TO CONTACT ALL COMPANIES USED ABOVE ABOUT MY EMPLOYMENT RECORD. THE COMPLETION OF THIS APPLICATION DOES NOT INDICATE THERE ARE ANY POSITIONS OPEN AND DOES NOT IN ANY WAY OBLIGATE THE COMPANY.

IN CONSIDERATION OF MY EMPLOYMENT, I AGREE TO CONFORM TO THE RULES AND REGULATIONS OF THE COMPANY, AND THAT MY EMPLOYMENT AND COMPENSATION MAY BE TERMINATED, WITH OR WITHOUT CAUSE, AND WITH OR WITHOUT NOTICE, AT ANY TIME, AT THE OPTION OF EITHER THE COMPANY OR MYSELF. I UNDERSTAND THAT NO REPRESENTATIVE OF THE COMPANY HAS AUTHORITY TO ENTER INTO AN AGREEMENT WITH ME FOR EMPLOYMENT FOR ANY SPECIFIED PERIOD OF TIME, OR TO MAKE ANY AGREEMENT WITH ME CONTRARY TO THE FOREGOING.

DATE	SIGNATURE

CASE 3.1

Offices "R" Us

Beth sat at her desk and reflected on the three job applicant resumes in front of her. She knew she would have to make a decision soon, but after narrowing the pool of applicants down to three, she couldn't decide which one to hire. Each had unique strengths and weaknesses. She knew her boss was getting anxious to fill the position, so Beth decided to review the job description again and go through the resumes one last time.

Beth is supervisor of Accounts Payable and Receivable for Offices "R" Us, a large manufacturer and distributor of office furniture and supplies. The company has recently added a full line of computer hardware and software to its product lines. Offices "R" Us, however, does not manufacture any of this computer equipment, but rather has a contract with a large, well-known electronics firm to produce computer hardware carrying the ORU brand.

Beth is trying to fill the position of an entry-level sales representative. The position carries with it an excellent fringe benefit package and a generous salary plus commission. Most ORU sales representatives were earning more than $50,000 per year; last year, the top sales representative earned $117,250. The primary responsibility of persons in this position is to call on organizations and businesses to market Offices "R" Us products. ORU has recently decided to emphasize computer hardware, software, and supplies and to market itself as the "complete office supply center." Turnover among sales representatives at ORU has been relatively high, averaging around 33 percent per year. Most of these employees have received job offers from larger firms and have moved on to bigger territories. Beth's boss told her to do what she can to reduce that turnover. She also recognizes that sales representatives will need more computer skills and knowledge than those of the past. Her boss told her to consider the management potential of job applicants, because ORU had just developed career paths for these sales representatives that move them into district management after only 2 to 3 years. With all of this in mind, Beth picked up the three resumes, each of which contained her interview comments. It is now August 5th, and Beth knows that she needs to hire someone by the end of the month.

Pete Leland
2134 Cameron Place
Charleston, Illinois 61920

EDUCATION

Associate Degree, Computer Technology, Lake Land Junior College, Mattoon, Illinois, 1986. 3.27 G.P.A. 36 hours in computer-related courses. Dean's list 5 semesters.

WORK EXPERIENCE

Data Processing Operations, Eastern Illinois University, 1986 to present. Responsible for operating mainframe computer, loading tapes and magnetic disks, servicing and maintaining high speed printers, and making minor repairs.

Retail sales clerk, Walker Hardware, 1983 to 1986 (part-time, approximately 25 hours per week). Responsible for assisting customers, ringing up sales, and restocking shelves.

Interview Notes

Very friendly and at ease during interview. Seems to handle meeting people very well. Good appearance. Worked himself through school. Hobby is personal computer systems. Has written programs to do various things such as balance a checkbook and print a telephone and address list. Has created several computer games.

Alice Louder
13 Trainer Court
Memphis, Tennessee 38152

EDUCATION

Associate Degree, Shelby County Community College, Memphis, Tennessee, 1980. Major in business administration. 32 hours in management, personnel, and marketing. 12 hours of computer science.

Bachelor of Science, Memphis State University, Memphis, Tennessee, 1988. Major in management, minor in management information systems.

Additional 12 hours coursework toward the Master of Business Administration (MBA) degree, Memphis State University.

WORK HISTORY

June 1978 to January 1980. Secretary/Receptionist, Stillwell Realty, Bartlett, Tennessee.

January 1980 to July 1984. Office Manager, Mid-South Office Products, Memphis, Tennessee. Responsible for bookkeeping and correspondence for largest office supply retailer in Memphis.

July 1984 to September 1986. Marketing consultant, Computer City, Memphis, Tennessee. Salesperson for large computer hardware and software retailer. Also responsible for setting up systems, and providing introductory training for persons purchasing computer systems.

September 1986 to present. Marketing consultant, Computer City, Memphis, Tennessee (part-time). Primary responsibility is sales of computer hardware and software.

Interview Notes

Somewhat nervous during interview, however, seemed to calm down about halfway through the interview. Very good appearance and well-groomed. Reason for seeking this job is that she is looking for a more challenging position.

Further, current employer does not have full-time position available. She is undecided about continuing work toward her master's degree. If she finds a position she likes, she will drop out of the MBA program. She freely offered the information that she is a single mother with two children, ages 7 and 9.

Howard Sawyer
117 Lindburgh Blvd.
Cedar Falls, Iowa 50614

EDUCATION

B.S. in business administration, major in marketing, Iowa State University, 1968.

Additional coursework, 15 hours in data processing and computer science at Cedar Falls Junior College, 1986 to 1988.

WORK EXPERIENCE

October 1976 to December 1988. Sales Manager, Midwest Region, Harriss Hospital Supply Corporation. Supervised twenty-five sales representatives who call on hospitals, nursing homes, clinics, and private medical practices. Full line of medical supplies.

January 1972 to October 1976. Sales representative, IBM Corporation. Marketing computer systems to large corporations throughout southwestern United States.

May 1968 to January 1972. Market Researcher, State Farm Insurance, Bloomington, Illinois. Primarily responsible for conducting marketing research on proposed advertisements for State Farm Insurance products.

Interview Notes

Howard was laid off from Harriss Hospital Supply due to cutbacks made by that company. Around 1,200 people were laid off from the headquarters alone. He is currently in an "outplacement program" being run by Harriss. He seems very sincere and energetic. He certainly knows sales. He also seems to know quite a lot about the new personal computer systems developed by the major competitors.

QUESTIONS

1. Which of the three applicants do you recommend that Beth hire? Explain your recommendation.
2. Was there any information contained, or implied, in the resumes or interview notes that may be illegal if Beth considers it in her decision?
3. Legality aside, was there any information included in the resumes or interview notes that you feel is irrelevant or inappropriate to consider?
4. What have you learned about selection from this exercise?

REFERENCES

[1] Wickliff, J. Beyond hiring: Staffing. *Personnel,* 1988, 65(5), 52–56.

[2] Bradshaw, D.S. Sexual Harassment: Confronting the troublesome issues. *Personnel Administrator,* 1987, 32(1), 51–53.

[3] Kohl, J.P. & Stephens, D.B. Expanding the legal rights of working women. *Personnel,* 1987, 64(5), 46–51.

[4] Feldman, D. Sexual harassment: Policies and prevention. *Personnel,* 1987, 64(9), 12–17.

[5] Bennett-Alexander, D. Sexual harassment in the office. *Personnel Administrator,* 1988, 33(6), 174–188.

[6] 29 U.S.C. Section 206(d)(1).

[7] Twomey, D.P. *A concise guide to employment law: EEO & OSHA.* Cincinnati: South-Western Publishing Company, 1986.

[8] Carrell, M.R. The "handi-capable" employee: An untapped resource. *Personnel,* 1987, 64(8), 40–45.

[9] Wagel, W.H. AIDS: Setting policy, educating employees at Bank of America. *Personnel,* 1988, 65(8), 4–8.

[10] Franklin, G.M. & Robinson, R.K. AIDS and the law. *Personnel Administrator,* 1988, 33(4), 118–121.

[11] Lutgen, L. AIDS in the workplace: Fighting fear with facts and policy. *Personnel,* 1987, 64(11), 53–57; Magnus, M. AIDS: Fear and ignorance still plague the workplace. *Personnel Journal,* 1988, 67(2), p. 28.

[12] Myers, P.S. & Myers, D.W. AIDS: Tackling a tough problem through policy. *Personnel Administrator,* 1987, 32(4), 95–108, 143; Masi, D.A. AIDS in the workplace: What can be done? *Personnel,* 1987, 64(7), 57–60.

[13] 29 U.S.C. Section 651(a).

[14] 29 U.S.C. Section 654(a).

[15] Sullivan, F.L. Immigration legislation: An update. *Personnel,* 1987, 64(12), 26–32.

[16] Novit, M.S. *Essentials of personnel management.* Second edition. Englewood Cliffs, NJ: Prentice-Hall, 1986.

[17] Novit, M.S. Employer liability for employee misconduct: Two common-law doctrines. *Personnel,* 1982, 59, 11–19.

[18] Novit, M.S. *Essentials of personnel management.* Second edition. Englewood Cliffs, NJ: Prentice-Hall, 1986.

[19] Scott, R.C. Negligent hiring: Guilt by association. *Personnel Administrator,* 1987, 32(10), 32–34.

[20] Baley, S. Recruitment: The legalities of hiring in the 80s. *Personnel Journal,* 1985, 64, 112–115.

[21] Bacon, D.L. & Gomez, A. How to prevent wrongful termination lawsuits. *Personnel,* 1988, 65(2), 70–72.

[22]Gilberg, K.R. & Voluck, P.R. Employee termination without litigation. *Personnel,* 1987, *64*(5), 17–20.

[23]Essex, N.L. Steering clear of defamation lawsuits. *Personnel,* 1988, *65*(5), 44–46.

[24]Dube, L.E. Employment references and the law. *Personnel Journal,* 1986, *65,* 87–91.

[25]Schneider, B. & Schmitt, N. *Staffing organizations.* Second edition. Glenview, IL: Scott, Foresman and Company, 1986.

[26]Ibid.

[27]Popovich, P.M. & Wanous, J.P. The realistic job preview as a persuasive communication. *Academy of Management Review,* 1982, *7,* 570–578; Premack, S.L. & Wanous, J.P. A meta-analysis of realistic job preview experiments. Columbus, Ohio: College of Administrative Sciences, The Ohio State University, 1985.

[28]Hollman, R.W. Let's not forget about new employee orientation. *Personnel Journal,* 1976, *55,* 244–250; Reed-Mendenhall, D. & Millard, C.W. Orientation: A training and development tool. *Personnel Administrator,* 1980, *25,* 40–43; St. John, W.D. The complete employee orientation program. *Personnel Journal,* 1980, *59,* 373–378.

[29]O'Reilly, C. & Weitz, B. Managing marginal employees: The use of warnings and dismissals. *Administrative Science Quarterly,* 1980, *25,* 467–484.

WHAT DO YOU THINK? NOTE

Edmund R. Hergenrather is the president of Hergenrather & Company, a large executive search firm located in Los Angeles. He has developed several criteria on which he rates each applicant he interviews.

- Overall appearance, grooming, and attire
- Appropriateness of dress for the interview
- Degree to which the applicant is polite and courteous
- Communication skills
- Degree to which the applicant is prepared for the interview (knowledge of company)
- Degree to which the applicant tries to control the interview compared to the degree to which the applicant listens
- Quality and quantity of questions asked by the applicant
- Knowledge of the organization, industry, competition, products and services
- Understanding of the requirements of the position
- Attitude toward present and past employers. Does applicant make many negative comments about these organizations? Does applicant disclose confidential information?*

---

*Based upon Hergenrather, E.R. 32 points no interviewer should miss. *Recruitment Today,* *1*(1), 28–32.

PART TWO

Individual Relationships

CHAPTER FOUR

Individual Differences

PROLOGUE

If we were to play a word association game, and I said to you "individual differences," a likely response would be "personality." When we think of how individuals are different from one another, personality is commonly used to explain these differences. Several types of personality dimensions will be discussed in the chapter. One dimension not discussed at length is the personality dimension of thrill seeking, or "Type T".

Type T personalities have strong needs for the thrills and excitement associated with taking risks and breaking the rules. Many entrepreneurs are believed to be Type T; they enjoy the risks associated with starting a new company. Aviators Dick Rutan and Jeana Yeager, who completed the first nonstop flight around the world, may also fit the Type T pattern.

One key to success for Type T's may be their ability to handle high levels of stress. Dick Rutan, for example, doesn't see his record-setting flights as stressful, "There are only two types of flying worth a damn—test pilot and combat. The rest is repetitive and boring and should be left to bus drivers."[1]

At the other end of the spectrum are Type t personalities. They are risk-avoiders; they prefer predictability and simplicity.

What implications do these personality types have for managers? What kinds of work do you think are best suited for Type T's? For Type t's?

LEARNING OBJECTIVES

After successful completion of this chapter, you should be able to

- Define perception,
- Explain how perception influences everything we do and say,

89

- Explain why managers need an understanding of individual differences to promote good human relations,
- Identify several important variables on which individual employees may differ,
- Recognize the importance of perception in an individual's ability to process information,
- Understand how individuals may respond to information overload,
- Identify several potential perception problems,
- Explain the attribution process,
- Differentiate between attitudes and values,
- Understand what personality is and how it influences human behavior in organizations, and
- Recognize the various ways that individuals can differ in terms of ability.

DIFFERENCES AT WORK

Explain why managers need an understanding of individual differences to promote good human relations.

Why don't all employees respond to the same motivational strategy? How can a reward that motivates one employee "unmotivate" another? Why do some employees really get turned on to their jobs and show up early every day, while others come in late, stretch their lunch hours and frequently call in sick? How can two people witness the same event and then give completely different descriptions of it? The answer, of course, is that people are different. Employees differ in a number of important variables which will be examined in this chapter. All of these variables have an impact on human relations within an organization as well as on the organization's performance and effectiveness in accomplishing objectives.

PERCEPTION

Identify several important variables on which individuals may differ.

A discussion of individual differences should logically begin with an examination of the perception process, since many of our beliefs, attitudes, and behaviors are influenced by how we perceive our environment. This study of perception will set the stage for an examination of a number of other variables on which individuals may differ. Perception will be discussed again briefly in Chapter 6, relating it to interpersonal communications within organizations.

Perception Defined

Define perception.

Perception is the process by which individuals receive and interpret information about their environment.[2] We are all constantly bombarded with a great deal of information and messages from a variety of sources. As you are reading this chapter, you may hear traffic sounds from outside the building. There may be a couple at the next table discussing a class project that you haven't started yet. Someone may be playing a radio across the hall. On the wall of the room in which you are diligently reading this chapter, there may be a number of posters of faraway places that you'd like to visit. Then, of course, there are the pages of the textbook in front of you. Which of these messages gets through to you? Which ones do you pay attention to, and which ones do you ignore?

CHAPTER FOUR: Individual Differences   91

Individuals are constantly bombarded with a great deal of messages from a variety of sources.

What meaning do you attach to the messages that you do receive? How accurately do you interpret the information contained in these messages?

Most of us perceive our environment somewhat uniquely. It is important to note that perceptions can, and often do, differ from objective reality. That is, our perceptions may often be inaccurate compared to objective reality. However, since each of us has only our perceptions to rely on, one important aspect of the perception process is that *individuals' perceptions are reality for them*. Different perceptions of reality result in different attitudes, values, beliefs, and behaviors.

An example of how perceptual reality can differ among individuals may occur in your class. Student evaluations of an instructor often differ substantially. In a single class, overall ratings of the instructor can range from "This is the worst instructor I've ever had. I'll never take another course from this person" to "This is without question the best instructor I've had in my college career. I will recommend this person to all of my friends." How can perceptions of an instructor vary so much? Students were exposed to the same number of classes, heard the same lectures, and took the same tests, yet their perceptions would suggest that they had two different instructors! As you will learn in this chapter, many things can influence an individual's perception. These factors can be divided into two primary categories, internal and external. Internal factors are those things that occur within an individual to influence perception. Many of these are related to the individual's limitations in processing information or in the individual's preference for certain types of information. External factors are characteristics of the object being perceived.

Explain how perception influences everything we do or say.

Internal Factors That Influence Perception

While it is true that we do not perceive all the information to which we are exposed, nor do we always perceive information accurately, perception serves a necessary purpose.[3] We simply cannot process and retain all of the information to which we are exposed. Thus, we need some means of dealing with excess information. In addition, we may from time to time be exposed to information we find distasteful or even painful. Therefore, we need a way to protect ourselves from unwanted information. Several distinct processes are known, in which individuals engage to help them deal with information from their environments. Each of these processes may cause perceptions to be inaccurate or incomplete. (Three of them—selective perception or filtering, expectations, and distortion—will be further discussed in Chapter 6 as they apply to interpersonal communication.)

Selective Perception

Recognize the importance of perception in an individual's ability to process information.

The first identifiable difference in perception is that individuals are capable of processing different amounts of information. For example, some employees may become overwhelmed by instructions on how to perform a new task. As a result, they experience *information overload,* and do not process all of the information to which they have been exposed. This reaction is known as **selective perception**. Some individuals may simply stop receiving information when they reach their information processing limit. Others may sort through all pieces of information, retaining the most important while screening out information that does not appear to be immediately useful. Other individuals may reduce the amount of information they have to process by *summarizing* messages (omitting details and focusing on the main idea). Regardless of the specific method of handling information overload, these people may miss some important pieces of information that were provided to them. Unless some effort is made to determine what information they did retain, it may be assumed that they received all of the information that was sent. It will not be obvious until they make a serious mistake that they missed a very important piece of information.

Understand how individuals may respond to information overload.

Individuals may also differ in the means by which they select information from their environment. Persons tend to select information consistent with their values, beliefs, and needs. Inconsistent information may simply be screened out or ignored, even though it may be important. Since different individuals have different needs, values, and beliefs, they will select different types of information. For example, in high school you may have been very sensitive to information regarding colleges and universities, since you had a strong desire to get a college education. A friend of yours, who had no plans to attend college, may have completely ignored this type of information. Instead, she may have been very sensitive to information concerning job openings in the community, information which you may have ignored since you were going on to college.

Stop reading for a moment and look up. Look and listen to your immediate environment. How many sounds and activities were being screened out by your perceptual process as you were concentrating on your reading? What implications does this have for managers and employees in organizational work settings?

Expectations

There is a familiar phrase which describes how expectations influence perception, "We all see (hear) what we want to see (hear)." While it suggests selective perception of information, it also suggests that we may unconsciously distort information so that it is consistent with what we expect. For example, instead of accepting information that suggests we are not performing well, we might distort the information so it is more in line with the level of performance we *want* to achieve. Anyone who has written a book or a lengthy paper has experienced the influence of expectations. Proofreading a document that you have written is a very difficult thing to do. It is extremely difficult to spot typographical errors since you know what is *supposed* to be there. As a result, you may miss rather obvious errors, which someone not familiar with the document might see immediately. You don't see these errors because you are *expecting* another word (the write one) to be there. The point is, expectations can distort your perceptions so that you see what you want to see. Did you perceive the misuse of the word *write* in a previous sentence?

Perceptual Defense/Distortion

Once we have developed a perception of something (or someone), we tend to hold on to that perception and even defend it against conflicting information. One primary **defense** is altering any conflicting information to which we might be exposed. We change information to make it more consistent with the perception already formed. Your high school friend, who was not interested in getting a college education, may have read a newspaper account of how college graduates with *certain* majors were having difficulty finding jobs. While the story may have focused on only two or three major courses of study, your friend may have unconsciously altered the information she received so that what she heard was that *all* college graduates were having difficulty finding jobs. This interpretation makes the information she received more consistent with her perception that a college degree isn't necessary.

Halo Effect

The **halo effect** is a tendency to perceive an individual on the basis of one extremely favorable or unfavorable characteristic which colors your perception. For example, an employee who is always punctual and well-dressed for work may be perceived as a top performer in all areas of job performance. On the other hand, an employee who is timid and has few social skills may be perceived as a below-average performer on aspects of the job totally unrelated to social skills. The halo effect **distorts** perceptions in the direction of the outstanding (either positive or negative) characteristic. Halo is a particularly difficult problem for managers when they are evaluating employees or job applicants. It can easily lead to erroneous employment-related decisions. Managers must make a conscious effort to avoid being influenced by one single

Identify several potential perception problems.

outstanding characteristic, and consider independently each aspect of an employee's job performance or an applicant's qualifications.

Stereotyping

Stereotyping occurs when someone is judged on the basis of a perception of the group to which she belongs. We all have preconceived ideas about the characteristics shared by members of a particular group. If another individual is judged to be a member of this group, we assume that she also has these characteristics. There are many commonly held stereotypes about women, the handicapped, and older employees. Several of these appear in Exhibit 4.1. A major problem arises when a manager makes a decision based on a stereotype. The manager is assuming, for example, that *all* women share the characteristics shown in Exhibit 4.1. This assumption is likely to limit employment and/or advancement opportunities for individuals who are perceived to be members of these groups.[4] Managers should treat applicants and employees as individuals, not as stereotypes.

Projection

Projection occurs when we perceive our own characteristics, attitudes, and beliefs in others. Without being aware of it, we see others as a reflection of ourselves. As a result, we may make serious errors in judgment based on our misperceptions of others. Projection often occurs when we project our own negative or undesirable characteristics onto others. For example, if we are very

---

Exhibit 4.1
Common stereotypes

Common Stereotypes of Women

- too emotional to make rational decisions
- not interested in careers
- content with dull, repetitive jobs
- have a low commitment to work

Common Stereotypes of Older Employees

- have high absenteeism and turnover rates
- inflexible and resistant to change
- accident-prone
- not interested in challenging, responsible assignments

Common Stereotypes of Handicapped Employees

- have high absenteeism and turnover rates
- accident-prone
- make other employees uncomfortable

Source: Compiled from Schnake, M. E. *Principles of supervision.* Dubuque, Iowa: Wm. C. Brown Publishers, 1987, 321–325.

aggressive and anxious to move up in the organization, we might project this characteristic onto our coworkers. Then we can rationalize our own aggressive behavior by telling ourselves that everyone else is that way, and we have to protect ourselves. (If this is a particularly strong perception, it may influence our personality. See the Human Relations in Action box later in this chapter.)

Denial

If we are exposed to information that is particularly painful, we may simply deny that the information ever existed. We are not lying to ourselves or others; we may really believe that we never saw the information. A similar process occurs sometimes when someone is in a particularly bad accident or receives a serious injury. The mind cannot cope with the situation and closes itself to the unpleasant information. **Denial** occurs with many people as they reach for their cigarettes with the warning from the Surgeon General of the United States printed conspicuously on the side of the pack. On the job, denial occurs when employees refuse to admit to themselves that they have a performance problem—or a substance abuse problem that is causing their job performance to deteriorate.

External Factors That Influence Perception

Several characteristics of an external object or piece of information may influence the degree to which it is perceived. These characteristics, presented in Exhibit 4.2, all pertain to the extent to which an object "stands out" from other objects.

Size

We are most likely to notice things that differ in size from other objects in the immediate environment. For example, in several pages of large-format maga-

Exhibit 4.2
External influences on perception

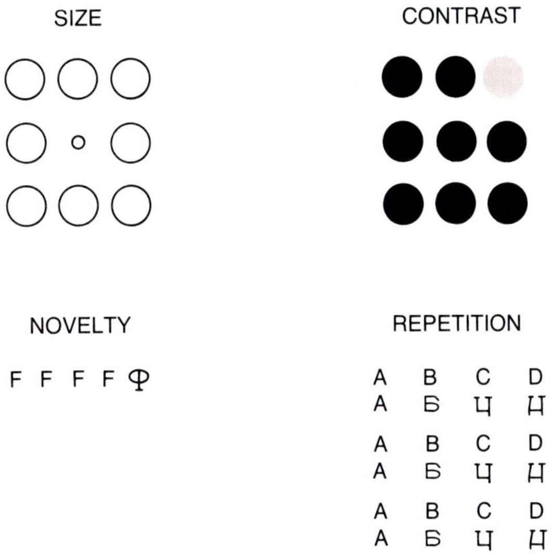

zine ads, we might notice a small 2-inch-square ad while ignoring many of the others. Similarly, objects much larger than surrounding objects will stand out.

Contrast
Objects which contrast with their immediate environment tend to be more noticeable. For example, objects which differ substantially in color or shape from other surrounding objects are likely to be perceived while other objects go unnoticed. Magazine advertisements are typically made up of many different, bright colors designed to catch the attention of the reader. However, occasionally you will see a black and white advertisement placed on a page containing full color advertisements. The black and white advertisement gets noticed because of contrast. How might contrast occur in a work setting?

Intensity
Objects may be conspicuous because they vary in intensity from their surroundings. Intensity includes color, depth, sound, and brightness. Television commercials are commonly much louder than the regular program to catch viewers' attention. However, occasionally a commercial will involve very little sound, or even silence. The viewer, expecting a loud commercial, may be drawn into paying attention to the commercial because the intensity is suddenly much different.

Movement
Objects moving in relation to their immediate surroundings tend to be noticed. When retailers began to suspect that their stationary billboard advertisements were not getting through the perceptual filters of passing motorists, they began using the mobile flashing arrow signs that now clutter some highways. In the army, recruits are taught to move extremely slowly across an open field to avoid detection. If they were to simply run across the field, they would be easily detected because of their motion against a stationary background.

Repetition
Repetition can increase the likelihood of perceiving an object. While we might not perceive the object initially, continued exposure may eventually result in our becoming aware of it. Again, many advertisers use repetition in their commercials to penetrate our perceptions. The next time you are watching a television commercial, count the number of times the name of the product is repeated. In Exhibit 4.2, the first four letters of both the English and Russian alphabets are repeated. At first, the Russian letters may be meaningless. After a number of repetitions, however, the Russian letters will be perceived and remembered.

Novelty
We are likely to notice an unusual or unfamiliar object before we recognize a familiar one. Think back to some of the people that you have recently met. Which ones do you remember? Generally, we remember individuals who have

something unusual about them. They were wearing unusual clothes, had an unusual name, or said or did something unusual. This novelty is different from contrast, in that contrast highlights an object different from surrounding objects, while novelty has to do with objects differing from objects in our experience. For example, in Exhibit 4.2, all of the letters under the word NOVELTY are the letter *F*. The last letter, however, is from the Russian alphabet. Since most of us are not familiar with the Russian alphabet, our attention is naturally drawn to this unusual letter. It is not expected in a series of *F*'s, and therefore catches our attention.

PERCEPTION AND HUMAN RELATIONS

It is clear that perception is an extremely complex process, influenced by a number of internal and external variables. However, it is extremely important for managers to understand the process because of its potential impact on human relations within the organization or work group. One significant fact about perception is that what people perceive is reality to them, even though others "know" (perceive?) that the objective situation is much different. Many human relations problems result from inaccurate (or simply different) perceptions by employees and managers. Managers must take great care that (1) important information is perceived as such by employees, and (2) the information is perceived as intended and not distorted or simplified. Managers must also be careful that their own perceptions of employees are not colored or inaccurate. One potential problem area for managers is in determining reasons for employees' behavior. This process is known as **attribution**.

Attribution

After observing some event, most of us have a need to decide on the cause of that event. If we see someone behaving in a particularly unusual manner, we must decide for ourselves why that person behaved as she did. Basically, the process of attribution consists of perceiving an individual's behavior and then deciding whether it was internally or externally caused.[5] Internally caused behaviors are those under the control of the individual—the individual has a choice as to whether or not to engage in the particular behavior. Externally caused behaviors are beyond the control of the individual—the individual has little choice, but is forced into the particular behavior by external forces beyond her control.

Explain the attribution process.

The importance of the attribution process is that managers base their actions toward, and decisions concerning, employees on their assessment of these employees' behavior. For example, how should you respond to an employee who is late for work? This question is difficult, unless you know whether the cause of the behavior was internal or external. If it was internal, you may speak to the employee about the importance of being at work on time. If it was external, you may ignore the behavior entirely. Three aspects of an employee's behavior influence managers' attributions of that behavior—distinctiveness, consensus, and consistency.

Distinctiveness

Distinctiveness relates to how unusual the behavior is for the employee. If a certain behavior (such as being late for work) is unusual, the manager will probably attribute it to external causes—something must have happened to prompt the employee's unusual behavior. If a certain behavior is not unusual, the manager will tend to attribute it to internal causes. Since this behavior has occurred previously, there is no reason to assume that something in the external environment caused it. Rather, the assumption is that the employee simply decided to repeat the behavior.

Consensus

Consensus refers to how others respond in the same situation. For example, if a number of employees are late for work, the lateness can be attributed to an external cause. However, only one employee being late for work leads to the conclusion (in the absence of any other information) that the cause of the behavior was internal.

Consistency

Consistency in an employee's behavior also influences managers' attributions, by the extent to which the same individual engages in the same behavior over time. If an employee, who has never before been late for work, is late one morning, it is rational to assume an external cause (something beyond her control) for the behavior. On the other hand, if an employee who has been frequently late for work in the past is late for work again, an internal cause will be blamed for the behavior.

As shown in Exhibit 4.3, the more distinctive, the higher the consensus, and the less consistent an employee's behavior, the more likely the manager will attribute the behavior to an external cause. The less distinctive, the lower

Exhibit 4.3
Attributions of behavior

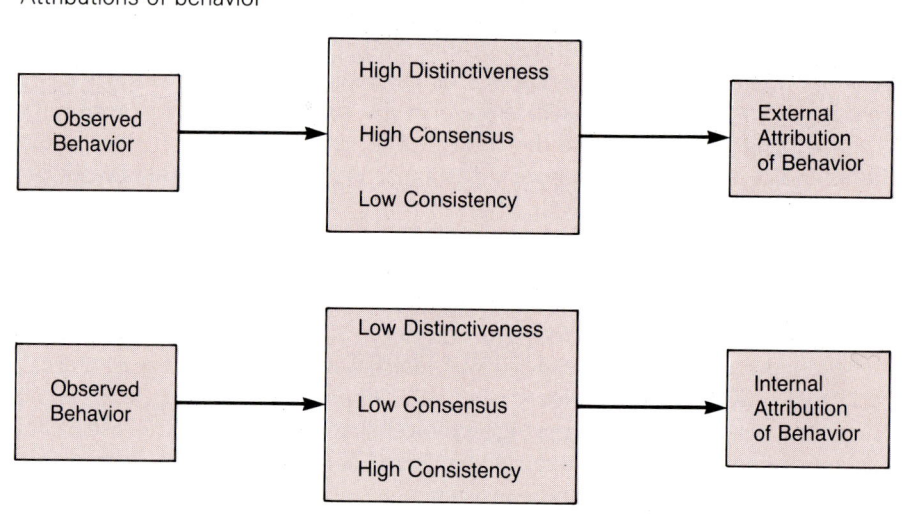

Observed Behavior → High Distinctiveness / High Consensus / Low Consistency → External Attribution of Behavior

Observed Behavior → Low Distinctiveness / Low Consensus / High Consistency → Internal Attribution of Behavior

the consensus, and the more consistent the behavior, the more probable it will be attributed to an internal cause. It is important to point out that attributions sometimes are based on *perceptions,* with very little factual input.

Managers who make inaccurate attributions about employees' behavior can damage human relations. Imagine how you would react if you were late for work because of an accident on the interstate. Then, your manager attributes your lateness to an internal cause and chews you out in front of your coworkers. It's bad enough to be reprimanded publicly, but your frustration and anxiety may be substantially magnified because the behavior was beyond your control. Managers must restrain the tendency to make decisions and judgments about employee behavior without knowing the facts.

VALUES AND ATTITUDES

Is it wrong to punish employees? Should people engage in sex before marriage? Should people work hard, or is it okay to take it easy on the job? Is it right to experiment on animals to advance medical care for human beings? Do we have an obligation to help those people less fortunate than ourselves? All of these questions involve value judgments; there are no clearly right or wrong answers. Each individual has to decide on the basis of her own system of values.

Differentiate between attitudes and values.

Values

A **value** is a general belief about some way of behaving or some end state that is preferable to the individual.[6] Values include an individual's sense of what is right or wrong, and good or bad. A **value system** is the entire set of an individual's values, prioritized in their order of importance to that individual. Values are important in understanding human relations because they guide individuals' decisions and behavior. They provide boundaries for behavior, in that an individual is generally not likely to engage in behavior that is inconsistent with her value system. Also, knowledge about an individual's value system will help predict how she will react in a given situation.

How Values Form

Values are formed as individuals mature and are influenced by a number of sources: family, friends, coworkers, managers, teachers, television, movies, newspapers, and radio. As we are growing up, we hear our parents tell us "That's not right" or "That's not good." As we grow older, we begin to get information from other sources about what is right or good. Over time, we develop our own value system. While individuals' value systems are largely formed and relatively stable by the time they reach adulthood, there may be some degree of change throughout life. When individuals join organizations as employees, their values may change to come more in line with those of coworkers or managers. Employees promoted to supervisory positions may change their values and beliefs to be more consistent with their new role in the organization.

Types of Values

Among the almost infinite number of specific values which individuals may form, six primary types of values have been identified.

1. Theoretical—emphasizes the discovery of truth through a critical and rational approach
2. Economic—emphasizes the useful and practical
3. Aesthetic—places importance on form and harmony
4. Social—places highest importance on the love of people
5. Political—emphasizes the acquisition of power and influence
6. Religious—places greatest importance on the understanding of the cosmos as a whole[7]

Value Differences Across Occupations

Research has determined that individuals in different occupations place varying degrees of importance on these six types of values. As shown in Exhibit 4.4, purchasing executives attached greatest importance to economic values, scientists in industry emphasized theoretical values, and ministers regarded religious values as most important.[8] Comparing the values rated least important by individuals in the three occupations, purchasing executives and scientists rated social values last, while ministers rated economic values lowest.

While values are likely to differ among occupations, age groups, geographic regions of the same country, and cultures, a set of *core values* for Americans, has been identified. This list, presented in Exhibit 4.5, summarizes ten values which many Americans have developed as a result of growing up in this country. What impact is each of these values likely to have on the behavior of an individual employee?

The results of a telephone survey illustrate how values influence behavior. More specifically, this study shows how values shape individuals' perceptions of what is ethical. Two groups of people, middle-level managers and the general public, were surveyed. Some of the results are presented in Exhibit 4.6.

Exhibit 4.4
Ranking of values by importance among three occupations

Ministers	Purchasing Executives	Scientists in Industry
1. Religious	1. Economic	1. Theoretical
2. Social	2. Theoretical	2. Political
3. Aesthetic	3. Political	3. Economic
4. Political	4. Religious	4. Aesthetic
5. Theoretical	5. Aesthetic	5. Religious
6. Economic	6. Social	6. Social

Source: Taguiri, R. Purchasing executive: General manager or specialist? *Journal of Purchasing,* August 1967, 16–21.

Exhibit 4.5
Summary of American core values

Value	General Features
1. Achievement and success	Hard work is good; success flows from hard work
2. Activity	Keeping busy is healthy and natural
3. Efficiency and practicality	Admiration of things that solve problems (e.g., save time and effort)
4. Progress	People can improve themselves; tomorrow should be better
5. Material comfort	"The good life"
6. Individualism	Being one's self (e.g., self-reliance, self-interest, and self-esteem)
7. Freedom	Freedom of choice
8. External conformity	Uniformity of observable behavior; desire to be accepted
9. Humanitarianism	Caring for others, particularly the underdog
10. Youthfulness	A state of mind that stresses being young at heart or appearing young

Source: Schiffman, L. G. & Kanuck, L. L. *Consumer behavior.* Second edition, Englewood Cliffs, N.J.: Prentice-Hall, 1987, p. 506.

Exhibit 4.6
Survey of ethics in America

	A	B	C	D	E	F
1. Taken work supplies home	74%	40%	26%	50%	33%	47%
2. Called in sick when not ill	14	31	18	40	—	—
3. Used company telephone for personal long-distance calls	78	15	—	—	—	—
4. Overstated income tax deductions	35	13	24	41	—	—
5. Driven while drunk	80	33	19	43*	46	21

*Under 30 years of age.

A = Business Executives
B = General Public
C = General Public Over Age 50
D = General Public Between Ages of 30 and 49
E = General Public, Women
F = General Public, Men

Source: Compiled from Ricklefs, R. Executives and general public say ethical behavior is declining in U.S. *Wall Street Journal,* October 31, 1983.

Note how responses to the questions differ, based on group membership. The general public showed a more ethical behavior pattern than did business executives, older people claimed more ethical behavior than did younger people, and women reported more ethical behavior than did men.[9] And, the differences *within* these groups of people are interesting. While executives' values did not prevent them from taking work supplies home, using company telephones for personal long-distance calls, or even driving while drunk, they did feel it was wrong to call in sick when they were not actually ill. Which of these activities do you believe are unethical? How do your beliefs compare to those of business executives?

Attitudes

Attitudes are opinions about people, objects, places, or events which reflect an individual's likes and dislikes. Attitudes may appear to be somewhat similar to values, but there are three important differences:

1. Attitudes are more specific than values. If you say "Hard work is good for you," you are expressing a value. If you say, "I hate my job," you are expressing an attitude.
2. Values focus on what is right or wrong and good or bad; attitudes focus on likes or dislikes. Thus, in the example, you were expressing a value (your belief that it is right to work hard) and an attitude (you do not like your current job).
3. Values are more stable than attitudes. Attitudes are easier to change than values. Without changing your belief that hard work is good, your attitude toward your job might change almost immediately, if you were given more challenging task assignments.

While values and attitudes are different, in most cases they are likely to be consistent.[10] This situation is desirable, because when values and attitudes are inconsistent, individuals may feel some degree of psychological discomfort or imbalance. They may become motivated to do something to restore balance between their values and attitudes. Does it appear consistent to believe that hard work is good, but that you dislike your job? Perhaps job conditions are so unfavorable that it is difficult for you to work as hard as you'd like. A person who believes that it is right to work hard might find herself in a job that doesn't provide much of a challenge. She wants to work hard and feel good about her job, but is prevented from doing so by the boring and repetitive nature of her job. Thus, she has a positive value about hard work, but a negative attitude toward her current job. She may become motivated to seek alternative employment.

Attitudes and Behavior

Jim said again and again that he would never own a major brand of personal computer. He said they were significantly overpriced, and not any better than the "generic" computers that cost about one-third of the price of a name brand. In addition, generic computers offered a number of additional features that would cost extra with a name brand. But when Jim stumbled across a good buy on a name brand computer, his story immediately changed. Now he argued that the quality of the name brand computer far exceeded that of any generic computer. The name brand computer system was worth its slightly higher cost, for the increased quality and dependability. Why did Jim's story change so quickly? People have a need for their attitudes and behaviors to be consistent. When they are not consistent, we experience some degree of psychological discomfort, called **cognitive dissonance**.[11] It is difficult for us to reconcile why we are behaving in a manner that is inconsistent with our attitudes, so something has to change. If we are locked into a behavior inconsistent with an attitude, then the attitude must change. This disparity confronted Jim, when he spent a great deal of money on a name brand computer and then had to change his attitude about name brand computers. It would have been uncomfortable for him to continue to express a negative attitude toward those computers while owning one.

Even with this tendency to strive for consistency, it is often difficult to use attitudes to predict how an individual will react in a particular situation.[12] Just as Jim did when he bought the name brand computer, people sometimes behave in a manner inconsistent with their attitudes. If someone who knew Jim and his attitude toward name brand computers had used this knowledge to predict Jim's behavior, that prediction would have been wrong! This misconception is not unusual, because a large number of situational variables may also influence an individual's behavior. In Jim's case, he happened to find a major name brand personal computer for sale at a price near the price of the generic computers he had always praised. Jim's case notwithstanding, it is clear that attitudes exert an important influence upon individual behavior.[13] In addition, as will be shown in Chapter 12, small groups often place pressures on individuals to behave in a certain manner.

Job Satisfaction

One of the fundamental types of attitudes that employees will form in organizational work settings is **job satisfaction**, which was discussed in Chapter 2. Job satisfaction is the set of attitudes that individuals develop toward their jobs. It includes the degree of satisfaction with several specific aspects of the job, including the work itself, supervision, coworkers, pay, promotions, fringe benefits, recognition, feelings of accomplishment, and working conditions.[14] Like any type of attitude, job satisfaction results in a tendency to behave in a certain manner. While researchers have had great difficulty establishing a direct relationship between job satisfaction and job performance,[15] satisfaction has been shown to influence a number of other important variables, including turnover, absenteeism, and interest in unions.[16]

From a manager's point of view, it would be helpful to understand what causes employees to be satisfied with their jobs. As suggested earlier, overall job satisfaction can be grouped into several more specific dimensions (e.g., pay, promotions, the work itself). Obviously, satisfaction with any one of these components is a matter of the degree to which the type and level of the item (e.g., pay) being provided by the job matches what the individual desires. As described in Chapter 2, when individuals accept employment, they form a number of expectations concerning that employment. To the extent that the organization meets these expectations, employees will experience job satisfaction. The manager's task is to determine, *for each employee,* those expectations that are most important, and create opportunities for the individual. Studies have attempted to ascertain, for employees in general, those aspects of their jobs most important to them. Exhibit 4.7 presents the results of a series of such studies between 1946 and 1975. It can be seen that over the years, job security has decreased in importance, especially for women, while interesting and challenging work has increased in importance. Possibly, rising educational levels have heightened employees' expectations about what jobs should provide. Based on recent data, the top three factors for men are type of work, security, and advancement; for women, the priorities are type of work, company, and supervisor.[17]

Exhibit 4.7
Ranks of 10 job factors over a 30 year time interval

Male Employees

Job Factor	1946–50	1951–55	1956–60	1961–65	1966–70	1971–75
Advancement	2	2	3	3	3	3
Benefits	9	8	7	8	8	8
Company	4	4	4	4	5	4
Coworkers	5	6	6	6	6	6
Hours	8	9	9	9	9	9
Pay	7	5	5	5	4	5
Security	1	1	1	1	2	2
Supervisor	6	7	8	7	7	7
Type of work	3	3	2	2	1	1
Working conditions	10	10	10	10	10	10

Female Employees

Job Factor	1946–50	1951–55	1956–60	1961–65	1966–70	1971–75
Advancement	3	3	4	6	6	7
Benefits	10	10	10	10	10	10
Company	5	4	2	2	2	2
Coworkers	4	5	4	4	3	4
Hours	9	9	9	9	9	8
Pay	8	7	7	7	5	5
Security	2	2	3	3	7	6
Supervisor	6	6	6	4	4	3
Type of work	1	1	1	1	1	1
Working conditions	7	8	8	8	8	9

Source: Compiled from Jurgensen, C. E. Job preferences (what makes a job good or bad?) *Journal of Applied Psychology,* 1978, *63,* 269–270.

When considering individual differences, perhaps the first thing that comes to mind for most people, is "what you are like." In other words, people develop a mental image of what their friends and associates are like, and how they typically behave. This illusive image of others is referred to as personality.

PERSONALITY

Everyone uses (and sometimes misuses) the term "personality." It is one of those common words which everyone assumes they understand. One of the leading researchers in the area of personality once said, "Personality is like love. Everyone agrees it exists, but disagrees on what it is."[18] Sometimes when a person misbehaves you hear someone say "That's just Tom." Everyone nods in agreement and accepts that statement as an explanation of Tom's behavior. The implication is that Tom generally behaves in the manner just observed. In other words, the behavior is consistent with Tom's personality. It is as if Tom didn't have any choice; his personality caused his behavior.

Actually, this description isn't too far off base. **Personality** is defined as a relatively stable pattern of reacting to people, ideas, or objects. One underlying implication of this definition is that personality is not something that you can see. It comprises the traits, characteristics, and tendencies which guide each individual's thoughts and behavior. It is what makes Tom likely to behave in a particular manner most of the time. Just as with values and attitudes, you must observe a person's behavior to characterize that person's personality. The importance of this statement is that too often, because of selective perception, filtering, and expectations, we make assumptions about an individual's personality from very limited information. Once the decision is made and we think we know what type of personality the individual has, we stop receiving any additional information. Unfortunately, even though these initial decisions are often incorrect, our classification of this person is unlikely to change.

Understand what personality is and how it influences human behavior in organizations.

Personality and Behavior

Another important aspect of personality lies in the phrasing of the definition, "*relatively* stable pattern." As mentioned earlier, situational variables may also influence an individual's behavior at any point in time. Therefore, even though an individual's personality is known, it cannot be used to predict that person's behavior 100 percent of the time. Instances of personality problems in the workplace are discussed in the Human Relations in Action box, "Personalities at Work."

Personality Development

Two major factors, heredity (nature) and environment (nurture), account for the development of an individual's personality. There is long-standing disagreement among scientists as to which of these factors is more important.[19] Heredity provides a starting point for personality development. The environment—family, friends, teachers, language, religion, culture, values, and work experiences—then influences individuals as they grow and develop.

HUMAN RELATIONS IN ACTION

Personalities at Work

Sometimes an individual's personality can be heavily influenced by an extremely strong need. When a need becomes too strong, it can cause problems in the workplace—even to the point of damaging human relations. Seven types of "problem personalities" based on overly strong needs have been identified.

1. Need for attention. This person would prefer to receive positive attention; however, negative attention is preferable to none. Over the years, he has developed a number of strategies for getting attention, including bragging about accomplishments, speaking in a loud voice, telling his personal problems in order to get sympathy, interrupting conversations, asking unnecessary questions, disagreeing after everyone else has agreed, or pretending to not understand something. This person believes that getting others to pay attention to him will induce them to know and like him. However, just the opposite often happens. If left unchecked, this personality can cause significant human relations problems, particularly when cooperation and teamwork are important.

2. Need to be successful. This person equates self-worth with success. Success makes her feel good about herself; a lack of success results in a lower perception of self-worth. She often sets relatively high goals for herself but realizes that hard work and excellent performance are not the only things on which rewards are based. Because of this belief, she feels it necessary to engage in relatively unethical behaviors to accomplish her goals and perceive herself as successful: (a) sabotaging the competition—she points publicly to the weaknesses of coworkers, creates or inflates damaging rumors about them, and withholds important information that might help them; (b) manipulating and exploiting people—she develops friendships with others who may help her succeed. When she feels they are no longer useful, she discards them; (c) dishonesty—she sees nothing wrong with telling lies that might make her look better, or cover up something that might make her look bad; (d) breaking the written and unwritten laws of society and the workplace—she sometimes ignores company policy and even the law, to advance her own interests. She believes "the end justifies the means."

3. Need to wage unfinished battles. This person feels that he has always been under his parents' control. Even though now an adult, his behavior is still very much influenced by his parents' expectations. He may feel guilty if he does something of which his parents would not approve. This feeling of being constantly controlled has created resentment toward any other attempts to control or influence his behavior. This person is likely to be oversensitive to being controlled so that helpful suggestions from managers are perceived as orders. In addition, this person may perceive that these "orders" are the manager's way of saying "I don't trust your ability to make decisions on your own," which feeds the resentment. When he receives orders from a superior that absolutely must be obeyed, he may obey them to the letter. For example, when told to pay attention to details in reports, he may pay so much attention to details that the paperwork is slowed to a standstill.

4. Need to be liked. This person has an extremely strong need to be liked. She learned that being nice to everyone minimized friction in relationships and caused everyone to like her. This personality type may be a more serious problem in managers than in employees. Employees with a strong need to be liked are likely to take the jobs no one else wants, work overtime when no one else wants to, and help others who fall behind in their work. However, in a managerial position, this person may try to please everyone. As a result, she may exert little control over

employees. When this doesn't work, she may try to make managerial decisions based upon the majority rule, or may simply go along with what the most forceful employees want. This may result in poor decisions and alienation of the better employees. She also gives undeservedly positive performance evaluations, and rarely confronts employees about poor performance. If she should confront an employee about her performance, it is unlikely that she will realize that she has been confronted, because of her indirect and apologetic manner.

5. Need to be strong. This individual needs to perceive himself as a strong person. This need translates into pushing himself to the limit. He works long hours, and sees social and recreational activities as a sign of weakness. He is also likely to have little compassion for his coworkers or employees, and expects them to work as hard as he does. He has difficulty understanding why someone would take time off from work to attend to personal matters, or how someone could let performance deteriorate because of a personal problem. This behavior often creates resentment among coworkers and/or employees who may begin to try and thwart his efforts. This pattern can develop into a vicious circle; the more coworkers or peers work against him, the more he exerts himself.

6. Need to be unhappy. This person learned early in life that it was easier to be unhappy than happy. When she was happy, she had higher expectations that sometimes didn't materialize. Rather than deal with this disappointment, it became easier to expect the worse. Then if something didn't materialize, it wasn't such a big disappointment. In addition, she found that since she was gloomy and pessimistic all of the time, people tended to leave her alone. This pattern of behavior was safer; she was placing herself in less of a position to be hurt, disappointed, or rejected by others. Over time, however, she began to actually enjoy it when things went wrong. Because she always expected the worst in a situation, she was actually somewhat pleased when it happened. On the job, this person is likely to be unhappy with just about everything: physical working conditions, coworkers, pay, fringe benefits, and company policies and actions. This chronic complaining is likely to create some tension among coworkers who have, or at least try to have, a more positive outlook on life.

7. Need to be right. This person's self-esteem depends on his being right on matters that are important to him. The idea that he could be wrong on an important matter causes him to experience anxiety and presents a very real threat to his perceived self-worth. To avoid this anxiety and threat to his self-esteem, he is capable of adjusting his perceptions (perceptual distortion/defense) so he is always correct, and anyone who disagrees with him is incorrect. This individual always presents information in a way that makes it difficult to disagree with him. For example, he may say "According to every source that we've been able to find, as well as several leading experts in this field, this is the conclusion. . ." He engages in selective perception by receiving only that information which supports his position, and screening out any conflicting information. Finally, this individual is likely to punish people who disagree with him. In a managerial position, he may deny employees pay increases and promotions, give them poor performance evaluations, and assign them to undesirable tasks. If he is not in an authority position over persons who disagree with him, he may ignore them, spread rumors about them, or even try to sabotage projects on which they are working. The result of this behavior is twofold: first, poor decisions are often made based on incomplete and/or distorted information; and second, conflict among coworkers or with employees may develop.

Source: Adapted from Cavanaugh, M.E. Personalities at work. *Personnel Journal*, 1985, *64*, 55–64.

> **WHAT DO YOU THINK?**
>
> Which exerts the greatest influence on an individual's personality, the environment or heredity? Are people born with their personality largely in place? Or, are they born with just the beginnings of a personality which is then molded and formed by the environment? Develop a position on this issue and be prepared to defend it. Some additional ideas on this issue are presented at the end of the chapter.

Personality Traits

Among the large number of identifiable personality traits, six have particularly important implications for managers concerned with the human relations climate within their department or organization. These are **authoritarianism**, **introversion/extroversion**, **neuroticism**, **achievement orientation**, **locus of control**, and **Type A/Type B**.

Authoritarianism

Authoritarianism is the extent of an individual's belief that there should be power and status differences within the organization.[20] Authoritarian people are more likely to obey orders from someone in a position of authority without questioning those orders. Nonauthoritarian people are more likely to question the orders or require explanation or justification before they obey. Managers who have some idea of the extent of this trait in their employees can treat each employee in a manner consistent with her personality. Strongly authoritarian individuals may experience stress and anxiety when placed in an ambiguous situation with little guidance. These people may feel more comfortable with clear, specific directions. Less authoritarian employees, on the other hand, may perform better without close managerial control and direction.

Introversion/Extroversion

This trait ranges from introversion, a tendency to be reserved and sensitive to one's own feelings, to extroversion, a tendency to be outgoing and gregarious. Some characteristics of both are presented in Exhibit 4.8. Extroverts need stimulation in their environments, and tend to respond negatively to simple, boring, repetitive jobs. They need work environments that provide variety, unpredictability, and excitement. Introverts, on the other hand, prefer work environments that are stable, predictable, and provide less stimulation.[21] From a manager's perspective, the biggest task with introverted employees is to control the stimulation in their work environments.[22] Thus, introverts are likely to perform better on repetitive tasks that provide them with the orderly, predictable environment they prefer. When extroverts are placed in repetitive jobs, they may quickly become bored and resort to horseplay or even sabotage to provide themselves with the stimulation they need. An automobile assembly line worker was observed welding a soft drink bottle inside an automobile door as it passed by on the assembly line. When asked why, the response was that working on the assembly line was boring and this provided some diver-

> **Exhibit 4.8**
> Characteristics of extroverts and introverts
>
> | Extroverts | Introverts |
> |---|---|
> | Like variety and action | Like quiet for concentration |
> | Tend to be faster, dislike complicated procedures | Tend to be careful with details, dislike sweeping statements |
> | Are often good at greeting people | Have trouble remembering names and faces |
> | Are often impatient with long, slow jobs | Tend not to mind working on one project for a long time uninterruptedly |
> | Are interested in the results of their job, in getting it done and in how other people do it | Are interested in the idea behind their job |
> | Often do not mind the interruptions of answering the telephone | Dislike telephone intrusions and interruptions |
> | Often act quickly, sometimes without thinking | Like to think a lot before they act, sometimes without acting |
> | Like to have people around | Work contentedly alone |
> | Usually communicate freely | Have some problems communicating |

Source: Reproduced by special permission of the Publisher, Consulting Psychologists Press, Inc., Palo Alto, CA 94306, from *Introduction to Type* by Isabel Briggs Myers, Copyright 1980. Further reproduction is prohibited without the Publisher's consent.

sion, something to increase the amount of stimulation in the work environment.

Neuroticism

Neuroticism is a measure of an individual's emotional maturity.[23] Individuals who are highly neurotic have a low tolerance for stress and anxiety. They are very sensitive to threat, whether real or imagined. From a manager's perspective, neurotic individuals cannot tolerate ambiguity in their jobs. They need clear instructions, rules, and procedures. They also need to be constantly reassured by their manager that they are performing adequately. But, managers must be careful how they provide feedback to neurotic employees; even a passing remark may be interpreted as a reprimand, and hence a threat, to these individuals.

Achievement Orientation

Employees with a strong need for achievement continually try to improve and do things better. However, they need to feel that these improvements or accomplishments were due to their own efforts. As a result, they prefer tasks of intermediate difficulty. Tasks that are too easy provide no challenge, since success may be due more to the ease of the task than to the employee's efforts. Extremely difficult tasks are avoided, since the achievement-oriented employee may feel that there is little chance of success. Or, if they are successful, given the difficulty of the task, they feel that the success may have been due to chance rather than to their efforts.[24] Thus, managers should attempt to assign employees with strong need for achievement to tasks that (1) provide a challenge to their abilities (although not too much challenge), (2) provide feedback so that employees know how they are doing, and (3) provide responsibility so that successes are attributable to their own efforts.

Locus of Control

Locus of control refers to the degree to which individuals believe their actions can influence what happens to them.[25] **Internals** believe their behavior is the primary determinant of what happens to them; **externals** believe forces such as fate, chance, luck, or powerful organizations are stronger influences. Internals have confidence in their own abilities and believe their performance determines their rewards; externals believe their level of performance is less important in determining rewards.[26] Externals are also likely to be more dissatisfied and less involved with their jobs than internals. Because internals believe that performance level determines rewards, they should be easier to motivate than externals. However, since externals look to others for direction, they may be more willing to follow directions than internals (who tend to be more independent and try to resist managerial control). Finally, internals may be more suited to jobs requiring initiative and independence, while externals may be more suited to unskilled, simple, repetitive jobs.[27]

Type A/Type B

This personality trait differentiates individuals' general behavioral tendencies as they react to their environments. Type A individuals try to accomplish the greatest number of things in the shortest possible time.[28] They are generally unable to relax, extremely active and energetic, perfectionists, very competitive, and aggressive. Type B individuals are generally the opposites of Type A's. They are more relaxed and more sociable.[29] Managers typically find that individuals with Type A personality traits perform well under tight schedules, time pressures, and challenging goals. Type B individuals may also work hard or fast to accomplish a difficult goal under time pressure, but they are more able than Type A's to relax once the goal has been achieved.[30]

Review each personality trait introduced in the preceding paragraphs. How would you rate yourself on each trait? Are you an internal or an external? What implications do these ratings have for you as a manager and as an employee?

ABILITY

Recognize the various ways that individuals can differ in terms of ability.

Individuals may vary in their ability to perform assigned tasks. Ability is a primary variable for managers to consider, because of its effect upon performance. Performance is said to be a function of both motivation and ability.[31] Motivation (discussed in Chapter 5) is the degree to which an employee is

> **RETURN TO THE PROLOGUE**
>
> A relatively new type of personality, the Type T discussed in the Prologue, is defined as one who seeks thrills, excitement, and stimulation. There is both a positive and negative side to Type T personalities. Actually, this personality type should be viewed on a continuum from Type "t" (risk avoiders) on one end, to Type "T" (risk seekers) on the other end. It has been suggested that the Type T personality may be at least partially responsible for some criminal behavior. Criminals such as Bonnie and Clyde may engage in such behavior in an attempt to seek thrills and excitement.
>
> | Type t | | Type T |
> |---|---|---|
> | Risk Avoiders | ├─────────────────────────┤ | Risk Seekers |
>
> The Type t–T personality continuum has clear implications in the world of work. It highlights the importance of matching employees' personalities to their work assignments. In organizational work settings, Type T's are not likely to perform well in routine, repetitive work assignments. Rather, they need substantial challenge and variety in their jobs. They need relatively high levels of control over their own jobs, and are likely to respond negatively to close supervision and managerial control. Type T's will generally prefer jobs where they can be creative and use their own initiative and judgment in making decisions about how to perform the work. Type T's who are assigned to jobs that provide little stimulation may begin to seek excitement—or even create their own. This may explain why automobile production workers sometimes engage in horseplay such as hiding a coworker's lunchbox, or sending some unusual object down the assembly line. Type t's prefer predictability, familiarity, simplicity, and low risk. Type t's who are assigned to fast-paced, exciting jobs may react negatively—by being absent from work or even quitting.[32]

willing to perform; ability is the degree to which an employee is *capable* of performing. Thus, holding motivational level constant, the employee with the greater ability will be the better performer, assuming of course that the employee's ability is in areas important to job performance. However, it is also true that an individual with little ability, even though highly motivated, is not likely to perform well. And, there are different types of ability; one individual may be good at some things but not at others. Thus, it is important for managers to be aware of different types of ability, both within a single individual, and among different individuals.

There are two primary categories of ability—**intellectual and physical**; each is made up of a number of subcategories.

Intellectual Ability

Intellectual ability comprises two basic dimensions, *verbal* and *numerical*. These dimensions consist of the following components:[33]

1. Verbal comprehension—the ability to effectively use words in spoken and written communication

2. Numerical comprehension—the ability to perform arithmetic calculations and mathematical analysis
3. Perceptual speed—the ability to discern small details rapidly
4. Visualization—the ability to envision objects in three dimensions
5. Inductive reasoning—the ability to identify relationships and principles by correlating pieces of seemingly unrelated information

Physical Ability

Individuals may differ in nine basic physical abilities. In Exhibit 4.9, these abilities are divided into three categories: strength, flexibility, and other.

Exhibit 4.9
Nine basic physical abilities

Strength Factors

1. Dynamic strength	Ability to exert muscular force repeatedly or continuously over time
2. Trunk strength	Ability to exert muscular strength using the trunk (particularly abdominal) muscles
3. Static strength	Ability to exert force against external objects
4. Explosive strength	Ability to expend a maximum of energy in one or a series of explosive acts

Flexibility Factors

5. Extent flexibility	Ability to move the trunk and back muscles as far as possible
6. Dynamic flexibility	Ability to make rapid, repeated flexing movements

Other Factors

7. Body coordination	Ability to coordinate the simultaneous actions of different parts of the body
8. Balance	Ability to maintain equilibrium despite forces pulling off balance
9. Stamina	Ability to continue maximum effort requiring prolonged effort over time

Source: Fleishman, E. A. Evaluating physical abilities required by jobs. *Personnel Administrator,* 1979, 24, 82–92.

DEVELOPING YOUR HUMAN RELATIONS SKILLS

The information presented in this chapter has important implications for you in your role as a manager as well as in your role as an employee. The ideas and theories are aimed at helping managers better understand their employees, and employees better understand themselves.

Comprehension of the ways in which individuals differ is important to managers for a number of reasons.

1. Individuals differ in their ability and willingness to perform certain tasks. Matching individual abilities and interests with job requirements will improve human relations and performance.
2. Individuals differ in terms of what will motivate them. Motivation will be discussed in detail in the following chapter, but it is important to realize that managers cannot use the same motivational strategy on all employees.
3. Individuals differ in the style of leadership to which they will respond. Some employees will need a great deal of guidance and direction, while others prefer to be left primarily on their own to get their work done. Managers must be able to display different leadership styles (discussed in more detail in Chapter 13).
4. Individuals differ in terms of the amount of communication and information they need. Some feel a need to be informed on nearly everything, while others might feel unnecessarily overburdened with that amount of information. Also, individuals may prefer different types of communications (e.g., verbal versus written).
5. Individuals differ in terms of the amount of social interaction they need. Some people might become depressed if they were not able to frequently communicate and interact with other people, while others may prefer to work alone most of the time.
6. Individuals perceive and interpret information and events differently. When a message or event carries a great deal of significance, managers must ensure that perceptions by employees are accurate. The manager may ask employees for their opinions or comments to determine that each employee perceived and interpreted the information accurately.

The difficult task of the manager is to accommodate these many individual differences while directing the activities of employees toward organizational goal accomplishment.

The following suggestions are provided for you to consider as you fulfill your role as an employee.

1. Remember that there are many sources of error in the perception process. Before making an important decision or reacting to an action taken by a manager or coworker, ask yourself if your perceptions are accurate. Don't react without making sure your actions are based upon fact and reality, not misperceptions.

(continued)

2. Keep in mind your own set of values, attitudes, and beliefs when considering courses of action or making decisions. Know whether your own values, rather than objective information, are influencing a particular decision.
3. Give some thought to how your personality affects others. Do you have a manner of behaving that annoys, inhibits, or intimidates other people? If you are having problems at work, consider whether your personality is at least partially to blame. Do you, for example, have an overwhelming need to be right, or a need for attention? While personality is a rather enduring characteristic, awareness of a specific problem can enable you to overcome, or at least minimize, such behavior.
4. Consider how your personality matches the requirements of your job and organization. Some organizations don't do a good job of matching employees to jobs. This places the responsibility almost entirely on your shoulders to get a job that fits your personality. Identify those job attributes that are most important to you, such as challenging work, responsibility, autonomy, feedback, recognition, and so forth. Then carefully evaluate the extent to which your current job provides these things. If you find your job lacking, talk with your manager about your situation, or begin looking for another job that better matches your personality.
5. Review your intellectual and physical abilities; tabulate your strengths and weaknesses. Use these qualities to guide your selection of occupations and jobs. Many colleges and universities have placement centers that provide testing to help you determine your abilities, interests, and personality. Some state employment agencies also provide testing services.

SUMMARY

Individuals differ in a number of important respects that may influence human relations and organizational performance. Some of the more important variables identified in the chapter were perception, values, attitudes, personality, and ability. Perception, defined as the process by which individuals receive and interpret information about their environment, is influenced by a number of internal and external factors. Internal factors include selective perception, expectations, perceptual defense/distortion, halo effect, stereotyping, projection, denial, and attribution. External factors include size, contrast, intensity, movement, repetition, and novelty.

A value is a general belief about some way of behaving or some end state that is preferable to the individual. A value system is the entire set of an individual's values, prioritized in the order of their importance to the individual. Attitudes are opinions about people, objects, places, or events which reflect an individual's likes and dislikes. Attitudes and values differ in three important respects: (1) attitudes are more specific than values; (2) values focus on what is right or wrong and good or bad, while attitudes focus on likes and dislikes; and (3) values are more stable than attitudes.

Personality is a relatively stable pattern of reacting to people, ideas, or objects. It is a set of traits, characteristics, and tendencies which guide each individual's thoughts and behaviors. Specific personality types of particular importance to human relations in organizational settings include authoritarianism, introversion/extroversion, neuroticism, achievement orientation, locus of control, and Type A/Type B. Finally, ability consists of two primary categories, intellectual and physical. Managers must, to the extent possible, match individuals to jobs based on these individual difference variables.

KEY TERMS

perception
selective perception
perceptual defense/
    distortion
halo effect
stereotyping
projection
denial
attribution
distinctiveness
consensus
consistency
value
value system
attitude
cognitive dissonance
job satisfaction
personality
authoritarianism
introversion/introverts
extroversion/extroverts
neuroticism
achievement
    orientation
locus of control
Type A/Type B
internals/externals
intellectual ability
physical ability

DISCUSSION QUESTIONS

1. Why do different individuals perceive the same situation, comment, or event differently?
2. Identify at least three internal factors and three external factors that influence perception.
3. Describe the selective perception process. What causes some information to get through and other information to be screened out?
4. How can your expectations influence what you perceive?
5. Explain how the halo effect and stereotyping can influence perception.
6. What is projection? Denial?
7. Explain the attribution process. What influences attributions of behavior?
8. What are values and attitudes? How are they different?
9. How can values differ, based upon occupation or age?
10. Explain cognitive dissonance. How does it influence an individual's behavior?
11. Define job satisfaction. What are some of the specific dimensions or aspects of job satisfaction?
12. What is meant by "personality"? How can the personality of individual employees influence human relations and organizational performance?
13. Which of the personality types discussed in the chapter would you hope your own employees would have? Which would you hope none of your employees would have? Why?
14. Can managers actually do anything about an employee's personality?

EXERCISE 4.1

Personality and Birth Order

Objectives

- To gain awareness of similarities and differences between individuals
- To explore the influence of birth order on personality

Process

I. Divide the class into four groups, dependent on birth order (5 minutes).
   A. Only children.
   B. Oldest children.
   C. Middle children. If this is a large group, it may be subdivided by: those with older brothers only; older sisters only; female middles; male middles; younger brothers only; younger sisters only; etc.
   D. Youngest children.
II. Share and compare factors that you think helped to mold who you are (25 minutes). You may want to include:

   - parental expectations
   - perceptions of self
   - personality traits
   - prospective careers

   Look for similarities and differences.
III. Have a spokesperson from each group summarize the discussion for the class. (10 minutes)

Discussion

1. What were the areas of similarity and differences among groups?
2. How similar were the conclusions of the different groups?
3. How important do you think birth order is in the development of an individual's personality? Why?

Source: Frantzve, J.L. *Behaving in organizations: Tales from the trenches.* Boston: Allyn and Bacon, Inc., 1983, p.41. (Exercise 4 - Birth Order).

CASE 4.1

Corporate Social Responsibility
by Thomas R. Miller, Memphis State University

Two manufacturing companies, Big Deal Corporation and Slinky Corporation, are engaged in the production and distribution of a popular consumer product, the Super Widget. Both firms sell in the same market area, have similar cost structures and scales of operations, and enjoy about the same annual dollar sales volume. Although each company has been successful over the years, enjoying substantial profits, this trend seems to be changing. Profits of both firms have been shrinking, and the competition between the firms has become increasingly intense.

There are several differences in the communities where the plants are located. Big Deal is located in the heart of Metro City, a regional industrial and commercial center of 275,000 population; Slinky is located near Acmeville, a rural town of 2,500 population situated about 150 miles south of Metro City. Metro City has for many years been the home of several large manufacturing plants. In contrast, Acmeville has little industry other than the Slinky plant.

An unfortunate byproduct of the manufacturing operations of both plants is air pollution. Both firms emit odorous, dirty gases into the environment. While there has been relatively little reaction to this condition in Acmeville (where Slinky is a major employer), the residents and community groups of Metro City are becoming alarmed with the situation at Big Deal. Spurred by the national interest in environmental safety, the pollution problem at Big Deal is a common topic of conversation throughout the city. Further, students from the campus of Metro State University have been demonstrating and picketing around the grounds of Big Deal's plant, generating a lot of attention from the local media.

Leonard Powell, the president of Big Deal, is deeply concerned. Recently, he has been bombarded with telephone calls from angry citizens. While he feels his firm should be a "good corporate citizen," he is uncertain about what he should do. Profit margins have been narrowing in recent years, largely due to the competitive actions of the Slinky Corporation. Big Deal is in trouble and Mr. Powell knows it. He is "under the gun" from the Board of Directors over the firm's lackluster profit performance. The pressure of adverse public opinion is mounting. Something must be done soon!

QUESTIONS

1. What is the "social responsibility" of business?
2. What major problems are facing Leonard Powell and the Big Deal Corporation?
3. How is the situation faced by Mr. Powell different from that of Slinky Corporation, his competitor? Explain. What role do values play in these differences?
4. What course of action do you recommend for Mr. Powell?
5. Is the action you recommended in question 4 socially responsible? Why or why not?
6. Will the action you recommended enhance the profitability of the Big Deal Corporation? Explain.
7. How did your own values influence your recommendation?
8. What relationship is there between an organization's social responsibility and human relations among employees and managers of that organization?

REFERENCES

[1] Slrzuclo, C., Horn, M., Moore, L.J., Golden, S.F., Linnon, N. & Dworking, P. Risk takers. *U.S. News & World Report,* January 26, 1987, 60–67.

[2] Levine, M.W. & Shefner, J.M. *Fundamentals of sensation and perception.* Reading, MA: Addison-Wesley, 1981.

[3] Schiff, W. *Perception: An applied approach.* Boston: Houghton-Mifflin, 1980.

[4]Pennar, K. & Mervosh, E. Women at work. *Business Week*, January 28, 1985, 80–85.

[5]Kelley, H.H. *Attribution in social interaction*. Morristown, NJ: General Learning Press, 1971.

[6]Rokeach, M. *Beliefs, values, and attitudes*. San Francisco: Josey-Bass, 1968; Rokeach, M. *The nature of human values*. New York: Free Press, 1973.

[7]Allport, G.W., Vernon, P.E. & Lindzey, G. *Study of values*. Boston: Houghton-Mifflin, 1951.

[8]Taguiri, R. Purchasing executive: General manager or specialist? *Journal of Purchasing*, August 1967, 16–21.

[9]Ethics in America: A *Wall Street Journal*–Gallup survey. *Wall Street Journal*, October 31, 1983.

[10]Rokeach, M. *The nature of human values*. New York: Free Press, 1973.

[11]Festinger, L. *A theory of cognitive dissonance*. Stanford, CA: Stanford University Press, 1957.

[12]Wicker, A.W. Attitude versus action: The relationship of verbal and overt behavioral responses to attitude objects. *Journal of Social Issues*, Autumn 1969, 41–78.

[13]Kahle, L.R. & Berman, H.J. Attitudes cause behavior: A cross-logged panel analysis. *Journal of Personality and Social Psychology*, 1979, *37*, 315–321.

[14]Smith, P.C., Kendall, L.M. & Hulin, C.L. *The measurement of satisfaction in work and retirement: A strategy for the study of attitudes*. Skokie, IL: Rand-McNally, 1969; Weiss, D.J., Dawis, R.V., England, G.W. & Lofquist, L.H. *Manual for the Minnesota studies in vocational rehabilitation*. Volume 22. Minneapolis, MN: University of Minnesota, 1967.

[15]Brayfield, A.H. & Crockett, W.H. Employee attitudes and employee performance. *Psychological Bulletin*, 1955, *52*, 396–424; Vroom, V.H. *Work and motivation*. New York: John Wiley & Sons, 1964; Lawler, E.E. & Porter, L.W. The effect of performance on job satisfaction. *Industrial Relations*, 1967, *7*, 20–28.

[16]Schriesheim, C.A. Job satisfaction, attitudes toward unions and voting in a union representation election. *Journal of Applied Psychology*, 1978, *63*, 548–552; Steers, R.M. & Rhoades, S.R. Major influences on employee attendance: A process model. *Journal of Applied Psychology*, 1978, *63*, 391–407.

[17]Jurgensen, C.E. Job preferences (What makes a job good or bad?) *Journal of Applied Psychology*, 1978, *63*, 267–276.

[18]Cattell, R.B. Personality pinned down. *Psychology Today*, 1973, *7*, 49–56.

[19]Allport, G.W. *Pattern and growth in personality*. New York: Holt, Rinehart & Winston, 1967.

[20]Price, R.A., Vandenberg, S.G., Iyer, H. & Williams, J.S. Components of variation in normal personality. *Journal of Personality and Social Psychology*, 1982, *43*, 328–340.

[21]Eysenck, H.J. (Ed.) *Readings in extroversion-introversion*. Volume 3. London: Staple Press, 1970; Eysenck, H.J. (Ed.) *Eysenck on extroversion*. New York: John Wiley and Sons, 1973.

[22]Weinstein, N.D. Individual differences in reaction to noise: A longitudinal study in a college dormitory. *Journal of Applied Psychology*, 1978, *63*, 458–466.

[23]Eysenck, H.J. *The biological basis of personality*. Springfield, IL: Charles C. Thomas, 1967.

[24]McClelland, D.C. *The achieving society*, New York: Van Nostrand Reinhold, 1961; Atkinson, J.W. & Raynor, J.O. *Motivation and achievement*. Washington, D.C.: Winston, 1974.

[25]Rotter, J.B. Generalized expectancies for internal versus external control of reinforcement. *Psychological Monographs*, 1966, *80*, Whole Number 609.

[26]Mitchell, T., Smyser, C. & Weed, S. Locus of control: Supervision and work satisfaction. *Academy of Management Journal*, 1975, *18*, 623–631.

[27]Spector, P.E. Behavior in organizations as a function of employee's locus of control. *Psychological Bulletin*, 1982, *91*, 482–497.

[28]Friedman, M. (Ed.) *Pathogenesis of coronary artery disease*. New York: McGraw Hill, 1969.

[29]Friedman, M. & Rosenman, R.H. *Type A behavior and your heart*. New York: Fawcett Crest, 1974.

[30]Glass, D.C. *Behavior patterns, stress, and coronary disease*. Hillsdale, NJ: Lawrence Erlbaum Associates, 1977.

[31]Mitchell, T.R. Motivation: New directions for theory, research, and practice. *Academy of Management Review*, 1982, *7*, 80–88.

[32]Farley, F. The big T in personality. *Psychology Today*, May 1986, *20*, p. 45.

[33]*The Employee Aptitude Survey*. Published by Psychological Services, Inc., Los Angeles, CA.

WHAT DO YOU THINK? NOTE

There is evidence that both environment and heredity play important roles in personality development. Consider the case of identical twins who were separated at birth and raised apart. Neither was aware of the existence of the other until they reached the age of 39. Both babies were named Jim by their adoptive parents. In school, both men did well in math and poorly in spelling. Both married, and then later divorced, women named Linda. Both married a second time. Both of the present wives are named Betty. Both men had sons. One named his son James Allan. The other twin named his son James Alan. Both twins have training in law enforcement and have worked as part-time deputy sheriffs. Both men have hemorrhoids and identical blood pressure, pulse, and sleep patterns. Both twins chew their fingernails. These rather surprising similarities provide some evidence that heredity exerts an important influence on personality development.

However, a number of differences in the behavior of the twins suggests that the environment also influenced each twin's personality. One twin wears his hair combed back with sideburns, while the other twin combs his hair over. One twin expresses himself better orally, while the other expresses himself better with the written word.

Holden, C. Identical twins reared apart. *Science,* 1980, *207* (4436), 1323–1328.

CHAPTER FIVE

Motivating Employees

PROLOGUE

Sandy reflected on her first six months as a supervisor in the Group Claims Division of a large insurance company. There were six supervisors in the division, all performing similar work. Their jobs consisted mainly of supervising several clerical employees who processed group health insurance claims. The supervisors handled all personnel matters within their respective departments such as interviewing, hiring, making salary decisions, training, and firing. The supervisors were also available for handling problems or special projects. While Sandy was somewhat apprehensive about her ability when she first took the job, she now had become somewhat bored. She had just finished college when she accepted the job and was excited about assuming supervisory responsibility right away. However, after about two months she had learned her job and had her department running smoothly. Now there just didn't seem to be much for her to do—at least not any tasks that she found challenging or interesting.

    Sandy thought about the other supervisors in the department. All but two were college graduates. One was working on a master's degree at night. One of the other supervisors seemed to live and breathe his job. He was always talking about the company and his department. He was especially fond of telling the other supervisors when his department processed an unusually large number of claims. Another supervisor seemed to be withdrawn and almost apathetic. He came to work and went through the motions, but it was almost as if he resigned himself to put in the required number of hours at work and do as little as possible. The supervisor who was working on her master's degree was "all business" while she was on the job, but she never spoke very enthusiastically about her work or her department. Somehow she always steered conversations around to graduate work. Another supervisor seemed somewhat overworked all the time. He was constantly coming to Sandy for help or advice. "It's interesting how several different people can be working in identical jobs and yet react so differently to them," Sandy thought.

LEARNING OBJECTIVES

After successful completion of this chapter, you should be able to:

- Understand the basic motivation process,
- Relate unsatisfied needs to motivation,
- Identify several important categories of needs,
- Explain what happens when people are unable to satisfy important needs,
- Explain the difference between extrinsic and intrinsic needs,
- Discuss several important theories of motivation,
- Understand the difference between direct and indirect reinforcement, and
- Develop strategies for motivating employees.

MOTIVATION IN ORGANIZATIONAL WORK SETTINGS

The word **motivation** comes from the Latin word *movere,* which means "to move." Thus, motivation is concerned with what "moves" people. In organizations, there are four aspects of motivation which managers must consider.

1. Managers must identify those factors that energize employees' behavior. What is it that gets employees' attention and causes them to be willing to exert effort?
2. Managers must also be concerned about the direction of employees' effort. What factors determine whether employees will channel their effort in organizationally desired directions rather than in undesirable directions?
3. Managers concerned with motivating employees to perform up to their capabilities must also consider what determines the level or strength of effort. What is it that determines how much effort an individual is willing to exert?
4. Managers must also consider what determines the persistence of the effort. What determines how long an individual is willing to continue to exert a given level of effort?

RETURN TO THE PROLOGUE

These four issues provide great insight into employee motivation. Asking the four questions of the supervisors described in the Prologue would help explain their behavior. (1) Why does one of the supervisors simply go through the motions on his job while another always talks enthusiastically about his department? (2) Why does one supervisor appear to direct more effort toward her master's degree than toward her job? (3) Why does one of the supervisors appear to exert maximum effort while another puts forth as little effort as possible? (4) How long will the supervisor who appears enthusiastic about his work continue to exert maximum effort? How long will the apathetic supervisor continue to exert minimal levels of effort? These four questions will be asked throughout the chapter, each time a theory or concept is presented which relates to one of these aspects of motivation.

The ideas and theories presented in this chapter will focus on these four aspects of motivation. Once you have information concerning these four factors, you should be able to develop motivational strategies to fit different situations and different employees. This information will also be helpful to you in understanding your own behavior. As the Prologue suggests, people differ from one another. They do not react to the same work environment in the same way. One of the first things to learn is that motivation is a highly individualized process. What you choose to motivate one employee may not work with another.

Discuss several important theories of motivation.

SATISFACTION OF NEEDS

Many theories of motivation are based on the idea that individuals are motivated to satisfy important needs. The simple model of motivation presented in Exhibit 5.1 shows that unsatisfied needs cause individuals to experience tension or feel uncomfortable. This tension energizes their behavior, and they are motivated to do something that will eliminate, or at least reduce, the tension. They begin searching their environment for something they believe will eliminate the tension. For one supervisor in the Prologue, the activity chosen was his work. Another supervisor chose graduate school. Still others may have chosen leisure activities or hobbies away from the workplace. Once individuals have chosen a particular course of action, they engage in the behavior they hope will satisfy the need, then evaluate the results of their behavior. If the need was satisfied, they have learned which behavior will satisfy that particular need; the next time a similar need is experienced, they will engage in that behavior. If the need remains unsatisfied, they will search for other behaviors, and repeat this trial and error process until they are able to satisfy the need. The difficult task of managers is to identify which needs are important to each employee and provide as many opportunities as possible for employees to satisfy these needs on the job.

Understand the basic motivational process.

Exhibit 5.1
Basic model of motivation process

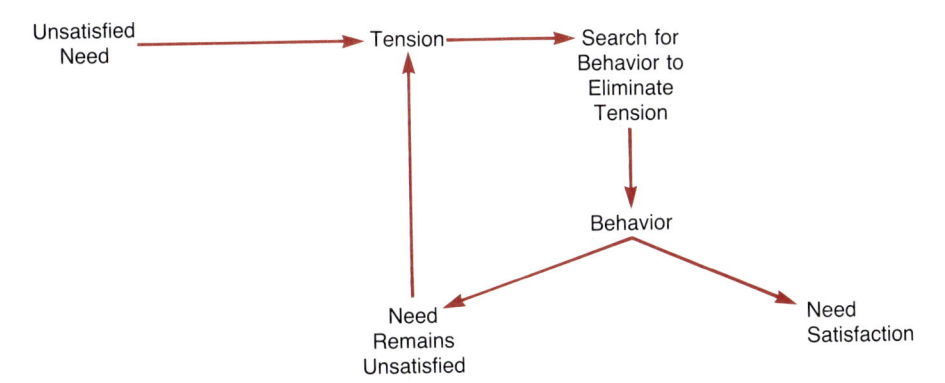

Unsatisfied Need → Tension → Search for Behavior to Eliminate Tension → Behavior → Need Satisfaction

Behavior → Need Remains Unsatisfied → Tension

Exhibit 5.2
Murray's manifest needs theory

Need	Characteristics
Achievement	Individual aspires to accomplish difficult tasks; maintains high standards and is willing to work toward distant goals; responds positively to competition; willing to put forth effort to attain excellence.
Affiliation	Individual enjoys being with friends and people in general; accepts people readily; makes efforts to win friendships and maintain associations with people.
Aggression	Individual enjoys combat and argument; easily annoyed; sometimes willing to hurt people to get his way; may seek to "get even" with people perceived as having harmed him.
Autonomy	Individual tries to break away from restraints, confinement, or restrictions of any kind; enjoys being unattached, free, not tied to people, places or obligations; may be rebellious when faced with restraints.
Endurance	Individual is willing to work long hours; does not give up quickly on a problem; perservering, even in the face of great difficulty; patient and unrelenting in his work habits.
Exhibition	Individual wants to be the center of attention; enjoys having an audience; engages in behavior that wins the notice of others; may enjoy being dramatic or witty.
Harm Avoidance	Individual does not enjoy exciting activities, especially if danger is involved; avoids risks of bodily harm; seeks to maximize personal safety.

CATEGORIES OF NEEDS

Motivation is complex, because there is an almost infinite number of needs which different individuals may find important. Several authors have identified those categories of needs they believe are most important to individuals.

Murray's Manifest Needs Theory

One of the more comprehensive listings was developed by Murray.[1] Murray's categories of needs appear in Exhibit 5.2, Murray's Manifest Needs Theory. Any of these needs may be *manifest* or *latent*. A **manifest need** is active, affecting

Exhibit 5.2 *(continued)*

Need	Characteristics
Impulsivity	Individual tends to act on the "spur of the moment" and without deliberation; given to readily vent feelings and wishes; speaks freely; may be volatile in emotional expression.
Nurturance	Individual gives sympathy and comfort; assists others whenever possible; interested in caring for children, the disabled, or the infirm; offers a "helping hand" to those in need; readily performs favors for others.
Order	Individual is concerned with keeping personal effects and surroundings neat and organized; dislikes clutter, confusion, lack of organization; interested in developing methods for keeping materials methodically organized.
Power	Individual attempts to control the environment and to influence or direct other people; expresses opinions forcefully; enjoys the role of leader and may assume it spontaneously.
Succor	Individual frequently seeks the sympathy, protection, love, advice, and reassurance of other people; may feel insecure or helpless without such support; confides difficulties readily to a receptive person.
Understanding	Individual wants to understand many areas of knowledge; values synthesis of ideas, verifiable generalization, logical thought, particularly when directed at satisfying intellectual curiosity.

Source: Adapted from Jackson, D. N. *Personality Research Form Manual.* Goshen, New York: Research Psychologists Press, Inc., 1967, 1974.

an individual's behavior; a **latent need** is inactive, currently exerting no influence on an individual's behavior. A need, however strong, is latent when there is currently no opportunity to satisfy that need and it has become inactive. This pattern makes it difficult to determine which needs are most important to individual employees. An individual may have a very strong need to participate in important decisions; however, his work environment may not have allowed him to do so. His need for participation may become latent and he may direct his energies toward other needs important to him which he is able to satisfy. Thus, his manager may see very little behavior which would suggest that he has a strong need to participate in important decisions. This

WHAT DO YOU THINK? Which of the need categories in Exhibit 5.2 are manifest for you right now? How do your manifest needs compare with those of your classmates? Your friends? Your parents? Your boss? Do you think that your needs will change over the next few years? Why and how? Do you currently have any latent needs which cannot be satisfied in your current environment, but if presented, would be a highly effective motivator for you?

apparent lack of interest does not mean that participation would be ineffective in motivating this employee. It may be extremely effective, but unfortunately the manager may never use it.

Maslow's Hierarchy of Needs

Identify several important categories of needs.

One important theory of motivation arranges categories of needs within hierarchies—specific orders or arrangements. Maslow's Hierarchy of Needs identifies five categories of needs.[2]

1. **Physiological needs**. These are basic physical needs such as those for food and water. On the job, these needs are satisfied by pay and fringe benefits such as paid vacation, and paid holidays.
2. **Safety needs**. These encompass the need for a safe physical and emotional environment. These needs are satisfied on the job by pay and fringe benefits such as disability pay, sick pay, and health insurance. They are also satisfied by management policies that provide for job security (such as a no layoff policy), as well as policies that provide for financial security (such as pension plans).
3. **Social needs**. This group includes the need to be accepted and liked by others. The work setting typically provides many opportunities for employees to develop relationships and interact with others. However, some work settings minimize or restrict the satisfaction of these important needs, due either to the technology or manner in which the work is performed, or to management rules and policies that restrict interaction during working hours. Managers should carefully evaluate these factors to determine whether policies and/or work methods can be altered to provide greater opportunities for employees to satisfy social needs.
4. **Esteem needs**. This category may be broken down into two types of esteem needs. **Self-esteem** has to do with the need to have a positive self-image. **Esteem of others** defines the need for recognition and attention from others whose opinions you respect. Both types of esteem needs may be satisfied on the job through interactions with coworkers and managers. Self-esteem may also result simply from good job performance, or from solving a difficult work-related problem.

Management at the General Foods plant in Dover, Maryland seems to have come up with a plan to provide opportunities for employees to satisfy both types of esteem needs. A "pride committee" comprising the plant manager, four supervisors, two union representatives, and seven hourly workers, receives and evaluates nominations for the winner of the company's monthly "Dover Pride Award." The award consists of a plaque and the choice between a day off with pay or dinner for the winner's family. Candidates for the award, which was implemented to improve employee morale and productivity, must exhibit the "Dover Pride." One winner pulled a small child from a burning automobile, another developed a plan for cutting inventory losses by 74 percent, and a third reduced the damage rate to the lowest level ever experienced at any General Foods plant. The major accomplishment of this program, according to one manager at the Dover plant, is that it has made "people feel better about working here."[3]

5. **Self-actualization needs**. These needs are exemplified by the need to grow, develop, and reach one's full potential. Many people have a relatively strong need to continually improve themselves, become better at the skills and abilities they have developed, and develop new skills and abilities. The opportunity to satisfy these needs can be built into many jobs by making the assigned work activities challenging and interesting, and by encouraging employees to participate in decisions and assume control of their own work activities.

   Quad/Graphics, one of the largest magazine printers in the country, prints more than 100 national magazines. Harry Quadracci, the owner, implemented an Employee Ownership Stock Plan, whereby employees can own a percentage of the company. The company makes contributions to a fund that buys the company's stock, which is then allocated to employees on the basis of seniority. However, Quad/Graphics has taken the idea of employee ownership and control much further than other companies. Employees are encouraged to be owners of the company in more than name only. Quadracci's philosophy, which he refers to as "Theory Q," focuses on making managers and employees indistinguishable. For example, every spring, Quadracci holds a "Spring Fling" managerial retreat that all managers attend. The company is left completely in the hands of the employees, who control all aspects of the company during this time. According to Quadracci, "Responsibility should be shared. Our people shouldn't need me or anyone else to tell them what to do."[4]

Which of these five categories of needs are manifest for you right now? Is any one category clearly more important to you than others? Are any of the categories latent? How likely is this to change in the near future?

Maslow arranges these five categories of needs in a hierarchy beginning with physiological needs and ending with self-actualization needs as shown in Exhibit 5.3. The arrangement in the hierarchy suggests the order in which the needs become manifest for most individuals. In other words, the lowest category of needs remaining unsatisfied will be the category of needs that influences an individual's motivation. There are some important implications in these statements. First, at any one point in time, only one category of needs will be manifest; and second, all individuals move through the hierarchy of needs in the same order, beginning with physiological needs, then safety needs, and so on.

Exhibit 5.3
Maslow's hierarchy of needs

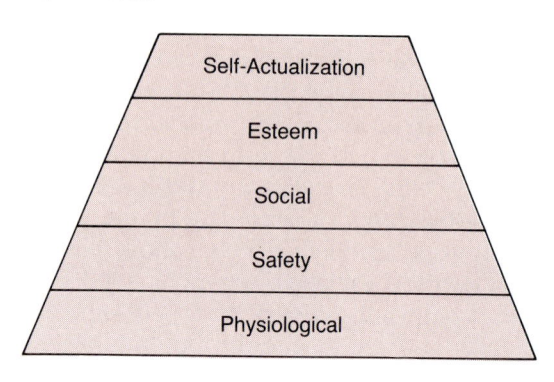

```
         Self-Actualization
            Esteem
            Social
            Safety
         Physiological
```

Modifications to Maslow's Theory

Relate unsatisfied needs to motivation.

Many scholars regard these two aspects of Maslow's theory as too restrictive. These critics suggest that the theory should be modified to take into account individual differences. Specifically, the theory should allow individuals to move through the categories of needs in different orders. It is hard to imagine that a person whose physiological or safety needs are not satisfied would be concerned with esteem or self-actualization. However, if we modify Maslow's Hierarchy so that only the first two needs (physiological and safety) are fixed, as shown in Exhibit 5.4, it may be more representative of individual behavior. This version suggests that once physiological and safety needs are satisfied, different individuals may move through the remaining three categories of needs in a different order. According to Maslow, the only need that can become manifest is an unsatisfied need. As the need begins to be relatively satisfied, its motivational force upon the individual diminishes. While this may be true for lower order needs such as hunger and thirst, it may not hold for higher order needs. What determines how much self-actualization will completely satisfy this need? The important point is, the motivational force of certain higher order needs may not diminish, but may actually become *stronger* as they are satisfied. As an employee begins to receive attention or esteem from others, or begins to grow and develop, these needs may become even more important to him.

Frustration–Regression Process

Explain what happens when people are unable to satisfy important needs.

Another important modification to Maslow's theory is the **frustration–regression** process.[5] This concept, illustrated in Exhibit 5.5, expands on the possibility that individuals may be unable to satisfy certain needs. A good example would be an individual who may have important self-actualization needs but is working in a routine and repetitive job for a manager who does not allow employee participation in important decisions. If this individual has satisfied all needs lower in the hierarchy, what happens? Maslow's theory really doesn't cover this situation. Since all needs lower in the hierarchy are satisfied, they would not exert any motivational influence on the individual. But the individ-

Exhibit 5.4
Modified hierarchy of needs

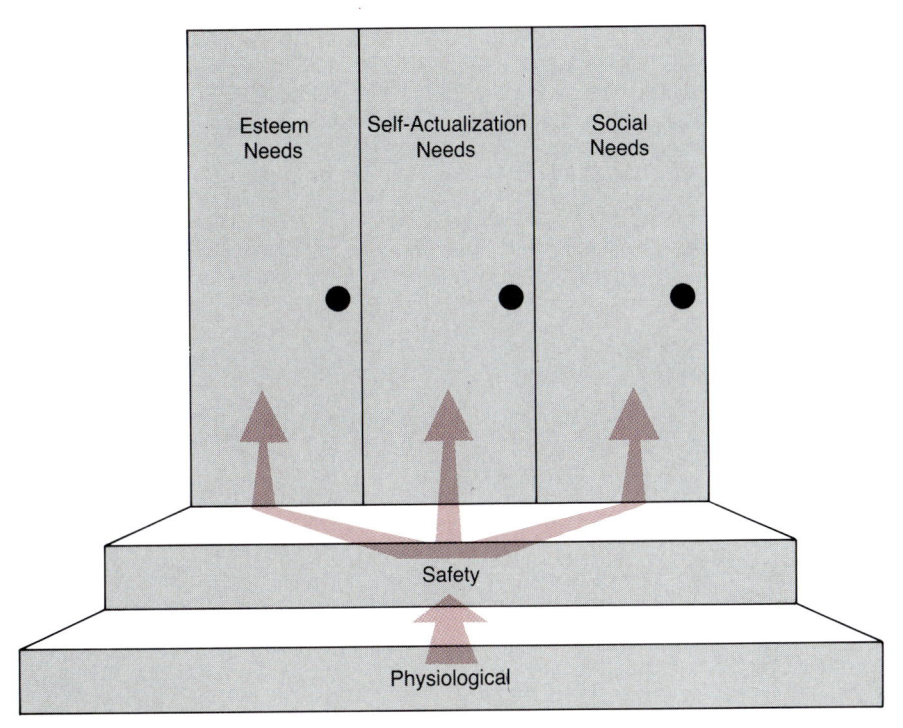

ual is not able to satisfy the needs at the next level. According to the frustration–regression process, previously satisfied lower level needs may again become manifest. The individual realizes that he cannot satisfy self-actualization needs and focuses again on satisfying esteem or social needs. Actually, individuals may follow any of several courses of action when they are prevented from satisfying important needs.

1. The individual may look for other ways of satisfying the need. For example, if the individual cannot satisfy growth and development needs on the job, he may enroll in classes at a local university, develop a challenging hobby, or do volunteer work. This may be one reason the supervisor in the Prologue enrolled in a graduate degree program. Perhaps she was unable to satisfy important growth and development needs at the workplace.
2. The individual may simply change jobs. If he is unable to satisfy important needs on the present job, there may be great incentive to seek alternative employment. This may be the strategy of the supervisor in the Prologue who is attending graduate school at night.
3. The individual may become withdrawn and alienated from the job and the organization. He may simply become resigned to "the way things are" and give up. He may do enough to keep from being fired, but is unlikely to do any more than is absolutely required. This may explain the behavior of the

Exhibit 5.5
Frustration–regression process

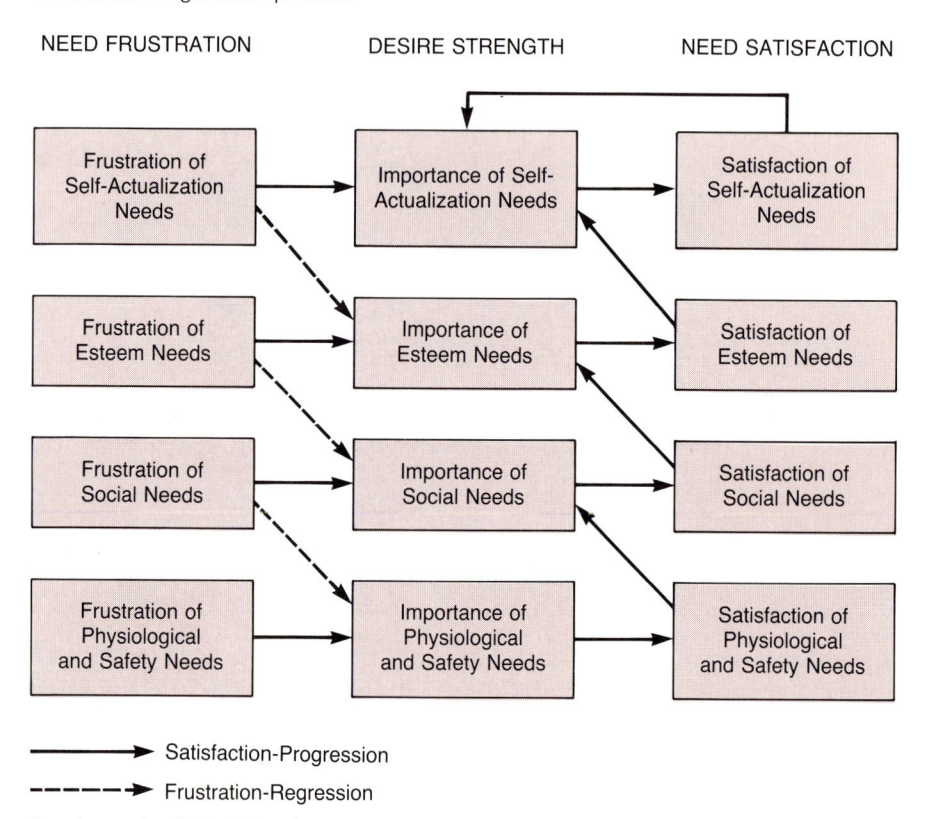

NEED FRUSTRATION	DESIRE STRENGTH	NEED SATISFACTION
Frustration of Self-Actualization Needs	Importance of Self-Actualization Needs	Satisfaction of Self-Actualization Needs
Frustration of Esteem Needs	Importance of Esteem Needs	Satisfaction of Esteem Needs
Frustration of Social Needs	Importance of Social Needs	Satisfaction of Social Needs
Frustration of Physiological and Safety Needs	Importance of Physiological and Safety Needs	Satisfaction of Physiological and Safety Needs

⎯⎯⎯→ Satisfaction-Progression
------→ Frustration-Regression

Based upon Landy, F. & Trumbo, D. *Psychology and work behavior.* Homewood, Illinois: Dorsey, 1980, p. 341.

supervisor in the Prologue who simply goes through the motions and tries to do as little as possible.

4. The individual may engage in dysfunctional behavior, spreading rumors, or even sabotage. While none of the supervisors in the Prologue exhibited these behavior patterns, it is a relatively common reaction for employees who are unable to satisfy important needs at work, and are unable to find alternative employment.

Two-Factor Theory

One theory of motivation, Herzberg's Two-Factor Theory, is based on the idea that unsatisfied needs motivate behavior, but does not adopt the hierarchical arrangement of those needs.[6] Herzberg's theory includes only two categories of needs. **Hygiene factors** are similar to Maslow's physiological, safety, and esteem of others needs. They are necessary for basic survival and well-being. **Motivators** are similar to Maslow's self-esteem and self-actualization needs. Hy-

Exhibit 5.6
Herzberg's Two-Factor Theory

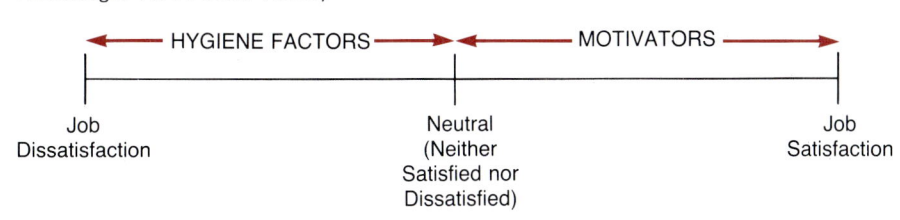

```
   ←——— HYGIENE FACTORS ———→  ←——— MOTIVATORS ———→
   |                            |                     |
   Job                        Neutral                Job
   Dissatisfaction           (Neither              Satisfaction
                            Satisfied nor
                            Dissatisfied)
```

giene factors include money, supervision, physical working conditions, interpersonal relations, status, security, and organizational policies. Motivators include achievement, recognition, challenging work, responsibility, autonomy, advancement, and growth and development.

According to Herzberg, managers cannot use hygiene factors to encourage employees to be highly motivated. Even if all organizational resources were diverted to provide employees with as many hygiene factors as possible, it is not likely that they would be highly motivated. On the other hand, if sufficient hygiene factors are not present, employees are likely to be highly dissatisfied with their job. Hygiene factors operate from a point of high job dissatisfaction to a neutral point where employees are neither satisfied nor dissatisfied. Hygiene factors can only attract employees to come to work and put in their time. Employees cannot be expected to be highly motivated and willing to put in extra effort or use their own initiative unless motivators are also provided. Motivators operate from the neutral point to a point of high job satisfaction and motivation, as shown in Exhibit 5.6.

Herzberg's theory is suggesting that managers cannot rely on *extrinsic needs*, (lower order needs, such as money) to motivate employees. To have highly motivated employees, managers must also provide *intrinsic needs*, (higher order needs, such as challenging and interesting work, recognition, responsibility, and opportunities for growth).

> Explain the difference between extrinsic and intrinsic motivation.

Herzberg's theory may partially explain the behavior of two of the supervisors described in the Prologue. The supervisor who seemed to live and breathe his job may be receiving adequate levels of both hygiene factors and motivators. However, the supervisor who did just enough to get by may be receiving adequate levels of hygiene factors, but inadequate levels of motivators. He was motivated to do enough to keep his job because of adequate levels of hygiene factors; he was not willing to exert any additional effort due to an absence of motivators.

> **RETURN TO THE PROLOGUE**

Job Enrichment

The ideas contained in Herzberg's Two-Factor Theory are implemented by various types of **job enrichment**. The purpose of job enrichment is to make a job more meaningful, challenging, and interesting, while providing employees with more responsibility, **autonomy** (freedom or self-control), and opportunities for growth. This concept is much different from *job enlargement,* which involves simply adding more of the same kind of work to employees' jobs, and *job rotation,* which involves rotating employees among similar jobs. Job enrichment adds different kinds of tasks and responsibilities to jobs. Methods of enriching jobs involve adding or increasing the motivating properties of tasks discussed in Chapter 2 and include the following:[7]

1. Combining tasks so that a job is more meaningful. Meaningful work measures the extent to which an employee is allowed to do a complete portion of the work, from start to finish.[8] Work is likely to be meaningful if an employee makes a complete item. For example, some automobile plants have changed the way the work was performed, to allow work teams to build a complete car from the ground up. This approach was in contrast to assembly-line methods where one person attached the rear view mirror, another person attached the hood, and so on.
2. Increasing skill variety, by offering the opportunity to use a large number of different skills. If an employee is good at 10 tasks, but his current job allows him to perform only 2 of these, how motivated would he be? Most people want to be able to use all, or at least most, of the skills and abilities they have developed.
3. Increasing autonomy, by giving an employee the freedom to determine the manner in which work is performed. Employees who are provided with a relatively high degree of autonomy are likely to experience responsibility, achievement, and recognition. Employees with autonomy are responsible for what happens. If a manager retains tight control and provides little freedom, he is largely responsible for what happens on a job. However, if an employee has autonomy, then *he* largely controls what happens on the job. These employees may feel that they "own the job." It is their job, as opposed to a job which someone else controls.
4. Assigning more difficult, challenging tasks provides employees with opportunities for growth, development, and self-actualization.

Perceptions of Inequity

Based on the motivation theories discussed so far, it is clear that managers must determine the specific needs which are most important to individual employees and then provide rewards or opportunities for employees to satisfy these needs. However, there is an aspect of motivation, related to administering rewards to employees, that complicates this process for managers—employee perceptions of reward equity or inequity.

Equity theory is concerned with employee perceptions of the fairness with which rewards are administered.[9] Employees commonly engage in a comparison process. They compare what they put into the job, called *inputs,* with what they get out of the job, called *outcomes.* The ratio of outcomes/inputs must be at least 1.0. That is, an employee must perceive that he is getting at least as much out of the job, in terms of rewards, as he is putting into it. However, this

---

HUMAN RELATIONS IN ACTION

Job Enrichment and Job Performance

In June of 1985, TWA flight 847 was highjacked on its way from Athens to Rome. The plane was forced to land in Beirut, Lebanon where it remained for 17 days. One passenger was shot and killed. What does this have to do with job enrichment? A lack of job enrichment may have contributed to the highjackers' ability to smuggle weapons aboard the plane.

Researchers have been examining what happens to people when they must engage in a monitoring task. Monitoring tasks include such jobs as airport security guards looking at X-rays of passenger baggage, intensive care nursing stations in hospitals, and airport control towers. The findings suggest that employee attentiveness declines rapidly when they must continually monitor equipment or other people. For example, airport security guards must sit behind an X-ray device and monitor passenger baggage for weapons and explosive devices. Fortunately, they do not see many of these items, called "critical signals." However, they must monitor extremely large numbers of "non-critical signals" to watch for a single critical signal. Since these critical signals occur so infrequently, the guards become bored and inattentive, lessening their ability to detect a critical signal when one is present. This boredom has been suggested as at least a partial reason for the highjackers' success in getting weapons aboard the TWA flight. The security guard simply did not detect a critical signal.

This decline in ability to detect critical signals occurs rapidly, perhaps after only 20 to 35 minutes of an employee's monitoring activity. Fortunately, several techniques have been found to maintain an employee's attentiveness at a high level. For most types of jobs, this involves some type of job enrichment. Making the task more complex and challenging may increase an employee's attentiveness and maintain it at a relatively high level. The challenging task provides the necessary stimulation to keep the employee alert at the monitoring activity.

Source: Warm, J.S. & Dember, W.N. Awake at the switch. *Psychology Today,* April 1986, *20,* 46–53.

---

isn't the only comparison being made. Employees compare their own outcome/input ratio to the ratios of other people, most commonly coworkers in similar jobs, as shown in Exhibit 5.7. According to equity theory, employees who perceive that their outcome/input ratio is not equal to that of the person they choose for comparison will experience tension. Since most people have

---

Exhibit 5.7
Equity theory comparisons

$$\frac{\text{Your perceptions of your outcomes from the job}}{\text{Your perceptions of your inputs to the job}} \quad \overset{?}{\underset{?}{=}} \quad \frac{\text{Your perceptions of other person's outcomes from the job}}{\text{Your perceptions of other person's inputs to the job}}$$

a need for being treated fairly, perceived inequity creates an unsatisfied need, leading to tension. As described earlier, in the simple model of motivation, this tension is a result of their belief that they are being treated inequitably. As a result, they will be motivated to do something to relieve this tension and restore equity. For example, if an employee feels underrewarded, he might simply lower his level of inputs to restore equity. If the inequity persists or is very strong, the employee might resort to absenteeism, tardiness, turnover, or even sabotage. It is rumored that when Herschel Walker joined the Dallas Cowboys football team and was paid an extremely high salary, Tony Dorsett, who had been the Cowboy's leading running back for several years prior to Walker's joining the team, demanded that he make at least $1.00 more than Walker.

Have you ever taken a course where at least one student seemed to have a much easier time with the material than you? This other student never seemed to study or take good notes, but always scored as well as you did on tests. You, on the other hand, had to study extremely hard to get the grade that you did. How did you feel about this situation?

Two aspects of this theory require further explanation. First, the comparison process is extremely subjective. It is *your* perception of *your* inputs and outcomes that you compare with *your* perception of another person's inputs and outcomes. Since you are not likely to have all the information you need concerning the other person's inputs and outcomes, you may have to rely on estimations in making your comparisons.

Second, not everyone will use the same set of inputs and outcomes. When you engage in an equity comparison, you decide which factors to consider. You might decide that level of effort, years of education, and experience are the only inputs worth considering. Another person might include these three factors, plus hours worked per week and age, in his comparisons. The importance of this exercise is that two employees could be putting exactly the same amount of inputs into the job, and be receiving the same level of outcomes, *yet both could perceive inequity*! This scenario suggests that it is important for managers to communicate their rationale for administering rewards to employees. Employees are going to make these kinds of comparisons. Managers can either provide them with accurate information about reward allocations, or they can allow employees to make comparisons with less accurate or incomplete information.

Recognize that the implication of equity theory is *not* that managers should reward all employees the same. Your inputs and outcomes do not have to match your comparison person's inputs and outcomes exactly. Only the *ratios* have to be equal. Employees will not perceive inequity if another person receives higher rewards than they do, as long as that person has to put more into the job. Returning to the earlier example, if the other student obviously worked harder than you did for a higher grade, you may be less likely to be upset. In this case, rewards (grades) are commensurate with outcomes. Exhibit 5.8 shows different combinations of inputs and outcomes which lead to perceptions of equity or inequity.

Exhibit 5.8
Perceptions of equity and inequity

Your Perceptions of Your Own Inputs and Outcomes		Your Perceptions of Other Persons' Inputs and Outcomes
Perceived Equity		
Low outcomes / Low inputs	=	Moderate outcomes / Moderate inputs
High outcomes / High inputs	=	Moderate outcomes / Moderate inputs
Perceived Inequity		
Moderate outcomes / High inputs	≠	Moderate outcomes / Moderate inputs
Low outcomes / Low inputs	≠	Moderate outcomes / Low inputs

Employee Expectations

Need-satisfaction theories and equity theory provide information concerning what energizes behavior. Managers must provide rewards that employees value and the rewards must be allocated equitably. Perceived inequity might energize behavior, but it is not likely to be behavior desired by the organization.

Expectancy theory is a popular concept of motivation that provides answers to the questions, what determines the direction of behavior? and what determines the strength of behavior?[10] Expectancy theory is based on the assumption that people will do things they believe will result in the highest payoffs for themselves. Three important components to the expectancy theory model are depicted in Exhibit 5.9.

Valence establishes the degree to which an employee desires a reward. Valence can be negative, neutral, or positive. Any activity or job is likely to

Exhibit 5.9
Model of expectancy theory of motivation

Effort ---- E_1 ----> Performance ---- E_2 ----> Outcomes NET VALENCE

have any number of rewards or outcomes associated with it. Some of these rewards will be desirable or have a positive valence, some will be neutral and some will be negative. A person might attach a high positive valence to additional responsibility and autonomy, and a negative valence to increased travel and relocating to a large city. Another person might attach a negative valence to additional responsibility and autonomy and a positive valence to travel and relocating to a large city. Of concern here is the net valence or summation of valences of all possible outcomes associated with the job or task. This bundle of outcomes must have a net positive valence, for the person to be willing to exert any effort to perform the activity. Managers must make sure they are offering rewards that employees desire, and are minimizing outcomes which employees find negative or neutral.

Performance→Outcome Expectancy (E_2) refers to the employee's perception that promised rewards will be delivered if he performs successfully. Employees ask themselves, "If I do what is asked will I get the rewards that were promised?" For an employee to be highly motivated, the answer to this question must be "Yes." An employee who is unsure that his manager will honor his promises of rewards will not be as highly motivated as an employee who is confident of receiving promised rewards. Managers must be careful that offhand remarks do not give employees the impression that a reward has been promised. Since rewards are so salient to most employees, a manager's offhand remark may be taken as a promise of a reward. Consider the effect of a manager's statement, "You've certainly performed well this past year. You'll be moving up in this organization soon." An employee could easily interpret this to mean that the manager has just promised to promote him. From the employees' perspective, such offhand remarks may lower their E_2.

A problem for managers is that many rewards are *system rewards,* administered just for being a member of the system (organization). They are not tied to specific levels of performance. Even salary, in many organizations, is only weakly tied to performance levels. This practice can make it difficult to use these rewards to motivate employees. Managers should be free to allocate *individual rewards* to individuals and/or groups solely on the basis of their level of performance. Managers must control the frequency and amount of rewards, to be able to truly motivate employees. Unfortunately, in some organizations, managers may completely control only intangible rewards such as praise and recognition.

Effort→Performance Expectancy (E_1) refers to the employee's confidence in his ability to successfully perform the task. The employee asks himself, "Am I capable of performing this job or activity successfully?" If the answer to this question is negative, it is unlikely that he will be highly motivated. For example, suppose you've just accepted a new job as a supervisor of Accounts/Payable and Receivable in a large retail organization. After a two-week orientation period, your boss gives you a special project. The assignment is to correlate several customer characteristics such as age, income level, number of dependents, and type of employment with the speed of payment. Your boss hypothesizes that several of these characteristics will show a relationship with speed of payment. He says something about using several statistical techniques such as regression and correlation to analyze this data. You have heard of these techniques but you really don't know much about them. How motivated are you likely to be to perform this assignment? Since your lack of familiarity with statistical techniques limits your ability to perform successfully, you may not be willing to exert much effort on this task, since you believe there is a good chance it will be wasted effort.

According to expectancy theory, three things must happen if an employee is going to be highly motivated to perform. First, the employee must have a high positive net valence for the outcomes associated with the activity. Second, the employee must have a high E_2. He must believe that the rewards will be forthcoming if he performs successfully. Rewards must be contingent upon performance; high performers must earn high rewards, low performers must earn low rewards, and so on. Finally, the employee must have a high E_1. He must believe that he can perform. A low E_1 may result because of the following.

1. The employee does not have the skill, training, ability, or experience to perform successfully. Managers must either provide the training or education necessary for the employee to perform the job or transfer him to a job for which he is prepared.
2. The employee *perceives* he does not have the skill, training, ability, or experience to perform successfully. In other words, the employee lacks confidence in his ability. In this case, managers must coach and counsel, to build the employee's confidence.
3. The employee isn't sure what "successful performance" is. In this case, it has not been made clear to the employee what is expected of him. To increase the employee's E_1, managers must clarify performance expectations and set clear and specific goals for the employee.

Reinforcement Theory

Need satisfaction and equity theories have suggested ways to energize behavior. Equity theory also has implications for the direction of the behavior—toward organizationally desired behaviors if equity is perceived, toward organizationally undesired behaviors if inequity is perceived. Expectancy theory provided information on ways to increase the strength of the behavior (level of effort), and to some degree the direction of the behavior, if desired outcomes are tied to specific behaviors. *Reinforcement theory* will provide additional information on determinants of the direction of motivated behavior, as well as on what causes behavior to persist over time.

Law of Effect
Reinforcement theory draws heavily upon the work of B.F. Skinner.[11] Other names for reinforcement theory are behavior modification, instrumental learning, and operant conditioning. The theory is based upon the law of effect—which states that behavior producing pleasurable consequences tends to be repeated, while behavior that results in unpleasurable consequences tends to be eliminated. The managerial implications of the law of effect are very simple:

Reward employees when they perform well, do not reward them when they do not perform well. However, implementing this rather straightforward suggestion is not so easy. There are two aspects of reinforcement theory—types of reinforcement and reinforcement schedules—that managers should clearly understand.

Types of Reinforcement
There are four types of reinforcement. Two are used to make behavior more likely to be repeated and two are used to make behavior less likely to be repeated.

Positive Reinforcement. **Positive reinforcement** involves administering a reward an employee desires after he engages in an organizationally desired behavior (high job performance or solving a difficult work-related problem). It is used to make the behavior likely to be repeated in the future. The reward must be made contingent on performance; the employee must clearly understand the reason for the reward. In addition, the reward should be administered as soon as possible after the desired behavior.

Negative Reinforcement. **Negative reinforcement** is the other type of reinforcement which makes behavior likely to be repeated. Negative reinforcement occurs when an employee engages in an organizationally desired behavior, to avoid an unpleasant outcome. Thus, when an employee exerts great effort to get back from lunch on time in order to avoid a reprimand in front of his coworkers, negative reinforcement is at work.

Extinction. **Extinction** basically involves ignoring a particular behavior. When an employee engages in a particular behavior, and is ignored, he has no incentive to repeat the behavior. Unfortunately, managers sometimes unintentionally extinguish the wrong behaviors. When employees devise better ways of doing their jobs and make suggestions to a manager who ignores them, this behavior is extinguished.

Punishment. **Punishment** is administering an unpleasant consequence or outcome to an employee engaging in an organizationally undesired behavior. Punishment is being administered when an employee is publicly reprimanded for returning from lunch 20 minutes late.

Suggestions for Using Reinforcement Theory
In most cases, scholars recommend positive reinforcement and extinction over negative reinforcement and punishment, in the belief that people react poorly to punishment or the threat of punishment (negative reinforcement). For example, publicly reprimanding an employee might embarrass that person to the point where he feels inequitably treated and becomes motivated to "get even." This action might be calling in sick when he really isn't or something even more serious. Several rules for using reinforcement theory ideas have been suggested.[12]

1. Differentiate rewards based on performance levels. High performers should receive high rewards; poor performers should receive low rewards. To reward all employees equally extinguishes the extra effort of high performers. There is no incentive for them to continue to perform better than their coworkers.
2. Ignoring employee behaviors will result in the extinction of those behaviors. When employees do something that merits attention, reinforce it. Failing to respond to employee behavior is not neutral; it modifies (extinguishes) behavior.
3. Make it clear to employees which behaviors will result in positive reinforcement and which may result in punishment. Employees must clearly understand the rules of the game before they go out on the court.
4. If an employee isn't performing adequately, tell that person immediately. It isn't fair to the employee to wait until the yearly performance/salary review to tell him there is a problem. Even extinction involves some action on the part of the manager. Extinction should be accompanied with clear communications about the performance problem and what can be done to correct it.
5. The outcomes or rewards should equal the behavior: high performers, high rewards; low performers, low rewards. In this way, high performers are reinforced and given an incentive to continue their level of performance. Low performers are given an incentive to improve. At least, they are not given an incentive to continue their low performance, which is often what happens when clear differentiation is not made between levels of performance.
6. Consider the manner in which the reward is administered.[13] A reward which is highly valued by employees may lose its potential to motivate if it is administered carelessly. How would you feel if the promotion you have been wanting for three years finally came through, and then you found that one of your best friends had been fired to create the opening? Or, suppose you developed a plan to save the company over $100,000 per year and when you met your manager in the hall he simply muttered something about "Pretty good work" almost as an afterthought. Perhaps he took the time to dictate a letter of commendation to be placed in your permanent personnel record, but when you received it, it contained several typographical errors. Now, on the other hand, suppose that instead of your immediate superior, the vice-president of the Division came down to your department to publicly thank you for your valuable contribution. Why is this last example likely to be much more effective than the previous ones? The reward, praise and recognition, is the same. Only the way the reward is administered has been changed.

Schedules of Reinforcement
Positive reinforcement can be administered in several different ways. On a *continuous reinforcement schedule* rewards are dispensed every time an employee engages in a correct behavior. This prompt response results in rapid learning of new behaviors, but rapid extinction if the continuous reinforce-

ment is discontinued. On a *variable reinforcement schedule* rewards are not dispensed after every correct behavior. It may take employees longer to learn new behaviors under variable reinforcement schedules, but once learned, these behaviors are likely to be more permanent. There are four types of variable reinforcement schedules. Two of these, **fixed interval** and **variable interval**, are based on time; and two, **fixed ratio** and **variable ratio**, are based on the number of correct behaviors.

1. Fixed interval reinforcement schedule. If employees continue to engage in desired behaviors, a reward is administered at fixed intervals, such as once a week or once a month. The problem with this schedule is that employees learn when to expect the reward, and improve their performance just before it is due. Once the reward is received, they may let their performance decline to minimally acceptable levels. Examples of this reinforcement schedule are the weekly pay check, or a supervisor checking on the shop floor at 2:00 every afternoon.
2. Variable interval reinforcement schedule, also based upon a time interval, varies the specific length of time between rewards. Obviously, this schedule could not be used for distributing paychecks, since employees must meet monthly bills. However, it could be used for rewards such as promotions, positive feedback, or bonuses. This schedule may make behavior more consistent, since it is more difficult to predict exactly when the reward will come. Thus, employees may be motivated to maintain their level of performance to be eligible when the reward is due. However, since this schedule is based on time rather than behavior, employees may associate the reward with spending a certain amount of time on the job rather than performing at specific levels.
3. Fixed ratio reinforcement schedule is based on the number of correct behaviors which the employee exhibits. For example, a personal computer salesperson may earn a $2,500 bonus for every 10 personal computers sold. This schedule ties the reward to a specific behavior, but since it is a fixed schedule, the reward is predictable.
4. Variable ratio reinforcement schedule makes it most difficult for employees to predict when rewards will be administered, and ties the rewards to specific behaviors. Under this schedule, rewards are administered after a certain number of correct behaviors, with the exact number of behaviors necessary for a reward varying around some average. Thus, the computer salesperson might earn a $2,500 bonus after every 10 computers sold, on average. He might actually receive the bonus after selling 5 computers, then 10 computers, then 15 computers, then 5 computers, then 15 computers, and so on. Exhibit 5.10 summarizes the characteristics of the 4 basic reinforcement schedules.

Vicarious Learning

There is a final aspect of reinforcement which managers should understand. Behavior modification covers only direct learning, which occurs when an employee actually engages in a behavior and receives a reinforcement (e.g., re-

Understand the difference between direct and indirect reinforcement.

Exhibit 5.10
Characteristics of partial reinforcement schedules

	Not Difficult to Predict Rewards	Difficult to Predict Rewards
Ties Rewards to Specific Behaviors	Fixed Ratio	Variable Ratio
Does Not Tie Rewards to Specific Behaviors	Fixed Interval	Variable Interval

ward or punishment). However, employees receive information that they use to make decisions about their behavior from another source—indirect, or **vicarious**, learning.[14] Employees observe the consequences of others' behavior and use this information to make decisions about their own behavior. Thus, a manager who rewards one employee for a certain behavior should be aware that other employees may begin engaging in that behavior in the hope of receiving a similar reward. If the manager doesn't recognize and reward the other employees, they may perceive that they are being inequitably treated.

Employees learn vicariously by observing the consequences of others' behavior.

DEVELOPING YOUR HUMAN RELATIONS SKILLS

This chapter has provided information that is important for you both as a manager and as an employee. As an employee, you can greatly assist your manager in effectively motivating your behavior.

1. Identify which needs are most important to you and how they might be satisfied on the job. For example, if esteem needs are particularly important to you right now, a promotion, challenging work assignment, or special project that receives a great deal of attention in the organization might satisfy these needs.
2. Communicate your needs to your manager. Managers typically have many responsibilities and sometimes are not able to spend enough time with employees to learn which needs are most important to each individual. In casual conversations, regularly scheduled counseling sessions, or performance evaluations, let your manager know which needs you value the most and how they might be satisfied on your current job.
3. Recognize that managers don't always have control over all rewards. It is not uncommon, particularly at lower levels in organizations, for managers to have very little control over rewards. Even pay raises may have to be approved by higher levels. Don't let this damage relations between you and your boss.

As a manager, there are several basic steps you can take to effectively motivate employees.

1. Recognize that all employees are different and have different needs. The same rewards will not work with all employees.
2. Recognize that what motivates employees is likely to change over time. Just because you know what motivates a particular individual right now, you can't become complacent and continue to motivate this person with the same rewards over time.
3. Keep in mind the idea of latent needs. Don't assume that because there is no indication that a specific reward would motivate a particular employee, it will automatically be ineffective. You must get to know your employees well enough to know if they have any strong latent needs which can be used to motivate them.
4. When administering rewards, remember that employees are likely to make equity comparisons. Linking rewards closely to performance levels and communicating openly about the reward administration process may help reduce equity comparisons.
5. To the extent that it is possible, tie rewards closely to performance levels. This means that the amount of rewards which are given to employees who perform at different levels must be meaningful. A one or two percent difference in salary increases for a top performer and an average performer is not a meaningful difference.
6. Remember that rewards given to one employee will influence the behavior of other employees who become aware of it. Employees pay close attention to rewards in organizational work settings, so rewards can be used to send strong messages to all employees. If rewards are highly contingent on performance, that message can be motivating. However, if rewards are not strongly linked to performance, the message can be that performing up to one's capabilities is not necessary.

While rewards must be individualized to satisfy a particular employee's needs, managers must realize their potential effects on other employees.

One organization that has reaped the benefits of an effectively implemented reinforcement program is the Union National Bank in Little Rock, Arkansas.[15] Positive reinforcement is being used to increase performance and reduce absenteeism and turnover in several areas within the bank. In one of the departments where impressive results have been achieved, the proof department, employees code the numbers on checks so they can be processed electronically. Accuracy and speed are essential. Checks which are not coded, or are coded incorrectly, do not get credited to the bank's account and the bank does not earn interest on these amounts.

Before the first experiment with positive reinforcement, employees in the proof department were coding an average of 1,065 checks per hour (industry average was about 1,000). The first attempt at positive reinforcement involved the weekly posting of a graph showing output and praising the employees with the highest performance. Output increased to 2,100 checks per hour. Later, a bonus was added to the program whereby employees could increase their earnings by producing up to a maximum of 2,800 checks per hour. Bonuses were not paid for output over this level. Within three months, output had reached the maximum. When the maximum was increased to 3,000 checks per hour, output went up again. Finally, no maximum level was stated and output increased to an average of 3,500 checks per hour where it remained. Some individuals, however, have produced as many as 4,460 checks per hour! Under this program employees are able to earn bonuses of 50 to 70 percent of their base salary.

Before the positive reinforcement program was implemented, turnover was 110 percent and absenteeism was 4.24 percent. After the program began, turnover dropped to 0 percent and absenteeism dropped to 2.23 percent. In addition, overtime declined from 475 to only 13 hours per year. The bank estimates savings due to faster and more accurate check processing of approximately $100,000 per year.[16]

Develop strategies for motivating employees.

SUMMARY

Motivation is defined as the force which determines (1) what energizes behavior, (2) the direction of the behavior, (3) the strength of the behavior, and (4) how long the behavior will persist. Many theories of motivation are based on the idea that unsatisfied needs motivate individual behavior. Therefore, one important task for managers is to identify those categories of needs most important to individual employees. The importance of various categories of needs will vary among individuals and over time. Theories which help identify important need categories are Maslow's Hierarchy of Needs and Herzberg's Two-Factor Theory. Equity theory suggests that managers must not only provide rewards which satisfy important needs of individual employees, but must administer these rewards equitably. Equitable does not mean equal.

Expectancy theory is based on employee perceptions of three aspects of their work situation. Valence refers to the desirability of a particular outcome or reward. Effort→Performance Expectancy refers to the individual's confidence in his ability to perform. Performance→Outcomes Expectancy refers to the individual's belief that rewards are contingent on performance. According to this theory, individuals must have a high positive net preference for outcomes, a high effort→performance expectancy, and a high performance→outcomes expectancy.

Reinforcement theory is based upon the law of effect—behavior that results in a pleasurable consequence tends to be repeated; behavior that results in unpleasurable or neutral outcomes, or behavior which is ignored tends to be eliminated. Managers must be aware of two types of learning: direct, and indirect or vicarious.

KEY TERMS

motivation
manifest needs
physiological needs
safety needs
social needs
esteem needs
self-actualization needs
frustration–regression
hygiene factors
motivators
job enrichment
autonomy
valence
performance→outcome
    expectancy
effort→performance
    expectancy
positive reinforcement
negative reinforcement
extinction
punishment
fixed interval schedule
variable interval
    schedule
fixed ratio schedule
variable ratio schedule
vicarious learning

DISCUSSION QUESTIONS

1. Describe how Maslow's Hierarchy of Needs predicts employee motivation.
2. How does the frustration–regression process work?
3. Explain Herzberg's Two-Factor Theory of motivation.
4. How are perceptions of inequity related to employee motivation?
5. What are the three components of the expectancy theory of motivation? According to expectancy theory, what is necessary before an individual becomes highly motivated?
6. Describe the four types of reinforcement. When is each most appropriate?
7. Describe the two primary schedules of reinforcement and the four types of variable reinforcement schedules. What are the advantages and disadvantages of each?
8. Differentiate between direct learning and vicarious learning.

EXERCISE 5.1

Listed below are several statements which have to do with a variety of needs. Rate each of these statements using the following scale:

3 = very much like me
1 = somewhat like me
0 = not at all like me

____ 1. I like to work hard.
____ 2. I enjoy a challenge.
____ 3. I like having a lot of friends.
____ 4. I enjoy belonging to many different groups and organizations.
____ 5. I enjoy influencing other people.
____ 6. I will often step forward and assume a leadership position.
____ 7. I prefer working with other people rather than working alone.
____ 8. If given a choice, I would prefer to be in charge.
____ 9. I prefer difficult assignments to easy ones.

Scoring

____ Need for Power score: Sum your ratings for items 5, 6, and 8.
____ Need for Affiliation score: Sum your ratings for items 3, 4, and 7.
____ Need for Achievement score: Sum your ratings for items 1, 2, and 9.

Your score for each of these types of needs can range from 0 to 9. Which category of need is dominant? What does this dominance mean to a manager interested in motivating you? Do you think these results have any implications for your ability to motivate your employees?

EXERCISE 5.2

Listed below are ten factors which are likely to be associated with most jobs. In Column 1, rank these items from 1 to 10 in terms of how important each is to you right now. In Column 2, rank the items from 1 to 10 in terms of how important you think these factors are to a particular group of employees. Your instructor will inform you which group of employees to consider.

Job Factor	My Ranking	Employee Ranking
1. Good wages and benefits	____	____
2. Job security	____	____

3. Tactful disciplining   ___   ___
4. Recognition and appreciation of good work   ___   ___
5. Interesting/challenging work   ___   ___
6. Understanding of personal problems   ___   ___
7. Good working conditions   ___   ___
8. Opportunity for growth and advancement   ___   ___
9. Participation in decision making   ___   ___
10. Friendly coworkers   ___   ___

CASE 5.1

Motivation Without Money
By John E. Oliver, Valdosta State College

Zeke Carter has been in state government for 5 years, since graduating from Southern State University with a degree in Clinical Psychology. His career in the Department of Human Resources has been intrinsically rewarding, because Zeke has gained a tremendous amount of personal satisfaction from working with the mentally retarded and with autistic children. In fact, Zeke was called by the producers of the movie "Rainman" to consult with the moviemakers on autistic behavior. He has a national reputation for breaking through to autistic children when others have been unable to do so. Just last year Zeke was able to communicate with a boy who had not spoken a word for twelve years.

Six months ago, Zeke was promoted to manager of a Mental Retardation Service Center for several counties in the southern part of the state. The center's goal is to "deinstitutionalize" the mentally retarded. Six county supervisors report directly to Zeke, and each of them monitors from five to forty social workers, behavior specialists, houseparents, home-providers, and community workers serving mentally retarded clients in their communities. At a meeting between Zeke and the county supervisors, the problem of motivating the social workers, specialists, and other first-line employees was discussed. Salaries in many of the jobs are low, set by the state merit system. Supervisors have little impact on people's pay. Promotion is slow and sometimes limited by the need for advanced degrees or license requirements. The work, while rewarding, is sometimes frustrating and difficult. Many of the people working directly with mentally retarded clients suffer "burnout," characterized by emotional exhaustion, loss of feeling and concern, loss of trust, loss of interest, and loss of spirit. Burnout sufferers have a negative reaction to others, an aversion to clients, a tendency toward irritability, and a loss of idealism. They feel helpless, depressed, and unable to cope. They may withdraw from people and feel that their own accomplishments are not worthwhile.

Since their control over raises and promotions is so limited, Zeke and his supervisors are in a quandary. How can they motivate these specialized employees while dealing with the burnout issue? Perhaps some of the theories of motivation Zeke read about in his Human Relations text can provide some ideas.

QUESTIONS

1. What advice would you give to Zeke to help him motivate employees in the Department of Human Resources?
2. Which theories of motivation discussed in the chapter seem to best fit Zeke's situation?

REFERENCES

[1] Murray, H.A. *Exploration in personality*. New York: Oxford University Press, 1938; Atkinson, J.W. *An introduction to motivation*. Princeton, N.J.: Van Nostrand, 1964.

[2] Maslow, A.H. A theory of human motivation. *Psychological Review,* 1943, *50,* 370–396; Maslow, A.H. *Motivation and personality*. New York: Harper and Row, 1954.

[3] General Foods pride committee salutes hero employees. *Management Review,* May 1984, p. 42.

[4] Rosen, C., Klein, K.J. & Young, K.M. When employees share the profits. *Psychology Today,* 1986, *21*(1), 30–36.

[5] Alderfer, C.P. *Existence, relatedness and growth*. New York: Free Press, 1972; Alderfer, C.P. An empirical test of a new theory of human needs. *Organizational Behavior and Human Performance,* 1969, *4,* 142–175.

[6] Herzberg, F., Mausner, B. and Snyderman, B. *The motivation to work*. New York: John Wiley, 1959.

[7] Herzberg, F. One more time: How do you motivate employees? *Harvard Business Review,* January-February 1968, *46,* 53–62.

[8] Plous, F.K. Redesigning work. *Personnel Administrator,* 1987, *32*(3); p. 99.

[9] Adams, J.S. Toward an understanding of inequity. *Journal of Abnormal and Social Psychology,* 1963, *67,* 422–436; Cosier, R.A. & Dalton, D.R. Equity theory and time: A reformulation. *Academy of Management Journal,* 1983, *8,* 311–319; Carroll, M.R. & Dittrich, J.E. Equity theory: The recent literature, methodological considerations, and new directions. *Academy of Management Review,* 1978, *3,* 202–209.

[10] Vroom, V.H. *Work and motivation*. New York: Wiley, 1964; Porter, L.W. & Lawler, E.E., III, *Managerial attitudes and performance*. Homewood, Illinois: Dorsey Press, 1968.

[11] Skinner, B.F. *The behavior of organisms*. New York: Appleton-Century, 1938; Skinner, B.F. *Walden Two*. New York: The Macmillan Company, 1948; Skinner, B.F. *Science and human behavior*. New York: The Macmillan Company, 1953; Skinner, B.F. Freedom and the control of men. *American Scholar,* 1956, *25,* 47–65.

[12] Hamner, W.C. Reinforcement theory and contingency management in organizational settings. From Tosi, H.L. & Hamner, W.C. (Eds.), *Organizational behavior and management: A contingency approach*. Chicago: St. Clair Press, 1974.

[13] Grant, P.C. Rewards: The pizzazz is the package, not the prize. *Personnel Journal,* March 1988, *67*(3), 76–81.

[14] Bandura, A. *Social learning theory*. Englewood Cliffs, N.J.: Prentice-Hall, 1977.

[15] Dierks, W. & McNally, K. Incentives you can bank on. *Personnel Administrator,* 1987, *32*(3), 60–65.

[16] Ibid.

WHAT DO YOU THINK? NOTE

There are obviously no correct or incorrect answers to these questions. It might be interesting to compare the needs which are most important to you right now with those of your classmates, and then to discuss why each person values each particular need. You should also be able to predict, at least over the near future, which needs are most likely to become less important and which ones will become more important. How will you be able to satisfy each of these needs on the job? Finally, for some individuals, there may be a category of need which is unimportant to them.

CHAPTER SIX

Interpersonal Communication: Getting Your Message Across

PROLOGUE

Ben was 25 minutes late for an important staff meeting. "I knew I should've purchased those new tires last weekend. I hope some of the others were late too." He knew that his boss would not hold the meeting up for him. He also knew that he would have to explain why he was late and ask him to repeat what was covered before Ben got there. "He absolutely hates to have to repeat himself," Ben thought.

As Ben walked into the conference room, he saw that he was right. The meeting had obviously been underway for several minutes. It took Ben a few more minutes to figure out exactly what they were talking about. Fortunately, no one called attention to his late arrival. However, Ben thought he noticed his manager's eyebrows lower as he walked in the room.

As soon as the meeting was over, Ben walked back to his office. On the way he stopped to speak to several of his employees. Ben had tried to explain to some of the other supervisors that it was a good idea to spend a couple of minutes in small talk with your employees. He believed that it let them know you are aware of what they're doing and that you do care about them. Most of the other supervisors teased Ben about this. They seemed to believe that they were too busy to waste their time in this manner.

As Ben approached Joe's desk, Joe appeared to be waiting for him. Ben said hello and asked how things were going. Joe responded with "Just fine." But there was something about the way he said it that made Ben think that everything wasn't "fine." Ben told Joe that he had to check in at his office, but that he would be back later that morning to talk with him.

As Ben approached his office, he could see that there were two people waiting to see him. His secretary introduced these people and told him that he had an important call on hold. He apologized to the visitors and went into his office to take the call. As he sat down at his desk he noticed that memorandum he had

145

been working on to announce the new company safety policy. He just had to get that finished today.

LEARNING OBJECTIVES

After successful completion of this chapter, you should be able to:

- Describe the communication process,
- Explain how perception influences communication,
- Identify several common perceptual problems and explain their influences upon the effectiveness of communications,
- Explain why meaning cannot be transmitted,
- Describe nonverbal communication and be able to identify several of its specific forms,
- Recognize the differences between destructive and constructive feedback,
- Engage in active listening,
- Compare the purposes, advantages, and disadvantages of upward versus downward communications, and
- Explain how the grapevine works.

COMMUNICATION IN ORGANIZATIONS

To say that communication is important in organizations is one of the greatest understatements of all time. Communication has been referred to as the "lifeblood of an organization."[1] Organizations depend on the communication process to collect information, both within and outside of the organization, and transmit this information to points within the organization where it is needed. Organizations communicate with other organizations, groups (e.g., competitors, suppliers, banks, consumer groups, employee groups), and individuals to acquire and provide information. Within the organization, managers depend on their ability to communicate to provide employees with guidance, direction, and encouragement. Employees depend on their ability to communicate to make managers aware of their needs, problems they are facing on their jobs, and suggestions for improving the way their jobs are performed. Many human relations problems can be traced to ineffective communications. In fact, the nature of communication (e.g., open, trusting, secretive, impersonal) has a significant impact on human relations within organizations.

Even though most people recognize the importance of communication in work settings, many organizations list communication difficulty as one of their top three problems. One of the reasons for communication problems is that we become complacent about communicating. We communicate so much that we forget to do it carefully. We don't plan our communications and we don't follow up on them to ensure that they were received and interpreted correctly. The "What Do You Think?" box contains a short quiz designed to help you assess your own communications effectiveness. Do not answer this quiz in terms of what you think is correct, but rather in terms of what you actually do most of the time.

CHAPTER SIX: Interpersonal Communication: Getting Your Message Across   147

For each statement below, rate yourself as follows:

    3 = excellent   2 = good   1 = fair

	WHAT DO YOU THINK?

IN SPEAKING:

____ My attitude is positive.
____ I analyze the situation and listener and adapt to these.
____ I plan my purpose related to listener interest and attitude.
____ I try to get on common ground.
____ My prejudices are submerged.

MY MESSAGE:

____ Is organized clearly.
____ Has a definite and clear purpose.
____ Adapts opening remarks to listener(s).
____ Presents points (not too many) in clear order.
____ Goes clearly from one point to another (transitions).
____ Has sufficient proof and support.
____ Holds interest and attention.
____ Uses appropriate language.
____ Shows clear thinking.

IN PRESENTING THE MESSAGE:

____ My manner is enthusiastic.
____ I look directly at listener(s).
____ My posture and gestures are appropriate.
____ I project my voice with emphasis and variety.
____ I speak clearly and distinctly.
____ I adapt to listener reactions.

AS A LISTENER:

____ I pay full attention to the speaker.
____ I look at the speaker.
____ I am openminded and empathetic.
____ I help establish a pleasant climate.
____ I try to understand the speaker's purpose.
____ I separate facts from opinion.
____ I evaluate, not jumping to conclusions.
____ I avoid daydreaming.
____ I listen fully before trying to talk back or refute the speaker.
____ I apply the message to my needs.
____ TOTAL SCORE

EVALUATION OF YOUR COMMUNICATION EFFECTIVENESS:

80–90 = EXCELLENT
70–80 = GOOD
60–70 = FAIR[2]

If you fall into the *good* or *fair* categories, there is room for improvement. Refer back to the individual items in the Communications Effectiveness Quiz for specific areas in which you need to improve.

MANAGERS AND COMMUNICATION

It has been estimated that managers spend approximately 80 percent of their time in some form of communication.[3] The manager described in the Prologue was exposed to several types and incidents of communication in just his first few minutes on the job. Nonmanagerial employees must also communicate extensively in carrying out their assigned tasks. Thus, learning to communicate effectively is one of the most important things you can do to ensure a successful career.

RETURN TO THE PROLOGUE

The prologue illustrates how frequently managers must engage in various forms of communication with a variety of individuals. Ben had only been at work a short time, yet had already been exposed to several instances of verbal communication, written communication, and nonverbal communication. To a great extent, a manager's job performance depends upon his ability to communicate effectively. Yet, when asked to name the three biggest problems faced by their organization, communication problems always make the list. As our economy continues to change from manufacturing-oriented to service-oriented, communication will become even more important. In a service-oriented economy, most of the jobs involve the collection, analysis, and dissemination of information rather than the production of physical output.[4] Communication is the primary means by which this information is transmitted.

This chapter will present a simple model of interpersonal communication and discuss potential problems or obstacles to effective communication. Suggestions to help you communicate more effectively will be given throughout the chapter.

INTERPERSONAL COMMUNICATION

Interpersonal communication may be defined as a transmission of signals or symbols from a sender to a receiver, with the intent of sharing meaning. The transmission can be either verbal (including nonverbal communication) or written. The focus of this chapter will be on verbal communication, since managers tend to most frequently engage in and prefer verbal communication. A simple model of interpersonal communication appears in Exhibit 6.1. The communication process begins when the sender becomes aware of a message she wishes to transmit to a receiver. The sender must then choose the symbols (e.g., words, pictures) to use in transmitting her message. Symbols are chosen

Exhibit 6.1
Model of interpersonal communication

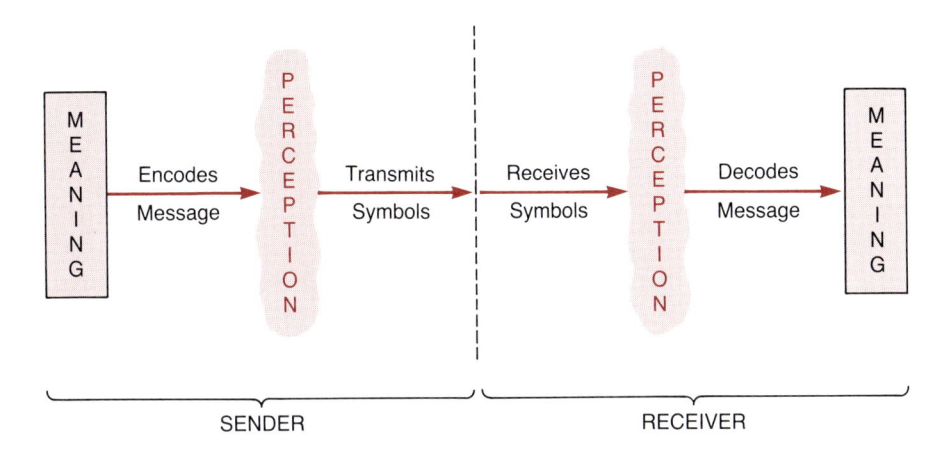

```
[MEANING] --Encodes Message--> [PERCEPTION] --Transmits Symbols--> | --Receives Symbols--> [PERCEPTION] --Decodes Message--> [MEANING]
           _____ SENDER _____/                  _____ RECEIVER _____/
```

which the sender believes the receiver will interpret in the desired manner. The sender must then choose a medium (e.g., spoken word, written word). Once the message has been transmitted, the recipient must receive the symbols and interpret meaning from them.

Several obstacles may prevent the symbols from being received; others may prevent the symbols from being interpreted correctly. The important point is that meaning cannot be transmitted.[5] Message senders can transmit only symbols, such as words, which have no inherent meaning. Communication is effective only when receivers interpret the correct meaning from the symbols. Differences in perception are the cause of many communication problems.

PERCEPTION

Perception was described in Chapter 4 as a process in which individuals interpret information about their surroundings. In simple terms, perception is how each of us sees reality. Perception can cause communication problems because each of us tends to view "reality" a little differently. Even though you and I might look at a wall in an office building and agree that its color is blue, the color blue you perceive may be different from the color blue that I perceive. These different shades of blue may cause us to interpret our surroundings differently. Perhaps the shade of blue that I perceive causes me to see a crisp, cool surrounding, while the shade of blue that you perceive causes you to see your surroundings as secure and comfortable.

Perception and Communication

Four major aspects of perception are potential causes of communication problems: *perceptual filtering, perceptual expectations, perceptual distortion,* and *closure.* These factors may cause communication problems because each of them can cause perceptions to be inaccurate or incomplete. Since we have no alternative but to communicate about the things we perceive, our messages are likely to be inaccurate to the extent that one of these perceptual problems is present. In addition, as message receivers, we all interpret symbols in light of our perceptions. Thus, if I told you that the color of your new office was blue, you might assume that the environment was secure and comfortable. Actually, I was trying to communicate to you that your new office environment was crisp and cool.

Perceptual Filtering

Perceptual filtering occurs when we purposely do not receive certain messages. Members of organizations are constantly being bombarded with messages and environmental stimuli (e.g., room color, temperature), but there are limits to the amount of information that they can process. For example, one of the reasons telephone numbers are seven digits long is because research has suggested that human beings have difficulty remembering more than seven items.[6] Thus, we have no alternative but to filter out some of these messages and stimuli so that we do not have to process all of them and can focus on those that are most important. From a communications perspective, the importance of perceptual filtering lies in what causes certain messages to make it through our filters and others to be filtered out.

As the Simon and Garfunkel song goes "We all hear what we want to hear and disregard the rest." Messages consistent with our basic beliefs and values, and those related to important needs, are likely to make it through our perceptual filters. Messages contrary to what we believe make us uncomfortable and are likely to be ignored if possible. Messages unrelated to important personal needs may not be viewed as important and may be ignored. Since we can deal only with a portion of the messages we are sent, we tend to choose those that support our beliefs and values as well as those that may help us satisfy important needs.

There are several things message senders can do to make it more likely that their message will not be filtered out. The first step is to consider the intended receiver. If you know this person, you may be able to construct your message so that it is of particular interest to her. At the very least you can make sure that you don't use symbols or terms that are likely to be unfamiliar to this person. In addition, intensity, repetition, and contrast may increase the chances that the message makes it past a receiver's perceptual filters. The louder, brighter, or stronger the message, the more likely we are to receive it. For example, the American Cancer Society use high-intensity commercials pointing out the potential harmful effects of smoking. The late Yul Brenner was filmed just before his death. In the commercial, he stated that the reason for his illness was cigarette smoking. His "don't smoke" message very likely penetrated the perceptual filters of many smokers.

Messages of lower intensity may penetrate perceptual filters through repetition. Over time, the message is received. It is difficult to continue to ignore something that is repeated over and over. Have you ever been in a room trying to read or study (or write a book) with some type of repetitious sound outside?

Messages which are substantially different (contrast) from other messages which are present may be received, while the others are filtered out. The fact that they are so much different from other messages present causes us to notice them. This is one reason why some commercials on television are so outrageous. They are trying to break through your perceptual filters.

Perceptual Expectation
Perceptual expectation is similar to perceptual filtering. This aspect of perception means that we hear or see what we expect. In other words, when we get set to see something, we may see it weather or not it is really there. Did you perceive the typographical error in the preceding sentence? Many people are set to see the word *whether* rather than the word which is really there—*weather*. The result is that not many people notice the error. This may cause problems in communication since we may hear (or see) a different message than the one actually sent. For example, an employee who is anxious about her performance on a particular assignment might "hear" a reprimand when the boss simply asks, "How are you doing on that assignment I gave you last week?" What the anxious employee may hear is, "Aren't you finished with that assignment yet?"

Perceptual Distortion
Sometimes we actually modify or **distort** a message so it is more consistent with our own beliefs or values. We may also distort a message so it is more consistent with our satisfying important needs. For example, suppose your manager says to you, "This company rewards for performance. You do your job well and you get rewarded." You may interpret this message to be a promise of a huge salary increase if you perform your job well. Your manager may have meant that if you don't make waves and work hard enough so that no one complains, you can be sure of keeping your job with the company. You obviously derived a much different meaning from the message than the one intended. What happens at the end of the year when you don't get the big raise you believe you were promised? Managers must be very careful to not send unintended messages containing implied promises of rewards they cannot deliver.

Closure
Closure occurs when we fill gaps in messages with what we expect or want to be there. Most of us are uncomfortable with things (e.g., messages, tasks, puzzles, games) that are incomplete. The importance of this concept for communication is that we may fill in missing information with incorrect information. This substitution decreases the likelihood that we will derive the correct meaning from the message. It also suggests that managers should take the time to determine whether or not their message is complete—from the perspective of the intended receiver. Try to put yourself in the receiver's shoes and imagine

how she is likely to react to it. Is it likely that she has the same information on the subject as you do? Or is it likely that she lacks certain information, which if you do not provide in your message, she may have to fill in herself with an educated guess? The key word here is guess. Since communication is not effective unless both receiver and sender derive the same meaning from a message, there is little room for guessing in the communication process.

NONVERBAL COMMUNICATION

Nonverbal communication is another aspect of interpersonal communication which, unfortunately, many people do not carefully consider. It may be defined as anything other than words that communicates. Nonverbal communication deserves a great deal of attention, since as much as 93 percent of our messages may be transmitted nonverbally.[7] If this figure is even approximately accurate, it is obvious that nonverbal communication can drastically alter a message. In fact, when the nonverbal portion of a message is in conflict with the verbal portion, most of us will believe the nonverbal portion. This selection comes about because nonverbal communication is harder to control than verbal. It may be that we reveal our true feelings through our nonverbal communications even when we carefully hide our feelings in our verbal message.

Managers can increase the likelihood of employees interpreting messages correctly by planning for the inclusion of nonverbal messages which reinforce the verbal message. At the very least, managers can ensure that their nonverbal messages do not contradict their verbal message or that they do not send unintentional messages to employees. Important categories of nonverbal com-

Managers spend approximately 80% of their time engaged in some form of communication.

munication include *proxemics, kinesics, vocalics, environmental factors,* and *time.*

Proxemics

Proxemics, the study of spatial relationships, looks at how each of us uses the space around us to communicate with others. Americans are very concerned about their private space or territory; we are reluctant to allow people to get close if we do not know them well. To measure the extent of our own space needs, four interpersonal space zones have been identified.[8] These are:

1. **Intimate space**—from physical contact to approximately eighteen inches. We typically allow only people we know and like extremely well to enter this zone. Communications are likely to be about personal matters.
2. **Personal space**—from eighteen inches to four feet. Communications within this range also tend to be personal. We must know a person well to let them get this close. Workers who belong to the same informal group may pass information along the grapevine in communications occurring within the personal space zone.
3. **Social space**—from four to twelve feet. Communications within social space typically occur with someone you know and you generally have a specific reason for the communication. Most task-related communications (e.g., manager–employee) occur within this range.
4. **Public space**—more than twelve feet. Very little communication occurs at this range, and we tend to feel safe even with strangers. In fact, as long as people stay more than twelve feet from us, we tend to not even notice them.

In organizational settings, proxemics can be used to identify status or authority. Persons with more authority in the organization are typically given more territory (i.e., bigger offices) than persons with less status. Territory of persons in authority also tends to be of higher quality (e.g., a plush, carpeted, private office). And, individuals with authority tend to be more comfortable invading the territory of those with less authority. Managers often walk into their employee's offices unannounced, but employees usually need appointments or must be announced by a secretary before invading the boss's territory. Thus, territory or space can be used to communicate status.[9]

From a human relations perspective, status may have a negative impact. Many people may feel uncomfortable or even threatened in the presence of persons they perceive to be of higher status. If this status is emphasized by the use of territory, their discomfort will increase. Some organizations are taking steps to de-emphasize status and other differences between managers and employees in the hope of improving human relations.

Kinesics

Kinesics are concerned with body motions that convey messages—facial expressions, eye movements, head movements, and movements of the arms, legs, and general body.

> ## HUMAN RELATIONS IN ACTION
>
> ### Communicating Through Executive Perks
>
> Does the use of space, territory, and executive perks such as private parking spaces and lunch rooms really communicate something to employees? Many of the Japanese-managed automobile plants in the United States believe that these practices communicate the wrong message—that employees are merely extensions of equipment.
>
> Japanese managers consider themselves to be the equals of employees. At several Japanese-managed plants in the U.S., there are no private parking spaces for managers, no executive dining rooms, no private offices, and no close control of employees. Instead, these managers use space and furnishings to communicate the idea that employees are important; they are the equals of management. At many of these plants, top executives wear the same white coveralls as other employees, with just their first name sewn on the pocket. Unbelievable as it may seem to many American managers, Honda President Shoichiro Irimajiri does not even have his own office. He has a desk in the same room as approximately 100 other white collar workers!
>
> These practices seem to have had an important effect upon the human relations climate in these plants. For example, in 1982, Toyota Motor Company took over the General Motors Corporation's Fremont, California auto-assembly plant. At the time, the absenteeism rate was around 20 percent, there were about 5,000 grievances filed each year, and frequent wildcat strikes stopped the production line. By 1986, the plant is producing at the same level (240,000 cars per year), but with about half the number of employees (2,500 as opposed to 5,000). The absenteeism rate has dropped to under 2 percent, and grievances have almost disappeared.
>
> Source: The difference Japanese management makes. *Business Week,* July 14, 1986, 47–50.

Eye movements are important nonverbal communicators. Many people convey their true feelings or beliefs through eye contact (or lack of eye contact). When a person avoids maintaining eye contact with you it is a good sign that she is uncomfortable with her message. It may be that she is trying to deceive you, convince you of something she knows is not true, or she simply is not confident of what she has to say. Downward glances and lowered eyes may also indicate discomfort with the message. Eye movements can also indicate fear, sadness, happiness, and surprise.[10]

Movements of the general body, arms, and legs may often indicate a person's openness or receptivity to the message you are sending. For example, if the person leans backward (away from you), with arms and legs crossed, you may want to wait and send your message to this person another time. This closed, protective posture indicates that this person is not particularly receptive to communications at this time. A more open stance (e.g., leaning toward the sender, with arms and legs uncrossed) may indicate receptivity to your message.

Vocalics

Vocalics have to do with characteristics of the voice, such as pitch, rate of speech, and volume. Generally, if senders are not confident in, or do not believe, their message, they speak softly, rapidly, and in a monotone. A slow monotone may also indicate that the message sender is actually quite bored with the message, which may in turn affect receivers in the same way. This analysis highlights an important point about all nonverbal cues—actions or movements that accompany a verbal message. Sometimes a receiver may become aware of them and decide there is something wrong with the verbal message. However, given the difficulty in interpreting some nonverbal cues, they may not provide the receiver with enough information to decide what the true message is. Interpretation of a message should not be influenced by a single cue, but rather by all the nonverbal cues and the verbal message itself.

Environmental Factors

Nonverbal cues can also include physical characteristics of the setting in which the communication takes place, such as color, temperature, and furniture arrangement. Different colors create different moods in people, as shown in Exhibit 6.2. The effects of temperature are obvious. If people are not comfortable, their minds will be on their discomfort and not on effective communication. Furniture and its arrangement can be used to facilitate or retard communications. It is rumored that Admiral Hyman Rickover used furniture to communicate status to new recruits. According to the rumor, he would saw off about two inches of the front legs of the chair to which he led the recruits. There was no way they could sit comfortably in the chair without sliding off onto the floor! It is doubtful that Rickover's recruits felt comfortable and willing to openly communicate with the Admiral. Similarly, offices which have barriers between people are not conducive to open communications.

Exhibit 6.2
The effect of color on moods

Color	Mood
Red	exciting, stimulating
Red	protective, defending
Red	defiant, contrary, hostile
Blue	secure, comfortable
Blue	tender, soothing
Blue	calm, peaceful, serene
Yellow	cheerful, jovial, joyful
Orange	distressed, disturbed, upset
Purple	dignified, stately
Black	despondent, dejected, unhappy, melancholy
Black	powerful, strong, masterful

Source: Wexner, L.B. The degree to which colors (hues) are associated with moodtones. *Journal of Applied Psychology,* 1954, *38,* 433–434.

Time

The nonverbal messages communicated by the use of time are of critical importance in maintaining good human relations. Aspects of time include how long an employee must wait to see you, the length of time which passes between contacts you initiate with the employee, the length of time you devote to meetings with the employee, and the quality of the time spent with the employee. In the employee's mind, these uses of time communicate very clearly what you think of her. It may be that you are simply very busy, but some employees may perceive a negative message from the fact that you don't spend much time with them. Over the long run, it pays to keep in touch with employees—not devoting long blocks of time to each employee, but using an occasional word or short conversation to keep the lines of communication open.

Providing feedback to employees is one of the most important, albeit difficult, types of planned communication in which managers engage. Whether it is done on a formal or informal basis, great care must be exercised to ensure that the feedback has its intended positive effects. Poorly done feedback can produce unintended negative effects such as alienating employees or lowering their motivation.

FEEDBACK

Earlier, communication was called "the lifeblood of an organization." Similarly, feedback is the lifeblood of manager-employee relations. There are two major categories of feedback problems: no feedback, and feedback which is not constructive. These problems are present, regardless of the employee's performance level. An absence of positive feedback to high performers may result in a deterioration in their performance. An absence of corrective feedback to a poor performer may result in the employee continuing the poor performance. Feedback which is carelessly administered may be destructive for both categories of employees. Unfortunately, often there is only a fine line separating constructive feedback from destructive feedback. Guidelines for making feedback constructive include:

1. Before providing any feedback, make sure the reason for the feedback is to help the employee correct or improve her performance. Feedback administered in haste, while the manager is angry or emotional, is not likely to be perceived by the employee as helpful.
2. The focus of the feedback should be on specific, performance-related behaviors that are under the employee's control. Criticizing an employee for things beyond her control will only cause the employee to experience stress, frustration, and resentment. The relationship between manager and employee can be severely damaged.
3. The feedback should be immediate, whether it is positive (praise) or constructive (suggestions for performance improvement or problem correction). Positive feedback often serves as an important reward for employees.

It should follow the episodes of high performance as closely as possible, to have the strongest motivational effects. Constructive feedback should also closely follow low performances, so the employee can correct the problem as soon as possible.
4. Constructive feedback should be impersonal and objective. It should focus on task-related behaviors and not on personalities or attitudes.
5. Positive feedback should be sincere. Remember, it is difficult to control many nonverbal cues. Unless you are a good actor, these nonverbal cues may give you away. Employees who perceive insincerity in your praise may begin to question your sincerity in other matters. This doubt can have a serious long-term negative effect on human relations.
6. Both positive and constructive feedback should be administered consistently among employees and across time. Every employee who does something to deserve feedback (either positive or constructive) should receive it.

LISTENING

Until recently, the focus of the study of interpersonal communication has been on message transmission and message senders. Most scholars now agree that listening and receiving should receive equal attention. Communication is a two-way process, even when only one person does all the talking. Communication is effective only when the receiver interprets the meaning that the sender intended. Thus, listeners should assume as much responsibility as the sender for the accuracy of the message. There are several approaches to improve listening effectiveness and become an "active listener." **Active listening** involves assuming responsibility for receiving the intended message, and becoming a contributor to the communication. Suggestions for becoming an active listener are:

1. Avoid distractions. If the communication takes place on your "territory," be sure there will be no distractions. For example, tell your secretary to hold all of your calls and appointments, close the office door, and arrange the seating so that no one is distracted by activities outside a window.
2. Concentrate on what is being said. Sometimes messages don't get through because we are not paying attention. We become bored or restless and our minds begin to wander. Research has shown that we can listen much faster than we can talk (over 600 words per minute compared to 125 words per minute).[11]
3. Listen to what is being said rather than how it is being said. Don't be turned off by a communicator who is rather dry and boring, or who has some annoying mannerism. Concentrate on message content, not delivery.
4. In a small-group or two-way communication setting, use feedback to make sure you are interpreting the message as intended. From time to time, summarize what you understand the message to be so far. This response gives the sender a chance to correct you if you have misinterpreted any part of

the message. It also gives the sender a chance to pause and reflect on the message, and make any necessary deletions or amplifications.
5. Pay attention to nonverbal cues. They are important to the communication, and should be included in the feedback used to ensure message accuracy. Remember, you are trying to determine the true meaning of the message—which is not necessarily the same as the obvious verbal content. Item 3 suggests that you should avoid being turned off by a poor delivery. This does not mean that you should ignore the delivery entirely, but you should ignore distracting nonverbal cues that contain no important information. Item 5 suggests that you must pay attention to those nonverbal cues that do contain important information.
6. Avoid argument, evaluation, or criticism of the message. This negative response may cause the sender to become defensive and reluctant to communicate openly.

MANAGER-EMPLOYEE COMMUNICATIONS

Feedback and listening are extremely important activities in manager-employee communications, which consists of both *upward* and *downward* communications. The purpose of **upward communications** is to apprise managers of performance problems, constraints, or possible improvements in the way work is performed.[12] Employees are often much closer to the action than their managers, and can be sources of valuable information. However, they will offer this information only if the manager has ensured open communications within the department or work group. Employees are not likely to initiate upward communications about problems if they perceive they may be reprimanded or punished as a result.[13] Employees are also unlikely to initiate upward communications concerning ideas for work-related improvements if their managers don't act on at least some of their ideas. The best way to create a climate of mediocre performance and "preserving the status quo" is to ignore employee suggestions for improvements. The accompanying Human Relations in Action box describes one organization's somewhat unusual approach to increasing upward communications, employee participation, and involvement.

Downward communications are intended to provide employees with information and instructions that will help them perform their jobs. Directives, guidance, rules, policies, procedures, and encouragement such as positive feedback are among the forms of this communication. Unfortunately, the research results presented in Exhibit 6.3 suggest that downward communications are not particularly effective in many organizations.

Downward communications can be either verbal or written. Exhibit 6.4 shows when each form is likely to be most effective. In general, however, verbal followed by written may be the most productive in most situations, because the advantages of both communication modes are realized. Face-to-face feedback and nonverbal cues are benefits of the verbal message, and the written summary provides a permanent record. This record can be useful if there is disagreement in the future as to what was said or agreed upon. It can

Exhibit 6.3
Effectiveness of downward communications

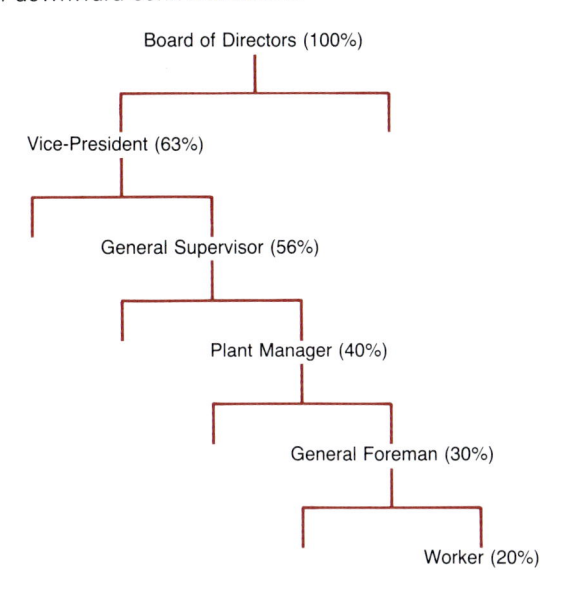

```
Board of Directors (100%)
    │
Vice-President (63%)
    │
    General Supervisor (56%)
        │
        Plant Manager (40%)
            │
            General Foreman (30%)
                │
                Worker (20%)
```

Source: Based upon Nichols, R.G. Listening is good business. *Management of Personnel Quarterly*, 1962, *1*, 2–9. Numbers in parentheses indicate the portion of the message that was received and interpreted correctly at each level.

also be used by employees as a reminder of what was said in the earlier communication.

The Grapevine

The **grapevine** is an informal communication system that evolves because employees have a need for more information than they are receiving from formal communications sources. Grapevines also satisfy important social needs for many employees, who feel "in the know" to be plugged into the grapevine and receive up-to-date information (or rumors) about the organization and its employees. Regardless of their size or scope, grapevines have several characteristics in common:

1. Messages typically travel much faster on the grapevine than through formal organizational communications channels.
2. Not everyone receives all messages that are transmitted on the grapevine. Some organizational members do not receive any. Others may be "plugged in" only for messages on certain topics.
3. Grapevines will emerge in all but the very smallest organizations. Once they emerge, they cannot be eliminated.
4. Not all of the information transmitted on the grapevine is accurate. There is disagreement on how accurate they are, with estimates ranging from 50 percent to 75 percent accuracy.

> **Exhibit 6.4**
> Effectiveness of different methods of downward communication
>
> **Written Only is Most Effective:**
>
> - To communicate information requiring future employee action.
> - To communicate information of a general nature.
>
> **Oral Only is Most Effective:**
>
> - To reprimand an employee for work deficiency.
> - To settle a dispute among employees about a work problem.
>
> **Oral Followed by Written is Most Effective:**
>
> - To communicate information requiring immediate employee action.
> - To communicate a company directive or order.
> - To communicate information on an important company policy change.
> - To communicate with your immediate supervisor about work progress.
> - To promote a safety campaign.
> - To commend an employee for noteworthy work.
>
> **Written Only is Least Effective:**
>
> - To communicate information requiring immediate employee action.
> - To commend an employee for noteworthy work.
> - To reprimand an employee for work deficiency.
> - To settle a dispute among employees about a work problem.
>
> **Oral Only is Least Effective:**
>
> - To communicate information requiring future employee action.
> - To communicate information of a general nature.
> - To communicate a company directive or order.
> - To communicate information on an important company policy change.
> - To communicate with your immediate supervisor about work progress.
> - To promote a safety campaign.

Based upon Level, D.A. Communication effectiveness: Method and situation. *Journal of Business Communication,* 1972, *9,* 19–25.

Managing the Grapevine

Although it is futile to attempt to eliminate the grapevine, some managers try. In doing so, they are attacking an important source of need satisfaction for these employees, and possibly attacking manager-employee relations as well. On the other hand, managers can use the grapevine strategically, by determining those individuals who seem to be informal leaders and who receive most informal messages. If they can develop trust and open communications with

HUMAN RELATIONS IN ACTION

Thank God, It's Friday

Executives at MeraBank's Human Resources Group were convinced that the department was facing a crisis. Turnover and conflict were both extremely high, while productivity and morale were extremely low. These problems were damaging to the group's reputation.

Executives realized that drastic action was necessary to improve human relations among the 35 employees in the group's five departments. Since most employees looked forward to the weekend so that they could get away from their jobs for a couple of days, executives decided to hold a TGIF (Thank God, It's Friday) party. The party was scheduled to begin one hour before the end of the work day; employees were paid to attend for at least one hour. The company arranged for an outside service to answer telephones during this hour. The invitations sent to employees promised them that the party would not involve any work, and the price of admission was "one idea, frivolous or serious, to improve human resources in the company." All employees submitted at least one suggestion and most of these suggestions focused on what appeared to be the company's core problem: a failure to communicate.

One of the suggestions was to publish a Human Resources newsletter to provide employees with additional information about the group and its five departments. Two other general principles which came out of the employee suggestions were to improve communications, and to get employees fully involved in the activities and decisions of the department.

Several other guiding principles have been identified since the TGIF parties began. Managers must create opportunities for employees in different departments to communicate. This may mean some social activity such as the TGIF party, a company softball team, or regular interdepartmental meetings. Organizations should also recruit managers who are effective communicators to serve as role models for all employees. Training in communication skills should be made available for all employees. Finally, interpersonal communications skills should be considered in performance evaluations. Evaluating employees and managers on their communication effectiveness clearly sends the message that good communication is a priority in the organization.

The TGIF party at MeraBank was extremely successful. Two years after the party was implemented, turnover and absenteeism had declined substantially, while productivity and morale had reached new highs. Employees were communicating with one another, sharing ideas and information, and working together as a team.

Source: Roarty, C.J. A party crashes the communication barrier. *Personnel Administrator,* 1987, *32*(11), 66–69.

---

these informal leaders, then they can provide accurate information to the grapevine, rather than allowing rumors to travel on it. Unchecked, some of these rumors can take on a life of their own. They can even be transmitted outside the organization. Case in point, McDonald's Restaurants spent an entire year fighting a false rumor that the company was using red worms in its hamburgers to increase the protein content. And, it cost Squibb approximately $100,000 to convince the public there were no spider eggs in its Bubble Yum bubble gum.[14]

Rumors which travel on a grapevine within a single organization can have a similar effect. Once negative information about an individual is transmitted on the grapevine, it becomes very difficult to counter it. Employees' careers may be damaged along with the human relations of entire departments and organizations. The negative information will affect not only the target individual but also all of that person's friends and supporters. If the source of the information becomes known, conflict and political infighting may develop between groups of employees.

While the grapevine may be an *important* source of information, particularly in an organization not committed to open communications, it is an *informal* source of information. There is little control over the accuracy of the information transmitted. It is not advisable to base important decisions on grapevine information until this information is verified from at least one other source.

ELECTRONIC COMMUNICATION

Advances in computer technology have made it possible to send "electronic messages" over an **electronic communications system**. These systems, also known as electronic message systems or electronic mail, consist of a network of personal computers or terminals, linked together electronically. An individual at one terminal can send an electronic message to an individual in a different part of the building simply by typing in the message on a keyboard and entering the code number of the individual to whom the message is to be sent. Since this is a relatively recent phenomenon, researchers have not yet assessed the impact such systems will have upon interpersonal communications.[15] However, **electronic communications** do not allow for the transmission of nonverbal cues. This shortcoming fosters a realistic prediction that electronic communications may run a greater risk of being misunderstood; the richness of a message cannot be transmitted electronically. Further, immediate face-to-face feedback is lost in electronic communications. There is no opportunity to engage immediately in active listening to ensure receipt of the message the sender intended. Another potential disadvantage of electronic communications systems is related to one of their major advantages. Given the ease and convenience of simply typing in a message and hitting a key to transmit it, electronic communications may contribute to an information overload problem.

Potential advantages of electronic communications are the speed with which messages can be transmitted, the ease of transmitting the same message to a large number of individuals, and the ability to print and/or store the message for later reference. If an individual is not at her desk when your message is sent, most electronic communications systems store the message in her terminal. When she returns to her desk, a message on the terminal screen tells her that there is a message waiting. Simply depressing a key will load the message on the screen. Exhibit 6.5 shows two elements of an electronic mail system, as they would appear on the screen of a desktop terminal.

Exhibit 6.5
Electronic communications systems

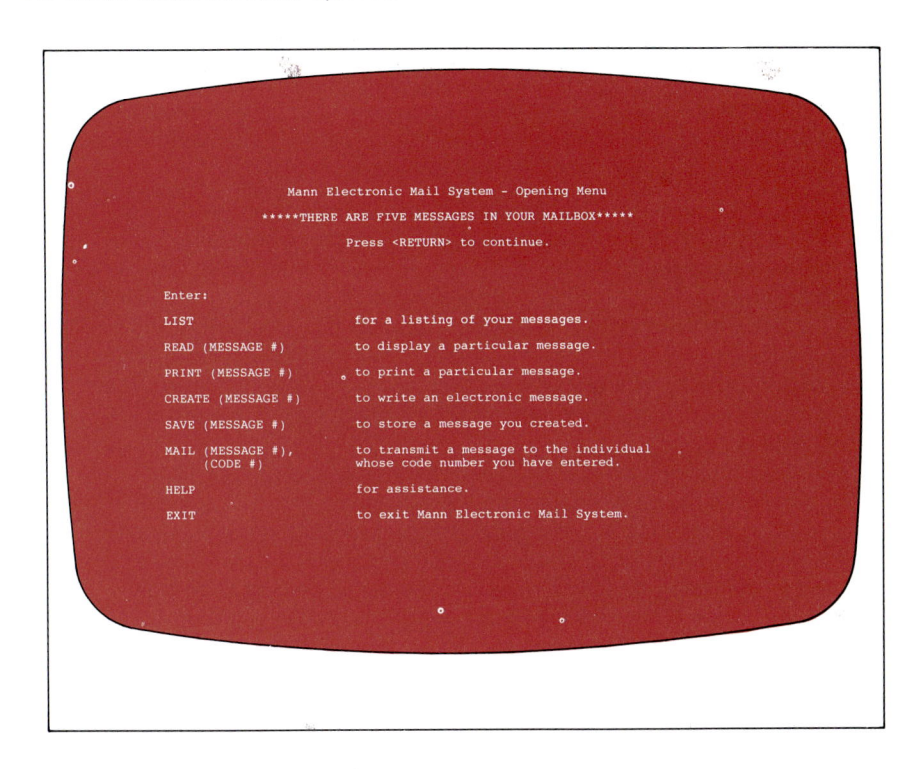

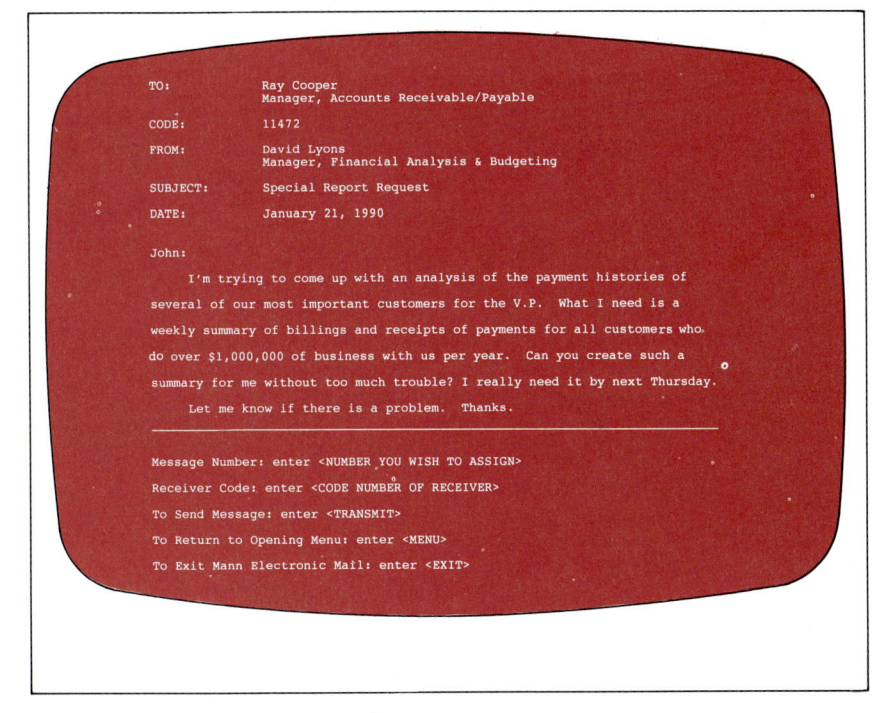

```
            Mann Electronic Mail System - Opening Menu
              *****THERE ARE FIVE MESSAGES IN YOUR MAILBOX*****
                       Press <RETURN> to continue.


  Enter:
  LIST                   for a listing of your messages.
  READ (MESSAGE #)       to display a particular message.
  PRINT (MESSAGE #)      to print a particular message.
  CREATE (MESSAGE #)     to write an electronic message.
  SAVE (MESSAGE #)       to store a message you created.
  MAIL (MESSAGE #),      to transmit a message to the individual
       (CODE #)          whose code number you have entered.
  HELP                   for assistance.
  EXIT                   to exit Mann Electronic Mail System.
```

```
  TO:         Ray Cooper
              Manager, Accounts Receivable/Payable
  CODE:       11472
  FROM:       David Lyons
              Manager, Financial Analysis & Budgeting
  SUBJECT:    Special Report Request
  DATE:       January 21, 1990

  John:
       I'm trying to come up with an analysis of the payment histories of
  several of our most important customers for the V.P.  What I need is a
  weekly summary of billings and receipts of payments for all customers who
  do over $1,000,000 of business with us per year.  Can you create such a
  summary for me without too much trouble? I really need it by next Thursday.
       Let me know if there is a problem.  Thanks.
  _____

  Message Number: enter <NUMBER YOU WISH TO ASSIGN>
  Receiver Code: enter <CODE NUMBER OF RECEIVER>
  To Send Message: enter <TRANSMIT>
  To Return to Opening Menu: enter <MENU>
  To Exit Mann Electronic Mail: enter <EXIT>
```

DEVELOPING YOUR HUMAN RELATIONS SKILLS

The Developing Your Human Relations Skills box at the end of each chapter has focused on guidelines for the two roles which you are likely to occupy throughout your work career; manager and employee. Most of the guidelines for communicating effectively are equally important in both roles; several of these "dual" guidelines are presented here:

1. Remember that individual perception exerts a strong influence upon the communication process. Perceptual filtering, perceptual expectations, perceptual distortion, and closure are all related to the receiver's background. To put it simply, we all hear what we want to hear, what we are prepared to hear, and what makes us feel comfortable. As a message sender, consider the receiver's background, interests, and values to determine how she is likely to interpret your message. Then you can formulate a message which is likely to be interpreted as you intend.
2. Always be aware of nonverbal communication. It is easy to become complacent about this aspect of communication and miss important messages. Nothing in most organizational work settings will remind you to pay attention to these nonverbal messages. However, since nonverbal communication makes up at least 50 percent of all messages, it is too important to ignore. To develop skills in identifying and interpreting nonverbal communications, practice with your friends and family.
3. Remember that sending a message is only half of the communication process. Listening, or receiving and interpreting the message, is the other half. Receivers should share the responsibility for effective communications. Active listening involves paying attention to nonverbal messages, avoiding argument and evaluation of the sender's message while it is being transmitted, and using feedback to ensure receiving and interpreting the message as the sender intends.

Suggestions specific to your role as a manager, summarized from the information presented in this chapter, are:

1. Encourage upward communication. It is a good source of information since employees are closer to the action. It also promotes good human relations, by encouraging employees to provide input into decisions that affect their jobs. When managers encourage employees to communicate openly, they send the message that employees are important and their ideas and opinions are valued.
2. Carefully plan feedback to employees to ensure that it is constructive, not destructive. Constructive feedback is intended to be helpful. It is specific and focuses upon job-related behaviors; it must be immediate, impersonal, and objective.

SUMMARY

Communication is the lifeblood of an organization. Critical information is transmitted throughout the organization by means of formal and informal communications systems. Interpersonal communication is a transmission of signals or symbols from a sender to a receiver, with the intent of sharing meaning. Senders cannot transmit meaning. They can only transmit symbols from which they hope the receiver derives the intended meaning.

Many communication problems can be traced to perception—the way each of us views the world. Unfortunately, from a communications perspective, we all see the world a little differently. The four major aspects of perception which can cause communications problems are perceptual filtering, perceptual expectations, perceptual distortion, and closure.

Research has determined that more of a message is transmitted nonverbally than verbally. Nonverbal communication is anything other than words that communicates. Its categories include proxemics, kinesics, vocalics, environmental factors, and time. When verbal and nonverbal messages are in conflict, people will frequently believe the nonverbal message, because nonverbal cues are more difficult to control than verbal messages, and can be more persuasive than the message itself.

Feedback is one of a manager's most important types of communication. Positive feedback is intended to praise employees and encourage them to continue high levels of performance. Constructive feedback is intended to help employees improve performance and/or correct performance problems. For feedback to be constructive, it must: be intended to be helpful; focus on specific, performance-related behaviors under the employee's control; be administered immediately after exceptionally good or poor performance; be impersonal and objective; show sincerity; and be administered consistently.

Communication is a two-way process; the effectiveness of any communication is as dependent on listening to a message as it is on sending that message. An active listener assumes responsibility for receiving the intended message, and becomes actively involved in the communication. Good listeners avoid distractions; concentrate on what is being said; refrain from judging the message by how it is being said; use feedback to ensure that they receive the intended message; pay attention to nonverbal cues; and avoid argument or criticism.

Upward communication and downward communication are fundamental to manager-employee communications. Upward communication makes managers aware of performance problems, constraints, and/or possible improvements in the way the work is performed. Managers must encourage employees to initiate upward communications. Employees are not likely to talk to managers concerning performance problems if they believe reprimand or punishment may result. They are unlikely to propose ideas for improving performance if they see many of their ideas being ignored. Downward communication provides employees with information that will help them perform their jobs. It can be either verbal or written; however, a verbal message followed by a written summary may be the most effective for most purposes.

Electronic communication is a relatively new approach to organizational communication. These systems (also called electronic mail or electronic message systems) are comprised of a network of personal computers or terminals. Individuals can enter messages at their own terminals and transmit them electronically to other individuals who are part of the network. Advantages of this form of communication include its speed and convenience; its primary disadvantage is that nonverbal cues and immediate feedback are lost.

KEY TERMS

interpersonal communication
perception
perceptual filtering
perceptual expectation
perceptual distortion
closure
nonverbal communication
proxemics
intimate space
personal space
social space
public space
kinesics
vocalics
active listening
upward communications
downward communications
grapevine
electronic communications systems
electronic communication

DISCUSSION QUESTIONS

1. Explain the statement "communication is the lifeblood of organizations." Explain why you agree or disagree with this statement.
2. It was stated in the chapter that "meaning cannot be transmitted." What is meant by this statement?
3. What can a manager do to ensure that feedback to employees is constructive rather than destructive?
4. How does one engage in "active listening"?
5. What is the "grapevine" and how does it work? Can managers use grapevines to improve communications in the organization?
6. What are four common perceptual problems that may hinder communication? What can be done to minimize these problems?
7. What is "nonverbal communication"? What can managers do about it?
8. How can a manager's use of time send messages (either intended or unintended) to employees?

EXERCISE 6.1

Meanings in Words or in People?

This exercise will demonstrate that meanings are not in words but in the people who use them. Based on our perceptions and experiences, we may interpret a word differently than it was intended. Your instructor will divide the class into groups and assign a word to each group. Each person will then list all the words brought to mind by the assigned word. Next, determine whether each of the listed words has a positive, negative, or neutral connotation. Then summarize your findings as a group.

Target Word	Word Associations	Value + − 0

Word List

rural	employee
urban	bureaucracy
rules	unusual
freedom	sophisticated
pride	alcohol
emotion	socialist
boss	procedures
civil servant	affair
learning	assertive
job	support
tradition	decisions
evaluation	risk
foreign	home
manager	regulations
politician	soft
experience	subordinate
profession	liberal
conventional	duty
adventure	discussion
instructions	fancy
independent	vacation

To close the exercise, the instructor leads a discussion of the experience, including:

1. How the different values associated with words illustrate that meanings are not in words, but in the people who use them.
2. How our perceptions of words affect our communication effectiveness.
3. How active listening might be used to ensure that receivers interpret words the way the sender intends.
4. What individual participants learned from the experience about themselves and their own use of words.
5. How participants plan to apply what they learned.

From Pfeiffer, J.W. and Jones, J.E. *A handbook of structured experiences for human relations training.* Volume VII. Exercise 250: Meanings are in people: Perception checking. San Diego, Cal.: University Associates Publishers and Consultants, 1979, 28–33.

CASE 6.1

A Simple Misunderstanding

Bob found himself in an uncomfortable position. He got along well with both his supervisor, Mary, and Chuck, a coworker. Unfortunately, Mary and Chuck did not seem to be getting along. It appeared to Bob that the conflict was the result of a simple misunderstanding on both sides. But Bob wasn't sure if he should get involved. "I guess I am involved already to some extent," Bob thought as he returned to his desk. "They each come to me and complain about the other. I wish they could each hear the other's story. Then they would see how senseless this disagreement is."

CHUCK'S SIDE OF THE STORY

I've worked in this department for six years. I've seen three supervisors come and go. Given what I've seen recently, I'd say that there will be a fourth before long. Mary took over as supervisor five months ago. Since I have been in the department longer than any of the other employees, I went to see her during her first week to offer my help. I've learned how to get things done in this company, and it's not always the way you would expect. You have to know where to go for answers and resources around here. Just because some document says you should have someone's help or support doesn't mean you'll get it in this company. Anyway, Mary was very cool and distant during our first meeting and didn't seem interested in what I had to say. She kept looking at her watch, and nervously shuffled papers. So I just told her that she should call on me if she needed any help and went back to work. If that meeting had been my annual performance evaluation, I'd have thought I was about to be fired.

I've seen her spend time at other employees' work stations, apparently trying to familiarize herself with what they do. She's never come to my desk. She's good at sending me memorandums with additional assignments in them, though.

Since that first meeting, Mary hasn't had much to say to me. It's been five months and things haven't changed much. We speak, say hello when we meet, but that's about it. I have no idea what I did to offend her, but I'm not used to getting treated like that by my supervisor.

MARY'S SIDE OF THE STORY

I don't know what to do about Chuck. He apparently thinks that he should be the supervisor of the department. He may need to find out the hard way that he's not. I hadn't been in the department for a full week when he came charging into my office, without an appointment, telling me how he thought things should be done! He's been here longer than anyone else, and no doubt he knows a lot about the way things work in this company, but he's not the supervisor of this department. I was polite during that first meeting, but I tried to end it as quickly as possible without just telling him to get back to work and that I'd run the department. However, since that day, he's had very little to say to me. We're polite when we meet, but that's about it. A senior employee like Chuck should really be working much closer with the departmental supervisor. I also believe that he has been saying some negative things to some of the other employees about my ability as a supervisor. No one has said anything specific, but the way Bob looked the other day when I mentioned Chuck told me everything I needed to know.

QUESTIONS

1. What types of communication problems exist here?
2. If you were Chuck, how would you have handled that first meeting?
3. If you were Mary, how would you have handled that first meeting?
4. Assume that you are the fourth supervisor of the department, as Chuck predicted, and you are aware of what happened with the previous supervisor. How would you manage communications in this department?

REFERENCES

[1] Dessler, G. *Organization and management*. Boston: Houghton Mifflin, 1984.

[2] Zelko, H.P. Rate your communication skills. *Personnel Journal* 1986, *66*(11), p. 133.

[3] Mintzberg, H. *The nature of managerial work*. New York: Harper and Row Publishers, 1973.

[4] Dizard, W.P. *The coming information age*. New York: Longman, 1982.

[5] Axley, S.R. Managerial and organizational communication in terms of the conduit metaphor. *Academy of Management Review,* 1984, *9,* 428–437.

[6] Miller, G.W. The magical number seven, plus or minus two: Some limits on our capacity for processing information. *Psychological Review,* 1965, *63,* 81–97.

[7] Mehrabian, A. Communication without words. *Psychology Today,* 1968, *3,* 53.

[8] Hall, E.T. *The hidden dimension*. Garden City, New York: Doubleday, Anchor, 1966.

[9] Baskin, O.W. & Aronoff, C.E. *Interpersonal communication in organizations*. Santa Monica, California: Goodyear Publishing Company, Inc., 1980.

[10] Henderson, P.E. Communication without words. *Personnel Journal,* 1989, *68*(1), 22–29.

[11] Nichols, R.G. Listening: What price inefficiency? *Office Executive,* April 1959, 15–22.

[12] McClelland, V.A. Upward communication: Is anyone listening? *Personnel Journal,* 1988, *67*(6), 124–131.

[13] Roberts, K.H. & O'Reilly, C.A. Failures in upward communication in organizations: Three possible culprits. *Academy of Management Journal,* 1974, *17,* 205–215.

[14] Rowan, R. Where did *that* rumor come from? *Fortune,* August 13, 1979, 130–137.

[15] Huseman, R.C. & Miles, E.W. Organizational communication in the information age: Implications of computer-based systems. *Journal of Management,* 1988, *14*(2), 181–204.

WHAT DO YOU THINK? NOTE

There are no right or wrong answers for this communications quiz. However, if you don't score as well as you had hoped, go back and look at the specific items on which you scored only good or fair. This will identify some specific areas in which you need to improve. Few people will score in the excellent category, if they are totally honest with themselves as they answer the quiz. Most of us become complacent about our ability to communicate and need to be reminded that effective communication takes planning and effort.

CHAPTER SEVEN

Appraising and Rewarding Performance

PROLOGUE

Joe knew he had a problem on his hands. Eight months ago he had replaced Tom Smythe as Supervisor of Financial Statement Analysis. In this position, he supervised the work of eleven clerical employees, Accounting Clerk II to Accounting Clerk V. He had just received the performance appraisal form from personnel for Diane Howser. In Joe's first week on the job, he had recognized a problem with Diane. Not only was her job performance below average, but she frequently took extended lunches and coffee breaks.

Joe had talked with her about these actions on four separate occasions during his first eight months on the job. Each time Diane promised that she would do better and gave some excuse about her health or family problems. She would seem to improve for a couple of weeks, but it wasn't long before things returned to "normal." Joe didn't see any way he could give Diane anything but a very poor performance appraisal this year. "Maybe that's exactly what she needs to motivate her to improve," Joe thought as he pulled out Diane's performance appraisal form. However, since she seemed to be so well liked by her coworkers, Joe wondered how they might react to her receiving a poor performance rating. "Besides," thought Joe as he began filling out the appraisal form, "if I give her a low rating, she'll be in my office in the morning arguing about it. I've got more important things to do."

LEARNING OBJECTIVES

After successful completion of this chapter, you should be able to:

- Recognize the multiple purposes of performance appraisals,
- Describe the various forms of performance appraisal,
- Identify several common problems or errors in performance appraisal ratings,

169

- Explain how to conduct an effective performance appraisal interview,
- Differentiate between system rewards and individual rewards,
- Discuss several constraints in administering rewards,
- Explain how to administer rewards effectively, and
- Understand how to administer merit pay.

PERFORMANCE APPRAISAL AND REWARD ADMINISTRATION

Two of the most important activities for managers at all levels are performance appraisal and reward administration. These two activities are frequently interrelated, since in most organizations, rewards are based on the results of performance appraisals. Both must be performed effectively if managers are going to be successful in building a motivating human relations climate. This chapter will discuss the purposes and types of performance appraisals, and will analyze several common errors by **raters**. A discussion of how to conduct an effective performance appraisal feedback interview will lead to an examination of administering rewards. The focus of this discussion will be on how to administer rewards so as to motivate employees, given the many constraints that exist within organizations.

PERFORMANCE APPRAISALS

Performance appraisals are *potentially* one of the most effective tools under a manager's control. They can send very strong messages (either positive or negative) to employees. As such, they can serve as a strong impetus to improve if performance is not up to par, or a strong incentive to continue good performance. Since performance appraisals are typically tied closely to reward administration, the process of administering rewards often reinforces the message contained in the performance appraisal. Unfortunately, several authors agree that "the measurement of human performance in work roles is, at best, fuzzy."[1] Performance appraisals continue to be fuzzy for at least two reasons: the accurate measurement of an individual's job performance or contribution is extremely difficult and often highly subjective, and many managers are uncomfortable conducting performance appraisals. Their discomfort leads them to "get it over with as quickly and painlessly as possible." In addition, some managers may not receive competent appraisals of their own performance from their managers. It may be difficult for these managers to exert extra effort in conducting performance appraisals of their subordinates if they are receiving inadequate appraisals themselves.

Purposes of Performance Appraisals

Recognize the multiple purposes of performance appraisal.

The predominant purpose of performance appraisals in organizations is as a basis for reward allocation.[2] Performance appraisals are primarily used as a justification for salary increase decisions. However, as Exhibit 7.1 shows, there

> **Exhibit 7.1**
> Multiple purposes of performance appraisal
>
> 1. Fostering improvements in work performance
> 2. Assigning work more efficiently
> 3. Meeting employees' needs for growth
> 4. Assisting employees in setting career goals
> 5. Recognizing potential for development to managerial position
> 6. Keeping employees informed of what is expected of them
> 7. Improving job placement (i.e., effecting better employee-job matches)
> 8. Identifying training needs
> 9. Validating selection procedures and evaluating training programs
> 10. Fostering a better working relationship between subordinate and supervisor
> 11. Fostering a better working relationship between work units

Source: Bernardin, H.J. & Beatty, R.W. *Performance appraisal: Assessing human behavior at work.* Boston: Kent Publishing Company, 1984, 8.

are many other purposes for which they could be used. It is unfortunate that most organizations do not use performance appraisals to their full potential. These appraisals can provide valuable information concerning areas in which employees need additional training, increase and possibly improve communications between managers and employees, provide valuable feedback to employees concerning areas of needed improvement in their job performance, and motivate employees to perform at higher levels. To accomplish these several purposes, however, performance appraisals must be accepted—by the employees whose performance is being evaluated and the managers who are conducting the evaluation. In addition, managers must be motivated to conduct accurate performance appraisals.

RETURN TO THE PROLOGUE

Joe, the supervisor described in the Prologue, is experiencing uncertainty and discomfort associated with rating the performance of one of his employees. As a result, he may not conduct an accurate and objective performance appraisal. He is likely to make two major mistakes. First, rather than trying to be as accurate as possible, he is likely to be very lenient in his rating of Diane. This will lead to problems in administering rewards, as she will receive more rewards than is really justified by her job performance. Second, he may not spend adequate time discussing the areas of her performance which need to be improved. In order for managers to be highly motivated to conduct accurate performance appraisals, they must have confidence in the organization's performance appraisal and reward systems.

Types of Performance Appraisals

Describe the various forms of performance appraisal.

There are a number of different types of performance appraisals from which managers can choose. They range from a simple ranking of employees to **trait-based appraisals** such as **graphic rating scales**, to **behavior-based appraisals** such as **behaviorally anchored rating scales** and **behavioral observation scales**, to **results-oriented appraisals** such as **management by objectives**. While research suggests that no one of these formats is clearly best, they each have advantages and disadvantages of which managers should be aware.[3]

Graphic Rating Scale

The most widely used form of performance appraisal is the trait-based graphic rating scale.[4] One of the reasons for its popularity is its simplicity. It is easy to understand and use, making it acceptable to both managers (raters) and employees (ratees). However, its simplicity makes it highly susceptible to many forms of rater errors. An example of a graphic rating scale appears in Exhibit 7.2. As the figure shows, this appraisal instrument consists of a set of traits or characteristics and a very simple measurement scale. The manager simply rates each employee on each of the traits. Obviously, this type of appraisal is highly subjective and dependent on the manager's judgment. On the plus side, these scales are easy to develop and can be used for a variety of jobs.

Behavior-Based Appraisals

Two popular forms of behavior-based appraisals are behaviorally anchored rating scales (BARS) and behavioral observation scales (BOS). Each of these scales places the emphasis of the rating on specific behaviors in which employees should engage to successfully perform their jobs. In addition, both BARS and BOS are job-specific instruments; they are developed for use in appraising employee performance only on specific jobs.

An example of a BARS for one behavior or factor to be rated appears in Exhibit 7.3. The complete BARS appraisal instrument would consist of several pages similar to the one in Exhibit 7.3—one for each job factor to be rated. An advantage of BARS is that examples of specific behaviors are used to rate each factor. This reduces some of the ambiguity present in graphic rating scales. In addition, BARS is less dependent on managers' subjective judgments. A major disadvantage of BARS is the difficulty and cost of preparing these instruments.

A behavioral observation scale (BOS) for an administrative assistant appears in Exhibit 7.4. Managers are asked to indicate the frequency with which employees engage in the behaviors included on the scale. Here, managers are placed in the role of observers rather than evaluators. They simply report on the frequency of behaviors that relate to successful job performance.

Results-Oriented Appraisals

The most popular form of results-oriented performance appraisal is management by objectives (MBO). The typical MBO process comprises the following steps.

Exhibit 7.2
Example of a graphic rating scale

NAME: _____

DEPARTMENT: _____ POSITION: _____

TIME PERIOD COVERED BY APPRAISAL: _____

1 = unsatisfactory   4 = above average
2 = below average   5 = superior
3 = average

1. Quantity of Work   6. Quality of Work
        1 2 3 4 5   1 2 3 4 5
2. Dependability   7. Cooperation
        1 2 3 4 5   1 2 3 4 5
3. Initiative   8. Communication Skills
        1 2 3 4 5   1 2 3 4 5
4. Potential   9. Job Knowledge
        1 2 3 4 5   1 2 3 4 5
5. Appearance & Behavior   10. Judgment
        1 2 3 4 5   1 2 3 4 5

Overall Performance Rating

         1   2   3   4   5
   UNSATISFACTORY   BELOW   AVERAGE   ABOVE   SUPERIOR
                    AVERAGE   AVERAGE

COMMENTS:

EMPLOYEE SIGNATURE: _____
APPRAISER SIGNATURE: _____
PERSONNEL DEPARTMENT: _____ DATE: _____

1. The manager and employee jointly agree on objectives for the employee. Proponents of MBO recommend substantial employee participation in the objective-setting process, to increase employee commitment to accomplishing the objectives which are set.
2. The employee is given freedom to accomplish the objectives as he sees fit.
3. The manager monitors the employee's progress, providing suggestions or guidance when needed. A large part of this monitoring process involves feedback to the employee on how well he is doing. Thus, MBO encourages an ongoing informal performance appraisal in addition to the typically infrequent formal appraisal.

> **Exhibit 7.3**
> Example of a Behaviorally Anchored Rating Scale (BARS)
>
> **Performance Dimension: Meeting Deadlines**
>
> In the job of department manager, how well does this person do in meeting deadlines? Consider only day-to-day or typical job behavior.
>
> Place a check mark on the line next to the statement which best describes this person's behavior in meeting deadlines when doing a usual or typical job.
>
> 1. Could be expected to meet deadlines comfortably by delegating an unusually high number of assignments to two highly rated associates. _____
> 2. Could be expected to meet seasonal deadlines within reasonable length of time. _____
> 3. Could be expected to fail to schedule additional help to complete assignments on time. _____
> 4. Could be expected to disregard due dates for assignments in his department. _____
> 5. Could be expected never to be late in meeting deadlines no matter how unusual the circumstances. _____
> 6. Could be expected always to get his or her associates' work schedules made out on time. _____
> 7. Could be expected to offer to do the assignments at home after failing to get them out on the deadline day. _____
> 8. Could be expected to be late all the time on weekly assignments for his department. _____
> 9. Could be expected to leave assignments in a desk drawer for several weeks even when they had been given by a superior and called to his attention after due dates. _____

Source: Klatt, L.A., Murdick, R.G., & Schuster, F.E. *Human Resource Management.* Columbus, Ohio: Merrill Publishing Company, 1985, p. 428.

4. The employee's performance is appraised in terms of the degree to which objectives were accomplished during the allotted time period.

Exhibit 7.5 is an example of a management-by-objective (MBO) performance appraisal form. MBO appraisals offer the advantages of focusing employee efforts on important activities, focusing employee attention on desired results (objectives), and increasing employee commitment. In addition, since performance is measured in terms of objectives or outcomes, MBO may be less subjective than trait-oriented or behavior-oriented appraisals. Consequently, employees may be more satisfied with the performance appraisal process. Reported disadvantages of MBO include manager complaints that it increases the amount of paperwork they must perform and the time they must spend counseling employees.[5]

Exhibit 7.4
Example of a Behavioral Observation Scale (BOS)

Administrative Assistant

1. Types minimum of 60 words per minute.
   Almost never   1   2   3   4   5   Almost always
2. Can take shorthand.
   Almost never   1   2   3   4   5   Almost always
3. Can type from a dictaphone machine.
   Almost never   1   2   3   4   5   Almost always
4. Answers the phone in a courteous manner.
   Almost never   1   2   3   4   5   Almost always
5. Smiles at all employees.
   Almost never   1   2   3   4   5   Almost always
6. Smiles at all customers.
   Almost never   1   2   3   4   5   Almost always
7. Gossips with employees about other employees.
   Almost always   1   2   3   4   5   Almost never
8. Complains in front of customers.
   Almost always   1   2   3   4   5   Almost never
9. Can use an adding machine.
   Almost never   1   2   3   4   5   Almost always
10. Can reconcile a bank account.
    Almost never   1   2   3   4   5   Almost always
11. Pays bills on time.
    Almost never   1   2   3   4   5   Almost always
12. Maintains and balances cash disbursements journal.
    Almost never   1   2   3   4   5   Almost always
13. Posts all journals in general ledger.
    Almost never   1   2   3   4   5   Almost always
14. Able to make adjustments in general ledger.
    Almost never   1   2   3   4   5   Almost always
15. Handles complete inventory function (includes physically counting purchases such as bowling balls).
    Almost never   1   2   3   4   5   Almost always
16. Gathers information (bowling scores, new records, bowling news, bowling tips) for monthly newsletter.
    Almost never   1   2   3   4   5   Almost always
17. Informs president/general manager of pressing matters.
    Almost never   1   2   3   4   5   Almost always
18. Knows how to trace all accounting and cash flows, thereby performing internal control checks.
    Almost never   1   2   3   4   5   Almost always
19. Tabulates employee performance appraisal reports three times a year.
    Almost never   1   2   3   4   5   Almost always
20. Keeps issues relevant only to the president/general manager confidential (refuses to discuss such information with employees).
    Almost never   1   2   3   4   5   Almost always

(continued)

> **Exhibit 7.4** *(continued)*
>
> **Administrative Assistant**
> 21. Prepares biweekly payroll (multiply hours X rate, make deductions, balance payroll).
>   Almost never   1   2   3   4   5   Almost always
> 22. Assists in the collection of amusement machine revenue.
>   Almost never   1   2   3   4   5   Almost always
> 23. Can operate the copying machine.
>   Almost never   1   2   3   4   5   Almost always
> 24. Assists in the preparation of trophy orders (assembling, engraving).
>   Almost never   1   2   3   4   5   Almost always
> 25. Allows people to congregate in front of her desk.
>   Almost always   1   2   3   4   5   Almost never
> 26. Must be repeatedly asked to do the same thing.
>   Almost always   1   2   3   4   5   Almost never
> 27. Can compose own letters as directed by president/general manager.
>   Almost never   1   2   3   4   5   Almost always
> 28. Organizes a filing system that is easily learned by the president/general manager and keeps it up to date on a daily basis (items are promptly filed).
>   Almost never   1   2   3   4   5   Almost always
> 29. Keeps executive offices clean (vacuum, dust, water plants).
>   Almost never   1   2   3   4   5   Almost always
> 30. Can drive all company vehicles for performing company business.
>   Almost never   1   2   3   4   5   Almost always
>
> | 30–96 | 97–111 | 112–126 |
> | :-------: | :-----------: | :----------: |
> | very poor | unsatisfactory | satisfactory |
> | | 127–141 | 142–150 |
> | | excellent | superior |

Source: Latham, G.P. & Wexley, K.N. *Increasing productivity through performance appraisal.* Reading, Massachusetts: Addison-Wesley Publishing Company, 1981, 221–223.

A basic characteristic of MBO appraisals is that they usually focus entirely on outcomes and ignore behaviors. Thus, unless managers specifically include guidelines on how objectives are to be accomplished, employees are free to accomplish objectives in any manner they choose. This emphasis on outcomes and not on methods may lead some employees to questionable or unethical behavior to accomplish objectives. During the objective-setting process, managers may want to make it a point to discuss exactly how objectives should and should not be accomplished.

Regardless of the particular form used, any performance appraisal that includes a rating or judgment of employee performance is subject to rater errors. Conversely, the objective performance appraisal systems are less susceptible to these rater errors. However, many of the most popular performance appraisals in use today are subjective to some degree.

Exhibit 7.5
Example of an MBO appraisal form

Sam Speedy		Date		General Manager		Progress Reviews		
Prepared by Manager				Position Title		1st _____		
Harry Slow				Production		2nd _____		
Reviewed by Supervisor		Date		Position Title		3rd _____ Date		

MAJOR JOB OBJECTIVES	% WORK TIME	MEASURES OF RESULTS	STD. OF PERF.	RESULTS TARGET	RESULTS ACTUAL	DATES TARGET	DATES ACTUAL
1. Product Delivery (May be broken down by products)	25%	a. % of on-schedule delivery	94%	Increase to 98%		8/31	
		b. Number of customer complaints as a % of monthly purchase orders	4%	Decrease to 3%		9/30	
2. Product Quality (May be broken down by products)	30%	a. % of rejects per total monthly volume	6%	Decrease to 4%		7/31	
		b. Ratio of factory repair time to total production hours/month	7%	Decrease to 4%		9/31	
		c. Number of units service-free during warranty period	73%	Increase to 86%		10/31	
3. Operating Efficiency	25%	a. Cost per unit of output per month	$35.75 /unit	Reduce to $35.50/unit		2/1	
		b. Equipment-utilization time as a % of monthly available hours	86%	Increase to 95%		11/15	
4. Other Key Objectives	20%						

Source: R.W. Beatty and C.E. Schneier, *Personnel Administration: An Experiential Skill-Building Approach,* p. 156, © 1981, Addison-Wesley, Reading, Mass. Reprinted with permission.

Rater Errors

Identify several common problems or errors in performance appraisal ratings.

Rater errors in performance appraisal are very similar to some of the problems in perception discussed in Chapters 4 and 6. While some rater errors may occur regardless of the particular type of performance appraisal instrument in use, most researchers agree that graphic rating scales are most prone to rater errors. These errors serve to reduce the accuracy, and therefore the usefulness, of appraisals. Rater errors are a serious problem because managers are typically not aware that they are making these errors. Several common rater errors have been identified.[6]

Halo Error

The most common type of rater error, **halo error**, occurs when a rater (manager) is so strongly influenced by one of the traits on the scale that he rates all other traits in a similar manner. Referring to Exhibit 7.2, assume that I am rating your job performance, and I determine that your appearance and behavior (item 9) are excellent. I am so impressed by your excellent appearance and behavior that it influences how I rate you on the other traits. In fact, I would most likely give you an excellent rating on most of the other factors as well, even though you might really be only average, or even below average, on one or more of these factors. Halo error, in effect, colors or clouds a rater's judgment, causing him to form an overall evaluation of performance before rating the individual factors. Then the manager rates each individual factor so that it is consistent with this overall evaluation. Once you have decided that a person is average (or excellent or poor) it becomes difficult to rate this person differently on any of the individual factors or traits. Ideally, the determination of an overall performance rating should occur *after* the individual is rated on the individual factors, and should reflect an average of the individual factors.

Of course, halo error is not always positive. It can be anywhere between highly positive to highly negative. If your appearance and behavior are extremely poor, this might influence me to rate you as extremely poor on most other factors. Halo can also be neutral or average. If your appearance and behavior are clearly average, I might be influenced to rate you approximately average on most other traits as well.

To reduce halo error, some authors recommend that each employee be rated on factor 1, then each employee is rated on factor 2 and so on, instead of rating each employee on all factors in sequence. While this procedure might reduce halo error, it is difficult to implement. Since most organizations conduct performance appraisals of their employees on their employment anniversary date, few employees will have their performance appraisal on the same day. Therefore, raters have to be constantly aware of halo error and make a conscious effort to rate each job factor independently.

Central Tendency

Another common rater error places all employees toward the center of the scale (from slightly below average to slightly above average). It occurs because managers are not comfortable conducting performance appraisals. This discomfort may be because they lack confidence in the performance appraisal instrument, or in their ability to accurately rate employee job performance. Managers may feel that this central rating of employees will result in the fewest complaints from employees about their performance appraisals. Assuming that most employees probably do fall somewhere around average performance levels, this judgement may be correct. Poor performers are rated higher than they deserve, so they are not likely to complain. The employees who are likely to be most upset are the top performers. However, managers respond that while these top performers may not have been rated as excellent, they were rated higher than most other employees. This response may appease some of the top performers, so that the number of complaints is minimized.

For managers who are motivated to rate employees in a manner that will produce the fewest complaints, **central tendency** is the answer. Joe, the supervisor in the Prologue, may use central tendency ratings to deal with his uncertainty and discomfort in conducting performance appraisals.

However, in terms of accomplishing all of the purposes of performance appraisal, central tendency is extremely damaging. Just as with halo error, central tendency reduces the accuracy of performance appraisals. Specifically, the *amount* of difference in various employees' performance is lost. While it still may be possible to identify the top performers, it is no longer possible to determine how much better they are.

Primacy/Recency

Primacy error occurs when a manager gives greater weight to an employee's performance during the first part of a rating period. This rating error may occur, for example, when an employee takes a new job, and the manager is attentive to the employee's performance during the first few weeks. The manager, in effect, conducts the performance appraisal during the initial period of employment. When the time for the formal appraisal arrives, the manager simply completes the appraisal instrument so that it is consistent with his initial appraisal. However, this formal appraisal may occur several months later!

Recency error is the tendency for managers to give greater weight to more recent employee job performance. The result is an improvement in employee job performance a short time before the annual performance appraisal is conducted. Then, once the appraisal has been performed and the employee has received his annual salary increase, performance declines to previous levels. Actually, performance appraisals should reflect the employee's performance during the entire rating period, not just the most recent period of time.

The point is, with either primacy or recency, for long periods of time the employee's performance is not being evaluated. What happens when an employee performs at extremely high levels during the first or last part of a rating period and then allows his performance to decline substantially during other times? Employees learn that the performance appraisal process is a game, and they also quickly learn how to play the game. It doesn't matter at that point what the manager *says* about performance appraisals. Managers may truly believe that they are conducting accurate performance appraisals and tell employees that "rewards are based upon performance," but the employees know better. They know they only have to perform during certain periods of time, because that's the only time the manager is paying attention.

Another bad situation develops when an employee does something particularly noteworthy during this period of managerial inattentiveness. The employee may have made a substantial contribution to the organization by using his own initiative. If it occurred during a period of managerial inattentiveness, it may go largely unnoticed, and therefore, unrewarded. The employee is not likely to do anything noteworthy again.

Harshness/Leniency

Harsh raters tend to rate everyone toward the negative or low end of the scale; **lenient raters** tend toward the positive or high end of the scale. Harsh raters may be sensitive to the need to accurately rate employees, and may simply be overcompensating. In their desire to not rate any employees higher than they deserve, they may actually underrate them. The lenient rater may be sensitive to the effect performance appraisals have on an employee's career and rewards, or may simply wish to avoid having to deal with employees unhappy with the results of their performance appraisals. Joe, the supervisor in the Prologue, seems to be moving toward giving one of his employees a lenient rating in order to avoid a confrontation. The effect of lenient ratings is similar to that of central tendency. It is possible to determine the better (poorer) performers, but it is not possible to determine how much better (or worse) their performance is, compared to other employees.

Ambiguity of Terms

Particularly when graphic rating scales are used, **ambiguity of terms** may lead various raters to different interpretations of traits and factors on the scale. Factors such as dependability, initiative, and flexibility are likely to be interpreted differently by different managers. In this situation, employees of one manager are, in effect, being rated on different factors than the employees of another manager. Since it may never be known that the managers are interpreting factors differently, comparisons of employees may be made assuming all employees are rated on the same factors. This assumption can lead to errors in decisions based on these appraisals. Ambiguity of terms may alter the value of the points on the scale. What is average performance to one manager may be poor performance to another. This is separate from harsh and lenient ratings; here, managers may simply define levels of performance differently.

Guidelines for improving performance appraisals are summarized in Exhibit 7.6.

Performance Appraisal Feedback Interview

Explain how to conduct an effective performance appraisal interview.

Perhaps a better title for this activity would be simply "performance appraisal interview" because, unfortunately, frequently very little feedback is provided. This is largely due to the fact that many managers are uncomfortable conducting performance appraisals. They are even more uncomfortable sitting down

> **Exhibit 7.6**
> How to improve performance appraisals
>
> 1. Appraisal factors should be critical job requirement identified through job analysis.
> 2. Appraisals should be behavior-oriented, not trait-oriented.
> 3. Employees should be told in advance what is expected of them.
> 4. Appraisers should be given specific written instructions that cover the purposes of the appraisal and how to conduct it.
> 5. Appraisals should be reviewed by higher levels of management.
> 6. Appraisals should be discussed with employees.
> 7. Employees should be given the right to appeal appraisals with which they disagree.

Source: Teel, K.S. Are merit raises really based on merit? *Personnel Journal,* 1986, 65, 88–95.

face-to-face with employees to discuss performance successes or deficiencies. There are several rules for managers to make this interview more effective:

1. Don't limit performance feedback to the formal appraisal interview. Feedback must be frequent, if it is to have an impact on employee behavior.

The feedback interview is a critical component of the performance appraisal process.

When employees do something worthy of recognition, give them positive feedback immediately. This praise reinforces the behavior and makes it more likely to be repeated. Conversely, when employees have performance problems, provide constructive feedback immediately.
2. Feedback must be explicit. Tell employees precisely what needs to be corrected. Don't assume that employees know and understand what aspects of their jobs are most important and should receive the most attention. Expectations of performance should be communicated explicitly to employees.[7] Focus on specific behaviors and not vague generalities (such as "You need to be more cooperative."), or personalities. Instead of telling an employee "I don't think you care about your work," tell him which specific behaviors are causing that feeling.
3. Begin the formal feedback interview with positive feedback. Reinforce those areas of the employee's performance that are acceptable or superior. Employees may be more receptive to constructive feedback after they have been recognized for examples of good performance. Again, *specific behaviors* should be emphasized.
4. Even while providing constructive feedback concerning performance deficiencies, criticism should be avoided. Be objective, not accusing or evaluative. Criticism will only cause the employee to become defensive and unreceptive to suggestions for improvement.
5. Once performance deficiencies have been identified and discussed, it is time to set clear and specific objectives that will produce improved performance. If the employee has had a 10 percent error rate and the ultimate goal is 3 percent, move the employee toward this goal in increments. Set an objective of 7 percent error rate and give the employee adequate time to reach this objective. If the employee reaches that error rate, the next objective should be closer to the ultimate goal, until by the next appraisal the employee's error rate is only 3 percent.
6. Give employees time to voice their opinion. There may be performance constraints or problems which are not evident. Employees need an opportunity to make known any problems they are facing. In addition, ask employees if there is any assistance they need in the performance of their jobs.
7. Be supportive and encouraging. The tone of the interview should be one of help and support. State openly that the purpose of this interview is to develop ways the employee can improve his performance. Involve the employee by asking for his suggestions or recommendations.

The effectiveness of the entire performance appraisal process is highly dependent on the effectiveness of the performance appraisal feedback interview. Even though performance ratings might be highly accurate and free of rater errors or bias, if this information isn't provided to employees in a manner acceptable to them, it will not have the desired effect. It may, in fact, have a negative effect upon employee performance. Many employees have departed from a feedback interview with much lower levels of motivation and commitment than when they entered. It is too important an activity for managers to neglect the attention and preparation it deserves.

An activity that is, or should be, closely related to performance appraisal is rewarding employees. Accurate performance appraisals make it possible to identify each employee's contribution to the organization or level of performance.

REWARDING EMPLOYEES

There should be a direct link between performance appraisal systems and reward administration. This rule is especially true for salary, since most employees attach great importance to this particular reward. For that reason, it is common practice for managers to discuss the performance appraisal and salary increase during the same feedback interview. However, some authors suggest that this practice be discontinued.[8] The following quotation illustrates this position.

> "Performance feedback to an employee has the greatest impact when the person giving the feedback adopts a tone of trying to help the individual, taking the role of counselor. In most performance appraisal systems, however, and particularly those where salary increases are based on the appraisal, the manager is placed in the role of being a judge. His tone becomes evaluative rather than helpful because he must justify the person's increase. This, in turn, reduces the effectiveness of the feedback"[9]

Several authors suggest that the performance appraisal and feedback interview occur at one time, focusing on correcting or improving employee performance. The salary increase is discussed in a separate interview some time later. This separation is intended to allow the manager to be a counselor during the performance appraisal feedback interview and a judge during the salary increase interview. However, this time lapse puts demands on managers' time in conducting two separate interviews. As a result, few companies have separated the performance appraisal from the salary increase. Wight has suggested that this separation can occur during a single interview.[10] He suggests structuring the feedback interview into four distinct steps or phases.

Phase 1: the manager is clearly a counselor. The focus in this stage is on clarifying performance expectations, as well as identifying areas of performance which need improvement.

Phase 2: the manager explains his evaluation (rating) of the employee's performance. Since areas of performance needing improvement were identified in Phase 1, the manager should now focus on translating these deficiencies into a performance rating.

Phase 3: the manager links the employee's overall performance rating to the amount of salary increase forthcoming.

Phase 4: the manager now discusses what kind of a salary increase the employee might receive by correcting the deficient areas of performance identified earlier. The focus here is on providing a clear incentive for the employee to improve his performance.

Employing this four-phase approach to feedback interviews requires planning and preparation on the part of the manager. It is absolutely critical to

HUMAN RELATIONS IN ACTION

Performance Appraisals at Xerox Corporation

In 1983, the Xerox Reprographic Business Group (RPG) decided to revise its performance appraisal process. Until that time, Xerox had been using a rather traditional approach to performance appraisals which included: an annual performance appraisal, the requirement that employees document their own accomplishments, a managerial rating of employee accomplishments, merit increase amounts directly tied to an overall performance rating, and a combination performance appraisal/salary increase interview.

Surveys conducted by Xerox showed that both managers and employees were dissatisfied with the performance appraisal system. Few employees could see a strong link between performance levels and the ratings or rewards. For example, in 1983, over 95 percent of the ratings were 3 (meets and sometimes exceeds expected level of performance) or 4 (consistently exceeds expected level of performance), on a 5 point scale! The resulting merit increases were within 1/2 percent of each other. Thus, while the company claimed it was "paying for performance," employees couldn't see much of a relationship.

The revised performance appraisal system incorporates many of the suggestions provided in the chapter. Specifically:

1. Managers and employees set objectives at the beginning of the appraisal period. These are put into writing and serve as yardsticks for the year-end appraisal.
2. After six months, the manager and employee are required to sit down face-to-face and discuss the employee's progress in meeting objectives. While this can be an informal discussion, both are required to sign the objectives document to show that the midyear review took place.
3. A final written performance appraisal occurs at the end of the year, and the results of the appraisal are discussed with the employee during a feedback interview. The emphasis of this interview is on performance correction. Merit increases are not discussed.
4. One to two months following the performance appraisal feedback interview, a second interview takes place where the merit increase is discussed. The focus of this interview is on how the amount of the merit increase was determined and how this employee's increase compares to his co-workers'.

In a follow-up survey of employee attitudes toward the new performance appraisal system, Xerox found that: 81 percent of the employees had a better understanding of their work group objectives, 84 percent of the employees felt the appraisal they received was a fair assessment of their performance, 72 percent said they understood how their merit increase was determined, and 77 percent of the employees said that they considered the new appraisal system a step in the right direction.

Source: Deets, N.R. & Tyler, D.T. How Xerox improved its performance appraisals. *Personnel Journal,* 1986, 65, 50–52.

---

avoid any mention of salary increases or other rewards during the first two phases of the interview. The early focus must be on specific, job-related behaviors. It is also critical that the manager be able to justify the overall rating and amount of increase to the employee. One way to accomplish this justification may be to keep a **critical incident file** on each employee. This record cites specific examples of job performance that are representative of the employee's overall job performance. From time to time throughout the appraisal period, the manager writes a short paragraph describing the situation and the specific behavior of the employee.[10] Managers should be sure to include examples of especially good, as well as especially bad, performance. However, the goal should be to have a record that is representative of the employee's performance.

While the most direct link may be between performance appraisal and salary, other rewards may be affected as well. For example, many organizations base promotion decisions, at least in part, on performance appraisals. Managers may informally administer other rewards, such as praise and recognition, on the basis of performance appraisal results. Therefore, it is important for managers to be aware of a wide variety of possible rewards, the purpose of organizational reward systems, and the varied effects different rewards may have on different employees.

Purpose of Reward Systems

The purpose of most organizational reward systems is to attract, retain, and motivate qualified employees.[11] Not all rewards will accomplish all three of these objectives. In other words, managers must be sure that the reward they are trying to use to motivate an employee is capable of doing so. Often managers seem to try and motivate employees to perform at higher levels by using rewards that are designed to attract or retain employees. Two categories of rewards, system and individual, can be identified.[12]

Explain how to administer rewards effectively.

System Rewards
System rewards are awarded to employees for simply being a member of the system (organization). These rewards have no tie to performance levels. Most fringe benefits, such as health and life insurance, vacation, pension plans, and sick pay are system rewards. Even pay is used as a system reward in many organizations, although not always intentionally. System rewards have very little effect on the motivational levels of employees. However, they may be able to attract and retain qualified employees if they are equal to or better than alternative employers' rewards.

Differentiate between system rewards and individual rewards.

Individual Rewards
Individual rewards are administered on the basis of a person's performance or contribution to the organization. One of the most important types of individual rewards, **merit pay**, will be discussed in detail later. Examples include salary, awards for excellent performance, bonuses, praise, and recognition. However, it is important to point out that even individual rewards will have an impact on employee motivation only to the extent that they are tied to performance. Think back to some previous jobs you have held. Was pay used as a system reward or an individual reward? What did the organization do right in allocating pay? What did they do wrong?

Criteria for Reward Allocation

The point has been repeatedly made that to motivate employees, rewards must be made contingent on performance. That is, high performers must receive substantially higher rewards than low performers. Anyone who has been a member of an organization realizes that this premise does not always hold in practice.[13] In fact, there are a number of **criteria**, other than levels of performance, which managers may use in their reward allocation decisions.

Discuss several constraints in administering rewards, and explain how to administer rewards effectively.

1. *Equality* was mentioned earlier in the discussion of central tendency error in performance ratings. Managers may try to reward everyone at similar levels, if they believe they can eliminate or reduce employee complaints and requests for explanations of reward decisions. When rewards are administered in this manner, they function more as system rewards than as individual or merit rewards; they are not likely to produce high levels of motivation. Rewards are often standardized in unionized organizations.
2. *Seniority* on the job is often a major factor in determining reward allocations. This approach is widespread in civil service systems as well as in unionized organizations. When rewards are heavily based on seniority, they are not likely to produce high levels of employee motivation. Rather, they operate more as system rewards that are intended to retain people in the system.
3. *Effort* is sometimes a troublesome area for managers. Should you reward effort or performance, or both?

WHAT DO YOU THINK?

Should your instructor reward you with a high grade because you put a great deal of effort into the class? How should your rewards relate to the student who put in less effort, but scored higher on the exams? Further, how should these rewards compare with those of another student who had to put in a great deal of effort to score well on the exams? What effect would these strategies have upon your motivation and performance? What effect would these strategies have on other students who become aware of the instructor's grade allocations?

Considering only low and high levels of both effort and performance, four combinations are possible; they are presented in Exhibit 7.7. How would you appraise the performance of employees in each of these cells? Cell 1 is relatively clear. Since both effort and performance are low, few would disagree that this person should receive few, if any, rewards. However, cells 2,

Exhibit 7.7
Combinations of effort and performance

		PERFORMANCE	
		Low	High
EFFORT	Low	1	2
	High	3	4

3, and 4 are more difficult. Cell 3 requires a decision on whether or not to reward for effort, since performance is low. What about cells 2 and 4? Since both individuals are high performers, should the employee who put in the most effort receive additional rewards, or should the employee who did not have to put in as much effort to achieve high performance? A good exercise is to think of the effects high rewards would have in each cell, then consider the effects of low rewards.

Managers are often heavily influenced by the effort they perceive an employee is putting into the job. There is a danger here that employees will confuse means (effort) with ends (performance). They may learn that it is more important to look good than to actually perform at high levels.

4. *Nature of the Job/Working Conditions* mandate that if the job is especially difficult or undesirable, it may be necessary to provide higher rewards to attract employees to this type of work. Similarly, if working conditions are especially unpleasant (e.g., hot, cold, noisy, dusty), greater rewards may be necessary than for jobs with more pleasant working conditions. However, including a consideration of working conditions may weaken the linkage between productivity and rewards in the minds of employees.

An interesting study was conducted to determine which factors were most closely associated with pay increases. The results for nonunion and union hourly employees are presented in Exhibit 7.8. The most important factors for nonunion employees were prevailing wage rates in the area and cost of living.

Exhibit 7.8
Factors determining pay increases

Factor	Nonunion Hourly Employee	Union Hourly Employee
Worker productivity	3	9
Company's financial results	5	7
Company's financial prospects	4	5
Internal equity among groups	6	8
Increases of industry leaders	7	4
Area surveys	1	6
Ability to hire	10	10
National bargaining settlements	8	2
Union demands	9	1
Cost of living index	2	3

Note: Survey of approximately 9,000 workers (management, salaried and hourly employees) in 493 companies (44 percent manufacturing, 38 percent banking and insurance, 15 percent utility, and 3 percent retail firms). Importance rating was determined by mentions in first, second, or third place in a ranking from 1 to 10.

Source: Adapted from Weeks, D.A. *Compensating employees: Lessons of the 1970s. Report No. 707.* New York: The Conference Board, 1976, 12–14.

Worker productivity was third. The most important factors for union employees were union demands and national bargaining settlements. Worker productivity was rated ninth, out of ten factors! This variance suggests that in practice, many organizations may lose sight of how to use pay increases to motivate employees. Or, perhaps these organizations have made conscious decisions against using pay as a motivator, concentrating instead on other types of rewards.

Pay Secrecy/Openness

Another aspect of salary/pay allocation that deserves managers' consideration is the issue of **pay openness** or **pay secrecy**. Organizations which have adopted a policy of pay secrecy do not openly provide information on employee salaries or publish the amounts of employee salary/pay increases. In the past, organizations would even fire employees if they were observed discussing or making public their salary levels! The courts have ruled that employers may no longer fire employees for discussing their own salaries. However, many organizations continue to make efforts to keep this type of information secret. The primary reason for adopting a policy of pay secrecy seems to be that it will result in fewer complaints or jealous employees who find out what their coworkers are being paid. In other words, many managers seem to believe that pay secrecy produces fewer problems as a result of employees' equity comparisons. (See Chapter 5 for a discussion of equity theory.)

However, a number of researchers and managers believe just the opposite—that employees will make equity comparisons regardless of the organization policy. And, under a policy of pay secrecy, employees may be making these comparisons with less than accurate information. Further, pay secrecy policies may create suspicion in the minds of employees that they are not being treated fairly. In this case, providing employees with accurate information about levels of employee salaries may produce fewer equity comparison-type problems. However, there is one major qualification to this last statement. Pay openness is likely to succeed only in those organizations which have developed an accurate method of appraising employee performance, which is accepted by managers and employees alike. In addition, salary increases must be highly contingent on performance, rather than on other factors (e.g., seniority). It is difficult for anyone to argue with a system that accurately appraises performance and gives greater rewards to higher performers. Which approach do you think is best, pay secrecy or pay openness? Why? Which would you prefer as a manager? As an employee?

Merit Pay

Understand how to administer merit pay.

The idea of merit pay is not new. However, organizations have begun to implement merit pay programs as a new management technique. Reasons for this renewed interest in merit pay are easy to understand.[14] First, many U.S. organizations are facing increased competition from abroad, where labor costs are cheaper. Any program that will improve productivity and/or decrease labor costs will help U.S. companies compete in the international markets. Second, there is a growing concern surrounding productivity levels of American workers. Again, many foreign countries, such as Japan and West Germany, have gained on the U.S. in terms of growth in productivity and productivity per worker. Merit pay plans are seen as a way of stimulating employee productivity and at the same time spending labor dollars more efficiently.

Traditional merit pay plans are relatively simple. Employees are paid a base salary determined primarily by what it takes to attract qualified employees to a particular position. Factors such as labor market conditions, competitor's salaries, and internal equity influence the base salary. Increases to base salary are determined on the basis of performance or productivity. These increases are typically percentages of, and are added to, the base salary.

It was pointed out earlier that several factors inhibit linking rewards to performance. Unfortunately, this restraint is also the case with merit pay. Other factors sometimes reduce the strength of the relationship between merit pay and performance. These factors include cost of living, difficulty in replacing employees who leave, seniority, and budget constraints.[15] Some managers believe that they have an obligation to protect employees' purchasing power, giving employees salary increases at least equal to the rate of inflation. These cost of living increases are not at all related to level of performance, but since most organizations have limited funds available for increases, funds allocated to cost of living increases reduce amounts available for true merit increases. Frequently, the amounts remaining after cost of living increases are not sufficient to give motivating pay increases to top performers.

It is clear that many organizations which *claim* they have merit pay, may not have effective systems. Some may not have merit pay systems at all, but rather may be allocating salary increase dollars as if they were system rewards, rather than individual rewards.

From the employees' perspective, there are two major problems to overcome in order to have a truly effective merit pay system. The first problem is the amount of the salary increase.[16] Many merit pay systems give salary increases that are too small to have any substantial effect upon motivation. Further, there is often little difference in the amount of salary increase given to poor performers and top performers. As pointed out earlier, the reason may be because of cost of living or other noncontingent salary increases. It is impossible to establish what level of salary increase is motivating (since individuals are likely to become motivated at different levels); increases in base salary of between 10 and 15 percent have been suggested.[17] Bank of America's merit pay program resulted in some top performers getting *40 percent* more than poor performers.[18]

Assume that you are just out of school and working on your first job at a salary of $18,000 per year. How much of a salary increase would it take to motivate you? What is the minimum percentage salary increase that would be motivational to you?

The second problem lies in how the amount of salary increase is determined. As discussed earlier in this chapter, the employees' salary increases are typically determined by performance appraisals. For the salary increases to be effective, however, they must not only be adequate in terms of amount, but they must also be accepted and perceived as fair by employees.[19]

WHAT DO YOU THINK?

Assume that your company has a true merit pay plan. Salary increases are highly dependent on level of performance. At some point, some of your top performers may actually be making more money than you are. Isn't it possible that under a true merit pay plan a few "star performers" would actually make more than their managers? Do you think this could work? Why or why not? What are the implications when employees make more money than their bosses?

A rather novel approach to merit pay was developed by Michael Dunaway, founder of PSICOR, a small manufacturer located in Michigan.[20] PSICOR manufactures equipment and supplies professional employees, known as "perfusionists," for open heart surgery. Perfusionists are in high demand and, as a result, are frequently lured to change jobs by higher salaries offered by competitors. Recognizing that even substantial rewards given at the end of the year may be too far removed from performance to be motivating, Dunaway developed the idea of "continuous raises." Perfusionists were given a salary increase in every paycheck, which added up to a total annual raise of at least 5 percent. In addition, up to 8 percent was added on as a lump-sum increase at the end of the year.

WHAT DO YOU THINK?

What do you think of this idea of "continuous raises"? What are its advantages and disadvantages? See the note at the end of the chapter for what happened at PSICOR.

Recent Developments in Organizational Rewards

Organizations seem to be constantly in search of better methods of rewarding employees. As a result, new methods and new rewards are constantly being developed and tried in organizations. Some of the newer approaches which seem to have met with some success are **cafeteria-style benefits, lump-sum salary increases, gainsharing, and pay for knowledge**.

Cafeteria Style Benefits

The traditional fringe benefit system provides exactly the same benefits (e.g., life insurance, health insurance, retirement pensions, vacations) to all employees. However, the recognition of the importance of individual differences has led many organizations to implement a cafeteria-style benefit system.[21] This benefit allows employees to make choices about the benefits they will receive. Usually, some maximum dollar amount is determined by the organization. Employees then have at least some degree of freedom in determining which benefits they will "purchase" with their allotment. Some organizations have set minimums in certain benefit categories such as life and health insurance to ensure that employees will have at least some protection in these areas. Other companies even allow employees to move dollars from fringe benefits to salary. The payoff an organization can expect to receive from cafeteria-style benefit systems is a more satisfied work force. Employee commitment to the organization may increase if employees feel the organization trusts them to make important decisions about their compensation. The primary disadvantage to the organization is the increased administrative expense of keeping track of an infinite number of individualized fringe benefit programs.

Lump-Sum Salary Increases

Lump-sum salary increases have become popular with managers in many organizations, and have been accepted by their employees' unions in place of the traditional salary increases. Managers see lump-sum increases as a cost-cutting tool, because these increases are not added to the employee's base salary. An example will help clarify the difference between traditional and lump-sum salary increases. If an employee were to receive a traditional salary increase of 5 percent for each of the next three years, the total increase received would not be 15 percent (5 + 5 + 5), but rather 15.76 percent (1.05^3). This difference occurs because the first 5 percent increase is added to the employee's base salary. If the employee were making $10,000 before the first salary increase, he would be making $10,500 after the increase. The second year's 5 percent increase would then be based upon $10,500 rather than the original $10,000, resulting in an increase for the second year of $525, rather than $500. Under a lump-sum salary increase of 15 percent, employees making $10,000 would receive a one-time payment of $1,500. Employees receiving a 5 percent traditional increase for each of the next three years would receive a total of $1,576. This may not seem like a large difference on the surface. However, in organizations that have thousands of employees, the difference in the two forms of salary increases can be substantial. Lump-sum salary increases may also make the salary increase more visible to the employee. Many plans allow the employee to choose between a one-time payment or spreading the increase over twelve months. A one-time payment of $1,500 may seem much greater than an extra $125 each month. Would you prefer to receive a traditional salary increase which is added to your base pay or a lump-sum salary increase? Why?

The major benefit to organizations of lump-sum salary increases is cost containment. Not only are salary costs held down since increases are not added to employees' base pay, but fringe benefit costs are contained as well. Since fringe benefits such as pensions are based directly on salary level, these costs will not escalate since lump-sum increases do not affect base salaries. Another potential benefit for organizations is that lump-sum salary increases may be perceived by employees to be more closely related to performance than traditional salary increases spread out over an entire year. Similarly, since the increase comes in a lump sum, the lump-sum salary increase may be perceived by employees to be more meaningful than traditional salary increases which are allocated in much smaller monthly increments.[22] The disadvantage to employees is that they receive a smaller amount of money under a lump-sum salary increase.

Gainsharing

Gainsharing is a pay system linking merit pay to group or team performance. Typically, monthly bonuses are paid to all employees within a department or work team based on a predetermined formula. These bonuses are paid when the department or team produces a measurable decrease in costs or improvement in company productivity.[23] When teamwork and cooperation are important elements of performance, gainsharing may be more effective than individualized systems. It may also be appropriate in situations where individual performance is difficult to measure.[24]

The Swedish firm Volvo implemented a gainsharing plant at its Kalmar auto assembly plant.[25] The plan involved sharing benefits in overall plant productivity with employees. It also involved substantial employee participation and attempted to increase the level of employee identification with the company. Both of these factors are seen as essential to the effectiveness of the gainsharing plan. Volvo attempted to increase employee identification with the company by focusing upon the common interests of both parties. This philosophy is illustrated in the following statement developed by Volvo management and local unions:

> Volvo's development depends on the efforts and personal involvement of the employees. Volvo needs employees prepared to work hard, accept responsibility, and play their part with initiative and ideas to stimulate development of the company.

To increase employee involvement, Volvo encouraged employees to participate in important decisions affecting the plant. The company supplied all employees with information about the plant's operations, such as spoilage rates, hours worked, and productivity levels. Production teams made up of employees from the same area of the plant discussed methods of improving productivity, reducing spoilage, and other specific production-related problems.

Bonuses paid to employees were based upon several production-related factors including spoilage, inventory costs, labor hours per car, materials and supplies consumption, a quality index, and the number of hours worked by office workers. Employees received 25 percent of the improvements made over a 1980 base level of these factors. This enabled most employees to earn a bonus of about 10 per cent of their base pay. The Volvo gainsharing plan produced positive results. In fact, several U.S. firms, such as the GM plant in Pontiac, Michigan implemented gainsharing plans very similar to the one used by Volvo.[26]

Pay for Knowledge

Pay for knowledge or pay for skill is a pay program in which employees earn salary increases based upon what they learn, rather than output or seniority. Some programs, however, base at least part of employees' pay increases on these factors. Typically, these pay programs are part of semiautonomous work teams. The Saturn plant in Smyrna, Tennessee which scheduled its first car production around 1990, had plans for semiautonomous work teams and pay for knowledge. Work teams would be responsible for such things as interviewing and hiring new employees, assigning work to employees, and deciding when pay raises are due. New employees hire in at a base pay. Employees will

CHAPTER SEVEN: Appraising and Rewarding Performance

DEVELOPING YOUR HUMAN RELATIONS SKILLS

The information and ideas presented in this chapter have important implications for you as a manager who is interested in promoting good human relations within your work unit. The following suggestions provide a summary of these ideas:

1. Before conducting a performance appraisal, become familiar with the areas of job performance to be rated. Make sure that you know how to use the particular rating scale employed by the organization and that all terms and performance factors are clearly understood.
2. Avoid making common rating errors by being constantly aware of them and how they occur. Be as objective as possible in your performance ratings and rate each factor independently.
3. Do not allow an overall impression or judgment of an employee cloud your ratings on individual performance factors.
4. Conduct informal performance appraisals regularly. When it is appropriate, informally let employees know how they are performing. Let them know when they perform a task particularly well or particularly poorly. There should never be any surprises during the formal performance appraisal.
5. Provide timely, objective, and specific feedback. Let employees know exactly what they can do to improve their performance ratings. Focus on specific behaviors, rather than attitudes or personalities.
6. To the extent possible, tie rewards to performance. Also, differentiate the rewards given to employees performing at different levels. Poor performers should receive appreciably less than average performers.

As an employee, the performance appraisal/reward administration process is typically beyond your influence. However, one thing that you can do as an employee is to ask your manager for specific suggestions on how to improve your performance. Remember that many managers are extremely uncomfortable conducting these appraisal/reward activities. They may have helpful suggestions for you, but their discomfort may prevent them from openly discussing them. They may welcome an employee who seeks out suggestions for improvement.

earn pay raises by learning new jobs. During their free time, employees are permitted to go to other work stations and learn those jobs. When employees feel they have a job mastered, they are tested by the work team responsible for that job. If they pass the test, the employees are eligible for a pay raise. In other organizations, employees earn pay raises by mastering specific skills such as machine maintenance and quality control.[27]

SUMMARY

Performance appraisals and reward administration are two of the most important activities of managers. Both of these activities are extremely important to employees and therefore are highly visible. In addition, both activities are highly interrelated, with reward decisions usually being based upon performance appraisals. It is important to remember that the degree to which reward allocations are effective in motivating employees is highly dependent on the effectiveness of the performance appraisal.

While most organizations tend to use performance appraisals primarily as a basis for reward allocations, there are a number of other purposes for which performance appraisals could be used. These include identifying training needs of employees, increasing/improving communications between managers and employees, providing valuable feedback to employees, improving performance, and motivating employees.

The most widely used form of performance appraisal is the graphic rating scale, primarily because of its simplicity. However, this simplicity also makes it susceptible to a variety of rater errors—halo error, primacy/recency, central tendency, harshness/leniency, and different interpretation by raters due to ambiguity of terms. Other popular forms of performance appraisal include behaviorally anchored rating scales (BARS), behavioral observation scales (BOS), and management by objectives (MBO). Graphic rating scales are trait-based appraisals; BARS and BOS are behavior-based appraisals; and MBO is a results-oriented appraisal method.

The effectiveness of the performance appraisal is highly dependent on the effectiveness of the feedback interview. Many of the purposes of performance appraisal are accomplished by providing positive and constructive feedback to employees concerning their job performance. Suggestions for the feedback interview include being objective and not critical and focusing upon specific, job related behaviors.

The purpose of most organizational reward systems is to attract, retain, and motivate qualified employees. However, not all types of rewards can accomplish all three of these goals. System rewards are designed primarily to attract and retain qualified employees, while individual or merit rewards are designed to motivate employees. However, it is a fact of organizational life that many rewards intended to be merit rewards are actually used as systems rewards. It is also true that managers are sometimes influenced to base their reward decisions on factors other than job performance. These factors include equality, seniority, effort, and the nature of the job or working conditions. An ongoing debate exists over whether organizations should adopt a policy of pay openness or pay secrecy. New developments in rewarding employees include cafeteria-style benefit programs, gainsharing, lump-sum salary increases, and pay for knowledge.

It would be difficult to argue against the idea that in organizational work settings, job performance should be emphasized and rewarded. Thus, an emphasis on, and rewarding employees for, good job performance would seem to be an element of a good human relations climate. Do merit based rewards influence performance? The evidence suggests that they do. The closer rewards are tied to performance, the higher that performance will be. Managers have to be sure they are emphasizing the right areas of performance in their performance appraisals and reward allocations.

KEY TERMS

rater errors
trait-based appraisal
graphic rating scale
behavior-based
 appraisal
behaviorally anchored
 rating scales
 (BARS)
behavioral observation
 scales (BOS)
results-oriented
 appraisal
management by
 objectives (MBO)
halo error
central tendency
primacy/recency
harshness
leniency
ambiguity of terms
critical incident file
system rewards
individual rewards
merit pay
criteria for reward
 allocation
pay secrecy/openness
cafeteria-style benefits
lump-sum salary
 increases
gainsharing
pay for knowledge

DISCUSSION QUESTIONS

1. Identify at least five specific purposes of performance appraisal. Explain why each is important.
2. Describe the graphic rating scale form of performance appraisal. What are its advantages and disadvantages?
3. Compare and contrast the BARS appraisal with the BOS appraisal. How are they similar? How are they different? Which do you prefer and why?
4. How do results-oriented appraisals differ from behavior-based appraisals? What effect will

each form have on human relations within an organization?
5. Describe how MBO can be used in appraising employee job performance.
6. What causes halo error? How can it be avoided?
7. What causes managers to engage in central tendency error?
8. Explain primacy/recency error and harsh/lenient rater problems. What effect does each have on the performance rating?
9. What are some suggestions for conducting effective performance appraisal feedback interviews? If you had to pick one of these suggestions as the most important, which would it be? Why?
10. Should the discussion of an employee's salary increase be separated from the performance appraisal feedback interview? Why or why not?
11. Explain the difference between system rewards and individual rewards. What are the objectives of each type of reward system?
12. What criteria, other than level of performance, do managers sometimes use in making reward allocation decisions? Which of these do you think are inappropriate?
13. What advantages and disadvantages are there to an organization adopting a policy of pay openness? Pay secrecy?
14. Explain how cafeteria-style benefit programs work. What advantages are there from the organization's perspective?
15. What are lump-sum salary increases? How might employees benefit from such programs? How might organizations benefit?
16. What are several problems or constraints that make it difficult for organizations to implement true merit pay plans?
17. What is pay for knowledge? How does it work? How does pay for knowledge compare with traditional merit pay plans?

EXERCISE 7.1

Appraising and Rewarding Performance

You are the manager of the following four employees. It is time to conduct their annual performance appraisal and determine the amount of their salary increase. The following information is provided concerning the nature of their jobs:

Accounting Clerks, Grade IV, are responsible for billing customers and recording customer payments for all credit sales. Nearly all of this work is done on personal computers at each employee's desk. For example, when a credit sale takes place, the sales slip is forwarded to your department where one of your employees enters the information into the computerized billing system which prints a bill which is mailed to the customer. When the customer makes a payment, the check is mailed directly to your department where an employee enters the amount paid into the computer system which reduces the amount due from the customer. The work load is steady, but usually not so heavy that your department falls behind in keeping customer accounts up to date.

As you sit down at your desk this morning, you see the note on your calendar that the performance appraisals are to be conducted today. In preparation, you pull out the files you keep on each employee's performance during the year. You have just enough time to review these before completing the performance appraisal forms on each employee and returning them to the personnel department for processing.

Steve. Steve is just finishing his first year in your department. He accepted this job after graduating from the local community college. Your assessment of Steve is that he's a pretty good employee. He certainly tries hard. There's no question but that he puts more into the job than the others. And he's always willing to do something extra, that the others sometimes aren't willing to do. He has made a few mistakes during the year. You recall talking with one angry customer who was billed $1,500 for a $15.00 wallet. You wonder if Steve made any mistakes in the other direction (billing a customer $15.00 for a $1,500 entertainment center!). You weren't likely to get customers' complaints about mistakes like that. Steve is never late nor absent without reason. If he could just improve his speed in processing billings and payments, and reduce those errors, he would be an excellent employee.

Mary. Mary has been with you for five years. In fact, she had already been in the department for three years when you took over as manager. Mary seems quite content with her job. She does an acceptable amount of work with few errors, but you think that someone who has spent eight years doing the same kind of work shouldn't make *any* errors. Your impression is that Mary could be a much better performer. She seems to have decided to put forth only so much effort for the salary she receives. It's as if she decided "For that amount of pay, I'm only willing to give this much effort." She's almost mechanical in her work. She comes to work on time and takes her breaks on time. She never stretches lunch or coffee breaks, but she never returns early, either. Nor is she willing to work overtime in those unusual cases when the department falls behind in its billings. Mary doesn't seem to be well accepted by the other employees. You're not sure if this is because she's older or because she is quiet. The others are pleasant toward her but they don't spend any time talking with her.

Tony. Tony has been working for you for three years. He is without question the best performer in the department. He consistently processes more billings and customer payments than any of the others, and you can't remember the last time he made a mistake. The only problem is, he knows he's much better. As a result, he frequently comes to work a few minutes late and will stretch his lunch and coffee breaks. Every time you say anything to him he replies "I'm only a couple of minutes late, and by the end of the day I will have done more work than the others anyway." He's always right about the output, but it still bothers you that he's frequently late. But you don't want to reprimand him because you want him to continue his present level of performance. If he dropped his performance to Mary's level, the department would have real trouble getting customers billed on time. However, there may be another problem arising. You overheard Mary complaining to Jane that Tony "gets away with anything he wants." The implication was that if Tony gets longer lunches and coffee breaks, so should the others.

Jane. There are no major problems with Jane's performance. However, it certainly isn't outstanding. You know she doesn't need the money she earns from this job. Her husband is an attorney in a well-established practice across town. They live in a more expensive neighborhood than you do. In fact, the only thing that you can see that Jane enjoys about her job are the lunch and coffee breaks. She really seems to enjoy sitting in the lounge, talking with employees from other departments about fashions or civic events. Her error rate is just about average, sometimes a little worse. It's not that she doesn't care at all about her job. It's more like there are many other things more important to her and she's constantly distracted. She can't keep her mind on her work, and when you sit at a computer keyboard all day long, it only takes a couple of keystrokes to make a major mistake. Steve learned that when he billed that customer $1,500 for a wallet!

Your instructor will pass out performance appraisal forms for you to use in rating each employee's performance. You may refer back to your files on each of these employees as you rate them on the following factors: quality of work, quantity of work, dependability, initiative, and cooperation.

When you have finished with the performance appraisal, determine a percentage salary increase for each employee. This should be an individual or merit increase. There is a space provided on the performance appraisal form for each employee's salary increase recommendation.

CASE 7.1

The Performance Appraisal Feedback Interview

You feel a great sense of relief. You have just finished conducting performance appraisals on all four of your employees. None of the supervisors enjoys appraising the performance of his employees. It is a constant subject of discussion among the supervisors this time of year. As you place the forms in the envelope to mail to the personnel department, that sense of relief disappears. You remember that a new company policy requires that you sit down with each employee and go over the results of their performance appraisal. Refer back to Exercise 7.1. Prepare an outline of topics to be discussed with each employee. Remember, the overall effectiveness of performance appraisals depends largely on what is said during the feedback interview. What will you say to each of these employees so that they become more highly motivated and better performers in the future?

REFERENCES

[1] Rowland, K.M. & Ferris, G.R. *Personnel Management*. Boston: Allyn & Bacon, 1982, p. 188.

[2] Locher, A.H. & Teel, K.S. Performance appraisal: A survey of current practices. *Personnel Journal,* 1977, *56,* 245–254; Teel, K.S. Performance appraisal: Current trends, persistent progress. *Personnel Journal,* 1980, *59,* 296–301, 316.

[3] Bernardin, J.H. & Smith, P.C. A clarification of some issues regarding the development and use of behaviorally anchored rating scales (BARS). *Journal of Applied Psychology,* 1981, *66,* 458–463.

[4] Locher, A.H. & Teel, K.S., 1980, Ibid.

[5] Carroll, S.J. & Tosi, H.L. *Management by objectives: Applications and research*. New York: Macmillan, 1973.

[6] Lowe, T.R. Eight ways to ruin a performance review. *Personnel Journal,* 1986, *65,* 60–62.

[7] Regel, R.W. & Hollman, R.W. Gauging performance objectively. *Personnel Administrator,* 1987, *32*(6), 74–78.

[8] Meyer, H.H., Kay, E. & French, J.R.P. Split roles in performance appraisal. *Harvard Business Review,* 1965, *43,* 123–129.

[9] Wight, D.T. The split role in performance appraisal. *Personnel Administrator,* 1985, *30,* 83.

[10] Wight, D.T. The split role in performance appraisal. *Personnel Administrator,* 1985, *30,* 83–87.

[11] Friedman, J.B. 10 steps to objective appraisals. *Personnel Journal,* 1986, *65,* 66–71.

[12] Gehrman, D.B. Beyond today's compensation and performance appraisal systems. *Personnel Administrator,* 1984, *29,* 21–33.

[13] Brennan, E.J. The myth and reality of pay for performance. *Personnel Journal,* 1985, *64,* 73–75; Rollins, T. Pay for performance: Is it worth the trouble? *Personnel Administrator,* 1988, *33*(5), 42–46.

[14] Kanter, R.M. From status to contribution: Some organizational implications of the changing basis for pay. *Personnel,* 1987, *64*(1), 12–37.

[15] Schuster, J.R. & Zingheim, P.K. Merit pay: Is it hopeless in the public sector? *Personnel Administrator,* 1987, *32*(10), 83–84.

[16] Kanter, R.M., 1987, Ibid.

[17] Kanter, R.M., 1987, Ibid.

[18] Kanter, R.M., 1987, Ibid.

[19] Lawler, E.E. New approaches to pay: Innovations that work. *Personnel,* 1976, *53*(5), 11–23.

[20] Kanter, R.M. From status to contribution: Some organizational implications of the changing basis for pay. *Personnel,* 1987, *64*(1), 12–37.

[21] Baker, C.A. Flex your benefits. *Personnel Journal,* 1988, *67*(5), 54–61.

[22] Minken, S.L. Does lump-sum pay merit attention? *Personnel Journal,* 1988, *67*(6), 76–83.

[23] Kanter, R.M., 1987, Ibid.

[24] Lawler, E.E. Whatever happened to incentive pay? *New Management,* 1984, *1,* 37–41; Kopleman, R.E., Reinharth, L. & Beer, A.A. The link between judgmental rewards and performance. *Personnel Administrator,* 1983, *28,* 78–79.

[25] Hauck, W.C. & Ross, T.L. Sweden's experiments in productivity gainsharing: A second look. *Personnel,* 1987, *64*(1), 61–67.

[26] Ibid.

[27] Tosi, H. & Tosi, L. What managers need to know about knowledge-based pay. *Organizational Dynamics,* 1986, *14,* 52–64.

WHAT DO YOU THINK? NOTE 1

There is no right or wrong answer here. Some managers and instructors obviously do reward for effort. This is a decision that each manager will have to make for himself. However, in making this decision, you should carefully consider the effect on employee motivation. If your objective is to encourage employees to perform up to their capabilities, it is difficult to argue that effort should be rewarded. Remember, performance is a function of both ability and effort. To reward employees for effort alone, in effect, punishes employees with greater ability. If you reward employees for effort, what effect will these rewards have upon employees who are better performers due to their greater ability? Do you expect that they will continue to perform at the same level? Remember equity theory from Chapter 5?

WHAT DO YOU THINK? NOTE 2

In PSICOR's continuous raises program, employees responded to the continuous raises very positively, but the accounting department became overloaded with paperwork. Even though the program produced positive results, the administration of the program proved to be too much. The company backed off the idea of continuous raises and now uses a combination of quarterly merit raises of up to 5 percent per year and a series of bonuses.

CHAPTER EIGHT

Disciplining and Counseling Employees

PROLOGUE

One of the most difficult, and unfortunately widespread, employee problems that managers must face is employee substance abuse. Some experts have estimated that as much as 50 percent of the absenteeism and work accidents which occur in organizations each year are related to drug or alcohol abuse. Organizations are quickly responding by developing employee assistance and counseling services, engaging in electronic surveillance of employees, and more carefully screening employees. IBM Corporation announced in January, 1985, that all new job candidates would have to undergo a urinalysis before being hired. In extreme cases, organizations have cooperated with local police departments to stage raids and "sting operations" on employees suspected of substance abuse, drug dealing, and theft. San Jose, California police found $250,000 worth of sophisticated electronics equipment which had been stolen by "high-tech" employees to support their drug habit. According to police, they also found "vice-presidents who were passing around sugar bowls full of cocaine."[1]

LEARNING OBJECTIVES

After successful completion of this chapter, you should be able to

- Recognize the importance of developing good discipline and counseling skills,
- Identify the variety of causes of performance problems,
- Describe a number of personal problems which might affect an employee's job performance,
- Discuss methods for dealing with controlled substance and alcohol abuse,
- Deal with employees who violate organizational rules,
- Understand the causes of absenteeism,

- Identify several ways of reducing absenteeism,
- Describe how to administer discipline effectively, and
- Identify several characteristics of effective employee counseling practices.

EMPLOYEE PROBLEMS AND HUMAN RELATIONS

Even in departments experiencing extremely good human relations and job performance, employee problems may develop from time to time. These problems may stem from a variety of sources, including personal concerns such as family trouble; alcohol and drug abuse; illegal acts such as theft and sabotage of organization property; rule violations; and tardiness, absenteeism, and turnover. To deal with these problems effectively, managers must have good skills in counseling and disciplining. Both of these activities can be emotional and stressful for managers and employees alike. As a result, many managers may delay or even avoid counseling and disciplining activities. Similarly, employees may avoid seeking assistance and may deny that a problem exists, even when confronted by their managers. Thus, the problem never gets resolved and may develop into an even more serious situation. This chapter will review several categories of problems that give rise to the need for discipline and counseling of employees. Causes and potential remedies for each category of problem will be discussed. The text also offers suggestions for effective disciplining and counseling of employees.

NEED FOR DISCIPLINE AND COUNSELING

Recognize the importance of developing good discipline and counseling skills.

Employee problems that call for discipline and/or counseling include **performance problems**; personal troubles; drug and alcohol abuse; illegal acts; rule violations; and tardiness, absenteeism and turnover.

Performance Problems

Job performance has been defined in terms of three components—*willingness* (motivation), *capacity* (ability), and *opportunity*.[2] **Willingness to perform** includes such variables as motivation, job satisfaction, job involvement, clarity of work assignments, and perceptions of equity. **Capacity to perform** encompasses ability, health, age, job knowledge, skills, education, and endurance. **Opportunity to perform** consists largely of environmental variables beyond the control of the individual employee. Tools, equipment, materials, supplies, working conditions, actions of coworkers, actions of leader, time pressure, and organizational policies, rules, and procedures are among these variables. Thus, the category includes potential constraints on performance from the work setting (i.e., working conditions, availability of supplies and materials, condition of equipment), and from other people in the work setting (actions of coworkers and leaders). Various combinations of these factors, and their effect on performance levels, are presented in Exhibit 8.1.

Exhibit 8.1
Predicted performance outcomes for different levels of opportunity, capacity, and willingness

ENVIRONMENTAL FACTORS

PERSONAL FACTORS

		Opportunity	
		Less Favorable	More Favorable
Lower Capacity	Lower Willingness	1 Very Low Performance	2 Low Performance
Lower Capacity	Higher Willingness	3 Low to Moderate Performance	4 Moderate Performance
Higher Capacity	Lower Willingness	5 Low to Moderate Performance	6 Moderate Performance
Higher Capacity	Higher Willingness	7 High Performance	8 Very High Performance

Source: Blumberg, M. & Pringle, C.D. The missing opportunity in organizational research: Some implications for a theory of work performance. *Academy of Management Review,* 1982, 7, 567.

Since all three factors (willingness, capacity, and opportunity) influence job performance, all must be present in some degree. For example, a willing employee with the capacity to perform will not perform well if the equipment on which she must work is outdated and in constant need of repair. Similarly, the most capable employee working on the most up-to-date and well-maintained equipment will not perform well if she lacks the motivation to do so. Consequently, managers must diagnose employee performance problems in terms of all three categories. Too often, performance problems are assumed to be caused by a lack of motivation or ability, disregarding the effect of constraints to the opportunity to perform. Managers are responsible not only for motivating employees, assigning them to jobs for which they have the ability to perform, and providing additional training so that they are capable of performing, but also for removing obstacles and constraints on employees' op-

Identify the variety of causes of performance problems.

portunity to perform. Depending on the exact cause of the performance problem, counseling and/or discipline might be appropriate. Managers must be able to determine which of these two responses is most appropriate in each situation. Engaging in discipline when counseling is most appropriate, or counseling when discipline is most appropriate, can be detrimental to human relations.

Personal Problems

Describe a number of personal problems which might affect an employee's job performance.

Personal problems involve emotional traumas such as family difficulties, divorce, death of a family member or close friend, and severe illness—all of which may serve to increase the anxiety and stress experienced by employees.[3] While alcohol and drug abuse might properly be placed in this category, they will be given separate treatment due to the increasing severity of these types of problems in organizations.

Personal problems are particularly difficult for managers to address. They are in one sense private matters and are unrelated to the work setting. On the other hand, severe personal problems may put an employee under an unacceptably high level of stress, which decreases the employee's ability to perform assigned tasks. When this happens, managers must become involved to help the employee bring performance back up to adequate levels.

Alcohol and Drug Abuse

It has been estimated that 10 percent of the labor force are alcoholics and another 10 percent are borderline alcoholics.[4] "Compared to workers who are not alcoholic, problem drinkers take two-and-one-half times more absences of eight days or more; receive three times as much sick leave and accident benefits and five times as many workman's compensation claims; are subject to garnishment seven times more often; and are repeatedly involved in job grievance proceedings. Other reports indicate that the overall productivity of the troubled employee is decreased by as much as 25 percent."[5] This productivity loss translates into a $30 billion annual cost to U.S. businesses in absenteeism, sick pay benefits, and decreased productivity.[6] It is difficult to develop similar numbers for drug abuse since it is illegal and employees are more likely to hide their use of illegal drugs. However, one estimate is that drug abuse at the workplace costs U.S. businesses $26 billion per year.[7]

Warning Signs

Managers must be familiar with several common symptoms of alcohol and **substance abuse**. Depending on the degree of the employee's problem, it may be difficult to detect. Several common warning signs of substance abuse are:

1. Sudden change in behavior
2. Sudden decrease in job performance
3. Increased absenteeism and tardiness
4. Slurred speech
5. Difficulty concentrating

CHAPTER EIGHT: Disciplining and Counseling Employees   203

The outcomes of employee drug abuse are similar to those of alcohol abuse—decreased productivity, absenteeism, turnover, accidents, and errors. These consequences are reason enough for organizations (such as IBM which was mentioned in the Prologue) to get involved in helping employees overcome their alcohol and drug abuse problems. But there is another reason; court rulings in at least three states suggest that employers may be held liable for negligent activities of off-duty employees, impaired by alcohol and/or drugs, which result in injury to a third party. A noteworthy case in Texas resulted in an employer being held responsible for a fatal motor vehicle accident caused by an intoxicated employee.[8] The employee was observed to be intoxicated on the job and was sent home by the supervisor, who asked the employee if he could make it home. When the employee stated that he could make it home, he was allowed to drive off the organization's property. The court reasoned that the company knew of the employee's intoxicated condition and should have restrained him from driving a motor vehicle while in that condition. To put it simply, "an employer has a duty, as a reasonably prudent employer, to exercise control over an intoxicated employee in order to prevent the employee from causing unreasonable risk of harm to others."[9]

RETURN TO THE PROLOGUE

6. Dilated pupils
7. Apathy and indifference
8. Suspicious behavior; appearance of hiding something
9. Glassy eyes
10. More frequent physical illness

Recognizing symptoms of substance abuse leads to a need to take corrective action. Important to that corrective action is a corporate substance abuse policy that includes confronting the employee with documentation that a problem exists.

Substance Abuse Policy

Many organizations have adopted similar procedures for controlling alcohol and drug abuse problems of employees. At the heart of these attempts is a carefully developed substance abuse policy.[10] Characteristics of an effective policy are listed below.[11]

1. General statement. The policy should include a general statement of the organization's position on substance abuse. This statement might include an expression of the organization's concern for the effects of substance abuse (e.g., decreased performance, accidents, absenteeism) and the belief that employees should report to work in a fit condition to perform their jobs effectively.
2. Organization's intent to take action. It should be made clear that the organization intends to take immediate action against employees who use, distribute, or possess controlled substances or alcohol while on the job.
3. Description of process. This section should include a relatively detailed explanation of what happens when an employee is suspected of controlled

Discuss methods of dealing with controlled substance and alcohol abuse.

HUMAN RELATIONS IN ACTION

EAPs—Employee Assistance Programs

Annual costs of alcohol and drug abuse quoted in the chapter were $30 billion and $26 billion respectively. Annual costs of absenteeism were estimated to be over $26 billion. Of course, some absenteeism can be expected to be the result of alcohol or drug abuse; however, some of the costs of absenteeism must be attributed to other types of personal problems, such as stress, family problems, financial difficulties, and so on. If half of the costs of absenteeism can be attributed to these other causes, the combined costs of employee problems amount to nearly $70 billion per year! This is probably a conservative estimate. In addition, other costs are incurred as a result of employee problems, but they are more difficult to measure. These include increased conflict, lower morale, workers' compensation claims, greater use of paid sick leave, more frequent accidents, and more grievances. In an attempt to control these costs and help employees resolve their problems and become more productive, approximately 5,000 organizations have implemented EAPs–Employee Assistance Programs.[1]

EAPs have begun as counseling programs for employees with alcohol problems. However, they now assist employees with all types of problems that may affect their work.[2] Case in point: the city of Phoenix, Arizona, reports that requests for counseling in their Project Concern EAP fall into the following problem categories: job-related, 42 percent; alcohol-drug, 21 percent; marital, 12 percent; family, 10 percent; financial, 4 percent; health, 3 percent; and miscellaneous, 8 percent.[3] The proportion of counseling which takes place within an organization, as opposed to outside agencies, varies across organizations. At one extreme, the organization employs a "counselor" who really does little counseling other than to find the cause of the employee's problem and refer her to the appropriate outside agency for counseling. At the other extreme, the organization may employee a staff of qualified counselors who perform in-house employee counseling.

If EAPs are to be effective, employees must be willing to use them. EAP counseling must be tied to the problem employee's work because employees may not take advantage of the EAP unless they recognize that their job depends on resolving their problem. Several other characteristics of effective EAPs have been identified:

1. Top management support
2. Support from labor union
3. Easy access
4. Supervisor training in counseling and referral to EAP
5. Confidentiality
6. Publicity about program to ensure employee awareness of its availability

Reported results from EAPs have been very positive. In one case, AT&T reported a conservative estimate of cost savings of $448,000.[4] The city of Phoenix estimates that it saved the taxpayers approximately $2.4 million dollars in one year alone.[5] United Airlines calculates that for every dollar it spends on its EAP, it gets back $16.35 in savings due to reduced absenteeism alone.[6]

EAPs offer great promise to both organizations and employees. A recent survey of subscribers to *Personnel Journal* found that 45.2 percent of the organizations who responded already offer some form of EAP to their employees.[7] Given the positive results of these programs, their growth is likely to continue.[8]

---

[1] Carr, J.L. & Hellan, R.T. Improving corporate performance through employee assistance programs. *Business Horizons,* 1980, *23,* 57–60.

[2] Scanlon, W. Trends in EAPs: Then and now. *EAP Digest,* May-June 1983, 38–41.

[3] Wagner, W.G. Assisting employees with personal problems. *Personnel Administrator,* 1982, *27,* 59–64.

[4] Gaeta, E., Lynn, R. & Greg, L. AT&T looks at program evaluation. *EAP Digest,* May-June 1982, 22–31.

[5] Wagner, Ibid.

[6] Employer assistance plans: Barriers to growth. Washington, D.C.: Bureau of National Affairs, Inc., *Daily Labor Report,* July 31, 1984, 2.

[7] Grossman, M.E. & Magnus, M. Benefits: Costs and coverage. *Personnel Journal,* 1986, *65,* 74–79.

[8] Hellan, R.T. Employee assistance. An EAP update: A perspective for the '80s. *Personnel Journal,* 1986, *65,* 51–54.

substance or alcohol abuse. If drug testing, such as urinalysis, is to be used, these procedures should be described. At least, employees should be warned that suspected substance abusers will be required to undergo testing. (In unionized settings, testing has to be negotiated with the union).
4. Employee assistance. Since the courts and many arbitrators seem to favor giving troubled employees a second chance, many organizations have adopted a general posture of trying to assist employees in overcoming their substance- and/or alcohol-abuse problems. Therefore, the policy statement may include an acknowledgment that the organization views drug and alcohol abuse as illnesses and wants to provide assistance to employees who want to overcome these problems. Some organizations offer **employee assistance programs,** described in the accompanying Human Relations in Action box, that provide employees with access to trained medical and counseling professionals.[12]
5. Employees who seek assistance. Employees who voluntarily come forward for assistance are often treated differently from employees who are discovered by managers or supervisors. The policy may include a statement that employees who voluntarily come forward for assistance will retain all job security or seniority and promotional opportunities, and will be guaranteed confidentiality. In contrast, employees who are discovered may be subject to disciplinary action.
6. Employee acknowledgment of policy. All employees should be required to read and sign a statement acknowledging their awareness of the organization's substance abuse control policy.

Documentation

One of the more important steps in the process of substance abuse control in organizations is gathering proof that there is a problem. Affected employees may not be fully aware that they have such a problem, or may deny it, even to themselves. Thus, it is often not enough to simply confront an employee with your suspicions. Confronting the employee is a necessary first step; however, the confrontation must include irrefutable evidence that there is a problem. This evidence can often be obtained by documenting a decline in performance, and/or increases in tardiness, absenteeism, and accidents. The employee must then be required to seek counseling to overcome the problem and must also be advised that a failure to do so will result in termination of employment.

Rule Violations

Both unionized and nonunion organizations are likely to have a set of rules and an associated list of penalties for successive violations. This list of rules and violations may appear in the Employee Handbook in nonunion settings and in the labor contract in unionized organizations. Most organizations have rules in a variety of areas including absenteeism, tardiness, controlled substance abuse, alcohol use, refusing to obey orders, refusing to obey safety rules, physical violence, and theft of company property. Exhibit 8.2 presents a list of topics on which organizations commonly develop rules.

> **Exhibit 8.2**
> Areas in which organizations commonly create rules
>
> 1. Tardiness
> 2. Performance inadequacy
> 3. Theft of company property
> 4. Working for a competitor
> 5. Dating coworkers
> 6. Safety
> 7. Sexual harassment
> 8. Punching another employee's time card
> 9. Sleeping on the job
> 10. Refusing to work overtime
> 11. Fighting
> 12. Divulging trade secrets
> 13. Absenteeism
> 14. Substance abuse
> 15. Misuse of company property
> 16. Moonlighting
> 17. Accepting gifts from suppliers
> 18. Use of alcohol or controlled substances on company property
> 19. Discrimination on the basis of race, color, religion, sex, or national origin
> 20. Falsification/omission on the employment application
> 21. Possession of a weapon on company property
> 22. Abusive or threatening language toward supervisor
> 23. Gambling
> 24. Refusing legitimate orders or assignments from supervisor

Underlying most sets of organizational rules is the idea of **progressive discipline**, which for now, will be defined as increasing the severity of the discipline or punishment for each successive violation of a particular rule. This concept will be discussed in more detail later in this chapter. Basically, once employees are informed of the organization's rules and the penalties attached to violations of these rules, the penalties are administered as called for in the labor agreement or employee handbook.

Many of these rules or problems have already been discussed; others will be examined in more detail later. Of interest now are violations of one particular type—employee theft—which seem to be increasing.

Employee Theft

It has been estimated that U.S. businesses lose $40 billion per year from theft by employees. Perhaps a more surprising statistic is that approximately 30 percent of small business failures each year can be directly attributed to employee theft.[13] Clearly, it is becoming more and more important for organizations to develop theft prevention policies. These policies should be more than simply trying to select employees who won't steal (which is extremely difficult) and carrying out surveillance of current employees (which may damage human relations). Close surveillance, polygraph tests, and close control and supervision of employees may create a climate of distrust and frustration. This state of mind may lead to other types of dysfunctional behaviors on the part of employees, such as absenteeism, turnover, and even increased theft.

A clear policy statement needs to be communicated, telling employees that the organization will take action against employees who violate the theft rule. However, the problem may be de-emphasized through good management practices. Employees who have challenging, interesting work assignments; who are included in important decisions; and who are respected and trusted by their supervisors are not likely to take a chance with theft of organization property. They have too much to lose. Other employees who may have a problem of an emotional or psychological nature may require professional counseling to offset any tendency toward theft. Finally, the organization and its managers can set a good example by actions in other areas. An organization which is known for shady dealings with suppliers and/or customers, or which engages in "creative accounting" when the auditors are on the premises may be indirectly encouraging employees to engage in similar activities.[14]

Deal with employees who violate organizational rules.

Bizarre Employee Behavior

No labor agreement or employee handbook can anticipate the sometimes unusual types of employee misconduct illustrated here:

> "An airline ground employee was terminated when, after completing his night shift, he "streaked" (ran naked) along a traffic island fronting the airport to win a $20 dare from his coworkers.
>
> While engaging in horseplay, an employee of an equipment company threw a pie at a management consultant."[15]

These behaviors (referred to by two authors as "**bizarre employee behavior**") are not likely to be covered in the rules, but represent rule violations nonetheless. They are particularly difficult problems for management to handle, since neither the rule nor the appropriate penalty has been specified in advance. Leap and Crino suggest eight questions for managers to ask themselves when deciding how to handle bizarre employee behavior. These questions appear in Exhibit 8.3.

In general, managers must be careful that they do not overreact and administer discipline more severe than the "crime" justifies. In other words, even in the case of bizarre behaviors which may be embarrassing to management, managers should probably not terminate the employee (unless the behavior could have resulted in injury to other workers or customers, or damaged the organization's public image).[16]

ABSENTEEISM AND TURNOVER

Contrary to popular belief, tardiness, absenteeism, and turnover are not just variations on a theme. While there is some relationship between these variables, researchers have recently been separating these forms of withdrawal from the organization into two general categories of behavior: absenteeism, which includes tardiness; and turnover. This separate treatment of absenteeism

> **Exhibit 8.3**
> Guidelines for dealing with bizarre employee behavior
>
> 1. Did the employee's action damage equipment or products? Intentional damage is generally dealt with more severely than is unintentional damage.
> 2. Did the employee's actions disrupt the workflow? If the actions were intentional and resulted in a relatively severe disruption of the workflow, the penalty of termination may be upheld by the courts and/or a labor arbitrator.
> 3. Did the employee's actions create a safety hazard? Employee behavior that resulted or could have resulted in serious injury generally receives relatively severe discipline.
> 4. Should the employee have known better? Employees who should have known the particular bizarre behavior was wrong are likely to be dealt with more harshly than employees who could not have been expected to make that judgment.
> 5. Is the behavior correctable? If counseling or discipline cannot be expected to correct the problematic behavior, termination of employment may be justified.
> 6. Did the behavior violate the law? Illegal behaviors clearly require discipline. Repeated illegal behaviors on the job typically result in termination.
> 7. Did the behavior damage the organization's image, customer relations, or competitive position? Organizations generally have the right to protect their public image by taking disciplinary actions to correct employee behavior which is harmful to that image.

Source: Based upon Leap, T.L. & Crino, M.D. How to deal with bizarre employee behavior. *Harvard Business Review,* 1986, *64,* 18–22.

and turnover evolved because research has determined that they are separate phenomena. They have somewhat different causes and therefore require different methods of control.[17]

Cost of Absenteeism and Turnover

The high cost of both absenteeism and turnover is reason enough for managers to be concerned with methods of controlling these problems. It has been estimated that absenteeism costs U.S. businesses between $8.5 billion (a highly conservative estimate) and $26.4 billion (a conservative estimate) each year.[18] According to a study conducted by the Bureau of National Affairs, Inc., 60 percent of the organizations surveyed considered absenteeism to be their most serious discipline problem.[19] There is also evidence that turnover represents a serious problem for many organizations. An earlier Bureau of National Affairs study found that turnover rates in organizations responding to their survey averaged 1.9 percent per month.[20]

Dollar estimates of the costs of turnover are more difficult to identify, but they would most likely include advertising the job opening, applicant expenses, relocation expenses, recruiters' expenses, direct hiring costs, employment agency fees, training and orienting new employees, and lost productivity. A survey of five organizations found that the average turnover cost for a nonexempt employee (i.e., hourly worker or nonmanagerial employee) was $3,136, while the average turnover cost for an exempt employee was $11,094.

In addition to economic costs, both absenteeism and turnover may have detrimental effects on the human relations within the work group or organization. Absenteeism seems to be highly contagious, and if left uncontrolled can spread rapidly.[21] The effects of turnover on employees who remain behind must also be considered. These remaining employees may begin to believe there must be something wrong with the organization if so many people are leaving. Over a longer time period, they may even begin to ask what's wrong with themselves if they choose to, or must, remain in the organization.

ABSENTEEISM

Whether studying causes and remedies for absenteeism, or trying to actually solve absenteeism problems in organizational work settings, there are two issues which must be resolved before proceeding; defining absenteeism and determining the specific type of absenteeism under consideration.

Absenteeism Defined

Defining **absenteeism** involves determining how absenteeism will be measured. A variety of methods have been identified, including:[22]

1. Frequency. This approach simply counts the number of employee absences. Often, under this method, a three-day absence counts as a single occurrence, just as a one-day absence.
2. Severity. Here, the days absent are totaled without concern for frequency.
3. Lateness. Depending upon the degree of lateness, the count might range from one quarter of a day's absence to three quarters of a day's absence.

Voluntary and Involuntary Absenteeism

The second issue in solving absenteeism problems is the determination of the specific type of absence involved. Two primary types have been identified; voluntary and involuntary. **Voluntary absences** represent a conscious choice by an employee to be absent from work. **Involuntary absences** result from factors beyond the employee's control (e.g., illnesses and accidents). Thus, absenteeism can be viewed as a function of two primary factors: (1) an employee's motivation to come to work, which is related most closely to voluntary absenteeism; and (2) an employee's ability to come to work, related most closely to involuntary absenteeism.[23] Both forms of absenteeism merit consideration and both forms can be controlled. Each form will be discussed separately.

Understand the causes of absenteeism.

Voluntary Absenteeism

When most people think of absenteeism, the voluntary type generally comes to mind. It has been referred to as attitudinal absenteeism since employees decide to be absent from work for a short period of time (most commonly a single day, usually on a Friday or Monday so as to extend the weekend) to improve their morale or "attitude." Employees have referred to this practice, which usually involves abuse of the organization's paid sick leave program, as an "attitude adjustment."

Identify several ways of reducing absenteeism.

In order to minimize voluntary absenteeism problems, employees must be motivated to come to work. This motivation can be because of an attraction (pull) to work, or because of the repercussions of not attending (push) (i.e., the costs of not coming to work are greater than the benefits associated with absenteeism). Both *pull* (positive) and *push* (negative) strategies are currently being employed in organizations.

Negative (push) control strategies for absenteeism are based on progressive discipline. The organization clearly states its policy on absenteeism and then develops a series of increasingly severe punishments for successive violations of this policy. Employees who continue to be absent from work will eventually be terminated. In order for this approach to work, several elements must be present. First, the organization must have a clearly written attendance policy which is communicated to all employees. It may also be a good idea to publish a reminder from time to time, so that employees cannot argue that it had been so long since they were informed of the attendance policy that they forgot its specifics. In addition, accurate attendance data must be collected. This activity involves a careful consideration of the type(s) of absenteeism the organization is attempting to control. Measuring the frequency of absences without considering the severity of those absences may encourage problem employees to be absent for extended periods of time. "If a three-day absence counts the same as a one-day absence, why not take three days off?" On the other hand, emphasizing the severity (number of days missed during a single occurrence) may encourage employees to take more single days off. The particular manner of absenteeism measuring must be carefully chosen so it does not lead employees to reduce one form of absenteeism while increasing another.

Progressive Discipline. Another necessary element in absenteeism control is **progressive discipline**. Basically, employees must first be informed that the organization expects them to be at work when scheduled (except of course for excused absences). Then employees should be told they will be penalized for violating this policy, will be given a chance to correct their behavior, but will be terminated if excessive unexcused absences continue. In addition, the organization must carefully document the absenteeism problem by recording the dates, times, lengths, and reasons given for the absences.[24] This approach to absenteeism control is clearly a *push* type of disciplinary strategy.

No-Fault Absenteeism Control. A strategy which falls between *push* and *pull* is the **no-fault absenteeism control** strategy. It recognizes that employees must be absent from their jobs on occasion. Managers and employees jointly establish an acceptable level of absences (and tardiness) which they feel will be adequate for employees to take care of minor emergencies, illnesses, and accidents. Surprisingly, in one case, employees set these acceptable limits much lower than management expected.[25] In some forms of no-fault absenteeism control, once an employee surpasses the allowable number of absences, she is immediately terminated, even if this last absence is for an illness or other acceptable reason![26] In other organizations, two levels of absences may be established. As an employee surpasses the first cutoff, she is counseled in an attempt to help her correct the absenteeism problem. After counseling, if the absenteeism continues and surpasses the second cutoff (say, three more absences), she is terminated.

The major advantage of no-fault absenteeism control programs is that the supervisor or manager does not have to determine whether an employee had a good excuse for missing work. Employees are treated like adults, and "the responsibility for being at work is placed squarely on the shoulders of the employee."[27] No questions are asked of the employee until she surpasses the acceptable number of absences during any time period.

The potential to eliminate a recorded absence is a feature of no-fault absenteeism control programs that rewards employees for good attendance. Employees who have no absences for some period of time (three to six months) get one absence "erased." Along this same line, employees who are not only absent, but do not call in to notify their supervisor, get charged double (two absences). The results of one such system are impressive. Absenteeism dropped from 6.7 percent before the no-fault program was implemented to 1.1 percent after one year of experience with the program.[28]

Positive Attendance Control. Another relatively recent approach to absenteeism control is the *pull* strategy that rewards employees for good attendance, rather than punishing them for poor attendance.[29] In these **positive attendance control** programs, various types of rewards are tied to good attendance. For example, employees who have no absences during a three-month period might receive two chances in a lottery for a color television set or a weekend trip. A recent simultaneous test of four positive attendance control programs found that the most effective one involved personal recognition of individual employees for good attendance. At the end of each three-month period, employees with no more than one absence received a card from their manager congratulating them for their attendance record. At the end of the year, employees who had missed no more than two days received a custom designed piece of engraved jewelry.[30] The other programs tested included:

1. A financial incentive program which gave $50 cash to each employee who had no absences during the year, and $25 to each employee who had only one or two absences during the same period.
2. A lottery program, which entered employees with perfect attendance in a lottery for a prize worth approximately $200. Every three months, employees with perfect attendance received two chances in the lottery, while employees with one absence received one chance.

3. An information feedback program, which functioned by placing a record of each employee's attendance in her pay envelope at the end of each month.

Interpreting the results of this competitive test of various positive attendance control methods should be done with caution. First, while the personal recognition program resulted in the largest decrease in absenteeism (36.9 percent), both the financial incentive and information feedback programs resulted in lower absenteeism (4.9 percent and 3.8 percent, respectively). Further, while the monetary aspects of the recognition program were not emphasized by the authors, the year-end prize was worth substantially more than the cash bonus in the financial incentive program. Perhaps a slightly higher cash bonus would have produced different results. Regardless, positive attendance control programs offer great promise. They represent relatively inexpensive methods for organizations to experience substantial cost savings due to decreased absenteeism.

Involuntary Absenteeism

Involuntary absenteeism may be particularly difficult for managers to handle. On the one hand, it is reasonable to expect employees to be on the job when scheduled. On the other hand, illnesses and accidents are legitimate reasons for employees to be absent. Problems develop when an employee has an extremely high level of legitimate absenteeism. Thus, involuntary absenteeism occurs because of a lack of ability to come to work, rather than a lack of motivation to do so.

WHAT DO YOU THINK?

As pointed out in the preceding paragraph, involuntary absenteeism is often a difficult problem for managers. Many managers seem unsure of how to handle it, and as a result, it is often ignored. Should managers attempt to manage involuntary absenteeism? What, if anything, can managers do to reduce involuntary absenteeism? Should an employee be fired for excessive involuntary absenteeism? Outline some specific steps which managers can take to deal with this problem. Remember that involuntary absenteeism occurs because of a lack of ability to come to work as scheduled, and not a lack of motivation to do so. Develop your own response to this issue before turning to the "What Do You Think? Note at the end of the chapter.

TURNOVER

The dysfunctional aspects of employee **turnover** have already been established. When employees leave their jobs there are economic costs to the organization in terms of replacing these employees and lost productivity as replacements learn their new jobs.[31] In addition, there may be damage to human relations within the department and organization as remaining employees question their own continued employment. Due to these generally high costs, many managers and researchers have simply assumed that turnover is dysfunctional and should therefore be reduced. However, more recently, authors have recognized the functional or positive outcomes associated with turnover.[32] For the organization, potential benefits of turnover depend on two factors; the performance of the employee, and the replaceability of the employee.[33] The higher the performance and the greater the difficulty involved in replacing the employee (due to the employee's specialized skill or training), the more dysfunctional the turnover of the employee. On the other hand, poorly performing or disruptive employees who can be easily replaced may actually benefit the organization by leaving. The benefits will be even greater if this employee is highly paid and the organization can replace her with a lower-paid entry-level employee with higher skills.

Avoidable and Unavoidable Turnover

We must distinguish between avoidable and unavoidable turnover. **Unavoidable turnover** is generally beyond the control or influence of the organization and includes employee separations due to retirements, promotions, deaths, or transfer of a spouse. All organizations will experience some degree of unavoidable turnover. In contrast, **avoidable turnover** is due to causes that are controlled by the organization. These turnovers would include terminations of poor performers initiated by the organization, as well as resignations of high performers. From the organization's perspective, turnover of poor performers would have to be classified as **functional turnover**. Avoidable turnover of average to excellent performers, particularly when replacement of these employees is expected to be difficult, is clearly **dysfunctional turnover**. Exhibit 8.4 illustrates the various combinations of replaceability and performance which result in either functional or dysfunctional turnover. The exhibit also includes suggested turnover management strategies. For example, employees in category F should be given additional training and/or counseling to increase their performance to acceptable levels. If this effort fails, they should be terminated. While employees in category E are difficult to replace, they are also poor performers. Retaining these employees may damage human relations in the department as average-to-excellent performers begin to question the strength of the relationship between performance and rewards. In this case, the management strategy would be to attempt to increase the performance of the employee, and search for a replacement in the event termination is necessary. Category D employees are average employees who are easily replaceable. If they are highly paid employees, their turnover may be functional, assuming the organization can replace them with lower-paid entry-level employees who have greater ability. On the other hand, if they are not highly paid, the appropriate strategy would be to retain them and perhaps try to increase their level of performance. The remaining categories (A, B, and C) all represent dysfunctional turnover. These categories represent average performers who are difficult to replace (C), high performers who are easy to replace (B), and high performers who are difficult to replace (A). The basic management strategy for these categories of employees is to expend resources or make changes in organizational policies or in the workflow that will result in retention of these employees.

Exhibit 8.4
Performance-replaceability turnover control matrix

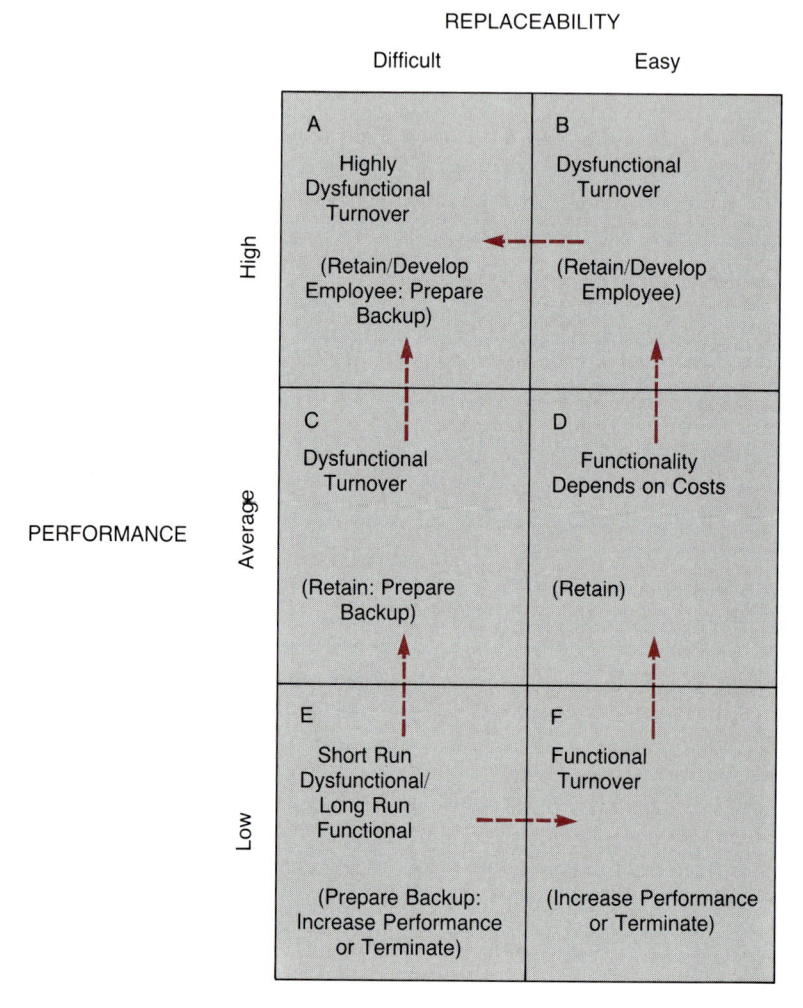

REPLACEABILITY

	Difficult	Easy
High	**A** Highly Dysfunctional Turnover (Retain/Develop Employee: Prepare Backup)	**B** Dysfunctional Turnover (Retain/Develop Employee)
Average	**C** Dysfunctional Turnover (Retain: Prepare Backup)	**D** Functionality Depends on Costs (Retain)
Low	**E** Short Run Dysfunctional/ Long Run Functional (Prepare Backup: Increase Performance or Terminate)	**F** Functional Turnover (Increase Performance or Terminate)

PERFORMANCE (High / Average / Low)

Source: Martin, D.C. & Bartol, K.M. Managing turnover strategically. *Personnel Administrator,* 1985, *30,* 63–73.

The importance of this discussion is the recognition that organizations should not focus on a single, overall turnover rate. Organizations experiencing what sounds like a very high overall turnover rate, say 12 per cent, may actually be experiencing a 9 percent functional turnover rate and only a 3 percent dysfunctional turnover rate. Expending great amounts of time and resources to reduce turnover in this instance would actually be counter-productive.

DISCIPLINING EMPLOYEES AND COUNSELING

No matter how effective your human relations and managerial skills, there will always be problem employees or employees with problems. The categories of

Exhibit 8.5
Typical organizational rules and violations

Rule	1st Offense	2nd Offense	3rd Offense
Theft of company property	Termination		
Use of alcohol or drugs on company property.	Termination		
Unexcused absence	Written warning	3-day suspension	Termination
Refusal to obey orders	3-day suspension	5-day suspension	Termination
Violation of safety rules	5-day suspension	Termination	
Intentional damage to company property	Termination		
Repeated tardiness	Written warning	3-day suspension	Termination
Working for a competitor	5-day suspension	Termination	

problems discussed earlier in the chapter all require either discipline or counseling, and sometimes both. When these problems are experienced, effective disciplining and counseling skills can prevent damage to human relations within the organization or department.[34]

Progressive Discipline

The traditional form of discipline in organizations is **progressive discipline**, which was mentioned earlier. A list of typical organizational rules and the discipline associated with their violation appears in Exhibit 8.5. For example, for a first violation of a minor rule such as tardiness, employees might receive an oral warning. For a second violation, employees might receive a written reprimand which is placed in their personnel records. For a third violation, employees might receive another written reprimand and a suspension without pay. A fourth violation might result in termination. In order for progressive discipline to be effective, several elements must be incorporated into the organization's discipline policy:

Describe how to administer discipline effectively.

1. Advance warning. The organization must develop a clearly written policy, listing rules and expected conduct along with the associated punishments for violations of these rules. Employees must be aware of the rules; holding employees responsible for following rules of which they were unaware is likely to lead to resentment and distrust. Advance warning is necessary if employees are to believe the discipline policy and resulting disciplinary actions are fair.
2. Immediacy. Managers should administer the discipline as soon as possible after the offense or rule violation. The longer the delay between the rule

violation and the discipline, the more likely the employee will react defensively or will resent the action. The only exception to this principle is when the manager is angry or emotional regarding the employee's action. In this case it is a good idea to not administer the discipline immediately, but wait until the anger has passed. However, even in this case the discipline should be administered within 24 hours of the offense.

3. Consistency. If employees are to perceive the discipline system as fair and equitable, discipline must be administered consistently. Consistency can vary in several ways: across time (e.g., you can't discipline an employee for a rule violation this week and ignore the same violation next week), across employees (e.g., you can't discipline one employee and ignore or administer a less severe punishment for another employee's violation of the same rule), and across managers (employees are likely to perceive they are being treated unfairly if you go by the book and administer discipline for rule violations while the manager in the next department does not). Consistency in all actions is necessary for the discipline program to be effective.

4. Impersonal. Administration of discipline must be objective and impersonal; the discipline must be directed at the *behavior* and not at the *person*. Managers must control their emotions and anger at all times. Employees must perceive that they are not being attacked personally. Rather, it is their behavior which is causing the problem, and this behavior can be changed. For example, instead of saying "You don't care about your work," managers should say "Your frequent tardiness is causing a problem. What can I do to help you correct it?" The first approach appears to be an accusation. It may appear to the employee that the manager is saying "There is something wrong with you." The second approach, more objective and impersonal, does not appear to be an attack on the person.

5. No apology. Managers should not apologize for having to administer discipline. This may at least partially dilute or offset the discipline. Further, it may cause employee resentment or perceptions of inconsistency. Since these two acts (discipline and then apologizing for it) are inconsistent, the manager may appear insincere.

6. Documentation. Every step of the process should be documented. For example, when an employee receives an oral or written warning, the manager should record the event and perhaps ask the employee to sign a statement acknowledging the warning. Documentation may be crucial if the behavior is not corrected and termination of the employee becomes necessary.[35]

One other characteristic of effective discipline deserves attention—the manager's or supervisor's *reasons* for administering discipline. Effective discipline is future-oriented and intended to correct behavior. There is really no other reason for discipline in organizational work settings. Unfortunately, many discipline systems in organizations today tend to be past-oriented or punitive in nature. If a manager's reason for administering discipline is to be punitive for a rule violation, the discipline is not likely to be effective. In fact, it may result in the employee becoming defensive or perceiving inequitable treatment. In turn, the employee may engage in some other undesirable behavior to retaliate. The result is a cycle of destructive behavior on the part of both manager and employee.

Positive Discipline

A number of organizations have adopted a modified version of the traditional progressive discipline system. This system, known as **positive discipline** or discipline without punishment, incorporates many of the characteristics of effective discipline systems described earlier. Positive discipline is clearly future-oriented and intended to correct employee behavior. Even the best traditional progressive discipline system may seem punitive to employees. What employees hear from managers is "Here's what you did wrong and here's what's going to happen to you." Positive discipline makes employees responsible for their own behavior. In addition, the entire tone of the discipline procedure is less punitive than in traditional programs. For example, instead of warnings after violations of rules, employees receive reminders. Perhaps the biggest difference between positive discipline and traditional discipline procedures is the inclusion of a *decision-making leave* in positive discipline programs. A decision-making leave is the final step before termination for successive rule violators. Employees receive a day off *with pay,* to decide whether they can, and are willing to, abide by the rules and expectations of the organization.

One company's experience with this program has been very impressive. In the first year of the positive discipline program, 3,565 informal counseling sessions were conducted with employees to discuss rule violations or areas of performance needing improvement. Only ninety formal reminders were necessary and only eleven employees had to be placed on decision-making leave. Of these eleven employees, only one was terminated. During the second year of the program, 3,295 counseling sessions were conducted and 65 reminders were issued. Seven employees were placed on decision-making leave and none were terminated.[36]

Counseling

Counseling is an important part of any manager's job. It can be viewed as an ongoing process of openly communicating with employees about how their job performance and behavior compares with organizational expectations. This process would include counseling sessions concerning specific problem behaviors, such as absenteeism, substance abuse, and tardiness. The counseling process consists of four steps: (1) confrontation, (2) constructive feedback, (3) active listening, and (4) goal setting.

Confrontation

The first step in counseling an employee concerning some job-related behavior or problem is confrontation. Employees must be confronted with evidence that a problem does exist. This result is often accomplished by presenting documentation of declining performance levels, or rising error and rejection rates. The evidence must be presented to the employee in a nonthreatening,

Identify several characteristics of effective employee counseling practices.

DEVELOPING YOUR HUMAN RELATIONS SKILLS

The information presented in this chapter has important implications for you in your role as a manager and your role as an employee. Several suggestions for dealing with employee problems, summarized from the chapter are:

1. When faced with an employee job performance problem, carefully diagnose the situation to determine which of the three components of job performance (willingness, capacity, or opportunity) is the cause of the problem. Accurately identifying the component of job performance which is causing the problem goes a long way toward determining the remedy.

2. When personal problems, such as the loss of a family member or divorce, begin to affect job performance, managers must get involved. Sometimes a sympathetic ear is enough. If it is sincere, simply showing the employee that you are concerned about her and value her contributions to the organization may help the employee to focus more upon job performance during working hours.

3. You must make sure that your employees are aware of the organization's substance abuse policy. Occasional reminders are generally a good idea. When dealing with an employee you suspect of a substance abuse problem you should first have documentation that there is a problem. Records of the employee's job performance ratings, output, or number of rejects over a period of time can prove a decline in job performance. This decline can be used to confront the employee. If the organization offers an employee assistance program or some other form of professional counseling, offer to help the employee enter the program. If the organization does not offer some type of employee assistance for these types of problems, document that you made the employee aware of the problem and give the employee adequate time to correct it. If the problem persists an additional warning may be appropriate; if the employee has not shown improvement after a reasonable period of time, termination may be necessary.

4. When dealing with employee rule violations, follow the progressive discipline process. If the organization has published a list of rules and the associated discipline, follow these guidelines. For problem behav-

objective manner. It should be made clear that the purpose of the counseling session is to correct a problem for the future, not punish past mistakes. The discussion should focus upon specific, objective, job-related information as opposed to subjective assessments of the reasons for the employee's behavior. In other words, focus upon behaviors, not personalities or attitudes.

Constructive feedback

Once employees accept that a problem does exist, they are likely to be more open to receiving suggestions on how to correct their behavior. The second

iors, such as bizarre employee behaviors described in the chapter, make the punishment fit the crime. It is generally not appropriate to terminate an employee on the spot for such behavior. Instead, warn the employee that this behavior is unacceptable and that if it occurs again, she may be terminated. Of course, this warning should be documented.

5. When dealing with voluntary and involuntary absenteeism, documentation and consistency in administration of discipline are important. Following the progressive discipline process is also good advice, even if the organization has no formal policy covering absenteeism. Generally, you must make the employee aware that there is a problem, state the specific nature of the problem, and give the employee time to correct it.

6. When counseling employees about problem behaviors, you should follow these steps: use documentation to confront the employee with the problem so that it cannot be denied or ignored; provide constructive feedback that will help the employee correct the problem; use active listening to make sure that the employee understands the problem and what must be done to correct it; and agree on goals the employee is to accomplish during some time period that will correct the problem or bring the employee's job performance up to an acceptable level.

As an employee, the most important implication of this chapter is that if you have a problem, even a sensitive one such as substance abuse, seek help from your employer. Many organizations today have formal, completely confidential programs designed to help employees with most personal problems. Don't ignore warnings from friends, coworkers, or your manager. It is often difficult for people to admit to themselves that they have a problem; however, this is a vital first step. Unless you admit that you have a problem, treatment of the problem is likely to be ineffective. Take advantage of whatever programs your organization offers. Or, you can contact an outside agency yourself, so that even your manager is unaware of the problem unless you ignore it until your job performance is affected.

step in the counseling process, constructive feedback, is intended to be helpful and corrective. Other characteristics of constructive feedback are that it occurs immediately after the problematic behavior and that it focuses upon specific, job-related behaviors that are under the control of the employee. It accomplishes little to encourage an employee to correct a behavior that she does not control. Further, non-specific suggestions such as "You need to show more initiative," do not provide employees with much guidance about what is really wanted. There are any number of ways an employee might show more initiative. Suggestions must be specific.

Constructive feedback and active listening are important components of the counseling process.

Active Listening

Active listening, discussed in Chapter 6, involves listening carefully to what the employee has to say. It involves listening to more than just the employee's words; it includes paying careful attention to nonverbal cues, and listening for meaning sometimes hidden in the words. Active listening techniques include summarizing what the employee has said, and asking clarifying questions. These techniques show the employee that you are really interested in what she has to say. Summarizing also allows the employee to hear what she has said so far, or at least how the message has been interpreted. It gives the employee a chance to cool off and tone down her comments somewhat, and correct any misinterpretations the manager may have made.

Goal Setting

The last step in the counseling process is goal setting. Toward the end of the session, the employee should be asked for suggestions on how to correct the problem. Then the manager and employee can jointly agree on objectives which hopefully will result in the elimination of the problem.

Counseling can be an extremely effective managerial tool. In addition to solving specific job-related problems, counseling may open communication channels between managers and employees, clarify performance expectations for employees, and reduce the stress and anxiety experienced by employees.[37]

SUMMARY

Employee problems will occur from time to time, even in organizations with excellent human relations. These problems stem from a variety of sources, including family situations; alcohol and drug abuse; illegal acts; rule violations; and tardiness, absenteeism, and turnover. These employee problems create the need for effective discipline and counseling by managers.

One corrective technique, progressive discipline, consists of increasingly severe punishments for successive rule violations. Basic to any discipline program are clear policies and rules, communicated to employees.

Managing absenteeism and turnover first requires managers to identify the specific type as well as level of absenteeism or turnover the organization is experiencing. Absenteeism can be measured on a variety of bases, including frequency, severity, and lateness. Voluntary absenteeism involves a conscious choice by an employee to be absent from work; involuntary absenteeism results from factors beyond the employee's control. A relatively new approach to controlling employee attendance is the no-fault absenteeism control strategy. Functional turnover is voluntary turnover of poor or ineffective performers and dysfunctional turnover is the voluntary turnover of the organization's top performers.

Positive discipline or discipline without punishment makes employees responsible for their own behavior. One important feature of positive discipline programs is the "decision-making leave" whereby employees are given a day off with pay to decide whether they can, and are willing to, abide by the organization's rules and policies.

Counseling employees is an important part of any manager's job. It is an ongoing process of openly communicating with employees about organizational expectations, performance standards, and the employee's actual performance. It also may cover correction strategies for specific employee problems such as tardiness, substance abuse, and absenteeism. Counseling consists of four steps: confrontation, constructive feedback, active listening, and goal setting.

KEY TERMS

performance problems
willingness to perform
capacity to perform
opportunity to perform
personal problems
substance abuse
EAPs—employee assistance programs
progressive discipline
bizarre employee behaviors
absenteeism
voluntary absenteeism
involuntary absenteeism
no-fault absenteeism control
positive attendance control
turnover
unavoidable turnover
avoidable turnover
functional turnover
dysfunctional turnover
progressive discipline
positive discipline

DISCUSSION QUESTIONS

1. Describe the three components of job performance and what managers can do to correct problems in each category.
2. Describe the characteristics of an effective substance abuse control policy.
3. Explain how managers can use progressive discipline to handle employees who continually violate organizational rules.
4. Can or should progressive discipline be used to handle situations of "bizarre employee behavior?" Why or why not?
5. What is the importance of clearly "defining" absenteeism? What are the different ways to define absenteeism?

6. Explain the difference between voluntary and involuntary absenteeism. Which is easier to control?
7. Explain how a negative or "push" absenteeism control policy might work.
8. Describe the characteristics of a "no-fault absenteeism control" program. What are the major advantages of this type of attendance control program?
9. Explain the difference between no-fault absenteeism control and positive attendance control.
10. Give an example of a hypothetical positive attendance control program.
11. What is involuntary absenteeism and how can managers control it?
12. Explain the difference between the following terms: avoidable turnover, unavoidable turnover, functional turnover, and dysfunctional turnover.
13. Describe the characteristics of "positive discipline."
14. What are the primary steps in the counseling process?

EXERCISE 8.1

Developing a Progressive Discipline Policy

In groups of three to five students, develop a progressive discipline policy for the rule violations listed here. Your policy should include specific disciplines (punishments) for each successive rule violation. You will need to consider also how many rule violations will be tolerated before termination is necessary. Typical violations are:

- Drinking or substance abuse on company property,
- Coming to work under the influence of alcohol or illegal drugs,
- Fighting with coworkers,
- Insubordination,
- Tardiness,
- Unexcused absences,
- Poor job performance,
- Sleeping on the job,
- Threatening coworkers,
- Threatening supervisor,
- Failure to follow safety rules (e.g., not wearing protective eyewear),
- Theft of company property (low dollar amount; for example, office supplies), and
- Refusal to obey a direct order from supervisor.

Compare your group's recommended progressive discipline policy with those developed by other groups in the class. Were there any major differences? Were you able to reconcile these differences after discussion? Consider the effects of your policy both upon the rule violator and on coworkers who become aware of the rule violation and penalty imposed.

CASE 8.1

Going to "The Top"

Dave rushed to catch the elevator at the end of the second floor hallway. He jumped in just as the doors closed and saw the three other department heads from his division. "Going up to 'the top' too, huh, Dave?" asked Mark, "Looks like we've all been summoned. This is definitely not a good sign. There are only two reasons I can remember for calling all four department heads upstairs. One is additional work that needs to be done. The other is some kind of major problem." "You're the eternal pessimist, Mark," said Terry. "There's always a first time. Maybe we're being summoned to 'the top' to be congratulated on our performance for last quarter. We did set new records, you know." "Well, we're about to find out," Dave announced as the elevator doors opened at the top floor.

Five minutes later, Steve Robinson, division vice-president called the meeting to order. He announced that the purpose of this meeting was to develop ways to reduce departmental absenteeism and turnover rates. The outside consultants that the president hired to conduct an attitude survey had also examined some internal records and found that turnover in the division was running around 17 percent per year. The industry average is around 9 percent. Further, absenteeism in the division, which had 125 employees, was averaging 1250 hours per month over the past year. The industry average for last year was 385 hours per month. "The president was appalled at these figures," Steve announced. "He wants corrective action taken right away. What can we do?"

Terry answered, "That's easy. We simply need tougher penalties for people who continually are absent without a valid reason. Right now, there really isn't much supervisors can do, except report them. If the absences get excessive, the employees may lose some pay, or in the extreme, be fired. But by the time this happens, the employee already has a severe attendance problem. I think we need some stiff penalties to apply immediately at the supervisory level."

"I'm not so sure we should jump right in with solutions until we examine the problem more carefully," Dave replied thoughtfully. "I suggest that we get the information that the consultant presented to the president, then maybe do some data collection of our own. We

REPORT COVERING JANUARY 1, 1989 TO JANUARY 1, 1990

Employee Number	Annual Salary	Last Performance Rating	Absences (in hours)	Turnover	Years with Company
0225	$17,450	3	96	—	17
0317	$21,930	4	37	V (3/7/89)	5
0048	$15,995	3	51	—	12
0572	$24,500	5	77	—	3
0186	$16,275	2	20	—	13
0889	$23,800	4	09	V (5/1/89)	2
0873	$21,000	1	98	I (8/19/89)	2
0915	$27,000	5	10	—	1
0133	$21,225	3	21	—	9
0231	$26,000	5	3	V (12/1/89)	1
0779	$17,180	3	154	—	21
0443	$19,300	4	101	—	14
0488	$16,655	3	84	—	11
0234	$14,980	3	189	R (12/31/89)	23
0772	$19,965	4	72	—	8
0505	$26,750	5	12	V (11/26/89)	1
0668	$24,355	4	132	—	14
0177	$19,200	3	65	—	16
0223	$18,320	4	88	—	9
0398	$15,775	3	177	—	18
0712	$25,500	5	21	V (10/2/89)	4
0419	$28,750	5	34	—	3
0301	$22,265	4	56	—	2
0904	$20,150	2	11	—	10
0900	$28,000	5	47	—	2

Performance Rating:
  1 = Poor 2 = Below Average 3 = Average 4 = Above Average 5 = Excellent
Absences: (unexcused absences only—excused absences recorded as use of paid sick leave). Recorded in hours per year.
Turnover: V = Voluntary I = Involuntary R = Retired
         (date of separation in parentheses)

must fully understand the problem before we can develop a solution." The vice-president nodded his head, "I agree, Dave. Let's do this. I'll have the information gathered by the consultants broken down by departments and send each of you the information on your own departments. Look at this information on your own and then the four of you get together to discuss what you find. Once you are in agreement, set up a meeting with me to discuss your proposed solutions. I'd like to have something to show the president in 30 days."

The meeting broke up and the four department heads walked back to the elevator. Jim broke the silence, "You were right, Mark. Either a major problem or more work. This time it was both!"

The next afternoon, the information collected by the consultants arrived on Dave's desk. A copy of that report, which covers only the 25 employees in Dave's department for the previous year, appears on page 223. Analyze this information to determine the types of absenteeism and turnover Dave's department is experiencing, and develop a corrective program.

QUESTIONS

1. Based on your analysis of the data, what type of problem exists in Dave's department?
2. What are your recommendations for dealing with this problem?

REFERENCES

[1] O'Connell, J.M. & Arnold, B. Companies are starting to sniff out cocaine users. *Business Week,* February 18, 1985, p. 37.

[2] Blumberg, M. & Pringle, C.D. The missing opportunity in organizational research: Some implications for a theory of work performance. *Academy of Management Review,* 1982, 7, 560–569.

[3] Miner, J.B. *People problems: The executive answer book.* New York: Random House, 1985.

[4] Peyser, H. Stress and alcohol. In Goldberger, L. & Breznitz, S. (Eds.) *Handbook of stress.* New York: Free Press, 1982, 585–598.

[5] Madonia, J.F. Managerial responses to alcohol and drug abuse among employees. *Personnel Administrator,* 1984, 29, 134–139.

[6] Shirley, C.E. Alcoholism and drug abuse in the workplace: There is a way out. *Office Administration and Automation,* 1984, 45, 24–27, 90.

[7] Flax, S. The executive addict. *Fortune,* June 24, 1985, 24–31; Lyles, R.I Should the next drug bust be in your company? *Personnel Journal,* 1984, 63, 46–49.

[8] Obdyke, L.K., Employee intoxication and employers' liability. *Personnel Administrator,* 1986, 31, 109–114.

[9] Obdyke, Ibid, p. 112.

[10] Muczyk, J.P. & Heshizer, B.P. Managing in an era of substance abuse. *Personnel Administrator,* 1986, 31, 91–103; Schein, D.D. How to prepare a company policy on substance abuse control. *Personnel Journal,* 1986, 65, 30–38; Good, R.K. A critique of three corporate drug abuse policies. *Personnel Journal,* 1986, 65, 96–101.

[11] Good, R.K. A critique of three corporate drug abuse policies. *Personnel Journal,* 1986, 65, 96–101.

[12] Ivancevich, J.M. & Matteson, M.T. *Stress at work: A managerial perspective.* Glenview, IL: Scott, Foresman, 1980.

[13] Taylor, R.R. A positive guide to theft deterrence. *Personnel Journal,* 1986, 65, 36–40.

[14] Taylor, Ibid.

[15] Leap, T.L. & Crino, M.D. How to deal with bizarre employee behavior. *Harvard Business Review,* 1986, 64, 18.

[16] Leap & Crino, Ibid, 18–22.

[17] Dalton, D.R. Personnel and human resource management perspectives on turnover and absenteeism. In Schuler, R.S. & Youngblood, S.A. (Eds.) *Readings in personnel and human resource management.* Second edition. St. Paul, MN: West Publishing Company, 1984.

[18] Steers, R.M. & Rhodes, S.R. Major influences on employee attendance: A process model. *Journal of Applied Psychology,* 1975, 63, 391–407.

[19] BNA (Bureau of National Affairs, Inc.) Trends and issues in discipline. Washington, D.C.: *Personnel Policies Forum,* Number 139, January 1985.

[20]BNA (Bureau of National Affairs, Inc.) Employee conduct and discipline. Washington, D.C.: *Personnel Policies Forum,* January 1973.

[21]Skubal, L.B. Getting back to basics is the way to control employee absenteeism. *Telephony,* July 16, 1984, *207,* 34–36.

[22]Muchinsky, P.M. Employee absenteeism: A review of the literature. *Journal of Vocational Behavior,* 1977, *10,* 316–340.

[23]Steers, R.M. & Rhodes, S.R. Major influences on employee attendance: A process model. *Journal of Applied Psychology,* 1978, *63,* 391–407; Muchinsky, P.M. Employee absenteeism: A review of the literature. *Journal of Vocational Behavior,* 1977, *10,* 316–340.

[24]Scott, D. & Markham, S. Absenteeism control methods: A survey of practices and results. *Personnel Administrator,* 1982, *27,* 73–84; Markham, S. & Scott, D. Controlling absenteeism: Union and nonunion differences. *Personnel Administrator,* 1985, *30,* 87–102.

[25]Olson, D. & Bangs, R. No-fault attendance: A real-world application. *Personnel Administrator,* 1984, *29,* 53–56.

[26]Redeker, J. Employee absenteeism: An unnecessary problem. *Personnel Administrator,* 1984, *29,* 4–10.

[27]Olson, D. & Bangs, R. Ibid.

[28]Olson, D. & Bangs, R. Ibid.

[29]Orpen, C. Effects of bonuses for attendance on the absenteeism of industrial workers. *Journal of Organizational Behavior Management,* 1978, *1,* 118–124; Pedalino, E. & Gamboa, V.U. Behavior modification and absenteeism. *Journal of Applied*

Courts and arbitrators recognize that organizations have a right to expect reasonable attendance from employees. "Employees may be subject to discipline, including termination, for excessive absenteeism, even in cases where the absenteeism may have been entirely involuntary, cases in which the individual had 'legitimate' reasons for being absent."[1] Further, one arbitrator recently wrote in an opinion that upheld management's termination of a chronically ill employee, "An employer cannot be required to hold a position open for an employee incapable of performing the job, regardless of reason."[2]

Thus, it seems clear that employers have the right to terminate employees for excessive absenteeism, even when the absenteeism is caused by illness or injury. However, the manner in which this policy is carried out can have a substantial effect on human relations within the organization. Since controlling involuntary (or long-term) absenteeism must involve a form of discipline—positive reinforcement would not be effective. An effective control policy would be similar to the voluntary absenteeism policy described earlier. That is, (1) the company must publish a clearly written attendance policy which includes involuntary as well as voluntary absenteeism; (2) the policy must include a specification of the exact amount of absenteeism that will be considered excessive and will result in discipline or termination; (3) the organization must warn employees approaching excessive absenteeism levels that termination is a likelihood unless attendance improves, and (4) the entire process must be carefully documented in the event of litigation or arbitration.[3]

WHAT DO YOU THINK? NOTE

---

[1]Dalton, D.R. Personnel and human resource management perspectives on turnover and absenteeism. In Schuler, R.S. & Youngblood, S.A. Readings in personnel and human resource management. Second edition. St. Paul, MN: West Publishing Company, 1984, p. 527.

[2]Lissy, W.E. Labor law for supervisors: Excessive absenteeism due to illness. *Supervision,* 1986, *48,* 19–20.

[3]Kuzmits, F.E. What to do about long-term absenteeism. *Personnel Administrator,* 1986, *31,* 93–101.

Psychology, 1974, *59,* 694–698; Wallin, A. & Johnson, R.D. The positive reinforcement approach to controlling employee absenteeism. *Personnel Journal,* 1976, *55,* 390–392.

[30]Scott, K.D., Markham, S.E. & Roberts, R.W. Rewarding good attendance: A comparative study of positive ways to reduce absenteeism. *Personnel Administrator,* 1985, *30,* 72–83.

[31]Blakeslee, G.S., Suntrup, E.L. & Kernaghan, J.A. How much is turnover costing you? *Personnel Journal,* 1985, *64,* 98-103; Hall, T.E. How to estimate employee turnover costs. *Personnel,* 1981, *58,* 43–52.

[32]Dalton, D.R. & Toder, W.D. Turnover turned over: An expanded and positive perspective. *Academy of Management Review,* 1979, *4,* 225–235.

[33]Martin, D.C. & Bartol, K.M. Managing turnover strategically. *Personnel Administrator,* 1985, *56,* 21–24.

[34]Beary, R.P. Discipline policy: A neglected personnel tool. *Administrative Management,* 1985, *56,* 21–24.

[35]Wohlking, L. Effective discipline in employee relations. *Personnel Journal,* 1975, *54,* 489–501; Arvey, R.D. & Ivancevich, J.M. Punishment in organizations: A review, propositions, and research suggestions. *Academy of Management Review,* 1980, *5,* 123–132.

[36]Bryant, A.W. Replacing punitive discipline with a positive approach. *Personnel Administrator,* 1984, *29,* 79–87.

[37]Pawlik, V. & Kleiner, B.H. On-the-job employee counseling: Focus on performance. *Personnel Journal,* 1986, *65,* 31–36.

CHAPTER NINE

Managing Organizational Stress

PROLOGUE

The cover story for an issue of *Newsweek* was entitled "Stress on the Job." The introductory story in this article highlights the drastic effects stress can have upon employees.

> For four years [Robert] Hearsch had been a successful supervisor for Hughes Aircraft. Then General Motors took over the company—and his career took a nose dive. As part of the restructuring, he was put in charge of buying pens and pencils. He found orders backlogged and records in disarray. He spent most of his days appeasing angry secretaries. He stayed on gamely, arriving early, leaving late, working through his breaks. But, as Hearsch tells the story, things only got worse. His supervisors hinted that his position might be phased out. They ignored his diligence and recorded small mistakes into his file. They even left him off the guest list for the department office party.
>
> The pressure took its toll. Hearsch lost 20 pounds. His marriage hit the skids. He suffered a minor nervous breakdown. The strain got to his colleagues as well. One day, Hearsch says, a coworker showed up at the office brandishing a handgun. Hearsch finally filed a workers' compensation claim, blaming his health and emotional problems on Hughes. Last week he accepted a $20,000 settlement from the company, which refuses to comment on the case. The money, he says, is small consolation. "I lost my wife, my house and my career."[1]

LEARNING OBJECTIVES

After successful completion of this chapter, you should be able to

- Precisely define work-related stress,
- Differentiate between stress and pressure,
- Understand what happens during the "General Adaptation Syndrome" (GAS),
- Describe several important outcomes of stress,
- Identify several categories of stressors,

227

- Recognize several primary work-related causes of stress,
- Discuss what employees can do to manage stress, and
- Describe how managers can help employees manage stress.

STRESS IN THE WORKPLACE

Precisely define work-related stress.

As the Prologue suggests, work-related stress is becoming a serious problem for many workers. Constant exposure to "fear of job loss, work overload, lack of control over one's work, nonsupportive supervisors or coworkers, limited job opportunities, conflict, and uncertainty" are major contributors to work-related stress.[2] Some believe that work-related stress has reached epidemic proportions in the U.S. The problem is that not only the numbers of stressors to which employees are exposed are increasing, but also their duration. Stressors are nearly always present. Several years ago, employees might get a break from exposure to stressors and be able to recover. But in today's complex work organizations, exposure to stressors is constant for many employees.

Organizations are beginning to pay increased attention to employee stress. There is good reason for this interest, other than just concern for employee welfare. Stress has been shown to affect many important organizational outcomes, such as job performance, absenteeism, turnover, accidents, and grievances. Several recent studies have highlighted the magnitude of work-related stress problems in the United States:

- Between 75 percent and 90 percent of visits to physicians are for stress-related problems.
- Seventy-eight percent of all U.S. employees report that their jobs cause them to experience stress.
- Forty-five percent of employees surveyed in both private and public sector organizations report suffering from psychological burnout.
- The cost of stress-related problems in terms of decreased performance, absenteeism, and turnover is estimated to be $150 billion per year![3]

Further, in 1986 twenty-six states permitted workers to file legal claims for mental disorders resulting from work-related stress. The number of such claims being filed, and won, is increasing dramatically. For example, in California approximately 1,300 stress-related claims were filed in 1980; in 1984, workers had filed more than 4,200 such claims for compensation.[4]

Trends in Society

Increased levels of stress can be traced to a number of general trends in our society. According to a clinical psychologist who assists executives with stress-related problems, "We are people for whom stress, incredibly busy and hectic schedules, and the necessity of getting home well past our children's bedtime serve as very real, albeit sometimes painful, badges of success."[5] The society of the latter part of the twentieth century can be characterized by fast pace and rapid change. Telecommunications and computers transmit information and news instantaneously. Technological developments, such as robotics and personal computers, continue to change the nature of work. Increased foreign competition and "internationalization" of business are sending many U.S. firms abroad and attracting foreign firms to this country. Increasing numbers of women are entering the work force, creating many dual-career families, and placing additional pressure on parents of small children. Some evidence suggests that women may experience greater levels of stress than their male counterparts, since women typically retain greater home and childcare responsibilities than their husbands. Further, many more women than men remain in lower-status, lower-paying jobs. Women may also experience isolation as they enter previously male-dominated occupations and working environments.[6]

There are no signs that either the pace or complexity of modern life will decline in the near future. Thus, stress will continue to be an important concern in society and organizational work settings.

Who is responsible for employees' stress? Do employers have some responsibility for assisting employees in reducing or managing stress? How far does this responsibility go? If employees experience debilitating stress on their jobs should organizations compensate them? Should organizations be expected to expend large sums of money for employee physical fitness centers and counseling services? Or should employees themselves assume total responsibility for stress?

WHAT DO YOU THINK?

WHAT IS STRESS?

Over the past decade, *stress* has become a household word. There is still confusion, however, over exactly what it means. Stress is not the same as pressure. **Stress** is caused by a state of tension resulting from a situation or event that places unusual or extreme physical or psychological demands on an individual. This event can be pleasant, such as the prospect of promotion to a more challenging job; or unpleasant, such as the prospect of being passed over for promotion. And, an event may have different meanings to different individuals. What is pleasant for one individual may be unpleasant for another; some people might view the prospect of a promotion to a more challenging and responsible job as stressful. For these individuals, being passed over for promotion might bring great relief. Further, small daily annoyances can build up to the point where individuals experience stress. Thus, events that bring on stress, called **stressors**, can be positive or negative. Also, the results of stress, which depend largely on how individuals cope with stressful events, may be positive or negative. Common myths about stress being negative in both cause and effect are not accurate.[7]

Stress is neither an event or condition which causes individuals to feel tension or anxiety nor the result (e.g., depression, decreased motivation, high blood pressure) of experienced tension or anxiety. Stress is a chemical reaction that takes place as the body prepares itself to deal with pressure. Thus, **pressure** occurs in the environment (outside of the body) in a form that causes

Differentiate between stress and pressure.

a stress reaction within an individual.[8] When individuals experience pressure due to stressors in the environment, their bodies undergo chemical reactions to deal with the pressure. This chemical reaction has been referred to as the *flight or fight* response.[9] That is, the body prepares itself to handle pressure or dangerous situations either by getting away from the source of the pressure, or by attacking and eliminating that source. This general chemical reaction process, called the **general adaptation syndrome (GAS)**, consists of three sequential steps.

> Understand what happens during the "General Adaptation Syndrome" (GAS).

1. **Alarm**. When an individual first experiences stress, the initial reaction is alarm. The heart begins to beat faster as the flow of adrenaline increases. Blood pressure rises and muscles become tense. The body prepares itself to handle the pressure.
2. **Resistance**. During the second stage, the body tries to resist the stress, either physically or psychologically. There are now increased hormones and chemicals in the bloodstream which give the body additional defenses.
3. **Exhaustion**. The third stage occurs if resistance is not successful. As energy is used up attempting to resist the stress, the individual simply becomes exhausted. It is at this point when physical and mental illness may occur.[10]

The GAS may lead to increased performance when managed effectively. Many athletes experience this response just before they begin an event. There are stories of professional football players who kick lockers and slam their helmets into walls to "psych themselves up" for a game. The increased adrenaline, faster blood flow, and muscle tension which results may help them perform at higher levels. However, when there is no outlet for the chemical and physical changes brought on by the syndrome, which is the case in many organizational work settings, individuals may suffer adverse effects.

OUTCOMES OF STRESS

While most attention has been paid to negative or dysfunctional outcomes of stress, stress can have positive outcomes. Stress which has positive outcomes is called **eustress**; stress which has negative outcomes is called **distress**.

Personal Outcomes

> Describe several important outcomes of stress.

Stress has been found to be related to several types of physical and psychological outcomes.[11] Physical illnesses found to be associated with stress include heart disease, hypertension (high blood pressure), ulcers, arthritis, cancer, asthma, diabetes, insomnia, and migraine headaches. Psychological outcomes from stress include anxiety, boredom, depression, low self-esteem, alienation, anger, apathy, and job dissatisfaction.[12] On the other hand, stress can also result in increased motivation, job satisfaction, and job performance.

Distress

Individuals vary in their ability to tolerate various types and levels of stress, as well as varying lengths of time they are exposed to stressful situations. *Distress* occurs when an individual has been exposed to a stressful situation for an extended period of time and has reached a state of exhaustion. It may also occur from an event of short duration, but one that has a particularly high level of stress associated with it. For example, many people find public speaking extremely stressful. Just before they are to speak, their hands begin to perspire, their heart rate increases and the general adaptation syndrome begins. Some people experience such high levels of stress just before speaking in front of a group that their description of what they are feeling likens it to sheer terror. Conversely, distress may occur because levels of stress are too low. Some employees assigned to routine, repetitive jobs report relatively high levels of stress, as do those who simply do not have enough to do to keep themselves busy.

Robert Hearsch's stress, which was described in the Prologue, may have been partially the result of being reassigned to a routine, unchallenging job. Having been a supervisor for four years, he experienced stress when he was relieved of his supervisory responsibilities. Further, the reassignment and comments from his superiors led him to believe that he might be laid off. Finally, the manner in which he was treated may have also contributed to the stress he experienced. Hints that his position was being phased out, not inviting him to the department office party, and recording small mistakes in his file were all likely contributors to Hearsch's level of stress.

RETURN TO THE PROLOGUE

Eustress
Eustress occurs when individuals experience levels of stress with which they feel comfortable. That is, there is enough stress to create a feeling of stimulation or exhilaration, but not enough to create a perception of great danger. As pointed out earlier, individuals vary in the levels of stress with which they are comfortable. People who seek out relatively dangerous activities such as skydiving, automobile racing, and karate, need a higher level of stress in their lives to keep themselves stimulated than do individuals who would normally avoid such activities.

Stress and Personality
An individual's *personality type* is also an indicator of his ability to handle stress. Type A and Type B personalities were discussed in Chapter 4. **Type A personalities**, however, may actually prefer high stress to low stress; they may not manage stress as well as Type B's. Type A's tend to be always moving. They eat, talk, and walk rapidly. They are impatient, constantly trying to do more than one thing at the same time. They are also aggressive and competitive, experiencing constant time pressure. They work long hours, frequently take work home, and have difficulty relaxing.[13]

Exhibit 9.1
Type A–Type B self-test

Am casual about appointments	1	2	3	4	5	6	7	Am never late
Am not competitive	1	2	3	4	5	6	7	Am very competitive
Never feel rushed, even under pressure	1	2	3	4	5	6	7	Always feel rushed
Take things one at a time	1	2	3	4	5	6	7	Try to do too many things at once; think about what I am going to do next
Do things slowly	1	2	3	4	5	6	7	Do things fast (e.g., eating, walking)
Express feelings	1	2	3	4	5	6	7	Suppress feelings
Have many interests	1	2	3	4	5	6	7	Have few interests outside of work

Total your score. ____. Multiply it by 3: ____. The interpretation of your score is as follows:

Number of Points	Type of Personality
Less than 29	B
29 to 33	B+
34 to 38	A–
39 to 43	A
44 or more	A+

Source: Adapted from Bortner, R.W. A short rating scale as a potential measure of Pattern A behavior. *Journal of Chronic Diseases*, 1966, *22*, 87–91.

Type B characteristics are basically opposite those of Type A. Type B's do not worry about time. They are relaxed, patient, and never in a hurry. Type B's generally prefer lower levels of stress than Type A's.

At the same time, Type A's tend to expose themselves to too much stress over long periods of time. As a result, they are more likely to develop some of the negative personal outcomes of stress mentioned earlier (e.g., heart disease, high blood pressure). The short test in Exhibit 9.1 will enable you to estimate your Type A or Type B profile.

Social Support

The *social support* available to individuals also affects how well they manage stress. **Social support** is simply the assistance received from others, or the availability of other people to turn to for help.[14] If you have friends, coworkers, family members, clubs, professional associations, a church, or neighbors you trust and to whom you can turn to for help or advice, you have social support.[15] Predictably, individuals who have substantial social support tend to be able to manage stress better than those who have very limited social support.

CHAPTER NINE: Managing Organizational Stress

The [...] s of social support. **Emotional support** provides reassurance [...] al is loved. **Esteem support** provides reassurance that the ind[...]t and valued. **Network support** provides reassurance that th[...]gs" to the group (e.g., friends, family, club) or network.[1] [...]encing stress know that they are not alone, and that there [...] help with problems.

Orga[...]

Neg[...]es of stress include increased absenteeism and turn[...]nts, grievance rates, and even sabotage. In one inst[...] edia Britannica reacted to the stress associated with [...] the company's computer system. Before he wa[...] ritten history by substituting the names of Britannica emp[...] nt names in history.[17]

Potential positive organizational outcomes of stress include increased employee motivation and job performance. However, the relationship between stress and job performance is not a direct one, because either extremely high or extremely low levels of stress may result in decreases in job performance. On the other hand, some degree of stress is necessary to prevent individuals from becoming bored or inattentive to their work. During the 1987 NCAA basketball tournament, several highly ranked teams lost to teams that were ranked much lower. Many observers believed that these highly ranked teams took their opponents too lightly and perhaps looked ahead to later games against other highly ranked teams. The levels of stress these players experienced going into games against supposedly weaker teams may have been too low. As a result, the players did not play up to their potential and lost to a weaker team. On the other hand, players from the weaker teams may have experienced moderate levels of stress, resulting in their performing at an unusually high level. Since they were not supposed to win against such a highly ranked team, the stress was not so high that it was debilitating. They were stimulated by the stress associated with playing a higher ranked team, but since they were not expected to win, the stress was not overwhelming. In other words, there were no punishments associated with losing since they were not expected to win. However, there were great rewards associated with beating a higher ranked team. As one sports announcer put it, "They have nothing to lose, and everything to gain."

Further, in the late stages of the game, players from the highly ranked teams, who at that point began to perceive their real danger of being knocked out of the tournament, may have experienced levels of stress so high, it negatively affected their performance. Apparently, there is some optimal level of stress for each individual which causes him to perform up to his potential. This relationship is presented in Exhibit 9.2. The difficult task of the manager is to ensure that employees operate in an environment that includes enough stress to provide stimulation and motivation, but not enough to be debilitating.

Exhibit 9.2
Relationship between stress and job performance

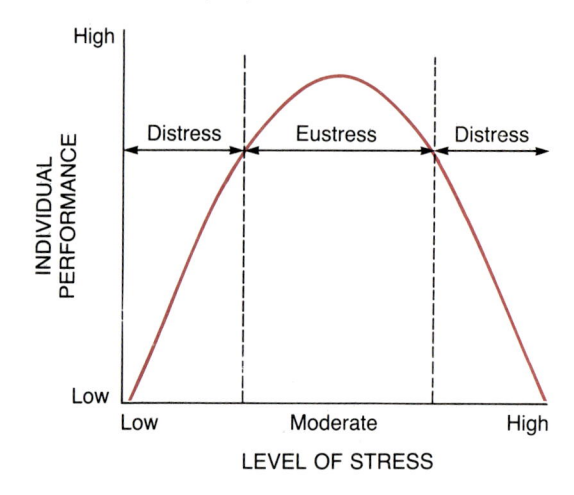

STRESSORS

Identify several categories of stressors.

Stress can be traced to a number of different sources, both work- and non-work related. One of the more complete listing of general stressors appears in Exhibit 9.3. Each event has a certain number of points assigned to it. Circle the number of points for each event you have experienced during the last year, to estimate your current level of stress. If your total is 150 points or less, you are experiencing generally tolerable levels of stress. If your score is between 150 and 300 points, there is a 35 to 50 percent probability of a stress-related illness. A score of over 300 points indicates an 80 percent probability of developing a stress-related illness.

Work-Related Stressors

Recognize several primary work-related causes of stress.

A number of work-related stressors have been identified. They include: conflict between departments and individuals, time pressure, performance deadlines, staff shortages, too much work, too little work, lack of job security, ambiguous work assignments, lack of recognition and acceptance, poor physical working conditions (e.g., temperature, noise, lights, pollutants, crowding, and privacy), work demands in conflict with family demands, poor relations with boss, and poor relations with coworkers. These characteristics are clearly more evident in some jobs than others, which suggests that certain jobs may be more stressful than others. A study of 130 job categories conducted by the National Institute for Occupational Safety and Health found that jobs do vary in their degree of stress. Exhibit 9.4 lists the twelve most stressful jobs found in this study. Several characteristics make these jobs particularly stressful—including negligible employee participation in important decisions, opportunity to use few skills and abilities, inherent conflict (e.g., between higher level management

Exhibit 9.3
The social readjustment rating scale

Life Event	Mean Value
1. Death of spouse	100
2. Divorce	73
3. Marital separation from mate	65
4. Detention in jail or other institution	63
5. Death of a close family member	63
6. Major personal injury or illness	53
7. Marriage	50
8. Being fired at work	47
9. Marital reconciliation with mate	45
10. Retirement from work	45
11. Major change in the health or behavior of a family member	44
12. Pregnancy	40
13. Sexual difficulties	39
14. Gaining a new family member	39
15. Major business readjustment	39
16. Major change in financial state	38
17. Death of a close friend	37
18. Changing to a different line of work	36
19. Major change in the number of arguments with spouse	35
20. Taking out a mortgage or loan for a major purchase	31
21. Foreclosure on a mortgage or loan	30
22. Major change in responsibilities at work	29
23. Son or daughter leaving home	29
24. In-law troubles	29
25. Outstanding personal achievement	28
26. Wife beginning or ceasing work outside the home	26
27. Beginning or ceasing formal schooling	26
28. Major change in living conditions	25
29. Revision of personal habits	24
30. Troubles with the boss	23
31. Major change in working hours or conditions	20
32. Change in residence	20
33. Changing to a new school	20
34. Major change in usual type and/or amount of recreation	19
35. Major change in church activities	19
36. Major change in social activities	18
37. Taking out a mortgage or loan for a lesser purchase	17
38. Major change in sleeping habits	16
39. Major change in number of family get-togethers	15
40. Major change in eating habits	15
41. Vacation	13
42. Christmas	12
43. Minor violations of the law	11

Source: Holmes, T.H. & Rahe, R.H. The Social Readjustment Scale. *Journal of Psychosomatic Research,* 1967, *11,* 213–218. Complete wording of Table 3, page 216. Reprinted with permission of Pergamon Press and Thomas H. Holmes, M.D.

> **Exhibit 9.4**
> The twelve most stressful jobs
>
> 1. Laborers
> 2. Secretaries
> 3. Inspectors
> 4. Clinical lab technicians
> 5. Office managers
> 6. Foremen
> 7. Managers and administrators
> 8. Waiters and waitresses
> 9. Machine operators
> 10. Farm owners
> 11. Miners
> 12. Painters

Source: Poe, R. Does your job make you sick? *Across the Board.* January 1987, pp. 34–43.

and employees or between the organization and customers), ambiguous performance standards and expectations, few opportunities for advancement, and uncertainty or job insecurity stemming from dramatic change (e.g., mergers, layoffs).[18] Several important work stressors are examined in more detail in the following paragraphs.

Properties of Physical Work Setting

The physical work setting may produce distress in some individuals. Extremes in temperature, lighting, pollutants in the air, noise, and crowding or lack of privacy have all been identified as stressors. Crowding and lack of privacy may make it difficult for employees to concentrate on their work and may contribute to the noise level.[19] Noise levels above 70 decibels arouse the sympathetic nervous system and stimulate the general adaptation response. Continued exposure to noise at this level without hearing protection may result in distress for some workers.

Similarly, continued exposure to lighting which is too bright or too dim and to temperatures above 80 degrees or below 60 degrees Fahrenheit may result in distress, which in turn, may result in decreased job performance, accidents, and errors. Improvements in lighting may produce substantial increases in productivity. For example, a large drafting office owned by Pennsylvania Power & Light Company implemented a new lighting system that produced an estimated $235,290 per year in increased productivity. The company also reported higher quality output and reduced sick leave.[20] Effective lighting is becoming more difficult to achieve with the increased use of video display terminals (VDTs) and personal computers. Offices must increasingly accommodate traditional tasks such as typing and filing and at the same time accommodate computer screens which are sensitive to glare from typical office lights. The accompanying Human Relations in Action box describes stress-related problems associated with the new electronic office.

Work Assignments

There are several ways in which employees' work loads may result in stress. **Quantitative overload** is the situation in which employees perceive that they

---

HUMAN RELATIONS IN ACTION

The Electronic Office

One outcome of the change from a manufacturing-based economy to a service-based economy combined with the rapid developments in computer technology is the electronic office. Paper is quickly being replaced by electronic displays and storage. Increasing numbers of managers and employees now spend a substantial portion of their work day in front of a video display terminal (VDT) or personal computer screen. It is estimated that by 1990, between 50 percent and 65 percent of all office workers will be using terminals. In total, around 40 million employees will be using some form of VDT on a daily basis.

Unfortunately, several stress-related problems have been found to be associated with prolonged use of VDTs. Employees who spend substantial portions of their workdays at VDTs experience the following stress-related problems more often than employees who do not work on VDTs: eyestrain; headaches; and shoulder, neck, back, arm, wrist, and hand pain. A study of VDT operators in Wisconsin showed the following differences between VDT operators and other employees:

	VDT Operators	Other Employees
Neck and shoulder pain	80%	45%
Backache	83%	54%
Burning eyes	75%	49%
Eyestrain	76%	51%
Headaches	82%	47%

In general, VDT operators experience the greatest stress when the pace of their work is controlled electronically (i.e., when employees must enter information in response to a request or "prompt" which appears on their VDT). Further, the more routine and repetitive the work (e.g., data entry), the higher the levels of stress experienced by employees.

Several areas must be examined in minimizing stress associated with the electronic office. First, physical working conditions must be examined. Office lighting is particularly important since many electronic displays are sensitive to glare. In addition, the furniture must be capable of adjustment by employees. Employees must be given frequent breaks to relax neck and back muscles and may even be provided with relaxation exercises to perform during these breaks. Finally, to the extent possible, employees' jobs must be redesigned to minimize boring, repetitive data entry tasks and to provide a measure of employee control over work pace.

Source: Chapnik, E. & Gross, C. Visual display terminals: Health issues and productivity. *Personnel,* 1987, *64,* 10–16; Galitz, W.O. & Crillo, D.J. The electronic office: How to make it user friendly. *Management Review,* 1983, *72(4),* 24–38; Henriques, V. & LeGates, C. A look at VDTs and their impact on the workplace and an overview of a new science called ergonomics. *Personnel Administrator,* 1984, *29(9),* 64–68.

---

have been assigned too much work. They believe that they simply cannot accomplish all of the work given to them. A similar, but slightly different work assignment stressor is *time pressure*. Here, employees have been assigned work which normally would not be perceived as a quantitative overload, but they have been given a very close deadline that creates a substantial amount of time pressure. **Qualitative overload** occurs when employees perceive that they do not have the ability to accomplish assigned work activities. **Quantitative underload** describes the situation in which employees do not have

Quantitative overload occurs when employees perceive they have too much work to complete.

enough work to perform. They may become bored and restless and over time experience stress due to the inactivity. **Qualitative underload** occurs when employees are assigned work activities that do not challenge and stimulate them; their jobs do not require them to use many of the skills and abilities they have developed.

Individuals differ in the degree to which each of these types of work loads results in stress. For example, Type A personalities will likely experience higher levels of stress than Type B's under qualitative or quantitative underload. In contrast, Type B's are likely to experience higher levels of stress than Type A's as a result of quantitative or qualitative overload.

One job, air traffic control, seems to include several types of work overload and time pressure, as well as the constant pressure associated with the consequences of making a mistake. Studies of air traffic controllers show that they experience stress-related outcomes such as hypertension at four times the rate of other jobs. Jules Masserman, a psychiatrist who has studied air traffic controllers, describes their job: "In the control tower, these [individuals] are guiding many planes at one time. They are communicating with pilots and copilots, they direct planes on the ground and keep intersections clear, and they take requests for landings and takeoffs. There is simply too much to do, and they are suffering from informational overload."[21] These problems are nowhere more prevalent than at Chicago's O'Hare International Airport, the busiest airport in the world. Takeoffs and landings occur at 20-second intervals. Approximately 75 percent of the controllers who go to O'Hare from other airports fail. Two-thirds of the O'Hare controllers have ulcers or show symptoms of ulcers. During one year, seven controllers were carried out of the control tower on stretchers.[22]

Other aspects of work assignments may lead to stress in some employees. *Shift work* has been shown to be related to increased levels of stress. Workers who rotate shifts (e.g., two weeks on the day shift, then two weeks on the evening shift, and so on) report relatively high levels of fatigue just after a shift change. Working different shifts may also interfere with family and leisure activities—absence from family activities can be a source of stress. Workers who work several consecutive nights also report higher levels of fatigue than day workers.[23] However, some individuals actually prefer night shifts and do not experience additional stress as a result of working at night. Several common reasons are given for the preference: there is usually a pay bonus for working the less desirable shifts; the workplace is usually quieter; and there are fewer supervisors looking over employees' shoulders (so these late-shift employees can experience greater freedom and control over their jobs).

Another work assignment source of stress is *unwanted overtime*. The effects of working overtime unwillingly are similar to those of shift work. It may interfere with family and leisure activities and result in employee fatigue.

Job Insecurity
Budget cuts and layoffs make employees insecure about their jobs. The economic difficulties faced in the 1980s resulted in many mergers and layoffs (downsizing). As a result, employees were unsure about their future with the organization. As they watched coworkers receive layoff notices, they wondered if their job would be the next to go.

Change
Changes in technology, organizational structure, management, and jobs may be very stressful for some employees, because change often creates uncertainty. As will be shown in Chapter 17, employees often resist change because they are uninformed about the nature of the change and how it will affect their jobs. Thus, they perceive a threat that the change may result in a loss of status, an inability to perform successfully after the change, and/or a change in social relationships (e.g., a change in technology may limit interaction during working hours).

Performance Evaluation
Evaluation of employee job performance can be an important source of stress for employees and their managers. As pointed out in Chapter 7, managers are often uncomfortable and reluctant to evaluate their employees' job performance. Employees are often equally uncomfortable when being evaluated and may become defensive when receiving negative feedback about their performance. The anticipation of employee defensiveness may create a source of

stress for managers.[24] Methods for reducing the level of stress created by performance evaluations were discussed in Chapter 7.

Isolation

Isolation refers to the perception of being alone and not accepted by coworkers, managers, or the organization as a whole. Women who enter traditionally male occupations frequently encounter this problem, and experience stress as a result. Increasingly, men are also encountering this problem as they enter traditionally female occupations (e.g., registered nurse). Management practices can also contribute to employees' perception of isolation by excluding them from important decisions that affect their jobs. Employees have a strong need to be involved in organizational decision making—or at least to be informed of important decisions which have been, or are about to be, made. Unfortunately, some organizations provide little information to employees until long after these decisions have been finalized. Such practices cause some employees to decide that they are not involved in organizational activities and decision making. To the extent that involvement is important to employees, they will experience stress.

A Model of Work-Related Stress

A model of work-related stress which summarizes the discussion above appears in Exhibit 9.5. This model traces the process by which stress develops from physical and psychological stressors to become either eustress or distress. Major organizational and individual outcomes of stress are also included.

MANAGING WORK-RELATED STRESS

Both individual employees and their managers are responsible for managing stress. Individual stress management strategies can be aimed at either reducing or increasing existing levels of stress and at preventing stress. These strategies include exercise, relaxation, meditation, and removing (or adding) stressors from the immediate environment.

Organizational stress management strategies can have the same goals. Some stress reduction and prevention occurs simply because of effective management. Selecting and assigning employees to jobs which match their skills, abilities and interests; making performance expectations clear to employees; keeping employees informed about the organization's plans and activities; resolving conflict between employees and departments; and communicating frequently with employees may all reduce ambiguity and uncertainty, and therefore stress. In addition, many organizations have implemented programs designed specifically to assist employees with stress management. For example, as described in the accompanying Human Relations in Action box, organizations are installing exercise facilities on company property. Other organizations make professional counseling available to assist employees with problems in diet, smoking, substance abuse, and other personal matters.

Exhibit 9.5
A model of work-related stress

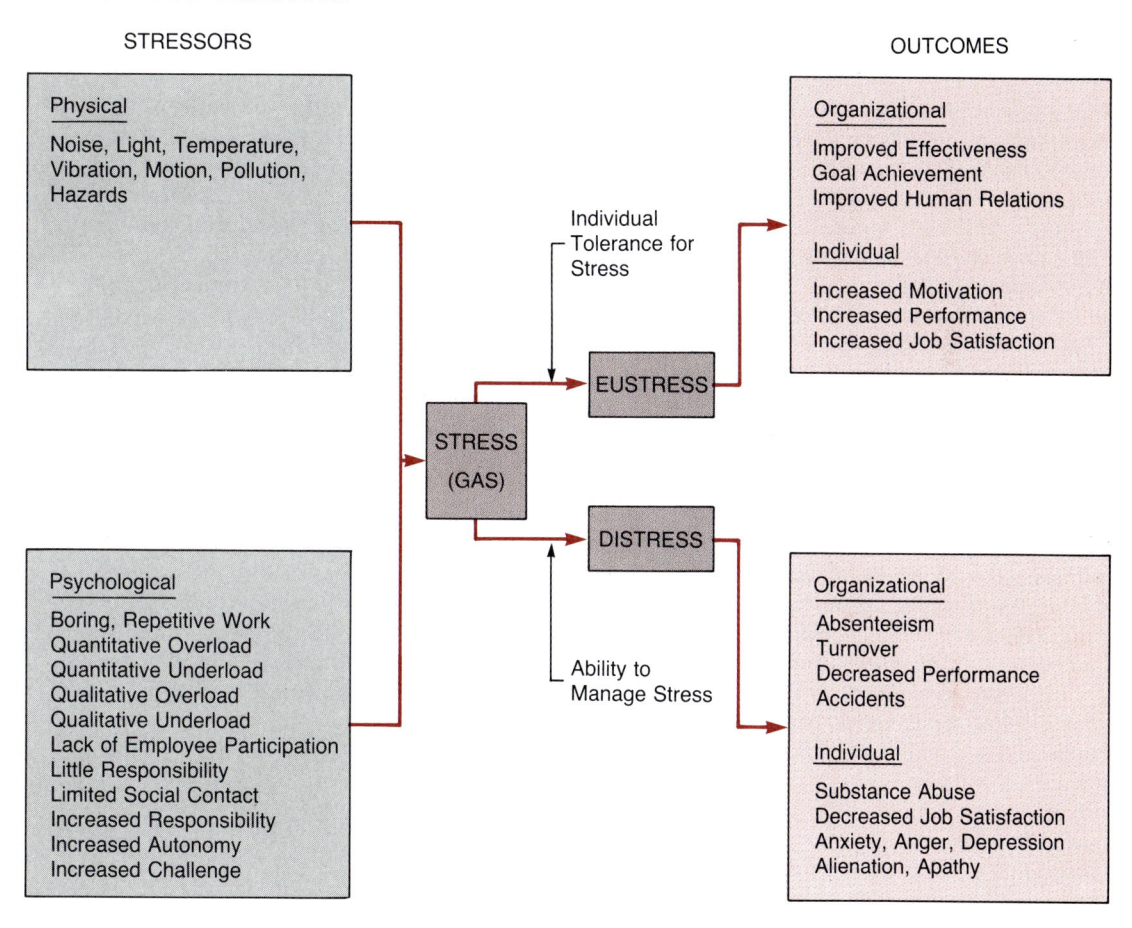

STRESSORS

Physical
Noise, Light, Temperature, Vibration, Motion, Pollution, Hazards

Psychological
Boring, Repetitive Work
Quantitative Overload
Quantitative Underload
Qualitative Overload
Qualitative Underload
Lack of Employee Participation
Little Responsibility
Limited Social Contact
Increased Responsibility
Increased Autonomy
Increased Challenge

STRESS (GAS) → **EUSTRESS** / **DISTRESS**

Individual Tolerance for Stress
Ability to Manage Stress

OUTCOMES

Organizational
Improved Effectiveness
Goal Achievement
Improved Human Relations

Individual
Increased Motivation
Increased Performance
Increased Job Satisfaction

Organizational
Absenteeism
Turnover
Decreased Performance
Accidents

Individual
Substance Abuse
Decreased Job Satisfaction
Anxiety, Anger, Depression
Alienation, Apathy

Individual Stress-Management Techniques

Whether or not the organization has implemented any stress management assistance programs for employees, individuals can take steps to reduce levels of stress they are experiencing. The importance of physical exercise has already been emphasized. Another easily adopted individual strategy is to develop hobbies and engage in recreational activities. These activities break the pattern of constant work and minimize work-related problems and pressures.[25]

Time Management

Time management is useful for employees who always feel pressure to complete assignments or who constantly perceive quantitative overload and/or time pressure.[26] Time management consists of two basic steps: (1) identifying precisely how time is spent, and (2) identifying ways to use time more effi-

Discuss what employees can do to manage stress.

> # HUMAN RELATIONS IN ACTION
>
> ## Organizationally-Sponsored Stress-Reduction Programs
>
> Many U.S. organizations have recognized the importance of helping employees manage work-related stress. One approach to the problem which many of these organizations have implemented is employee fitness centers. Research has shown physical fitness to be one way to reduce stress significantly.
>
> PepsiCo implemented a program called "Pepfit," which includes supervised jogging, cycling and aerobic exercise. Tenneco recently built an $11 million, 100,000-square-foot fitness facility at its Houston, Texas headquarters. The facility includes racquetball courts, dressing rooms, Nautilus exercise equipment, saunas, whirlpools, and a jogging track. There are even indoor gardens with simulated rainfall, employee and executive dining rooms, and a conference center. The facility is staffed by an executive chef, a doctor, a nurse, a physiologist and several trainers. Employees in the fitness program are monitored by a computer that evaluates each workout for its caloric benefits, prepares a profile for each employee, and monitors his progress toward his fitness goal. At T. Boone Pickens' Mesa Petroleum Company headquarters, employees and their spouses may work out in a health complex which features a gym, an indoor track, steam rooms, Nautilus equipment, whirlpools, saunas, racquetball courts, and a health food snack bar. Employees who work out get a free lunch or breakfast.
>
> Results of these companies' experiences with employee fitness have been positive. According to one employee at Mannington Mills, a producer of vinyl flooring, ceramic tiles, and carpeting, "Using the (fitness) center makes me feel better. It wakes me up and gets me going, particularly in the afternoon when you tend to slow down. It improves my job performance tremendously." Research conducted at Tenneco shows that health claims were substantially reduced for employees who regularly exercise. Other companies report decreases in accidents, absenteeism and turnover, and increases in morale and productivity. A study by the Equitable Life Assurance Society estimated that each dollar spent on helping employees with stress-related problems returned $5.52 in increased productivity and reduced absenteeism.
>
> ---
>
> Source: Gatty, B. How fitness works out. *Nation's Business*, July 1985, *73* (7), 18–24; Levy, R. Everybody into the company gym. *Dun's Review*, 1980, *116* (5), 115–118; Poe, R. Does your job make you sick? *Across the Board*, January 1987, 34–43.

ciently. Step 1 typically involves keeping a time log. This is a record of activities, usually recorded in 15- to 30-minute intervals for a period of two weeks. Analysis of the time log identifies any recurring activities or situations that make inefficient use of time. People are often surprised as they look back over their time logs. For instance, small talk with coworkers is a common time-waster. During the day, 20- to 30-minute conversations with coworkers may not appear significant, but a written record of these activities looks substantially different. When an employee totals up the time spent in this manner and finds that he spent a total of 240 minutes (four hours!) talking with a coworker during the past two weeks, it may be a shock to him. Think how much he could have accomplished in those four hours! Thus, an analysis of the time log includes identifying activities which should be eliminated or minimized.

The second step in time management involves identifying ways to make better use of time. After eliminating time-wasters from the time log, only necessary activities should remain. Setting goals and priorities will help accomplish the most important of these activities first. Developing a "To Do" list each morning prioritizes each activity to be performed as either: A, high priority; B, moderate priority; or C, low priority. No C activities should be begun before all A and B activities are completed.

Relaxation

Relaxation is another important stress management technique that individuals can learn. The **relaxation response** is a reaction (similar to meditation) which is the opposite of the general adaptation syndrome (GAS).[27] Individuals can learn to initiate this response through **biofeedback** techniques, as they feel levels of stress becoming too high. Biofeedback involves the use of equipment which measures physical and chemical changes within the body. For example, one outcome of the GAS is an increase in heart rate. Biofeedback equipment may elicit a tone which varies with heart rate. As heart rate increases the tone becomes higher, and as heart rate decreases the tone becomes lower. Individuals can learn to lower their heart rate by concentrating on lowering the tone. Over time, they can learn to lower their heart rate without the biofeedback equipment. Actually, what these people are learning is to initiate the relaxation response. Exhibit 9.6 presents instructions to elicit the relaxation response.

Exhibit 9.6
Instructions to elicit the relaxation response

1. Sit quietly in a comfortable position.
2. Close your eyes.
3. Beginning at your feet and progressing up to your face, deeply relax all your muscles. Keep them relaxed.
4. Breathe through your nose. Become aware of your breathing. As you breathe out, say the word *one* silently to yourself. Continue the pattern: breathe in . . . out, "one"; in . . . out, "one"; and so on. Breathe easily and naturally.
5. Continue for 10 to 20 minutes. You may open your eyes to check the time, but do not use an alarm. When you finish, sit quietly for several minutes, first with your eyes closed and later with your eyes open. Do not stand up for a few minutes.
6. Do not worry about whether you are successful in achieving a deep level of relaxation. Maintain a passive attitude and permit relaxation to occur at its own pace. When distracting thoughts occur, try to ignore them by not dwelling on them and return to repeating *one*. With practice, the response should come with little effort. Practice the technique once or twice daily but not within two hours after any meal, since the digestive processes seem to interfere with eliciting the relaxation response.

Source: Peters, R.K. & Benson, H. Time out from tension. *Harvard Business Review*, 1978, *56*(1), p. 124.

> **Exhibit 9.7**
> Indicators of individual stress
>
> 1. Feeling of unrelenting pressure and tension
> 2. Significant loss of personal self-confidence
> 3. Significant loss of energy
> 4. Loss of perspective and objectivity with regard to oneself and one's ability
> 5. Periods of intense preoccupation with business or personal matters
> 6. Imbalance in life—For example, all one's satisfactions come from work
> 7. Physical illnesses
> 8. Denial of illness or personal problems—defensiveness
> 9. Advice from a friend or family member that there is a problem
> 10. Personality changes

Source: Based upon Axline, L.L. Identifying and helping the troubled executive. *Personnel,* 1987, *64*(11), 40–47.

Indicators of Stress

The first step in the individual stress management process is to determine when such a program is needed. Many authors suggest that it is not really a question of *if* workers will ever need stress management activities, but *when.* Nevertheless, individuals may not immediately recognize the symptoms of stress or admit they are experiencing stress related problems. Exhibit 9.7 presents some general indicators of stress which individuals can use to determine if they are in need of stress management.

Organizational Stress Management Techniques

Describe how managers can help employees manage stress.

Organizations and managers can take steps to reduce or eliminate stressors from employees' work environments. For example, managers should attempt to create physical working conditions which are free of the stressors mentioned earlier in the chapter (e.g., noise, pollution, lack of privacy). Great care should be taken to match employees to jobs which fit their skills and abilities. Remember, work assignments which are both too demanding and under-demanding (both quantitatively and qualitatively) can cause stress. Jobs should provide adequate challenge and interest to employees. Further, employees should be provided with autonomy and control over their jobs to the greatest extent possible. Similarly, employee participation and involvement also increase the degree to which employees perceive that they own or control their own jobs. Further, flexible work schedules, where they are appropriate, may reduce stress experienced by employees attempting to meet both work and family responsibilities. Some organizations are implementing day care facilities and providing additional fringe benefits such as paternity leave for new fathers, and elder care.[28] Other important organizational/managerial stress management strategies include encouraging employee participation, career planning, communication, and team building.

An employee's participation in making decisions that affect her job may help reduce stress for several reasons. First, participation increases the amount of

---

DEVELOPING YOUR HUMAN RELATIONS SKILLS

This chapter has presented information which has important implications for you as an employee as well as for you as a manager. As an employee, you should immediately assume responsibility for your own stress, regardless of whether or not your organization has any stress-reduction programs to assist you. At a minimum, you should perform the following activities:

1. Determine your current level of stress. Questionnaires such as those presented in this chapter are available to help you determine the level of stress you are currently experiencing. Remember that assessing your stress level is an ongoing activity. In today's work environment, things change so rapidly that you should regularly monitor your stress.
2. Identify those stressors contributing most to your stress. Deal with these first.
3. Develop and maintain regular activities, such as hobbies and exercise, to help maintain manageable levels of stress. Exercise is particularly effective.
4. Develop good time-management skills. Ineffective use of time is one of the major stressors in organizational work settings. Effective use of time can substantially reduce stress for most employees.

As a manager, assume some responsibility for your employees' stress. You can be of great assistance to employees trying to manage stress. Consider these guidelines:

1. Be on the lookout for signs of stress in each of your employees. This is a continual activity since employees are exposed to changing circumstances at work.
2. Carefully consider how your treatment of employees and task assignments will affect each employee's stress. Don't carelessly assign additional tasks to an already overstressed employee. Don't place any unnecessary stress on employees by being careless in assignments or supervisory techniques.
3. Counsel employees in stress management techniques. Suggest time management, hobbies, and leisure activities. If your organization has fitness facilities or counseling programs, encourage stressed employees to take advantage of them. As a wise manager, you will undoubtedly already be taking advantage of these facilities. Invite your employees to join you to get them started.

information made available to employees. As employees participate in discussions regarding decisions they become more aware of the reasons for the decisions and how their jobs will be affected. This knowledge may foster a substantial reduction in uncertainty and job insecurity. Participation can also increase communication between managers and employees as well as among the employees themselves. This change may result in some employees becoming less isolated and more involved in organizational activities. Finally, employee participation may serve as a form of *social support*. Other employees and managers may provide increased social support as participation increases understanding and improves interpersonal relations within the work group.[29]

Career Planning

Organizations may be able to reduce uncertainty and stress experienced by employees by conducting formal career planning programs, which will be discussed in detail in Chapter 10. Important aspects of career planning include the realistic job previews and career paths discussed in Chapter 2. Realistic job previews provide job candidates with substantial information (the good and the bad) about the job and organization with which to make an informed decision. Career paths send a message to employees that the organization has given some thought to their growth and advancement. And, employee training and development programs may help reduce uncertainty and job insecurity. Training designed to prevent obsolescence and/or to provide employees the opportunity to develop new skills can increase chances of advancement.

Team Building

Team building may help reduce employee stress in many of the same ways as increased employee participation. It can increase understanding, expand communications, broaden social support and improve interpersonal relations, as well as decrease uncertainty and anxiety.[30] The process of team building will be discussed fully in Chapter 13.

Stressors in the work environment and in society in general are not likely to decline in the foreseeable future. It is becoming increasingly important that managers develop ways to help employees manage the levels of stress they are experiencing. Stress management not only facilitates the development of good human relations and employee welfare, but also increases productivity and organizational effectiveness.

SUMMARY

Work-related stress continues to be a significant organizational problem. Stress has been found to be related to several negative outcomes such as heart disease, high blood pressure, depression, ulcers, cancer, insomnia, and migraine headaches. Further, levels of stress which are too high or too low may result in decreased job performance, employee job dissatisfaction, and increases in absenteeism, turnover, and accidents. Whether stress has positive or negative effects depends on how individual employees and their organizations manage stress. Stress which has positive outcomes has been labeled eustress, while stress which has negative outcomes is referred to as distress.

Stress is caused by a state of tension that results from a situation or event placing unusual or extreme physical or psychological demands on an individual. Thus, stress is a chemical reaction which takes place as the body prepares itself to deal with these demands. This chemical reaction is called the general adaptation syndrome (GAS), also referred to as the "flight or fight" response. The GAS consists of three steps: alarm, resistance, and exhaustion. Stress should be distinguished from pressure; the event or situation which causes the individual to experience stress represents pressure.

Several events in day-to-day life can serve as stressors (events which lead to stress). These include the death of a spouse, divorce, marriage, major personal illness or injury, retirement from work, being fired, a major change in one's financial condition, taking out a mortgage or loan, son or daughter leaving home, a vacation, and even Christmas. Additional stressors which are more closely related to work include time pressure, job insecurity, poor physical working conditions (e.g., noise, uncomfortable temperature, inadequate lighting, pollutants, crowding, lack of privacy), quantitative and qualitative work overload and underload, shift work, unwanted overtime, and conflicting work and family responsibilities.

Organizations have begun taking a greater role in assisting employees in managing stress. Individual stress management strategies include exercise, relaxation, time management, and removing (or adding) stressors from the work environment. Organizational stress management strategies include: matching individuals to jobs that make use of their skills and abilities, job enrichment, increasing employee autonomy and responsibility, career planning, and team building.

KEY TERMS

stress
stressors
pressure
general adaptation syndrome
eustress
distress
Type A personality
Type B personality
social support
emotional support
esteem support
network support
quantitative overload
qualitative overload
quantitative underload
qualitative underload
relaxation response
biofeedback

DISCUSSION QUESTIONS

1. Distinguish between stressors and stress.
2. Describe what happens during the general adaptation syndrome.
3. Give several examples of organizational and individual distress.
4. Give several examples of organizational and individual eustress.
5. What is social support? Identify its three types.
6. What are the relationships between stress, motivation, and job performance?
7. Exhibit 9.4 presented a list of the twelve most stressful jobs. Are there other jobs you believe should be added to this list? What makes these jobs so stressful?
8. Distinguish between quantitative and qualitative work overload and underload.
9. Which of the work-related stressors identified in the chapter do you believe presents the greatest threat in terms of increasing employee stress levels? Why?
10. Which of the work-related stressors identified in the chapter do you believe are most difficult to bring under control? Explain.
11. Why do women sometimes experience greater levels of stress than their male counterparts?
12. Explain the relaxation response and how an individual might use it to reduce stress.
13. How does increased employee participation in decision making reduce stress?

EXERCISE 9.1

Stress Vulnerability Test

Two scales in the chapter enabled you to determine the level of stressors which you experienced during the last year and whether you have a Type A personality. This scale is designed to assess the degree to which your lifestyle makes you vulnerable to stress. Using the following scale, rate yourself on the items below.

1	2	3	4	5
Almost Always	Frequently	Sometimes	Infrequently	Almost Never

_____ 1. I eat at least one hot, balanced meal a day.

_____ 2. I get seven to eight hours sleep at least four nights a week.

Source: "Vulnerability Scale" from the *Stress Audit,* developed by Lyle H. Miller and Alma Dell Smith. Copyright 1983, Biobehavioral Associates, Brookline, MA 02146. Reprinted with permission.

___ 3. I give and receive affection regularly.

___ 4. I have at least one relative within fifty miles on whom I can rely.

___ 5. I exercise to the point of perspiration at least twice a week.

___ 6. I smoke less than half a pack of cigarettes a day.

___ 7. I take fewer than five alcoholic drinks a week.

___ 8. I am the appropriate weight for my height.

___ 9. I have an income adequate to meet basic expenses.

___ 10. I get strength from my religious beliefs.

___ 11. I regularly attend club or social activities.

___ 12. I have a network of friends and acquaintances.

___ 13. I have one or more friends to confide in about personal matters.

___ 14. I am in good health (including eyesight, hearing, teeth).

___ 15. I am able to speak openly about my feelings when angry or worried.

___ 16. I have regular conversations with the people I live with about domestic problems, e.g., chores, money, and daily living issues.

___ 17. I do something for fun at least once a week.

___ 18. I am able to organize my time effectively.

___ 19. I drink fewer than three cups of coffee (or tea or cola drinks) a day.

___ 20. I take quiet time for myself during the day.

___ TOTAL

To arrive at your stress vulnerability score, add up the figures and subtract 20. Any number over 30 indicates a vulnerability to stress. You are seriously vulnerable if your score is between 50 and 75, and extremely vulnerable if it is over 75.

EXERCISE 9.2

Diagnosing Stress Levels Inherent in Jobs

Examine the list of high-stress jobs in Exhibit 9.4. Determine exactly what makes these jobs so stressful. Make a list of stressors for each of these jobs. Then suggest specific strategies that managers might use to reduce levels of stress associated with each of these jobs.

CASE 9.1

Stress in the ICU

Fran walked back to the third floor nurses' station clenching her fists. "Who do those doctors think they are anyway? They waltz in here for an hour or two every day to see their patients and then return to their private offices. They boss nurses around as if we weren't really people. It's the nurses who put in at least eight hours a day in this hospital. We know the patients better than the doctors do."

Fran was coming to the end of her third day of twelve-hour shifts. She was one of the first nurses to agree to try the experimental 3/12 shift—working three days in a row for twelve hours each day and then having four days off. While she worked only thirty-six hours, she received a full forty hours' pay per week. Initially, Fran really enjoyed having four days in a row to spend with her family. They had been able to take several long weekend trips during the last three months. Lately, however, she preferred to stay at home and rest during her four days off.

Wanda Yokish was standing at the nurses' station desk, reading a chart as Fran walked up. "Oh great, all I need is to have to talk to Wanda today," thought Fran as she approached the desk. Wanda was the very demanding Third Floor Nurses' Supervisor. She and Fran had never gotten along well. Wanda likes to be in control of things and wants to know exactly what each nurse is doing. In contrast, Fran feels that she has been a registered nurse long enough to know what she is supposed to do.

She would prefer that Wanda simply leave her alone to do her job. Wanda looked up, saw Fran and said, "Fran. Just the person I wanted to see. I want to ask you about Mr. Robinson in 302." "Great!" thought Fran. "I'm about to be told how to do my job again. I thought that I would enjoy working in the Intensive Care Unit because nurses can have such a major impact upon patient care. Only ER (Emergency Room) and ICU (Intensive Care Unit) require nurses to constantly be on their toes. When physicians aren't around and a patient is in trouble, it's a nurse who provides care." Fran had saved two "Code Blues" (cardiac arrest) this week alone. "Now I'm not so sure I made a good decision in transferring here from the children's ward."

Fran continued to reflect on her work. "Now they're computerizing everything. I didn't get into this business to become a computer expert. I wanted to work with people, not machinery." All ICU patient monitors are linked to a central computer with monitors located at the Third Floor Nurses' Station. Further, all patient records, including medications, must now be entered into the computerized data base. When physicians make additions or modifications to a patient's treatment, or simply record comments about the patient's progress, the attending nurse is required to enter this information into the computerized data base within one hour. While the computer system has clearly cut down on the amount of paper which the nurses had to process, many nurses have complained about the new system. "Of course, the doctors want this information entered immediately. Last week I was attending nurse during Dr. Ramsey's rounds. She saw five patients and then went back to her office. Twenty minutes later she called the nurses' station to complain that this information wasn't in the computer yet!"

QUESTIONS

1. Identify the specific stressors to which Fran is exposed.
2. Assume that you are a consultant hired to help employees of this hospital reduce stress. What would you recommend in Fran's case?

REFERENCES

[1] Miller, A., Springen, K., Gordon, J., Murr, A., Cohn, B., Drew, L. & Barrett, T. Stress on the job. *Newsweek,* April 25, 1988, p. 40.

[2] Smith, E.T., Brott, J., Cuneo, A. & Davis, J.E. Stress: The test Americans are failing. *Business Week,* April 18, 1988, pp. 74–75.

[3] Noe, R. Does your job make you sick? *Across the Board,* January 1987, 34–43.

[4] Ibid.

[5] Axline, L.L. Identifying and helping the troubled executive. *Personnel,* 1987, *64*(11), 40–47.

[6] Chusmir, L.H. & Durand, D.E. Stress and the working woman. *Personnel,* 1987, *64*(5), 38–43.

[7] Pesci, M. Stress management: Separating myth from reality. *Personnel Administrator,* 1982, *27*(1), 57–67.

[8] Albrecht, K. *Stress and the manager: Making it work for you.* Englewood Cliffs, NJ: Prentice Hall, 1979.

[9] Cannon, W.B. *The wisdom of the body.* New York: W.W. Norton, 1932.

[10] Seyle, H. *The stress of life.* New York: McGraw-Hill, 1956; Wallis, C. Stress: Can we cope? *Time,* June 6, 1983, 48–54.

[11] Behling, O. & Darrow, A.L. *Managing work related stress. Modules in Management.* Chicago: Science Research Associates, 1984.

[12] Siwolop, S., Rhein, R. & Weber, J. The crippling ills that stress can trigger. *Business Week,* April 18, 1988, 77–78.

[13] Friedman, M. & Rosenman, R.H. *Type A behavior and your heart.* New York: Fawcett Crest, 1974.

[14] McLean, A.A. *Work stress.* Reading, MA: Addison-Wesley, 1979.

[15] Brief, A.P., Schuler, R.S. & Van Sell, M. *Managing job stress.* Boston: Little, Brown and Company, 1981.

[16] Cobb, S. Social support as a moderator of life stress. *Psychosomatic Medicine,* 1976, *38*(5), 300–314; Cobb, S. Social support and health through the life course. In Riley, M.W. (Ed.) *Aging from birth to death: Interdisciplinary perspectives.* Washington, D.C.: American Association for the Advancement of Science, 1979, 93–106; House, J.S. *Work stress and social support.* Reading, MA: Addison-Wesley, 1981.

[17] Miller, A., Springen, K., Gordon, J., Murr, A., Cohn, B., Drew, L. & Barrett, T. Stress on the job. *Newsweek,* April 25, 1988, 40–45.

[18] Noe, R. Does your job make you sick? *Across the Board,* January 1987, 34–43.

[19] Oldham, G.R. & Rotchford, N.L. Relationships between office characteristics and employee reactions: A study of the physical environment. *Administrative Science Quarterly,* 1983, *28,* 542–556; Sundstrom, E., Burt, R.E. & Kamp, D. Privacy at work: Architectural correlates of job satisfaction and performance. *Academy of Management Journal,* 1980, *23,* 101–117.

[20] Improving the quality of light and work performance. *Office Administration and Automation,* 1984, *55*(5), 38–48.

[21] Tower of stress: The plight of air traffic controllers. *Behavioral Medicine,* 1979, *6*(4), 38–41.

[22] Ibid

[23] Hood, J.C. & Milazzo, N. Shiftwork, stress and wellbeing. *Personnel Administrator,* 1984, *29*(12), 95–105.

[24] Quick, J.C. & Quick, J.D. *Organizational stress and preventive management.* New York: McGraw-Hill, 1984.

[25] Kreitner, R. Personal wellness: It's just good business. *Business Horizons,* 1982, *25*(3), 28–35; Hoffman, J.J. & Hobson, C.J. Physical fitness and employee effectiveness. *Personnel Administrator,* 1984, *29*(4), 101–104.

[26] Schuler, R.S. Time management: A stress management technique. *Personnel Journal,* 1979, *58,* 851–854.

[27] Benson, H. Your innate asset for combating stress. *Harvard Business Review,* 1974, *52*(4), 49–60.

[28] Friedman, D.E. Work vs. family: War of the worlds. *Personnel Administrator,* 1987, *32*(8), 36–38; Hunsaker, J.S. Work and family life must be integrated. *Personnel Administrator,* 1983, *28*(4), 92–98.

[29] Jackson, S.E. Participation in decision making as a strategy for reducing job-related strain. *Journal of Applied Psychology,* 1983, *68*(1), 3–19.

[30] Markowich, M.M. Using task forces to increase efficiency and reduce stress. *Personnel,* 1987, *64*(8), 34–38.

WHAT DO YOU THINK? NOTE

Many of the answers to the questions presented in the What Do You Think? box depend on your own set of values. However, most experts agree that both employers and employees have at least some responsibility for employees' stress. Since the work environment exposes employees to so many stressors, organizations have some responsibility to help employees manage their stress. At a minimum, managers must try to minimize the number of stressors in the work environment, and the length of time employees are exposed to the stressors which are present. Employees, however, must assume primary responsibility for managing their own stress. Several suggestions for doing this were presented in the chapter.

CHAPTER TEN

Managing Your Career

PROLOGUE

Ray hurried across campus to the Business Building. He hoped he could catch his former management professor before she left for the day. As he reached the fourth floor where faculty offices were located, he could see Dr. Williams just entering her office after her last class for the day. Ray called out to her, "Dr. Williams, remember me? Ray Stoner. I took several management classes from you a few years ago. I graduated in 1978." He was pleased when she indicated that she remembered him. "Sure, Ray. How are you?" "Do you have a few minutes, Dr. Williams? I need some advice." Dr. Williams glanced at her watch. "Of course, Ray. I have two hours until the faculty meeting. Come on in. What can I do for you?"

Ray proceeded to explain to Dr. Williams that he was facing some important decisions that would affect his future. He summarized his work experience for Dr. Williams. He had graduated from State University with a bachelor's degree in accounting. He had gone to work as an auditor for one of the "Big Eight" accounting firms right out of school. After six months as an auditor, he began to realize that he wasn't suited for that type of work, but he stuck with it for two years. He found auditing to be rather tedious and not particularly challenging. Further, he disliked being on the road three to four days per week. Then a job as manager of Accounts Receivable/Payable for a large retail store opened up. He applied for and received this job, at a substantial increase in salary. In addition, this new job did not require any travel. The work was interesting and challenging initially, since he had no previous experience in the field of retailing. However, after about a year and a half this job also lost its appeal; it was no longer challenging. He had four accounting clerks who reported to him, but their work was, for the most part, routine and repetitive. They all knew their jobs well and rarely sought his assistance. However, this job permitted him to be home by 6:00 P.M. every night and on the weekends. He enjoyed this time with his wife and new daughter.

After four years with the retail firm and a promotion to general manager of accounting, Ray was contacted by a managerial search firm (commonly called "headhunters") about a job as store manager of a retail chain in a moderate-sized city in the south. The recruiter felt that his accounting and retailing experience were perfect for this job. After long discussions with his wife and a close friend, he took the job and moved his family to the south. He has remained in this job until the present time. Again, he has reached the point where the job no longer provides a challenge, and he is considering moving on to another position.

"I just don't know which direction to go," Ray explained to Dr. Williams. "I'm trained as an accountant, but I really don't enjoy that type of work. I have several years experience in retailing; however, I don't enjoy it much more than I did accounting. I'm making a great salary and we live comfortably, but I keep getting the feeling that there should be something more to it than that. I have the feeling that something is missing. Do I expect too much from my job? Should I go back to school and retrain in another field? I'm really mixed up about what to do."

Dr. Williams took a deep breath and leaned back in her chair. She would need a minute to reflect on everything Ray told her before she answered him.

LEARNING OBJECTIVES

After successful completion of this chapter, you should be able to:

- Explain why individuals must assume responsibility for their own careers,
- Define the following terms: career, career management, career planning, career path, and career development,
- Describe the relationship between career planning and career development,
- Explain what individuals can do to plan their careers,
- Know how to conduct a self-assessment,
- Discuss several common reasons why job applicants do not get hired,
- Identify the characteristics of a good resume,
- Discuss how job applicants can increase the effectiveness of their interviews,
- Understand the advantages of mentoring,
- Identify the problems of balancing career and family responsibilities,
- Describe several things organizations can do to help employees balance work and family responsibilities, and
- Discuss what organizations can do to help individuals manage their careers.

IMPORTANCE OF CAREER MANAGEMENT

The world of work is continually undergoing change. Changes in an organization's environment creates pressure for change within the organization. For example, as the U.S. economy continues to switch from manufacturing-based to service-based, important changes will continue to occur in the work place. New jobs created by the growing service sector of our economy are much different from the manufacturing jobs they replaced. These new jobs generally require specific skills, such as operating a computer, which workers previously did not need to get a job. Whereas "work" used to mean physical labor to a

Robotics have replaced workers in some industries.

majority of workers in this country, it now means mental activity—over 80 percent of U.S. employees now work with their minds rather than their hands.[1]

Technological advances also create changes in the workplace. Robotics and other forms of new technology have replaced workers in some industries. Technological changes also create new jobs, often requiring skills much different from the jobs they replace. To illustrate, factories that have implemented robotics on the assembly line need employees to set up and maintain this new equipment.

Employment Contract

For many years, there was an unwritten employment contract that the organization would continue to provide a job and promotional opportunities for employees who performed their jobs adequately. A recent *Business Week*/Harris poll of middle managers at 600 corporations found that 56 percent of these managers assumed that if they continued to do a good job they could keep their job as long as they liked.[2] However, in the 1970s and 80s this agreement was set aside as many corporations, facing difficult economic conditions, laid off thousands of employees. Between January 1985 and June 1986 several well-known companies laid off thousands of employees. Some of these well-known companies and the numbers of employees they laid off are: Apple Computer, 1,200; AT&T, 35,251; CBS, 1,175; Du Pont, 12,000; Eastman Kodak, 13,700; General Electric, 26,000; and Union Carbide, 8,000.[3]

As corporations "downsized," unemployed workers had to begin searching for work in this new environment. Many of these people found that they did not have the skills necessary to find adequate employment. One author has suggested that employees are making a serious mistake if they passively rely on their employer to provide job security and career advancement. "To count on any particular employer to ensure we will have a meaningful, higher paying job next year or the year after is a big mistake. . ."[4]

You Are Responsible for Your Career

Explain why individuals must assume responsibility for their own careers.

These trends highlight the importance of **career management**. Individuals must take primary responsibility for the management of their careers. The new agreement between employees and employers seems to be: ". . .the employee will assume full responsibility for his own career, for keeping his qualifications up to date, for getting himself moved to the next position at the right time, for salting away funds for retirement, and, most daunting of all, for achieving job satisfaction. The company, while making no promises, will endeavor to provide

---

RETURN TO THE PROLOGUE

Ray apparently has assumed little responsibility for his own career. He seems to have assumed that his employer was primarily responsible for ensuring that he had a challenging and satisfying job, that he continued to grow and develop new skills, and that he would progress within the organization. Ray also seems to have given little thought to career planning. That is, he seems to view employment more as a "job" than as a "career." He has moved from job to job as opportunities presented themselves, with little thought to how each job would help him achieve personal objectives. A **job** is merely the formally assigned tasks that an individual employee must perform. In contrast, a career is much more than the specific tasks performed for the organization. A **career** is the sequence of work-related experiences over the life of the individual.[5] Thus, a career covers a much longer time span than a job, and will probably include a series of jobs. The term career also includes a consideration of the degree to which individuals become involved in their work.[6] Individuals tend to become much more involved with careers than with jobs. Apparently, Ray has taken a short-term view of work, and has been more interested in holding a job than developing a career. He now finds that after working for several years, "something is missing." He is paid well and his family has a good standard of living, but he is not completely satisfied with his work experiences. Career management, which consists of the related activities of career planning and career development, is designed to help individuals avoid situations like the one facing Ray. These activities can also be used to guide people like Ray toward a more challenging and satisfying career instead of just another job. How much thought have you given to your career?

a conducive environment, economic exigencies permitting."[7] Thus, career management is just as important to the 20-year veteran as it is to the recent college graduate.

CAREER MANAGEMENT

Career planning, which is one phase of career management, is primarily the individual's responsibility. It involves self-assessment, exploration of career opportunities, goal setting, and monitoring. The other phase, **career development**, is the responsibility of both the individual and the organization. It comprises activities designed to help the individual grow, develop new skills, and continue to progress within her chosen profession or occupation. It is worth emphasizing that while some organizations have implemented a variety of programs designed to assist employees manage their careers, *individuals must assume primary responsibility for managing their career*. Exhibit 10.1 illustrates the process of career management.

Define the following terms: career, career management, career planning, career path, and career development.

Describe the relationship between career planning and career development.

CAREER PLANNING

Career planning consists of self-assessment, exploration of opportunities, goal setting, marketing yourself, and monitoring. This process should begin at least several months before beginning a search for your first job.

Career planning should continue throughout your career. Given the remarkable changes that are occurring in our society and within the workplace, never become complacent about your career. Career planning will assist you in advancing within your current organization, as well as in searching for other employment opportunities should the need arise.

Explain what individuals can do to plan their careers.

Exhibit 10.1
The career management process

```
                        CAREER MANAGEMENT
                    ┌──────────┴──────────┐
           CAREER PLANNING          CAREER DEVELOPMENT

           Self-Assessment          Organizational
           Explore Opportunities
           Goal Setting             Training Programs
           Marketing Yourself       Performance Appraisal
           Follow-up                Career Paths
                                    Human Resource Planning
                                    Pre-retirement Programs

                                    Individual

                                    Mentoring
                                    Retraining
```

Self-Assessment

Self-assessment is one of the more difficult, yet one of the most important, steps in career planning. It provides the bases on which the rest of the career planning process builds. A good way to begin is by writing an autobiographical summary describing your life, your interests and values, and your feelings about the future.[8] You may also wish to keep a diary, for several 24-hour periods, to provide a record of the specific activities in which you frequently engage. Careful analysis of the diary can provide insight into your likes and dislikes.[9] While you may think you know what you like and dislike without keeping a diary, how you spend your time and the amount of time you spend on certain activities may surprise you.

Know how to conduct a self-assessment.

A number of questionnaires have been developed to assist individuals in self-assessment; several are used frequently during career planning. Three of the most popular are the Allport, Vernon, and Lindsey Study of Work Values Questionnaire; the Work Values Inventory; and the Strong-Campbell Interest Inventory.[10] Counselors in college placement centers or in state employment agencies will assist you in obtaining, completing, and scoring these questionnaires.

The objective of self-assessment is to determine your most important values, abilities, and interests—then match these with the characteristics of successful individuals working in various occupations. These comparisons should enable you to identify the occupation which best matches your personality. The adjacent What Do You Think? box is designed to get you started on your own personal self-assessment.

Exploration of Opportunities

The exploration of career opportunities should begin with the information collected during the self-assessment stage. Determine which jobs and occupations require qualifications similar to your own. Again, the college placement office or state employment agency will help you with this process. Many firms send materials to college placement centers and employment agencies so that prospective job applicants may become familiar with their operations. In addition, annual reports and articles in leading business magazines may provide useful information. You may also wish to write to the public relations departments of organizations in which you are interested, requesting information on these organizations' operations.

The next step is to assess how closely these jobs and occupations are likely to match your interests and enable you to satisfy important personal needs. Once you have identified specific jobs and occupations for which you seem suited, you must identify organizations with employment opportunities in these fields. Notices in the college placement office, newspaper advertisements, advertisements in professional or industry publications, public and private employment agencies, and direct contact with employers are among a variety of methods which will enable you to identify employment opportunities.

> **WHAT DO YOU THINK?**

In answering these questions, be objective. Your self-assessment will be more useful if you are as honest with yourself as possible. Write a short response to each question, then carefully analyze your responses to identify strengths and weaknesses.

1. Do I work better in a large or small group?
2. How important is geographic location to me? to my family?
3. Am I a loner, or do I work better as a member of a group?
4. Am I more comfortable following than leading?
5. Do I analyze better than I execute?
6. Am I an innovator?
7. Do I work more successfully under pressure?
8. Am I a good planner?
9. Am I a good listener?
10. Do I think well on my feet?
11. Do I express myself well orally? in writing?
12. What characteristics do I admire in others?
13. Which function of my job do I perform most effectively?
14. Which do I perform least effectively?
15. What do I most enjoy doing?
16. In the last six months, what accomplishment has most satisfied me? Which has been the most difficult?
17. What have I done to correct my shortcomings?
18. To what level of responsibility do I aspire in five years?
19. What should I be earning then?
20. How will I achieve these levels?[11]

Networking

Another technique for identifying employment opportunities, **networking**, is all too frequently overlooked. Networking makes use of personal contacts such as friends, professors, family members, classmates, and parents of classmates as sources of employment information. Networking is important since the majority of positions, especially at the entry level, are never advertised or listed with employment agencies. The only way to become aware of these positions is through an informal network.

Goal Setting

Once you have gathered information on yourself, occupations, and specific organizations, you are in a position to set specific goals for yourself. What exactly do you want to accomplish in your work life? Over the long term, what do you hope to accomplish by the end of your career? What do you want to accomplish in the short term, say, in the next year? In the next three years? Which of the jobs, occupations, and organizations you identified in Step 2 will enable you accomplish these objectives?

An important question for you to ask at this point is, "what do I want to get out of work?" Is it challenge, responsibility, and recognition? Or is it high pay and fringe benefits? While everyone says they want high pay, you must really try to determine which things are most important to you.

RETURN TO THE PROLOGUE

In the Prologue, Ray was being paid very well, but he kept getting the feeling that something was missing. His work wasn't satisfying his important needs for challenging work and recognition. In order to avoid finding yourself in Ray's dilemma after several years of work, be as objective with yourself as possible in matching your job/career opportunities with the results of your self-assessment.

Marketing Yourself

Successful job searchers are able to market themselves effectively. Unfortunately, the selection process is not perfect, and the most qualified job applicant does not always get the job. Particularly in cases where applicants' qualifications are similar, the successful applicant is generally the one who best presents herself to the prospective employer. The accompanying Human Relations in Action box lists the twenty most common reasons job applicants aren't hired, according to a recent survey of personnel managers. Many of these interviewer reactions can be avoided with careful planning and preparation by the applicant.

Two particularly important activities in marketing yourself are preparing a resume and interviewing. You can take steps to ensure that both of these activities are performed effectively.

Preparing a Resume

No particular resume format is best for all applicants. The format of your resume should reflect on your background, your qualifications, and the type of job for which you are applying. There are, however, several suggestions which are appropriate for most types of resumes.

Appearance. While it may seem obvious, the overall appearance of your resume should be immaculate. Sometimes job applicants will carelessly send poor copies of their resume or copies which are smudged. Remember that each copy of your resume that you mail to a prospective employer is likely to be the first contact this employer has with you. Your resume must present your qualifications in the best light possible; it must get you in the door for an interview where you can market yourself personally. Therefore, as a minimum, each copy of your resume mailed to a prospective employer must be neat, typed or printed clearly, showing no typographical errors or other faults which

HUMAN RELATIONS IN ACTION

20 Reasons Why Job Applicants Aren't Hired

To identify specific reasons why job applicants are not hired, Northwestern University's placement director, Fran S. Endicott, surveyed 153 personnel managers. The most commonly reported reasons why job applicants don't get the job are listed here in order of their importance.

1. Poor personal appearance
2. Overaggressiveness
3. Inability to express information clearly
4. Lack of interest and enthusiasm
5. Lack of career planning; no purpose and no goals
6. Nervous, lack or confidence and poise
7. Overemphasis on money
8. Unwillingness to start at the bottom
9. Makes excuses
10. Lack of tact and courtesy
11. Immaturity
12. Condemns past employers
13. No genuine interest in company or job
14. Fails to look interviewer in the eye
15. Sloppy application form
16. Little sense of humor
17. Arrives late at the interview
18. Fails to express appreciation for interviewer's time
19. Fails to ask questions about the company and the job
20. Vague responses to questions

Source: *The Northwestern Endicott Report,* published by The Placement Center, Northwestern University, Evanston, IL.

---

might send the message that you are careless or don't care much about a job with this particular employer. Further, avoid the use of gimmicks, such as colored paper. Remember, most often an employer wants to hire only one person. This means that she is looking for ways to screen *out* applicants.

Discuss several common reasons why job applicants do not get hired.

Format. A sample format for a resume appears in Exhibit 10.2, but no single format will work for everyone. When preparing your resume, carefully consider the firm to which you are applying, and which of your qualifications you want to emphasize. You may wish to prepare several different resumes for different employers or occupations, stressing different qualifications to better match different jobs.

Identify the characteristics of a good resume.

Interviewing

The interview may be the most important test of a job applicant. Although interviewing is a subjective process and its effectiveness depends heavily on the interviewer, U.S. organizations have historically placed great emphasis on the interview in selecting employees.

The best advice for job applicants regarding interviews is *be prepared*. At the minimum, be prepared in two general areas—*content* and *appearance*. Content involves being prepared for the questions the interviewer is likely to ask, and being prepared to ask questions yourself.

Be Prepared to Ask Questions. First, you must have done your homework on your potential employer. You should have a good understanding of the

> **Exhibit 10.2**
> Suggested format for resumes
>
> Name
Address
Telephone Number
>
> **CAREER OBJECTIVES**
> A short statement describing specific career objectives. Be careful to not be so narrow or specific as to exclude yourself from positions in which you may be interested. The statement should cover a period of time longer than just the job for which you are applying.
>
> **EDUCATION**
> List degrees and the schools from which they were awarded. If you have a particular concentration or major field, you may want to list specific courses to give the reader an idea of your training. This is particularly appropriate if your major course of study is directly applicable to the job for which you are applying. If you have a good grade point average, list it, as well as any awards or scholarships you received or professional organizations of which you were a member (such as the Society for the Advancement of Management or the American Society of Personnel Administrators). You may also wish to include a statement of the number of hours you worked each week for each degree, or the percentage of your educational costs that you paid.
>
> **WORK EXPERIENCE**
> List all work experience, both full- and part-time, in reverse chronological order. It is important to list specific activities, training, assignments, accomplishments, and/or experience that you received. Job titles can be misleading. Don't make the reader guess about what you learned or what skills you developed.
>
> **MISCELLANEOUS**
> List any other organizations to which you belong that might show that you can do the job. For example, if you held any offices in a fraternity or sorority, this may show leadership potential and drive. You may also list other extracurricular activities which, while perhaps not directly job-related, show energy and balanced interests.

organization's history, its major accomplishments and setbacks, exactly what the organization does (its major products or services), and where the organization seems to be going. Also, be sure you know who are its owners or top managers. You must be prepared to ask questions of the interviewer. Use this approach as an opportunity to let the interviewer know that you are interested enough in the position to have done research on the company, and also to find out some specific information about the organization and the job. Do not ask questions about such things as salary, fringe benefits, and promotional opportunities. This approach may give the interviewer the impression that you are more interested in the rewards than in the job.

Prepare to Answer Commonly Asked Questions. You should also prepare for several questions which interviewers commonly ask. If you do not give some prior thought to these questions, they can cause difficulty during the interview, making you appear unsure of yourself.[12] Exhibit 10.3 presents a list of questions commonly asked by interviewers. You should not appear to have predetermined answers to these questions; however, you should think about them carefully to avoid being surprised by them during an interview.

Your Appearance. The second general area in which you should prepare involves your appearance during the interview. Do you appear comfortable and sure of yourself? Do you appear confident? Do you express yourself clearly? Do you have any annoying mannerisms? In other words, how will you appear to an interviewer? An excellent way to prepare for this part of interviewing is to videotape yourself in a mock interview. Many college and university placement offices are equipped to provide this service for students. You might, for example, give your resume to the placement director who then interviews you as if she were a company recruiter. An assistant videotapes the interview for you to view later. This videotape provides one of the few chances you have to see yourself as others see you. It can be of substantial benefit as you interview. By carefully examining the tape, you can improve your appearance and more effectively market yourself to a prospective employer.

If videotaping is not available, you should at least take part in mock interviews with a friend or coworker who is also interviewing. Have another friend act as observer, carefully watching for mistakes or areas in which you can improve.

Monitoring

Monitoring is a strategy for keeping track of your career progress. As stated earlier, career planning is a never-ending process. You must continually reassess how well you are progressing toward your career objectives. Decide whether these objectives remain optimal or whether you should develop new ones. And, decide whether the specific activities you have chosen to accomplish these career objectives are still most appropriate or whether there is a better approach to achieving your objectives. You may wish to make an annual self-assessment to determine whether the career goals you have set for yourself remain appropriate. If they are not, you are ready to go to the next stages of the career planning process.

Career Stages

Most people change as they progress through their working careers. Their values, needs, and expectations change, causing them to set new career objec-

> **Exhibit 10.3**
> Questions interviewers comonly ask
>
> 1. Tell me about yourself. Use this opportunity to sell yourself. Having researched this organization and the job, you are in a position to emphasize the abilities and skills you have developed that suit you for this job.
> 2. What are your strengths? (Or "What is your greatest strength?") Again, emphasize the strengths which match the job for which you are interviewing.
> 3. What are your weaknesses? (Or "What is your greatest weakness?") Never simply state a major weakness. Instead mention an area where you would like to improve. Ideally, you will be able to (honestly) state that you have already begun a program to eliminate this weakness. For example, "I'd really like to improve my math skills. I have taken an evening math course at the local community college for the last two semesters. I believe that one more course will make me about as strong as anyone in this area."
> 4. Why do you want to work for this organization? Give an honest response here. If the organization has a particular strength or advantage, mention it—letting the interviewer know that you are familiar with the organization. For example, "During my research, I've found that your organization has introduced three new products every year for the past eleven years. That's the kind of innovative, progressive organization I want to work for."
> 5. What did you like best about your previous job (or manager or school)? Try to pick out something other than salary or working conditions. Mention the training or experience that you received. Here is a chance to mention some special achievement or accomplishment. For example, "My previous employer gave me an opportunity to learn about advertising from the ground up. I was responsible for the entire advertising campaign of four major product lines."

tives. Most careers go through the four distinct **stages** shown in Exhibit 10.4.[13] Individuals must deal with specific issues associated with each stage if they are to continue to progress and be satisfied with their careers.

Stage 1: Exploration and Trial. This stage takes place between the ages of 15 and 25. Individuals begin thinking about jobs and careers and may hold down their first real job, such as part-time employment while they finish school. This experience helps individuals form images of work and decide what type of career they would like to pursue. Individuals also accept their first (or first few) full-time jobs during these years. This stage is characterized by individuals trying different types of jobs and making decisions about staying with particular organizations or seeking employment elsewhere.

CHAPTER TEN: Managing Your Career 263

Exhibit 10.3 *(continued)*

6. What did you like least about your previous job (or manager or school)? *Never* say anything negative about a previous manager or employer. While what you have to say may be completely true, it gives an interviewer the impression that you are a problem employee or complainer.
7. Where do you want to be in five years? In ten years? Your career planning process should have enabled you to identify specific career objectives that you can share with the interviewer.
8. Why do you want to leave your present employer? Again, don't mention a negative reason. Instead, focus on the positive. Mention career advancement, opportunity to continue to grow and develop.
9. What are your salary expectations? Try to avoid giving a specific salary figure. Instead, you might state that salary is only one aspect of a job and you are also interested in challenging work and an opportunity to grow and develop. If pressed for a figure, state a range rather than a single salary level. It will help if you have researched the job market to get an idea of what salary organizations have offered for similar jobs. Your college placement center may have this information.
10. How would other people describe you? Use this as another opportunity to stress your strong points, especially those which are particularly appropriate for the job for which you are interviewing.
11. Why should we hire you instead of another applicant? Be prepared to emphasize your strengths that match the particular job for which you are interviewing.
12. Describe your ideal job. You had better make this sound as close as possible to the job for which you are interviewing.

One significant event which many individuals experience during this stage of their career is called **job shock**. This shock occurs when your job does not meet your expectations in important ways.[14] Individuals often begin their careers with unrealistically high expectations of what their jobs and employers will provide to them. They may, for example, expect that their work assignments will always be challenging and interesting, they will generally be permitted to exert some influence over their work environments, they will regularly be provided with promotional opportunities, they will be treated fairly by their managers and coworkers, and their rewards will always be commensurate with their job performance. For a variety of reasons, these expectations are seldom completely met in any organization. Sometimes employees have difficulty coming to terms with the realization that their job is not everything

Exhibit 10.4
A model of career stages

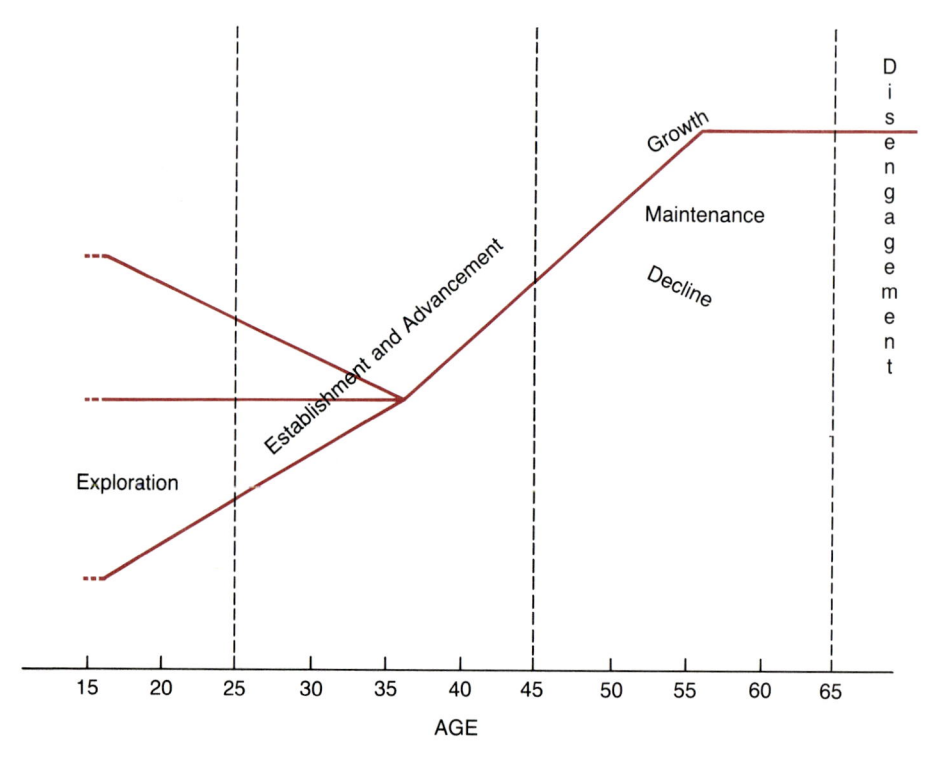

Source: Adapted from Hall, D. T. *Careers in organizations.* Santa Monica, CA: Goodyear, 1976, p. 57.

they expected it to be. They become disappointed, frustrated, and may begin seeking alternative employment. This job shock is one reason for the relatively high levels of turnover during the first few years of employment.

To avoid this misfortune, you must develop realistic expectations of your job, your occupation, and your employing organization. Careful research of occupations and organizations before accepting a job offer is a must. Further, talking with persons who are currently working in your occupation as well as employees of the organization you are considering joining may provide insight into what your job will *really* be like. Finally, thorough consideration of exactly what you expect from your work experience may help you reassess the expectations you have formed. Those which are based on hope or desire may need to be adjusted downward to be more in line with what might happen to you in the real world.

Stage 2: Establishment and Advancement. During this stage, between the ages of 25 and 45, individuals progress within an organization. They are promoted and transferred and begin to carve out a niche for themselves in their organization.

Stage 3: Mid-Career. This stage occurs for most individuals between the ages of 45 and 65. This stage represents a turning point. It is a period of time where some individuals begin to experience uncertainty and doubts about their careers or the direction their life has taken. Commonly referred to as a midlife crisis, it represents a major hurdle for individuals who experience it. Individuals who reach this stage can move in three directions; growth, maintenance, or decline. The success with which individuals handle the crisis is an important determinant of the path they take.

Some individuals continue to grow and progress in their careers. They are interested in, and challenged by, their work; they regularly receive promotions to positions of greater responsibility. Other individuals may choose to simply maintain what they have achieved. They may no longer be concerned with moving higher in the organization and may instead devote more energy to family or community projects. These individuals continue to perform their jobs well, but they prefer job security and status quo to additional promotions. Finally, some individuals may actually decline. They have allowed their skills to become obsolete due to a lack of career management. Others have simply lost the motivation to continue to work at the same pace as they did previously. These individuals must face the reality of no longer being part of the mainstream in their organization, eventually to face demotion, early retirement, or termination.

Stage 4: Disengagement. This stage occurs toward the end of every career, when individuals begin to prepare themselves and their families for retirement. An important part of this process is disengaging from their organizations and their occupations. This step is extremely difficult for some individuals since they have spent a substantial amount of their time in these environments. Organizations often provide preretirement counseling programs, which will be discussed later, to assist employees through this difficult time. Individuals can help themselves prepare for retirement by developing hobbies or other interests totally unrelated to their work.

Mentoring

A **mentor** is a higher-level manager who acts as a sponsor and counselor to a new employee.[15] A study published in the Harvard Business Review found that two-thirds of the executives studied had a mentor at some time during their careers. The study also found that executives who had mentors reported greater satisfaction from their career and work, and earned more money at a younger age than executives who did not have a mentor.[16]

The benefits of mentoring to a young employee are obvious. Mentors help their *proteges* learn the ropes and fit into the organization. New employees are able to learn what elements are most important to the organization and thus begin making a contribution and advancing their careers faster than employees without these advisors. Mentors can also directly advance the careers of their proteges by making them aware of promotional opportunities, nominating them for promotions, and making other executives aware of the protege's

Understand the advantages of mentoring.

work. Mentors may also provide their proteges with information that helps them improve their job performance. Finally, mentors often counsel and advise proteges on how to succeed in the organization.

The organization, too, can benefit from mentoring relationships, since they often enable new employees to perform their job more effectively, thus increasing productivity. Mentors may also reduce absenteeism and turnover as new employees adjust more quickly to their new work environments. Having a senior manager to turn to reduces the uncertainty and stress associated with accepting a new position.[17]

The mentor-protege relationship may be initiated by either party; however, often it is the senior manager who notices the potential of a new employee. The relationship typically goes through at least three stages: *initiation, cultivation,* and *separation.*[18] During the initiation stage, which lasts approximately six months, the mentor and protege get to know each other. The protege identifies with a senior manager who can provide support and encouragement; the senior manager identifies with a young employee showing potential, with whom it is enjoyable to work.

During the cultivation stage, the mentor coaches, advises, protects, and sponsors the new employee. The relationship during this stage has been described as teacher/student or master/apprentice, and during this period, the protege's work may not be recognized on its own merit. Others may discount the contributions of the protege since she received substantial assistance from the mentor.

For the protege's work to be recognized, she must eventually break away from the mentor. This action occurs during the separation stage, and is often initiated by the promotion or transfer of the protege. If the mentor can accept the protege as a peer, the separation need not be the end of the relationship. If the mentor cannot accept the former protege as an equal, the relationship may end at this point.[19]

Work and Family

Identify the problems of balancing career and family responsibilities.

Increasing emphasis is being placed on balancing work and family, partly because of a generally rising awareness of the importance of quality of work life. Rising educational levels and experience have produced employees who are becoming more concerned about the quality of their work experience. Today's employees expect more out of their jobs or careers than just a salary and fringe benefits.

The additional emphasis on balancing work and family has resulted from several major changes in the work force. One of the most important of these changes is the increase in the numbers of women who have entered the work force. This has resulted in increased numbers of dual-career families. In addition, increased numbers of single-parent families headed by women has also drawn attention to the relationship between work and family. In 1986, fifty-four percent of women with a child under six held jobs.[20] These changes to the work force have raised issues such as child care, elder care, parental leave, flexible working hours, **flexible time off**, and job sharing.

> **WHAT DO YOU THINK?**
>
> You have been working for five years in a middle-management job at a large industry leader located in the midwest. You expect a big promotion within the next three years. Your spouse has just finished an M.B.A. at a leading university and has a tremendous job offer with a large firm in a different industry located in a large southern city. Now you and your spouse have two careers to manage. What factors do you consider when making the decision as to whose career gets placed on "hold" while the other career progresses? Do you give up your career and move with your spouse? Do you insist that your spouse give up this opportunity and look for a position locally? What factors should be considered in this decision? What factors should not be considered?

Progressive organizations realize that their employees benefit from a balanced life, rather than a life that places too much emphasis on work. These same organizations may also be recognizing that most employees cannot easily separate their work life from their family life. Problems at home are carried to the office, and vice versa.[21] Surveys at several well-known companies such as AT&T and Honeywell show that between 30 and 60 percent of employees of both sexes have difficulty managing their work and family responsibilities.[22] Organizations can help employees balance their work and family responsibilities in a number of ways.

Dependent Care

Dependent care includes both **child care** and **elder care** (e.g., dependent grandparents, parents or other relatives). Some organizations help employees pay for these services; others provide in-house dependent care facilities for their employees.

Describe several things organizations can do to help employees balance work and family responsibilities.

Parental Leave

Parental leave grew out of the common practice of providing maternity leave for female employees who became pregnant. Some organizations provide extended parental leave for female employees, while others provide paternity leave to expectant or new fathers as well.

Flexible Work Scheduling

A study of full-time employees found that **flexible work scheduling** was rated as one of the organizational practices most helpful to employees trying to balance work and family demands.[23] Flexible work scheduling allows employees to schedule their own work hours, within certain guidelines. For example, it is common to set a *core time* at which all employees must be at work. This is often toward the middle of the day, between 10:00 A.M. and 2:00 P.M., or whenever the worksite is busiest. Outside this core time, employees are free to set their own hours as long as they work the required number of hours per week or per month. This scheduling flexibility enables employees to better meet family demands. A similar program combines vacation days and sick days into one pool. Employees may take off the days they have earned (based on seniority) for any reason, and in any increment.

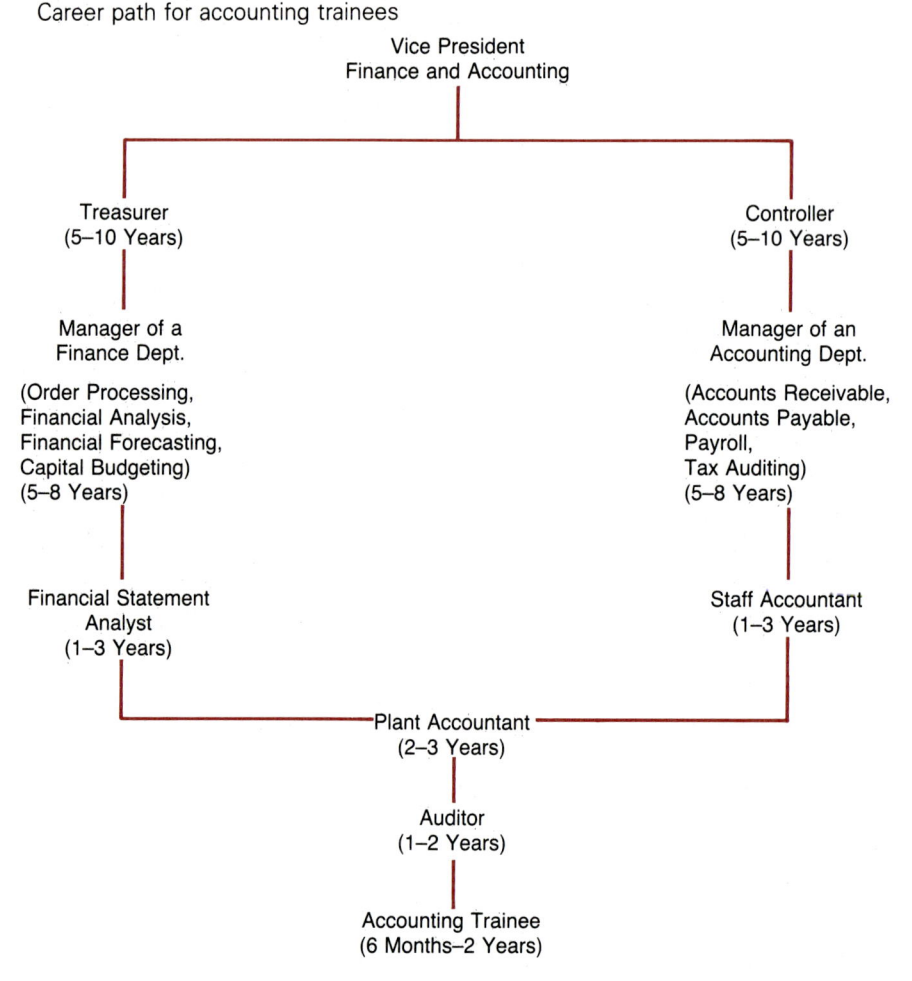

Exhibit 10.5
Career path for accounting trainees

```
                    Vice President
                  Finance and Accounting
                    /           \
           Treasurer            Controller
          (5–10 Years)         (5–10 Years)
              |                     |
        Manager of a          Manager of an
        Finance Dept.         Accounting Dept.
      (Order Processing,    (Accounts Receivable,
       Financial Analysis,   Accounts Payable,
       Financial Forecasting, Payroll,
       Capital Budgeting)    Tax Auditing)
        (5–8 Years)           (5–8 Years)
              |                     |
       Financial Statement     Staff Accountant
            Analyst             (1–3 Years)
         (1–3 Years)
              _____/
                     |
              Plant Accountant
                (2–3 Years)
                     |
                  Auditor
                (1–2 Years)
                     |
             Accounting Trainee
           (6 Months–2 Years)
```

Job Sharing

Job sharing involves two or more individuals sharing one full-time job. This arrangement gives employment to employees whose family responsibilities prevent them from holding a full-time job. It also allows the organization to retain top employees who otherwise might have had to quit due to family responsibilities.

ORGANIZATIONAL CAREER DEVELOPMENT

Several programs which organizations can undertake to help employees balance work and family responsibilities have been described. Organizations may also offer a number of other programs to help employees develop their careers. These activities include human resource planning, career paths, training and development, job posting, performance appraisal, and preretirement counseling.

Human Resource Planning

From the organization's perspective, employee career development activities must begin with **human resource planning**—a formal process of predicting the organization's personnel needs. It begins by determining the specific types and numbers of employees the organization will need in the future, then matches this data with projections on the supply of these types of employees. The organization must have a clear picture of the future supply and demand of human resources to assist employees with career development. Employee career development activities sponsored by an organization must be consistent with its own objectives. Thus, helping employees develop their careers must also help the organization accomplish its objectives. Case in point: the organization would not likely spend substantial amounts of money on training and developing certain skills if human resource planning projected no need for these skills.

> Discuss what organizations can do to help individuals manage their careers.

Career Paths

One important way organizations can assist employees in their careers is by developing career paths for entry-level positions. **Career paths** are series of positions through which individuals in particular jobs are likely to progress. An example of a career path for accounting trainees in a large organization appears in Exhibit 10.5. All accounting trainees followed a similar career path until their fourth promotion. At that point, depending on their interests and organizational needs, they began to specialize in either finance or accounting.

Career paths let employees know what they can expect in terms of advancement within the organization. The presence of career paths lets employees know that the organization has thought about employees' careers and views them as important. Both the organization and employees should look at career paths as guidelines, not inflexible contracts.

Training and Development

Organizations also contribute to employees' career development through training and development programs. Training generally refers to nonmanagerial technical skills training while development generally connotes management-related activities. Training programs focus on improving employees' technical capabilities and include on-the-job training, technical job skills training programs, and classroom instruction. Management development programs focus on long-term managerial attributes such as communication, counseling, motivation, and leadership. While some of these seminars are conducted by the organization's in-house training and development personnel, outside consultants are frequently used.

> **DEVELOPING YOUR HUMAN RELATIONS SKILLS**
>
> This chapter has established that individuals must assume primary responsibility for their own careers. Employees must be concerned with their careers for obvious reasons. Managers who assist employees in their careers can benefit from that effort, in terms of improved employee performance, increased motivation, and reduced absenteeism and turnover. As a manager, you should consider the following suggestions:
>
> 1. Become a mentor. Managers are in a unique position to guide a new employee through the uncertainty of the first several months (or years) on the job. In addition to providing technical job-related information and advice, managers can counsel employees on how to succeed in the politics which are present in any organization.
> 2. Use performance appraisals as a performance improvement, motivational, and career development technique. This employee review is an ideal time to set performance objectives jointly with employees; and to provide advice, counseling, and encouragement.
> 3. Remember, employees cannot consider your organization in their career planning without information on career paths and promotional opportunities. Discussions with employees regarding their career objectives and interests—perhaps during the performance appraisal—are essential to provide employees with information for career planning. Such discussions also keep managers apprised of employees' objectives, which should be considered when job openings occur. Finally, these discussions let employees know your interest in their development and advancement and your willingness to assist them in their careers. Career development is most effective when managers and employees work together.[24]

Promotions and transfers can also be important tools for development of both employees and managers. Promotion and transfer decisions should consider the development of the employee being considered for the move. Similarly, changing the current jobs of employees, by expanding responsibilities or encouraging employees to assume more control over their jobs, can be an excellent training and development tactic.

Job Posting

Job posting usually implies a preference for promoting employees from within the organization. Descriptions of open jobs are posted on a bulletin board for employees to review. Employees who feel they are qualified and who have an interest in a posted position can nominate themselves for the job. In some situations, an employee can directly contact the manager who has the job opening; in others, the response must be made through the employee's current manager.

In your role as an employee, you must assume responsibility for your own career. Specifically, you should:

1. Engage in career planning on an ongoing basis. Each year you should conduct a self-assessment and reconsider your career objectives. You should also assess the degree to which you are making progress in your current position and with your current employer. Virtually all material on career management suggests that you should not waste time in a dead-end position. If the prospects for advancement seem minimal, consider seeking alternative employment that will better enable you to accomplish your career objectives.
2. Seek out a successful senior manager as your mentor. Your approach must be done with common sense and tact since not all senior managers are interested in becoming a mentor. The mentor/protege relationship should develop naturally, but you should be looking for suitable mentors and go out of your way to cultivate a working relationship with them.
3. Seek out special projects, assignments, and committees that will provide visibility for you. Make sure that you work extremely hard on conspicuous assignments that will establish a record of success. The only way to progress within an organization is to make recognized contributions to that organization.
4. Career planning should consider family responsibilities. Organizations are increasingly aware that most employees cannot completely separate work and family. You should not even attempt to do so in your career planning. If your family or leisure life is unsatisfactory, it will affect your work life. When establishing career objectives, make sure that you will be able to accomplish nonwork objectives as well.

Performance Appraisal

As mentioned in Chapter 7, one of the potential benefits of performance appraisal is in its use as a career development tool. To assist employees in developing their careers, performance appraisals must measure objective, job-related behaviors rather than attitudes or personalities. Managers must carefully identify areas of each employee's job performance which need improvement and suggest corrective approaches. Objectives that will bring about the necessary improvements in performance should be set jointly with employees.

Preretirement Counseling

An organization's career development activities should also serve those employees in the disengagement stage of their careers. **Preretirement programs** can be offered to assist employees in the transition from work to retirement.

These programs typically include counseling on such topics as financial planning for retirement, benefits provided by the organization (pensions and/or health and life insurance), psychological adjustment to retirement, part-time employment, and second careers.[25]

Summary

Individuals must assume primary responsibility for their own careers. The relationship between employer and employee is no longer one of "if I do an adequate job, my employer will take care of me." The environments of today's complex organizations are constantly changing. This change creates the need for adjustment within organizations and within the workplace. This instability places increased importance on career development.

A *job* is a set of tasks assigned to an employee. A *career* is the sequence of work-related experiences over the life of an employee. Thus, a career has much broader scope than a job. Individuals are likely to be more involved in careers than in jobs.

Career management involves two interrelated sets of activities—career planning and career development. Career planning is the responsibility of individual employees; it comprises self-assessment, exploration of career opportunities, goal setting, marketing yourself, and monitoring. Two extremely important elements in marketing yourself are resume preparation and interviewing. Career development is the responsibility of both individual employees and their employing organizations. Career development activities are aimed at helping employees grow, develop new skills, and continue to progress in their chosen occupation.

Most people go through several identifiable career stages. In the exploration and trial stage, individuals begin thinking about jobs and careers and may try several different lines of work. Job shock often occurs during this stage. In the establishment and advancement stage, individuals prove themselves as solid employees and receive promotions. In the midcareer stage, they experience uncertainty about their career. They may question their choice of occupations or the direction their career has taken. Depending on how individuals handle this stage, they may take one of three paths: continued growth, maintenance, or decline. Finally, in the disengagement stage, individuals prepare themselves and their families for retirement.

A mentor is a senior manager who acts as a sponsor and counselor to a new employee. The typical mentor/protege relationship moves through at least three stages; initiation, cultivation, and separation.

Organizations are increasingly recognizing the difficulty many employees have in separating their work life from their private life. As a result, a number of programs have evolved which are designed to help employees balance work demands with family responsibilities. These include dependent care, parental leave, flexible work scheduling, flexible time off, and job sharing.

Several programs have been used by organizations to assist employees in career development. These include human resource planning, career paths, training and development, job posting, performance appraisal, and preretirement counseling.

Key Terms

career management
job
career
career planning
career development
self-assessment
networking
career stages
job shock
mentor
flexible time off

dependent care
parental leave
flexible work scheduling
job sharing
human resource planning
career path
job posting
preretirement programs

Review Questions

1. Distinguish between a job and a career.
2. What is job shock? How does it occur? What can individuals do about it?
3. What are the advantages to developing career paths? Disadvantages?
4. Think ahead to when you begin actively interviewing for a job. What exactly will you do in preparation for these interviews?
5. What career planning steps have you taken? What steps do you plan to take between now and graduation?
6. Do employees have to depend on a mentor to be successful? Explain.

7. Should you actively search for a mentor, or should you wait until a senior manager picks you as a protege?
8. Of all the organizational career development activities discussed in the chapter, which one or two do you consider most effective in assisting employees develop in their careers? Explain.

EXERCISE 10.1

Analyzing a Company

Pick out a major company in which you have an interest as a potential employer. Go to the library and research this company as you would if you were preparing for an interview. Prepare a short written summary of your research and be prepared to share it with the class. Based on your research, write at least six questions that you intend to ask during the interview. Remember that one of the things you are trying to accomplish by asking these questions is to display real interest in the company and the employment opportunity. Another objective is to gather additional information that will help you decide if you really want to accept employment with this organization.

CASE 10.1

Preparing a Targeted Resume

It is impossible to identify the best format for all resumes. As pointed out in the chapter, the exact format of your resume depends on the nature of the job for which you are applying and the specific qualifications that you want to stress. Therefore, it is generally a good idea to prepare several resumes, each of which is targeted to a particular occupation, company, or job. This case is designed to provide you with an opportunity to practice tailoring your resume for a specific job. A description of the two jobs and background information on the organization is presented in the following paragraphs. Select one of these jobs and redesign your own resume to target this particular job and organization.

BACKGROUND INFORMATION: ARENZ COMPUTER PRODUCTS, INC.

Arenz Computer Products is a rapidly growing computer manufacturer and supplier located in central Illinois. The company markets a full line of personal computer systems and software. In addition, Arenz has recently added a full line of office supplies, including diskettes, paper, ribbons, and storage cases for diskettes. The company has been in existence for only seven years, yet reached sales of $57 million last year. It has built its reputation on high-quality and low-cost computer systems, compatible with the major brands. The company originally operated only within the Great Lakes states; however, demand for its products has recently caused Arenz to expand nationwide. After this rapid expansion, there is a tremendous need for new employees, particularly marketing representatives.

JOB DESCRIPTION: RECRUITER, PERSONNEL DEPARTMENT

This position in the personnel department is entry-level. Primary responsibilities include recruiting and conducting screening interviews of job applicants. A major part of this recruiting is conducted during the fall and spring, at college campuses throughout the United States. Recruiting activities take place during college-sponsored "job fairs" and screening interviews are conducted in the college placement center. During the screening interviews, candidates are selected for more in-depth selection interviews at the company's headquarters.

JOB DESCRIPTION: MARKETING REPRESENTATIVE, COMPUTER PRODUCTS

The primary responsibility of individuals in this Sales Department position include calling on major corporations throughout the United States to market the company's line of personal computer hardware, software, and supplies. Marketing representatives must spend six months in the company's training program learning to set up and service the equipment they sell. In addition, they must conduct training programs for first-time buyers.

REFERENCES

[1] Hallett, J.J. Worklife visions. *Personnel Administrator,* 1987, *32*(5), 56–65.

[2] Jackson, S. (Ed.) *BW*/Harris executive poll: No job is forever. *Business Week,* August 4, 1986, p. 49.

[3] Nussbaum, B., Failla, K., Eklund, C.S., Beam, A., Norman, J.R., & Deveny, K. The end of corporate loyalty. *Business Week,* August 4, 1986, p. 45.

[4] Hallett, J.J. Worklife visions. *Personnel Administrator,* 1987, *32*(5), p. 63.

[5] Kiechell, W. Your new employment contract. *Fortune,* 1987, *116*(1), p. 109.

[6] Gutteridge, T. *Career planning and management.* Boston: Little, Brown, 1987.

[7] Hall, D.T. *Careers in organizations.* Santa Monica, CA: Goodyear, 1976.

[8] Kotter, J.P., Faux, V.A., & McArthur, C.C. *Self-assessment and career development.* Englewood Cliffs, NJ: Prentice-Hall, 1978.

[9] London, M., & Stumpf, S.A. *Managing careers.* Reading, MA: Addison-Wesley, 1982.

[10] Allport, G.W., Vernon, P.E., & Lindsey, G. *Study of values: A scale for measuring dominant interests in personality.* Third edition. Boston: Houghton Mifflin, 1960; Campbell, D.P. *Manual for the SVIB-SCII.* Stanford, CA: Stanford University Press, 1977; Super, D.E. *Work Values Inventory.* New York: Houghton Mifflin, 1970.

[11] Anderson, R.S. Marketing a "new product." *MBA Magazine,* October 1975, *9*, p. 28.

[12] Challenger, J.E. 10 tough interview questions. *Business Week Careers,* April/May 1988, 24–25.

[13] Hall, D.T. *Careers in organizations.* Santa Monica, CA: Goodyear, 1976.

[14] Fader, S.S. Job shock. *Business Week Careers,* Spring/Summer, 1988, 68–69.

[15] Kram, K.E. *Mentoring at work: Developmental relationships in organizational life.* Glenview, IL: Scott, Foresman, 1985.

[16] Roche, G.R. Much ado about mentors. *Harvard Business Review,* 1979, *57,* 14–28.

[17] Zey, M.G. A mentor for all reasons. *Personnel Journal,* 1988, *67*(1), 46–51.

[18] Kram, K.E. Phases of the mentor relationship. *Academy of Management Journal,* 1983, *26*(4), 608–625.

[19] Hunt, D.M., & Michael, C. Mentorship: A career training and development tool. *Academy of Management Review,* 1983, *8*(3), 475–485.

[20] Friedman, D.E. Work vs. family: War of the worlds. *Personnel Administrator,* 1988, *32*(8), 36–38.

[21] Hallett, J. Work life and family life: Separate but equal. *Personnel Administrator,* 1988, *32*(8), 22–24.

[22] Friedman, D.E. Work vs. family: War of the worlds. *Personnel Administrator,* 1988, *32*(8), 36–38.

[23] Schmidt, V.J., & Scott, N.A. Work and family life: A delicate balance. *Personnel Administrator,* 1988, *32*(8), 40–46.

[24] Gilley, J.W. Career development as a partnership. *Personnel Administrator,* 1988, *33*(4), 62–68.

[25] Morrison, M.H., & Jedrziewski, M.K. Retirement planning: Everybody benefits. *Personnel Administrator,* 1988, *33*(1), 74–80.

There are, of course, no right or wrong answers for these questions. They are designed to help you systematically analyze yourself and your career aspirations. As you look back over your responses to these questions, look for patterns or areas of agreement. Try to identify several things that you do well, and several things that you enjoy. One question which you should be able to answer is whether you prefer to work alone or with other people. In other words, do you prefer to have complete control of a project or work assignment, or are you able to share control with others? Another activity you may wish to try is writing a description of the ideal job. List the characteristics of this job in detail, then compare them with the characteristics you have identified about yourself. Does there appear to be a match? If not, you should carefully evaluate why not. Were you honest with yourself during the self-assessment?

> **WHAT DO YOU THINK? NOTE 1**

Unfortunately, there are no right or wrong answers to this dilemma. However, as the number of dual-career families increases, it is a situation that more and more employees will have to face during their careers. Some couples have solved this problem in the short term by commuting. This solution is likely to be more successful if one or both employers permit flexible work scheduling. Some organizations may assist the relocated spouse in a job search.

> **WHAT DO YOU THINK? NOTE 2**

CHAPTER ELEVEN

Decision Making and Creativity

PROLOGUE

Art Fry, a scientist at 3M's Commercial Office Supply Division, enjoyed singing bass in his church choir. He was frustrated, however, in his attempts to mark pages in his hymnal with scraps of paper. The scraps frequently fell out, leaving Art to search back through the hymnal for the pages he needed.

Suddenly Art remembered an adhesive developed by a coworker at 3M. Everyone had concluded that this adhesive was a failure since it didn't stick very well. Art coated his scraps of paper with some of this adhesive, and "Post-it Notes" were created. These notes are great for writing notes and sticking them up so they would be remembered, or for use as bookmarks. They can be removed without damage to the pages.[1]

Art developed a unique and creative solution to a problem he was facing. But where did this creative solution come from? Is Art a genius, or one of those people who are born with a creative instinct? Can everyone learn to be more creative? Can managers and organizations do anything to encourage employees to be more creative? These and other questions about creativity will be addressed in this chapter. One thing most people can agree on—creative approaches to problems and decisions are becoming increasingly important as organizations find themselves facing stiff competition at home and abroad.

LEARNING OBJECTIVES

After successful completion of this chapter, you should be able to:

- Describe the decision-making process,
- Identify several barriers to problem recognition,
- Explain the importance of accurate problem definition,

277

- Determine whether situations call for group or individual decision making,
- Discuss advantages and disadvantages of group decision making,
- Develop strategies for effective group decision making,
- Suggest how individuals can become more creative, and
- Identify ways organizations can encourage employee creativity.

DECISION MAKING IN ORGANIZATIONS

Decision making is an important component of the activities of all organizational members. Some authors consider decision making synonymous with management, since it permeates the management process. Decision making is clearly an important part of many managerial activities such as planning, organizing, motivating, communicating, coordinating, and controlling. However, decision making is also a component of the activities of nonmanagerial employees. They must constantly make decisions regarding their effort and performance, compliance with organizational policies, and interactions with others. To put it simply, every conscious act involves decision making. Thus, decision making exerts considerable influence upon human relations in organizations. As organizational members make decisions regarding how they will behave and interact with other organizational members, the human relations climate is formed.

Unfortunately, many managers and employees are not highly effective decision makers. Two authorities on decision making have estimated that personnel in U.S. companies use effective decision skills only about 12 percent of the time.[2] Managers, who frequently must operate under time pressure and amid distractions, may make decisions hastily, place undue emphasis on negative information, and ineffectively process information relevant to the decision.[3] There is no reason to believe that nonmanagerial employees make decisions under dissimilar conditions. Have you ever experienced difficulty in making a decision? Have you ever made a decision only to regret it later? Fortunately, behavioral science research has determined that people can learn to become better decision makers. The focus of this chapter is on techniques and suggestions for improving decision-making effectiveness.

THE DECISION-MAKING PROCESS

Describe the decision-making process.

The decision-making process, shown in Exhibit 11.1, consists of six interrelated steps: problem recognition, problem definition, developing and evaluating alternatives, selecting an alternative, implementation, and follow-up. Thus, decision making involves much more than simply selecting one solution from a set of alternatives. It begins with the sometimes very difficult tasks of **problem recognition** and **problem definition**.

Problem Recognition

Identify several barriers to problem recognition.

The decision-making process begins with the recognition that a *problem* or *performance gap* exists. A **problem** is a current or potential occurrence or

Exhibit 11.1
The decision-making process

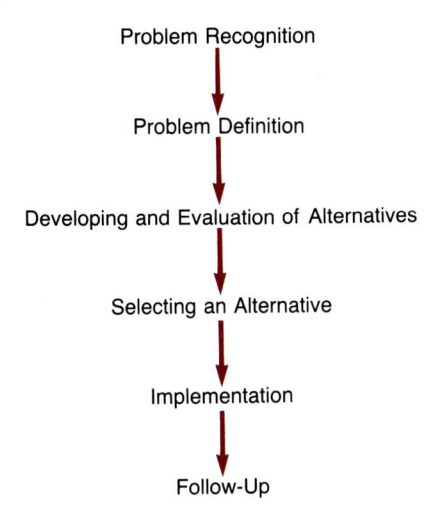

Problem Recognition
↓
Problem Definition
↓
Developing and Evaluation of Alternatives
↓
Selecting an Alternative
↓
Implementation
↓
Follow-Up

situation that may prevent the organization from accomplishing its goals. A **performance gap** is a difference between current conditions and desired conditions. Unfortunately, many individuals are not particularly good at problem recognition. Some people develop the attitude that "I've got enough problems right now to keep me busy. I certainly don't need to look for any more." However, this attitude will not enable managers to avoid dealing with problems that arise. In contrast, managers and employees who develop this attitude may not become aware of problems until it is too late to effectively deal with them. Individuals who are sensitive to their surroundings and who are constantly on the lookout for problems get a head start in dealing with them. They turn potential problems into opportunities for improving the organization. In a continually monitored environment, potential problems can become opportunities, not only for the organization to improve its performance, but also for an individual to make a valuable contribution to the organization. Managers who stick their heads in the sand and attempt to ignore problems will eventually have to deal with them. And, during the time they are being ignored, problems can become more serious.

Sources of Information
Recognizing that problems or potential problems exist is often difficult, since the process typically requires integration of information from a variety of sources. Formal information sources prepared by the organization consist of financial and accounting summaries, production reports, customer surveys, and employee surveys. Informal sources provide information gathered outside the formal information/communication system. For example, casual conversations with employees or customers are often excellent informal sources of information. Sometimes, these two sources of information provide conflicting information. Production reports may show adequate levels of production, but

informal conversations with employees suggest a severe morale problem with the potential of damaging production. Managers who are sensitive to their environments, and who are consciously looking for problems and potential problems, are in a better position to determine which source of information should be given greater emphasis. Managers who attempt to avoid new problems may not even be aware of potential problems suggested by the informal information system.

Problem Definition

Explain the importance of accurate problem definition.

Defining the problem accurately and specifically is critical to effective decision making. How the problem is defined determines, in large part, its possible solutions. Narrow problem definitions may exclude some feasible solutions from further consideration; broad definitions may be so general that they provide little direction in searching for potential solutions. Finally, inaccurate definitions may lead decision makers to solve the wrong problem! The accompanying What Do You Think? box illustrates the importance of accurate problem definition.

WHAT DO YOU THINK?

A Matter of Choice

During the Fall of 1988, the United States was preparing for the annual outbreak of influenza. Unfortunately, the U.S. Health Service couldn't be sure which strain of influenza would be most prevalent. They were fearful, however, that one or more unusually lethal strains of flu might develop. As a result of the indecision regarding the most prevalent type of flu, the pharmaceutical companies couldn't prepare vaccine for shipment to hospitals, clinics, and county health departments until much later than usual.

Assume that you are the director of a hospital in a small town of 100,000 people. If one of the more virulent flu strains hits your town, it could kill as many as 1,000 people. You generally administer flu shots to half the town's population, and they must be administered by the end of November to be effective. It is now November 15, and you must place an order for the flu vaccine.

Scenario 1—If you order Vaccine A, 300 people will be saved from severe illness and possible death. If you order Vaccine B, there is a 30 percent chance that 1,000 people will be saved, and a 70 percent chance that no one will be saved (1,000 people will come down with the flu and may die). Which vaccine do you order?

Now, look at the same problem defined somewhat differently.

Scenario 2—If you order Vaccine C, 700 people will die. If you order Vaccine D, there is a 30 percent chance that no one will die and a 70 percent chance that 1,000 people will die.[4]

Make a decision for both scenarios, then check the analysis in the WHAT DO YOU THINK? Note at the end of the chapter.

Defining a problem means identifying the precise nature and magnitude of the gap between desired conditions and actual conditions. An important part of problem definition involves determining the true **cause**(s) of the problem. Often, when the underlying cause of the problem can be identified, decision makers can gain greater insight into the problem. Further, potential solutions to the problem are often easier to identify. One common mistake made by decision makers in defining the problem is confusing *symptoms* with *causes*. A **symptom** is an observable event or condition that indicates a problem. A cough or a sneeze indicates that a person has a cold. The cough or sneeze is not the cause of the problem, and it is not the problem; it is simply evidence (symptom) that a problem exists. The problem is the cold. The cause of the problem may be a virus. Treating the symptoms usually does little to solve the underlying problem.

Similarly, in organizational work settings, decision makers must take care not to confuse symptoms, problems, and causes. Performance problems stem from a variety of causes such as employee ability, employee motivation, physical working conditions, lack of supplies, out-of-date equipment, organizational policies, lack of clear performance standards, and so on. Careful information gathering and analysis is imperative in uncovering the causes of a problem. Only when the underlying causes are identified can a lasting solution to the problem be developed.

Developing and Evaluating Alternatives

Once the problem has been identified, defined, and its causes determined, decision makers can begin considering alternative solutions. Ideally, all feasible alternative solutions should be identified and examined. Generally, decision makers first generate a list of all alternatives, and then eliminate those that are infeasible. A feasible alternative is one that, if chosen, could produce at least a minimally acceptable solution to the problem—but, the organization must have the ability and resources to implement it. An infeasible solution is one not expected to produce the desired outcomes, or which the organization cannot implement. Decision makers who search for all possible alternatives before making a choice are said to be **optimizers**—searchers for an optimal decision alternative.

Unfortunately, decision makers sometimes do not process all of the information that is available, but stop short of considering all possible decision alternatives. This tendency has been called *satisficing*.[5] **Satisficing** is choosing the first acceptable alternative, instead of continuing to search for all feasible alternatives in an attempt to ensure that the best alternative is chosen. Satisficers search only until they find an alternative which meets the minimal criteria that have been set.[6]

Decision makers become satisficers primarily because of the limitations of human information processing and perception. One of the problems associated with perception (discussed in Chapter 4) is that individuals sometimes do not receive or accept all of the information they are sent. They tend to try and reduce or simplify the information they must process by summarizing, condensing, modifying, and excluding certain pieces of information. Further, once an acceptable alternative has been identified, it becomes even more difficult to justify additional time and expense for a continued search for additional alternatives.

Selecting an Alternative

As a result of the previous step, decision makers are now faced with selecting the best alternative from a set of feasible decision alternatives. This task is not always easy. Sometimes the best alternative stands out from the others, but other times there is no clear-cut best alternative. How do you pick the best alternative?

At this point, decision makers should consider the objectives of making this particular decision. What exactly is to be accomplished? Comparing alternatives on the basis of objectives to be accomplished may reduce the set of feasible alternatives. In addition, decision makers should consider all possible outcomes of implementing each alternative. Sometimes an alternative that appears to be the best in terms of accomplishing objectives, also produces some undesirable side effects. Decision makers should attempt to forecast how implementing each alternative will affect different parts of the organization as well as elements in the organization's environment (e.g., customers, suppliers, unions, stockholders). For example, decision makers commonly use a computer simulation program that forecasts results for different decision alternatives.

Implementation

The implementation stage of the decision-making process involves putting the chosen decision alternative into effect. Decision makers must not develop the mindset that once an alternative has been selected their responsibility is ended. Even the best alternative, if it is implemented haphazardly, may be ineffective. Thus, an important part of decision making is implementing the chosen alternative.

Careful planning is critical to implementation. These plans must include consideration of exactly how the alternative will be introduced, what effects the implementation will have on other parts of the organization—as well as segments of its external environment, and how employees will react to the change. One potential major problem with implementing decision alternatives is the natural tendency for human beings to resist change. Generally, this resistance results from a fear of the unknown and can be overcome by providing information about the change to employees and involving them in the implementation process.[7] Resistance to change will be discussed in more detail in Chapter 17.

Follow-Up

Organizational decision making occurs in an environment that is constantly changing and exerting pressure for change upon the organization. Therefore, decision making must be a flexible, dynamic process rather than a fixed, inflexible process. This changing environment means that the conditions and assumptions on which decisions are based may change, rendering a decision ineffective. This possibility suggests the need for continual follow-up to check on the degree to which decisions are producing desired outcomes. Decision makers must evaluate their decisions in light of the results expected or objectives set. Then, if the problem or performance gap remains, a different alternative can be selected the next time the decision must be made.

Decision makers should attempt to evaluate their decisions *before* the final results are in; that is, before and during implementation of the alternative. Decision makers should continue to evaluate the chosen alternative to determine if it appears that the change will have the intended effect. This provides decision makers with an opportunity to make slight modifications in the decision or its implementation, to increase chances that it will be effective.

INDIVIDUAL VERSUS GROUP DECISION MAKING

Decisions in organizations are commonly made by both individuals and groups. One important task of managers is to determine whether individual or group decision making is most appropriate. The behavioral scientists have identified a number of characteristics of group decision making to assist managers in comparing individual versus group decision making.

Advantages of Group Decision Making

One of the greatest advantages of groups is the variety of experience, education, skills, viewpoints, and ideas which members bring to decision-making situations. More specifically, advantages of group decision making include:[8]

1. A diversity of viewpoints. This dissimilarity allows the group to consider a variety of approaches to a problem.
2. Diversity of knowledge and experience. Each individual brings unique knowledge and experience to the group, providing more complete information on which to base a decision. This cooperation typically results in a more accurate decision than would be made by an individual. However, it usually takes much longer for a group to make a decision than it takes for an individual, because of the greater amounts of information that must be processed.
3. Acceptance of the decision. People who are involved in making a decision are more likely to accept that decision and be committed to ensuring its successful implementation.

Determine whether situations call for group or individual decision making.

Discuss advantages and disadvantages of group decision making.

Disadvantages to Group Decision Making

There are some situations when individual decision making might be more effective than group decision making. Disadvantages to group decision making include:

1. Time consumption. As mentioned earlier, groups typically take longer than individuals to reach a decision.

PART TWO: Individual Relationships

2. Social pressure. There is a danger that those members who feel insecure or who want to be accepted by the group may simply go along with the majority—even when they have a better solution or when they are convinced the proposed decision will result in disaster. It can be very unpleasant being a single dissenting opinion in a group. It is much easier to simply conform to the wishes of the group, than to voice disagreement.
3. Reluctance by some to participate. Not every member of a group may feel comfortable voicing his opinions in front of the other members; some people become timid or shy in the presence of other people. However, the major advantage of group decision making is the inclusion and consideration of the knowledge, experience, and viewpoints of all members. Thus, group leaders have a responsibility to encourage all members to voice their opinions and concerns, to take advantage of group decision making. The nominal group technique, which will be discussed later, is one way to encourage participation.

Two other potential problems associated with group decision making, *groupthink* and *groupshift,* require attention.

Groupthink

When individuals are more concerned with reaching agreement or consensus than they are with making a high-quality decision, **groupthink** occurs.[9] In fact, the group probably does not even consider the possibility that it is not making a high-quality decision. This concern for agreement places a great deal of pressure on members to go along with the group, even though they may disagree

As groups increase in size, it becomes more difficult for members to participate in decision making.

> **Exhibit 11.2**
> Causes and symptoms of groupthink
>
> ### Causes of Groupthink
>
> - Group is isolated from outsiders
> - High group cohesiveness
> - Highly directive leader
> - Poor use of group decision-making techniques
>
> ### Symptoms of Groupthink
>
> - **Illusion of invulnerability**—The group emphasizes its strengths and minimizes its weaknesses. Reluctance to admit any weaknesses. Feeling group can do no wrong.
> - **Illusion of morality**—Belief that what the group is doing is good and right. Allows group members to label any criticism aimed at the group as simply incorrect.
> - **Rationalization**—Group explains away any criticism or conflicting information.
> - **Stereotyping**—Critics of the group or rival groups are labeled as wrong or evil.
> - **Pressure for conformity**—Group members are pressured to go along with the group's illusions and stereotypes. Any member who might express dissent or question the group's actions would be pressured by the other members to get in line or get out.
> - **Self-censorship**—Group members suppress any doubts or reservations they have about the group's actions or decisions to preserve the closeness and cohesiveness of the group.
> - **Illusion of unanimity**—Because of self-censorship and pressure for conformity, even those members who disagree are likely to remain silent. This silence is interpreted as agreement. Thus, members perceive that unanimity exists.
> - **Self-appointed mindguards**—Some members take it upon themselves to screen (protect) the group from conflicting information and critics.

with the group's present course. Have you ever been in a group where you felt pressure to "go along"? What happened, exactly? Causes and symptoms of groupthink are presented in Exhibit 11.2.

Overcoming Groupthink

The task facing the manager or group leader is to minimize the effects of groupthink. There are several approaches:

1. Encourage criticism. Members should be encouraged to voice disagreement with proposed decisions. Ideas should be discussed openly with careful consideration of any possible drawbacks to proposed decisions.

2. Encourage development of several alternatives. Group members can get locked into thinking in one particular direction. They hear a proposal that appears to meet their needs and do not consider any alternatives. Group leaders should try and prevent members from making a final decision until several alternatives have been proposed and discussed in detail.
3. Assign members to play "devil's advocate." One or more group members may be assigned to challenge all proposed decisions. This person must consider every possible drawback to each proposal. Sometimes decisions cause problems in the long term because all of the possible effects were not carefully considered. Case in point: several years ago, a major airline company developed a plan to encourage businesses to use its airline instead of the competition. The airline announced that business travelers could take their spouse along on overnight business trips for one-half of the regular fare. The promotion was a great success. The airline was so pleased with the results that it wrote a nice letter to the spouse of each passenger, to thank them for flying on that particular airline, and encourage them to choose the airline the next time they were invited along on a business trip. The airline was then bombarded with angry letters from former passengers whose spouse had received one of their letters, but hadn't been on any business trip with their mate for quite some time!
4. Include outsiders. It is often a good idea to bring in an outsider's point of view. Sometimes people unfamiliar with a decision can look at it differently and see things that group members, who have been involved in detailed discussions on the matter, cannot see. Outsiders may be able to see potential problems that insiders have overlooked.
5. Hold last-chance meetings. Once a decision has been made, it is prudent to wait for a few days and then hold a *last-chance meeting*. This delay gives group members a few days to think about their decision and one last chance to reconsider before the decision is implemented. Sometimes a decision will look different after a few days.

Groupshift

Groupshift is a process whereby group members exaggerate their initial positions. That is, if most group members come into a meeting prepared to make a somewhat risky decision, the final decision will tend to be even more risky (risky shift). If members come into a meeting with a relatively conservative attitude toward the decision, the final decision will tend to be even more conservative (conservative shift).[10]

There is some evidence to suggest that groups move toward risk more often than they move toward a more conservative position.[11] This trend may be because individual group members are able to hide their responsibility in a group. That is, it would be difficult hold any single group member entirely responsible for a bad group decision.

Minimizing groupshift is extremely difficult since group members are generally not aware that it is occurring. Managers or group leaders should keep the group focused on objectives during discussion of alternatives, to keep the group on target. They must discourage members reinforcing one another's initial positions.

Group Decision-Making Techniques

Typical group decision-making involves little structure. A leader calls a meeting, presents the problem, moderates a discussion, and eventually calls for a vote or agreement on which alternative should be selected. This traditional group decision-making process provides many opportunities for difficulties (e.g., groupthink, groupshift, lack of participation by some members) to arise.

Nominal Group Technique (NGT)

The **nominal group technique (NGT)** was designed to overcome many of these problems. All group members convene—just as in traditional group decision making—but interaction and communication among members are restricted. The name "nominal group technique" is appropriate because NGT groups are groups only in the nominal sense of the word (i.e., members are physically present and working on the same problem). The nominal group process follows these steps:

Develop strategies for effective group decision making.

1. The group leader presents the problem to the group, including any assumptions or constraints on the solution.
2. Members then silently and independently generate ideas, questions, and comments; they are written down and turned in to the group leader.
3. The leader summarizes the written comments and presents this information to the group.
4. Each member presents one idea, which the group leader records on a flip chart or chalkboard. No discussion is held until all ideas have been presented.
5. The group discusses and evaluates the ideas in front of them.
6. Each group member then silently and independently ranks the ideas. The final decision is determined by the alternative with the highest aggregate ranking.
7. Return to step 2 and repeat the cycle, if necessary (i.e., if no alternative clearly emerges as best).

The primary advantage of the NGT is that it overcomes member reluctance to participate since much of the process is completed individually. It may also stimulate creative thinking since there is typically less criticism of ideas in the NGT process than in the traditional decision-making process. Thus, the full advantages of group decision making may be realized. Research suggests that the NGT compares favorably with other forms of decision making in terms of number of ideas, quality of ideas, time and cost, and in providing group members with feelings of accomplishment.[12]

CREATIVITY

Creativity is becoming increasingly important in organizations as they, and the environments in which they operate, become more and more complex and dynamic. Further, the external environments of many organizations are also becoming more uncertain. This makes flexibility and adaptability critical to organizational success—even survival. Creativity is needed to help the organization adjust to its complex and rapidly changing environment. Several of these environmental forces have been, or will be, discussed in this book. These influences include the movement away from a manufacturing-based economy to a service-based economy, the dramatic increase in computer and communications technology, and the internationalization of business. All of these factors make creativity a necessity to remain competitive. Also, creativity is needed at all levels of the organization.

Several leading corporations have recognized the importance of creativity. Kodak and Goodyear have implemented innovation committees in each division. 3M encourages its research scientists to devote 15 percent of their time to whatever interests them. One of the outcomes of the 3M program, mentioned in the Prologue, was the development of Post-it Notes, one of the company's most successful products.[13] The notes developer used this time to develop a solution to his problem of marking pages in his hymnal.

What Is Creativity?

Creativity has historically been viewed as somewhat mysterious and even magical. For many years, it was believed to be a gift; some people were born with creative ability, others were not. As a result of the mystique, creativity has remained a nebulous concept, eluding precise definition. Until recently, only limited research examined the creative process to aid in our understanding of this phenomenon. Fortunately, recent research in the behavioral sciences has begun to uncover some of its mysteries. It now appears that individuals can learn to become more creative.

RETURN TO THE PROLOGUE

How did Art Fry come up with the idea to use an adhesive which everyone viewed as a failure, in developing "Post-it Notes"? Was this some type of magical insight, or light bulb flashing on as is commonly depicted in comic strips? Actually, most creative acts involve a great deal of preparation and hard work. Creative individuals do seem to have an ability to integrate seemingly unrelated ideas or information. However, they have developed an expertise or knowledge background in the area in which they are working.

Creativity has been defined as "the process of developing original, imaginative, and innovative perspectives on situations."[14] For example, a creative decision maker might develop an entirely new solution to an existing problem. Another popular definition of creativity says that creativity is "the reorganization of experience into new configurations."[15] Combining these two definitions gives a picture of what is currently believed about creativity. It does result in a unique or innovative solution or perspective. However, it is not a magical bolt of lightning; it is based on an individual's existing experience and knowledge. According to one author,

Creativity is a function of knowledge, imagination, and evaluation. The greater our knowledge, the more ideas, patterns, or combinations we can achieve. But merely having the knowledge does not guarantee the formation of new patterns; the bits and pieces must be shaken up and interrelated in new ways. Then the embryonic ideas must be evaluated and developed into new usable ideas.[16]

This view of creativity suggests that creative individuals have substantial knowledge or experience with the problem they are facing. In addition, they are able to combine information at their disposal in new and unusual ways to arrive at an innovative solution.

The Creative Process

The creative process consists of four stages: preparation, incubation, insight, and verification.[17] The description of this process is consistent with the view of creativity described above.

Preparation
Preparation involves education, learning, gathering and storing information, and acquiring experience. A professor of management is not likely to wake up one morning with a cure for cancer. He does not have the background or information to integrate in new ways to arrive at a solution to the problem. However, a biomedical researcher who has been working in cancer research for years may actually do just that some day. He does have the background. If this person also has the ability to integrate the information in new ways, such a breakthrough may come.

Incubation
During the incubation stage, the mind does not consciously focus on the problem. Incubation may take place during relaxation, sleep, exercise, or socializing with friends. Particularly after an intense period of preparation, individuals need some time to allow the information to fall into place. If individuals were to continue to focus on the problem, they might not be successful in developing an innovative solution. The mind needs time to sort out all of the information that has been collected, store it in various categories, and find relationships among these categories.

Insight
The insight stage follows incubation. During incubation, the subconscious mind has processed the information relevant to the problem. Insight is the point at which the conscious mind becomes aware of a new idea or solution resulting from the incubation stage. It is a sudden moment of inspiration where relationships between pieces of information fall into place and a feasible, innovative solution becomes apparent. The accompanying Human Relations in Action box describes one example of insight which not only helped keep a company from going bankrupt, but also substantially improved a common consumer product.[18]

HUMAN RELATIONS IN ACTION

Insight at Aquanautics Corporation

Aquanautics Corporation began research in 1981 to develop an artificial gill that would enable people to live and work under water. They tried a number of different chemical substitutes for hemoglobin, which is the substance in blood that attaches itself to oxygen and carries it throughout the body. After five years of research, they had not developed a chemical that was effective. The company was near bankruptcy, having spent substantial sums on this research project. Then a group of food packagers became aware of Aquanautics research on pulling oxygen out of sea water. The food packagers were interested in exactly the opposite process—how to keep oxygen out of food products. As a result, Aquanautics has developed a product, Longlife, that is used to coat the inside of food containers. The product, which looks like "rusty sand," soaks up oxygen from inside the container and extends the shelf life of the food products. Further, since Longlife changes color when saturated with oxygen, it indicates spoilage or tampering.

Source: Hamilton, J. O'C. A startup stumbles onto a solution to spoilage. *Business Week,* June 27, 1988, p. 91.

Verification

During the verification stage, decision makers search for evidence that their innovation solution will actually work. More traditional decision-making techniques such as cost-benefit analysis are used to determine if the proposed solution is feasible. For example, using surplus corn produced by America's farmers to manufacture gasohol (an alcohol and gasoline mixture) was a creative solution to the energy crisis of the 1970s. However, the cost of the process along with the small modification necessary to automobile engines, makes this process infeasible until the price of gasoline increases substantially.

Learning To Be More Creative

Suggest how individuals can be more creative.

One of the keys to more creative thinking is to overcome narrow thinking patterns—called **mental locks** by one expert on creativity.[19] Creative thinkers tend to be able to see beyond convention or "the way we always do things around here." Creativity can be stifled if we become accustomed to handling problems and decisions in a structured, routine manner. Exhibit 11.3 presents several mental locks that can stifle creativity. Overcoming these mental locks can open the door to more creative decision making.

Increasing Your Creativity

Several techniques for increasing creativity have been developed. Most of them are designed to overcome rigid thinking and unlock the creativity that already exists in everyone. Two of the more popular creativity-enhancing techniques are brainstorming and idea checklists.

Exhibit 11.3
Mental locks which stifle creativity

1. Looking for the "right" answer. Any problem or decision may have several right answers. Looking for a single right answer may lead the decision maker to neglect other answers which are equally right, and which may result in a slightly different or even better solution.
2. Always trying to be logical. Organizations are not always completely logical. They are made up of emotional and political human beings. Sometimes decisions are influenced by these illogical factors. To understand organizational decision making, one cannot always be logical.
3. Strictly following the rules. Strict adherence to rules limits decision making. Rules place boundaries around solutions. If the rules are restrictive, innovative solutions may be ruled out without even being considered.
4. Insisting on being practical. Impractical ideas and solutions to problems can sometimes trigger new ideas and perspectives which, in turn, can lead to practical creative solutions.
5. Avoiding ambiguity. Ambiguity is part of the creative process. Creativity implies entering new and unfamiliar territory. Avoiding ambiguity can stifle creativity.
6. Fearing and avoiding failure. Fear of failure can cause decision makers to avoid ambiguous and risky solutions. Since creative solutions are unique, they involve a certain amount of risk.
7. Forgetting how to play. Playful experimentation may lead to creative insights. Adults too often forget how to play.
8. Becoming too specialized. Over-specialization may lead to narrow thinking. Learning about unfamiliar things (such as jobs, departments, and organizations other than your own) may lead to creative insight.
9. Not wanting to look foolish. Decision makers often avoid asking questions which they fear may make them look foolish. Unfortunately, the answers to such questions may stimulate thinking and lead to creative insight. As some wise individual once said, "The only foolish question is the one which is not asked."
10. Saying "I'm not creative." If you tell yourself you are not creative, you are not likely to be motivated to try to become more creative. Everyone is creative and can learn to become even more creative.

Source: Based upon von Oech, R. *A whack on the side of the head.* New York: Warner, 1983.

Brainstorming

Brainstorming is a simple, yet effective, technique. A group of six to eight people is presented with a problem and asked to generate as many ideas as possible. One of the keys of brainstorming is the focus on idea generation, not

> **Exhibit 11.4**
> Four rules for brainstorming sessions
>
> 1. No criticism of others' ideas.
> 2. The wilder the idea the better.
> 3. Emphasize quantity of ideas over quality of ideas.
> 4. Suggestions for combining/improving/extending others' ideas are encouraged.

idea evaluation. In fact, criticism of others' ideas is prohibited, since it is believed that criticism might cause members to become defensive and stop the free flow of ideas.[20] Four rules for brainstorming sessions appear in Exhibit 11.4.

Idea Checklists

Several different versions of **idea checklists** exist.[21] One of the most popular is a list of "idea-generating questions." These general questions can be applied to any problem or decision, to generate additional ideas. A sample of such questions appears in Exhibit 11.5.

Creative Organizations

Identify ways organizations can encourage employee creativity.

Organizations can provide a work environment that stimulates creativity among employees. Creative organizations tend to be open and flexible. They do not provide rigid rules for employees or engage in close supervision.[22] Employees are encouraged to take calculated risks with the knowledge that they will not be punished for failure. Communications in creative organizations tend to be open and are not required to follow formal lines of authority.[23] Employees are encouraged to make contacts with people outside the or-

> **Exhibit 11.5**
> Sample questions from an idea checklist
>
> 1. Is this product similar to something else?
> 2. How is it different from other similar products?
> 2. Can it be made smaller? Larger? Shorter? Taller? Lighter? Heavier? Different shape?
> 3. Can it be rearranged?
> 4. Can different materials be used?
> 5. Can it be put to other uses?
> 6. Can other materials/processes/ingredients be substituted?

DEVELOPING YOUR HUMAN RELATIONS SKILLS

Managers and employees alike can benefit from paying increased attention to their decision-making activities. Similarly, both can benefit from efforts designed to increase their creativity. These guidelines apply:

1. Concentrate on problem recognition and problem definition. These critical steps are often overlooked. Carefully investigate problems so that you can clearly differentiate between symptoms of problems and their causes.
2. Consider whether the problem is important enough for you to be an optimizer, rather than a satisficer. If it is important, then do not allow yourself to accept the first reasonable solution that comes along. Continue to gather information until you are sure that you have identified all feasible alternatives. If the problem is not extremely important, the cost of gathering additional information may outweigh the benefits of identifying the optimal solution.
3. When implementing solutions to problems, remember that people have a natural tendency to resist change. Implementation involves plans for overcoming employees' resistance to change by providing information about the change and involving employees in the decision-making process.
4. Don't tell yourself that you are not creative. Everyone is creative. Some individuals need to overcome mental blocks or patterns of rigid thinking to unleash their creativity.
5. When faced with a problem or decision that requires a creative solution, make sure you adequately prepare. Research the problem carefully, gathering as much information as possible.
6. Don't attempt to force a creative solution. After preparation, you must allow time for incubation. In other words, relax! Engage in your favorite hobby or athletic activity. Let the subconscious mind have time to integrate the information you have collected.

Managers can take additional steps to provide an environment that encourages and supports employee creativity.

1. Encourage open communications. Don't insist that communications follow formal lines of authority.
2. Give employees adequate autonomy and control over their work. Substantial freedom is necessary for creative activities.
3. Do not create rigid rules, regulations, policies, or procedures. Do not engage in close supervision. Employees must have the flexibility to branch out in different directions.
4. Creativity must be part of the organization's culture. Employees must perceive that top management views creativity as important. Reward creative individuals. Monetary rewards are important and effective, but so are recognition and praise.

ganization as sources of new ideas and perspectives. Finally, creative organizations tend to hire employees with substantially different backgrounds who can bring new insights into the decision-making process.[24]

If creativity is valued by the organization, it must be rewarded. Individuals who develop creative solutions to problems must be provided with rewards that equal their contribution to the organization. Further, employees must perceive that creativity is a part of the organization's culture that top management believes is important. Finally, organizations must not stifle creativity with unnecessary rules, regulations, policies, and management actions.

SUMMARY

Decision making is an extremely important activity at all levels of an organization. As employees make decisions regarding how they will behave and interact with other organizational members, the human relations climate is formed.

The decision-making process consists of six interrelated steps: problem recognition, problem definition, developing and evaluating alternatives, selecting an alternative, implementation, and follow-up. A problem is a current or potential situation that may prevent the organization from accomplishing its objectives. A performance gap is the difference between actual performance and desired performance. Managers may be more effective at selecting alternatives than recognizing and defining problems. One common mistake made by decision makers when defining the problem is confusing symptoms with causes.

Decision makers do not always process all of the information available to them. Decision makers who diligently search for all possible alternatives in an attempt to find the absolute best solution are said to be optimizers. Decision makers who accept the first acceptable alternative rather than continuing to search for the best alternative are referred to as satisficers.

Decisions in organizations are made by both individuals and groups. One important task of managers is to determine when individual or group decision making is most effective. Attributes of group decision making include a diversity of viewpoints, a diversity of knowledge and experience, and facilitation of acceptance of the decision. Disadvantages of group decision making include a reluctance by some group members to participate, social pressure, and time requirements. Groupthink occurs when group members are more concerned with reaching agreement than with making a high-quality decision. This misdirection may lead to ignoring information which contradicts the proposed decision, and making inappropriate and ineffective decisions. To overcome groupthink, managers should encourage criticism, encourage the development of several alternatives, assign a member to play devil's advocate, include outsiders in the decision-making process, and hold last-chance meetings. Groupshift is a process whereby group members exaggerate their initial positions. If individuals come to the group prepared to make a somewhat risky decision, interaction with other group members reinforces this position, leading the group to make an even riskier decision. If group members come prepared to make a conservative decision, interaction leads to an even more conservative position.

Traditional group decision making occurs when a group leader calls a meeting, presents a problem, moderates a discussion, and then calls for a vote on which alternative to select. This process provides many opportunities for groupthink, groupshift, social pressure, and other problems to affect decision making. The nominal group technique (NGT) was designed to overcome these problems and encourage all members to participate in the decision-making process.

Creativity is the process of developing original, imaginative, and innovative perspectives on situations by reorganizing experience into new configurations. The creative process consists of four stages: preparation, incubation, insight, and verification. To become more creative, individuals must overcome mental locks, which stifle creativity by restricting decision making to conventional methods. Organizations that encourage employee creativity are open and flexible, do not use rigid rules and close supervision, encourage employees to take calculated risks, encourage employees to make contacts with outsiders, and hire employees with different backgrounds. Organizations must not stifle creativity with rigid rules, procedures, policies, and management actions. In addition, it must be clear to employees that top management believes that creativity is important. Finally, creativity must be rewarded.

KEY TERMS

decision making
problem recognition
problem definition
problem
performance gap
causes
symptom
optimizers
satisficing
groupthink
groupshift
nominal group technique (NGT)
creativity
mental locks
brainstorming
idea checklists

DISCUSSION QUESTIONS

1. Describe the problem-recognition stage of the decision-making process. Why are managers not particularly effective at this stage?
2. Why is problem definition such a critical step in the decision-making process?
3. Differentiate between symptoms and causes.
4. What are optimizers and satisficers? When is each style most appropriate?
5. What are some advantages to group decision making?
6. What are some disadvantages to group decision making?
7. What is groupthink? Why does it occur? What effect does it have? What can be done about it?
8. What is groupshift? Why does it occur and what can be done about it?
9. Describe how managers can use the nominal group technique to make group decision making more effective.
10. Explain creativity and the creative process.
11. What can individuals do to become more creative?
12. What can organizations do to encourage employee creativity?

EXERCISE 11.1

Are You Creative?

PURPOSE: To measure different aspects of creativity.

GROUP SIZE: Any number
TIME REQUIRED: 15–25 minutes.
INTRODUCTION: Carefully consider each of the following statements. Place an "A" by each statement with which you agree, a "B" if you are undecided or don't know, and a "C" if you disagree.

_____ 1. I place relatively greater values on rewards such as salary and status than on "job interest" and "challenge."

_____ 2. I always work with a great deal of certainty that I'm following the correct procedures for solving a particular problem.

_____ 3. I like work that has regular hours.

_____ 4. One of my primary concerns is to discover the kind of work that would be most natural for me, most inclusive of and challenging to all my capacities.

_____ 5. I prefer specific instructions to those which leave many details optional.

_____ 6. I concentrate harder than most people on whatever interests me.

_____ 7. I usually work things out for myself rather than get someone to show me.

_____ 8. I apply myself longer and harder in the absence of external pressure than do most people.

_____ 9. I seldom get behind in my work.

_____ 10. I don't enjoy tackling a job that might involve many unknown difficulties.

_____ 11. I seldom begin work on a problem that I can only dimly sense and not yet express.

_____ 12. I am more inclined to derive my major satisfactions from people than from my work.

_____ 13. I don't mind routine work if I have to do it.

_____ 14. I sometimes get so involved with a new idea that I forget to do the things I ought to be doing.

_____ 15. I regard myself more as a specialist than a generalist.

_____ 16. I prefer tackling problems for which there are precise answers.

_____ 17. When a certain approach to a problem doesn't work, I can easily drop it.

___ 18. Intuitive hunches are unreliable guides in problem solving.
___ 19. I have never felt very inspired.
___ 20. I don't like to ask questions that show ignorance.
___ 21. I get irritated when somebody interrupts me when I'm working on something I really enjoy.
___ 22. I often get my best ideas when doing nothing in particular.
___ 23. Ideas often run through my head, preventing sleep.
___ 24. In evaluating information, its source is more important to me than its content.
___ 25. I feel that a logical step-by-step method is best for solving problems.
___ 26. People who are willing to entertain "crackpot" ideas are impractical.
___ 27. Complex problems and situations have no appeal to me.
___ 28. I have vivid imagery.
___ 29. I cannot get excited about ideas that may never lead to anything.
___ 30. Daydreaming has provided the impetus for many of my more important projects.
___ 31. If I were a college professor, I would rather teach fact courses than those involving theory.
___ 32. I sometimes "get lost" in the library for hours on end, just browsing and looking at interesting books.
___ 33. I have broader interests and am more widely informed than are most people of equal intelligence and educational background.
___ 34. I have many hobbies.

Scoring Key

Attitudes Toward Work

	A	B	C
1.	−1	0	+1
2.	0	+1	0
3.	0	+1	0
4.	+2	0	−2
5.	−1	0	+1
6.	+2	0	−2
7.	+1	+2	0
8.	+1	0	−1
9.	−1	0	+1
10.	−1	0	+1
11.	−1	0	+1
12.	−1	0	+1
13.	0	+1	+2
14.	+1	0	−1
15.	−1	0	+1
16.	−1	0	+1
17.	+1	0	−1
18.	−2	0	+2
19.	−2	0	+2
20.	−1	0	+1
21.	+1	0	−1
22.	+1	0	−1
23.	+1	+2	0
24.	−2	0	+2
25.	−2	0	+2
26.	−1	0	+1
27.	−1	0	+1
28.	+1	0	−1
29.	−1	0	+1
30.	+2	0	−2

Interests

	A	B	C
31.	−1	0	+1
32.	+1	0	−1
33.	+2	0	−2
34.	+1	0	−1
35.	+1	0	−1
36.	−1	0	+1
37.	−1	0	+1
38.	+1	0	−1
39.	−1	0	+1
40.	+1	0	−1
41.	−1	0	+1
42.	+1	0	−1

Your Total Score

43 to 53—Especially Creative
27 to 42—Very Creative
12 to 26—Above Average Creativity
5 to 11—Average Creativity
−2 to −4—Below Average Creativity
−3 to −38—Non-Creative

_____ 35. I can learn more from self-instruction than through taking courses.

_____ 36. I like hobbies that involve collecting things.

_____ 37. I always consider carefully the consequences of each of my actions.

_____ 38. People often say that I'm somewhat absentminded.

_____ 39. I keep my things well organized.

_____ 40. I like to stick my neck out even if risk-taking is not warranted.

_____ 41. I resent things being uncertain and unpredictable.

_____ 42. The room in which I work is quite cluttered and messy.

Part II: Characteristics of the Creative Person.

1. Fluency: the ability to generate and juggle a large number of ideas when confronting a problem.
2. Flexibility: the ability to explore a wide variety of approaches to the problem and to adapt quickly when necessary.
3. Sensitivity to Problems: the ability to see the challenges that have escaped the attention of others.
4. Originality: can think of more unique solutions, with thoughts not jammed up with stereotypes.
5. Curiosity: exhibits high imagination, fantasy-making and interest beyond one's own specialization (intellectually restless).
6. Openness to Feelings and the Unconscious: more expressive and more responsive to emotions.
7. Motivation: has a strong desire to create.
8. Persistence and Concentration: has enormous capacity for taking pains in the face of difficulties and frustrations.
9. Ability to Think in Images: can readily envision thought.
10. Tolerance of Ambiguity: is open to the intricate, confusing and paradoxical qualities of most situations.

CASE 11.1

Mike's Restaurant

Mike Dumler is a Professor of Management at Illinois State University, which is located in the twin cities of Bloomington/Normal, Illinois. Bloomington/Normal is a rapidly growing area of around 100,000 people. Unemployment has always been lower than in most Illinois cities, and recently, with the opening of the Diamond-Star automobile manufacturing plant, a new IRS facility, and several new shopping malls, more people are working than ever before.

Mike has accumulated around $75,000 and is considering various investments. He has always wanted to open a restaurant. The recent increase in the population of the twin cities and the number of dual-career couples suggest that the time could be right for a new restaurant. Since there are two universities (one with 25,000 students and one with 2,500 students) and several major white-collar and professional employers in Bloomington/Normal, Mike believes that a very classy restaurant, catering to the "Yuppie" (young upwardly mobile professional) would have the best chance of success. There are a few nice restaurants in the twin cities, but nothing on the order of Arnaud's of New Orleans or Daley's of Atlanta. One thing Mike is sure of—he wants his restaurant to be *different*.

QUESTIONS

1. What type of information should Mike gather in order to make an effective decision about his restaurant?
2. Develop several alternatives (types of restaurants) to present to Mike for consideration. BE CREATIVE!
3. Select and recommend one of the alternatives you identified in question 2. Justify your recommendation.
4. Present your recommendation to the class for evaluation. Analyze your decision making process. Were you a satisficer or an optimizer?

CASE 11.2

A Chance to Be Creative

In class, your instructor will assign some of you to work alone, while others will be assigned to groups. Your assignment is to develop as many different uses as possible for the empty clear plastic housing of a Bic ball point pen. Your instructor will tell you how much time you have to complete the assignment. No other instructions or guidance will be given.

QUESTIONS

1. Compare the results of individuals' decisions with those of the groups. Did individuals or groups develop the most uses? Did individuals or groups develop the most creative uses?
2. What does this case illustrate about individual versus group decision making?

---

11. Background of Fundamental Knowledge: generalists rather than specialists.

Part III: Discussion (15–25 minutes).

How important is creativity in today's society? In today's workplace? Justify your response. Consider the following questions:

1. In what situations is creativity most useful?
2. How can you enhance your own creativity?
3. Are there times when creativity may be a hindrance?
4. Who "fits in" better—a creative person or a noncreative person? Why?

Adapted from Raudsepp, E. *How creative are you?* New York: G.P. Putnam, 1981, pp. 23–39 and 103–138.

REFERENCES

[1] McCormick, J. The wisdom of Solomon. *Newsweek*, August 17, 1987, 62–63.

[2] Wright, P. The harassed decision maker: Time pressures, distractions, and the use of evidence. *Journal of Applied Psychology*, 1974, 59, 555–561.

[3] Decision-making exercise based on the work of Tversky, A. & Kahneman, D. The framing of decisions and the psychology of choice. *Science*, 1981, 211, 453–458.

[4] March, J.G. & Simon, H.A. *Organizations*. New York: John Wiley & Sons, 1958.

[5] Lawrence, P.R. How to deal with resistance to change. *Harvard Business Review*, 1969, 47(1), 4–12 and 166–176; Nord, W.R. & Durance, D.E. Beyond resistance to change: Behavioral science on the firing line. *Organizational Dynamics*, 1975, 4, 2–20; Sagie, A., Elizur, D. & Greenbaum, C.W. Job experience, persuasion strategy and resistance to change: An experimental study. *Journal of Occupational Behavior*, 1985, 6, 157–162.

[6] Maier, N.R.F. Assets and liabilities in group problem solving: The need for an integrative function. *Psychological Review*, 1967, 89, 239–249; Hill, G.W. Group versus individual performance: Are N + 1 heads better than one? *Psychological Bulletin*, 1982, 91, 517–539.

[7] Simon, H.A. *Administrative Behavior*. Third edition. New York: Free Press, 1976.

[8] Janis, I.L. Group think. *Psychology Today*, 1971, 5, 43–46, 74–76.

[9] Myers, D.G. & Lamm, H. The group polarization phenomenon. *Psychological Bulletin*, 1976, 85, 602–627.

[10] Clark, R.D. Group-induced shift toward risk: A critical appraisal. *Psychological Bulletin*, 1971, 80, 251–270.

[11] Delbecq, A., Van de Ven, A. & Gustafson, D. *Group techniques for program planning*. Glenview, IL: Scott, Foresman and Co., 1975; Hoffman, L.R. Improving the problem-solving process in managerial groups. In Guzzo, R.A. (Ed.) *Improving group decision making in organizations*. New York: Academic Press, 1982, 95–126.

[12] Creativity: A special report. *Success!* March 1985, 32, 55–61.

[13] Whitney, C.S. *Creative thinking*. New York: Reinhold, 1958.

[14] Maier, N.R.F., Julius, M. & Thurber, J. Studies in creativity: Individual differences in the storing and utilization of information. *The American Journal of Psychology,* 1967, *80,* 492–519.

[15] Parnes, S.J. Learning creative behavior. *The Futurist,* 1984, *18,* 30–31.

[16] Wallas, G. *The art of thought.* New York: Harcourt Brace Jovanovich, 1926; Busse, T.V. & Mansfield, R.S. Theories of the creative process: A review and a perspective. *Journal of Creative Behavior,* 1980, *4,* 91–103.

[17] von Oech, R. *A whack on the side of the head.* New York: Warner, 1983.

[18] Hamilton, J. O'C. A startup stumbles onto a solution to spoilage. *Business Week,* June 27, 1988, p. 91.

[19] Meehan, R.H. Programs that foster creativity and innovation. *Personnel,* 1986, *63*(2), 31–35.

[20] Osborn, A.F. *Applied imagination: Principles and procedures for creative problem-solving.* Third edition. New York: Scribner, 1963.

[21] Davis, G.A. *Creativity is forever.* Dubuque, IA: Kendall/Hunt Publishing Co., 1983.

[22] de Chambreau, F.A. & Mackenzie, F. Intrapreneurship. *Personnel Journal,* 1986, *65*(7), 40–45.

[23] Steiner, G.A. (Ed.) *The creative organization.* Chicago: University of Chicago Press, 1965.

[24] Delbecq, A. & Mills, P. Managerial practices that enhance innovation. *Organizational Dynamics,* Summer 1985, 24–34.

WHAT DO YOU THINK? NOTE

This exercise illustrates the effect of how a problem is defined or framed. In the first scenario, you are faced with two somewhat risky alternatives. Most people choose Vaccine A, since the chance of saving 300 people is more acceptable than a high chance of saving no one. Most people tend to be risk-averse when faced with a problem defined in this manner.

The same basic problem is defined as a risk-taking problem in Scenario 2. Ordering Vaccine C, which results in 700 people dying, is the same as ordering Vaccine A and saving 300 (out of 1,000) people. Ordering Vaccine D, which results in a 70 percent chance of 1,000 people dying, is the same as ordering Vaccine B, which results in a 30 percent chance of saving 1,000 people.

In Scenario 1, the problem is a risk-avoiding problem while in Scenario 2, the problem is a risk-taking problem. Most people choose Vaccine D in Scenario 2 since a 30 percent chance of saving all 1,000 people seems more acceptable than allowing 700 people to die.

Remember, the problem in Scenario 1 is identical to the problem in Scenario 2; it is simply defined differently. However, the manner in which the problem was defined led people to make different decisions.

PART THREE

Group Relationships

CHAPTER TWELVE

Relationships Within Groups

PROLOGUE

One of the points to be emphasized in this chapter is that groups often change the behavior of individuals. That is, individuals often do things in groups that they would never do on their own. Consider the following example. . .

Tom works as a machinist in a large manufacturing plant which pays its employees on a "piece-rate with bonus" system. For every unit produced up to the standard of 60 units per day, Tom earns $1.88. Thus, just by meeting the standard of 60 units per day (one unit of output every eight minutes), Tom could earn $564 per week. For every unit of output over the standard, the company pays at the rate of $2.05 per unit. Therefore, if Tom produced at the rate of just under one unit every seven minutes, he would produce approximately 70 units per day and earn an additional $102.50 per week. Tom just bought a new house and his oldest daughter just left for college, so he could really use the additional income. Besides, he knows that he could produce around 80 units per day if he really worked at it. However, like the other employees, Tom takes his time as he works and makes sure that he never produces more than 65 units per day.

LEARNING OBJECTIVES

After successful completion of this chapter, you should be able to:

- Understand the importance of groups in organizations,
- Identify several important types of groups,
- Know why individuals join groups,
- Describe how groups develop,
- Recognize how roles and norms operate to influence the behavior of group members,

303

- Explain the effects of size, homogeneity of membership, and cohesiveness on group functioning,
- Identify several factors that cause group cohesiveness to increase, as well as several factors that cause group cohesiveness to decrease, and
- Provide a number of suggestions for managing groups effectively.

GROUPS IN ORGANIZATIONS

An examination of the influence of groups is essential to our understanding of human relations in organizations for several reasons. There are four key implications of groups in organizations.

First, most individuals are members of a number of different groups both inside and outside their employing organization. These groups may place significant demands on members' time as well as constraints on their behavior. In addition, some of these groups may make demands on individuals that are in conflict with the demands made by other groups—creating anxiety and stress for the individual.

Second, groups are a major source of influence on the behavior of individuals in organizations. They encourage members to engage in certain behaviors conducive to accomplishing the group's goals. In addition, groups provide constraints on members by identifying those activities the group has determined are incompatible with continued group membership.

Groups are a major source of influence on the behavior of individuals in organizations.

Third, all organizations are made up of groups of individuals. Employees are placed together in various work groups to perform tasks that will contribute to organizational goal attainment. In addition, a number of groups may arise naturally, not initiated by the organization. Each of these groups has its own set of goals and expectations of its members.

Fourth, groups sometimes provide a shield or buffer between management and employees. While managers are responsible for directing the activities of organizational members, they cannot ignore the influence of employee groups. These groups may allow employees to resist managers' attempts to influence their behavior. An understanding of human relations in organizations requires an understanding of how these various groups affect the behavior of their members.

Thus, human relations within organizations cannot be fully understood by examining only individual variables. Individuals are members of, and are greatly affected by, the groups to which they belong. In how many groups do you currently hold membership? Why are you a member of each of these groups?

Understand the importance of groups in organizations.

Definition of a Group

Not every collection of people is a **group** (as we will use the term). A number of people sitting in the departure gate area at an airport, waiting for their flight to board, is not a group. A crowd at a football or basketball game is not a group. For the purposes of studying group dynamics in organizations, some specific conditions must be met before a collection of people is considered a *group*. "A group is defined as two or more persons who are interacting with one another in such a manner that each person influences, and is influenced by, each other person."[1] Several aspects of this definition require further explanation.

Interaction and Influence

Employees may be working side-by-side in the same department, but if they do not interact with one another, they are not a group. Further, even if there is interaction, the employees must influence one another. One-way influence between two or more individuals does not constitute a group. An employee may be strongly influenced by another employee due to the second employee's skill, personality, or status. However, unless this second employee's behavior is also influenced by the first, they are not a group. Thus, the two key requirements of a group are interaction of all individuals, and mutual influence.

Goals

While not explicitly included in the definition of a group, there are other common characteristics of groups in organizations. Group members typically share some common goal or goals. The interaction process described in the definition is usually for the purpose of accomplishing a goal or goals shared by most members of the group.

Perceptions

Group members typically perceive themselves to be a group, banded together to accomplish some purpose. Each member of the group performs some activity or function necessary to accomplish that purpose. In other words, group members think of themselves as a group, which affects the behavior of individual members. They can no longer consider only their own needs and goals. They must now also consider those of the group.

Roles

Each group member generally occupies some specific position or role within the group. Just as in formal organizations, all types of groups assign particular tasks to members so that they may efficiently accomplish group goals. We will examine roles in more depth later.

Types of Groups

Identify several important types of groups.

There are two primary types of groups in organizational settings—formal groups and informal groups. **Formal groups** are initiated by the organization to accomplish organizational goals. They can be either command groups or task groups.[2] **Command groups** are relatively permanent groups, typically represented on the organization chart such as the one shown in Exhibit 12.1. Most employees are assigned to a command group, such as the Finance Division, the Accounts Payable/Receivable Department, or a smaller work group. A **task group** is usually temporary and will not generally appear on the organization chart. Task groups are initiated when there is a specific project to be completed or problem to be solved. Once the problem is solved or project completed, the task group is dissolved and members return to their command groups. For example, a large insurance company located in the midwest in-

Informal groups arise naturally as employees interact.

stalled a new computerized billing system. Since output of the billing department affected the finance, accounting, and claims processing departments, representatives from all of these departments were placed on a planning and implementation committee to assist in switching to the new computer system. As soon as the system was installed and employees were familiar with it, the committee was disbanded.

Exhibit 12.1 illustrates formal and informal groups. Formal groups are shown encircled on the organization chart; informal groups are in boxes at the bottom of the chart.

Informal groups are not initiated by the organization but rather evolve naturally among employees. Employees join informal groups to satisfy important individual needs which they would otherwise be unable to satisfy. The primary reasons why employees join informal groups will be examined in more detail in the following paragraphs. Two primary types of informal groups are friendship groups and interest groups.[3] **Friendship groups**, which are rel-

Exhibit 12.1
Formal and informal groups in organizations

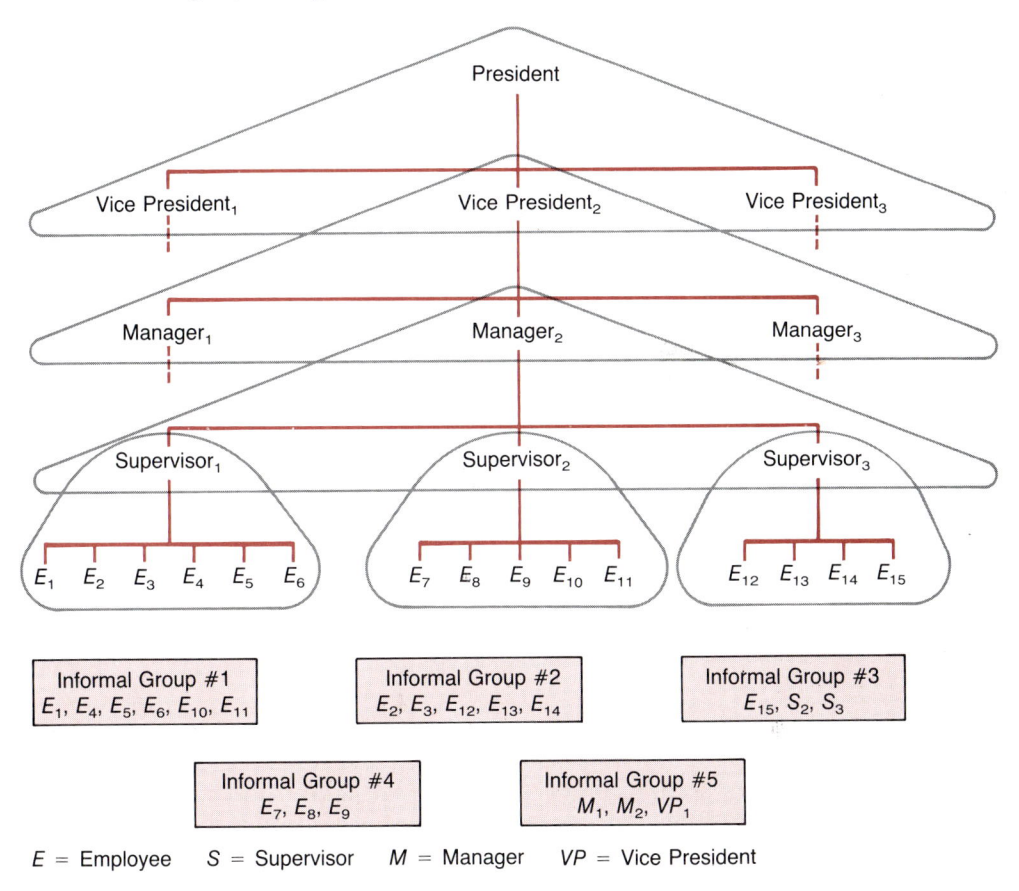

President

Vice President$_1$ Vice President$_2$ Vice President$_3$

Manager$_1$ Manager$_2$ Manager$_3$

Supervisor$_1$ Supervisor$_2$ Supervisor$_3$

E_1 E_2 E_3 E_4 E_5 E_6 E_7 E_8 E_9 E_{10} E_{11} E_{12} E_{13} E_{14} E_{15}

| Informal Group #1 | Informal Group #2 | Informal Group #3 |
| $E_1, E_4, E_5, E_6, E_{10}, E_{11}$ | $E_2, E_3, E_{12}, E_{13}, E_{14}$ | E_{15}, S_2, S_3 |

| Informal Group #4 | Informal Group #5 |
| E_7, E_8, E_9 | M_1, M_2, VP_1 |

E = Employee   S = Supervisor   M = Manager   VP = Vice President

atively permanent, form because members enjoy interacting with the other members. There are not necessarily any work-related goals to be accomplished or tasks to be performed. The primary reason for the friendship group's existence is to provide an opportunity for the members to interact. **Interest groups**, which tend to be temporary, form because of a common interest, activity, or problem. For example, interest groups often develop when an organization announces it is considering employee layoffs to reduce operating costs. Then, employees will band together to deal with the problem of the potential loss of jobs. Once the problem is solved or the worst occurs, the interest group is dissolved.

Sometimes the distinction between friendship groups and interest groups becomes blurred, because friendships may develop between some members of an interest group. When the interest group dissolves, a friendship group, made up of some or all of the members of the original interest group, may remain.

WHY EMPLOYEES JOIN GROUPS

Know why individuals join groups.

There is no single overriding reason why employees join groups. Different people will join the same group for different reasons, or different groups for the same reasons. It is clear that formal groups arise in order to help perform the tasks and activities that will ultimately contribute to the achievement of organizational objectives. While employees make a voluntary decision on whether to join the organization, they may have little choice on which specific command or task group they are assigned by the organization. Thus, the discussion of why employees join groups focuses upon informal groups.

Need Satisfaction

People often join groups to satisfy important individual needs such as security, status, self-esteem, affiliation, and power.

Security

Everyone has heard the saying, "There's safety in numbers." Informal group membership will often increase employees' feelings of security. Employees may join a group in response to some real or imagined threat, such as the firing of a coworker, layoffs, or a harsh manager. It is safe to say that poor human relations increase employees' needs for informal group membership. When trust and open communication do not exist between managers and employees, employees may feel the need for informal group membership.

Status and Self-Esteem

Membership in a group that is admired and respected can contribute to an employee's status in the organization and add to that person's self-esteem. Being a member of an important group means that each member is "somebody." Individuals take great pride in belonging to certain prestigious groups.

Affiliation

Individuals have strong needs for affiliation or to interact with others. For some people, interactions on the job are their primary means of satisfying these social needs. Case in point: the janitor who won several million dollars in a state lottery. At a news conference, when asked about his plans for the future, he replied that he would buy a new house and a car and take a short vacation before returning to work. Several of the reporters expressed great surprise that this new millionaire would continue working as a janitor. However, it is likely that this person had developed many important friendships at his place of work. He may have had few other opportunities to satisfy important social needs. Even though he could easily afford to stop working, to do so might have meant giving up these relationships—which would have been unthinkable to him.

Power

Sometimes employees join informal groups to acquire power that they did not have on their own. Employees may band together to improve working conditions, because the complaints and/or suggestions of a single employee often go unnoticed. However, management may hear and act on the complaints of a number of employees banded together. The need for bargaining strength is often a reason employees join unions.[4]

Support, Guidance, and Information

Employees will also frequently join informal groups for the support, guidance, and information they can provide. This benefit is especially important for new employees looking for clues as to how to become successful in the organization. Sometimes employees may be reluctant to go to their immediate supervisor or manager with questions or problems, for fear of being viewed as incompetent. However, asking another member of the informal work group for assistance or advice is typically not as threatening. An example of a relatively new form of interest group, which actually started out as a friendship group, appears in the accompanying Human Relations in Action box. This group now provides invaluable support, guidance, and information to women who find themselves working in male-dominated organizations.

Managers can minimize the need for informal group membership (they can never eliminate it) by encouraging employees to communicate openly about their problems or concerns. Employees who perceive that they may be punished or reprimanded for making mistakes or requesting help are likely to look to the informal group for assistance before they go to their manager. Managers should be supportive and show a willingness to help employees not only in performing their immediate tasks, but also in growing and developing within the organization.

Common Interests, Activities, and Goals

Another reason individuals may choose to join an informal group within an organization is because the group engages in activities of interest to the indi-

HUMAN RELATIONS IN ACTION

Networking: Interest Groups for Women

Everyone has heard or complained of the "good old boy's network." This was typically an all-male informal (friendship and/or interest group) that was used to help members advance in their careers. These groups provided very important and useful contacts for its members. A member had the opportunity to meet and get to know higher ranking managers of a number of organizations. More importantly, these higher ranking managers got to know *you*. When these managers had positions open up, they might think of someone they met at a group function. Unfortunately, as women began to enter management positions in organizations, they found these important sources of contact closed to them.

Networking is defined as "the process of developing and using your contacts for information, advice, and moral support as you pursue your career."[1] As the above paragraph suggests, men have been using such networks for years. Men's networks have developed from a number of social groups (e.g., social clubs, civic organizations, athletic clubs). As a result of women managers' exclusion from these all-male networks, predominantly female networks have arisen. While the primary purpose of the "good old boy's network" was social interaction with career advancement as a by-product, women's networks have the advancement of members' careers as their primary mission. Women's networks are deliberate attempts to link women from a number of organizations, to expand contacts for all members. In addition to making new contacts, women may find successful role models, exchange information, and help solve members' problems.

The popularity of women's networking groups is illustrated by a network established by four local professionals in a large midwestern city. The first meeting drew about seventy participants. In a short time, the mailing list had grown to over 500. While not all of these members regularly attend meetings, they retain their membership to be plugged in to this rich source of information. A survey of members' reasons for participating in the network showed that the primary reason was to receive information. The next most frequently mentioned reasons were to meet other women, get career guidance, and attend educational programs offered by the network.

Source: DeWine, S. & Casbolt, D. Networking: External communication systems for female organizational members. *Journal of Communication Systems,* 1983, 20, 57–67.

[1] Welch, M.S. *Networking: The great new way for women to get ahead.* New York: Harcourt Brace Jovanovich, 1980, 15.

---

vidual, and/or the group is engaged in accomplishing goals important to the individual. For example, many people join other volunteers to help solicit contributions to charities such as the Heart Fund, the Cancer Society, the American Lung Association, the March of Dimes, the Muscular Dystrophy Association, and the United Way. While not a charity per se, many individuals have recently joined Mothers Against Drunk Driving (MADD) and Students Against Drunk Driving (SADD) in an attempt to get drunk drivers off the roads. A primary reason individuals join these groups is that they identify with the goals of the group. It is not likely that an individual, acting alone, would have much of an impact in accomplishing these goals, but many of these groups of individuals have made substantial contributions to their respective organizations.

Interpersonal Attraction

One of the strongest reasons individuals join groups is interpersonal attraction. While obviously related to needs for affiliation, interpersonal attraction refers to individuals wanting to join a particular group in order to associate with certain members. Several factors influence interpersonal attraction; similarities in attitudes, beliefs, sex, age, race, and personality; physical proximity; and opportunity for interaction.

Similarity of Members

Individuals are more likely to be attracted to and join groups with members who are similar to themselves. Many of us feel more comfortable when we are around others who are like us. Interaction and communication may develop much quicker in a group of similar people than in a group made up of people who are very different from one another.

Physical Proximity

People tend to join with others who are located in close physical proximity to themselves, although this is not necessarily the case. Individuals who are located near one another have greater opportunities to interact with and get to know one another.[5] However, if individuals located near one another have much different beliefs, or appear different to one another, they are unlikely to form an informal group. Rather, informal groups are likely to be made up of individuals who share similar beliefs and attitudes toward important issues, from various locations within the organization.

Opportunity for Interaction

While physical proximity obviously contributes to the opportunity employees have to interact, there are other factors which must be considered. Sometimes there are constraints placed on employees that prohibit their ability to interact, even though they are in close physical proximity to one another. For example, some organizations may develop rules that prohibit employees from interacting during working hours. In other cases, the task itself might be so noisy or complex and difficult that it prevents employees from interacting. The ability to interact on a regular basis is a primary factor in the development of informal groups.

Identity

Identity refers to the process by which we compare ourselves with other group members to "make sure we are all right." We all tend to compare ourselves, our behaviors, our attitudes, and our beliefs with other group members, to determine if others share our perception of the world, or if perhaps there is something wrong with us. In most cases, we find that others are relatively similar to ourselves, which contributes to our identity. We simply need to reassure ourselves that our perceptions and beliefs are correct.[6] Interactions with the group helps us to find out who we are, or at least, that who we are isn't bad at all.

PROCESS OF GROUP DEVELOPMENT

Describe how groups develop.

The **process of group development** is dynamic; most groups are in a constant state of development. While there is always some degree of change taking place within a group, there is a relatively stable pattern of development through which most groups pass. This development pattern can be divided into four distinct stages—**forming**, **storming**, **norming**, and **performing**—as shown in Exhibit 12.2.[7]

Forming

This first stage is characterized by a great deal of uncertainty. There is uncertainty regarding the exact purpose of the group, the group's goals, and who will be the leader of the group. In addition, potential members are trying to determine which types of behavior are acceptable. They are still somewhat unsure they are willing to give up some independence to become a group member. It may not yet be clear to these potential members that the advantages of group membership outweigh the costs of giving up some independence and individuality.

Storming

This second stage of group development is characterized by conflict. Members may have begun to accept the group's purpose and goals, but there is still some resistance to giving up one's individuality and independence. In addition, there is conflict over who will control the group as leader. There may be a struggle among several members to assume the leadership role. Expected patterns of behavior, standards, and rules may begin to develop during this stage. As the conflicts are resolved, some individuals will leave the group. Those who remain will begin to occupy particular roles within the group.

Norming

In this third stage, the remaining members begin to develop close relationships with other group members. A strong sense of group identity develops

Exhibit 12.2
Stages of group development

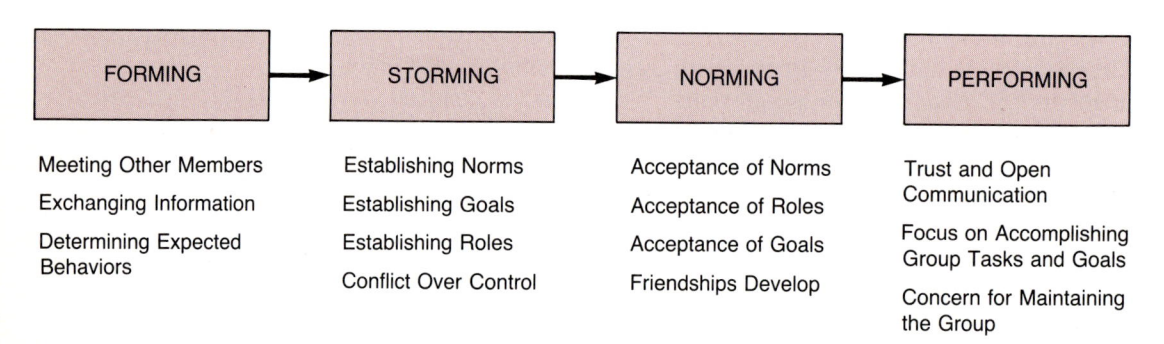

FORMING	STORMING	NORMING	PERFORMING
Meeting Other Members	Establishing Norms	Acceptance of Norms	Trust and Open Communication
Exchanging Information	Establishing Goals	Acceptance of Roles	Focus on Accomplishing Group Tasks and Goals
Determining Expected Behaviors	Establishing Roles	Acceptance of Goals	Concern for Maintaining the Group
	Conflict Over Control	Friendships Develop	

and members begin to accept roles and patterns of expected behavior, which are called *norms*. Group norms will be examined in more detail later.

Performing

The fourth and final stage of group development is performing. At this point, the structure of the group is fully developed. That is, all necessary roles have been assumed and members are now directing their energies to the accomplishment of group goals, rather than to engaging in conflict. Group members now work well with one another, and communicate openly with other members. The focus of the group at this point is two-fold: (1) performing the activities necessary to achieve group goals, and (2) maintaining the group. Both of these activities are critical. Even though the group may have developed into a high-performing team, since group development is a dynamic process, it faces the difficult challenge of staying at this stage. Without efforts to maintain the group, it might slip back into an earlier stage, which would require energies and resources to be devoted to managing conflict rather than accomplishing goals. In the constantly changing environment in which most groups must operate, group development is a never-ending process.

Groups which make it through the developmental process to Stage 4, develop an identifiable structure. This structure enables the group to ensure that necessary activities are performed and goals are accomplished.

GROUP STRUCTURE

Group structure is defined as those variables which make one group different from another group: norms, roles, status, size, and cohesiveness.

Group Norms

A **norm** is an acceptable pattern of behavior that is shared by a group's members. Norms tell group members how they are expected to behave if they hope to continue as a member of the group. Informal groups develop their own norms regarding normal working hours, production standards and performance levels, dress, and methods of dealing with conflict between members. Several characteristics of norms have been identified.[8]

1. Norms make it easier for leaders to monitor and control member behavior.
2. While norms often include expected attitudes and values in addition to expected behaviors, it is more important for group members to engage in expected behaviors. As long as the observable behaviors are consistent with the norms, it is not necessary for members to accept or agree with the norms, or hold certain values and beliefs.
3. Norms are generally developed only for those behaviors considered extremely important to the group.
4. Norms develop and change slowly; radical changes are infrequent.
5. Not all group members must adhere to all norms. Leaders or other high-status group members may be permitted to violate some norms.

Conformity, Compliance, Obedience, and Internalization

Once norms are established, groups must ensure that members conform to these expected behavioral patterns. Four processes explain why group members adhere to norms; these are *conformity, compliance, obedience,* and *internalization*. **Conformity** is defined as "a change in behavior or belief . . . as a result of a real or imagined group pressure."[9] However, this pressure is implied (not actually exerted). Conformity occurs when members voluntarily decide to go along with the group. There may be real or imagined pressure for them to do so, however, they are still free to make the decision. In contrast, **compliance** occurs when there is overt pressure to go along with the group. "In conformity, the pressure is invisible; in compliance, it is obvious."[10] Thus, with compliance, members are not entirely free to make their own decision. They often comply with requests in order to receive a highly valued reward, to avoid a severe punishment, or because they are indebted to someone. As a result, compliance often comes with at least some degree of resistance. Even though the pressure is more overt with compliance, individuals may still refuse to comply. It may be more difficult to say "No" than in the case of conformity, but it is still possible.

RETURN TO THE PROLOGUE

Tom, the machinist in the Prologue, decided that he would not produce over 65 units per day even though the additional income would have been welcome. He was sure that he had the ability to produce approximately 80 units per day if he tried. What makes Tom produce five units over the company standard, yet far below what he is capable of producing? The answer is informal group norms. The informal group of which Tom is a member has decided that 65 units per day is the appropriate level of output for employees in Tom's department. This output allows employees to earn a few dollars bonus each day. However, it prevents management from deciding that employees are capable of producing far more than the current standard and raising it to, say, 70 units per day. Then employees would not begin earning a bonus until after the seventieth unit.

If Tom simply became aware of the informal group norm and began adhering to it, he *conformed*. On the other hand, if Tom initially produced above the informal group norm and began adhering to it only after being pressured by members of the informal group, he *complied* with the norm.

Obedience occurs when one person has enough power over another person to demand submission to requests. If the person fails to obey, power is exercised in the form of punishment. One of the most powerful forms of punishment in informal groups is the **threat of ostracism**. Because individuals voluntarily joined the group and have remained members suggests that they have been able to satisfy important individual needs. Therefore, they would like to continue their membership. This is what makes the threat of ostracism so powerful. If members don't obey, they may be expelled from the group. The more highly satisfied members are with group membership, the more likely they are to conform to group norms.[11]

CHAPTER TWELVE: Relationships Within Groups

Tom may have *obeyed* the informal group productivity norm because he wanted to remain a member of the group and was being threatened with expulsion if he decided to break the norm. Finally, Tom may have adhered to the informal group norm because he really believed that it was the right thing to do. In this case, Tom *internalized* the norm because it was consistent with his own values and beliefs.

RETURN TO THE PROLOGUE

Internalization occurs when group goals are consistent with the beliefs and values of group members. Thus, very little external influence is necessary to get members to abide by norms designed to facilitate the accomplishment of group goals. Internalization is not the same thing as conformance, since conformance implies that the group is ready to use some form of pressure to force members to adhere to its norms.

From a human relations perspective, internalization followed by conformance are the desired methods of influencing members. Individuals conform due to a felt obligation, not an overt use of force or pressure. For example, because they believe the goals of the group are worthwhile, individuals may feel an obligation to attend a group meeting when they really would rather stay at home and watch the football game. They also know that other group members will be at the meeting. Even though there may be not overt threat of punishment if they were to miss the meeting, they feel pressure to conform because they would feel guilty knowing other members are there working to accomplish group goals. Internalization leads members to abide by group norms because doing so provides them with a sense of satisfaction. Since group norms are consistent with their values and beliefs, adhering to these norms really does not require a change in their normal behavior.

Group Roles

Groups that reach a Stage 4 (Performing) level of development typically assign individual members to specific roles. A **role** is a set of expected behaviors associated with a particular position within a group, whereas a norm was a general set of expected behaviors for all group members. To illustrate, members typically have a set of expectations of their group leader. The leader is expected to call meetings, resolve conflict, collect and distribute information, and represent the group to other groups.[12]

As shown in Exhibit 12.3, there are three primary categories of roles which members may fill in informal groups; *task* roles, *maintenance* roles, and *individual* roles.[13]

Recognize how roles and norms operate to influence the behavior of group members.

Task Roles

Task roles, which are concerned with getting the job done, include:

Initiator-Contributor. This individual proposes new ideas, goals and solutions; gets discussions started, and defines problems. This person's concern is

Exhibit 12.3
Types of roles within groups

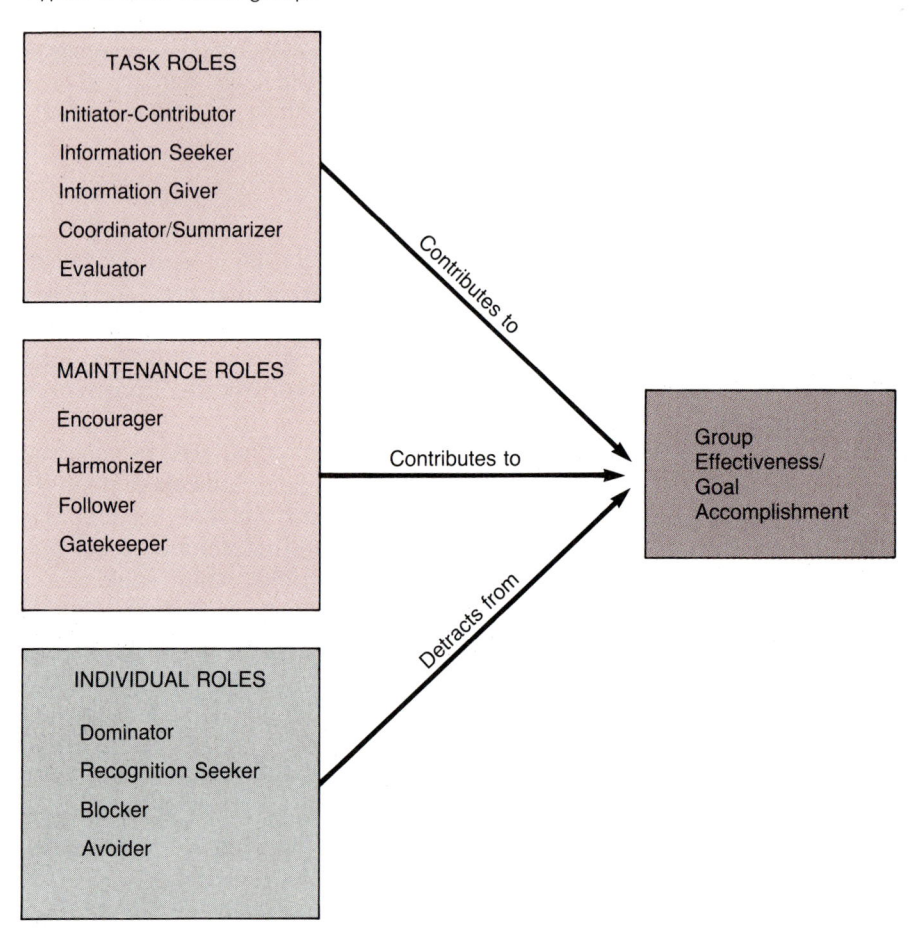

TASK ROLES
- Initiator-Contributor
- Information Seeker
- Information Giver
- Coordinator/Summarizer
- Evaluator

Contributes to →

MAINTENANCE ROLES
- Encourager
- Harmonizer
- Follower
- Gatekeeper

Contributes to → **Group Effectiveness/Goal Accomplishment**

INDIVIDUAL ROLES
- Dominator
- Recognition Seeker
- Blocker
- Avoider

Detracts from →

with getting the group moving in the right direction toward a solution to a problem or toward accomplishment of a goal.

Information Seeker. This person seeks out data and/or information by asking experts for their opinions or advice. She may also ask experienced members of other groups for suggestions. In addition, this individual may solicit suggestions, ideas, values, and/or beliefs from her own group members.

Information Giver. This individual is concerned with offering facts or other relevant information and experience to the group so that it has more information on which to base a decision. This person might, for example, offer examples from her own experience to clarify a problem or situation with which she is familiar.

Coordinator-Summarizer. This role involves assimilating ideas, suggestions, and opinions. This person may summarize and restate the group discussion and then offer a conclusion. She focuses on pulling all available information together to facilitate a decision by the group.

Evaluator. A person occupying the role of evaluator appraises the ideas, suggestions, or solutions discussed by the group. If this assessment is seen as an attempt to determine whether or not the group has reached the best possible decision, other group members may accept this person's actions. However, there is a danger that they may become defensive if they see this person as being unnecessarily critical or as a threat to the group.

Maintenance Roles

Maintenance roles are aimed at building and maintaining the group. This effort is necessary to prevent valued group members from becoming dissatisfied with their membership and leaving the group. Maintenance roles include:

Encourager. The person occupying this role is supportive of other members, praises efforts and ideas, and encourages members to continue to participate in group activities and to contribute to the group.

Harmonizer. This individual tries to reduce conflict and tension and reconcile any differences which may develop. Keeping peace in the ranks enables the group to avoid expending resources and energy dealing with internal conflict. Instead, the group can focus on accomplishing its goals.

Follower. This person simply goes along with the group, accepting the ideas and suggestions of others, and compromising for the sake of the group. This person is likely to volunteer for tasks that no one else wants to perform.

Gatekeeper. This role involves getting all members to participate and offer their ideas and suggestions by controlling communication (e.g., "opening and closing the gate"). This may involve suggesting procedures that will encourage everyone to participate, such as going around the room for comments, or simply asking for response from members who haven't yet participated.

Individual Roles

While task and maintenance roles are both necessary for the efficient and effective functioning of groups, **individual roles** are dysfunctional (e.g., they prevent or make it difficult for the group to accomplish its goals). It is important for the group leader to recognize when an individual is engaging in disruptive activity and try to limit that person's influence on the group. The approach to the situation may involve limiting that person's access to the group. Individual roles include:

Dominator. This person tries to control the group by preventing others from participating, or by interrupting other members who are speaking. Dominators attempt to direct group members toward working on tasks that will assist the dominator accomplish personal goals.

Recognition Seeker. The recognition seeker tries to get attention from group members by doing things to call attention to herself. This person may engage in loud or unusual behavior or boast about her accomplishments or skills.

Blocker. The individual engaging in this role will attempt to block the group's progress by arguing, getting the discussion off track, or focusing on personal concerns.

Avoider. This person acts indifferently to the group's activities and/or discussion. She may appear to be daydreaming, or may talk to others about subjects unrelated to the matters before the group. This individual does not really accept the goals of the group and may be disruptive.

Group Leader

In addition to these three primary categories of group roles, one additional role could be identified—the group leader. This person may have to perform some of the task and maintenance roles just described, to ensure that the group accomplishes its goals and continues to exist. It is also the responsibility of the group leader to minimize the occurrences of group members engaging in individual roles.

Earlier, you were asked to identify the groups to which you currently belong. Now consider which specific roles you occupy in each of these groups. What activities do you commonly perform within each group? How did you come to occupy these roles? Did you volunteer or did the group encourage or pressure you to accept a particular role?

Role-Related Problems

Several problems exist that are directly related to the roles an individual occupies. These problems are partly the result of individuals occupying more than one role in a group, or roles in several different groups. Other problems arise that are the result of a lack of information concerning the role.

Role ambiguity exists when individuals are not sure exactly what is expected of them. **Role conflict** occurs when an individual occupies two roles (within the same group, or more probably in separate groups), placing conflicting demands on the individual. That is, satisfying the expectations of one role could prevent satisfying the expectations of the other. For example, an individual might occupy certain work-related roles that demand long hours spent on the job, even on weekends. This same individual may also occupy family roles that place demands on the individual to spend more time at home.[14] Two specific forms of role conflict are role overload and role underload. **Role overload** occurs when individuals perceive that the demands placed upon them in their role(s) exceed their abilities. **Role underload** occurs when individuals perceive that their abilities exceed the demands of their role(s). That is, they are not being challenged by the roles they currently occupy. Severe role ambiguity and/or role conflict that lasts for extended periods of time can cause anxiety, stress, and dysfunctional behavior such as absenteeism and turnover.[15]

Status

Individuals within groups do not all have the same rank. **Status** is a measure of an individual's rank or prestige within a group. Status determines (at least partially) the appropriate behaviors for individuals within groups. Individuals with higher status within a group are generally afforded some privileges that lower-status members are not. For instance, high-status members are not required to adhere to all group norms. In addition, high-status group members typically have more power and influence within the group and may occupy important roles, such as leader or gatekeeper.

A group member can acquire status by the role she occupies within the group. For example, leaders nearly always have more status than other members. In addition, roles occupied in one group may contribute to an individual's status in a second group. For example, leading local business executives often have high status in the college of business of the nearby university. Status in a group is also related to an individual's status in the community. For example, a wealthy young entrepreneur from one of the community's leading families may have relatively high status in any group. Status is also related to one's educational level, accomplishments or performance level, expertise, experience, job knowledge, personality, or simply associating with other people who have high status.

One way that organizations and informal groups display status is through the use of *status symbols*. Status symbols can be nearly anything that displays an individual's status. Some of the more common include expensive clothing; company car; large, plush office; impressive job titles; private secretary; access to company jet, mountain cabin, etc.; club membership; and desirable office location (e.g., top floor with a view of the city).[16]

Group Size

Group size can have an important effect on performance. From the definition proposed earlier in the chapter, a group can have as few as two members, or it may be quite large. There are both advantages and disadvantages to large groups. A large number of members allows a group to engage in many activities and complete many tasks. When faced with decisions, a group with many members may draw upon the diverse knowledge and experience of those members. As a result, large groups are generally able to propose more ideas and solutions and bring more information to bear on the problem or decision.

The primary disadvantage of a large number of members is that interaction among members becomes more difficult. This can make it harder for the

Explain the effects of size, homogeneity of membership, and cohesiveness on group functioning.

Exhibit 12.4
Effects of size on groups

	Group Size	
Category	Small	Large
Leadership		
1. Demands on the leader	Low ←——————————→ High
2. Differences between leaders and members	Few ←——————————→ Many
3. Direction by leader	Low ←——————————→ High
Members		
4. Tolerance of direction from leader	Low ←——————————→ High
5. Domination of group activities by a few members	Low ←——————————→ High
6. Inhibition in participation by some members	Low ←——————————→ High
Group Process		
7. Formalization of rules and procedures	Low ←——————————→ High
8. Time required to make decisions	Short ←——————————→ Long
9. Tendency for subgroups to form within the group or for group to break into several smaller groups	Low ←——————————→ High

Source: Based upon Hare, A.P. Group size. *American Behavioral Scientist,* 1981, *24,* 695–708; Markham, S.E., Dansereau, F., Y Alutto, J.A. *Group size and absenteeism rates: A longitudinal analysis.* Academy of Management Journal 1982, 25, 921–927.

group to reach a decision and to communicate important information to all members. Some members may be prevented from participating as much as they would like and may therefore become dissatisfied with their membership. In the worst case, the group may actually dissolve, or split into smaller groups. Exhibit 12.4 presents other possible effects of size upon group functioning. While it is difficult to say exactly how many members constitute a small group or a large group, as a rule of thumb two to seven members are classified as a small group, eight to twelve members are a moderate-sized group, and thirteen to sixteen members make up a large group. When groups reach approximately sixteen members they have reached the size where the tendency for the group to dissolve or break into several smaller groups is increased. When groups increase in size from moderate to large, it is difficult for all members to continue participating in group activities and discussions as much as they would prefer.[17]

> **Exhibit 12.5**
> Factors which affect group cohesiveness
>
> | Factors that Increase Cohesiveness | Factors that Decrease Cohesiveness |
> |---|---|
> | • Small group size | • Large group size |
> | • Homogeneity of members | • Heterogeneity of members |
> | • Success in accomplishing group goals | • Failure in accomplishing group goals |
> | • Mature stage of development (performing) | • Immature stage of development (forming through norming) |
> | • Competition with or isolation from other groups/External threat | • Disagreement and conflict among group members/Internal threat |
> | • Organizational rewards based upon group performance | • Organizational rewards based upon individual performance |

Group Cohesiveness

Cohesiveness is the strength of group members' desire to remain in the group.[18] This implies that members are highly satisfied with their membership and want the group to continue in its present form.[19] A number of factors that affect group cohesiveness are identified in Exhibit 12.5. Most of these factors have to do with member satisfaction or the ability of members to interact and participate.

Groups whose members are similar (homogeneous) in terms of beliefs, values, experience, and demographics (e.g., age, sex) tend to become more cohesive than groups whose members are dissimilar. In addition, agreement on the basic purpose and goals of the group will tend to increase cohesiveness. Group size influences cohesiveness because groups could be too small or too large for good interaction among members.

Other factors include the group's success in accomplishing important goals and its stage of development. Success in accomplishing important goals is directly related to member satisfaction; most people identify more strongly with a group that is competent and successful. Groups which have matured to a Stage 4 level of development are likely to be more cohesive than groups that have not yet reached this level. Because groups at Stages 1–3 are engaging in substantial amounts of conflict over group goals, roles, norms, and structure, their development is slow.

External factors that can affect cohesiveness include intergroup competition and any external threat. When a group engages in competition with another group, members of each group tend to band together and become more

> Identify several factors that cause group cohesiveness to increase, as well as several factors that cause group cohesiveness to decrease.

> ### DEVELOPING YOUR HUMAN RELATIONS SKILLS
>
> It is important for you to understand the development and influence of groups on individuals from your perspective as a manager and as an employee in an organizational work setting.
>
> As a manager of a formal group, which may include one or more informal groups, there are several things you can do to promote work group effectiveness.
>
> 1. Determine the size and composition of the formal and informal groups. Group variables can be more easily changed in formal groups to match situational requirements. For example, to increase cohesiveness, you can reduce the size of the group.
> 2. Determine the stage of group development. Neither formal nor informal groups will be able to concentrate on the task at hand until they reach Stage 4. Managers can sometimes help groups mature by encouraging cohesiveness, making suggestions concerning which tasks need to be performed, and managing conflict between members.
> 3. Identify and communicate with the informal group leader. Building a good relationship with this group leader may be beneficial in terms of acceptance of the formal organization's goals, and acceptance of organization-initiated change.
> 4. Encourage open communication and trust within your work group. Be receptive when employees come to you with problems, suggestions, and/or mistakes. If you are not receptive to such communications, you are, in effect, punishing employees who do come forward. They will not continue to do so if they are met with discipline and reprimands. They will continue to communicate openly with you if they are met

cohesive. Similarly, when group members perceive an external threat, members pull together to protect the group and ensure its survival. To some extent, competition with another group may be perceived as a mild form of external threat. More severe forms of these threats sometimes come from the management of organizations. Arbitrary decisions (such as announcing layoffs or the plant moving), harsh treatment by superiors, and the termination of a

WHAT DO YOU THINK?

Would you rather manage a work group that is highly cohesive or one that is not at all cohesive? Which type of group do you believe would outperform the other? From the perspective of a manager, which type of group would be easier to manage? What are the advantages and disadvantages of managing cohesive versus noncohesive groups? The relationship between group cohesiveness and productivity is discussed in the "What Do You Think? Note" at the end of the chapter.

with understanding and support. If employees receive information and support from you, they are less likely to seek it from an informal group. While it is not the intent to eliminate informal groups, it is desirable that the manager keep open the lines of communication with employees.

5. Remember that groups must go through several stages of development. Different management techniques may be required for each stage. Be aware that until the internal structure of the group has been developed, pushing members to accomplish goals is likely to be ineffective.

As an employee, your success in any group, formal or informal, depends upon several things:

1. As you enter any group, it is important that you learn the norms as quickly as possible. Remember that these may differ from explicitly stated norms of the group. The best way to learn group norms is to carefully observe the behavior of group members whom you consider to be successful.
2. As new members enter your group, make sure that they understand important group norms. It is much easier to help new members learn positive group norms initially than to change negative norms later.
3. Remember that most people belong to several groups, all of which may have conflicting norms. Individuals are likely to identify most strongly with the group that understands this premise, rather than the group that places a great deal of pressure on individuals to conform, regardless of the stress and anxiety it may cause.

group member are examples of actions which might be perceived as external threats.

Effects of Cohesiveness

It is not possible to make a blanket statement that cohesiveness is either desirable or undesirable. However, several things are known to be a result of group cohesiveness. As implied earlier, members of cohesive groups tend to be highly satisfied with their membership in the group. As a result, both the quality and quantity of interactions are higher for members of cohesive groups than for members of groups which are not cohesive. In addition, cohesive groups tend to be more successful in accomplishing their goals. They capitalize on their ability to work together and direct their energy and resources toward goal accomplishment rather than resolving internal conflict. Thus, within the group, human relations are likely to be good. However, this success does not guarantee that good human relations exist between the informal group and the formal organization.

> Exhibit 12.6
> Characteristics of effective groups
>
> 1. Well-established working relationships exist among all group members.
> 2. Group members are skilled in their various roles.
> 3. Members of the group are attracted to it and are loyal.
> 4. Each group member is motivated to make every effort to help the group accomplish its goals.
> 5. There is a supportive atmosphere in the group.
> 6. When necessary, group members willingly help one another accomplish tasks.
> 7. Members communicate freely and openly.
> 8. The goals and values of the group are clearly understood and accepted by all members.

Source: Based upon Likert, R. The nature of highly effective groups. In Kolb, D.A., Rubin, I.M. & McIntyre, J.M. (Eds.), *Organizational psychology: Readings on human behavior in organizations.* Fourth edition. Englewood Cliffs, N.J.: Prentice-Hall, 1984, 153–166.

Another consequence of group cohesiveness is directly related to the group decision-making process. Cohesiveness may actually result in poorer decisions due to an unwillingness to consider information in conflict with the consensus of the group. However, steps can be taken to ensure the quality of decisions in highly cohesive groups. Group decision making was discussed in more detail in Chapter 11.

MAKING GROUPS EFFECTIVE

Provide a number of suggestions for managing groups effectively.

Characteristics of effective groups are presented in Exhibit 12.6. Managers can promote these qualities in several ways. First, there are some relatively obvious ways in which groups (both formal and informal) can become more effective. Through additional training, they can increase their knowledge and update their skills, to improve task performance. They can remove obstacles to performance, by techniques such as revitalizing aging equipment. However, human relations is the area in which greatest progress can often be made. Unfortunately, this may also be the most difficult area for many groups. Promoting good human relations requires leaders and group members with good human relations skills in areas such as communication, negotiation, and conflict resolution.

Several other ideas for assessing and managing group effectiveness are presented in Exhibit 12.7—A Checklist for Group Effectiveness. This checklist can be used to determine specific areas needing attention. Both group leaders and members should complete the checklist then compare their answers. Areas of disagreement should be examined carefully.[20]

Exhibit 12.7
Work group effectiveness checklist

	Mostly Yes	Mostly No
1. The atmosphere is relaxed and comfortable.	_____	_____
2. Group discussion is frequent, and it is usually pertinent to the task at hand.	_____	_____
3. Group members understand what they are trying to accomplish.	_____	_____
4. People listen to each others suggestions and ideas.	_____	_____
5. Disagreements are tolerated and an attempt is made to resolve them.	_____	_____
6. There is general agreement on most courses of action.	_____	_____
7. The group welcomes frank criticism from inside and outside sources.	_____	_____
8. When the group takes action, clear assignments are made and accepted.	_____	_____
9. There is a well-established, relaxed working relationship among the members.	_____	_____
10. There is a high degree of trust and confidence among the leader and subordinates.	_____	_____
11. The group members strive hard to help the group achieve its goal.	_____	_____
12. Suggestions and criticisms are offered and received in a helpful spirit.	_____	_____
13. There is a cooperative rather than a competitive relationship among group members.	_____	_____
14. The group goals are set high but not so high as to create anxieties or fear of failure.	_____	_____
15. The leaders and members hold a high opinion of the group's capabilities.	_____	_____
16. Creativity is stimulated within the group.	_____	_____
17. There is ample communication within the group on topics relevant to getting the work accomplished.	_____	_____
18. Group members feel confident in making decisions.	_____	_____
19. People are kept busy but not overworked.	_____	_____
20. The leader of the group is well suited for the job.	_____	_____

Source: DuBrin, A.J. *Contemporary applied management: Behavioral science techniques for managers and professionals.* Second edition, Plano, Texas: Business Publications, Inc., 1985, 169–170.

SUMMARY

It is impossible to study human relations in organizations without considering the many effects that groups have on individual behavior. Most people are members of a number of different groups both inside and outside their employing organization. All of these groups make demands of, and place constraints on, individual members.

The term group is defined as two or more persons who are interacting with one another in such a manner that each person influences, and is influenced by, each other person. Thus, the two key requirements are interaction of all individuals and mutual influence. In addition, most group members typically share a common goal or goals, and will perceive themselves to be a group.

Two primary types of groups exist in organizations. Formal groups are initiated by the organization to accomplish organizational goals. The two types of formal groups are command groups and task groups. Informal groups are not initiated by the organization, but arise naturally among employees. The two types of informal groups are friendship groups and interest groups.

A major reason employees decide to join informal groups is to satisfy some important individual need, such as the need for security, status, self-esteem, affiliation, or power. In addition, informal groups often provide support, guidance, and information to members. Individuals also join groups because the activities of the group are of interest to them, or because they believe the goals of the group are important and want to help accomplish them.

Most groups go through a similar process of four distinct development stages: forming, storming, norming, and performing. It is not until a group reaches Stage 4 that it concentrates its energies on accomplishing its goals. Up to that point, substantial energies and resources are devoted to conflict.

Group structure is defined as those variables that make one group different from another group. These variables include norms, roles, status, size, and cohesiveness. Norms are acceptable patterns of behavior, shared by a group's members, and which members must not violate if they wish to remain a member of the group. Groups can encourage members to abide by group norms through several processes; conformity, compliance, obedience, and internalization.

Groups that reach a Stage 4 level of development typically assign individual members to specific roles. A role is a set of expected behaviors associated with a particular position within the group. Three categories of roles have been identified: task roles, maintenance roles, and individual roles.

Other structural variables include status, size, and cohesiveness. Status is a measure of an individual's rank or prestige within a group. Individuals with higher status are generally afforded certain privileges that lower-status members are not. In addition, high-status group members typically have more power and influence within a group.

Group size has a definite impact upon group performance. Groups can be either too small or too large. Too few members, and too many as well, can make interaction and open communication between members difficult. As groups become too large and members are no longer able to participate as freely as they wish, the group may split into several smaller groups.

Cohesiveness refers to the strength of group members' desire to remain members of the group. Several factors contribute to group cohesiveness: similarity of members, isolation of the group, competition with other groups, perceived external threat, success in accomplishing important goals, and a Stage 4 level of development.

One of the primary advantages of groups is the variety of experience, education, skills, viewpoints, and ideas which members bring to decision-making situations. However, while group decisions tend to be more accurate than decisions made by most individuals, they tend to take much longer. And, there is a danger that some members may feel reluctant to participate or be influenced by other more dominant members.

KEY TERMS

group	conformity
formal group	compliance
command group	obedience
task group	ostracism
informal group	internalization
friendship group	roles
interest group	task roles
group development process	maintenance roles
	individual roles
forming	role ambiguity
storming	role conflict
norming	role overload
performing	role underload
group structure	status
norms	cohesiveness

DISCUSSION QUESTIONS

1. What is the definition of a group?
2. Describe the different types of groups found in organizations.
3. Why do employees join informal groups?

4. Explain the group development process.
5. What is a group norm and how does it affect the behavior of group members?
6. What specific processes cause group members to abide by group norms?
7. What is a group role? Identify the three categories of group roles and give an example of each.
8. What are some potential problems associated with roles?
9. What is status and what effect does it have on groups?
10. How does group size affect the performance of a group?
11. What is group cohesiveness and how does it influence groups? As a manager would you prefer to supervise a group which was cohesive or noncohesive? Why?

EXERCISE 12.1

Group Performance

The purpose of this exercise is to demonstrate the benefits of group membership in performing a task. You will first be asked to perform the task on your own. Later, your instructor will assign you to a group where you will perform the task again.

Procedure

Step 1: Write the letters of the alphabet in a vertical column along the left side of a sheet of paper.

Step 2: Your instructor will randomly select a sentence from the textbook and read aloud the first 26 letters in that sentence. Write these letters in a second vertical column just to the right of the first column. You now have a single column of two-letter combinations.

Step 3: On your own, think of a famous person whose initials correspond to each pair of letters on your paper and write the name of that person next to the initials. You have only ten minutes to accomplish this task. Your instructor will stop you at the end of the work period. You earn $100 (hypothetical) for each legitimate name. Your name, the name of your instructor, your cat's name, and so on, do not count. Thus, the maximum pay possible for this task is $2,600.

Step 4: Your instructor will now divide the class into groups of five to ten people each. Perform the task again, beginning with Step 1. Your instructor will read a second set of 26 letters from a randomly selected sentence in the text. You have an additional ten minutes to perform this task in your group.

Step 5: In your groups, calculate the average individual score of your members. Compare this average individual score with the group score. Did individuals or groups perform better? What could account for these differences?

Source: Adapted from Jones, J.E. & Pfeiffer, J.W. (Eds.) *The 1979 Annual Handbook for Group Facilitators*. San Diego, CA: University Associates, 1979, 19–20.

REFERENCES

[1] Shaw, M.E. *Group dynamics: The psychology of small group behavior*. Second edition. New York: McGraw-Hill Book Company, 1976, p. 11.

[2] Sayles, L.R. Work group behavior and the larger organization. In Arensburg, C., et al. (Eds.) *Research in industrial relations*. New York: Harper & Row, 1957, 131–145.

[3] Sayles, 1957, Ibid.

[4] Brett, J.M. Why employees want unions. *Organizational Dynamics,* 1980, 8, 47–59.

[5] Huckfeldt, R.R. Social contexts, social networks, and urban neighborhoods: Environmental constraints of friendship choice. *American Journal of Sociology,* November 1983, 651–669.

[6] Festinger, L. A theory of social comparison. *Human Relations,* 1954, 7, 114–140.

[7] Tuckman, B.W. Developmental sequence in small groups. *Psychological Bulletin,* 1965, 63, 384–399.

[8] Hackman, J.R. Group influence on individuals. In Dunnette, M.P. (Ed.) *Handbook of industrial and organizational psychology*. Chicago: Rand McNally, 1976.

[9] Kiesler, C.A. & Kiesler, C.B. *Conformity*. Reading, MA: Addison-Wesley, 1969.

[10] Napier, R.W. & Gershenfeld, M.K. *Groups: Theory and experience*. Third edition. Boston: Houghton-Mifflin, 1985, p. 143.

[11] Festinger, L. & Thibaut, J. Interpersonal communication in small groups. *Journal of Abnormal and*

Social Psychology, 1951, *16,* 92–99; Janis, I.L. Group think. *Psychology Today,* 1971, *5,* 43–46, 74–76.

[12]Manz, C.C. & Sims, H.P. Searching for the "unleader:" Organizational member views on leading self-managed groups. *Human Relations,* 1984, *37,* 409–424.

[13]Benne, K.D. & Sheats, P. Functional roles and group members. *Journal of Social Issues,* 1948, *4,* 41–49; Feldman, D.C. The development and enforcement of group norms. *Academy of Management Review, 9,* 47–53.

[14]Greenhaus, J.H. & Bentell, N.J. Sources of conflict between work and family roles. *Academy of Management Review,* 1985, *10,* 76–88.

[15]Fisher, C.D. & Gitelson, R. A meta-analysis of the correlates of role conflict and role ambiguity. *Journal of Applied Psychology,* 1983, *68,* 320–333; Jackson, S.E. & Schuler, R.S. A meta-analysis and conceptual critique of research on role ambiguity and role conflict in work settings. *Organizational Behavior and Human Decision Processes,* 1985, *36,* 66–78.

[16]Davis, K. *Human behavior at work.* Sixth edition. New York: McGraw-Hill, 1981, p. 37; Konar, E., Sundstrom, E., Brady, C., Mandel, D., & Rice, R.W. Status demarcation in the office. *Environment and Behavior,* September 1982, p. 571.

[17]Davis, J.H. *Group performance.* Reading, MA: Addison-Wesley, 1964, 82–86.

[18]Cartwright, D. The nature of group cohesiveness. In Cartwright, D. & Zander, A. (Eds.) *Group dynamics: Research and theory.* Third edition. New York: Harper & Row, 1968; Jewell, L.N. & Reitz, H.J. *Group effectiveness in organizations.* Glenview, IL: Scott, Foresman & Co., 1981.

[19]Piper, W.E., Marrache, M., Lacroix, R., Richardson, A.M. & Jones, B.D. Cohesion as a basic bond in groups. *Human Relations,* 1983, *36,* 93–108.

[20]DuBrin, A.J. *Contemporary applied management: Behavioral science techniques for managers and professionals.* Plano, TX: Business Publications, Inc., 1985.

CASE 12.1

The New Employees

Joe settled back into the seat of the L1011 aircraft and waited for takeoff. He had just spent five days at a software developers' convention in New York City and was glad to be returning home. Joe had not been able to get much rest during the convention since his primary reason for attending was to recruit software engineers through the convention's job placement center. As Manager of New Product Development for TKD Software, Joe has found himself dealing more with "people issues" than computer software. He doesn't really mind, however, since he has found managing people to be at least as rewarding as developing a new piece of software.

The convention had been a success for Joe. He had interviewed over 25 people for three positions which were open at TKD. He felt that he had three very strong candidates for these positions who had expressed strong interest in TKD. He was sure that he would be able to hire these individuals. All had extremely strong records, having graduated from impressive computer science programs at prestigious universities. Further, all three had several years' experience with competitors of TKD, and all had developed at least one highly successful piece of software. As expected, upon seeing the three applicants' credentials, Joe's boss told him to make formal offers of employment immediately. When all three applicants accepted the offers, Joe felt both excitement and relief. He was relieved that he had filled all open positions in his department and they could now focus their energies upon software development. He was also relieved that the workload in the department would not be so heavy. The department had been operating understaffed for several months and employees were beginning to complain about the frequent long hours and lost weekends. "Hiring these three hotshots should permit everyone to work normal hours," thought Joe as he sent the final employment documents to the personnel department. "By next week, everything will be back to normal around here."

Four months after the three new software engineers began working at TKD, Joe was confused about conditions in his department. On the one hand, these three new employees had performed very well. They had been assigned as a team to develop a new word-processing program for use in elementary and secondary schools. The program they developed has all the signs of being a market leader. Joe's boss was so pleased that at a recent staff meeting he complimented Joe on his success at attracting and hiring such high-quality people.

However, there seemed to be something going on in his department that Joe just couldn't put his finger on. On the surface, everything seemed to be going well. However, Joe had noticed that the three new employees did not interact much with the other employees. The new people usually ate lunch alone, took breaks alone and he never saw them with the others at the local "watering hole" after work. He also noticed that the others did not seem to make much effort to include the new employees in anything. For example, the annual TKD "Duffers Golf Tournament" was only two weeks away and when Joe asked the new employees if they were planning to play, they told him that they hadn't heard about the tournament. Apparently, they hadn't been sent any announcements or application forms by the planning committee.

Joe didn't know what the problem was, but he was concerned. This situation wouldn't create any difficulties for the department if the three new employees could always work as a team on software development projects, but this wasn't possible. Many projects that Joe's department worked on needed much larger teams than just three individuals. Further, with the advanced training the three new employees had received, there would be a real advantage in spreading this expertise around by assigning each of the newcomers to different teams of long-time employees. As things stood now, Joe wasn't sure how this would work. However, he knew he had to do something by the end of the summer, since the workload always picked up during the fall and winter months.

QUESTIONS

1. What kinds of things can explain the apparent lack of acceptance of the new employees?
2. What could Joe have done prior to hiring these people to prevent such problems from developing?
3. What should Joe do now to resolve the problem?

To answer the question "Is cohesiveness desirable from the organization's perspective?" the goals and norms of the group must be considered. While it is true that cohesive groups tend to be more productive and able to accomplish their goals, these are not necessarily the goals of the organization. For example, it is very common for groups to have a norm which sets what the group believes to be a fair level of productivity. This norm is often in conflict with organizational goals of high productivity. In fact, the organization may have developed its own norm or performance standard, higher than the group norm. In this case, high cohesiveness would limit productivity, from the formal organization's perspective. Therefore, to the extent that group norms and goals are consistent with those of the formal organization, cohesiveness will contribute to organizational performance and good human relations. To the extent that group norms and goals are inconsistent with those of the formal organization, group cohesiveness will limit productivity. This suggests that managers may want to try to stimulate cohesiveness in groups whose members have accepted, and are committed to, the goals of the organization. However, managers may want to try and cause cohesiveness to decline in groups whose goals and norms are substantially different from those of the formal organization. This can be done by managing the factors listed in Exhibit 12.5.

WHAT DO YOU THINK? Note

CHAPTER THIRTEEN

Leadership and Team Building

PROLOGUE

It is difficult to say exactly what makes someone a good leader, particularly at top levels of management. Sometimes the profitability, goal accomplishment or success of the organization is a measure of leadership effectiveness. The morale and opinions of employees are also evidence of good leadership. In still other cases, innovative solutions to difficult problems, or seeing the organization through difficult times, is evidence that someone is a good leader. In truth, effective leadership is probably a little of all of these things, plus a great deal more.

George A. Schaefer, Chief Executive Officer of Caterpillar, Inc. of Peoria, Illinois seems to exhibit all of the factors mentioned above. During the early 1980s, Caterpillar faced some of the most difficult times of its history due to high oil prices, foreign competition, and high interest rates. The company faced a loss of $258 million for the nine months ending in March, 1987. However, Caterpillar began to turn things around. Between March and June, 1987, Caterpillar recorded a $118-million profit which sent the price of its stock to the highest level in six years.

The turnaround has not been painless. Schaefer had to initiate some drastic cost cutting in order to meet foreign competitors' prices. Part of this cost cutting has meant a reduction of the workforce by about 40 percent. However, while Schaefer has had to make some tough decisions, he has a reputation for being "laid back." He and Caterpillar President Peter P. Donis regularly eat breakfast in the Caterpillar cafeteria with five or six middle and lower level managers. During these breakfast meetings, the managers can talk about anything they wish. Further, Schaefer recognizes the importance of maintaining a balance between work and family and leisure activities. He typically stops work at 5:30 each day and tends garden during summer months at his seven acre home near Peoria. During winter months when time and commitments permit he makes trips to a retreat in Jackson Hole, Wyoming where he enjoys skiing. He stresses this balance between work and outside interests with his employees as well. "I don't want workaholics working for me."[1]

LEARNING OBJECTIVES

Upon successful completion of this chapter, you should be able to:

- Differentiate between leadership as a process and leadership as a set of personal characteristics.
- Define leadership,
- Explain the Life Cycle Theory of Leadership,
- Relate categories of leader behaviors to situational variables,
- Understand the primary leadership styles, and determine when each is appropriate,
- Recognize the relationship between leadership and team building,
- State the characteristics of effective quality circles (QCs),
- Discuss recent approaches to team building, such as quality circles and semiautonomous work teams, and
- Understand how to build effective work teams.

LEADERS AND LEADERSHIP

If you were asked to list ten individuals you considered to be highly effective leaders, you would very likely be able to provide a list in just a couple of minutes. While it is relatively easy to determine *who* effective leaders are, it is much more difficult to determine *what* makes people effective leaders. In fact, it is difficult to precisely define *leadership* so that it is distinct from other concepts such as motivation, communication, politics, and power.[2]

Most likely, the individuals on your list of effective leaders were included for a variety of reasons. Some perhaps were chosen for their personality and ability to deal with other people. Others may have been included for their ability to influence the behavior of others. Those in positions of authority may have made your list not for their personalities, but for their power, which you perceived to be exercised fairly and impartially. One of the best-known leaders in the world is the person who occupies the office of president of the United

WHAT DO YOU THINK?

At this point, it would be a good exercise for you to actually compile the list just described. Whom do you consider to be effective leaders—high government officials such as U.S. presidents, governors, members of Congress? Does your list include a coach you once had, or a boss, or a teacher? Once you have completed this first list, start a second one stating the attributes of these highly effective leaders. Do they share a set of common characteristics? In other words, think of exactly why you consider each individual on your list an effective leader. Is the reason the same for each individual?

CHAPTER THIRTEEN: Leadership and Team Building 333

HUMAN RELATIONS IN ACTION

A Leadership Profile

One of the most highly publicized leaders in this country is the President of the United States. Each president brings his (perhaps in the future, her?) own leadership style to that position. A 1986 *Fortune* article described former president Ronald Reagan's leadership style as well as his philosophy of managing.

President Reagan's management philosophy might be described by his statement that "I believe that you surround yourself with the best people you can find, delegate authority, and don't interfere as long as the overall policy that you've decided upon is being carried out." This statement implies that President Reagan prefers to set policy or objectives, and then use a participative leadership style (perhaps even low task/low relations orientation) to allow subordinates to use their own initiative in accomplishing these objectives. It is clear that, perhaps more than any other president, President Reagan encourages subordinates to speak their minds, even when they disagree with the president. While the president generally reserves the right to make the final decision, he does seem to be more concerned than many previous presidents with hearing everyone's point of view. However, when discussions in meetings become heated or subordinates with different points of view engage in conflict, President Reagan seems to have the ability to vary his leadership style to a supportive or even directive style in order to resolve these differences. In another sense, President Reagan seems to occasionally exhibit an achievement-oriented leadership style to the general population. His speeches are noted for their positive vision of what the country is and how it can become even better.

Source: Doud, A. R. What managers can learn from manager Reagan. *Fortune,* September 15, 1986, 33–41.

States. As described in the accompanying Human Relations in Action box, a recent president was well known for his participatory leadership style.

Actually, there are various reasons why people come to be considered leaders. Some may have been considered leaders because of certain traits or characteristics they possess—intelligence, insight, originality, and judgment. In fact, the earliest leadership theories, called trait theories, emphasized traits of effective leaders. The basic idea was to determine the specific set of traits that all effective leaders exhibited, so individuals who were likely to be effective leaders could be identified and placed into leadership positions. Those who did not have the "right stuff" could also be identified and placed into positions not requiring leadership. Unfortunately, researchers soon found it very difficult to identify a set of traits that could be used to accurately predict who would be a successful leader. First, there is an almost infinite list of traits to be considered. Second, research findings were conflicting. While one study showed intelligence; for example, to be related to effective leadership, a second study might show intelligence to be totally unrelated to effective leadership.[3] Exhibit 13.1 presents some of the traits that were considered in trying to separate leaders from nonleaders. Which traits do you think effective leaders should have?

Japanese businessman Hisao Tsubouchi is considered an effective leader by many of his peers and employees. If you did not know that he was the head

Differentiate between leadership as a process and leadership as a set of personal characteristics.

> **Exhibit 13.1**
> The "right stuff" of leaders
>
> | | |
> |---|---|
> | Age | Height |
> | Weight | Physique |
> | Athletic ability | Energy |
> | Health | Appearance |
> | Fluency of speech | Intelligence |
> | Scholarship | Knowledge |
> | Judgment and decision | Insight |
> | Originality | Adaptability |
> | Introversion/Extroversion | Dominance |
> | Initiative | Persistence |
> | Ambition | Responsibility |
> | Integrity | Strength of conviction |
> | Self-confidence | Mood control/Mood optimism |
> | Emotional control | |
> | Social activity and mobility | Social and economic status |
> | Social skills | Daring/Adventurous/Active |
> | Prestige | Popularity |
> | | Cooperation |

Source: Developed from Stogdill, R.M. *The handbook of leadership*. New York: The Free Press, 1974, Chapter 5.

of one of the largest industrial fortunes in the world, what would you think of his leadership style? Tsubouchi begins his day at 5:00 A.M. He visits at least three of his companies every day. At the age of seventy, he commonly wears faded, loose-fitting clothes to his office. He has earned a reputation as a tough, autocratic manager. He has fired large numbers of employees and broken several unions. Employees, who have been told that bonuses come directly out of his pocket, have learned to fear him. Training sessions involve grueling self-criticism sessions which are intended to teach employees the "joy of working." He expects employees to call him "Owner Tsubouchi." According to Tsubouchi, "I did some investigating to find what employees like in a boss, and I found they like someone who lives frugally, is serious, treats employees well, and has no mistresses. I have done my best to become the model boss."[4]

Leaders and Leadership Defined

Two primary forms of leaders have been identified—*appointed* (formal) leaders and *emergent* (informal) leaders. **Appointed leaders** are individuals placed in positions of authority by the organization. The organization has given them the authority to "lead" other members of the organization. **Emergent leaders** are individuals able to influence others by means other than formal authority, such as personality, interpersonal skills, expertise, and knowledge. Emergent leaders are not appointed to their positions by the organization. Rather, they assume (emerge into) leadership roles due to their charisma or expertise. We are primarily interested in appointed leaders (managers) in this chapter; however, many appointed leaders may have become emergent leaders had they not been placed in a position of authority by the organization. Also, many appointed leaders may also develop interpersonal skills, expertise, knowledge, or have magnetic personalities and thereby become even more effective as leaders.

Leadership in organizational work settings is the process of influencing members of an organization to engage in activities that will contribute to organizational goal accomplishment. This definition implies the use of some form of power to influence the behavior of others.

Define leadership.

Bases of Power

There are five primary **bases of power** on which managers may rely to influence employees.[5] Later discussion will show that the power base a manager uses directly influences his leadership style which, in turn, influences the human relations climate within the organization.

1. **Reward Power**. The authority or ability to reward employees provides a certain degree of power. To the extent that a manager controls rewards the employees desire, they will submit to his attempts to influence their behavior.
2. **Coercive Power**. The authority or ability to punish employees or withhold rewards provides a certain degree of power. To the extent that employees wish to avoid sanctions that a manager controls, or to the extent that they desire rewards he is able to withhold from them, they will submit to his attempts to influence their behavior.
3. **Legitimate Power**. Legitimate power stems directly from the manager's formal position. The organization has placed him in a position of authority over other organizational members. To the extent that employees view his position of authority as appropriate or legitimate, they will be willing to be influenced by him. To illustrate, if a manager makes requests of employees, they may willingly comply because they view his requests as legitimate by virtue of his position.
4. **Expert Power**. To the extent that a manager is regarded as an expert in a particular area, employees are likely to submit to his attempts to influence their behavior. For example, assume that the department has just installed microcomputers on everyone's desk. If the manager is regarded as a microcomputer expert, then employees probably will follow his directions in matters pertaining to microcomputers. However, his influence may not extend to other areas in which employees do not regard him as an expert.
5. **Referent Power**. To the extent that employees like and respect a manager, and identify with him (want to be like him), they are likely to submit to his attempts to influence their behavior. This is similar to the idea of the "charismatic leader," such as John F. Kennedy, Paul "Bear" Bryant, and Lee Iacocca. **Charismatic leaders** seem to be able to exert unusually strong in-

fluence on employees.[6] This ability is undoubtedly due to the great willingness of employees to follow a charismatic leader.

Every manager, at least to some degree, has reward, coercive, and legitimate power based upon his position within the organization. Thus, managers can exert at least some degree of influence on employees by drawing on these power bases. However, managers can be more effective leaders to the extent that they work to develop referent and expert power bases. The first three bases of power (reward, coercive, and legitimate) are related to formal authority. While employees may submit to the influence of managers using these forms of power, their willingness to be influenced may decline over time. Employees are likely to be influenced voluntarily for longer periods of time by attempts based at least in part on the manager's use of informal authority (expert and referent power) along with explanations of any requests of employees.[7] Which of the five bases of power do you think Japanese businessman Hisao Tsubouchi, described earlier in the chapter, relies on most heavily?

A manager who functions through reward, coercive, and legitimate power may create a climate in which employees feel they are being closely controlled. This may give rise to feelings that the manager doesn't trust or have confidence in them. The human relations climate in this manager's department is likely to be one of distrust, suspicion, and alienation. Employees may do what they are specifically asked to do—but no more. On the other hand, a manager who relies also on expert and referent power creates a much different human relations climate in the department. Here, employees willingly submit to the manager's influence attempts. Since such a manager is likely to be more participative, employees are more involved in important decisions that affect their jobs. As a result, the human relations climate is one of trust, confidence, and involvement. Thus, the most effective leaders are those who draw on all five bases of power, not just those directly related to their managerial position within the organization.

Managers at Squibb Corporation determined that they were relying too heavily on formal power in managing their employees. As a result, a training program entitled "Insights to Productive Leadership" was developed to help Squibb managers improve, and place more emphasis on, their interpersonal skills. The workshop emphasizes to managers how the way they interact with others impacts the human relations climate within the organization. Interpersonal skill improvement training is provided in several areas including communicating with employees, providing feedback, resolving problem situations, recognizing individual differences, and negotiating with employees.[8]

Leadership Behaviors

The most popular leadership theories describe two categories of leader behaviors, *task-oriented* and *relations-oriented*. These theories focus on identifying situations where each type of leader behavior would be most effective. In other words, the presence of certain situational variables will call for task-oriented leader behaviors, while the presence of other situational variables will call for relations-oriented leader behaviors. In addition, certain situations may require leaders to engage in both types of leader behaviors. Finally, although perhaps less frequent, there may be some situations that call for few behaviors of either type on the part of the leader.

The two categories of leader behaviors are not "either-or" ends of the same continuum. Rather, they are separate and independent categories of behaviors that may be exhibited simultaneously. While many managers may have a **dominant leadership style** (e.g., a style they prefer or feel more comfortable exhibiting), it is not true that leaders have to be either task-oriented *or* relations-oriented.[9] They may vary their style according to the particular situation. First, let's identify the specific behaviors included in these two categories of leader behaviors, and then turn our attention to the situational variables that affect the type of leader behavior likely to be most effective.

Task-Oriented Leader Behaviors
A leader who engages in **task-oriented behavior** is not an autocratic, inflexible, taskmaster. Rather, task-oriented behaviors are related to completing tasks effectively and on time. Examples of task-oriented leader behaviors include:

1. Emphasizing quality and quantity of output,
2. Scheduling the work to be done,
3. Encouraging employees to perform up to their capabilities,
4. Emphasizing the importance of meeting deadlines,
5. Setting high performance standards, and
6. Instructing employees in how to perform tasks.

Relations-Oriented Leader Behaviors
Relations-oriented behaviors are linked to employee welfare, morale and motivation. Examples of relations-oriented behaviors include:

1. Treating employees as equals,
2. Being friendly and accessible to employees,
3. Encouraging employees to participate in important decisions that affect their jobs,
4. Keeping employees informed about what is going on in the organization,
5. Encouraging employees to communicate openly about their problems and concerns,
6. Giving employees some freedom in deciding how to perform their jobs,
7. Complimenting and rewarding employees for good work, and
8. Exhibiting trust in employees and respecting them.

Since these two categories of leader behaviors are independent, a leader may exhibit a low or high degree of both types of behaviors. Further, behaviors may change with the situation, so that in one situation a leader may exhibit many behaviors from both categories, while in another case that leader may exhibit several relations-oriented behaviors and few task-oriented behaviors. Thus, there are four primary combinations of these categories of leader behaviors: (1) low-task, low-relations; (2) low-task, high-relations; (3) high-task, high-relations; and (4) high-task, low-relations. The appropriateness of each of these combinations depends on a number of situational variables.

LEADER BEHAVIORS AND SITUATIONAL VARIABLES

As mentioned earlier, a number of the most popular leadership theories focus on identifying those situational variables that determine which leader behaviors are most appropriate. Rather than detail each of these theories, this chapter will present a modified version of one of the most popular situational leadership theories, then expand it to include a summary of the suggestions of other situational leadership theories.

The Life Cycle Theory of Leadership

Hersey and Blanchard have proposed the Life Cycle Theory of Leadership, which is based on one important situational variable, task-relevant maturity.[10] A modified version of this theory is presented graphically Exhibit 13.2. While this theory has received some criticism, it continues to be one of the most popular theories of leadership.[11]

Explain the Life Cycle Theory of Leadership.

Task-relevant maturity consists of two components: (1) *psychological* maturity, or motivation to perform, and (2) *job* maturity, or ability to perform.[12] Employees lacking job maturity need guidance and structure to enable them to perform their jobs. Thus, a lack of job maturity calls for task-oriented leader behaviors. Employees lacking in psychological maturity need coaching and encouragement to increase their motivation to perform. Here, relations-oriented leader behaviors are most appropriate. Employees who are both psychologically mature and job mature do not require a particular emphasis on either task-oriented or relations-oriented leader behaviors. When employees' job maturity begins to increase, less emphasis can be placed on task-oriented leader behaviors and more emphasis should be placed on relations-oriented leader behaviors so that these employees are encouraged to continue to mature. These four situations are represented in Exhibit 13.2 by four sections on the maturity curve and four quadrants representing the four leadership styles.

The bell-shaped curve in Exhibit 13.2 represents an employee's task-relevant maturity, including both job maturity (ability) and psychological maturity (motivation). Beginning at the lower right-hand corner, the employee has low task-relevant maturity due to low levels of both ability and motivation. Task-oriented leader behaviors are required in this situation, to get the employee to perform at an acceptable level as soon as possible. As the employee begins to learn how to perform (increased job maturity), the leader can begin to add relations-oriented behaviors to increase the employee's motivation (psychological maturity). Moving up the maturity curve to Quadrant 2, it is apparent that an emphasis on both task-oriented and relations-oriented leader behaviors is most appropriate. If the employee continues to mature, both ability and motivation continue to increase. Moving to Quadrant 3, the employee now has a relatively high ability level, while motivation is still increasing. Thus, task-

Exhibit 13.2
Modified Life Cycle Theory of Leadership

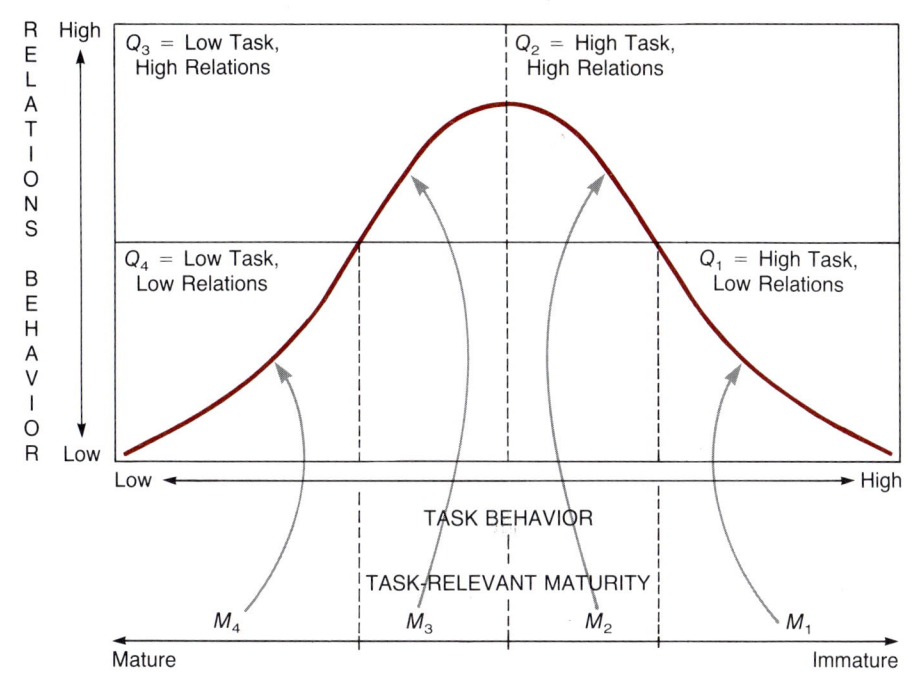

EFFECTIVE LEADERSHIP STYLES

RELATIONS BEHAVIOR (High/Low) vs. TASK BEHAVIOR (Low/High)

- Q_3 = Low Task, High Relations
- Q_2 = High Task, High Relations
- Q_4 = Low Task, Low Relations
- Q_1 = High Task, Low Relations

TASK-RELEVANT MATURITY: M_4 (Mature) — M_3 — M_2 — M_1 (Immature)

M_1 = Low Ability and Low Motivation.
M_2 = Low-Moderate Ability and Low Motivation.
M_3 = High Ability and Low-Moderate Motivation.
M_4 = High Ability and High Motivation.

Source: Adapted from Hersey, P. & Blanchard, K.H. *Management of organization behavior: Utilizing human resources.* Third edition. Englewood Cliffs, N.J.: Prentice-Hall, 1982, p. 96. Adapted by permission of Prentice-Hall, Inc.

oriented behaviors become less important; however, relations-oriented behaviors are still needed so that the employee's motivational level will continue to increase. Once the employee becomes highly motivated to perform (Quadrant 4), relations-oriented leader behaviors become less important. At this point, the leader does not need to emphasize either task-oriented or relations-oriented behaviors. In this ideal situation, the employee not only clearly knows how to perform and has the ability, but is also highly motivated to do so.

Individuals do not move in only one direction along the task-relevant maturity curve. After moving into Quadrant 4, for example, an employee who experiences a failure might move backward along this curve all the way to Quadrant 1. In other words, the employee's job maturity has decreased as a result of the failure. This employee is now likely to respond best to task-oriented leader behaviors until his confidence returns. Other factors might impact psychological maturity. The important point here is that managers must be constantly aware of their employees' levels of maturity in order to engage in the leader behaviors that will be most effective with each employee.

Summary of Other Situational Leadership Theories

Task-relevant maturity is clearly an important situational variable for managers to consider when deciding upon an appropriate leadership style. However, a number of other important situational variables have been identified. Exhibit 13.3 presents the four primary combinations of the two categories of leader behaviors and the situational variables that have been included in other popular situational leadership theories.[13] These situational variables can be categorized as either employee-related, manager-related, or organization-related.[14]

Relate categories of leader behaviors to situational variables.

Employee-Related Situational Variables. Exhibit 13.3 can be used to interpret employee-related situational variables by locating a point on one of the situational variables continuums, then finding the box at the top to determine which leadership style is most appropriate. For example, employees who have a low tolerance for ambiguity are likely to perform best under a high-task, low-relations leadership style. These employees will not perform well in a situation where the task, performance standards, or objectives to be accomplished are unclear. They need the structure that high-task, low-relations leader behaviors provide. These employees may prefer to be told precisely what to do and how to do it. In contrast, employees with a high tolerance for ambiguity may perform well under a leader exhibiting low task-oriented behaviors.

Employees with high levels of skills, abilities, experience, and job knowledge do not need the structure of high task-oriented leader behaviors. They know what needs to be done and also how to do it. Emphasizing task-oriented behavior may actually have an adverse affect on the performance of these employees. Imagine yourself about to perform a task with which you are very familiar. You have performed this task successfully numerous times. How would you react to someone standing over you, telling you precisely how to perform this task? Probably, you would be annoyed. Highly skilled employees may respond more positively to relations-oriented leader behaviors if they lack motivation, or to low-task/low-relations behavior if they are both highly skilled and motivated.

Employees who display high interest in their task are likely to be concerned with the quality and quantity of their performance. This high interest acts as somewhat of a substitute for task-oriented leader behaviors.[15] Whether or not these employees will perform best under low-task/high-relations behavior or low-task/low-relations behavior depends on their motivation and whether team building or conflict resolution is needed. Employees who are motivated and who are already working well together may perform best under low-task/low-relations leader behavior. On the other hand, employees with little interest in their tasks may require task-oriented behaviors to keep them performing up to standard.

Employees who have a high need for independence may feel unnecessarily constrained working for a leader who frequently engages in high task-oriented behaviors. Low-task/high-relations or low-task/low-relations behaviors

Exhibit 13.3
Summary of major contingency theories of leadership

Low Task/ Low Relations	Low Task/ High Relations	High Task/ High Relations	High Task/ Low Relations

Employee-Related Characteristics

Tolerance for Ambiguity
High ←--------------------------------------→ Low

Skills, abilities, experience, job knowledge
High ←--------------------------------------→ Low

Interest in the task
High ←--------------------------------------→ Low

Employee independence
High ←--------------------------------------→ Low

Acceptance of decision by employees needed
Low ←----------→ High ←----------------→ Low

Employee motivation
High ←----------→ Low ←----------------→ High

Manager-Related Characteristics

Confidence/trust in employees
High ←--------------------------------------→ Low

Relations with employees
Good ←--------------------------------------→ Poor

Manager has sufficient information to make decision
Yes ←----------------→ No ←----------------→ Yes

Organization-Related Characteristics

Organizational culture/history
??? ←--------------------------------------→ ???

Task uniqueness/complexity
Low ←--------------------------------------→ High

Time pressure
Low ←--------------------------------------→ High

Simple/repetitive task
No ←----------------→ Yes ←----------------→ No

Number of employees supervised
Few ←--------------------------------------→ Many

Degree of task structure
High ←--------------------------------------→ Low

are more likely to provide the freedom these employees need. However, this assumes that they know how to perform the task and are willing to do so.

When the acceptance of a decision by employees is important, high relations-oriented leader behaviors may be most appropriate. If employees are afforded a high degree of participation in the decision-making process, they will be more likely to accept the decision. And if they accept the decision, they will be more likely to ensure that it is implemented properly. Using task-oriented leader behaviors and shutting employees out of the decision-making process when their acceptance of the decision is needed may result in low employee commitment in implementing the decision successfully. In extreme cases, employees may actually sabotage a decision and prevent it from being carried out according to plan.[16]

The level of an employee's motivation will also affect which leader behaviors are likely to be most effective. Employees who lack motivation may respond to a leader who emphasizes relations-oriented behaviors. If these employees have the knowledge, skills, and experience to perform effectively, the leader is likely to be most effective by engaging in low task-oriented/high relations-oriented behaviors. On the other hand, if these employees lack job knowledge, experience, or ability, in addition to motivation, the leader also may need to engage in task-related leader behaviors (high task-oriented/high relations-oriented behaviors).

Manager-Related Characteristics. Managers who lack confidence and trust in their employees are likely to emphasize task-oriented behaviors. Such behaviors provide the close control necessary to ensure that tasks are performed successfully and on time. Managers who have high levels of confidence and trust in employees may be more comfortable exhibiting relations oriented behaviors or low-task/low-relations behaviors since they believe that close control of employees is not necessary. When their relations with employees are poor, managers often feel the need to control work activities closely. They tend to emphasize such task-oriented leader behaviors as setting performance standards, scheduling the work, and enforcing adherence to deadlines. When relations with employees are good, managers may feel more comfortable emphasizing low-task/high-relations or low-task/low-relations behaviors, allowing employees more freedom.

When a manager has sufficient information to make a decision, he can make the decision alone (high-task/low-relations or low-task/low-relations behaviors). However, when a manager has insufficient information to make a decision, employee participation associated with high relations-oriented leader behavior is needed.[17]

Organization-Related Characteristics. Many organizations have a culture or history that favors a particular set of leader behaviors. For example, in some organizations, encouraging employees to participate in important decisions may be viewed as weakness. In these organizations, managers are expected to run the show and employees are expected to follow. Other organizations may value a high level of employee participation in policy-making or setting standards. In these organizations, managers who are unable to engage in relations-oriented behaviors may be viewed with disfavor. This is not to suggest that either of these organizations represents the correct corporate culture. However, to be a successful manager in an organization, you must exhibit the type of leader behaviors expected of you. Earlier in the chapter, Squibb Corporation's leadership training program was described. This program was designed to help managers rely less on formal power and more on informal power and social skills. It is likely that managers at Squibb are expected to emphasize a relations-oriented leadership style over a task-oriented one.

The uniqueness and complexity of a task directly influence the type of leader behavior which will be most effective. When a task is highly complex or unique, task-oriented leader behaviors may be called for because employees would not have the experience for performing a unique task or the job information they need for a complex task. Furthermore, if conditions are constantly changing, new problems may develop that employees lack experience in solving. In contrast, for simple and repetitive tasks, task-oriented leader behaviors will probably not be necessary, but, relations-oriented behaviors may be needed to keep employees motivated.

When there is a great deal of time pressure, there may not be time to engage in relations-oriented behaviors (encouraging employees to participate in decision making and allowing them freedom on the job). The leader may have little choice but to emphasize task-oriented behaviors.

When the number of employees supervised is large, managers may not have the time to engage primarily in relations-oriented behaviors. Thus, holding all other variables constant, task-oriented leader behaviors may be required. However, when a leader supervises only a few employees, there may be adequate time to allow them freedom on the job and encourage their participation in important decisions.

When a task is highly structured, with methods and procedures clearly detailed, task-oriented leader behaviors become less appropriate. If employees are highly motivated and work well together, low-task/low-relations leader behaviors may suffice. If employees lack motivation or do not work well together, low-task/high-relations behaviors may be most effective.[18] On the other hand, tasks that are less structured may require an emphasis on task-oriented leader behaviors.

Combining Situational Variables

So far, each of these situational variables has been considered individually. In a real work setting, however, managers have to consider all of these situational variables together to determine the type of leader behaviors needed in a given situation. Let's say, for example, the manager is contending with (a) a task that is highly structured; (b) employees who are skilled and experienced; (c) employees with a high tolerance for ambiguity; and (d) a rush schedule that allows no room for errors. In this situation, what type of leader behavior would you choose? The first three variables call for relations-oriented behaviors; the last variable calls for task-oriented behaviors. The difficulty for the leader is to determine which of these variables dominate (are most important) in that particular situation, or if any are unimportant. Even though there is extreme time pressure in the example, a highly structured task and highly skilled, experienced employees may make task-oriented behaviors unnecessary.

LEADERSHIP STYLES

Leadership style may be defined as the leader's predominant pattern of behavior toward employees. It is closely related to the four primary combinations of leader behaviors discussed earlier. For example, a leader who engages primarily in task-oriented behaviors displays a *directive* leadership style. A leader who engages primarily in relations-oriented behaviors exhibits a *supportive* leadership style. There are, in addition, two other primary leadership styles: *participative* leadership and *achievement-oriented* leadership.[19]

> Understand the primary leadership styles and determine when each is appropriate.

Directive Leadership Style. A leader exhibiting this style provides specific instructions for performing tasks, sets performance standards, schedules work to be done, and develops rules and regulations.

Supportive Leadership Style. A leader engaging in this style shows concern for the personal needs of employees and works to develop good interpersonal relations among members of the work group.

Participative Leadership Style. A participative leader keeps employees informed about organizational activities and plans, asks employees for suggestions, and includes employees in decision making.

Achievement-Oriented Leadership Style. With this style, the leader sets challenging goals and high performance standards, encourages employees to continually improve their performance, and maintains high expectations of employees.[20]

Exhibit 13.4 shows the relationship between these leadership styles and types of leader behaviors. Exhibit 13.5 presents the relationship between the four primary leadership styles and several situational variables. It shows that (1) a supportive leadership style involves an emphasis on relations-oriented behaviors and is appropriate for employees working on simple/repetitive jobs; (2) a directive leadership style involves an emphasis on task-related behaviors and is appropriate when the task is unique, complex, and not highly structured; (3) an achievement-oriented leadership style involves an emphasis on *both* task- and relations-oriented behaviors, and is appropriate when the task does not provide a challenge to motivate employees; and finally (4) a participative leadership style involves low to moderate levels of both task- and relations-oriented behaviors, and is appropriate when the task is not clearly defined. The participative leader does not emphasize either type of leader behavior, but rather encourages employee participation. Through participation in the decision-making process, employees obtain increased information about their jobs and the organization. The participative leader engages in only enough task-oriented behaviors to keep employees on track and in only enough relations-oriented behaviors to keep them motivated.

Comparison of Leadership Styles

Do not be misled that any one of these leadership styles is necessarily better than the others. Consider that while at first glance a supportive style might

Exhibit 13.4
Relationship between leadership styles and behaviors

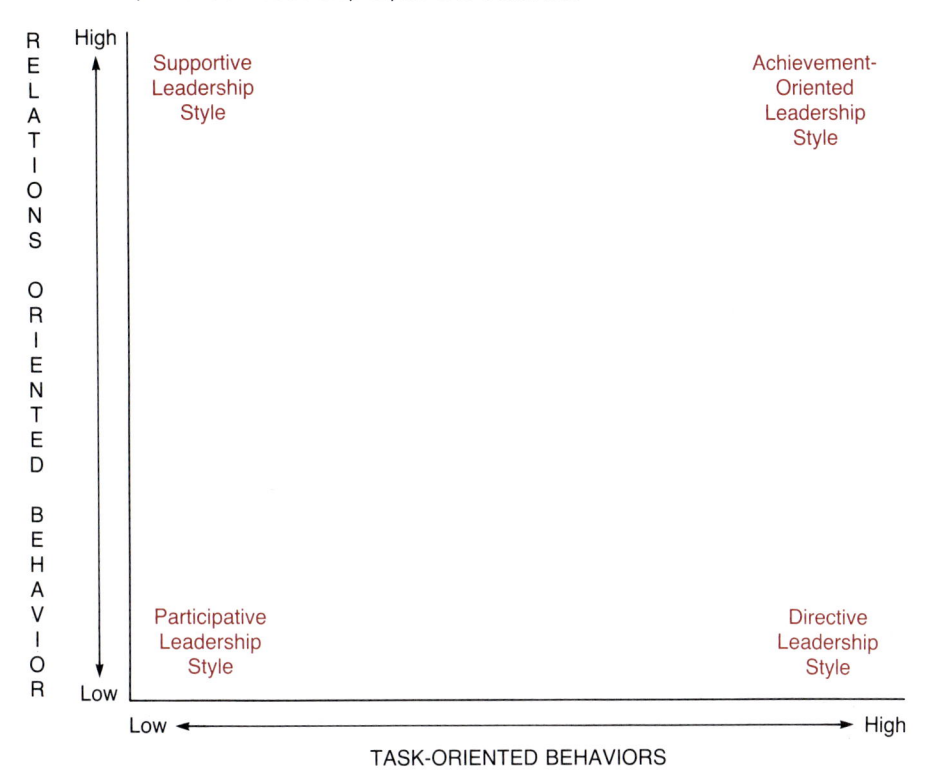

```
RELATIONS ORIENTED BEHAVIOR
High
  │  Supportive                    Achievement-
  │  Leadership                    Oriented
  │  Style                         Leadership
  │                                Style
  │
  │
  │
  │
  │
  │  Participative                 Directive
  │  Leadership                    Leadership
  │  Style                         Style
Low└─────────────────────────────────────────
   Low ←───── TASK-ORIENTED BEHAVIORS ─────→ High
```

seem more closely related to a good human relations climate, this is not necessarily the case. In a situation where the task is unique and complex and employees have had little experience, a supportive leadership style is not appropriate, and could actually damage human relations within the work group.

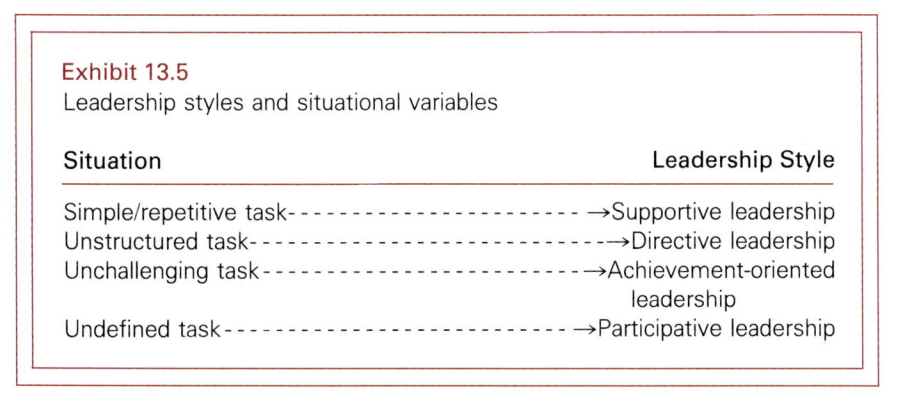

Exhibit 13.5
Leadership styles and situational variables

Situation	Leadership Style
Simple/repetitive task	→Supportive leadership
Unstructured task	→Directive leadership
Unchallenging task	→Achievement-oriented leadership
Undefined task	→Participative leadership

Source: Adapted from Yukl, G.A. *Leadership in organizations.* Englewood Cliffs, N.J.: Prentice-Hall, 1981, 146–152.

RETURN TO THE PROLOGUE

The CEO of Caterpillar, George A. Schaefer, was discussed in the Prologue. He apparently has the flexibility to be tough when necessary—as when he had to lay off a large number of Caterpillar employees. Yet he has also earned a reputation for being "laid back." He also appears to be achievement-oriented in his determination to turn things around for Caterpillar, and participative in his breakfast meetings with Cat employees. Schaefer's flexibility to exhibit all of the primary leadership styles when called for has helped him bring Caterpillar back to profitability.

These employees need information and structure regarding their task and performance expectations; therefore, supportive leadership style in this situation might be viewed as incompetence. Employees may perceive they are being unfairly held responsible for a task they cannot possibly complete successfully. Few things can damage human relations faster than a perception of unfair treatment. On the other hand, human relations may be improved in this situation by a leader displaying a directive leadership style. Employees could perceive that they can count on their leader to provide whatever is necessary to enable them to perform their tasks successfully. It is evident that good human relations are enhanced by engaging in the leadership style called for by the situation.

Conclusions About Leadership

Two primary conclusions from current leadership theory are: (1) managers must first carefully diagnose each situation to determine the specific leadership style needed to help employees perform their jobs successfully; and (2) managers must develop the flexibility to vary their leadership style to match situational variables. This versatility may be difficult for those managers who have a dominant leadership style with which they are most comfortable. However, several theories are based on the assumption that managers can learn to vary their leadership style.[21] Even those managers with a highly dominant style can learn to exhibit other types of leader behaviors when they are required.

LEADERSHIP AND TEAMWORK

While it is established that managers may have to use a slightly different leadership style with each individual employee, leadership does have a direct effect on the work group as a whole. This influence is particularly strong when the tasks are interdependent (i.e., the output of one employee's job becomes the input for another employee's job; the second job cannot begin until the first job has been completed successfully). However, even when employees work independently on their jobs, poor human relations within the work group can develop into conflict and dysfunctional behavior that can impact on employees' job performance. Further, there is a trend to combine previously independent jobs into work teams such as semiautonomous work groups or quality circles.

A Quality circle (QC) is a small group of employees who meet regularly to develop solutions to work-related problems.

Thus, one important aspect of leadership, and good human relations, is **building teamwork**. These newer forms of work teams or work groups will be examined in this chapter, together with a discussion of what leaders can do to enhance teamwork within their work group.

Quality Circles

A **quality circle (QC)** is a small group of employees, usually from the same department or division, who meet regularly to discuss and develop solutions to work problems. While QCs vary considerably from organization to organization, a typical QC consists of 3 to 15 members who meet voluntarily, on company time, at least once per month. A manager or supervisor typically serves as the QC leader.[22] Exhibit 13.6 presents some of the characteristics of effective QCs—many of them directly related to leadership. For example, the QC leader must instill in the members an acceptance of high standards of performance—by developing high expectations of their performance and encouraging employees to perform up to their capabilities.[23] Further, employee satisfaction and commitment depend heavily on the leader's ability to diagnose the situation and provide structure and/or support as it is needed. QC activities are often quite different from employees' primary jobs. Thus, directive leadership may be needed initially as employees learn their new QC roles, while supportive or participative leadership may be appropriate with an experienced QC.

Recognize the relationship between leadership and team building.

> **Exhibit 13.6**
> Characteristics of effective quality circles
>
> | Characteristic | Definition |
> | --- | --- |
> | Cohesion | The extent to which the individual members want to continue participating in their QC. |
> | High performance norms | Standards of performance developed by the group. |
> | Satisfaction with leader, coworkers, and job | Leader refers to formal manager, coworkers refers to everyday coworkers, job refers to employees' regular job (not QC activities). |
> | Intrinsic and extrinsic satisfaction | Intrinsic satisfaction is the satisfaction with rewards that come from performing a task. Extrinsic satisfaction is the satisfaction with rewards that are external to the task, such as pay. |
> | Organization's commitment to the QC | The extent to which QC members believe that the organization is committed to the QC program. |
> | Self-esteem | Extent to which an individual respects his own abilities, competencies, and skills and the degree of confidence the person has in approaching new problems. |

Source: Wayne, S., Griffin, R.W. & Bateman, T.S. Improving the effectiveness of quality circles. *Personnel Administrator,* 1986, *31,* 79–88, 84.

Semiautonomous Work Groups

State the characteristics of effective quality circles.

Semiautonomous work groups are similar to QCs in that both increase employee participation and autonomy. While specific applications of these groups vary among organizations, several characteristics can be identified. Members (usually about eight to fifteen employees) of semiautonomous work groups decide how tasks are to be performed and which members will perform them; interview job applicants; establish goals; train new employees; set vacation schedules; control costs; conduct quality inspections; and develop better methods of performing tasks.[24] The accompanying Human Relations in Action box illustrates one organization's approach to semiautonomous work groups.

Discuss recent approaches to team building, such as quality circles and semiautonomous work teams.

Encouraging Teamwork

These new forms of work groups (QCs and semiautonomous work groups) are but two forces making teamwork critical to an organization's success. Even in the absence of such new forms of work groups, teamwork is becoming more and more important if organizations are to react and adapt to their changing environments. Several ways of encouraging teamwork have been identified:

CHAPTER THIRTEEN: Leadership and Team Building   349

Members of semiautonomous work groups check the quality of their own work.

1. Develop an expectation of teamwork. Leaders should make it clear through their behavior, reward practices, and communications that working together is an expected form of behavior. Teamwork should be emphasized as an expectation; failure to work together should be treated as a failure to accomplish an objective.
2. Encourage and provide emotional support. Employees should be encouraged and supported for expressing ideas and suggestions for improving task performance. The leader should also encourage members of the group to provide encouragement and support for each other.
3. Emphasize a common goal. Conflict tends to be minimized and work group members tend to pull together when they are working toward a common goal. Leaders should encourage employees to take part in determining goals for their work groups. When employees participate in goal setting, they may be more committed to accomplishing these goals, since they are at least in part, the employees' goals. The basic idea here is that goals, rather than a manager, guide their behavior.
4. Support the work group. Leaders must be willing to stand up to higher management on behalf of the work group. Employees tend to pull together behind a leader who is willing to fight for the team, especially with higher levels of management. This does not mean that the leader is in constant conflict with management. It means that the leader is constantly aware of the group's needs, and works to provide those things. If a leader is willing to go to bat for the work group, employees are more likely to stand behind this leader and work together to make the group successful.

Understand how to build effective work teams.

HUMAN RELATIONS IN ACTION

One Company's Approach to Semiautonomous Work Groups

General Motor's Saturn Plant at Spring Hill, Tennessee received a great deal of attention in the news even before it was built, due primarily to its plans for relatively unusual semiautonomous work groups. While semiautonomous work groups are not particularly unusual, Saturn's plans for implementation of these groups is unusual to the extent the basic idea is being carried. One of the most unusual elements of these plans is the degree to which assembly line employees will be involved in the decision-making process. Saturn's employees are considered to be full partners of management. As such they will perform many activities previously considered to be solely managerial. For example, there will be no foremen to supervise these work teams of six to fifteen employees. The teams will supervise their own work. They will also decide which team member will perform each job, maintain their own equipment, order their own supplies, and even interview job applicants for membership in their work team. Distinctions between assembly line employees and managers will be further lessened by: paying all employees a salary rather than an hourly rate, eliminating time clocks, eliminating reserved parking places, and doing without an executive cafeteria. Saturn employees will experience autonomy not found in many other organizations. The union representing Saturn employees (United Auto Workers–UAW) will even have the power to veto decisions made at all levels of the plant. The Saturn Plant will truly be "co-managed" by Saturn executives and assembly line employees.

Source: Maynard, M. A labor deal that clears way for GM's Saturn. *U. S. News and World Report,* August 5, 1985, 22; Edid, M. How power will be balanced on Saturn's shop floor. *Business Week,* August 5, 1985, 65–66.

---

5. Engage in competition with another workteam. Supervisors at an Oscar Mayer meat packing plant in the midwest used to place a large sign above the employees' entrance to the plant. The only thing printed on the sign was the number representing the productivity of the best performing shift for that week and the number of that leading shift. Nothing else had to be said. Employees on each shift worked together to beat the record of the other shift. The only way they could beat the record was to work together; individual efforts could not do it. Employees who began to fall behind were immediately helped by other employees until they caught up. The supervisors did not have to ask employees to help one another. They did it on their own so that their shift wouldn't be outperformed by any other shift.
6. Orient new workteam members. The importance of good orientation programs was discussed in Chapter 3. In terms of building teamwork, new employees must be made to feel they are an important part of the workteam as soon as possible.
7. Encourage employee participation. All employees should be encouraged to participate in making decisions that will affect their jobs. Employee participation often results in a perception of "ownership" of the job, which translates into increased commitment and teamwork.
8. Encourage open communication. Employees have a need to be kept informed about the organization's and department's activities and plans. Sim-

DEVELOPING YOUR HUMAN RELATIONS SKILLS

The information presented in this chapter has several important implications for you, both as an employee and a manager. As an employee, a knowledge of leadership can help you understand and get along with your manager. You should become aware of the following characteristics of your manager:

1. Does your manager have a dominant leadership style? If so, what is it and how does it fit your own personality? Recognition of your manager's dominant style may make it easier to tolerate his task-oriented behaviors, when you really needed relations-oriented behaviors.
2. Among the many situational variables that determine the most appropriate leadership style, there may be several variables of which you are unaware. One or more of these influences may account for managers using one leadership style when you were expecting another. If your manager seems particularly task-oriented when you would prefer relations-oriented behaviors, be tolerant. It may be that there is a crisis or unusual time demand that requires a task-oriented style.
3. If your manager has the flexibility to engage in a variety of leadership styles, help him get to know which style you work with most effectively. Provide positive feedback to him when he leads in the style you prefer. For example, if you currently prefer a task-oriented style, you might let your boss know by saying "I really appreciate the way you let me know how to handle that last job."

This chapter also has several important implications for you as a leader:

1. The first step is to get to know yourself. Learn whether you have a dominant leadership style and what it is, or whether you are flexible and can engage in a variety of leadership styles. Do you tend to rely on only one or two bases of power, or have you developed all five?
2. Become aware of the many situational variables which determine the effectiveness of leadership—and when each leadership style is most appropriate.
3. Carefully observe and model your behavior after other managers who appear to be effective leaders. You may not be able to copy exactly the behavior of another leader since you are likely to face situations somewhat different from those faced by this individual. However, if you have a particularly difficult time with a particular leadership style or situation, you may gain insight in how to improve in this area by observing other leaders.
4. You may also wish to ask for feedback about your leadership style from superiors, coworkers, and employees. Many times other people who observe your behavior have valuable insights of which you are unaware, but, they may be unwilling to provide feedback unless it is requested.

ilarly, managers have a need for employees to keep them informed on how various aspects of the work are going. This interchange requires open two-way communication between the leader and employees, and also among employees, to ensure that information gets to the place it is needed in time to be useful.[25]

General Foods has had great success with its approach to teamwork called "interfunctional" work teams. These teams are made up of individuals from various disciplines and departments such as finance, accounting, and marketing. They are similar to quality circles and semiautonomous work teams in that their focus is on improving the performance of their product. A major difference, however, is that interfunctional team members are expected to contribute to the product outside their own specialty. A marketing representative, for instance, would be expected to contribute to solving financial problems. General Foods expects to realize several benefits from these teams. One major benefit will come from accessing the previously untapped skills and resources of employees. This leads to greater creativity and innovation and more ideas for use in problem solving. Employees also become more motivated and excited about their work when working in a team than when working alone. A second benefit is that the increased participation by employees may lead to feelings of job or product ownership. Employees may begin to feel that Minute Rice, for example, is "their product." This attitude, in turn, leads to greater employee involvement, commitment, jobs satisfaction, and motivation.[26]

SUMMARY

While it is relatively easy to identify those persons whom most people would agree are effective leaders, it is much more difficult to identify precisely what it is that makes them good leaders. Two primary forms of leaders have been identified. Appointed leaders are placed in positions of authority by the organization. Emergent leaders are able to influence others by means other than formal authority or position within an organization. Emergent leaders are not appointed to their positions, but rather just "emerge" as leaders.

Leadership is defined as the process of influencing members of an organization to engage in activities that will contribute to organizational goal accomplishment. Leadership, as a form of influence, is related to five bases of power: reward, coercive, legitimate, referent, and expert. The most effective leaders generally develop and use all five.

Two primary categories of leader behaviors have been identified. Task-oriented behaviors emphasize completing tasks effectively and on time. Relations-oriented behaviors emphasize employee welfare, morale, and motivation. Situational variables determine which specific combination of these two categories of leader behaviors is likely to be most effective.

One of the most popular situational leadership theories is Hersey and Blanchard's Life Cycle Theory of Leadership. It uses task-relevant maturity of employees as the situational variable that will determine the right combination of leader behaviors. Task-relevant maturity consists of two components: job maturity or ability to perform, and psychological maturity or motivation to perform. An absence of job maturity calls for task-oriented leader behaviors, while an absence of psychological maturity calls for relations-oriented leader behaviors. Other situational leadership theories have identified a number of additional situational variables that must be considered. These variables fall into three categories: employee-related, manager-related, and organization-related.

Leadership style is defined as the leader's predominant pattern of behavior toward employees. Four primary leadership styles are: directive, supportive, participative, and achievement-oriented. It is important to understand that there is generally no "one best leadership style." The best leadership style is determined by the situation, and therefore will be different for different situations and different employees. Human relations within the department will be improved to the extent that managers exhibit the leadership style most appropriate in each situation.

One significant aspect of leadership and human relations is encouraging teamwork. Two relatively new forms of teamwork arrangements that many organizations have implemented are quality circles and semiautonomous work groups. Even in those organizations that have not implemented formal work group relationships, teamwork is becoming more and more critical if the organizations are to be able to react and adapt to their changing environments. Managers/leaders are primarily responsible for encouraging teamwork within their departments.

KEY TERMS

appointed leaders
emergent leaders
leadership
bases of power
reward power
coercive power
legitimate power
expert power
referent power
charismatic leader
dominant leadership style

task-oriented behavior
relations-oriented behaviors
directive style
supportive style
participative style
achievement-oriented style
building teamwork
quality circles (QCs)
semiautonomous work groups

DISCUSSION QUESTIONS

1. Explain the differences and similarities between appointed leaders and emergent leaders.
2. How are the bases of power used by a manager related to that manager's leadership style?
3. If you were somehow limited to using only one base of power, which one would you choose? Why?
4. Identify at least four specific task-oriented leader behaviors. Four specific relations-oriented behaviors.
5. Briefly explain the Life Cycle Theory of Leadership.
6. Do you think that many employees ever progress to the point where a low task/low relations leadership style is most effective?
7. What do you think would happen if a manager engaged in a supportive leadership style (high relations-oriented behaviors and low task-oriented behaviors) for an employee at an M1 maturity level (low job maturity and low psychological maturity)? How would you expect this employee to react? Be specific.
8. Can you think of any other important situational variables not included in Exhibit 13.3?
9. Explain quality circles and semiautonomous work groups. What are the advantages to the organization? To the employees? To the manager?
10. What can leaders do to build teamwork in their departments?

EXERCISE 13.1

Analyzing Leaders

A very popular business magazine, *Business Week,* often publishes stories about managers who have been effective leaders. A list of several recent articles appears here. Your instructor may assign you or your group one specific article or ask you to read them all. Your task is to look for behaviors, qualities, characteristics, and activities which the manager(s) in these articles exhibited which made them effective leaders. Then write a short summary of what it takes to be an effective leader. Most of the individuals in these *Business Week* articles are high-level managers. Would the factors you identified also be required at lower levels of management? Make a list of these factors and be prepared to compare your results with those of other individuals or groups in class.

"The King of Cable." *Business Week,* October 26, 1987, pp. 88–90.

"The Miracle Company." *Business Week,* October 19, 1987, pp. 84–86.

"Disney's Magic: It's back!" *Business Week,* March 9, 1987, pp. 62–68.

"Do you know me?" *Business Week,* January 25, 1987, pp. 72–81.

"Sony's challenge." *Business Week,* June 1, 1987, pp. 64–69.

"AT&T's comeback." *Business Week,* January 18, 1988, pp. 56–60.

"GE's Jack Welch." *Business Week,* December 14, 1987, pp. 92–102.

CASE 13.1

Choosing a Leadership Style

Dana was nervous as she drove into the company's south parking lot. The butterflies in her stomach grew more active as she walked in the employees' entrance and neared her new office. She had just accepted a job as supervisor of one of the new, somewhat experimental, work teams at the newly built automobile manufacturing plant. This plant was a joint venture by a major U.S. automobile manufacturer and a large Korean manufacturing firm.

The newly built plant was extremely modern and featured a relatively heavy use of robotics and electronic computer-assisted manufacturing (CAM) technology. In addition, supervisors and employees had received thorough training in company methods and philosophy—which were modeled after well-known "Japanese management" practices. Nonsupervisory employees spent three months in Korea and received extensive training in the newer technology and equipment that they would be using in the new U.S. plant. Employees were assigned to semiautonomous work groups responsible for performing several tasks as opposed to the traditional automobile assembly line where workers performed one or only a few simple, repetitive tasks. For example, instead of simply installing a headlight as might be done in a traditional automobile assembly line, these work groups might install the entire electrical system. Further, the work groups were given substantial freedom and control over their own work activities. For instance, work groups interview their own job applicants and made recommendations to the group supervisor. These work groups also evaluate their own performance and make pay increase recommendations to the supervisor.

After hearing a description of the new work group she was to supervise, Dana remembered thinking "They don't really need a supervisor. The work group seems to make all of the decisions and the formal supervisor simply 'rubber stamps' them." Dana had taken several courses in leadership in college and had also attended three management training seminars. With that experience, she felt she had a good understanding of leadership and had developed the flexibility to use a number of different leadership styles. However, she wasn't sure which style was most appropriate for her new assignment. Using the information on situational variables and the descriptions of leadership styles presented in the chapter, determine the most appropriate leadership style for Dana to use in her assignment as supervisor of a semiautonomous work group. Be prepared to justify your answer.

REFERENCES

[1] Deveny, K. For Caterpillar, the metamorphosis isn't over. *Business Week,* August 31, 1987, 72–74.

[2] Pfeffer, J. The ambiguity of leadership. *Academy of Management Review,* 1977, *2,* 104–112.

[3] Stogdill, R.M. *The handbook of leadership.* New York: The Free Press, 1981.

[4] A Japanese boss whose "consensus" is an iron fist. *Business Week,* November 9, 1984, 176–178.

[5] French, J.R., & Raven, B. The bases of social power. In Cartwright, D., & Zender, A. (Eds.), *Group Dynamics,* New York: Harper & Row, 1968.

[6] Conger, J.A., & Kanungo, R.N. Toward a behavioral theory of charismatic leadership in organizational settings. *Academy of Management Review,* 1987, *12*(4), 637–647.

[7] Hinkin, T.R., & Schriesheim, C.A. Power and influence: The view from below. *Personnel,* 1988, *65*(5), 47–50.

[8] Wagel, W.H. Developing productive leadership at Squibb. *Personnel,* 1987, *64*(5), 4–8.

[9] Allcorn, S. Leadership styles: The psychological picture. *Personnel,* 1988, *65*(4), 46–54.

[10] Hersey, P., & Blanchard, K.H. Life cycle theory of leadership. *Training and Development Journal,*

1969, 23, 26–43; Hersey, P., & Blanchard, K.H. So you want to know your leadership style? *Training and Development Journal*, 1974, 28, 22–37.

[11]Graeff, C.L. The Situational Leadership Theory: A critical view. *Academy of Management Review*, 1983, 8, 285–291.

[12]Hersey, P., & Blanchard, K.H. *Management of organization behavior: Utilizing human resources*. 4th edition. Englewood Cliffs, NJ: Prentice-Hall, 1982.

[13]Fiedler, F. *A theory of leadership effectiveness*. New York: McGraw-Hill, 1967; Hersey, P. & Blanchard, K.H. *Management of organizational behavior*. Second edition. Englewood Cliffs, NJ: Prentice-Hall, 1972, 150–175; House, R.J. A path-goal theory of leader effectiveness. *Administrative Science Quarterly*, 1971, 16, 321–338; Tannenbaum, R., & Schmidt, W.H. How to choose a leadership pattern. *Harvard Business Review*, 1958, 36, 95–101; Vroom, V.H., & Yetton, P.W. *Leadership and decision making*. Pittsburgh: University of Pittsburgh Press, 1973.

[14]Tannenbaum, R., & Schmidt, W.H. How to choose a leadership pattern. *Harvard Business Review*, 1958, 36, 95–101.

[15]Kerr, S., & Jermier, J.M. Substitutes for leadership: Their meaning and measurement. *Organizational Behavior and Human Performance*, 1978, 22, 375–403.

[16]Vroom, V.H., & Yetton, P.W. *Leadership and decision-making*. Pittsburgh: University of Pittsburgh Press, 1973; Vroom, V.H., & Jago, A.G. On the validity of the Vroom-Yetton model. *Journal of Applied Psychology*, 1978, 63, 151–162.

[17]Ibid.

[18]Hersey, P., & Blanchard, K.H. *Management of organizational behavior*. Second edition. Englewood Cliffs, NJ: 1972.

[19]Yukl, G.A. *Leadership in organizations*. Englewood Cliffs, NJ: Prentice-Hall, 1981.

[20]House, R. A path-goal theory of leader effectiveness. *Administrative Science Quarterly*, 1971, 16, 321–338.

[21]Blake, R.R., & Mouton, J.S. *The new Managerial Grid*. Houston: Gulf Publishing Company, 1978; Blake, R.R., & Mouton, J.S. *The versatile manager: A Grid profile*. Homewood, IL: Irwin, 1981.

[22]Wood, R., Hull, F., & Azumi, K. Evaluating quality circles: The American application. *California Management Review*, 1983, 26, 37–53; Marks, M.L. The question of quality circles. *Psychology Today*, 1986, 20, 36–46.

[23]Wayne, S., Griffin, R.W., & Bateman, T.S. Improving the effectiveness of quality circles. *Personnel Administrator*, 1986, 31, 79–88.

[24]Hoerr, J., Pollack, M.A., & Whiteside, D.E. Management discovers the human side of automation. *Business Week*, September 29, 1986, 70–79; Edid, M. How power will be balanced on Saturn's shop floor. *Business Week*, August 5, 1985, 65–66.

[25]DuBrin, A.J. *Contemporary applied management*. Plano, Texas: Business Publications, Inc., 1985; Lefton, R.E. The eight barriers to teamwork. *Personnel Journal*, 1988, 67(1), 18–24; Shonk, W., & Shonk, J.H. What business teams can learn from athletic teams. *Personnel*, 1988, 65(6), 76–80.

[26]Bassin, M. Teamwork at General Foods: New and improved. *Personnel Journal*, 1988, 67(5), 62–70.

There is no correct answer to this exercise. Students typically list well-known world figures, such as the current U.S. and Soviet Presidents, Martin Luther King, Adolf Hitler, Coach Paul "Bear" Bryant, Coach George Halas, and so on. It is more difficult to identify exactly what makes each of these persons "leaders." However, this is a good exercise to go through since it requires careful thought about precisely what leadership is. Try not to concentrate on traits such as intelligence or communications ability, but rather focus on observable behaviors or activities that make these people "leaders."

| WHAT DO YOU THINK? NOTE |

CHAPTER FOURTEEN

Managing Conflict Between Individuals and Groups

PROLOGUE

Conflict is common in today's complex world. One has only to listen to the evening news, scan a daily newspaper, or just look around to find a number of examples of conflict. It is extremely common in organizational work settings. One well-known study of top- and middle-level managers reported that top-level managers spend approximately 18 percent of their time dealing with conflict, while middle-level managers spend as much as 26 percent of their time in conflict-handling activities. Further, these managers rated conflict of equal or higher in importance than such managerial activities as planning, communication, motivation, and decision making.[1] Managers in today's complex organizations must be prepared to deal with conflict, to prevent damage to human relations within their department or work unit. Everyday examples of conflict abound.

In 1987, at Reykjavik, Iceland, President Ronald Reagan and Soviet Premier Mikhail Gorbachev disagreed over terms of a nuclear arms control treaty. Agreement on nuclear arms control had nearly been reached. However, toward the end of negotiations Gorbachev demanded limits on President Reagan's Strategic Defense Initiative (SDI, better known as "Star Wars"). Reagan refused, and the summit ended in a stalemate.[2]

During the 1987 NCAA Championship Tournament, the National Association of Basketball Coaches announced that it was considering forming a union because, as Georgetown University Coach John Thompson put it, "The coaches feel they're tired of being the scapegoats for everything evil existing in college athletics today."[3]

On March 19, 1987, Reverend Jim Bakker resigned as chairman of the PTL Ministry, claiming that he had been blackmailed by former friends. On March 24, 1987, Oral Roberts accused Jimmy Swaggart of trying to take over PTL. Swaggart denied the allegations.[4]

Two middle-level managers in a large insurance company disagree over which of them has responsibility for preparing a report recently requested by the vice-president of their division that summarized sales of a new type of insurance policy the company has just begun to offer.

357

A supervisor of a financial analysis department in a medium-sized agricultural supply company received a request for a summary report of the company's last five years' financial ratios. The report was requested by a former financial analysis supervisor who had recently been promoted to a middle-level management position in the treasurer's office. The supervisor who received the request had also applied for that middle-level management position. She placed the request on the bottom of her "in" basket.

In a college classroom at a large university in the midwest, two students argue with their professor about the quality of a question on a multiple-choice exam. The manner in which the students phrased their comments causes the professor to stop the discussion and refuse to consider their argument.

LEARNING OBJECTIVES

After successful completion of this chapter, you should be able to:

- Describe the process of conflict,
- Understand what happens at each stage of the conflict process,
- Identify the several types of conflict that occur in organizations,
- Recognize the most common sources of conflict,
- Explain several common reactions of individuals and groups to conflict,
- Understand what typically happens both within and between groups in conflict,
- Describe both the dysfunctional and functional outcomes of conflict,
- Suggest several conflict management techniques and when each is appropriate, and
- Distinguish between competition and conflict.

WHAT IS ORGANIZATIONAL CONFLICT?

The first detail to understand about organizational conflict is that it is not a "thing"; rather, it is a process which may take place over a relatively long period of time. In fact, it may continue indefinitely unless something is done to resolve the underlying causes of the conflict. Conflict is not the causes or events which lead up to observable behaviors that indicate two parties are in conflict. Nor is it the behaviors of the two parties to a conflict. The behaviors that you might observe are only a part of the conflict process. This process has begun before any observable behaviors were exhibited, and may continue long after observable behaviors have ended. Therefore, conflict is really all of these things, and more.

To describe the conflict process, there must be a definition of the term *conflict*. **Conflict** has been defined as "the process which begins when one party perceives that the other has frustrated, or is about to frustrate, some concern of his."[5] In other words, one or both of these parties (individuals or groups) is blocking, or is about to block, the other's path to accomplishing important goals or satisfying important needs. This action usually results in the other party attempting to remove the obstacles, and a struggle ensues.

THE CONFLICT PROCESS

At some point, the struggle between the two parties typically produces observable behaviors. Many people use this point to define conflict, but it is only a part of the conflict process. As suggested earlier, conflict is a dynamic, ongoing process which may occur over relatively long periods of time—even as long as several years. The **conflict process** consists of five stages, which may be repeated in situations of long-term conflict.[6]

Describe the process of conflict.

Latent Conflict

At this stage, the parties are not yet aware of any blockage or potential blockage of goals. However, the potential for conflict exists; one or more of the many potential sources or antecedent conditions of conflict (e.g., stress, misunderstanding, unclear responsibility), to be discussed later, is present. For example, two employees may each have plans for a special project they would like to work on during the coming year, but their department has only enough resources to fund one of these projects.

Understand what happens at each stage of the conflict process.

Perceived Conflict

During this period, one or both of the parties to the conflict become aware of a controversy. Conflict may be perceived because there is a true difference of opinion or incompatibility of the two parties' positions. It may also be perceived to exist when the positions of the two parties are not incompatible (i.e., as a result of a misperception or misunderstanding). For example, one or both of the parties described here may become aware that there are two special projects being planned and the department has only enough resources to fund one. Of course, **perceived conflict** could also exist if the department really did have sufficient resources for both projects but one or both parties *perceived* that there were only enough resources to fund one project.

Felt Conflict

Perceived conflict is not necessarily *felt conflict*. A person may perceive that there is conflict, but may not feel strongly enough to do anything about it. In other words, a person or group may be aware that their goals are incompatible with those of another party, however, they do not perceive any threat from the other party. In the project funding conflict, one of the employees may feel that her special project request is so superior that it will surely be funded. Thus, even though there are two parties competing for limited resources, one party really doesn't feel threatened. When the perceived conflict is strong enough or important enough to cause one or both parties to experience tension or anxiety, it is **felt conflict**. The party or parties experiencing felt conflict are likely to be motivated to react to the source of the conflict, leading to the next stage of the conflict process, *manifest* conflict.

Manifest Conflict

It is at this point in the process that the conflict may become observable. During the **manifest conflict** stage, individuals engage in behavior designed to eliminate or reduce the conflict. These attempts may be overt, such as arguing, withdrawal, and various aggressive or defensive actions; they may be covert, such as gossiping about the other party to the conflict, withholding important information or assistance, and sabotage. Thus, the conflict manifests itself in some type of action. However, not all actions are readily observable.

Conflict Aftermath

The complete five-stage process is known as a **conflict episode**. There may be several conflict episodes in an ongoing conflict between two or more parties. Until the conflict is actually resolved and its underlying causes eliminated, there is likely to be a continual sequence of conflict episodes. If the conflict is not resolved, after each conflict episode there is an aftermath, that is, an effect.

One likely effect or result of an unresolved conflict episode is suppression and aggravation of the underlying reasons for the conflict. Then, during the next conflict episode, the behaviors that occur during the manifest conflict stage may be stronger and more aggressive. For example, you might physically separate two of your employees who are engaged in conflict. This may temporarily stop observable behavior since it is now more difficult for the two parties to interact. However, even though separated, one or both parties may begin thinking about the conflict and how they feel they were inequitably treated or harmed by the other party. At some point this tension may build to the point where this party seeks out the other, and the conflict surfaces or becomes manifest again. The party experiencing psychological tension as a result of her perceptions of being harmed or inequitably treated becomes motivated to remove this tension and seeks out the other party to correct the situation.

The sequential nature of conflict episodes is portrayed in Exhibit 14.1. This sequence of stages is likely to continue until some action or intervention removes the underlying source(s) (latent conflict or antecedent conditions) of the conflict.

Conceptualization of Conflict

One additional point about the process of conflict needs to be made. Once the parties become aware of the conflict, they begin to try and understand it and determine why it exists. This involves the attribution process described in Chapter 4. In other words, one or both parties may try and decide upon the reasons or causes of the conflict. This is referred to as *conceptualization*.[7] The manner in which the parties conceptualize the conflict may determine the manner in which they react to it.

To illustrate, if you decide that Ed is responsible for a conflict and the conflict is primarily due to Ed's attempts to discredit you, you are likely to react defensively and perhaps aggressively. On the other hand, if you believe

CHAPTER FOURTEEN: Managing Conflict Between Individuals and Groups 361

Exhibit 14.1
Sequential nature of the conflict process

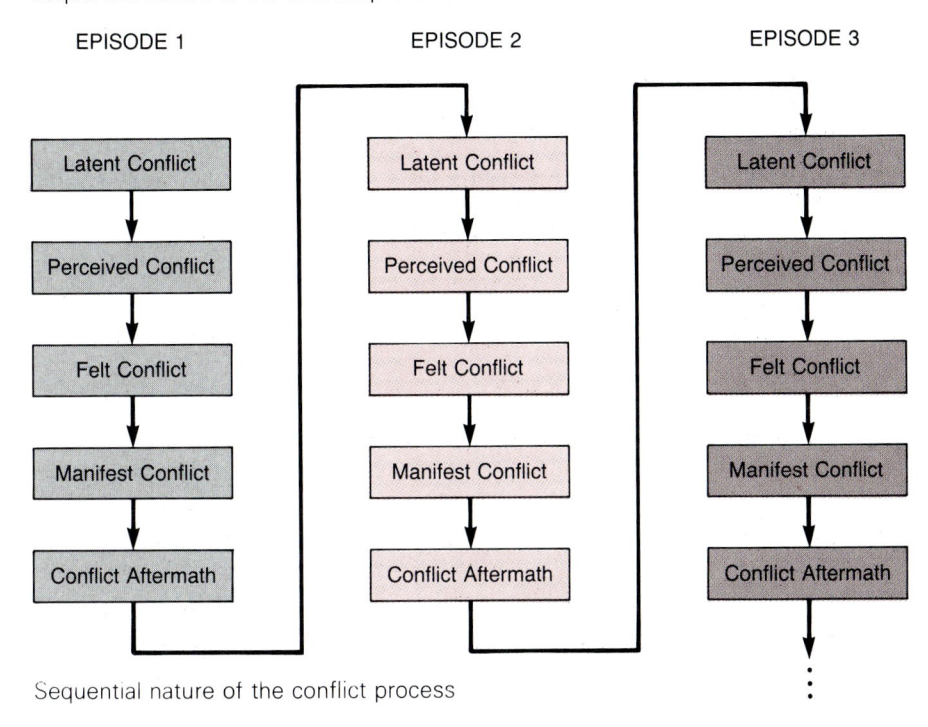

EPISODE 1	EPISODE 2	EPISODE 3
Latent Conflict	Latent Conflict	Latent Conflict
↓	↓	↓
Perceived Conflict	Perceived Conflict	Perceived Conflict
↓	↓	↓
Felt Conflict	Felt Conflict	Felt Conflict
↓	↓	↓
Manifest Conflict	Manifest Conflict	Manifest Conflict
↓	↓	↓
Conflict Aftermath	Conflict Aftermath	Conflict Aftermath

Sequential nature of the conflict process

that the conflict is due to Ed's behavior, but you also decide that the problematic behavior is a result of Ed's not fully understanding the situation, you may react to the conflict in a more cooperative fashion.

Reaction of the Other Party

When conflict reaches the manifest stage, one or both parties may observe the other party engage in certain behaviors. How each party chooses to respond to the conflict will affect how the other party responds. For example, if you react aggressively to the conflict, Ed is likely to react aggressively as well. If you react in a cooperative manner, Ed is likely to be more cooperative.

TYPES OF CONFLICT

There are several types of conflict that occur with some frequency in organizational work settings. Conflict may occur between both individuals and groups, as shown in Exhibit 14.2. **Inter-individual conflict** occurs between two or more individuals. Group membership and group goals have little to do with the reasons for the conflict. Prevalent reasons for inter-individual conflict are that the individuals are trying to accomplish goals which would prevent the accomplishment of the other's goals and they are competing for limited re-

Identify the several types of conflict that occur in organizations.

Exhibit 14.2
Types of organizational conflict

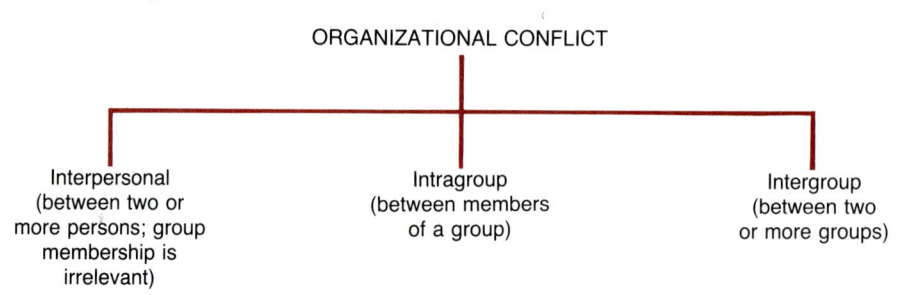

```
                    ORGANIZATIONAL CONFLICT
                              |
        ┌─────────────────────┼─────────────────────┐
   Interpersonal           Intragroup            Intergroup
  (between two or       (between members       (between two
  more persons; group     of a group)          or more groups)
  membership is
  irrelevant)
```

sources. **Intragroup conflict** occurs when members within a single group are engaged in conflict. A prevalent cause of this type of conflict is a difference of opinion on what the group's goals should be, or how already determined goals should be accomplished. Finally, **intergroup conflict** is between two or more groups. A common source of intergroup conflict is competition for limited resources. All of these forms of conflict occur relatively frequently in organizational work settings. Before examining the effects of conflict in organizations, several specific sources of conflict should be discussed.

SOURCES OF CONFLICT

Several common sources of organizational conflict have been identified. Each of these can contribute to any or all of the three forms of conflict just discussed.

Scarce Resources

Recognize the most common sources of conflict.

Few organizations have unlimited amounts of all types of resources (e.g., supplies, salary dollars, promotional opportunities, additional employees). Thus, individuals and groups must compete for these limited resources. This competition is not necessarily bad for an organization. If it focuses on factual reasons why each party should get additional resources, the competition may result in resources being allocated in the most effective way. However, if the competition escalates into conflict, facts may play a lesser role in the process. Not only may resources be allocated ineffectively, but also the resulting conflict may damage human relations within the organization. Differences between competition and conflict will be examined in more detail later in the chapter.

RETURN TO THE PROLOGUE

The examples of conflict described in the Prologue stem from a variety of sources. As you read through the common sources of conflict in the following paragraphs, consider which of them are likely causes for each situation in the Prologue. Are there any sources which are most common?

CHAPTER FOURTEEN: Managing Conflict Between Individuals and Groups

---

HUMAN RELATIONS IN ACTION

U-Haul is Hauling Itself into Court

U-Haul, a national truck rental company, was founded over forty years ago by Leonard S. Schoen. Now in his seventies, the company is run by some of his twelve children. Other children, while heirs to part of the fortune, have been prevented from participating in the running of U-Haul. These children have filed suit in court to reverse several management actions their brothers who are running U-Haul have taken. The children who have been excluded from running the company are seeking to free up their wealth, which may mean selling the company or at least some of its assets. The children who are currently in power want to continue down the same path since U-Haul's financial situation has recently taken a turn for the better. Statements by some of the children who filed suit illustrate their frustration. One brother, who had been U-Haul's CEO said, "We're very frustrated. We're entitled to be heard." Another stated, "I don't want the door to my future, my fortune, my inheritance slammed in my face." The future of U-Haul will likely have to be settled in the courts.

Source: Toy, S. & Dobrzynski, J.H. The family that hauls together brawls together. *Business Week,* August 29, 1988, 64–66.

Incompatible Goals

Individuals and groups may engage in conflict because they have goals that are incompatible. A classic conflict in organizations occurs between production departments and sales departments. Production wants to operate smoothly with few interruptions. They do not want to have to stop production in order to change settings on machines or retool in order to produce different forms of the basic product. Sales, on the other hand, would generally prefer to have many different versions of the product available to appeal to as many customers as possible. This would require many interruptions to the production process. The accompanying Human Relations in Action box describes how incompatible goals may result in the breakup of a well-known U.S. company.

Role Ambiguity

Role ambiguity is, by definition, uncertainty about an individual's or group's role (assignment) in the organization. To put it more simply, the individual or group is not sure of task assignments or responsibility. This uncertainty can lead to conflict when two or more parties disagree on areas of responsibility. The disagreement can occur in two directions: both parties may want responsibility in a specific area, or both parties may want to avoid it. The result in either case is a territorial struggle.

Values and Beliefs

Both individuals and groups develop values and beliefs. Over time, individual members either begin to adopt group values and beliefs, or they leave. Thus, conflict may develop as a result of differences in parties' values and beliefs.

Two groups which often express somewhat different values and beliefs are managers and union leaders. Whereas managers often believe that they should have considerable flexibility in running the organization, union leaders frequently attempt to limit that flexibility. Further, individuals may have values which conflict with organizational practices. For example, an employee who is told to give expensive gifts to suppliers' representatives to get favorable terms on purchases may experience conflict between her own values and those reflected by the organization's practices.

Perception and Communication

The relationship between perception and communication was discussed in Chapter 6. You'll recall that the way we perceive the world has a great influence on what and how we communicate. Perception and communication may also serve as sources of conflict. Some conflict which occurs in organizations results from misunderstandings that are often traceable to problems with perceptions and/or communication. You are much less likely to engage in conflict with someone who perceives the world much as you do than with someone who has substantially different perceptions. You are also less likely to engage in conflict with someone you openly communicate with, than with someone you communicate with infrequently. In addition, you'll recall the many potential problems inherent in the perception and communication processes. There are simply many opportunities for misunderstandings to develop between individuals and/or groups as a result of these problems. Recall the process of conceptualization, which occurs in every conflict episode. This is a very subjective process in which errors in perception may lead one party to believe that the other party to the conflict intends damage. This perception may result in the first party reacting very aggressively, producing a rapid escalation to the conflict.

REACTIONS TO CONFLICT

Explain several common reactions of individuals and groups to conflict.

Once individuals and/or groups become aware of conflict, they may react to it differently. Kenneth Thomas has proposed a model of reactions to conflict based on two dimensions:[8] (1) *assertiveness,* the degree to which an individual or group focuses on satisfying their own needs and accomplishing their own goals; and (2) *cooperativeness,* the degree to which an individual or group considers the needs and goals of the other party. The combination of these two factors results in five primary modes of reacting to conflict episodes, as shown in Exhibit 14.3.

Competing

Individuals and groups react to conflict **competitively** when they are assertive and uncooperative. These parties are likely to attempt to satisfy their own needs at the other party's expense. This strategy is clearly "win–lose," where only one party can accomplish its goals.

Exhibit 14.3
A two-dimensional model of conflict behavior

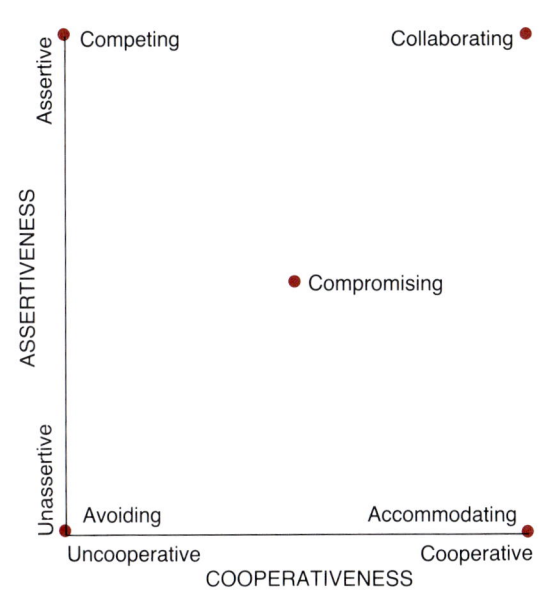

```
          Competing                Collaborating
    Assertive●                              ●
  A
  S
  S
  E
  R
  T
  I
  V
  E
  N                   ● Compromising
  E
  S
  S

  Unassertive
          ●                                 ●
          Avoiding              Accommodating
          Uncooperative           Cooperative
                    COOPERATIVENESS
```

Source: Thomas, K.W. Conflict and conflict management. In Dunnette, M.D. (Ed.) *Handbook of industrial and organizational behavior.* New York: Wiley, 1976, 900.

Accommodating

At the other extreme from competing is **accommodating**, which involves putting the needs and goals of the other party ahead of your own. Accommodators are unassertive and highly cooperative. This strategy is also "win–lose"; however, the accommodator does not focus on winning.

Avoiding

Individuals and groups who **avoid** conflict are both unassertive and uncooperative. These people are prone to being uncomfortable and emotional when faced with conflict. Their preference is to simply ignore the conflict in the hope that it will go away. Unfortunately, this fading away is not likely to happen. An avoidance reaction may result in the conflict being suppressed after a conflict episode—which may further reinforce the avoiding behavior. This strategy might be viewed as "lose–lose," at least in the long run, since this method of reaction does nothing to deal with the underlying causes of the conflict.

Compromising

People who react to conflict in a **compromising** fashion tend to exhibit moderate assertiveness as well as moderate cooperation. They are willing to consider the needs and goals of the other party, but are not willing to completely ignore their own. If both sides react to the conflict in a compromising manner, the result is likely to be a compromise in which neither party accomplishes all of its goals, but neither party comes away with nothing. Both sides have to "give something to get something." It is difficult to classify this reaction behavior, since both sides win and lose.

Collaborating

People who react to conflict in a **collaborating** manner tend to emphasize both assertiveness and cooperation. They are willing to consider the other party's needs and goals, but at the same time, are willing to assert themselves to ensure that their own needs and goals are considered. Collaboration is considered to be a "win–win" behavior since the ultimate goal of collaboration is that both parties accomplish all of their goals and satisfy all of their needs.

Comparison of Types of Reactions to Conflict

While compromise and collaboration may seem to be the most desirable ways of reacting to a conflict, each of these reactions may be appropriate depending upon the particular circumstances of the situation. Exhibit 14.4 presents situational circumstances that determine when each form of reaction to conflict may be most appropriate. As the table shows, even avoiding may be an effective reaction to conflict, at least in the short run. It is appropriate when the issue is not important to you, when the damage to human relations may outweigh the benefits of recognizing and dealing with the conflict, when you need time to gather information to support your position, or when the parties to the conflict need a cooling-off period. An examination of Exhibit 14.4 will help develop an understanding of when each method of reacting to conflict is likely to be most effective.

INTERGROUP CONFLICT

Intergroup conflict is an extremely important form of conflict in organizational settings for three basic reasons: (1) most work in organizations is performed in groups rather than by individuals working completely on their own; (2) inter-individual conflict not quickly resolved can turn into intergroup conflict as other individuals are drawn in and forced to take sides; and (3) severe conflict between groups can damage organizational performance and effectiveness. Thus, managers must thoroughly understand intergroup conflict and what happens both within and between groups as this type of conflict is occurring.

Understand what typically happens both within and between groups in conflict.

What Happens to Groups During Intergroup Conflict

Research has discovered several things which commonly occur within and between groups as they engage in conflict with another group(s).[9]

Exhibit 14.4
Situations in which each reaction to conflict is appropriate

Conflict Mode	Situation	Conflict Mode	Situation

Competing

1. When quick, decisive action is vital—e.g., emergencies.
2. On important issues where unpopular actions need implementing—e.g., cost cutting, enforcing unpopular rules, discipline.
3. On issues vital to company welfare when you know you're right.
4. Against people who take advantage of noncompetitive behavior.

Collaborating

1. To find an integrative solution when both sets of concerns are too important to be compromised.
2. When your objective is to learn.
3. To merge insights from people with different perspectives.
4. To gain commitment by incorporating concerns into a consensus.
5. To work through feelings which have interfered with a relationship.

Compromising

1. When goals are important, but not worth the effort or potential disruption of more assertive modes.
2. When opponents with equal power are committed to mutually exclusive goals.
3. To achieve temporary settlements to complex issues.
4. To arrive at expedient solutions under time pressure.
5. As a backup when collaboration or competition is unsuccessful.

Avoiding

1. When an issue is trivial, or more important issues are pressing.
2. When you perceive no chance of satisfying your concerns.
3. When potential disruption outweighs the benefits of resolution.
4. To let people cool down and regain perspective.
5. When gathering information supercedes immediate decision.
6. When others can resolve the conflict more effectively.
7. When issues seem tangential or symptomatic of other issues.

Accommodating

1. When you find you are wrong—to allow a better position to be heard, to learn, and to show your reasonableness.
2. When issues are more important to others than yourself—to satisfy others and maintain cooperation.
3. To build social credits for later issues.
4. To minimize loss when you are outmatched and losing.
5. When harmony and stability are especially important.
6. To allow subordinates to develop by learning from mistakes.

Source: Thomas, K.W. Toward multi-dimensional values in teaching: The example of conflict behaviors. *Academy of Management Review*, 1977, *2*, 487.

Increased Group Cohesiveness

You'll recall from Chapter 12, that when members of a group perceive an external threat, their group tends to become more cohesive. When a group is engaged in intergroup conflict, the external group is certainly perceived as a threat. Differences between members of the group tend to be forgotten as group loyalty and group goals are emphasized and attention is focused upon the "enemy."

"We–They Attitudes" Form

While differences *within* the conflicting groups tend to be minimized, differences *between* conflicting groups tend to be emphasized. Group members focus on these differences and may even magnify them. The opposing group tends to be viewed as the enemy, and contact with members of the other group is minimized.

Distorted Perceptions and Communications

Group members tend to view the opposing group with suspicion. Information which supports the opposing group's position may be ignored or unconsciously distorted so that it is more consistent with the position of the first group. Information that is damaging to the opposing group is sought out and perhaps even enhanced to show how unreasonable this group has been. It is often difficult for members of one group to recognize the contributions or importance of a second group. For example, in the classic conflict between sales and production departments mentioned earlier, production may lose sight of the importance of the sales department's activities to the overall performance of the organization. Thus, requests for different versions of the basic product may be seen by the production department as unreasonable.

Managers must carefully monitor and actively manage the conflict episodes so that the results of the conflict are beneficial to the conflicting groups as well as to the organization as a whole. Before suggesting ways of managing conflict, the potential positive and negative outcomes of conflict will be examined.

OUTCOMES OF CONFLICT

Describe both the dysfunctional and functional outcomes of conflict.

Conflict can result in positive (functional) or negative (dysfunctional) outcomes for the conflicting parties and the organization.[10] Whether the conflict results in functional or dysfunctional outcomes depends largely on how effectively managers control the conflict.[11]

Dysfunctional Outcomes of Conflict

Several dysfunctional outcomes of conflict were discussed in Chapter 8: tardiness, absenteeism, turnover, substance abuse, anxiety, and stress. Other potential dysfunctional outcomes include the following three.

Damaged Human Relations

Severe conflict may result in a climate of distrust and suspicion among organizational members. When one party wins and the other loses, relationships between the two may be damaged for a long time. Even the winning party may continue to be suspicious, and mistrust the other. The losing party may not only continue to be suspicious of the winning party, but also of any managers who took part in resolving the conflict. When managers must make decisions on how the conflict is to be resolved, and these decisions result in one side winning and the other losing, the losers often view the managers as biased and unfair.[12]

Lower Task Performance
In times of conflict, energy and resources are diverted away from accomplishing important organizational goals to dealing with the conflict. Severe conflict may become more salient to, and occupy more time of, individuals and/or groups.

Restricted Interaction, Communication, and Information
Because of the mistrust and suspicion that typically develop between conflicting parties, the two sides usually restrict interaction and communication. The result is a slowing or even a complete stop of the flow of information between the two parties to the conflict. This can be very harmful to the organization in situations where the work of the two parties is interdependent. One side may intentionally withhold information, to weaken their opponent.

Functional Outcomes of Conflict

For many years, functional or positive outcomes of conflict were not widely recognized. Recently, however, conflict management has been defined more broadly than in the past. Currently, conflict management involves not only conflict resolution or reduction, but also conflict stimulation—to take advantage of the several positive outcomes from functional conflict.[13] Functional outcomes from conflict are described in the next paragraphs.

Motivation and Stimulation of Organizational Members
A complete absence of conflict would probably result in a very stagnant and boring work environment. Moderate levels of conflict may actually motivate employees as they search for ways of resolving conflicts.

Clarified Issues
Conflict episodes will bring the problem out into the open. Both sides may describe their position and exchange information about the conflict. The result may be greater understanding of the opponent and the reasons for the conflict. As the issues become clearer, solutions to the conflict can be more readily developed.

Increased Communication and Information Flow
Many conflict episodes result in increased communication and exchange of information as the two parties seek a solution. Sometimes this benefit continues after the conflict has been resolved.

Managers Made Aware of Problems

While some conflict may occur for reasons not related to the goals of the organization (e.g., personality clashes, differences in values), a great deal of conflict relates to task performance or how organizational goals should be accomplished. Conflict therefore may make managers aware of matters needing managerial attention—which might have otherwise gone unnoticed.

Change Initiated, Facilitated

Conflict is an important source of change in organizations. Conflict over organizational goals, ways to accomplish organizational goals, and how organizational resources should be divided, may often uncover ways in which the organization needs to change to be more effective or to adapt to changing environmental conditions.

Clarified Authority and Responsibility

A common cause of conflict in organizational work settings is unclear authority and responsibility. When managers and employees aren't sure who is responsible for certain activities, they may engage in conflict to either assume or reject responsibility for these activities. Conflict, when managed effectively, may resolve unclear authority and responsibility, without damaging relations between the parties to the conflict.

Innovation and Creativity Trigger

As parties seek ways of resolving conflict, they may become more highly motivated and also more innovative and creative.[14] When old methods of ending conflict do not work, new methods are sought.

Better Decisions

Because information is exchanged between the conflicting parties, conflict can result in better decisions and solutions to problems. As the communication increases, the effectiveness of decisions and solutions to problems also typically increases, at least up to a point. That point is reached when so much information is available, it cannot all be processed. Important pieces of that information could be overlooked, and lower quality decisions would result. However, up to this point of information overload, increasing amounts of information typically produce better decisions.

Reduced Stagnation and Obsolescence

An absence of conflict may cause stagnation and obsolescence in the organization and its work force. Moderate levels of conflict can increase the motivation of organizational members and can also uncover ways in which the organization needs to change to overcome stagnation and obsolescence.

Greater Understanding and Cooperation

Depending on how the conflict is managed (e.g., resolved, avoided, suppressed) greater understanding and cooperation may emerge between the two conflicting parties once the conflict is over. Open communication and exchange of information concerning the conflict may lead the two parties to a greater appreciation of each other. This rapport may pave the way to greater cooperation.

On the other hand, avoiding or suppressing the conflict may let it build and become more serious. As a result, there may be even less understanding and cooperation between the parties in the future.

MANAGING CONFLICT

The management of conflict has historically been viewed as synonymous with the resolution or reduction of conflict. Today, this concept is no longer valid. Managing conflict today includes both conflict resolution and conflict stimulation. Conflict which is severe or results in dysfunctional outcomes for the organization must be resolved. However, in cases where conflict is absent or only minimal, conflict stimulation can prevent organizational stagnation and decline. "Opposition to others' ideas, dissatisfaction with the status quo, concern about doing things better, and the desire to improve inadequacies" are all necessary forms of conflict for modern organizations.[15]

Suggest several conflict management techniques and when each is appropriate.

Conflict Resolution

Techniques for conflict resolution are aimed at reducing or eliminating the reasons for the conflict. Several such techniques have been identified. Each of the five reactions to conflict discussed earlier may be a conflict resolution strategy. In fact, an individual's preferred form of reaction to conflict may lead that person to engage in a related conflict resolution strategy. Each strategy could be appropriate in particular situations.

Avoidance

Avoidance should be viewed as a temporary or short-term managerial strategy. If all of the facts are not available, or if tempers and emotions run high, avoidance may provide time to collect additional information or for the parties to the conflict to cool off. Unfortunately, since many people are understandably uncomfortable dealing with conflict, avoidance is used as a conflict management technique much more than is appropriate. A study of middle-level managers showed that avoidance was the second (tied for second place with problem solving) most frequently used conflict resolution strategy.[16]

Forcing

Another method of resolving conflict calls for managers to rely on their formal authority and impose a decision on the two parties to the conflict. While this action may appear to resolve the conflict, it will probably not eliminate the underlying causes for the conflict. Although it may stop the two parties from engaging in manifest conflict, the conflict may surface again later in another form. In other words, the two parties may find another area of conflict. In the study of middle-level managers mentioned previously, forcing was the most frequently used method of resolving conflict.[17]

Problem solving requires both parties to openly exchange information, beliefs, and feelings.

Problem Solving

Individuals and groups whose preferred means of reacting to conflict is collaboration are likely to use a problem-solving strategy for conflict resolution. Problem solving involves the following steps:

1. Parties openly exchange information, beliefs, and feelings to determine the true causes of the conflict.
2. Parties focus on facts and objective information rather than on personalities.
3. Parties search for a solution which will satisfy the goals of both parties (a "win–win" solution).

During problem solving, the parties confront the reasons for the conflict and negotiate a mutually acceptable solution. Exhibit 14.5 presents some basic guidelines for confrontation. Basically, the parties must openly communicate their feelings, problems, fears, perceptions, and opinions. In addition, great emphasis should be placed on reaching agreement on the true underlying cause(s) of the conflict. Unless the two parties can agree on the cause of a conflict, little progress can be made toward resolving that conflict.[18] Problem solving and confrontation appear to be most appropriate when the parties must work together to accomplish their assigned jobs, both parties are open-minded about possible means of resolving the conflict, and both parties are willing to ignore personalities and emotions and focus on facts.[19]

The major advantages of a problem-solving approach to conflict resolution are: (1) it tends to result in a permanent, or at least long-term, solution to the conflict, and (2) it sets the stage for a more cooperative relationship between the parties. The major disadvantage of problem solving is that it takes a considerable amount of time for the two parties to exchange information and find a

> **Exhibit 14.5**
> Guidelines for conflict confrontation
>
> 1. Determine whether the issue is important and whether both parties are open and skilled enough to make the discussion useful.
> 2. Find a suitable time and place—private, if possible.
> 3. Establish a joint cooperative context. Both parties should realize that they are responsible for both the problem and its solution.
> 4. Present opening arguments—the parties express their feelings, ideas, and thoughts.
> 5. Definition of the problem—participants try to define the problem as specifically as possible.
> 6. Generate problem solutions—examine the problem from different perspectives and encourage new ways of looking at it.
> 7. Evaluation—those involved should evaluate the gains and costs to each of the solutions and determine whether it is practical to implement them.
> 8. Reflection—the parties should share their feelings about how the procedures of cooperative problem solving were followed.

Source: Tjosvold, D. Making conflict productive. *Personnel Administrator,* 1984, *29,* 121–130.

solution. Further, confrontation and problem solving is not likely to be appropriate in cases where the conflict stems from a personality clash or differing value systems. It should be effective when the conflict stems from differing goals, competition over scarce resources, or disagreements over areas of responsibility.

Conflict Stimulation

Much more has been written about conflict resolution than about conflict stimulation. However, since levels of conflict can be too low in organizations, conflict stimulation deserves increased attention. One author has suggested that "yes" responses to the following questions suggest a need for conflict stimulation.[20]

1. Are you surrounded by "yes men" and "yes women"?
2. Are your employees afraid to admit mistakes or that they need assistance?
3. Do decision makers concentrate more heavily on reaching agreement than on reaching the best decision?
4. Do managers emphasize cooperation and getting along with others more than accomplishing objectives?
5. Do decision makers place more emphasis on not hurting others' feelings than on quality decisions?
6. Is popularity more important to managers than competence and high job performance?

DEVELOPING YOUR HUMAN RELATIONS SKILLS

The information presented in this chapter has important implications for you both in your role as a manager and in your role as an employee. In general, as a manager, you must remain alert for instances of conflict between your employees or work groups that could be damaging to human relations. You must also be alert to the possibility that in certain situations human relations and productivity might be *improved* by increasing conflict.

More specific suggestions for managers include the following:

1. Remember that conflict that goes unresolved is likely to return, perhaps even stronger. While avoidance and forcing may be temporary solutions to a conflict, only problem solving and collaboration get at the real underlying reasons for the conflict. Unless the true reason for the conflict is identified, agreed to by the parties to the conflict, and resolved, the conflict is likely to resurface.

2. Role ambiguity, one common reason for conflict in organizations, is at least partially under the control of managers. There is little excuse for conflict to result from role ambiguity. If it does occur, the manager has not effectively communicated responsibilities to employees. You should ensure that your employees clearly understand their responsibilities, as well as those of their coworkers. Ask for feedback from employees to check their understanding of their responsibilities.

3. When faced with the problem of scarce resources, clearly communicate the goals you are trying to accomplish and the priorities among these goals. Employees must understand which goals are most important, to avoid conflict over scarce resources. This knowledge provides a rationale for the allocation of these scarce resources. To return to an example used earlier in the chapter—if two employees are competing for resources to fund a special project they have developed, knowing which project would contribute most to the organization's highest-priority goal would substantially resolve that dispute. It would be difficult for an employee to continue to engage in conflict once it was clear that her project would contribute little to the organization's most important goal.

4. Another common reason for organizational conflict is incompatible goals. Conflict over goals may be functional if it is managed effectively. Such conflict can create greater understanding between the parties, result in new and perhaps creative solutions to problems, and set the stage for greater cooperation between these parties in the future. However, if ignored or managed ineffectively, this conflict can result in dysfunctional outcomes for the organization. One reason conflict over goals can become dysfunctional is that the parties to the conflict have

7. Are managers overconcerned with getting everyone to agree on and accept their decisions?
8. Are employees highly resistant to change?
9. Do managers and employees propose few new ideas?
10. Is employee turnover unusually low?

lost sight of overall organizational goals. When two departments engage in conflict over goals, they have generally become somewhat shortsighted and have begun to focus on their own department rather than the overall organization. They have lost sight of the fact that their departmental goals are intended to contribute to the accomplishment of overall organizational goals. Managers may need to remind employees of the organization's goals and point out how departmental goals are not an end in themselves, but rather a means to an end, namely, accomplishing overall organizational goals.

As an employee, there are several things that you can do to become more effective at handling conflict:

1. Recognize that perceptions and conceptualizations can play a large part in the conflict process. Don't be quick on the trigger. When you believe you are faced with a conflict, take the time to examine it carefully. Make sure that you are not basing your conclusion on a misperception or misunderstanding. Make sure that you are faced with a real threat before taking any action.
2. Remember that your reaction to the conflict will influence the other party's reaction. If you wish to engage in problem solving and find a permanent solution to the conflict as quickly as possible, you may want to react in a cooperative manner. Many people find it difficult to respond aggressively to cooperative behavior. Your cooperative reaction may help to defuse the emotional nature of the conflict and allow the other party to objectively consider the facts of the situation.
3. Communication tends to make conflict less likely. Get in the habit of exchanging information with others, especially those with whom you recognize an opportunity for conflict to develop. Ask for their suggestions. Ask what problems they are facing and if there is anything that you, or your department, could do to make their jobs easier. In time, they may reciprocate with offers to help your department. Establishing this type of relationship makes conflict less likely.
4. Understand how you naturally tend to react to conflict. Are you an avoider? A competitor? Do you always react to conflict in the same way? If so, consider some situations where another reaction might have been more effective. You can learn to react differently to conflict with a little careful planning and practice. As suggested earlier, don't react too quickly. Give yourself time to plan your reaction. Consider the possible reaction of the other party and what you want to accomplish. A review of Exhibit 14.4 will help you decide when each type of reaction is most appropriate.

The greater the number of "yes" responses to the above questions, the greater the need for conflict stimulation to prevent stagnation and stimulate creativity, innovation, and adaptability. Conflict stimulation techniques may be placed into three primary categories: implementing communication techniques, altering organizational structure, and changing behavior.[21]

> **WHAT DO YOU THINK?**
>
> Two terms that are frequently confused are "conflict" and "competition." Are these terms synonymous? Is one more desirable than the other? Is one more likely to lead to undesirable consequences than the other? Can you identify important distinctions between conflict and competition, or should managers treat them as if they were the same thing? Develop your own answers to these questions before reading further.

Distinguish between competition and conflict.

Implementing communication techniques involves either altering the message that is sent or altering the channel through which it is transmitted. Altering the message includes withholding information, transmitting too much information, and transmitting ambiguous or threatening information. Altering the communication channel might involve transmitting information through the informal grapevine, rather than through formal organizational communication channels.[22]

Altering organizational structure requires changing the manner in which people are assigned to departments or to work groups within the organization. Since increased group size tends to reduce group cohesiveness and therefore increase conflict potential, managers might add employees to work groups to stimulate conflict. Heterogeneous groups are more likely to experience intragroup conflict, so managers may assign members to existing groups whose backgrounds differ from those of the other group members. Similarly, groups whose members are substantially different from the members of other groups are more likely to experience intergroup conflict. Thus, managers may create groups with members who are similar internally, but different from those of external groups. Making work groups dependent on one another is likely to stimulate conflict. To illustrate, if group A depends on group B for information or assistance, conflict becomes more probable. Similarly, if the output of group A becomes the input for group B, conflict potential increases. Rearranging the physical layout of the plant or office so that it is more difficult for groups to interact with one another also increases the tendency toward conflict.

Assigning goals to individuals or groups that are somewhat incompatible will increase the likelihood of conflict.[23] Similarly, reward systems tied to individual or small-group performance levels stimulate competition and increase conflict potential.

Regardless of the method of conflict stimulation chosen, managers must exercise great care that the conflict does not become too severe and therefore dysfunctional. This control requires a constant monitoring of the conflict, and should include plans for reducing or resolving the conflict should it escalate to a harmful level.

SUMMARY

Conflict is common in today's modern organizations. In fact, organizations depend on a certain amount of conflict to identify problems needing attention. And, conflict stimulates change, which helps organizations better adapt to their rapidly changing environments.

Conflict is the process which begins when one party perceives that the other has frustrated, or is about to frustrate, some concern of hers. Conflict is a dynamic, on-going process which consists of the following stages: (1) latent conflict, (2) perceived conflict, (3) felt conflict, (4) manifest conflict, and (5) conflict aftermath. This complete five-stage process is known as a conflict episode. When conflict becomes perceived, one or both parties try to determine causes of the conflict. This investigation is known as conceptualization. The manner in which the parties conceptualize the conflict will determine, at least in part, how they choose to react to it.

Three important types of organizational conflict are inter-individual conflict, intragroup conflict, and intergroup conflict. Inter-individual conflict occurs between two or more individuals, where group membership is not an issue. Intragroup conflict is actually inter-individual conflict within a single group, and is related to group membership. Finally, intergroup conflict occurs between two or more groups. Several common causes (or antecedent conditions) of these forms of conflict include scarce or limited resources, incompatible goals, role ambiguity, different values and beliefs, and perception and communication problems.

Individuals and groups commonly develop preferred or dominant reactions to conflict situations. Five primary forms of reaction to conflict have been identified; they are based on two dimensions: assertiveness, the degree to which an individual or group focuses on satisfying their own needs and accomplishing their own goals; and cooperativeness, the degree to which an individual or group considers the needs and goals of the other party to the conflict.

The five forms of reaction to conflict are: competing (high assertiveness and low cooperativeness), accommodating (high cooperativeness and low assertiveness), avoiding (low assertiveness and low cooperativeness), compromising (moderate assertiveness and moderate cooperativeness), and collaborating (high assertiveness and high cooperativeness). Each of these forms of conflict reaction may be appropriate in particular situations.

Intergroup conflict is a significant form of organizational conflict, since most work in organizations is performed in groups. When groups are engaged in conflict, several things commonly occur: (1) cohesiveness within each group increases; (2) "we–they attitudes" form; and (3) perceptions and communications between conflicting groups become distorted.

Outcomes of conflict may be functional or dysfunctional, depending on how the conflict is managed. Dysfunctional outcomes of conflict include: damaged human relations; lower task performance; and restricted interaction, communication, and information exchange between participants. Functional outcomes include: motivation and stimulation of employees; clarification of issues; increased communication and information flow; increased managerial awareness of problems; initiation of innovation, creativity, and change; clarified authority and responsibility; better decisions and solutions to problems; prevention of stagnation and obsolescence; and greater understanding and cooperation between conflicting parties.

KEY TERMS

conflict
conflict process
latent conflict
perceived conflict
felt conflict
manifest conflict
conflict episode
conflict aftermath

inter-individual conflict
intragroup conflict
intergroup conflict
competing
accommodating
avoiding
compromising
collaborating

DISCUSSION QUESTIONS

1. Why is conflict more accurately defined as a process than a "thing"?
2. Describe the stages of the conflict process and what happens at each stage.
3. At which stage of the conflict process should managers attempt to intervene with conflict resolution? Explain.
4. Explain the difference between "felt conflict" and "manifest conflict."
5. What are some of the most common forms of "conflict aftermath"?
6. Explain the process of "conflict conceptualization" and show why it is important to managers in resolving conflict.
7. Describe the three main types of organizational conflict and give an example of each.
8. What are the primary forms of reactions to conflict? Describe how individuals would behave in each reaction form.
9. Explain when each form of reaction to conflict is likely to be most effective. Are any of these forms of reacting to conflict likely to be more effective than the others in most situations?

10. Explain what happens *within* groups during intergroup conflict.
11. Explain what happens *between* groups during intergroup conflict.
12. Identify several functional and dysfunctional outcomes of conflict.
13. Suppose a newly hired manager comes to you for advice concerning how to resolve conflict. She tells you that she wants to confront the conflict and develop a solution that both parties will accept. What advice for using confrontation and problem solving would you give her?
14. When should conflict be stimulated or increased?
15. How can managers stimulate conflict?

EXERCISE 14.1

Conflict Resolution

The purpose of this exercise is to provide an opportunity to gain experience in conflict resolution. Your instructor will divide the class into groups based on some characteristic that should produce conflict between these groups. Examples are: female/male, business majors/liberal arts majors, town/gown, liberal/conservative, younger/older.

Using chalkboards or large sheets of paper (e.g., newspapers), each group is to make three lists. For example, using the business major/liberal arts major classification, business majors would make the following lists:
1. Business majors are:
2. Liberal arts majors think we are:
3. Liberal arts majors think we think they are:

Liberal arts majors would make three similar lists:
1. Liberal arts majors are:
2. Business majors think we are:
3. Business majors think we think they are:

Each group should complete these three sentences as many ways as possible. When the groups are finished with the lists, post them around the room. Then everyone is to walk around the room and read the lists. No discussion is allowed during this activity.

When everyone has finished reading the lists, two members from each group are chosen as spokespersons, to sit in a central location so they can easily be seen and heard by other members. Only the spokespersons may speak, but the role of spokesperson may be alternated within groups. Questions to be addressed are:
1. What areas of commonality exist between the groups?
2. What are the bases for the perceptions of each group?
3. How accurate are the groups' perceptions of one another?
4. How does it feel to read perceptions of you that you think are incorrect?
5. What effect do these perceptions have on conflict between the groups?
6. What does this exercise suggest about conflict resolution between groups?

Source: Based upon Frantze, J.L. *Behavior in organizations: Tales from the trenches.* Boston: Allyn & Bacon, 1983, p. 147.

CASE 14.1

Farm-Towne Supply Store
By Michael P. Dumler, Illinois State University

On July 15, 1984, Peter Jones decided to purchase a gas-powered weed-eater. A price-sensitive consumer, Mr. Jones had made thorough price comparisons, and had concluded that the General-88 model, while at the low end of the quality scale, was the best bargain. And, since the weed-eater was on sale for $20.00 off its regular price of $99.95 at the local Farm-Towne Supply (FTS) store, the choice was obvious. FTS had long been a favorite store of Mr. Jones. When he purchased the weed-eater, he was informed that it carried a one-year warranty on the engine and drive shaft; that convinced him that his investment had been a good one.

CHAPTER FOURTEEN: Managing Conflict Between Individuals and Groups 379

During the following year while Mr. Jones was cutting a rather thick cluster of stalky weeds, the weed-eater abruptly stopped running. Several attempts to restart it were useless; in fact, the pull start cord was jammed and inoperable. He took the weed-eater to his garage and began to disassemble it, and when he removed the spark plug, several roller bearings fell to the floor. The engine was completely destroyed; the bargain-priced unit had lasted less than a year.

Realizing that the warranty was still in effect, Mr. Jones went to Farm-Towne the next morning, put the weed-eater on the counter and asked to see the manager. Unfortunately, it was the manager's day off, and the assistant manager was on vacation, so Mr. Jones was served by a young man who was on loan from another FTS store, acting as temporary assistant manager.

Mr. Jones was told that a mechanic would have to examine the weed-eater to determine the problem. In a very short time, the mechanic verified Mr. Jones's diagnosis that the engine was ruined and would have to be replaced. What didn't please Mr. Jones was the fact that it would take a month to get a new engine from the manufacturer. He was most indignant, but was somewhat appeased when the mechanic told him in confidence that in previous situations, the store manager had replaced a defective weed-eater with a new one from stock, to placate a disgruntled and vociferous customer.

With that, Mr. Jones went back to the visiting assistant manager to present his argument for a replacement unit. The response was that although a month was a long time to wait, there was no alternative; current store policy prohibited any in-store replacement of manufacturer-defective merchandise.

Infuriated by the change in store policy from the replacement policy that had been indicated by the mechanic, Mr. Jones demanded a full refund. The assistant manager informed Mr. Jones that under the terms of the warranty, the FTS had the option of fixing the defective product or refunding its cost—and that since the weed-eater could be fixed, it should be fixed. Seeing that he was getting nowhere with the 'rude young newcomer,' Mr. Jones decided to wait to see the store manager on the following day.

Early the next morning, Mr. Jones reviewed the events of the previous day with the store manager, including what he considered the inept handling of the problem by the visiting assistant manager. The manager agreed that a month was indeed a long wait, but the store policy dictated that defective merchandise was to be fixed, if at all possible. That, FTS would do.

Again, Mr. Jones registered his strong dissatisfaction, and requested a refund of his $79.95 purchase price. Again, he was rebuffed. Mr. Jones then asked the manager if he had ever settled similar situations with an in-stock replacement. The manager replied that FTS policy had changed, and customers were no longer provided with immediate replacements.

With that, Mr. Jones threatened to take his business elsewhere, including the pending purchase of a $2,500 lawn tractor. The store manager reluctantly insisted that store policy made it clear—repair defective merchandise whenever possible. Mr. Jones left FTS, vowing never to set foot in any Farm-Towne store again.

Later that day, the store manager called Mr. Jones. He said that when he had called the factory to order the repair parts, he had related his conversation with Mr. Jones, and the factory representative had authorized the immediate replacement of the defective weed-eater. So, Mr. Jones could come in at his convenience to pick up a new weed-eater.

The next day, Mr. Jones presented his year-old receipt to the clerk, only to be told that the procedure was that FTS would refund the original purchase price ($79.95) of the weed-eater, and the customer could purchase the new unit with the refund. To his astonishment, Mr. Jones learned that the current price of the weed-eater was only $59.95. Pleased with the arrangement, Mr. Jones completed the refund procedure and bought a new General-88 weed-eater. After leaving the store, he found that he had a new weed-eater with a one-year warranty, and $20 in his pocket. During the drive home, he pondered the events of the past several days, wondering how an organization's policies and procedures could be so inconsistent and aggravating to its customers? In the final analysis, Farm-Towne had almost lost a good customer and had unintentionally given the customer more than he had originally asked.

QUESTIONS

1. Summarize the specific nature of the conflict between Mr. Jones and FTS store management.
2. List all of the participants in the conflict episode and their contribution to the conflict.
3. In your own words, list all the "store policies" that contributed to the conflict, as they were discussed in this case.
4. How did the conflict episode end?
5. As a manager at FTS corporate headquarters, what would you do to remove the potential for future conflict between customers and FTS store managers with regard to warranty claims?

REFERENCES

[1] Thomas, K.W. & Schmidt, W.H. A survey of managerial interests with respect to conflict. *Academy of Management Journal*, 1976, *19*, 316–318.

[2] Watson, R. Deadlock in Iceland. *Newsweek*, October 20, 1986, 20–26.

[3] Coaches may unionize. *Times-Courier*, Charleston, Illinois, March 30, 1987, B–1.

[4] Ostling, R.N. TV's unholy row. *Time*, April 6, 1987, 60–67; Lord, L.J. An unholy war in the TV pulpits. *U.S. News and World Report*, April 6, 1987, 58–65; Martz, L. God and money. *Newsweek*, April 6, 1987, 16–22.

[5] Thomas, K.W. Conflict and conflict management. In Dunnette, M.D. (Ed.). *Handbook of Industrial and Organizational Psychology*, Chicago: Rand McNally, 1976.

[6] Pondy, L.R. Organizational conflict: Concepts and models. *Administrative Science Quarterly*, 1967, *12*, 296–320.

[7] Thomas, 1976, Ibid.

[8] Thomas, 1976, Ibid.

[9] Sherif, M. *Group conflict and cooperation*. London: Routledge & Kegan Paul, 1966; Blake, R.R. & Mouton, J.S. Reactions to intergroup competition under win–lose conditions. *Management Science*, 1961, *4*, 420–435.

[10] Deutsch, M. Conflicts: Productive and destructive. *Journal of Social Issues*, 1969, *25*, 7–41.

[11] Welds, K. Conflict in the work place and how to manage it. *Personnel Journal*, 1979, *58*, 380–383.

[12] Blake, R.R., Shepard, H.A. & Mouton, J.S. *Managing intergroup conflict in industry*. Houston: Gulf, 1964.

[13] Robbins, S.P. Conflict management and conflict resolution are not synonymous terms. *California Management Review*, 1978, *21*, 67–75.

[14] King, D. Three cheers for conflict! *Personnel*, 1981, *58*, 13–22.

[15] Robbins, 1978, Ibid.

[16] Phillips, E. & Cheston, R. Conflict resolution: What works? *California Management Review*, 1979, *21*, 76–83.

[17] Phillips & Cheston, 1979, Ibid.

[18] Stamatis, D.H. Conflict: You've got to accentuate the positive. *Personnel*, 1987, *64*(12), 47–50.

[19] Stimac, M. Strategies for resolving conflict: Their functional and dysfunctional sides. *Personnel*, 1982, *59*, 54–64.

[20] Robbins, 1978, Ibid.

[21] Robbins, 1978, Ibid.

[22] Robbins, 1978, Ibid.

[23] Van De Vliert, E. Escalative intervention in small-group conflict. *Journal of Applied Behavioral Science*, 1985, *21*, 19–36.

CHAPTER FOURTEEN: Managing Conflict Between Individuals and Groups

Functional conflict may be closer to "competition" than to traditional uses of the term "conflict." While both conflict and competition include goal incompatibility and/or limited resources, the terms may be distinguished. Competition occurs when individuals or groups are both trying to accomplish goals that are incompatible with those of other individuals or groups, or are trying to acquire limited resources. Conflict may include the process of competition, but also includes blocking the other parties' attempts to accomplish goals or acquire resources.[1] Thus, competition involves a simultaneous striving for goals or resources *without* attempts to block the progress of the opponent.[2] Attention is focused on facts and objective reasons why one party's goals should be given priority or why one party deserves more of the limited resources than the other party. This type of opposition can be healthy for an organization, because it assists managers in allocating resources and assistance most effectively. Competition also contributes to good human relations and helps establish a climate and culture (to be discussed in Chapter 13) that emphasizes high performance and goal accomplishment. Human relations in this type of organization also minimize the role of subjectivity and political behavior which can have disastrous consequences for an organization.

WHAT DO YOU THINK? NOTE

---

[1] Deutsch, M. Conflict: Productive and destructive. *Journal of Social Issues,* 1969, *25,* 7–41.
[2] Schmidt, S.M. & Kochan, T.A. Conflict: Toward conceptual clarity. *Administrative Science Quarterly,* 1972, *17,* 359–370.

PART FOUR

Organizational Relationships

CHAPTER FIFTEEN

Managing Organizational Politics

PROLOGUE

Sam and Amy had worked together as supervisors in the local automobile assembly plant for the last five years. They had started work there within a week of each other. Sam had graduated from the city university, while Amy had graduated from a small out-of-state college. They both have similar backgrounds, both were from small towns, both majored in business administration, both jog regularly and love professional ice hockey. Each Friday after work, they stop for a drink to compare notes about work and their careers. As they walked to Amy's car she could tell that something was bothering Sam. Sam didn't wait for Amy to ask him what was wrong. As soon as they got into the car, Sam began, "Jerry got promoted to that new division they're opening across town. He's only been here two years. Almost everyone else who started working here around the time we did has gotten a promotion. I've had it with this company. I've worked on several special projects, came up with that idea to make the line more efficient last year, and I haven't gotten more than a polite 'thank you.' The output of my unit has been in the top three since I started working here. This weekend I'm going to revise my resume and begin looking for a new job."

Amy began slowly. "Sam, this doesn't sound like the right time to tell you this, but I was called up to the vice-president's office this afternoon and offered a promotion as Manager of Accounts Receivable/Payable at the headquarters office. I hate to think about you leaving the company. Do you want to know what I think?" Sam replied that he valued Amy's opinion and would welcome any advice she could give him.

"Sam, there's no question that you and your department have been the best performers since you began working for the company. Everyone respects your extremely high motivation and hard work. But there's more to success in this company than just performing your job better than anyone else. What I think has held you back is your dealings with your coworkers and superiors. You never hang around after work and socialize with us. I've never seen you at the company picnic in the summer or at parties at any of the bosses' houses. I think that some of the other managers have developed the impression that you think you're better than everyone else."

Sam replied angrily, "I don't think any such thing! But even if I did believe that, what difference should it make? I just don't see those social activities as part of my job. I do better work than anyone else in a similar job and I can't believe that the company would promote people over me just because they go to parties."

Amy didn't want to argue the point. However, she had heard Sam's superiors say that he just didn't seem to fit in. They had decided that Sam seemed to like his current job since he did so well in it, and were content to let him stay in that job. They were reluctant to promote him since he didn't appear to have good human relations skills.

LEARNING OBJECTIVES

After successful completion of this chapter, you should be able to:

- Understand why power is necessary in organizations,
- Define organizational politics,
- Explain how individuals acquire power,
- Explain why politics arise in organizations,
- Discuss potential outcomes of organizational politics,
- Explain why individuals must be concerned about organizational politics,
- Describe what managers can do to manage organizational politics, and
- Explain how individuals can protect themselves from others' political behavior.

ORGANIZATIONAL POLITICS

For many people, **organizational politics** is a dirty word. It brings to mind unethical, unfair, and selfish behavior. As a result, few persons admit to engaging in political behavior. Further, many individuals try to avoid coworkers they believe to be highly political. However, this view of organizational politics may be dysfunctional since it may lead individuals to ignore politics within their organizations. Trying to ignore and remain separated from organizational politics may be damaging to your career.

Understand why power is necessary in organizations.

Politics are a natural outcome of organizations assigning different amounts of power and authority to individuals. Power is the ability to get others to do what you want. Authority is given to individuals by the organization and gives them the right to issue orders to other organizational members. Organizational structure places individuals in positions of varying degrees of formal authority or legitimate power. Thus, the very process of organizing implies that power will be exercised over certain organizational members. Some degree of political behavior typically develops from this imbalance of power and authority.[1] Sometimes, this power is used in ways not intended by the organization, or for purposes not approved by the organization. An individual developing the ability to "play politics," or at least protect himself from the political activity of others, may be helping himself advance within the organization.

Further, all political behavior is not "bad." Sometimes it is necessary to engage in various forms of political behavior to perform a job.[2] A certain amount of cooperation from other people is necessary in nearly any job. Often, the only way to get the cooperation of others is through political behavior.[3] When an individual needs the assistance or cooperation of others but lacks formal authority to demand it, some type of political behavior may be the only avenue open to him.

This chapter will examine the relationship between power and organizational politics, the conditions that lead to the development of political behavior, and the positive and negative outcomes of organizational politics. It will also present strategies for managing organizational politics.

In the Prologue, Sam appeared to be uncomfortable engaging in organizational politics. He had the opinion that employees who were top performers would be recognized and rewarded for their contributions. However, in his organization, it takes more than excellent job performance to receive promotion to more responsible positions. It also takes an ability to deal with other powerful individuals' needs and goals. In many organizations, you cannot simply be the best performer and expect to receive all the rewards you desire. You must also develop the ability to recognize and adapt to the political activities of others, particularly superiors. As John Crocker, III, an investment banker on Wall Street, says, "You can be the brightest person in the world and work your tail off, but if you aren't playing the game of organization, it may not get you anywhere."[4] You must be able to make your contributions and successes known to those in a position to reward and/or promote you, and you must become visible by volunteering for difficult assignments. But you must be able to engage in these political behaviors without appearing to be political. The "first rule of office politics" is to pretend that politics do not exist.[5]

RETURN TO THE PROLOGUE

WHAT IS ORGANIZATIONAL POLITICS?

Organizational politics is any use of power which is not sanctioned or authorized by the organization.[6] Notice that this does not necessarily mean that the use of power is illegitimate or used only for selfish reasons. While this use of power is certainly one type of political behavior, our definition of organizational politics includes the possibility of using power that, while not formally approved by the organization, is used to accomplish organizational goals. When Martha uses praise and flattery to get Joe, who works in another department, to complete reports she needs in her job, she is using organizational politics. Similarly, when Rob seeks out friendships with and does favors for employees in his department so that these employees will support him when he applies for the job of department manager, he is playing organizational politics. And, when George inflates his departmental budget projections for next year by 20 percent because he knows his boss typically cuts department manager's projections by 10 percent and he legitimately needs a 10 percent increase in his budget, he is playing organizational politics. In the first and last instances, political activity is undertaken to help accomplish organizational ob-

Define organizational politics.

jectives. In the second example, organizational politics are being used to further individual objectives.

> **WHAT DO YOU THINK?**
>
> Is it necessary to play politics to get ahead in most organizations? Can someone who is a top performer, but who refuses to play politics, advance as far or as rapidly as someone who is both a top performer and a good "politician"? What types of political behaviors, if any, do you believe are necessary for employees to learn to advance within their organizations?

Organizational Politics and Power

Most political behavior is aimed at acquiring, maintaining, or increasing power.[7] **Power** is the ability to get others to do things they would not otherwise do, or refrain from doing things that one does not want to do. To put it more simply, power is "the ability to get things done the way one wants them to be done."[8] According to this definition, managers and employees have power to the extent that they can, for example, set objectives, get others to perform activities, make decisions, define problems, select solutions to problems, choose to engage in some activities and refrain from engaging in others.

Bases of Power

Explain how individuals acquire power.

Five bases from which individuals may acquire power were briefly discussed in Chapter 13. One more base will be added to this list in this chapter. The six primary **power bases** that affect political activity are:

1. **Legitimate Power**. Legitimate power stems from one's formal position in the organizational hierarchy. Managers, who occupy positions higher in the organizational hierarchy than their employees, are generally seen as having a certain amount of legitimate power. That is, most employees perceive that it is legitimate for these managers to issue orders to their employees regarding departmental work activities.
2. **Reward Power**. Individuals also acquire power based on their ability to administer rewards which others desire. Employees often willingly submit to their manager's use of power to acquire rewards the manager controls.
3. **Coercive Power**. Employees also comply with requests from their managers to avoid punishments. Thus, managers have coercive power to the extent that they administer punishments or withhold rewards.
4. **Referent Power**. Managers have referent power to the extent that employees admire and identify with them. Individuals who are extremely likable or who have strong, pleasant personalities often acquire referent power. Employees willingly comply with such managers' attempts to influence their behavior because they like and respect these managers.
5. **Expert Power**. Individuals have expert power when they have expertise which others lack, but which is important to the organization. This expertise may be technical, such as statistical analysis or computer programming, or nontechnical, such as how the "organizational system" works. Low-level

employees often acquire expert power by learning how the system works—in other words, how to get things done. In the popular television show *M.A.S.H.*, "Radar" O'Reilly, the company clerk, was only a corporal, but had relatively high power due to his knowledge of the system and his network of contacts. He could often accomplish things by going outside formal channels that higher ranking officers could not accomplish.[9]

6. **Information Power**. Individuals' access to, and control of, scarce and important information is another significant base of power. Sometimes an individual's position within the organization provides access to unique information. Case in point: an employee who regularly interacts with customers or suppliers often acquires information not available from other sources. Of course, top level executives often receive information not available to other employees.[10] To the extent that others need information which a person controls, he has at least some power to influence their behavior.

Individuals may draw on any or all of these bases of power in their attempts to acquire, maintain, or increase their power. When the use of power is not sanctioned or approved by the organization, that use of power is considered political. When power is used in a formally approved manner for approved purposes, it is not considered political.

Relative Effectiveness of Power Bases

One important consideration in choosing a base of power is the probable effect on the person on whom the power is used. In any use of power, three outcomes are possible: *resistance, compliance,* and *commitment*. Resistance occurs when individuals ignore or fight an attempt to influence their behavior. Compliance occurs when individuals allow themselves to be influenced, but they are not enthusiastic and exert only minimal effort. Commitment occurs when individuals agree with the goals of the person attempting to influence their behavior. These individuals are willing to exert maximum effort to accomplish these goals. As shown in Exhibit 15.1, expert and referent power

Exhibit 15.1
Outcomes that result from different power bases

Power Base	Commitment	Compliance	Resistance
Legitimate	Possible	LIKELY	Possible
Reward	Possible	LIKELY	Possible
Coercive	Unlikely	Possible	LIKELY
Expert	LIKELY	Possible	Possible
Referent	LIKELY	Possible	Possible
Information	POSSIBLE	POSSIBLE	POSSIBLE

Based upon Yukl, G & Taber, T. The effective use of managerial power. *Personnel*, March–April 1983, *60*, 37–44.

tend to foster commitment; legitimate and reward power tend to encourage compliance; while coercive power tends to spawn resistance.[11] Power based on control of information may result in any of the three outcomes, depending on how the individual who controls the information behaves toward others. If the individual uses his control of information as a club or weapon to achieve individual goals at the expense of others, compliance is likely when others must have that information. If other organizational members can survive without the information, resistance is probable. Finally, if the information controller behaves in a helpful and supportive fashion toward others who seek information he controls, commitment will be the result.

CONDITIONS WHICH GIVE RISE TO ORGANIZATIONAL POLITICS

Explain why politics arise in organizations.

Organizations vary in the degree to which political behavior is present. Perhaps you have overheard students about to graduate discussing employment alternatives. A frequently overheard comment is "I don't want to work for that corporation. It's too political there." Several conditions facilitate the development of organizational politics. These include uncertainty, ambiguous or nonexistent objectives, ambiguous or nonexistent job performance standards, and competition for scarce resources or rewards.

Uncertainty

Uncertainty is a term often used to refer to external environmental conditions.[12] Managers may be uncertain about the activities of important components in their organization's external environment, such as federal legislators or active environmental protection groups. Conversely, they may have adequate information about groups in the organization's external environment, but lack information about how to respond to these groups.[13] Of course, uncertainty can occur at any level within an organization. Each department or subunit has its own external environment, even though this external environment may exist primarily within the organization.

Uncertainty facilitates the development of organizational politics mainly because it makes events and conditions subject to interpretation.[14] In uncertain environments, there are seldom right or wrong answers. High levels of uncertainty, whether at the overall organizational or departmental level, make it difficult to set clear goals, determine which activities should be undertaken, and set priorities. Since the importance of activities determines in large part how formal power in the organization should be divided, uncertainty makes it difficult to allocate power to organizational members. If power has already been allocated, if a structure exists creating authority and responsibility relationships, uncertainty makes people begin to question this allocation of power. Thus, the stage is set for individuals who are interested in acquiring additional power. During times of uncertainty, individuals and groups can attempt to win support for objectives that will benefit themselves. Since uncertain situations may be interpreted in several ways, individuals interested in increasing their power may attempt to define situations in ways that serve their own interest.

Ambiguous or Nonexistent Objectives

While environmental uncertainty may lead to ambiguous or nonexistent objectives, this is not necessarily the case. Managers in environments characterized by certainty sometimes neglect to set clear and specific objectives for their organization or department. A lack of objectives creates uncertainty. Since it has not been determined what the organization or department wants to accomplish, the door is open for individuals to engage in political maneuvering to establish objectives that are in their own best interest. Anyone who can set objectives for an organization or department has substantial power. Objectives can be set so that the activities deemed most important are those activities that the individual setting the objectives performs. Similarly, objectives can be set so that the skills and knowledge thought to be most important to the organization are the skills and knowledge possessed by the individual setting the objectives.

Ambiguous or Nonexistent Performance Standards

The effects of ambiguous or nonexistent performance standards are similar to those of ambiguous or nonexistent objectives. Without clear performance standards, individuals and groups are free to set their own. Usually, this practice results in individuals and groups trying to sell others on the idea that the most important aspect of performance is whatever they are good at. A perfect example of this exists in many colleges and universities. Most universities have defined the performance of faculty in terms of three factors: teaching, research, and service. Faculty who get the highest student classroom evaluations tend to argue that teaching should be given greater weight in performance evaluations, while faculty who do more research and publication tend to argue that this activity should be given greater weight. This jockeying for position will continue until some manager (administrator) sets clear performance standards not subject to varying interpretations.

Competition Over Scarce Resources

Chapter 14 established that competition over scarce resources is a primary cause of organizational conflict. Competition and conflict are, in turn, primary causes of organizational politics. Individuals with power can acquire scarce resources. Thus, scarce resources often set off competition among groups or individuals interested in acquiring these resources. For example, a department manager may attempt to convince the boss that customer relations are critical to the firm's success. Since his department has more customer contact than any other, if his argument is successful, he will acquire additional power, and therefore have greater access to scarce resources.

Outcomes of Organizational Politics

Organizational politics may have either positive or negative outcomes for organizations and individuals. When power is used to further individual interests at the expense of others or the organization, politics are likely to result in

Discuss potential outcomes of organizational politics.

WHAT DO YOU THINK?

The conditions that give rise to organizational politics are liable to differ across organizational subunits and activities. Consider the activities in the following list. Which are apt to be most political? Which are apt to be least political? Rank these activities in terms of how probable you believe it is that politics would be involved. (1 = least political and 11 = most political.)

___ Promotions and transfers
___ Hiring
___ Pay
___ Budget allocation
___ Facilities, equipment allocation
___ Delegation of authority
___ Interdepartmental coordination
___ Personnel policies
___ Disciplinary penalties
___ Work appraisals
___ Grievances and complaints[15]

negative outcomes for the organization. When power is used to enhance one's job performance or help accomplish organizational objectives, politics will probably result in positive outcomes for the organization. Organizational politics will have negative results for individuals when they either play politics poorly, or try to ignore the political behavior of other organizational members.

Several possible outcomes of politics are summarized in Exhibit 15.2. Playing politics may actually help individuals perform their jobs. When individuals must seek cooperation or assistance from others over whom they have no formal power, politics may have positive outcomes for both the individual and the organization. Further, political behavior aimed at performing one's job or accomplishing organizational objectives may result in greater communication and understanding among individuals and groups. The increased interaction and communication required to play politics may help these organizational members develop a better understanding of one another's jobs, problems, and roles in the organization. Increased communication and understanding may lead to increased cooperation, teamwork, and performance.

Explain why individuals must be concerned about organizational politics.

However, in some organizations, it is more important to "fit in" than to perform at your maximum ability, and individuals must play politics to be accepted. In these organizations, political behavior designed to make others feel influential and believe that you agree with them and their ideas may be more important than job performance. In fact, concentrating on job performance, at the expense of socializing with coworkers and superiors, may be damaging to your career. Since it is usually necessary to perform only to some minimally acceptable or average level to succeed in these organizations, politics has a positive outcome for individuals, but a negative outcome for the organization. In this situation, the ability to play organizational politics may help individuals achieve career goals such as salary increases, promotions, and desirable job assignments.

There are also negative or dysfunctional outcomes of organizational politics. Politics may increase divisiveness and conflict among organizational subunits or individuals, create a climate of distrust and suspicion, and damage the organization's image. Organizations that develop reputations for being highly

> **Exhibit 15.2**
> Possible outcomes of organizational politics
>
> ### ORGANIZATIONAL OUTCOMES
>
> **Positive**
>
> Greater cooperation/teamwork
> Improved communications
> Improved performance
>
> **Negative**
>
> Increased divisiveness/conflict
> Create climate of distrust/suspicion
> Damage organization's image
> Incompetent employees promoted over more capable performers
> Divert employee effort and organization's resources from goal accomplishment to political behavior
>
> ### INDIVIDUAL OUTCOMES
>
> **Positive**
>
> Increase job performance
> Acquire assistance/cooperation of others
> Career advancement, promotion
> Salary increases
> Desirable job assignments
>
> **Negative**
>
> Loss of prestige/credibility
> Demotion
> Loss of job

Based upon Madison, D.L., Allen, R.W., Porter, L.W., Renwick, P.A. & Mayes, B.T. *Human Relations,* 1980, *33*(2), p. 92.

political may have difficulty recruiting and hiring highly qualified job applicants. Further, in some cases, incompetent or marginal employees may be promoted over more capable employees. Finally, when employees are engaged in organizational politics, their effort and at least some organizational resources are being diverted from accomplishing objectives.

For individuals, organizational politics could have disastrous effects. When they ignore the political behavior of others, or play politics poorly, their careers can be severely damaged. They may be viewed with suspicion by others in the organization, and in extreme cases may suffer demotion or even termination.[16]

TYPES OF POLITICAL BEHAVIORS

It is impossible to generate a comprehensive list of political behaviors, since any behavior that uses power in a way unintended by the organization, or to accomplish objectives not sanctioned by the organization, is considered political. However, there are a number of relatively common political behaviors which have been identified by behavioral science researchers. These include scapegoating, character assassination, withholding or distorting information, image building, ingratiation, building alliances/coalitions, and creating obligations.[17]

Scapegoating

There are two versions of scapegoating, which involves attacking or blaming others.[18] The first is impersonal and involves protecting oneself. Typically, the individual has made a mistake or suffered a failure and tries to disassociate himself from the act. If a mistake or failure has occurred, someone will be blamed or associated with the problem when superiors become aware of it. However, the "politician" will take steps to ensure that it is someone other than himself—"covering his tracks" so there is no evidence that he was involved with the incident. One tactic would be withholding or destroying incriminating information or evidence.

The second version of scapegoating is personal and involves attempting to affix blame to another person or persons. Whereas the impersonal version of scapegoating may have allowed someone else to be blamed, this version actively tries to blame an individual or group. This may involve lying and/or falsifying information to incriminate others.

Character Assassination

Character assassination is intended to damage the image or credibility of another person. Usually, the politician plants bits of negative information about that person during casual conversations with others. Rumors transmitted over the grapevine are the primary means of carrying out character assassination. Since many people are intrigued by negative information, it does not take a great deal of effort to use this political tactic. In addition, the original rumor may be augmented and inflated as it travels on the grapevine. Typically, the politician attributes the negative information to another source by saying something like, "I hate to pass on negative information about a coworker, but I heard this from a very reliable source, and I thought you had a right to know." In this manner, it appears that it was someone other than the politician who began the rumor. Further, the politician appears to have the best interests of the other person at heart.

Withholding or Distorting Information

The increasing importance of information and information processing to today's organizations has been mentioned in several chapters. In this chapter, access to or control of information has been identified as a primary base of power. Thus, it should be no surprise that a significant and powerful political tactic is withholding or distorting information. This tactic can be used to make an opponent look bad or even cause him to fail in the performance of his task. Often, information which is extremely important to another person can be made to simply disappear, or a small "typographical error" may lead another person to make a serious mistake in calculations that costs the organization thousands of dollars. Sometimes this tactic might involve providing too much information to an opponent. The required information is buried in a mountain of paperwork, and by the time it is retrieved, it may be useless. The politician can argue that he provided every scrap of information available in an attempt to be helpful. "It's not my fault that Jerry didn't know what he was looking for!"

Image Building

Image building should be viewed as a continuum ranging from acceptable to unacceptable. Acceptable image building encompasses such activities as taking great care in one's grooming and dress.[19] As several self-help books put it, "To be successful, look successful." It is important to present a good image in

---

HUMAN RELATIONS IN ACTION

Suggestions for Dressing to Maintain a Positive Image

The importance of presenting a good first impression is widely accepted. However, maintaining a positive image or image of success is also extremely important in an organizational work setting. Here are several suggestions for men and women in dressing for success in the business world.

WARDROBE FOR MEN

SUIT: Conservative two-button suit with narrow lapels, in navy or grey, solid pinstripes, or shadow plaid.
TIE: Contrasting tie: maroon, rust, or brick-red; small patterns, bias stripe, club tie, or dots. Width must be current fashion.
SHOES: Basic lace-up, tassel loafers, or wingtips, black, brown, or oxblood in one color.
SHIRTS: 100 percent cotton, solid white, narrow pointed, round, or button-down collars.

ACCESSORIES: Gold pen and solid-color leather briefcase.
HAIR: Short haircut, no sideburns or beard.

WARDROBE FOR WOMEN

SUIT: Conservative suit: navy, grey, black, burgundy, or brown; pinstripe or solid.
DRESS: Coatstyle with the look of the suit, with white collar and cuffs; double-knit one-piece, solid color, accented with necklace or scarf.
SHOES: Plain pumps with medium-high heels in solid color; navy, black, brown, grey, or burgundy.
ACCESSORIES: Gold pen and solid-color briefcase.
HAIR: Short hair away from the face.

Source: How to establish a power presence. *Business Week's Guide to Careers,* Fall/Winter 1983, Volume 1 (2), pp. 68–70.

organizations. The accompanying Human Relations in Action box provides suggestions for building a positive image.

At the other end of the continuum, however, many people would argue that image building is inappropriate. This other extreme of image building activities includes such things as taking credit for things you did not do and trying to create an image that you are something you are not. For example, the politician may drop hints from time to time that he has had experience in a certain activity that is currently important to the organization. This fabrication might result in the politician being given a desirable job assignment or promotion. Taking credit for the activities of others may occur covertly; the politician may simply pass on another person's idea as his own. If the idea is accepted, the politician may simply remain silent about its true source. Once a number of people begin to attribute the idea to the politician, it will be difficult for the true originator of the idea to come forth and claim credit. Of course, if the idea turns out to be a bad one, the politician will immediately give "credit where credit is due."

Ingratiation

Ingratiation involves using flattery and praise to influence others.[20] The politician may also attempt to make others feel important, highly skilled, or knowledgeable—but for his own purposes. For example, the politician may praise a coworker's skill at financial analysis, then admit his own weakness in this area. Once the coworker believes the politician's "sincere" admiration of his financial analysis skills, the politician asks for help on a financial analysis project that he has been assigned. Having been the subject of so much praise and admiration, the coworker finds it difficult to refuse the politician's request for help. In the end, the coworker may complete most, if not all, of the politician's project.

And, the politician will attempt to use friendship to influence the behavior of another person, in the belief that individuals with whom he can build close friendships (or at least what appear to be close friendships) will support the politician's activities and ideas.

Creating Obligations

A tactic frequently used by effective politicians is **reciprocity**, or creating obligations. When using this ploy, a politician goes out of his way to do something for a coworker. Usually, this action is something that does not cost the politician anything of importance, such as time, effort, or other resources, but is of value to the coworker. Later, when the politician needs assistance or support, the coworker is reminded of the earlier favor by the politician, and is expected to reciprocate. This technique is highly effective, since most people have a need for equality. If someone does something for us, we generally feel a need to restore balance by doing something for them. What makes this a political tactic is that the politician may know in advance what he wants the coworker to do for him; he is building up credits to be used at a later date.

Building Alliances/Coalitions

This tactic involves establishing friendships and networks of relationships to get assistance, support, and information. Most effective politicians maintain direct access to the informal communications grapevine, because they need more information, or at least more timely information, than most formal organizational communication systems provide. An effective way of establishing entry into the grapevine is to create a network of contacts. This network can be initiated by identifying individuals who are likely to have access to important information and providing them with information that may be of use to them.

Another version of this tactic is building support for an idea or decision before it actually comes to a vote. Preceding a vote, politicians often spend considerable time visiting with individuals who will be involved in the decision. Politicians try to present their position in the best possible light and encourage others to vote for that position. This approach is particularly effective when the politician finds out about a vote or decision before the opposition does. Then the politician can get to the decision makers before the opposition has a chance to present its side of the story. This plan may involve the use of other tactics such as reminding individuals of obligations, promising reciprocity, and ingratiation.

MANAGING ORGANIZATIONAL POLITICS

One of the most important steps managers can take to minimize the amount of negative organizational politics is to set a good example. In short, don't engage in negative political behaviors. And, you should make it clear to all employees that you disapprove of such activities. Further, do not ignore negative political activities when you become aware of them. Speak to employees about their political activities, and consider punishments if their behavior has been particularly dysfunctional to the organization. In addition, managers should consider the following suggestions:

Set Clear Objectives

Each organizational subunit or department, as well as the organization as a whole, should have clear, unambiguous objectives to guide employee behavior and decision making. In addition, employees should be reminded of these objectives from time to time through informal and formal communications. If possible, employees' performance should be evaluated on the basis of how well they accomplished their objectives.

Describe what managers can do to manage organizational politics.

Develop Clear Performance Standards

Employees should know exactly what is expected of them. Some jobs lend themselves to objective performance appraisal; others do not. When it is impossible to measure employee performance objectively, managers can com-

Setting clear objectives and performance standards will reduce political behavior.

municate their expectations to employees. It is perhaps most effective to spend time communicating expectations to employees who work on jobs where their performance cannot be objectively measured.

Encourage Employee Participation in Decision Making

Employees become motivated to engage in political behavior when they believe that their interests are not being represented. By encouraging employees to participate in making important decisions that affect their jobs, you are giving them an opportunity to have a voice in decisions that have an impact on their lives. This participation must be legitimate, where good suggestions from employees are acted on—not merely apparent participation where employees' suggestions and opinions are heard, but are then ignored.

Confront Conflict and Problems Openly

When conflict, problems, or disagreements are ignored or swept under the carpet, they have a chance to grow and be used by organizational politicians. Politicians may have the time to redefine the nature of a problem or in some manner manipulate it to make it work to their advantage. To prevent this conflict recurrence, openly confront problem situations by trying to identify the true cause and by including all affected parties in discussions and decision making. Focus on objective information and facts—and on reaching a solution that all parties can live with.

SHOULD YOU ENGAGE IN ORGANIZATIONAL POLITICS?

Many individuals would immediately respond "No!" to this question because they are uncomfortable playing politics. They believe that organizational decisions should be based on objective, impersonal facts and not on emotional or biased opinions and feelings. They also believe that their rewards should be based solely on their job performance, not on whether they are liked by their superiors and coworkers. While this view represents what most people believe organizations *should* be, many organizations are not always characterized by impersonal, objective decision making. Instead, decisions are based on a combination of objective, impersonal information and organizational politics.

Exhibit 15.3
A decision tree for incorporating ethics into political behavior decisions

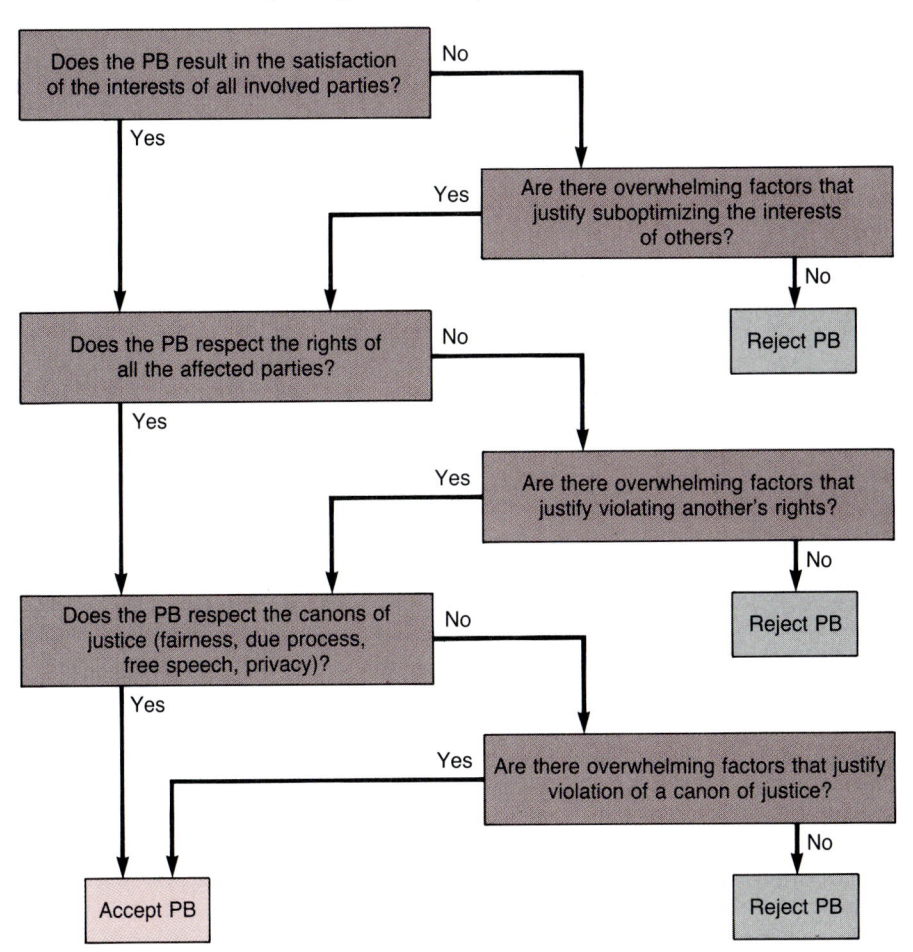

- Does the PB result in the satisfaction of the interests of all involved parties?
  - Yes → Does the PB respect the rights of all the affected parties?
  - No → Are there overwhelming factors that justify suboptimizing the interests of others?
    - Yes → (continue)
    - No → Reject PB

- Does the PB respect the rights of all the affected parties?
  - Yes → Does the PB respect the canons of justice (fairness, due process, free speech, privacy)?
  - No → Are there overwhelming factors that justify violating another's rights?
    - Yes → (continue)
    - No → Reject PB

- Does the PB respect the canons of justice (fairness, due process, free speech, privacy)?
  - Yes → Accept PB
  - No → Are there overwhelming factors that justify violation of a canon of justice?
    - Yes → Accept PB
    - No → Reject PB

Source: Adapted from Cavanagh, G.F., Moberg, D.J. & Velasquez, M. The ethics of organizational politics. *Academy of Management Review,* 1981, 6, p. 368.

DEVELOPING YOUR HUMAN RELATIONS SKILLS

The information presented in this chapter has important implications for both individual employees and managers. As an employee, you should:

1. Recognize that politics will develop in most organizations. You cannot afford to ignore it.
2. Recognize the dangers of developing a reputation as an organizational politician. While you cannot ignore politics, you cannot allow it to become more important than performing your job.
3. Realize that excellent job performance is not enough in some organizations. To get the rewards you want, you must develop the ability to play politics to a certain extent. You must at least identify individuals who have power, recognize the type of power they have, and determine what is important to them. Then you can avoid doing anything that might antagonize or anger these powerful individuals.
4. Identify what is truly important to your boss, or the individuals who control your rewards. Sometimes it is not what they *say* that is most important. You might find that while it might be more socially acceptable to give lip service to the idea that job performance is "really what matters around here," the way to get ahead is performing at an average level, expressing loyalty to the organization, and "fitting in."
5. When joining an organization, do not make close alliances too soon. Active politicians will try to win over new employees before they have a chance to make other friendships. If you unknowingly become associated with a person who has a reputation for playing politics, your career may be damaged.

Therefore, to be highly successful, you must engage in some degree of organizational politics.

This chapter has provided a great deal of information on why politics arise, the outcomes of organizational politics, and the types of political behavior. It is up to you to determine the specific type of political behavior in which you will engage and the degree to which you will participate.

Explain how individuals can protect themselves from others' political behavior.

The decision tree in Exhibit 15.3 can guide you in making ethical decisions about your own political behavior. A particular political activity is considered ethical when (1) it results in the greatest good for the greatest number of people; (2) it respects the rights (e.g., privacy, due process, free speech) of others; and (3) it represents justice (i.e., fairness, impartiality) for all individuals involved.[21]

SUMMARY

To many people, organizational politics is a dirty word. Consequently, they try to ignore politics. This attempt in itself may be damaging to their careers, because political behavior is a natural part of organizational life. Organizational politics is defined as any use of power that is not sanctioned or authorized by the organization. It is generally aimed at acquiring, maintaining, or increasing one's power. Politics can have either positive or negative outcomes for both individuals and organizations. It may result in increased job performance, communication, teamwork, and cooperation, but if it is not

> As a manager, the primary approaches to managing organizational politics are related to the factors that give rise to politics, namely, uncertainty, ambiguous or nonexistent objectives, ambiguous or nonexistent job performance standards, and competition for scarce resources or rewards. To manage politics effectively, you should:
>
> 1. Reduce uncertainty, by setting clear objectives and performance standards and communicating these regularly to employees. When employees know exactly what is expected of them, it is less probable that they will interpret unclear objectives or performance standards in ways that will benefit themselves.
> 2. Tie rewards and resources as closely as possible to objective measures of job performance.[22] You must accurately appraise employee performance and differentiate rewards and resources among employees who perform at different levels.[23] Top performers must receive more than average performers, who must receive more than poor performers. These differences in rewards and resources must be *meaningful*. It must be clear to everyone that the way to get more, is by performing at a higher level—not engaging in political behavior.
> 3. Communicate frequently and openly with employees. One reason people engage in political behavior is that a lack of information about what is going on in the organization creates uncertainty. If individuals are unsure about their future, they may be motivated to engage in politics to protect themselves. Providing employees with information about organizational plans and decisions may help reduce organizational politics. Further, it will help remind employees of organizational objectives.

managed effectively, it may foster increased divisiveness, conflict, distrust, and suspicion. It may also divert organizational resources and employee energy away from accomplishing organizational objectives.

Power is an important part of organizational politics. In this context, it is the ability to get others to do things they would not otherwise do, or refrain from doing things that one does not want to do. The six primary bases of power are reward, coercive, legitimate, expert, referent, and information. Use of power can result in resistance, compliance, or commitment. Expert and referent power tend to promote commitment. Legitimate and reward power tend to encourage compliance. Coercive power tends to incite resistance. Information power may result in any of these three outcomes, depending on how the individual uses his control of information.

Conditions which facilitate the development of organizational politics include uncertainty, ambiguous or nonexistent objectives, ambiguous or nonexistent performance standards, and competition for scarce resources or rewards. Several common types of political behaviors are scapegoating, character assassination, withholding or distorting information, image building, ingratiation, building alliances/coalitions, and creating obligations.

Managers can minimize negative organizational politics by setting clear objectives, developing clear performance standards, encouraging employee participation in decision making, communicating regularly and openly with employees, and confronting conflict and problems openly. In addition, managers should set a good example by not engaging in political activities themselves and by making it clear that they do not approve of such activities.

You cannot afford to ignore organizational politics, but you cannot become known as a "politician." The first rule of organizational politics is to pretend that it does not exist. Organizational political behavior is likely to be considered ethical if (1) it results in the greatest good for the greatest number of people, (2) it respects the rights of others, and (3) it represents justice for all individuals involved.

KEY TERMS

organizational politics
power
power base
legitimate power
reward power
coercive power
referent power
expert power
information power
character assassination
image building
ingratiation
reciprocity
building alliances/coalitions

DISCUSSION QUESTIONS

1. How is power related to organizational politics?
2. How do politics arise in organizations? Is it inevitable?
3. What political skills do you think it is absolutely necessary that you develop before entering the workplace?
4. What are some potential negative outcomes of organizational politics?
5. What are some potential positive outcomes of organizational politics?
6. How can managers minimize negative outcomes and maximize the positive outcomes of organizational politics?
7. When are organizational politics likely to be judged ethical?
8. Why do you think the "first rule of organizational politics" is to pretend that politics do not exist?

EXERCISE 15.1

Assessing Your Beliefs About Organizational Politics

The purpose of this exercise is to examine your own beliefs about organizational politics and compare these beliefs with those of actual managers. Using the five-point scale below, rate each of the following statements to reflect the degree to which you agree/disagree with each statement.

Strongly Agree	Slightly Agree	Neither Agree Nor Disagree
1	2	3

Slightly Disagree	Strongly Disagree
4	5

____ 1. The existence of workplace politics is common to most organizations.

____ 2. Successful executives must be good politicians.

____ 3. The higher you go in organizations, the more political the climate becomes.

____ 4. Only organizationally weak people play politics.*

____ 5. Organizations free of politics are happier than those where there is a lot of politics.

____ 6. You have to be political to get ahead in organizations.

____ 7. Politics in organizations are detrimental to efficiency.

____ 8. Top management should try to get rid of politics within the organization.

____ 9. Politics help organizations function efficiently.*

____ 10. Powerful executives don't act politically.*

---

*Reverse scoring.

Source: Gandz, J. & Murray, V.V. The experience of workplace politics. *Academy of Management Journal*, 1980, *23*(2), p. 244.

CASE 15.1

Politics at Bendix Corporation

In June 1979, William Agee, chairman of Bendix Corporation, hired Mary Cunningham out of the Harvard Business School to serve as his executive assistant. Only twenty-eight, she was described as an unusually brilliant, uncommonly ambitious, politically astute, sophisticated, and poised woman with high ideals. Almost immediately after joining the company, Agee decided to make use of her extensive financial and analytical skills to work on some major Bendix acquisition leads. One of her major projects was an analysis of the possible acquisition of the Warner and Swasey Company, a machine-tool business. Mary Cunningham completed her analysis with a strong recommendation that the company be acquired, and Bill Agee followed through in what became a very profitable investment for Bendix. Within a year, Agee promoted Cunningham to vice-president for corporate and public affairs, and the time they spent with each other in the office and on business trips increased. It soon appeared that Mary Cunningham had more access to Bill Agee's office than any other Bendix executive.

Although Mary's first year at Bendix was a dazzling success, executives were getting nervous. Conflicts between Agee and William Panny, Bendix president, began to appear over several important strategic decisions. In addition, rumors were circulating that Agee intended to implement a significant reorganization of Bendix's internal operations. Amid this turmoil, gossip spread about the relationship between Bill Agee and Mary Cunningham. It was noted that both soon separated from their spouses. There were stories about a more-than-professional relationship between the two. The fact that Mary was given the assignment of evaluating the strategic issue that had caused the rift between Panny and Agee did little to improve this climate of opinion. Her seven-person task force became known as "Snow White and the Seven Dwarfs," and their report was widely criticized by those opposed to its recommendation.

The climax grew closer. In early September 1980, Agee fired Panny over a policy disagreement, and the vice-president for strategic planning resigned within hours of that action. The stage was set for the final act. Bill Agee prepared to announce that Mary Cunningham was to become the new vice-president for strategic planning. As he did, he and Mary learned that someone was sending anonymous letters to the Bendix board of directors making "malicious references" to the pair's conduct. Agee acted quickly. He arranged meetings with Bendix's top managers and with the Board's executive committee. To each group he said the same thing: The rumors were false; he and Cunningham had no romantic involvement. Shortly before he was to announce Mary Cunningham's promotion, a newspaper reporter informed him that some Bendix people who were unhappy with Agee had contacted the reporter. They were planning to "leak" Agee's statement to the press. It might be better, the reporter suggested, if Agee allowed him to be present at the meeting. Agee acquiesced.

The following day William Agee announced Mary Cunningham's promotion to a gathering of 600 Bendix employees. His announcement included the following statement:

> I know it has been buzzing around that Mary Cunningham's rise in this company is very unusual and that it has something to do with a personal relationship we have. Sure it's unusual. Her rise in this company is unusual because she's a very unusual and very talented individual. It is true that we are very close friends and she's a very close friend of my family. But that has nothing to do with the way that I and others in this company evaluate performance. Her rapid promotions are totally justified.

The day after the meeting, the reporter printed the story, rumors and all, on the front page of a Detroit newspaper. By evening, the story had hit the news wires; over the next few days it became national news. The pressure on Mary Cunningham became too much. On October 9, 1980, she resigned from the Bendix Corporation.

QUESTIONS

1. What political mistakes did William Agee make, if any?
2. What political mistakes did Mary Cunningham make, if any?
3. What should Agee have done to manage organizational politics in this situation?
4. Is there anything Mary Cunningham could have done to prevent this situation?

Source: Cavanagh, G.F., Moberg, D.J. & Velasquez, M. The ethics of organizational politics. *Academy of Management Review*, 1981, *6*, 363–374.

REFERENCES

[1] Zaleznik, A. Power and politics in organizational life. *Harvard Business Review*, 1970, *48*(3), 47–60.

[2] Young, S. Politicking: The unsung managerial skill. *Personnel*, 1987, *64*(6), 62–68.

[3] Mondy, R.W. & Premaux, S.R. Power, politics, and the first-line supervisor. *Supervisory Management*, January 1986, *31*, 36–39.

[4] Buell, B. & Cowan, A.L. Learning how to play the corporate power game. *Business Week*, August 26, 1985, p. 56.

[5] Playing "office politics"–How necessary? *U.S. News & World Report*, January 12, 1981, 35–36.

[6] Mintzberg, H. The organization as a political arena. *Journal of Management Studies*, 1985, *22*(2), 133–154.

[7] Schein, V.E. Individual power and political behaviors in organizations: An inadequately explored reality. *Academy of Management Review*, 1977, *2*(1), 64–72.

[8] Salancik, G.R. & Pfeffer, J. Who gets power—and how they hold on to it: A strategic-contingency model of power. *Organizational Dynamics*, Winter 1977, *5*, 3–21.

[9] French, J.R.P. & Raven, B. The basis of social power. In Cartwright, D. (Ed.). *Studies in social power*. Ann Arbor: Institute for Social Research, University of Michigan, 1959, 150–167.

[10] Pettigrew, A.M. Information control as a power resource. *Sociology*, 1972, *6*, 187–204.

[11] Yukl, G. & Tabor, T. The effective use of managerial power. *Personnel*, 1983, *60*, 37–44.

[12] Duncan, R.B. Characteristics of organizational environments and perceived environmental uncertainty. *Administrative Science Quarterly*, 1972, *17*, 313–327.

[13] Milliken, F.J. Three types of environmental uncertainty about the environment: State, effect, and response uncertainty. *Academy of Management Review*, 1987, *12*, 133–143.

[14] Madison, D.L., Allen, R.W., Porter, L.W., Renwick, P.A. & Mayes, B.T. Organizational politics: An exploration of manager's perceptions. *Human Relations*, 1980, *33*(2), 79–100.

[15] Gandz, J. & Murray, V.V. The experience of workplace politics. *Academy of Management Journal*, 1980, *23*, 237–251.

[16] Madison, D.L., Allen, R.W., Porter, L.W., Renwick, P.A. & Mayes, B.T. Organizational politics: An exploration of manager's perceptions. *Human Relations*, 1980, *33*(2), 79–100.

[17] Allen, R.W., Madison, D.L., Porter, L.W., Renwick, P.A. & Mayes, B.T. Organizational politics: Tactics and characteristics of its actors. *California Management Review*, 1979, *22*(1), 77–83;

[18] Ibid.

[19] Tedeschi, J.T. & Melburg, V. Impression management and influence in the organization. *Research in the Sociology of Organizations*, 1984, *3*, 31–58.

[20] Kipnis, D., Schmidt, S.M. & Wilkinson, I. Intraorganizational influence tactics: Explorations in getting one's way. *Journal of Applied Psychology*, 1980, *65*, 440–452.

[21] Cavanagh, G.F., Moberg, D.J. & Velasquez, M. The ethics of organizational politics. *Academy of Management Review*, 1981, *6*, 363–374.

[22] Beeman, D.R. & Sharkey, T.W. The use and abuse of corporate politics. *Business Horizons*, 1987, *30*(2), 26–30.

[23] Longenecker, C.O., Sims, H.P., Jr. & Gioia, D.A. Behind the mask: The politics of employee appraisal. *Academy of Management Executive*, 1987, *1*, 183–193.

There are no right or wrong answers to these questions. However, surveys of managers in a variety of organizations have found strong opinions regarding organizational politics. Three interesting findings of these studies are that: (1) 93 percent of the managers surveyed believe that politics is common in most organizations, (2) 89 percent believe that successful managers must be "good politicians," and (3) 70 percent believe that "you must be political to get ahead." While it is clear that these managers believe organizational politics is widespread and necessary, they do not necessarily enjoy it. Nearly 60 percent of these same managers reported that organizations which are free of politics are happier and 55 percent reported that they believe that politics is detrimental to efficiency.* Almost half (49 percent) agree that managers should try to get rid of politics.

| WHAT DO YOU THINK? NOTE 1 |

*Gandz, J. & Murray, V.V. The experience of workplace politics. *Academy of Management Journal,* 1980, *23,* 237–251; Murray, V. & Gandz, J. Games executives play: Politics at work. *Business Horizons,* 1980, *23* (6), 11–28.

Researchers asked 428 current part-time MBA students and graduates of a large metropolitan business school to rate how political they perceived these activities to be in their own organizations. Their ratings are given below.

Activity	Rank
Interdepartmental coordination	11 (most political)
Promotions and transfers	10
Delegation of authority	9
Facilities, equipment allocation	8
Work appraisals	7
Budget allocation	6
Grievances and complaints	5
Pay	4
Personnel policies	3
Hiring	2
Disciplinary penalties*	1 (least political)

| WHAT DO YOU THINK? NOTE 2 |

Notice that activities likely to have fewer rules, procedures, or guidelines are rated the most political. Activities likely to have guidelines or policies to guide decision making, such as pay decisions, personnel policies, hiring decisions, and disciplinary penalties are rated the least political.

*Gandz, J. & Murray, V.V. The experience of workplace politics. *Academy of Management Journal,* 1980, *23,* 237–251.

CHAPTER SIXTEEN

Organizational Culture: Making Sense of Your Surroundings

PROLOGUE

Nearly everyone in the United States is familiar with Hershey Foods Corporation in Hershey, Pennsylvania—makers of such candy products as Hershey's Cocoa, Hershey's Kisses and Hershey Bars. In fact, when many people think of chocolate, they think of Hershey. Hershey has been so successful in the manufacture of chocolate products that for many people the name Hershey has become a synonym, or generic term, for chocolate. Part of this success may be due to Hershey's culture, which emphasizes the values of honesty, integrity, and ethics.

Hershey Foods recently completed a *values study* to identify the core values and beliefs of employees.[1] Employees were asked such questions as "What do you think is important to this company?" and "What values do you have to identify with in order to succeed at Hershey?" The results of the study showed that Hershey employees identified four primary categories of values they felt were important to Hershey; people orientation, consumer- and quality-consciousness, honesty and integrity, and results orientation. Management at Hershey feels these values are so important that they printed them on a card for each of the approximately 20,000 Hershey employees to carry. However, instilling a particular culture in an organization takes more than management statements that certain values or activities are to be emphasized. These values must be *exhibited* in all organizational activities and communications. John Rawley, director of corporate planning, summarizes this idea: "You can have a little piece of plastic in your wallet that says what you are. But it's really what you *do*—how you demonstrate care for each and every employee. Management has to think about this all the time—it must seep down throughout the company." Chairman and CEO Richard Zimmerman echoes this sentiment. He says, "We must *demonstrate,* over a long period of time, that we are serious. You can't preach ethics and integrity and be a little sloppy in your own habits."[2]

The values that characterize Hershey's culture today may be traced back to the company's beginnings. Hershey Chocolate Company was founded in 1903 by

Milton Snavely Hershey, whose lifestyle has been described as "high moral and religious principles; truth, honesty, and integrity; thrift, economy, and industry; the golden "do unto others" rule; the value of education; very high quality standards; the rewards of doing good and benefiting others; and an emphasis on the family and the community." Hershey expressed his values when he donated part of his fortune to a school for deprived boys. Support for this school continues today, with Hershey Foods owning 50.1% of the shares of the Milton Hershey School.

The Hershey story highlights three important aspects of culture which will be explored in more detail in this chapter: the role of the founder of an organization in determining its culture, the importance of identifying and managing culture, and the importance of actually living culture rather than merely talking about it.

LEARNING OBJECTIVES

After successful completion of this chapter, you should be able to:

- Precisely define organizational culture,
- Understand how culture forms in organizations,
- Discuss how employees learn culture,
- Differentiate between dominant culture and subculture,
- Understand how culture affects human relations,
- Explain why subcultures develop in an organization,
- Identify ways the culture of an organization is expressed, and
- Know how managers can manage organizational culture.

ORGANIZATIONAL CULTURE

Precisely define organizational culture.

One of the most important influences on human relations in organizational work settings is an organization's culture. **Organizational culture** is defined as "a fairly stable set of taken-for-granted assumptions, shared beliefs, meanings, and values that form a kind of backdrop for action."[3] The essence of culture is a set of shared assumptions that encompasses beliefs, meanings, priorities, and understandings, and is based on an agreed-upon set of values. These shared assumptions help employees learn the answers to two very important questions: (1) What things are important in this organization? and (2) How are things done around here? Organizational culture, therefore, identifies those things that employees should pay attention to, while it provides information concerning how they should behave. It tells employees what they need to do to be successful in their organization; that is, which activities have a high priority and which activities can be ignored or placed on the back burner. Think of the organizations of which you are a member as an employee, student, etc. How would you describe the culture of those organizations? What things are important to those organizations?

Another important characteristic of organizational culture is that these messages are generally implicit. In fact, employees may not even be aware of the culture or that they are being influenced by it. One author has suggested that culture exerts its strongest influence when employees are unaware of it.[4]

CHAPTER SIXTEEN: Organizational Culture: Making Sense of Your Surroundings   409

Employees may not always be aware of culture or its influence because, by the earlier definition, the essence of culture is a set of taken-for-granted assumptions. They become so familiar with "the way we do things around here" that they are no longer aware of the influence. They don't consciously think about how to perform familiar activities or tasks; they perform them in the same ways which led to success in the past. Nevertheless, the influence of organizational culture is generally one of the strongest and most important influences on human relations in organizational work settings.

HOW CULTURE FORMS

Organizational culture is an outcome of the process of employees interacting to solve problems and make sense of their working environment. This process begins with, and is heavily influenced by, the founder of the organization or a powerful top-level manager.

Understand how culture forms in organizations.

The Founder

The founder of an organization brings values, beliefs, assumptions, priorities and understandings to that organization.[5] In fact, the organization is initially built around these values and during its early life, the culture may be heavily influenced by the founder.

The influence of the founder's values on an organization is illustrated by the case of Mary Kay Cosmetics, founded by Mary Kay Ash. Before founding her company, she was a sales representative for Stanley Home Products. After winning a sales contest, she was terribly disappointed to find that her reward was a "flounder light," used by fishermen. According to Mary Kay, "I made up my mind that if I ever ran a company, one thing I would never do is give someone a fish light."

Mary Kay Ash went on to set up a company with a sales force primarily of women. Company meetings are called Pageant Nights. Sales awards include

---

As the Prologue illustrated, Hershey Foods Corporation was built on the values of its founder. More than eighty years later, the company's culture still revolves around this same basic set of values, modified somewhat to fit the current situation facing the firm. This modification of the culture created by the founder is due to the interaction of employees as they solve problems and perform assigned activities. Through their experience in the organization, they learn what is important and how things should be done. What they learn as a result of their interaction may lead to a modification of the original culture. In Hershey's case, the environment in which the firm operates today is much different than it was when Hershey was founded in 1903. The rules of the game are different; there are new laws, new technologies, and different economic conditions to be considered. Employees have to find new solutions to old problems, even as they find solutions to problems never even imagined in 1903.

RETURN TO THE PROLOGUE

HUMAN RELATIONS IN ACTION

Top Level Managers' Influence on Corporate Culture

The succession of CEOs at Xerox Corporation between 1961 and the present time provides an excellent example of the often substantial influence top-level managers exert on an organization's culture. Joseph C. Wilson was the founder and CEO at Xerox between 1961 and 1968. During this time Xerox was a high-growth company. It was still relatively small, so employees tended to know one another. The culture could be described as: informal, aggressive, encouraged risk-taking, and entrepreneurial. Employees were highly motivated and morale was high.

C. Peter McColough was CEO from 1968 to 1982. He inherited the controls of Xerox during a period of tremendous growth. During his reign, Xerox clearly dominated the copier market. The tremendous growth led to greater financial controls and clear lines of authority; in other words, Xerox became bureaucratic. In addition, Xerox's tremendous success made managers overconfident. For example, they didn't consider Japanese copier manufacturers a real threat until it was too late and Xerox had already lost a significant portion of the copier market to these foreign competitors. Xerox's culture during this period of time could be described as: formal, impersonal, discouragement of risk taking, and resistant to change. In addition, organizational politics and conflict over "turf" were widespread.

In 1982, David T. Kearns became Xerox's CEO. Kearns had joined Xerox in 1971 and had witnessed many of the changes in its culture. He immediately recognized the need for dramatic change. His emphasis was on quality products and service, reduction of the many layers of management which had developed under the previous CEO, and delegation of decision making. Under Kearns, Xerox eliminated 15,000 jobs between 1982 and 1983 and diversified into financial services, such as insurance and mutual funds. In many ways, Kearns was attempting to move Xerox's culture back to that which existed under its founder, Joseph C. Wilson. It will be several years until his success can be determined.

Source: Byrne, J. A. Culture shock at Xerox. *Business Week,* June 22, 1987, 106–110.

---

pink Cadillacs, furs, jewelry, and trips. A *Wall Street Journal* report in 1984 stated that Mary Kay employed more women earning over $50,000 per year than any other company in the United States.[6]

Interactions Among Employees

The fact that culture develops partially as a result of interactions among employees also suggests another aspect of organizational culture—while it is a relatively stable and enduring phenomenon, culture is never completely static. It is constantly changing and being modified by employee interactions. The changing environment in which the organization operates is constantly requiring employees to solve new problems. This movement, in turn, affects the shared assumptions on which culture is based. Thus, managers can never become complacent about their organization's culture. Managing culture is an ongoing, continuous activity.

It should be noted that the founder will not always have such a long-term effect on an organization's culture. At least two factors may make the current culture of an organization substantially different from that initiated by its founder. First, environmental conditions (e.g., laws governing commerce, economic conditions, foreign competition, technology) may be so radically different that the culture was modified as employees interacted to solve problems and perform assigned activities. Second, a powerful or charismatic top-level manager may exert so much influence on the organization that its culture begins to reflect this person's values more than those of the founder. The accompanying Human Relations in Action box illustrates the effect of top-level managers on organizational culture.

HOW EMPLOYEES LEARN CULTURE

An organization's culture must be expressed, if employees are to learn it. Since culture cannot be observed directly, behaviors which can be observed must carry the message of the organization's culture. It should be remembered that this learning process is not always explicit. Sometimes the messages are so subtle that employees learn culture without being aware of it.

Discuss how employees learn culture.

Exhibit 16.1 presents a model of the process by which organizational culture is developed, expressed, and maintained. The figure shows four primary means by which culture is expressed; shared things (e.g., physical work setting), shared sayings (e.g., jargon, annual reports, company newsletters, stories), shared doings (e.g., rites, rituals, ceremonials, meetings), and shared feelings (e.g., job satisfaction, organizational commitment, loyalty, job security). Some of the means by which a culture is expressed are examined in more detail in the following paragraphs.

Heroes

Organizational heroes are individuals who exemplify the core values of the culture and who serve as role models for others. Lee Iacocca, chairman of Chrysler Corporation, is an example of a modern-day organizational hero. He brought Chrysler back from near bankruptcy and an unprecedented loan from the federal government, to record profits in just a few years. Founders and top-level managers who solve a major problem or crisis facing the organization often become organizational heroes. Lower-level employees may also become heroes if they help the organization solve major problems or overcome formidable obstacles. Deal and Kennedy, in their book *Corporate Cultures,* identify several types of heroes.[7] **Visionary heroes,** such as Lee Iacocca, are leaders who serve as models for all employees. These heroes exemplify the organization's culture and transmit the core values of that culture to other employees by their words and actions. **Situational heroes** are the "Employees of the Month." They may influence only a few employees (e.g., a department or division) through their exceptional performance or problem solving. The organization draws attention to situational heroes through some type of award or recognition because these employees have performed in manner consistent with the culture of the organization. This recognition of situational heroes sends a message to other employees that one road to success is to model the

Exhibit 16.1
Model of the process by which culture is developed, expressed, and maintained

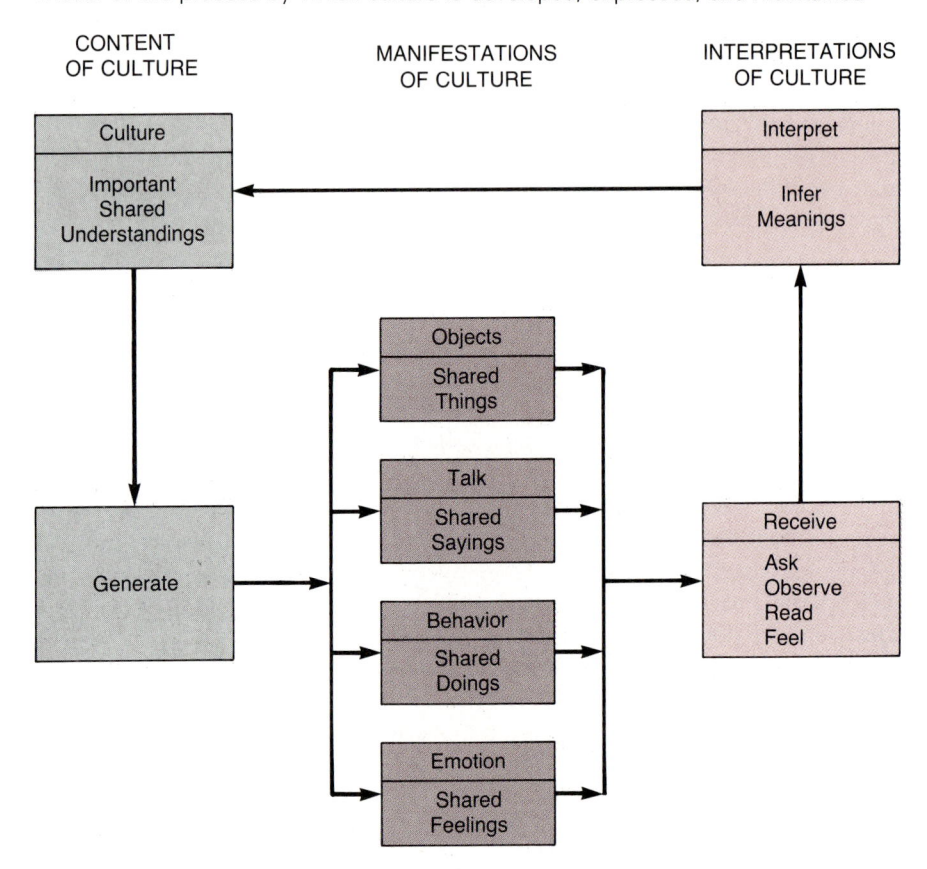

CONTENT OF CULTURE	MANIFESTATIONS OF CULTURE	INTERPRETATIONS OF CULTURE

Culture — Important Shared Understandings → Generate → Objects (Shared Things), Talk (Shared Sayings), Behavior (Shared Doings), Emotion (Shared Feelings) → Receive (Ask, Observe, Read, Feel) → Interpret (Infer Meanings) → Culture

Source: Sathe, V. Implications of corporate culture: A manager's guide to action. *Organizational Dynamics*, 1983, *12*, p. 8.

behavior of these situational heroes. Finally, **outlaws** are heroes who bring about needed change or creativity in the organization. While outlaws may violate some of the rules of the organization's culture, the organization chooses to ignore the infractions because of their contributions to the organization. Outlaws are often extremely high performers or creative individuals who are capable of making a unique contribution to the organization.

Rites/Ceremonials/Rituals

Identify ways the culture of an organization is expressed.

Rites are dramatic activities usually performed before an audience.[8] One example is the reception that is invariably held for a new dean or president of a university. Rites provide an opportunity to reinforce the core values of the culture at important times, such as celebrations of organizational heroes, retirements, promotions, and awards for outstanding performance. Rites enable an organization to recognize and award individuals who have exemplified the core values of the culture. This recognition sends a message to other employ-

Rites, such as awards for outstanding performance, transmit the organization's culture to employees.

ees concerning behavior. For example, during the presentation of the department's "Employee of the Month Award" the manager will likely stress those things that the recipient has done which are consistent with the core values of the organization's culture. The manager is sending a subtle message to all other employees to engage in these same behaviors.

Ceremonials are a set of several rites connected by a single occasion or event.⁹ An example of a ceremonial is the entire series of rites which are conducted as a new university president takes office or retires (e.g., receptions, meetings, lunches, convocations).

Rituals are relatively small events aimed primarily at reducing anxiety before a rite or ceremonial. Perhaps the most well-known example is the singing of the national anthem before sporting events. In organizational work settings, a ritual can be something as simple as waiting until everyone is seated or serving coffee before beginning a meeting. The ritual is familiar to everyone and helps ease the tension and anxiety before beginning an unfamiliar activity.

Stories

Stories are anecdotes which describe some event in the organization's history; they can be a blend of truth and fiction. They may, for example, describe how the founder or top-level manager overcame formidable odds to bring the organization out of a crisis. The longer the time from the actual event to the present story, the more likely the story has been embellished or modified. An example of a story which reinforces the core values of an organization's culture is the description of Milton Hershey's life. He and his wife had no children of their own, so Hershey donated part of their fortune to start a school for deprived boys.[10] This story reinforces the culture of Hershey Corporation which is characterized by concern for people, consumer- and quality-consciousness, integrity, honesty, and results orientation. Of course, employees may also tell stories that conflict with the expressed core values of the organization's culture. This inconsistency is likely to occur when managers express one set of values, yet they behave in a manner at odds with the stated values. For example, an organization publicly stressed the importance of its employees, saying that one major goal was to help employees grow and develop. However, this company expended resources on training programs for only its top-level managers. On one occasion, two highly motivated lower-level managers approached their boss with a request to attend a management development seminar being held at a local university. Their request was denied without explanation. These two examples were combined to form a story containing the message that regardless of what the organization said, it was not truly concerned about the growth and development of its employees.

Communications

Both formal and informal communications can reinforce and transmit (or perhaps modify) the core values of an organization's culture. Formal communications include company newsletters, annual reports, employee handbooks, formal plans, meetings, and memoranda.[11] Informal communications consist primarily of the countless conversations which take place every day—in the hallways, over desks, in the lunchroom, in the parking lot, and so on. Any communication that includes a message concerning what things are important to the organization or how things should be done has the potential of influencing organizational culture. When an employee tells her coworkers "I don't think this organization really cares much about its employees," or "It doesn't matter how well you do your job, just make sure you don't make any waves," culture is potentially influenced. Managers should take great care to ensure that the messages they send to employees during casual conversation reinforce and support the core values of the desired organizational culture. Culture will express those things that are truly emphasized by the organization, regardless of what is contained in various forms of communications. Employees cannot be fooled; they will quickly learn which things are truly valued by the organization and its managers and focus on these things. Other activities will receive much less, if any, attention regardless of whether or not managers say these excluded activities are important. Unless employees can observe managerial behavior that is consistent with the verbal and written messages they receive, efforts at reinforcing or changing culture through communications will be ineffective.

An important part of both formal and informal communications is jargon—created words, or familiar words used in a way unique to a group or organization. Organizations and work groups tend to develop a language of their

CHAPTER SIXTEEN: Organizational Culture: Making Sense of Your Surroundings   415

own when existing words and phrases do not communicate the exact meaning desired. To illustrate, look at academia. With the increased importance placed upon research and publishing, the word "hit" has taken on a new meaning. Professors frequently talk about getting a "hit" in various scientific journals (meaning an article was accepted for publication). Thus, since jargon tends to develop for things the organization gives high priority, its frequent and common use helps reinforce what the organization considers to be important. The Human Relations in Action box which appears later in the chapter illustrates the use of jargon at Domino's Pizza franchises.

Manager Behaviors

Edgar H. Schein, who has written extensively about organizational culture, suggests that the three concepts with the greatest influence on organizational culture are; (1) what managers pay attention to (and what they ignore), (2) managers' reactions to critical events or crises, and (3) managers' behavior (since employees tend to model their own behavior after that of their managers).[12] Employees are not fooled by managers who reinforce one set of values through communications, but a different set through their behavior. Managers cannot, for example, stress the importance of open and honest communications in their words, and at the same time hold secret meetings to make important decisions regarding the future of the company.[13] The importance of consistency in statements about an organization's culture and its managers' behavior cannot be overemphasized. Recall the words of John Rawley and Richard Zimmerman of Hershey Foods Corporation that were quoted in the Prologue, . . . it's really what you *do*—what you demonstrate for each and every employee over a long period of time.

LEVELS OF ORGANIZATIONAL CULTURE

Most of what has been written about organizational culture has focused on **dominant culture**—the culture of the overall organization. However, most organizations also have several subcultures. **Subcultures** develop around subunits or groups within an organization; each division, department, work team, and informal group within an organization may develop its own culture. In many cases, an organization's subcultures reflect primarily the core values of the dominant culture. Earlier, the process by which organizational culture forms was described as an outcome of employees interacting to solve problems and make sense of their environment. Just as some of this interaction takes place from the perspective of the overall organization, some interaction takes place from the perspective of organizational subunits. Thus, employees have experience as members of the overall organization, but they also have experience as members of a department or work team. While there is generally some degree of overlap between subcultures and the dominant culture, organizational subunits may produce an identifiable subculture somewhat different from the dominant culture. Exhibit 16.2 illustrates the relationship between an organization's dominant culture and subcultures.

Differentiate between dominant culture and subculture.

Explain why subcultures develop in an organization.

Exhibit 16.2
Relationship between organizational culture and subcultures

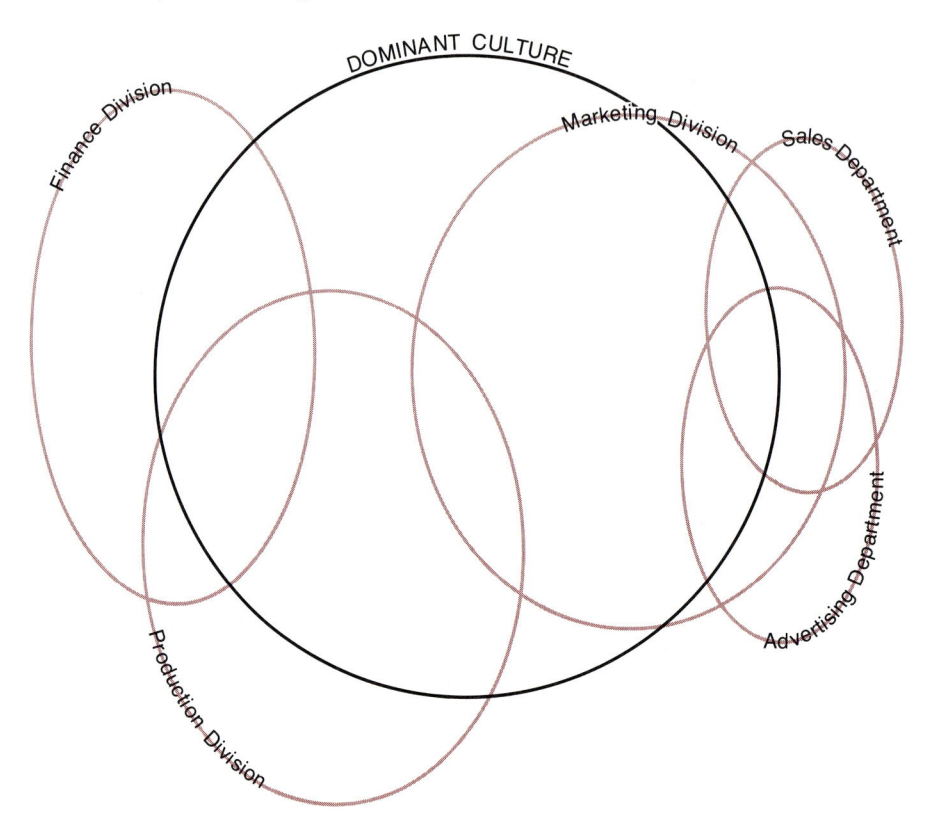

[Diagram: A large circle labeled "DOMINANT CULTURE" overlapping with ellipses labeled "Finance Division," "Marketing Division," "Sales Department," "Advertising Department," and "Production Division."]

Subcultures vary in the degree to which they reflect the organization's dominant culture. Subcultures in organizations with particularly strong dominant cultures will probably differ only slightly from the dominant culture. On the other hand, subcultures in organizations with weak dominant cultures may differ dramatically, and perhaps even conflict with, the organization's dominant culture.[14] Thus, in organizations with weak dominant cultures, the key to understanding employee behavior is identification of the core values of the subcultures.

STRENGTH OF A CULTURE

The **strength of a culture** (both dominant culture and subculture) is determined by four factors:[15]

1. Homogeneity of group membership. Groups and organizations made up of individuals with similar beliefs and values come into existence with the basis for a culture already in place. These individuals are already predisposed to value the same things and behave in a similar manner.

2. **Length of group membership.** Groups and organizations which remain together for long periods of time have a tremendous amount of "shared history." This history is used to understand what has happened to them, as well as what is likely to happen to them in the future. Further, long periods of interaction tend to reduce differences as individuals conform their behavior to remain a member of the group.
3. **Stability of group membership.** High levels of turnover of group members prevent individuals from establishing close relationships with one another. This lack of contact, in turn, reduces the likelihood of a strong culture developing, since frequent interactions among group members may not take place. Further, the group is joined frequently by new members who may not share the same beliefs and values as current members are frequently joining the group. Thus, stable membership is vital to the development of a strong culture.
4. **Intensity of group experience.** Groups which share intense experiences, such as overcoming seemingly insurmountable obstacles or solving extremely difficult problems, tend to develop relatively strong cultures. Through their experience, they found what it took to be successful in a very difficult situation. Therefore, their values and beliefs are likely to be widely accepted among group members.

The presence of subcultures suggests that managers of all organizational subunits must assume responsibility for managing culture (subculture). To the extent that subcultures holding values in conflict with those of the dominant culture are allowed to develop unchecked, managing or changing the dominant culture will become more difficult.

CULTURE AND HUMAN RELATIONS

It should be pointed out that strong cultures are not necessarily associated with good human relations or organizational performance. Unfortunately, a culture that emphasizes "doing just enough to get by" or "protecting your turf" could be widely shared by organizational members. Thus, the extent to which a culture benefits an organization depends not only on the strength of the culture, but also on the degree to which the culture emphasizes the accomplishment of organizational goals and the development of good human relations.

Understand how culture effects human relations.

Types of Cultures

Several types of dominant cultures, good and bad, have been identified. Five *dysfunctional* types of culture are *paranoid, avoidance, charismatic, bureaucratic,* and *politicized*.[16]

Paranoid Culture. This culture is characterized by distrust, suspicion, and a focus on identifying enemies. There is a lack of trust between managers and employees, which often results in close supervision and elaborate rules and procedures. Employees are quickly and sometimes harshly punished for mistakes. The result is a decline in employee's motivation and initiative. Top performers are likely to leave the organization, while those who remain become defensive and possibly even aggressive toward their manager and the organization.

Avoidance Culture. Employees in avoidance cultures share the belief that "what they do really doesn't make any difference." They have learned (correctly or incorrectly) that they can't make much of a difference. This culture is characterized by: high absenteeism, unmotivated employees, delays, buck passing, apathy, and "doing only enough to get by."

Charismatic Culture. Charismatic cultures develop around particularly strong, charismatic leaders. Employees become extremely dependent on this leader and follow directions unquestioningly and enthusiastically. This type of culture is characterized by risk taking, impulsiveness, and submission to the charismatic leader. The inherent danger is that employees continue to blindly follow this leader regardless of the outcomes or effects upon the organization.

Bureaucratic Culture. In this culture, top managers are preoccupied with exerting their control over employees. Organizations with bureaucratic cultures tend to develop many detailed formal policies, rules, and procedures. The culture can be characterized as depersonalized and inflexible. The result is that employees cannot use their own initiative and judgment and be involved in the operation of the organization. Employees are therefore likely to become uninvolved, disinterested, and unmotivated.

Politicized Cultures. Politicized cultures develop in organizations with weak leaders. This lack of leadership allows lower-level managers to try and gain additional power and control. The result is an organization with problems in several areas: communications, conflict, cooperation, coordination, and responsibility.

Potentially Functional Cultures

The grid in Exhibit 16.3 presents four types of culture that may be functional or dysfunctional, depending on the degree to which they facilitate the accomplishment of organizational goals.[17] This grid is based on two variables: the degree of risk associated with the organization's activities, and the speed with which the organization and its employees received feedback on their performance.

Tough-Guy, Macho Culture. In this culture characterized by high risk and quick feedback, employees operate in a climate of fast pace, intense pressure, and internal competition. These organizations tend to value short-term success over long-term prosperity. Individual performance is valued over teamwork and cooperation. In fact, the heroes in this culture are the individuals willing to make decisions quickly, take huge risks, and live with the consequences. Individuals can expect big rewards when the risk pays off, termination when it doesn't. Thus, the primary value of this culture is winning, and winning big.

Exhibit 16.3
Types of organizational cultures

	ENVIRONMENTAL RISK	
FEEDBACK	High	Low to Moderate
Fast	Tough-Guy, Macho Culture	Work-Hard, Play-Hard Culture
Slow	Bet-Your-Company Culture	Process Culture

Source: Based on Deal, T.E. & Kennedy, A.A. *Corporate cultures: The rites and rituals of corporate life.* Reading, MA: Addison-Wesley, 1982.

Management consulting, advertising, publishing, and sports are examples of organizations which fall into this category.

Work Hard/Play Hard Culture. This culture is characterized by low risk and fast feedback. The internal environment of the organization is one of fast pace, continuous activity, and persistence. There is a heavy emphasis upon customer needs. The way to success is through high volume and repeat sales. Examples of organizations which fall into this category are fast food restaurants (McDonalds, Domino's Pizza), real estate (Coldwell Banker, Century 21), door-to-door selling (Mary Kay Cosmetics, Avon). This culture places more emphasis on teamwork, cooperation, and interpersonal relations, and the organizations use a variety of games, conventions, competitions, and parties to keep employee motivation at high levels. The accompanying Human Relations in Action Box illustrates this process at Domino's Pizza.

Bet-Your-Company Culture. This type of culture is characterized by high risk and slow feedback. These types of organizations must invest large sums of money and resources and wait many years to find out whether they were successful. Organizations typical of this category are oil companies (Mobil, Exxon) and aerospace companies (McDonnell–Douglas, Boeing). For example, it might require an investment of billions of dollars to develop a new commercial aircraft. However, it may take 20 to 30 years before the aircraft has reached the breakeven point and the organization can begin to estimate its level of success. Since a single decision can seriously damage the organization, there is a substantial amount of constant pressure on employees to be correct. This typically results in a very slow, tedious, and deliberate decision-making process. Experience and technical expertise are highly valued in this type of culture.

Process Culture. This culture type is distinguished by low risk and slow feedback. Government agencies, banks, insurance companies, and schools are representative of this category, where the emphasis is on doing things the "right

HUMAN RELATIONS IN ACTION

TMS, FFF, HTA, PRP, and PEP

After getting out of the Marine Corps in 1960, Tom Monoghan enrolled at the University of Michigan and, with his brother and a $500 loan, bought DomiNick's Pizza in Ypsilanti, Michigan. After losing two partners, surviving a fire at corporate headquarters, and undergoing a name change, Monoghan has turned Domino's Pizza into the fastest-growing fast food franchise in the world, with revenues of $721 million in 1986.

The organizational culture at Domino's Pizza can be characterized in one word: "hustle." In fact, Domino's has written its own definition for this word: "hustle is a winning attitude of Domino's Pizza employees characterized by working quickly and efficiently." The pace in Domino's Pizza franchises is, at times, unbelievable. This is largely due to the fact that 80 percent of the customers call during only 20% of the store's hours. Performance standards seem rigorous. For example, order takers must answer the telephone within three rings, and take a complete order within 45 seconds. Pizza makers have only one minute to make a pizza and get it into the oven. Oven tenders must be able to load one pizza and unload another within five seconds, and also to slice and box the finished pizza by the count of 15. To meet the heavy demand, Domino's has developed its own language to reinforce the core values of its culture. There is even a company-published dictionary of company slang to help new employees learn the language. Some of the terms are:

TMS—thirty-minute service. Domino's guarantees your pizza will be delivered within 30 minutes or you get $3 off your next pizza.

FFF—fast, friendly, and free delivery.

HTA—heightened time awareness. Employees are encouraged to make wise and efficient use of their time.

PRP—pre-rush preparation.

PEP—a new motivational program designed to instill "passion, enthusiasm, and pride" in employees.

These terms help reinforce the core values of Domino's culture: hustle, customer service, and quality. Employees are also reminded of these values through contests between stores for the fastest service, fastest delivery time, and highest sales. The results of these contests are reported as "box scores" in the company newspaper, "The Pepperoni Press."

Source: Feuer, D. Training for fast times. *Training*, 1987, *24*, 25–30.

---

way." For many employees, *how* they do something is at least as important as *what* they do. As a result, employees pay a great deal of attention to detail and paperwork that documents things were done correctly. Conformity, respect for authority, caution, and thoroughness are highly valued. There is also a strong preference for the status quo, manifested in a resistance to change. To be successful in this culture, employees must not make waves, carry out their routine tasks exactly as spelled out in their job descriptions, and show respect for authority.

It should be noted that no single organization will fit perfectly into one of these four culture categories. Further, subunits within a single organization may display different types of culture. Case in point: the Finance and Accounting Division, which faces low-to-moderate risk and relatively slow feedback, may exhibit a process culture, while a Research and Development Division facing high risk and slow feedback might display more of a bet-your-company culture.

MANAGING ORGANIZATIONAL CULTURE

Given the subtle and shadowlike nature of organizational culture, it is unlikely that it can be managed precisely. Nevertheless, managers can have a substantial impact on their organization's or subunit's culture. If Schein is correct regarding those things which have the strongest effect upon culture (i.e., what managers pay attention to, what managers do, and how managers react to crises), managers have no choice in whether or not they will affect their organization's culture. Their only choice is whether to do it involuntarily and haphazardly through their everyday behavior, or to attempt to systematically install and reinforce the set of core values most beneficial to the organization. Managers will strongly influence what employees come to believe about the organization, its operating policies, and its priorities. Several techniques can be used to install and reinforce a desired culture, but the first step in managing culture is to determine the nature of the existing culture.

Know how managers can manage organizational culture.

Mapping the Existing Culture

The most difficult part of the entire culture management process may be to identify the existing culture. Managers must be able to look objectively at their organization—not an easy task, if they have been saying one thing, while doing another. Their organization may have been stressing the importance of open communications, but excluding employees from participating in important decision making. Or their organization might have stressed the importance of good performance and the rewards linked to that performance, but they administered basically equal rewards to all employees. In this latter case, the words say that performance is important and that employees should strive to perform to their capabilities. However, the behavior tells employees to just do enough to get by, since everyone will receive approximately the same reward anyway. It is often difficult for managers to see what is really emphasized in their organizations.

Another reason that culture is difficult to manage is its tendency to perpetuate itself. Organizations hire and socialize new employees to fit into the existing culture; members who cannot or will not fit in are frequently terminated. In addition, the communications and behaviors of employees who have been successfully socialized reinforce the core values of the existing culture. Fortunately, just as each of these activities may reinforce an existing culture, it also provides a point where managers can intervene and modify the organization's culture.[18] These points are illustrated in Exhibit 16.4.

Culture Management Techniques

Several techniques have been identified for managers to modify or manage organizational culture. Many of the means by which culture is expressed and learned can be used; for example, communications, appraising and rewarding

Exhibit 16.4
How culture perpetuates itself

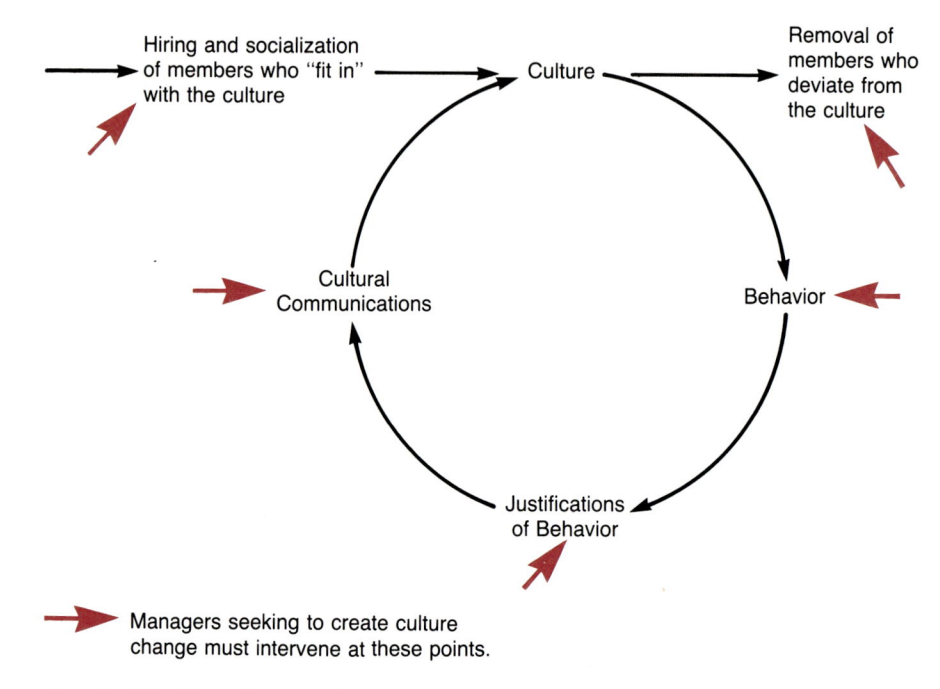

Hiring and socialization of members who "fit in" with the culture → Culture → Removal of members who deviate from the culture → Behavior → Justifications of Behavior → Cultural Communications → Culture

→ Managers seeking to create culture change must intervene at these points.

Source: Sathe, V. Implications of corporate culture: A manager's guide to action. *Organizational Dynamics*, 1983, *12*, p. 18.

performance, **modeling** (setting an example), socialization, and stories. Several of these techniques are discussed in detail in the following paragraphs.

Modeling

This may be the most effective way that managers can influence organizational culture. Employees carefully monitor the behavior of their managers for signals as to "what's important around here" and "how things should be done." Unfortunately, managers sometimes say one thing and do another, sending confusing signals to employees. It is not long, however, before employees decide that what's really important can be learned from managers' behavior, not their words.

Performance Appraisal and Reward Administration

Another highly effective culture management tool is the performance appraisal and reward system. "The reward system—who gets rewarded and why—is an unequivocal statement of the corporation's values and beliefs."[19] Unfortunately, managers' words and actions are often at odds. Take the case that one author reported after a study of the performance appraisal and reward practices of the group claims department of a large insurance company.[20] Managers said that their goal was the accurate payment of claims. However, any employee who received more than a certain number of customer complaints was repri-

CHAPTER SIXTEEN: Organizational Culture: Making Sense of Your Surroundings 423

manded and sometimes even docked pay. To avoid this punishment, employees would pay out the maximum amount when faced with an uncertain or ambiguous claim. It is not surprising that this practice reduced the number of customer complaints and also produced higher performance ratings for employees. In this case, management was saying it valued accurate claim processing, but the behavior of managers in the group claims department told employees that what managers really valued was a minimum of customer complaints.

Communications

Both formal and informal communications can help reinforce the core values of the desired organizational culture. Company newsletters, annual reports, internal memoranda, and speeches by top-level managers can all be used to good advantage. Managers should also take great care that their casual conversations with employees reinforce cultural values.

One interesting aspect of communications by which culture is expressed and reinforced is the use of **stories**. Some managers make it a practice to repeat stories that support desired cultural values. The founder of IBM, Thomas J. Watson, Jr., frequently used stories to send messages to employees. One of his better-known anecdotes was from the writing of Soren Kierkegaard.

> A nature lover enjoyed watching wild ducks fly south in vast flocks each fall. Feeling sorry for them, he began to place food in a nearby pond. After a while, some of the ducks no longer bothered to fly south and wintered in the pond on the food left for them. Over time they flew less and less . . . and after several years they grew so fat and lazy that they found it very difficult to fly at all.

The story above was one of Watson's favorites. He repeated it frequently whenever he felt it necessary to make this same point. How do you interpret this story? What message was Watson trying to send to his employees? Develop your own answer before turning to the note at the end of the chapter for the answer.

WHAT DO YOU THINK?

Stories describing some important event in the organization's history can reinforce the core values of the organization's culture. Such stories might, for example, relate the experience of a visionary or situational hero—much like the stories about Milton Hershey in the Prologue. Another story from IBM relates the time Watson was touring an IBM facility with a group of managers. A young security guard stopped them as they attempted to enter a secure room, and upon finding that Watson did not have the correct security badge, prohibited him from entering. One of the managers on the tour said "Don't you know who this is?" whereupon, Watson simply raised his hand to silence the managers and sent someone for the correct badge. The message sent to employees by this story is "*no one* breaks the rules—not even the founder of the company."[21]

DEVELOPING YOUR HUMAN RELATIONS SKILLS

This chapter presented information which is important in both your role as a manager and as an employee. As an employee, organizational culture helps you learn what the organization considers important and how you should behave. To put it more simply, learning an organization's culture helps you determine what it takes to be successful in that organization. Specific suggestions for you, as an employee learning an organization's culture, are offered here:

1. While it is important to listen to what managers and other employees tell you is important, pay particular attention to their actions. Sometimes a value or behavior is professed to be important when, in fact, the organization really doesn't value it at all. Certain values and behaviors may be given a great deal of lip service, to appeal to outsiders such as shareholders, government agencies, consumer groups, and so on. For example, many organizations who have been found guilty of some form of environmental pollution had publicly expressed goals of keeping the environment clean and healthy.
2. Become familiar with the ways a culture is expressed or learned, and pay particular attention to these activities in your own work setting.

Managers often have a tremendous influence on organizational culture, primarily the subculture in that manager's department or work unit. In your role as a manager, therefore, you must ensure that your communications, and even more importantly, your actions, establish the type of culture you desire. You should pay particular attention to the following activities:

1. First, determine the type of culture most appropriate for the type of work your unit performs and the goals you are trying to achieve.
2. Make sure that your actions and communications are consistent. You simply cannot say one thing and do the opposite, because employees will tend to believe actions over words in the long run. Both must reinforce the type of culture that you have identified as most appropriate for your work unit. Actions here refers to formal managerial behavior—such as performance appraisal and reward administration—as well as everyday informal interactions with employees.
3. From time to time, consider staging events such as rites and ceremonies that reinforce the desired organizational culture. Since culture is constantly evolving, it cannot be left to chance. Without constant attention and reinforcement, the culture may become inappropriate for your organization or work unit.
4. Provide clear, specific, and detailed guidelines to new employees as to what is expected of them. Establish the desired culture in the minds of new employees from the outset. If your organization does not have a formal orientation program for new employees, consider developing your own informal orientation program for employees coming into your work unit. Let these employees know from the first day what you consider important and how you want things done.

Managers considering the use of a story to reinforce or change cultural values should carefully consider the answers to the following questions:[22]

1. What did the person or people in the story do that our organization values?
2. Why is the person's behavior an example of desirable ways of doing things around here?
3. What other actions could people have taken that would also be desirable ways of doing things?
4. What additional actions could people have taken to be even more effective in this situation?
5. What are some examples of undesirable actions that people might have taken?

Socialization

Socialization is the process by which newcomers are "taught the ropes." In this chapter's context, socialization is the process by which new employees learn the culture.[23] New employees are particularly sensitive to information about what things are important and how things should be done. Consequently, they pay careful attention to what others say and do. Managers can take greater control of this process, rather than just letting it happen. They might temporarily pair a new employee with an experienced employee who displays the core values of the desired culture. This pairing would expose the new employee to the cultural values managers want to reinforce, as it minimized exposure to other employees who perhaps have not completely accepted these values. Further, any formal new employee orientation program should emphasize core values of the desired culture.

Perhaps the best advice for managers interested in managing their organization's culture is to remind them of the three elements that appear to be most important in influencing organizational culture: (1) what managers do, (2) what managers pay attention to (and what they ignore), and (3) managers' reactions to critical events. If these are indeed the three elements that have the most impact on new employees, managers have a tremendous responsibility in shaping and reinforcing the culture of their organizations. Through managers' behaviors, employees learn which things are *really* valued by the organization.

SUMMARY

Organizational culture is defined as a fairly stable set of taken-for-granted assumptions, shared beliefs, meanings, and values that form a kind of backdrop for action. Put more simply, organizational culture tells employees how to be successful in the organization. Culture provides employees with information regarding: (1) what things are important, and (2) how things should be done. A dominant culture is the culture of the overall organization. Subcultures form around subunits or groups (e.g., departments, divisions, work teams) within an organization. The strength of a culture is determined by four qualities of group membership: homogeneity, length, stability, and experience intensity.

Organizational culture evolves as a result of employees interacting to solve problems and make sense of their working environment. It can be strongly influenced by the founder or powerful top-level manager of an organization who brings personal values, beliefs, and priorities to the organization.

Employees learn organizational culture through a very subtle process including shared sayings, shared things, shared doings, and shared feelings. Organizational heroes also help pass along the culture to employees. Three categories of organizational heroes are designated visionary, situational, and outlaws. Other ways of introducing culture to employees include stories, ceremonials, rituals, rites, and communication. Methods of managing organizational culture include: diagnosing the existing culture, modeling appropriate behavior and values, conducting performance appraisal and reward programs, communicating, and socializing.

KEY TERMS

organizational culture
organizational heroes
visionary heroes
situational heroes
outlaws
rites
ceremonials
rituals
dominant culture
subculture
strength of culture
paranoid culture
avoidance culture
charismatic culture
bureaucratic culture
politicized culture
tough-guy, macho culture
work hard/play hard culture
bet-your-company culture
process culture
modeling
organizational stories

DISCUSSION QUESTIONS

1. What is an "organizational culture" and why is this concept important to understanding human relations in organizations?
2. How does a culture form in an organization?
3. How do employees learn an organization's culture?
4. Differentiate between a dominant culture and a subculture. Why do subcultures emerge in organizations?
5. Describe several ways in which organizational culture is expressed.
6. What effect does organizational culture have on human relations in organizations?
7. Is there any such thing as an "ideal culture"? Explain.
8. How can organizational stories be used to modify or reinforce an existing culture? Are you aware of any such stories from your experiences in organizations?
9. What is an "organizational hero"?
10. What factors influence the strength of an organization's culture? Is a strong culture always desirable? Why or why not?
11. Refer back to the Prologue at the beginning of this chapter. What type of culture do you think exists at Hershey Foods Corporation?
12. Assume you are to address a group of new first-line supervisors. What advice would you give to them regarding how to manage organizational culture?

EXERCISE 16.1

Diagnosing Organizational Culture

Popular magazines such as *Business Week* and *Fortune* often run detailed stories about various organizations. Very often, there are several stories about the same organization over the course of one or two years. Look back through several issues of these, or other similar publications, and find an organization you are curious about or which catches your attention. Collect several articles about this organization and diagnose its culture. You should answer the following questions:

1. What things are important in this organization?
2. What things do managers emphasize or focus their attention upon?
3. What basic values underly the activities and culture of this organization?
4. What should new employees do to be successful in this organization?
5. How would you feel about working in this organization?

REFERENCES

[1]Blank, S.J. Hershey: A company driven by values. *Personnel,* 1987, *64,* 46–51.

[2]Ibid, p. 49.

[3]Smircich, L. Is the concept of culture a paradigm for understanding organizations and ourselves? In Frost, P.J., Moore, L.F., Louis, M.R., Lundberg, C.C. & Martin, J. (Eds.) *Organizational culture.* Beverly Hills, CA: Sage Publications, 1985, p. 58.

[4]Schein, E.H. Coming to a new awareness of organizational culture. *Sloan Management Review,* 1984, *25,* p. 4.

[5]Schein, E.H. The role of the founder in creating organizational culture. *Organizational Dynamics,* 1983, *11,* 13–28.

CHAPTER SIXTEEN: Organizational Culture: Making Sense of Your Surroundings

CASE 16.1

A New Organizational Culture at GE

Since Jack Welch took over as chief executive officer of General Electric in 1981, the company has undergone a number of substantial changes. One of the most drastic has been the change in GE's organizational culture. Before Welch's tenure, GE had been a classic bureaucratic organization, with many layers of management, many staff departments, and a formal, stable organizational structure. The culture which grew out of this type of organization emphasized formal relationships between employees and managers, risk avoidance, stability, centralized decision making, conformance, and intense loyalty.

The culture at GE is now much different. To change its culture, Welch had to take a number of drastic, and sometimes difficult, actions. He eliminated approximately 100,000 jobs, and along with them, several layers of management. Previously, business heads reported to a group that reported to the CEO. Now, business heads report directly to the CEO. Welch also sold some of GE's old-line businesses such as housewares and television and has acquired new, less traditional businesses in such fields as broadcasting (NBC), investment banking, and high-tech manufacturing.

The culture at GE is now less bureaucratic; it has been decentralized. Increased authority has been delegated to lower-level managers. Employees are encouraged to use their own initiative and to take calculated risks. Teamwork, openness, and trust are emphasized. According to Welch, "You want to open up the place so people can flower and grow, expand, hit the home run. When you're tight-bound, controlled, checked, nitpicked, you kill it."

While managers appear to have accepted the changes and the new culture, nonmanagerial employees have not responded so positively. Some observers say that the intense employee loyalty which formerly characterized GE no longer exists. According to Tom Peters, co-author of *In Search of Excellence,* "Loyalty here is twenty-four hours deep. Welch has lost the dedication of a couple of hundred thousand people. He's done a remarkable job of changing the emphasis of the company. But is the price bigger than the company should be paying?" Employees have voiced relatively high levels of disenchantment and dissatisfaction. One employee suggested that workers at GE are "paralyzed by fear." Part of the reason for the negative employee reaction may be the large number of jobs that have been eliminated since Welch took over. In addition, remaining employees have had to pick up the slack. Performance expectations are now higher than they were previously. According to one observer, "A lot of people are burning out at GE." However, looking only at the "bottom line," one would have a hard time arguing that Welch was wrong. Since he took over, GE's revenues have grown 48 percent, and operating profits are up 61 percent!

QUESTIONS

1. Do you think the new culture is more appropriate for GE than the old one? Why or why not?
2. Why have nonmanagerial employees responded to the changes and the new culture less positively than managerial employees?
3. What could Welch have done to make the cultural change more effective?

Source: Mitchel, R. & Dobrzunski, J.H. Jack Welch: How good a manager? *Business Week,* December 14, 1987, 92–103.

---

[6]Wiley, K.W. Cold cream and hard cash. *Savvy,* June 1985, 36–41.

[7]Deal, T.E. & Kennedy, A.A. *Corporate cultures.* Reading, MA: Addison-Wesley, 1982.

[8]Trice, H.M. & Beyer, J.M. Studying organizational cultures through rites and ceremonials. *Academy of Management Review,* 1984, 9, 653–669.

[9]Ibid.

[10]Blank, Ibid.

[11]Corbett, W.J. The communication tools inherent in corporate culture. *Personnel Journal,* 1986, *65,* 71–74.

[12]Schein, E.H. The role of the founder in creating organizational culture. *Organizational Dynamics,* 1983, *11,* 13–28.

[13]Reynolds, P.C. Imposing a corporate culture. *Psychology Today,* 1987, *21,* 33–38.

[14]Martin, J. & Siehl, C. Organizational culture and counterculture: An uneasy symbiosis. *Organizational Dynamics,* 1983, *12,* 52–64.

[15]Schein, E.H. Coming to a new awareness of organizational culture. *Sloan Management Review,* 1984, *25,* 3–16.

[16]Kets de Vries, M.F.R. & Miller, D. Personality, culture, and organization. *Academy of Management Review,* 1986, *11,* 266–279.

[17]Deal, T.E. & Kennedy, A.A. *Corporate cultures.* Reading, MA: Addison-Wesley, 1982.

[18]Sathe, V. Implications of corporate culture: A manager's guide to action. *Organizational Dynamics,* 1983, *12,* 5–23.

[19]Kerr, J. & Slocum, J.W. Managing corporate culture through reward systems. *Academy of Management Executive,* 1987, *1,* p. 99.

[20]Kerr, S. On the folly of rewarding A, while hoping for B. *Academy of Management Journal,* 1975, *18,* 769–783.

[21]Rogers, W. *Think,* New York: Stein and Day, 1969.

[22]Albert, Ibid, p. 73.

[23]Louis, M.R. Surprise and sense making: What newcomers experience in entering unfamiliar organizational settings. *Administrative Science Quarterly,* 1980, *25,* 226–251.

WHAT DO YOU THINK? NOTE

After telling this story, Watson would make his point by saying, "You can make wild ducks tame, but you can never make tame ducks wild. The duck who is tame will never go anywhere anymore. We are convinced that business needs its wild ducks and at IBM we try not to tame them."* The message to employees was that IBM valued initiative, individuality, and creativity.

*Albert, M. Transmitting corporate culture through case stories. *Personnel,* 1987, *64,* 71–73.

CHAPTER SEVENTEEN

Managing Organizational Change

PROLOGUE

"This is great!" Ben thought to himself as he drove home from the job interview. "I haven't even graduated from school yet, and I've already got a good job." Ben had just received a job offer from a large insurance company whose headquarters were located in his home town. As soon as he graduated from Central State University, where he majored in data processing and business, Ben was to begin work as Supervisor, Group Claims Division. The division employed twelve clerks who checked group health insurance claims for accuracy and completeness and entered the information into the company's computerized claims processing system, which caused checks to be issued to customers. Ben was excited about this opportunity and decided that he would show this company what he could do. He was sure that his job performance would get him a promotion within the first two years.

Ben's first objective after beginning work was to get to know the work flow and computerized claims processing system inside out. He spent long hours studying documents and watching his employees perform their assigned tasks. He even worked alongside his employees for several weeks to ensure that he knew exactly what their jobs entailed. The employees thought it was great that their new boss would roll up his sleeves and help them out.

After studying the department's operations for several weeks, Ben decided he knew a way to make everyone more productive. Dividing up the claims into categories based on major clients (e.g., Central State University, Northern Utilities, Richard's Department Stores), he would assign teams of employees to process only the claims from one of these major clients. Employees could become more proficient and process substantially more claims. As it was, employees had to process a number of different types of claims which came in on all types of claim forms. According to Ben's calculations, the department's productivity should increase by as much as 30 percent.

The following Monday morning, Ben called a short departmental meeting and announced the changes. His announcement was met with complete silence as employees looked at one another to see who would respond. Finally, Mary, who had the most seniority in the department, responded. "We all thought you were doing a great job—until now. We're doing just fine the way things are. We process more claims than any other department in this company. Besides, I don't think your plan will work anyway." Ben was startled and somewhat angered by this reaction. After all, he was the supervisor and he would decide how the work was performed. Ben's response was, "I've got the numbers here to back up my plan. There is no question that this change will help us increase productivity. I'd really appreciate it if you would support me in this. However, the change has been made. You have your assignments. If there are any problems, please let me know."

Ben thought that after a week or so everyone would see just how much productivity had improved and go along with the changes. After the first week, productivity levels were just about where they were before the change. However, during the second through the fifth weeks following the change, productivity levels steadily declined. Two months after the change, productivity had declined by 20 percent. Ben called Mary into his office and asked what had happened. Mary said, "See? I told you your plan wouldn't work."

LEARNING OBJECTIVES

After successful completion of this chapter, you should be able to:

- Recognize the need for organizational change,
- Identify several primary types of change,
- Discuss different levels of "people change,"
- Understand the importance of organizational culture in any change effort,
- Understand the change process,
- Explain why employees resist organizational change,
- Describe how managers can overcome resistance to change, and
- Identify characteristics of successful change interventions.

ORGANIZATIONAL ENVIRONMENTS AND ORGANIZATIONAL CHANGE

Recognize the need for organizational change.

Anyone who lived through the 1970s and 1980s does not have to be convinced of the need for change in organizations. During these two decades, a number of unprecedented deviations from the economic norm took place, such as the Arab oil embargo and the accompanying high oil and gasoline prices, declining farm prices and foreclosures on family farms, double-digit inflation, prime interest rate over 20 percent, increased foreign competition, a stock market crash, and finally an oil surplus and the resulting fall in oil and gasoline prices. These changes affected organizations differently; some prospered and grew, others faced hard times and went out of business. For example, during the Arab oil embargo of the 1970s, many oil companies benefited from the rapidly rising oil prices while other organizations (such as motels and airlines) faced rising costs, higher prices for their products and services, and declining demand. In contrast, during the oil surplus of the late 1980s, oil companies (along with banks that financed their operations and states which depended on them for revenue) faced severe economic threats. While these economic gyrations affected organizations differently, few organizations went untouched. These effects were felt not only by businesses operating in the private sector, but also by many public organizations and governmental agencies. For example, many states that depend upon farmers and oil producers for revenue in the form of income and sales taxes have faced serious financial crises along with these businesses. Business declines translated into lower revenues for states which forced many of these states having to cut back on services offered. State-supported colleges and universities have experienced budget cuts, and regional offices of several governmental agencies (e.g., the Veterans Administration, county health services) have been closed.

In looking back over the 1970s and 1980s, one thing stands out—*change*. As we enter the 1990s, some of the drastic changes experienced in the previous two decades (e.g., double-digit inflation, extremely high interest rates) do not appear to present immediate threats. However, given the variety of changes we experienced since 1970, one has to wonder whether there aren't new changes, which we cannot even imagine, on the horizon. One thing unlikely to change is that we will continue to experience change. Someone once said, "The only thing certain about the external environments of today's organizations is that they are uncertain." Another way of stating this idea is, "The only thing about the external environments of organizations that won't change, is that they will continue to change!" As Frank T. Carey, chairman of IBM during the turbulent 1970s has stated, "One mark of every great organization is its willingness to change—to adapt to new needs and to new opportunities."[1] Stop for a moment and consider all of the changes you have experienced just within the last three to five years.

Strategies for Dealing with Change

Change is a basic fact of organizational life. No organization can escape it. Therefore, managers and administrators must be prepared to manage change effectively. As a manager or administrator, you have basically three choices with respect to handling change:

1. **Reactive strategy**—you can wait until a change occurs in the organization's environment and begins to exert pressure on the organization, before developing strategies for dealing with it. This reaction represents unplanned change. No attempt is made to predict environmental change; the organization passively responds only to those environmental forces that force it to change.
2. **Proactive strategy**—you can develop strategies for dealing with a number of expected changes, then implement the strategy associated with the change that actually occurs. This program involves continuous monitoring of the external environment and gathering of data regarding environmental

forces. Managers have to know exactly how the organization will respond to a number of possible changes, so when a specific environmental change occurs, the organization can respond immediately.

3. **Aggressive strategy**—you can develop strategies and implement them before any change occurs. This approach actually attempts to exert pressure on the external environment. For instance, organizations may lobby Congress to oppose legislation that will unfavorably impact their business operations. Organizations employing an aggressive strategy attempt to: (a) create favorable change in their external environments, or (b) prevent unfavorable change in their external environments.

No one can predict the future with 100 percent accuracy. In fact, some well-known individuals' predictions have come back to haunt them. For example, "following the great industrial expansion of the 1880s, the U.S. Commissioner of Patents predicted there would be no more inventions 'because everything has already been invented,' and he recommended the closing of the Patent Office."[2] In 1914, Orville Wright stated that it might be possible for a one-person aircraft to make it across the Atlantic Ocean, but that transatlantic passenger flights were out of the question.[3] The inability to accurately predict the future makes it necessary for managers to occasionally use a reactive strategy in response to environmental change. However, this type of response is generally the least effective, since it is unplanned change. Both proactive and aggressive strategies for dealing with change are generally preferred over a reactive strategy since planning for change occurs in advance of the actual change.

Organizational Environments

Most of the pressure for organizational change comes from the organization's **external environment**; organizations are in constant interaction with their environments. There is likely to be continuous, gradual organizational change as a result of this interaction. Occasionally, a more drastic change will occur in response to a stronger environmental pressure.

As shown in Exhibit 17.1, environments can be broken down into a number of segments, each of which may exert pressure on an organization to change. For example, a change in the legal/political segment of the environment was the Supreme Court ruling making employment of illegal aliens unlawful. Previously, there were no penalties imposed on organizations for employing illegal aliens. Organizations now have to carefully determine whether job applicants have the legal right to work in this country. If they do not, organizations employing them may face stiff penalties. Organizations must now also maintain detailed records on their alien employees. Another well-known organizational change initiated by pressure from the external environment is described in the accompanying Human Relations in Action box.

TYPES OF CHANGE

Identify several primary types of change.

In reaction to, or (ideally) in preparation for, an environmental pressure, organizations must determine the most appropriate form of response. Initially,

HUMAN RELATIONS IN ACTION

Organizational Change at Southwestern Bell Telephone

One of the most dramatic cases of organizational change took place in the early 1980s when a federal court ordered AT&T to divest itself of many of its holdings as part of the settlement of antitrust proceedings. The ramifications of the settlement were far-reaching, affecting approximately one million employees and $103 billion in assets. Divestiture created seven independent regional telephone companies, and a smaller AT&T Corporation which now concentrated on the long-distance telephone business.

One of these new regional companies is Southwestern Bell. Managers at Southwestern Bell identified 2,000 major activities which had to be performed to effectively deal with the divestiture. One frequently quoted description of the magnitude of the change was that "divestiture was like taking apart and reassembling a jumbo jet while in flight." One of Southwestern Bell's immediate concerns was dealing with the questions and anxiety of its 90,000 employees, a great number of whom were opposed to the divestiture. Many of these employees had been part of the AT&T family for a number of years, and were experiencing uncertainty regarding their future. They also felt a personal loss at the prospect of no longer being a member of the "Ma Bell family."

Southwestern Bell implemented two major programs to help employees deal with the change. Recognizing the change was highly emotional for employees, Southwestern used some of the AT&T satellite technology to hold a "gigantic get-together" for 55,000 employees and their spouses in 57 locations. This get-together was one big electronic party, with music, dancing, and jokes. It served as a kind of pressure release for employees, as they shared the fun with others who had shared the emotional breakup of AT&T.

A longer-term program implemented a Quality of Work Life (QWL) program emphasizing employee participation and involvement. Managers at Southwestern Bell realized that employees often had great ideas for improving operations. To take advantage of employee suggestions and to help employees feel a sense of ownership of the new regional company, Southwestern Bell encourages employees to contribute their ideas and suggestions to make "their company" more productive and a better place to work. The Southwestern experience was summarized by Michael Beer, Professor of Management at Harvard University, "It would appear that when change is mandated by clear and unalterable external forces, the job of managing change starts with helping employees accept their sense of loss as a first step in developing readiness to change."

Source: Barnes, Z.E. Change in the Bell System. *Academy of Management Executive,* 1987, *1*(1), 43–46; Beer, M. Revitalizing organizations: Change process and emergent model. *Academy of Management Executive,* 1987, *1*(1), 51–55.

---

the most appropriate *type of change* must be identified from among the three primary types of organizational change; structural, technological, and people.[4]

Structural Change

Organization structure is the formal authority and responsibility relationships among individuals and departments within organizations. It also embodies communication channels, work flows, and organizational policies and procedures. To cite an example, the structure of General Motors Corporation has been well known for many years as a divisional structure, with the major divisions being organized around product lines; Chevrolet, Cadillac, Pontiac, Olds-

Exhibit 17.1
Organizational environment

Arrows pointing to ORGANIZATION from: Domestic Competitors, Employees, Foreign Competitors, Stockholders, Unions, Suppliers, Legal/Political, Government, Society, Local Community.

mobile, and Buick. These divisions operated relatively autonomously with division managers making most decisions about their own product line. Divisional structures tend to be relatively **decentralized**, with important decisions made at lower levels in the organizational hierarchy (structure).

In centralized organizations, decisions (at least the important ones) are usually made near the top of the organizational hierarchy by top-level managers. In 1984, faced with declining market share and profits, General Motors (GM) implemented a substantial modification of its previously autonomous divisional structure, as illustrated in Exhibit 17.2. One of the major changes of this restructuring was a centralization of decision making. Unfortunately, this change all but isolated product managers from rapidly changing consumer tastes, which led to customer complaints that all GM cars looked alike. GM quickly reorganized again, moving back to a more decentralized structure. However, by now, managers were confused and uncertain about the direction of the company, as well as their own job security.[5] GM's experience illustrates the importance of careful planning before implementing change. Suggestions for effectively implementing change will be discussed later in the chapter.

Lines of Communication and Information

Notice that the change in GM's organizational structure also resulted in a change in the lines of formal communication and flow of information within the company. Whereas five automobile managers previously had direct access to all information within their divisions, now they do not. Only two division managers (Small Car and Large Car) have such access. Product managers must

Exhibit 17.2
Structural change at General Motors

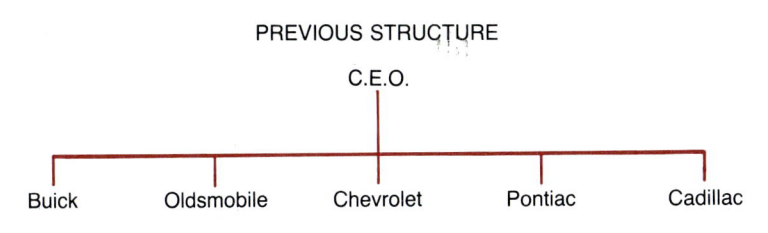

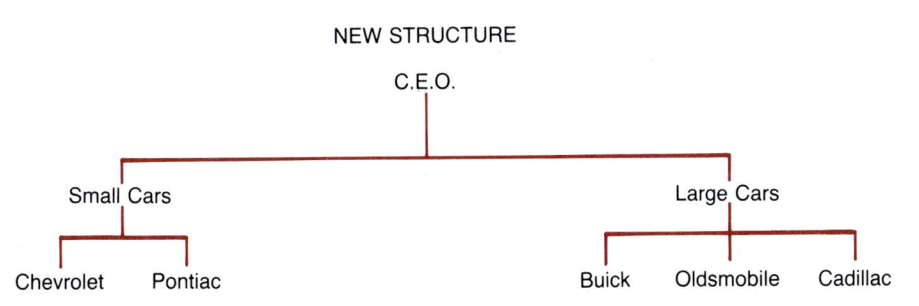

PREVIOUS STRUCTURE

C.E.O.
- Buick
- Oldsmobile
- Chevrolet
- Pontiac
- Cadillac

NEW STRUCTURE

C.E.O.
- Small Cars
  - Chevrolet
  - Pontiac
- Large Cars
  - Buick
  - Oldsmobile
  - Cadillac

Source: Based upon Hampton, W.J. & Norman, J.R. General Motors: What went wrong. *Business Week*, March 16, 1987, 102–110.

depend on their division managers for the information they need to manage their product lines.

Job Design

Structural change is not limited to upper echelons of management. It is also reflected in the structure or design of jobs. One form of structural change at the job level, job design or job enrichment, was discussed in Chapter 2. Job enrichment involves building into employees' jobs the motivating properties of work, such as autonomy and task identity. A newer form of job restructuring, discussed in Chapter 13, is the semiautonomous work group. This approach empowers teams of workers to make decisions on how the work is to be performed and to assume responsibility for the quality and quantity of the groups' outputs. Semiautonomous work groups typically produce a complete product or major component of the product. "Most groups are responsible for setting, adjusting, maintaining, and repairing their own equipment. They requisition and order their own materials, and they inspect incoming material and finished goods and rectify any product defects. They report and record their own output and work in progress. And they are responsible for maintaining safety in their own areas."[6]

Technological Change

Technology refers to the process used to produce an organization's basic unit of output (i.e., product or service). It is obvious that an automobile manufac-

Office automation often requires employees to learn new skills.

turer employs a technology much different than that used by a commercial bank or insurance company. Technological advances often result in dramatic and rapid change. Two recent forms of technological change are office automation and robotics.

Office Automation

Dramatic advances in computer and communications technology have made **office automation** possible. Automated offices are not just rooms full of clerical employees typing away on word processors. Office automation also includes electronic mail, teleconferencing, and computerized information processing systems.[7] One effect of office automation is that office workers are having to learn new skills (e.g., computer, word processing). Another potential effect of such change is that managers will become more effective and will handle many activities via the personal computer sitting on their desk. Some middle-level management and "assistant-to" positions may be eliminated. Further, employees who remain are likely to become much more efficient.[8] For example, in the early 1980s Hercules, Inc. implemented office automation which included word processing terminals, personal computers, and satellite dishes for video-conferencing. In three years, Hercules estimates that the automation resulted in a 40 percent reduction in secretarial work hours, a savings of over $3 million in employees' time (which previously had been wasted in less efficient typing and telephone calls), over $1.5 million savings in travel expense, and a 6.6 percent reduction in the work force (1,800 jobs).[9]

Robotics

Robotics is primarily the use of robots to perform repetitive tasks. Automobile manufacturers are increasingly using robots on their assembly lines. Other U.S. manufacturers are using robots to perform a variety of tasks including spray painting, welding, assembling, and materials handling. Not only do robotics free employees from boring, repetitive tasks, but robots can often perform precision movements or adjustments more accurately than humans can. Whereas human beings often become bored and fatigued when performing repetitive tasks, robots continue to perform programmed tasks until reprogrammed or turned off. Further, robots can perform many unpleasant or dangerous tasks.[10]

Many employees perceive robotics as a threat. Since robots can be operated for approximately $4.20 per hour while the average employee in the U.S. makes between $15 and $20 per hour, it is clear that organizations will continue to make increased use of robotics, which may eliminate many jobs.[11] There is substantial disagreement over the extent to which jobs will be lost. Some experts argue that robotics will actually increase the number of jobs since people will be needed to install, program, and repair robots. It is too early to determine whether robotics will actually reduce the number of jobs or whether the nature of the jobs will simply change.

People Change

People change involves changing attitudes or behaviors of either individuals or groups. Of the three types of change, people change has probably received the most attention. Part of the reason for this interest is that the other two types of change often include or result in people change. Implementing structural or technological change will often require changing employees' attitudes or behaviors as well.

Levels of People Change

Four levels of people change that have been identified are shown in Exhibit 17.3. They are progressively more difficult to implement and include changes in *knowledge, attitudes, individual behavior,* and *group behavior.*[12] Knowledge change is the easiest to carry out, since it involves simply presenting new information to individuals.

Attitudes are more difficult to change, since they include an individual's likes and dislikes, and beliefs about right and wrong. Attitudes contain more

Discuss different levels of "people change."

Exhibit 17.3
Levels of people change

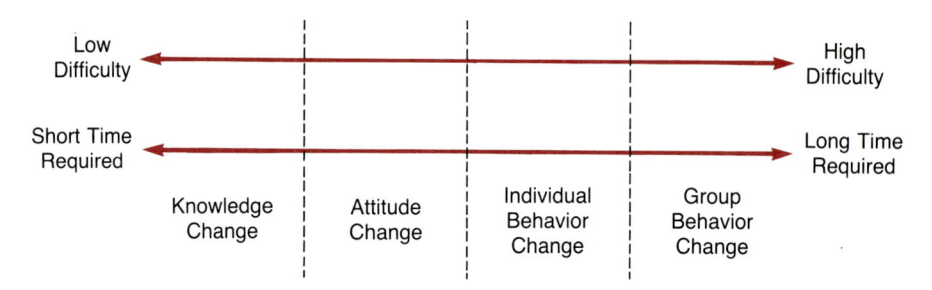

Low Difficulty				High Difficulty
Short Time Required				Long Time Required
Knowledge Change	Attitude Change	Individual Behavior Change	Group Behavior Change	

Source: Based upon Hersey, P. & Blanchard, K.H. The management of change. *Training and Development Journal,* June 1980, *36,* 80–98.

emotion than knowledge and usually will be defended strongly against conflicting information; individuals may not be receptive to information in conflict with their attitudes.

Accomplishing changes in individual behavior tends to be even more difficult than changing an attitude. People tend to be creatures of habit, at least to some degree. Anyone who has tried to lose weight or quit smoking, knows how difficult behavior change can be. Even if attitudes are inconsistent with behavior, it is difficult to change behavior. Case in point: many people in the U.S. are overweight. Even though they know that losing weight would improve their health, they find it a struggle to change their eating habits. The same thing occurs in organizational work settings. While it is not impossible to change, behavior that is comfortable and familiar to individuals may be difficult and time-consuming to change.

Finally, group behavior is even more difficult to change than individual behavior. The reason for this resistance is that groups tend to take on a life of their own. They develop their own structures, rules, and objectives. Group

WHAT DO YOU THINK?

The manner in which individual behavior change has been viewed so far is that new information or knowledge is presented, which changes attitudes. Changed attitudes then produce changes in behavior, as shown in the diagram below.

KNOWLEDGE ⟶ ATTITUDES ⟶ BEHAVIORS

While this is not necessarily incorrect, there may be another equally correct way of looking at individual behavior change.

ENVIRONMENT ⟶ BEHAVIORS ⟶ ATTITUDES

This view reverses the order of attitudes and behaviors.[13] The environment is changed to bring about a change in behavior. Over time, individuals adjust their attitudes to make them consistent with their behavior. Which do you think is the more accurate model of behavioral change? Do attitudes change first, followed by behaviors? Or do behaviors change first, followed by attitudes? Be prepared to explain your position.

behavior is therefore more than just the sum of the behavior of the group's members. Changing the behavior of groups must take into account the group's goals, beliefs, and expectations. Changing individual behavior without changing group behavior may be ineffective. Individuals will return to their groups where they may be reinforced for returning to old behaviors.

ORGANIZATIONAL CHANGE AND ORGANIZATIONAL CULTURE

In the previous chapter, organizational culture was defined as a relatively stable set of assumptions, shared meanings, beliefs and values which form a backdrop for action. In other words, an organization's culture determines what things are important to the organization and what things employees should emphasize. Organizational change cannot be effectively brought about without taking culture into consideration. In fact, to implement any of the types of change just discussed, it is often necessary to also change organizational culture.[14] Many attempts at individual and group change have failed because the organization's culture was not considered. Individuals or groups may be exposed to new information and learn new attitudes and behaviors and have every intention of applying these new ideas and behaviors back on the job. However, when they return to work they are immersed in the same old culture, emphasizing the same old behaviors. It is doubtful that they will sustain the new attitudes and behaviors very long when the culture encourages them to continue the old ways of doing things.[15] Thus, managers interested in truly effective and long-term individual and group change must carefully evaluate the organization's culture to determine whether it emphasizes the types of behaviors associated with the change, or whether cultural change is also necessary. Employees should return to a culture which tells them that the changes are important and encourages them to engage in the new behaviors.

Understand the importance of organizational culture in any change effort.

PROCESS OF PLANNED CHANGE

The most popular model of planned change was developed by Kurt Lewin and consists of three steps; unfreezing, moving, and refreezing. The model recognizes the general human tendency to resist change. It includes steps aimed at reducing this resistance and then, after implementing the change, making the change relatively permanent.

Understand the change process.

Unfreezing

Unfreezing involves preparing individuals for the change. An important part of the process is convincing individuals and groups of the need for change. This activity may require obtaining objective measurements of some problem (e.g., scrap rates, rejection rates, output rates) that is the target of change. Objective measures make it difficult to deny that there is a problem or there is room for improvement. Basically, individuals and groups must be convinced that the old ways of doing things are no longer the most effective.

RETURN TO THE PROLOGUE

In the case presented in the Prologue, employees were not prepared for the change and the results were disastrous. Employees not only did not support Ben's change, but actually worked to ensure that it would fail. Had they been presented with information that showed how ineffective the current work methods were, they may have been more receptive to the change.

Moving

Moving involves actual implementation of the change. The new organizational structure is implemented or jobs are redesigned. Employees are exposed to new information through training and development programs. This step should not be attempted until you are sure that employees are prepared for the change. In other words, sources of resistance must be eliminated or at least minimized, to make employees receptive to the change. Employees must be convinced that the proposed change is in their best interest as well as being good for the organization.

Refreezing

The **refreezing** stage functions to make the change permanent. Careful planning and effective management of this stage will go a long way toward facilitating refreezing. However, in addition, all organizational policies, rules, and procedures—as well as management practices—should reinforce the change. To the extent possible, employees should be positively reinforced for supporting the change. As pointed out earlier, it is also critical that the organization's culture supports the change.

EMPLOYEE RESISTANCE TO CHANGE

Crucial to successful organizational change is the managing of employee **resistance to change**. Reasons for resistance to change must be identified and ei-

RETURN TO THE PROLOGUE

Ben, the new supervisor described in the Prologue, may have developed a substantially better method of processing claims; one which would not only increase productivity but also make everyone's job easier. However, he neglected to consider employee reactions to change. He did not consider whether there would be any resistance to his proposed change or try to predict the source of that resistance. If he had, he could have taken steps to minimize resistance and gain the support of employees to help bring about the change. Developing a new work method, policy, or any type of change is only half of a manager's task. The other half is winning the support of people who have to actually implement the change and work under the new conditions.

ther eliminated or minimized. Resistance generally occurs because employees perceive some type of threat associated with the change. While a number of specific reasons for resistance have been identified, they may be placed in three categories of perceived threats: economic, psychological, and social.[16] It is important to anticipate and prepare for possible sources of resistance to change *before* any change is actually implemented.

Economic Reasons for Resistance to Change

Change that substantially affects employees' jobs can create a great deal of uncertainty and anxiety for them—particularly when they have not received much information regarding the change. This uncertainty may grow until employees actually fear loss of their job as a result of the change. Similarly, employees may perceive that the change has reduced the importance of their job in the organization. This perception leads them to the belief that they will receive fewer salary increases or promotions in the future. Another form of economic threat is the employees' apprehension that they may have to work harder or longer for the same amount of pay.[17]

Social Reasons for Resistance to Change

One important perceived threat that can encourage employees to resist change is the fear that the change will damage existing social relationships. In one situation, employees in a large office building strongly resisted the implementation of a new computerized order entry/customer billing system. Employees in this company had operated for years by taking orders over the phone and writing them up by hand. The work environment was very relaxed, permitting a great deal of socializing between phone calls. Employees saw the arrival of the new computer system as the end of the work world as they knew it. They had heard that everyone would have their own computer terminal on their desk and that the desks would have to be moved apart somewhat to make room for them. The employees' perception was that this physical separation meant they would no longer be able to talk to one another during working hours. Since most of these employees had relatively strong needs for social interaction—their jobs had been a major source of satisfaction of these important needs—resistance to the new computer system was vigorous.

Another reason for resistance to change in the social aspects of the work environment is the norms (rules of behavior) of informal groups. Chapter 12 pointed out that these informal groups can wield strong influence on the behavior of individual employees. In fact, employees will often conform to the norms of their informal groups even when it means breaking organizational rules. For example, a change that includes a higher standard of output or performance may be resisted by employees in an informal group that has adopted a lower standard of performance. Group members who exceed the informal group's standard of performance may be expelled from the group or disciplined in some other manner.

Explain why employees sometimes resist organizational change.

Psychological Reasons for Resistance to Change

One basic psychological reason for resistance to change is the fear of the unknown. Employees who lack information regarding the nature of the change and how it will affect them are likely to experience uncertainty. Few of us are comfortable with uncertainty and ambiguity surrounding our jobs. It is therefore, perfectly rational for employees to resist change when they do not know the reasons for the change or the outcomes expected.[18] The answer here, of course, is increased communications to employees, to provide detailed information about the reasons for the change, the expected outcomes of the change, and how it will affect each employee's job and working environment.

Closely related to a fear of the unknown is the fear of failure. Employees who do not fully understand the change may be unable to assess how their abilities match up with the restructured work environment. In the computerization of the office setting described earlier, one employee who had poor typing skills and no experience with computers was extremely fearful of the proposed change. His reason for resisting the change was simply that he did not think he could learn how to operate a personal computer. As a result, he frequently disparaged the new computer system to other employees. Every time there was a computer problem or the system "went down," he used it as an opportunity to turn other employees against the system. He frequently made remarks such as, "This wouldn't have happened under the old system," and "If we were doing things the old way we would be done by now." Over time, he did have an affect on the other employees, who also began to show more resistance to the new computer system. The organization probably could have prevented this resistance by providing this employee with information about the change and assurances that he would receive any training necessary to perform his changed job. In fact, providing such training before the actual change to the computerized system would have been more effective than providing the training after the computer system had been installed. Assessments of employees' typing and computer skills could have determined the amount of training needed for employees to feel confident that they could perform their changed jobs.

Human beings tend to be creatures of habit. We all have a relatively strong need for balance or **homeostasis** (equilibrium). As we spend time in a work setting, we become familiar with the work flow, rules and procedures, our coworkers, and the physical environment. In other words, we tend to become adjusted to our work setting and experience balance. Change often disrupts this balance and makes our familiar work setting unfamiliar. As a result, even when employees know that the change is in their best interests, they will sometimes continue to resist the change.

This unfamiliar–familiar tendency is put into practice in labor-management negotiations. Unions will often ask for an unusual item (such as paternity leave) that they know management will not approve. However, they have now planted the seed; when it is raised again in the next round of contract negotiations, it will no longer be unfamiliar to management. We tend to be more comfortable with, and accept, things and ideas with which we are familiar, while we tend to resist change with which we are unfamiliar.[19]

Fear of a loss of status is another form of psychological resistance to change. As pointed out in Chapter 2, individuals often achieve certain levels of status—at least partially due to the job they hold. Individuals who receive status in the organization or community as a result of their job may fear that any change within their department or work unit may diminish that status. Before the implementation of the new computer system in the office setting described earlier, Ron held the position of data processing liaison officer in the Order Processing Services (OPS) Department. In this position, he was responsible for serving as an interface between the Order Processing Department and the Data Processing Department. Since few employees (including other managers) within OPS were familiar with computers, everyone had to approach Ron with their requests and questions. Everyone seemed to look up to Ron as someone who had a great deal of expertise in a very important area—computerized data processing. Ron was afraid that the new computer system would eliminate this source of status. While OPS would still require a computer liaison officer, as soon as other employees began learning more and more about computers, they would no longer look to Ron for answers to their questions and help with their problems. Secretly, Ron hoped that the new computer system would present severe problems and he could continue his role as a computer expert.

Yet another psychological reason for resistance to change is **sunk costs**—employees' energy, time, effort and experience invested in learning their job and maximizing their skills. Once their efforts have raised their job performance to a high level, they are understandably reluctant to change to other methods and behaviors. To visualize their feelings, imagine that you have spent several months, working long hours each day, to learn the details of a particular word processing program used on the personal computer at your desk. How would you react to an announcement by your manager that the department's word processing software was to be discarded, and replaced by a product just introduced to the market? Even if this new software offered several advantages over the old one, you may not be very receptive to this change. You have too much investment in the old word processing software.

MANAGING RESISTANCE TO CHANGE

Managers can take several actions to reduce employee resistance to change; none of the reasons for employee resistance just discussed are insurmountable.

Managing resistance to change begins with careful planning of the change. This planning should involve not only the introduction of the structural or technological change itself, but also the employees' probable reaction to the change. As suggested earlier in the chapter, most structural and technological change also involves people change.

Describe how managers can overcome resistance to change.

Communication

One of the most important initial steps in managing resistance to change is communicating plans for the change to employees. This communication

> **Exhibit 17.4**
> Topics to be communicated to employees
>
> - Make clear the *needs* for change, or provide climate in which group members feel free to identify such needs.
> - Permit and encourage relevant group participation in clarifying the needed changes.
> - State the *objectives* to be achieved by the proposed changes.
> - Establish broad *guidelines* for achieving the objectives.
> - Leave the *details* for implementing the proposed changes to the group or to the personnel in the organization most affected by the change.
> - Indicate the *benefits* or rewards expected to accrue to the individuals or groups because of the change.
> - *Materialize* the benefits or rewards: i.e., keep the promises made to those who made the change.
>
> Source: Watson, G. & Glaser, E.M. What we have learned about planning for change. *Management Review,* November 1965, pp. 34–46.

should begin well in advance of any change implementation, and ideally, even before a final decision has been made regarding a change. The topics for the information that should be communicated to employees are listed in Exhibit 17.4.

Employee Participation

Encouraging employee participation in making decisions about the proposed change may help reduce employee resistance.[20] Employee participation will increase understanding of the reasons underlying the change and the need for it. Employees who have helped identify reasons for change, determine the type of change needed, and select the manner in which the change will be implemented are likely to work hard to ensure a successful change.[21] Employees tend to support change they helped to create. In contrast, employees who have not participated in creating change may see little reason to support it. Thus, two important outcomes of employee participation are: (1) increased knowledge about the change and the need for it, and (2) employee commitment to change they helped create.

Gradual Change

Another technique for minimizing employee resistance to change works particularly well when the primary reasons for resistance are a fear of the unknown or a preference for the status quo. This approach involves implementing change in stages, so employees can become familiar with new work methods, relationships, and behaviors a little at a time. As employees become familiar and comfortable with one stage of the change, another change is implemented. However, to use this technique, managers must have the luxury of little or no time pressure to implement the change. Early planning for change can reduce or eliminate this time pressure, and expedite managers' use of this technique.

Support and Encouragement

In addition to any techniques managers use to reduce resistance to change, they should provide *support* and *encouragement* for the change. Support involves training and education that will prepare employees to perform successfully in their new work environments, and making any required supplies and resources available to employees. Encouragement comes from recognition of those employees who are making an honest effort to assist in making the change successful.[22]

More specific suggestions for managers to consider when planning or implementing change appear in Exhibit 17.5. These recommendations are all related to providing information about the change to employees, inviting employee participation, and providing support and encouragement to employees.

Identify characteristics of successful change interventions.

Exhibit 17.5
Suggestions for implementing change

1. Encourage employee participation in the planning of the change.
2. Provide employees with a picture of what the proposed change is to accomplish.
3. Provide as much information to employees as possible about the change and its likely effects.
4. Divide a big change into smaller, more manageable stages.
5. Avoid surprises. Give employees advance warning about any change which affects them.
6. Give employees time to digest information about the proposed change.
7. Demonstrate, repeatedly and visibly, managers' commitment to the change.
8. Make any new performance standards, requirements, and expectations clear to employees.
9. Positively reinforce employees for engaging in the new behaviors.
10. Reward employees who successfully perform under the changed conditions. These employees will serve as models for others.
11. Compensate employees for extra time and effort the change requires (e.g., financial reward, time off, recognition).
12. Create excitement about the future of the organization or work unit.

Source: Based upon Kanter, R.M. Managing the human side of change. *Management Review,* April, 1985, pp. 52–56.

DEVELOPING YOUR HUMAN RELATIONS SKILLS

The information presented in this chapter has important implications for you in both your role as a manager and in your role as an employee. In order to manage change effectively, you should remember:

1. People naturally resist change. Even though the change might make their jobs easier or provide greater earnings, employees may resist the change for economic, social, or psychological reasons. You must determine the exact source of employee resistance and provide information to employees that supports the need for the change. Encouraging employees to participate in making decisions about the type of change proposed, and how the change is to be implemented, may help them become more committed to the change.
2. Employees must be prepared for change. They should be provided with specific information on how the proposed change will affect their jobs.
3. Once the change is implemented, your job as a manager is not finished. You must continue to provide encouragement and support until the change is no longer viewed as "a change," but rather as the normal condition.

As an employee, you will be faced with change from time to time during your work career. You must accept the fact that some organizational change is inevitable and be prepared to help the organization accomplish that change. More specifically, you should consider your own typical reaction to change. Do you tend to resist change, even before you know exactly what's involved? Does change in general make you uncomfortable? If so, you may wish to try the following exercise the next time you are faced with a change. First, refer to the common reasons people tend to resist change, as discussed in the chapter. These fall into three categories; economic, social, and psychological. Which of these seem to account for your resistance to change? Second, compare the projected outcomes of the proposed change to your reasons for resisting the change. Which make more sense? Try to be as objective as possible when comparing your reasons for resistance and the projected outcomes of the change.

SUMMARY

Organizational change is inevitable. As organizations continue to grow more complex and operate in increasingly unstable external environments, change will become even more common. Managers can adopt one of three strategies for reacting to change: reactive, proactive, and aggressive. The reactive strategy is generally the least effective, since it involves unplanned change. Planned change consists of three stages—unfreezing, moving, and refreezing. Three primary types of organizational change are; structural, technological, and people-oriented. Structural change affects the organization's structure and the structure or design of jobs. Technological change is exemplified in office automation and robotics. People change includes both attitude change and behavior change. Four levels of people change represent increasingly more difficult and time-consuming changes: knowledge change, attitude change, individual behavior change, and group behavior change.

Employees resist change for a number of reasons which can be categorized as: economic, social, and psychological. Numbered among the psychological reasons for resistance are fear of the unknown, fear of failure, preference for the status quo, fear of a loss of status, and sunk costs. Managing resistance to change involves communicating information about the change to employees, encouraging employee participation, and implementing change gradually.

KEY TERMS

reactive strategy
proactive strategy
aggressive strategy
external environment
structural change
decentralization
technological change
office automation

robotics
people change
unfreezing
moving
refreezing
resistance to change
homeostasis
sunk costs

DISCUSSION QUESTIONS

1. Why is change so common in organizations?
2. What types of forces in an organization's external environment create pressures for organizational change?
3. Describe the three-stage process of planned change. What happens at each stage?
4. What are the three types of strategies managers may use in responding to change? Which is the most effective? Why?
5. Why is organizational culture an important consideration when implementing organizational change?
6. Should managers change attitudes in an attempt to change behavior, or should they change behaviors in an attempt to change attitudes? Explain.
7. Why do some employees resist change?
8. What can managers do to overcome employee resistance to change? Be specific.
9. Refer back to the Prologue which opened this chapter. What would you do now if you replaced Ben as supervisor of group claims?
10. If Ben had come to you before he implemented the change, how would you have advised him to proceed?

EXERCISE 17.1

Analyzing Forces for Change

Colleges and universities are sometimes viewed as very stable, slow-to-change organizations. However, a closer analysis reveals many environmental factors exerting pressure on these organizations to change.

Part 1: In small groups, identify as many of these external environmental forces for change as possible for your own college or university. Then consider whether there are any forces for change coming from within the organization (i.e., the internal environment). After identifying the major forces for change, rate them on the following scale:

1–Extremely important force for change. Either an excellent opportunity or severe threat. Requires immediate action.

2–Moderately important force for change. Does not require immediate action, but planning for ways of dealing with this change should begin immediately.

3–Relatively unimportant force for change. Action and planning for dealing with this force for change may be postponed until forces in categories 1 and 2 have been adequately managed.

Part 2: For categories 1 and 2, identify the type of change (e.g., technological, structural, people) required by the organization. Develop a specific plan for dealing with each force for change. Include in your plan possible sources of resistance to the change as well as how you plan to overcome this resistance.

REFERENCES

[1] Much, M. Company structures respond to change. *Industry Week,* August 2, 1976, p. 45.

[2] Kent, J.L. Backing into the future. *PEOPLExpress,* August 1986, *1*(8), 46–47.

[3] Ibid, pp. 46–49.

[4] Powell, G.N. & Posner, B.Z. Managing change: Attitudes, targets, problems, and strategies. *Group and Organization Studies,* 1980, *5*(3), 310–323.

[5] Hampton, W.J. & Norman, J.R. General Motors: What went wrong. *Business Week,* March 16, 1987, 102–110.

[6] Fotilas, P.N. Semi-autonomous work groups: An alternative in organizing productive work? *Management Review,* July 1981, *70*(7), p. 51.

WHAT DO YOU THINK? NOTE

A student recently described the second process, where behavior change is followed by attitude change. Adam said that he was working at a part-time job while attending school. Since he had no intention of keeping this job after he graduated, and did not particularly enjoy his assigned tasks, he had what he described as a "bad attitude" toward his job. This attitude was reflected in his relatively low level of performance. One day his boss told him that he realized Adam's situation and understood that he would leave as soon as he graduated. "However, if you want to keep this job until you graduate, you had better substantially improve your performance." Instead of attempting to change Adam's attitudes toward his job, his boss focused upon his behavior. He was in effect saying, "I don't care what your attitudes toward the job are, I want your behavior to improve." According to Adam, he did improve his performance, since he needed the income from this job to finish school. In addition, Adam said that his attitude toward his job gradually improved. As he became more involved in the work and put more into it, he began to view the job more positively. The important point is that over time, Adam's attitude toward his job also improved. In other words, a change in behavior led to a change in attitudes. A detailed explanation of this phenomenon is beyond the scope of this book. However, a simple explanation is that people have a need for consistency. Once Adam's behavior was forced to change, his attitudes were inconsistent with his behavior. He was performing well in a job he did not like very much. Since he couldn't alter his behavior without losing his job, over time, he unconsciously adjusted his attitudes to match his behavior. It is also important to point out that Adam was not aware of this process until a discussion in class pointed it out to him. We all tend to adjust our attitudes and perceptions so that they are consistent with our behaviors, but it occurs subconsciously.

It is not a question of which of these views of individual behavior change is correct. They are both correct. It is sometimes possible to change behavior by first changing attitudes. It is also sometimes possible to change attitudes by first changing behavior. From a manager's perspective, it is equally important to consider what the converse of these statements implies. It is not always possible to change behavior by first changing attitudes. Further, not all types of behaviors are likely to be affected by changes in attitudes. As pointed out in Chapter 2, job satisfaction (an attitude) is not strongly related to job performance (a behavior). However, job satisfaction is strongly related to other types of behaviors (e.g., attendance, accidents). Thus, depending on the exact type of change desired, there are times when managers must focus on changing employee attitudes (e.g., job satisfaction) in order to change behaviors (e.g., absenteeism, accidents, grievances). There are other times when managers must focus on changing behaviors (e.g., job performance) since changing attitudes (e.g., job satisfaction) is not likely to produce the desired behavior change.

---

[7]Office automation restructures business. *Business Week*, October 8, 1984, 118–125.

[8]Hoerr, J., Pollock, M.A. & Whiteside, D.E. Management discovers the human side of automation. *Business Week*, September 29, 1986, 70–79.

[9]Beefing up on electronics makes Hercules leaner. *Business Week*, October 8, 1984, p. 125.

[10]Foulkes, F.K. & Hirsch, J.L. People make robots work. *Harvard Business Review*, January-February 1984, 67(1), 94–102.

[11]Pierson, R.A. Automation. *Management Review*, July 1985, 74, 33–35.

[12]Hersey, P. & Blanchard, K.H. The management of change. *Training and Development Journal*, June 1980, 36, 80–98.

[13]Wohlking, W. Attitude change, behavior change.

California Management Review, Winter 1970, *13*(2), 45–50.

[14]Walters, R.W. Organizational change — A new model. *Personnel Journal,* 1975, *54,* 573–574.

[15]Kilmann, R.H. Getting control of the corporate culture. *Managing,* 1982, *2,* 11–17.

[16]Brown, D.R. Ch-Ch-Ch-Change!? *Management World.* November-December 1986, *15,* 24–25.

[17]Berry, W. Overcoming resistance to change. *Supervisory Management,* February 1983, 26–30.

[18]Kerr, S. & Kerr, E.B. Why your employees resist perfectly rational changes. *Hospital Financial Management,* 1972, *26,* 4–6.

[19]Student, K.R. Managing change: A psychologist's perspective. *Business Horizons,* 1978, *21*(6), 28–33.

[20]Stanislav, J. & Stanislav, B.C. Dealing with resistance to change. *Business Horizons,* July-August 1983, *26,* 74–78.

[21]Coch, L. & French, J.R.P. Overcoming resistance to change. *Human Relations,* 1948, *1,* 512–532; Lawrence, P.R. How to deal with resistance to change. *Harvard Business Review,* May-June 1954, *32*(3), 49–57.

[22]Kotter, J.P. & Schlesinger, L.A. Choosing strategies for change. *Harvard Business Review,* March-April 1979, 1-6-114.

CHAPTER EIGHTEEN

Human Relations in Unionized Organizations

PROLOGUE

One recent development in relations between unions and organizations is an increase in attempts at labor-management cooperation. Both sides have incentives to put aside the traditional labor-versus-management adversarial relationship and replace it with a more cooperative one. As will be discussed in the chapter, the 1970s and 1980s have not been particularly good to unions; union membership has declined substantially. On the other side, however, the past twenty years have not been particularly good to certain organizations either, as evidenced by the number of business failures, downsizings, and mergers. A result of these hard times for both management and labor has been an effort to work together to increase productivity for the organization and job security for employees.

A common form of labor-management cooperation is the implementation of work teams to replace individualized work stations on the factory floor. These work teams are similar to quality circles that involve increased employee participation and autonomy. Employees meet regularly in groups of about ten to discuss work-related problems and develop ways to perform the work more efficiently, effectively, and safely. Another characteristic of many work teams is that workers learn to perform more than just their primary job. This capability increases the flexibility of the organization in rotating employees to cover for employees who are absent, or during periods of unusually heavy workloads. Some employees suggest that rotating jobs reduces the boredom they generally experience working at a single station all day.

However, teamwork has not been readily accepted by everyone on either side. Some labor leaders and unionized employees see work teams as simply another management trick for squeezing more work out of employees. Other employees are afraid that the work teams, by developing more efficient ways of performing the work, may bring about the elimination of some jobs. Some lower-level managers have also resisted the implementation of work teams since some work team programs have eliminated supervisory jobs. These lower-level managers have been replaced by a team leader, typically elected from the work team. Further, in those cases where supervisors continue to manage the work of these employees, some managers see the increased participation and control given to employees as a step toward reducing their own power in the organization. Regardless, interest in teamwork is likely to increase, given the widely publicized successes experienced by many well-known companies such as General Electric, Goodyear, Procter & Gamble, and Toyota.[1]

LEARNING OBJECTIVES

After successful completion of this chapter, you should be able to:

- Discuss the current state of unions in the United States,
- Understand why employees join unions,
- Summarize the major federal labor relations laws,
- Explain a manager's role during the organizing process,
- Describe a typical grievance procedure,
- Discuss how a union can affect human relations,
- Understand the decertification process,
- Discuss how managers can help the organization remain union-free,
- Explain how managers can improve human relations in unionized organizations, and
- Describe examples of union-management cooperation.

LABOR UNIONS AND HUMAN RELATIONS

Is it necessary to include an entire chapter on human relations in unionized organizations? Are relationships in unionized organizations likely to be different from relationships in nonunion organizations? The answer to both questions is "Yes." Unionized organizations present some unique constraints on behavior not found in nonunion organizations. Human relations in unionized organizations are not necessarily better or worse than human relations in nonunion organizations—but they are likely to be different. This chapter will examine the current state of **unions** in the United States, why employees join unions, and the process by which organizations are unionized. A review of important labor law which provides the blueprint for labor-management relations will identify required and prohibited activities on the part of both labor and management. Once an organization becomes unionized, the labor agreement specifies many aspects of the relationship between the organization (management) and the employees (labor). These constraints will be examined, followed by a discussion of how unionized organizations become nonunion and how nonunion organizations can remain union-free. Finally, a brief analysis of how unions and management are attempting to increase cooperation with one another will complete the discussion of human relations in unionized organizations.

CHAPTER EIGHTEEN: Human Relations in Unionized Organizations

Unionized organizations present some unique constraints on behavior not found in nonunion organizations.

Current State of Unions in the United States

The news media have been filled with stories of declining union membership, loss of union power, indictments of labor leaders on charges of corruption and racketeering, and the general poor image the public has of labor unions. However, it would be a mistake to assume from this that labor unions are no longer a force with which managers need be concerned.[2] While many of the ideas contained in these news stories are true, unions still represent a substantial number of employees in the United States (approximately twenty million). In unionized organizations (and also during union organizing campaigns) managers who are unfamiliar with fair and unfair labor practices may unknowingly damage human relations within the organization. Thus, managers of both union and nonunion organizations must be aware of how to manage in a unionized organization, and how to manage so that the organization remains nonunion.

Discuss the current state of unions in the United States.

Declining Union Membership

It is true that union membership has been declining. The percentage of the labor force belonging to a union has declined from a high of around 35 percent in 1954, to around 19 percent in 1986.[3] Projections are that unless unions are able to develop new strategies for organizing nonunion organizations and preventing unionized organizations from becoming nonunion, union membership may decline to around 13 percent of the labor force by the year 2000.[4]

Reasons for the Decline in Union Membership

Several reasons for this decline in union membership have been identified.[5] Unions have traditionally been strong in manufacturing (e.g. automobile industry, steel industry). These industries employ large numbers of the blue-collar workers who make up most of the union membership in this country. However, the United States is moving from a manufacturing-based economy to a service-based economy. This change means that the number of blue-collar jobs is not only not increasing, it is also actually decreasing—a major reason for the decline in union membership. In addition, while the number of white-collar jobs is increasing, unions have not been very successful in organizing these workers. White-collar workers may not see themselves as union members, since the stereotypical union member is a hard-working, blue-collar factory worker. Perhaps white-collar workers don't believe that the traditionally blue-collar unions can represent their needs and interests. This thinking doesn't mean that unions will never be successful in organizing white-collar workers or professionals. Several of these groups (e.g., actors, airline pilots, professional athletes) have been unionized for many years. Others, such as college professors, attorneys, nurses, and even physicians, are beginning to form and join unions. Union membership can be increased in only two ways: organizations which are already unionized can increase the number of jobs, or unions can organize nonunion organizations.

Two other important reasons for the decline in union membership are employment-related laws and increased participatory management practices. Laws such as those discussed in Chapter 3 are providing job security and other forms of protection that employees previously received only by joining a union. In addition, managers in many organizations have begun using more participatory management styles and involving employees more in important decisions that affect their jobs. This approach by management, at least to some degree, offsets a need for the presence of unions to ensure that employees have a voice in matters that concern their jobs.[6]

WHAT DO YOU THINK? Some people might argue that because of the employment laws which protect employees' rights and prohibit discrimination, increased use of employee participation by managers, and the changing nature of jobs, unions are no longer necessary. Do you think that unions are still necessary? Why or why not? What exactly can unions do for employees in today's modern work organizations? Are they necessary only in certain types of jobs? If so, which ones and why? Be prepared to take a position on this issue and defend it.

Why Do Employees Join Unions?

Understand why employees join unions.

Part of the reason for joining a union is that employees are dissatisfied with some aspects (particularly pay and job security) of their jobs.[7] Several authors have suggested that organizations that become unionized deserve it. This statement implies that these organizations did not treat employees well or there would have been no need for a union. Had these organizations paid more attention to human relations, employees may not have felt the need to bring in a union to improve their situation. In organizations such as these, human relations may actually improve after unionization, since the **labor agreement (contract)** will specify many areas of required or prohibited managerial activity. However, there is another aspect to the answer to the question, "why do employees join unions?" Research has determined that job dissatisfaction is generally not enough to cause employees to actually join a union. But, coupled with the perception that employees are powerless to do anything about its source, job dissatisfaction may be enough to encourage employees to vote for union representation.[8] This suggests the need to listen to employee complaints and suggestions and include employees in decision-making that affects their jobs. Dissatisfied employees who perceive they are powerless to change their situation are prime candidates for labor unions.

HOW DO ORGANIZATIONS BECOME UNIONIZED?

The **organizing process** is a sequence of activities by which unions come into an organization and ask employees to decide whether or not they want to be represented by the union in negotiations with management. This process consists of **initial contact**, the **organizing campaign**, a **representation election**, and **certification of election results** by the **National Labor Relations Board (NLRB)**.

Initial Contact

Initial contact with a union is usually made by a dissatisfied employee or group of employees. Unions might initiate contact with employees of an extremely large organization where unionization would add significant membership. Unions may also initiate contact with the employees of the last of a particular type of organization in the area that has managed to remain union-free. However, in most cases, employees initiate contact with the union.

Organizing Campaign

Once contact has been made, the union will usually send **organizers** to the organization to determine how much interest there is in the union and try to increase that interest. Often the early stages of organizing will be conducted covertly. Unions want to generate as much interest as possible in the union before management becomes aware that an organizing campaign is underway. Once management realizes that a union is trying to organize its employees, the organization will often begin a campaign of its own to keep the union out. Since union organizers who are not employees may be prevented from entering the work site, the union organizer will often identify employees who are highly supportive of the union and ask them to serve as the **organizing committee**. Non-employee union organizers cannot enter the work site if the organization has a **no-solicitation rule** that prohibits all forms of solicitation on the premises (i.e., charities). If the employer has allowed other groups to solicit on the organization's property, union organizers must be allowed to do

> **Exhibit 18.1**
> Example of an authorization card
>
> _____
> Date of Signing
>
> I, _____, an employee of
>   (print your full name here)
> _____, authorize the
>   (name and address of company)
> SOUTHEAST INFORMATION WORKERS UNION (SEIW) to act as my collective bargaining representative for wages, hours, and working conditions. I understand that this card may be used either to support a demand for recognition or to request an NLRB election, at the discretion of the union.
>
> HOME ADDRESS _____
> CITY _____ STATE _____ ZIP _____
> TELEPHONE _____
> JOB TITLE _____ DEPARTMENT _____
> SHIFT _____
> SIGNATURE _____
>
> RECEIVED BY _____
>   (name and title of union official)

so. However, non-employee union organizers may not solicit members during working time.

Once the union organizer determines sufficient interest in the union, the organizing committee will begin asking employees to sign **authorization cards** such as the one shown in Exhibit 18.1. Authorization cards state that employees want the union to represent them in negotiations with the employer. However, employees who sign authorization cards are free to vote either for or against union representation in the election. Unions must get 30 percent of the employees to sign authorization cards to petition the NLRB for a representation election. If the union gets 50 percent plus one employee to sign authorization cards, it can demand that the organization recognize it as the employees' bargaining agent without a representation election. Management will often refuse this request, after which the union will present the cards to the NLRB and ask that a representation election be held.

Representation Election

Once authorization cards have been submitted to the NLRB and a representation election requested, the NLRB will often conduct a hearing to determine if such an election is appropriate. Among other things, the NLRB verifies that at least 30 percent of the employees in the bargaining unit signed authorization cards. In addition, the NLRB will determine the appropriate bargaining unit. A **bargaining unit** is a group of employees, having similar interests and working conditions, who will be represented by the union. Often not all of the organization's employees will be members of the same bargaining unit, or of any bargaining unit. Clerical employees may belong to one bargaining unit, while production employees belong to another. The Taft-Hartley Act requires that a separate bargaining unit be created for guards and professional employees, unless a majority of the professional employees vote to be included in a bargaining unit with nonprofessional workers. In addition, the Wagner Act excludes supervisors, managers, confidential employees, agricultural workers, and independent contractors from representation. If the NLRB determines that a representation election is appropriate, it sets the date for the election, usually within thirty days of the hearing. The NLRB is responsible for conducting the election and certifying the results.

Certification of Election Results

If the union is to be certified as the employees' bargaining agent, at least 50 percent plus one employee of the employees voting in the election must vote for union representation. If this majority occurs, the NLRB certifies the union as the employee's bargaining agent, and the employer is required by law to bargain in good faith with the union. If fewer than 50 percent plus one employee vote for the union, the NLRB certifies the results of the election and the organization remains union-free. Once election results have been certified, another election cannot be held for twelve months.

LABOR LAW

To understand human relations within unionized organizations, it is necessary to be aware of the provisions of several major federal **labor laws**. These laws specify many things which both labor and management can and cannot do. The major federal laws covering labor-management relations in the private sector are the National Labor Relations Act of 1935 (Wagner Act), the Labor-Management Relations Act of 1947 (Taft-Hartley Act), and the Labor-Management Reporting and Disclosure Act of 1959 (Landrum-Griffin Act). Employees in the railroad and airline industries are covered by the **Railway Labor Act**. The provisions of the Railway Labor Act are very similar to those of the Wagner Act, as amended by the Taft-Hartley and Landrum-Griffin Acts.

Summarize the major federal labor relations laws.

Wagner Act

The **Wagner Act** was aimed at ensuring employees' rights to form and join unions. Prior to its passage, management used a number of tactics designed to prevent unions from entering their organizations. Many of these tactics prevented employees from making their own decisions about union representation. The major provisions of the Wagner Act are:

Explain a manager's role during the organizing process.

1. Employees are guaranteed the right to form and join unions, to engage in **collective bargaining** through their chosen representatives, and to participate in strikes and picketing.
2. Employers are prevented from:
    a. interfering with, restraining, or coercing employees in the exercise of their rights outlined in (1) above.
    b. discriminating against employees because of union membership or activity.
    c. dominating or interfering with the formation of a union.
    d. threatening employees with reprisals for participating in union activity.
    e. promising benefits (e.g., a pay increase) to employees for rejecting the union.
    f. questioning or surveillance of employees to determine their union activities.[9]
3. Employers are required to bargain in good faith with the chosen representatives of employees.
4. An independent federal agency, the National Labor Relations Board (NLRB), was created to enforce the provisions of the Act.

Taft-Hartley Act

While the Wagner Act was aimed primarily at managerial activities, the **Taft-Hartley Act** focuses on union activities. Important provisions of the Act include:

1. Guaranteed employees the right to *not* join unions as well as to form and join them.
2. Identified several unfair (illegal) labor practices on the part of unions:
    a. restraining or coercing employees to force them to join the union.
    b. causing the employer to discriminate against employees, thus encouraging them to join the union.
    c. refusing to bargain in good faith with the employer over wages, hours, and other conditions of employment.
    d. engaging in secondary strikes and secondary boycotts.
    e. charging excessive initiation fees and dues.
    f. engaging in **featherbedding**,—requiring the employer to pay for work not actually performed, or to pay for more workers than are actually needed for a job.
3. Prohibited the **closed shop** (employees must join the union before being hired) and allowed individual states to pass **right-to-work** legislation. These laws make it illegal for collective bargaining agreements to include maintenance of membership, union shop, or any clause that requires employees to join the union. The twenty states which currently have passed such laws are Alabama, Arizona, Arkansas, Florida, Georgia, Iowa, Kansas, Louisiana, Mississippi, Nebraska, Nevada, North Carolina, North Dakota, South Caro-

lina, South Dakota, Tennessee, Texas, Utah, Virginia, and Wyoming. In all other states, labor agreements may include various forms of union security, such as:

a. **Union shop.** Employees must join the union within a specified time period (usually thirty to ninety days) after being hired.
b. **Agency shop.** Employees who choose to not join the union must contribute to the union in an amount equal to union dues.[10]
c. **Maintenance of membership.** Employees are not required to join the union, but those who do join must remain members for the length of the labor agreement (contract).

An absence of any of these forms of union security is known as an **open shop**. In an open shop, employees are not required to join the union or contribute to the union. However, unions are required to bargain for *everyone* in the bargaining unit and to represent them at grievances and arbitration whether or not they are union members.

Landrum-Griffin Act

The **Landrum-Griffin Act** responded to publicity of widespread corruption within labor unions. This Act is designed to protect the rights of union members. Important provisions of this Act include:

1. A bill of rights for union members. This provision guarantees members the right to participate in the nomination of union officials, vote in union elections, attend meetings, and generally participate in union activities. This bill of rights also places limits on charges that can be made for dues, and gives employees the right to sue the union.
2. Reporting and disclosure requirements for unions. Labor unions must file reports of their finances and internal activities with the Secretary of Labor.
3. Eligibility requirements for union officials. Persons prohibited from holding office in labor unions include anyone who has been convicted of robbery, bribery, extortion, embezzlement, grand larceny, burglary, arson, violation of narcotics laws, murder, rape, assault with intent to kill, assault which inflicts grievous bodily injury, a violation of the provisions of Landrum-Griffin, or conspiracy to commit any such crimes. A provision in the law that prohibits past or present members of the Communist Party from holding office has been ruled unconstitutional.

Public Sector Labor Law

Employees in the public sector (e.g., employees of the federal government) are covered by the **Civil Service Reform Act of 1978**. This Act, modeled after the Wagner Act, created the **Federal Labor Relations Authority (FLRA)** to enforce its provisions. The FLRA performs a function similar to the NLRB's (e.g., conduct representation elections, investigate unfair labor practice charges).

Employees of state and local governments are not covered by any of the laws discussed so far. However, approximately two-thirds of the states have enacted legislation covering state, county, and local employees (e.g., police, firefighters, teachers).

MANAGING UNDER A LABOR AGREEMENT

Labor agreements are intended to specify the rules of the game for management-labor relations. Since they cover many work-related issues, they have a significant effect on human relations within organizations. Labor and management negotiators meet and approve the terms of the agreement and the contract language which describes these terms. Labor agreements vary a great deal in terms of length and specificity; however, most contain the clauses presented in Exhibit 18.2.

Disagreements in Interpreting the Contract

Two basic reasons underly disagreements that often occur even with a well-written labor agreement. First, negotiators can never foresee all possible problems or areas of potential conflict. Thus, no labor agreement can cover every problem that may occur as management and labor work together in an orga-

---

Exhibit 18.2
Clauses commonly found in labor agreements

1. Recognition: Recognizes the union as the bargaining agent for employees.
2. Management rights: States that management retains the right to perform all activities not specifically given to the union in this agreement.
3. Hours of work: Defines normal working hours, starting and stopping times, and how changes in work schedules are to be made.
4. Wage schedule and premium pay: Describes the wage schedule for each job classification and also overtime rates, holiday and vacation pay, shift differentials, and reporting or call-in pay.
5. Seniority: Defines the method of seniority used to determine promotions, transfers, and layoffs. Also specifies how seniority is earned and lost.
6. Grievance procedure and arbitration: Describes the procedure to be used in resolving grievances. Also describes the arbitration process, how the arbitrator is to be selected, and whether both sides agree to be bound by the arbitrator's decision.
7. Discipline and discharge: Specifies the procedures to be used when disciplining or discharging an employee.
8. Duration of contract: Identifies the period of time that the contract will be in force.
9. Fringe benefits: Describes the benefits management has agreed to provide, such as retirement pension, life and health insurance, paid holidays, dental and eye care, and paid vacations.

nization. The second reason for disagreements has to do with contract language. It is extremely difficult to write contract language so clearly that everyone interprets it in the same manner. Thus, disagreements are likely to occur. These disagreements are not necessarily damaging to human relations within the organization, if they are handled effectively. Most labor agreements include a **grievance procedure** to handle disagreements over interpretation of the contract or matters not covered by the contract.

Grievance Procedures

A grievance procedure is a specified sequence of events for resolving grievances. While formal grievance procedures originated in (and are still most common in) unionized organizations, a number of nonunion organizations have also developed such procedures. A typical grievance procedure is shown in Exhibit 18.3.

Exhibit 18.3
Typical grievance procedure

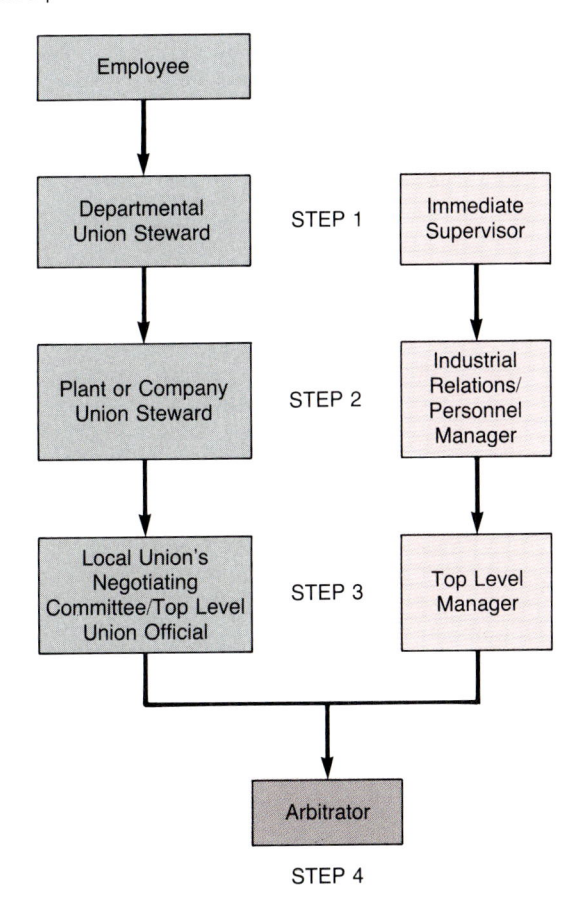

```
                    Employee
                       │
                       ▼
         Departmental              Immediate
         Union Steward   STEP 1   Supervisor
                │                      │
                ▼                      ▼
                                   Industrial
         Plant or Company          Relations/
         Union Steward   STEP 2    Personnel
                │                  Manager
                │                      │
                ▼                      ▼
         Local Union's
         Negotiating              Top Level
         Committee/Top Level STEP 3  Manager
         Union Official
                │                      │
                └──────────┬───────────┘
                           ▼
                       Arbitrator

                         STEP 4
```

Most grievances begin when an employee believes a manager has acted in a manner inconsistent with the terms of the labor agreement. The employee files a grievance and it is processed through the grievance procedure. Thus, most grievances are union-initiated. Management does not typically file grievances. If an employee's conduct is disruptive, or she behaves in a manner inconsistent with the labor agreement, management will generally just take action (e.g., discipline the employee). If the union feels that management's actions were not fair or were inconsistent with the labor agreement, a grievance will be filed. The most common areas of labor agreements in which grievances are filed include discipline, pay, work assignments, hours of work, supervisors doing production work, work standards, working conditions, and subcontracting.[11]

Employee Discipline

Employee discipline is one area of contract administration that presents potential problems in terms of grievances. Most labor agreements call for progressive discipline, which was discussed in Chapter 8. **Progressive discipline** is the administration of increasingly severe punishment for successive rule violations. An example of an organization's rules and the punishments for violations appears in Exhibit 18.4.

Describe a typical grievance procedure.

When an employee believes that management has violated the labor agreement, she first contacts the departmental or shop steward who helps her file a written grievance report. At Step 1 of the grievance process, the employee, the union steward, and the employee's immediate supervisor meet to discuss the grievance. If they reach agreement, the process stops here. If they cannot reach agreement, the grievance moves on to Step 2. There, the grievance is discussed by the plant or company steward and a representative from the industrial relations or personnel department of the organization. If no agreement is reached, the grievance proceeds to Step 3, where the local union's negotiating committee and a top-level manager meet to discuss the grievance. If they cannot reach a mutually acceptable resolution of the grievance, the grievance moves to the last step in the process, arbitration.

Arbitration

Arbitration involves bringing in a neutral third party (an arbitrator) to hear the positions of both labor and management and reach a decision regarding the grievance. This process is commonly referred to as **binding arbitration** since most labor agreements specify that the decision of the arbitrator will be binding upon both parties.

Grievance Procedures and Human Relations

Both the number of grievances filed and the number resolved during early stages of the grievance procedure are directly related to human relations within the organization. An organization with a poor human relations climate (e.g., mistrust between employees and managers, poor and infrequent communication, a "we–they" mentality, and little employee participation or in-

Exhibit 18.4
Example of organization's rules and penalties for violation

Rule	Penalties for: 1st Violation	2nd Violation	3rd Violation	4th Violation
1. Completing another employee's time card	oral warning	written warning	1-day suspension without pay	termination
2. Repeated tardiness	oral warning	written warning	1-day suspension without pay	termination
3. Stopping work before scheduled stopping time	oral warning	written warning	1-day suspension without pay	termination
4. Unsatisfactory work	oral warning	written warning	1-day suspension without pay	termination
5. Fighting on company property	written warning	2-day suspension without pay	termination	
6. Three days' unexcused absence within any 30 day period	written warning	2-day suspension without pay	termination	
7. Insubordination	termination			
8. Theft of company property	termination			
9. Possession of firearms, alcohol, or narcotics on company property	termination			
10. Sabotage	termination			
11. Reporting for work under the influence of alcohol or illegal drugs	termination			
12. Violation of safety rules	termination			

An arbitrator is a neutral third party who listens to both sides and then issues a decision regarding a grievance.

Discuss how a union can affect human relations.

volvement) is going to face many grievances. Further, employees are likely to be resistant to compromise regarding these grievances. Therefore, few will be resolved at the early stages of the grievance procedure. Instead, many may be forced all the way through the grievance procedure to arbitration.

There is somewhat of a vicious cycle at work in these organizations. An existing poor human relations climate may trigger the filing of a large number of grievances. The filing of grievances may contribute to a worsening of human relations within the organization as both sides fight to win at the other's expense. This poor human relations atmosphere contributes to a filing of even more grievances, and so on.

Work Stoppages

Poor human relations can carry over to all areas of labor-management relations. When the current labor agreement expires and the two sides begin negotiating over a new contract, it may be very difficult to reach an agreement. Strikes and lockouts become much more likely under such circumstances. A **strike** is a work stoppage initiated by a union; employees walk off the job and refuse to work. A **lockout** is a work stoppage initiated by management; management locks the doors and refuses to let employees work. Both forms of work stoppages can be extremely costly, financially and in terms of human relations, to both sides. The accompanying Human Relations in Action box describes a strike which had serious consequences for not only union and management, but also an entire town!

On the other hand, good human relations can facilitate cooperation between labor and management. In organizations where employees and manag-

HUMAN RELATIONS IN ACTION

Labor-Management Conflict

What can happen when labor and management choose to engage in conflict rather than cooperation? One or both parties can cease to exist! An extremely bitter strike began in August 1985 at the Hormel meat packing plant in Austin, Minnesota. Economic conditions had led many meatpackers to reduce the wages of their employees as demand for pork continued to decline. When Hormel reduced the wages of the employees at its Austin plant, the local union decided to fight to restore them. The position of the local union was that Hormel had had record earnings of $38 million in 1985 and could therefore afford wage increases. The company responded that the overcapacity (low demand) in the industry meant that the company could not afford higher wages. Even the national union with which the local was affiliated agreed that industry overcapacity meant it would be difficult to pay higher wages. If Hormel were forced to pay higher wages at the Austin plant, some of the work might be shifted to plants paying lower wages, resulting in a loss of jobs for the workers in Austin.

After the approximately 1,500 Hormel workers went out on strike, the plant reopened, hiring nonunion replacement workers. However, there was such violence on the picket lines by striking union members that the Governor of Minnesota had to call out the National Guard to ensure the safety of the replacement workers as they attempted to enter the plant. Ironically, Mayor Tom Kough of Austin, Minnesota, who asked Governor Rudy Perpich to call in the National Guard, was himself a striking meat-packer.

Source: Houston, P. & Bernstein, A. The pork workers' beef: Pay cuts that persist. *Business Week,* April 15, 1985, 74–76; Pitzer, M.J. & Bernstein, A. The union vs. the union at Hormel. *Business Week,* February 17, 1986, 36; National Guard called to protect meat plant. *Charleston Times-Courier,* January 21, 1986, B–5.

---

ers trust each other and communicate openly about problems, the two sides will usually work together to reach agreement. Instead of viewing a problem or grievance as an opportunity to "beat the other side," it is viewed as an opportunity to clarify, and perhaps improve, the relationship between labor and management. Exhibit 18.5 presents some guidelines for managers when handling grievances.

Administering the Labor Contract

Effective contract administration requires that everyone who is involved in interpreting the contract (e.g., supervisors, managers, employees, union stewards) has carefully read and understands the provisions of the contract. There is no reason for grievances to be filed simply because an employee or steward is unfamiliar with the portion of the labor contract that covers the pertinent situation. Similarly, there is no reason for the grievance to progress through several steps of the grievance procedure simply because supervisors and managers are not familiar with the contract clause that covers this particular grievance. A good understanding of the labor agreement by all parties will prevent the filing of unnecessary grievances, and ensure the rapid resolution of legitimate grievances—both measures that contribute to good human relations.

> **Exhibit 18.5**
> Guidelines for handling grievances
>
> 1. Treat each grievance seriously. Sometimes employees may file a grievance simply because they are frustrated or upset. They may have no intention of actually winning the grievance, but may just want someone to listen to their problem. Managers who are willing to listen to their employees contribute to good human relations and a climate of trust and support.
> 2. Carefully review the relevant provisions of the labor contract. Make sure that you thoroughly understand what the labor contract has to say about the situation.
> 3. Get the facts. Interview witnesses, gather documents and information concerning the case. Try to separate emotion from facts.
> 4. Present your findings and evidence to the steward in an objective, professional manner. Nothing will be served by becoming emotional or engaging in an argument with the steward. The grievance should be discussed objectively, and the discussion should focus upon the facts of the case and what the labor contract has to say about such matters.

Supervisors and Union Stewards

The relationship between supervisors and union stewards is particularly important to contract administration. These people are on the "front lines." They are involved in day-to-day contract interpretation and administration. The job of the steward is to represent the union, with the primary responsibilities to make sure that management lives up to the terms of the labor agreement, and to assist employees with their requests and problems. As pointed out earlier, the department or shop steward is usually the first person contacted by an employee who wishes to file a grievance. Then the supervisor and steward meet to try and resolve the problem. The substantial amount of interaction between supervisors and stewards necessary to administer a labor agreement requires a good working relationship between these two parties. While there is some degree of an adversarial relationship, there are advantages to both parties in developing a relationship of trust and mutual respect.

THE DECERTIFICATION PROCESS

Understand the decertification process.

Unionized organizations do not always remain so. Labor law provides a process, the **decertification election**, by which employees may remove a union as their bargaining representative. In recent years, not only have decertification elections become more common, but also unions have been losing more and more of them.[12]

The **decertification process** is similar in many ways to the certification process.[13] It begins when employees feel that the union no longer represents the interests of a majority of the employees in the bargaining unit. After a labor agreement has been in force for twelve months, employees may file a petition with the NLRB requesting that a decertification election be held. This election is virtually identical to that of the representation election, including the signing of authorization cards to indicate sufficient employee interest. If at least 30 percent of the employees in the bargaining unit sign authorization cards, the NLRB will set a date for an election. If a majority of employees *who vote* cast their ballots against representation, the union is decertified as the employees' representative. If a majority of voting employees cast their votes for the existing union, it is again certified as the employees' bargaining agent. Managers are prohibited from certain activities during this period of time:

1. Managers may not obtain forms from the NLRB for employees interested in decertification, and they may not provide any clerical services (e.g., typing, photocopying) or supplies (paper, typewriters, use of telephone) to these employees.
2. Managers may not initiate conversations with employees concerning how to decertify the union, or promote or encourage the decertification process.
3. Managers may not promise increases in wages or benefits if the union is decertified, or threaten employees with decreases if the union is not decertified.
4. Managers may not engage in surveillance or interrogation of employees regarding their union interests or activities.[14]

On the other hand, managers are permitted to engage in these activities:

1. Managers may refer employees to the NLRB if they ask about decertifying the union.
2. Managers may answer specific questions from employees.
3. Managers may provide employees with a current list of employee names and addresses.[15]

REMAINING UNION-FREE

Many organizations prefer to operate without a union representing its employees.[16] The primary reason—many managers perceive that a labor agreement will cause a loss of flexibility in their ability to manage. They will have fewer choices in how to manage, since many aspects of employment will be specified in the labor contract.

Discuss how managers can help the organization remain union-free.

A consideration of how to remain nonunion must begin with a reexamination of the reasons employees become interested in and join unions—dissatisfaction and a perceived lack of power to change their environment. Managerial strategies designed to keep the organization union-free must be aimed at preventing employee dissatisfaction and offsetting employees' perceived lack of power.

To prevent employee job dissatisfaction, non-union organizations will often choose to provide pay and benefits at least comparable to unionized organizations.[17] Many non-union organizations will purposely exceed unionized organizations' pay and benefits rates to avoid employee job dissatisfaction. Another aspect of minimizing dissatisfaction has to do with supervision. Employees must feel that they are treated equitably by supervisors. Thus, supervisors must be encouraged and perhaps trained so that they treat all employees fairly and impartially.

To avoid perceiving lack of power, employees must feel that they are an important part of the organization and that management is interested in them. Employees must perceive that managers are not only willing to listen to what they have to say, but also are actually interested in employee suggestions and complaints and will act on them. Thus, it is important that nonunion organizations have some form of grievance procedure that provides employees with a way of changing things that are problems for them. In addition, supervisors and managers should be trained to encourage employee participation in important decisions that affect employees' jobs. Finally, the organization needs to develop effective communication programs (e.g., newsletters, meetings) to keep employees informed of current activities of the organization, as well as those activities planned for the future.[18] All of these manager-employee interactions are consistent with developing and maintaining good human relations within the organization.

LABOR-MANAGEMENT COOPERATION

Explain how managers can improve human relations in unionized organizations.

Good human relations in a unionized organization is possible only through labor-management cooperation, such as the use of teamwork discussed in the Prologue. Labor and management must see themselves more as partners rather than opponents. While the nature of labor-management relations has always had at least some degree of adversarial tone to it, there are some signs that labor and management have recognized the advantages of cooperation.

The impetus for this cooperation may have come from recent hard economic times. High inflation and interest rates translated into high prices and unemployment. This, in turn resulted in lower demand for the products and services of many organizations. The outcome was that many organizations faced bankruptcy or drastic cost-cutting. Unions were presented with a choice between maintaining current levels of wages and benefits and losing some jobs, or givebacks or concessions (lower wages and benefits) to maintain the current number of employees. Many unions chose concessions as a way of preserving the jobs of their membership. While these were hard times and the concessions were often difficult to make, there were many instances of such labor-management cooperation.[19]

Describe examples of union-management cooperation.

Labor-management cooperation is being exemplified by relatively unusual labor agreements, such as the one at the General Motors' Saturn Plant in Spring Hill, Tennessee.[20] Saturn is the new subcompact car that GM hopes will compete with the highly successful Japanese imports. The labor agreement negotiated by General Motors and the United Auto Workers provides for a combination of provisions not commonly found in labor agreements—all

HUMAN RELATIONS IN ACTION

"NUMMI"

Given the relative recency of experimental labor contracts which provide for increased cooperation between labor and management, it is too early to assess their effectiveness. However, there is some evidence from one General Motors facility suggesting that labor-management cooperation provides benefits to both sides.

The New United Motor Manufacturing, Inc. facility in Fremont, California was known as a "grievance mill." To say that relations between labor and management were not good might be something of an understatement. As evidence of the poor human relations within the plant, absenteeism ran between 20 and 25 percent, and at any point in time there were approximately 1,000 unresolved grievances in the system.

In 1983, a joint venture was announced between General Motors, Toyota, and the United Auto Workers. A labor agreement covering the 2,200 employees was signed in July 1985. This labor agreement is similar to the Saturn agreement in that teams of six to eight workers are responsible for production, quality, cost, and safety at their work stations. Has the increased worker autonomy and responsibility, and labor-management cooperation paid off? By 1985, absenteeism had dropped to between 2 and 3 percent, and the number of unresolved grievances in the system dropped to around three. Further, the plant is producing Chevrolet Novas both effectively and efficiently, so that they will compete with the Japanese imports that have hurt the U.S. automobile industry over the last several years. The success of the plant has led Toyota to announce that a Toyota model will be produced at the Fremont, California facility.

Source: Perspective: NUMMI revisited. *What's new in collective bargaining: Negotiations and contracts*. Washington, D.C., The Bureau of National Affairs, June 5, 1986, 4.

As mentioned in the Prologue, there have recently been cases of union and management cooperation in organizations where these two parties had previously been antagonists. These cases of cooperation take many different forms, from implementing semiautonomous work teams to union leaders and managers working side by side to solve problems facing the organizations. One example of the new mood of cooperation and teamwork is the United Auto Worker (UAW)/General Motors (GM) Human Resource Center (HRC). The UAW/GM HRC is a national program developed by the union and the automaker to assist laid-off GM employees. Since it is improbable that auto assembly line workers will be able to find similar jobs after their plant closes, the HRC provides a wide range of services to help displaced workers find new jobs. These services include initial testing and evaluation to determine skills and interests, a library stocking occupational guides, seminars on interviewing and career planning, and a bank of ten telephones that former employees can use without charge to make calls anywhere in the United States on job-related matters. The employee response to the HRC has been very positive. According to one employee who used the HRC, "Some companies have no compassion at all. They give severance pay and that's all. UAW-GM is going out of its way to help families cope with what they are facing and give them a ray of hope that there is some place to go."[21]

RETURN TO THE PROLOGUE

DEVELOPING YOUR HUMAN RELATIONS SKILLS

One important implication of the information presented in this chapter affects your role as a manager as well as your role as an employee. That implication—there are several significant labor laws governing the relationships between unions and employers, and both managers and employees must have a good understanding of the provisions of these laws. Otherwise, you could unknowingly commit an unfair labor practice that could damage human relations within the organization.

Another important implication has to do with the labor agreement providing the ground rules for managing employees within the organization. Both managers and employees should have a clear understanding of the terms and intended interpretation of the clauses that make up the labor agreement. As long as the provisions of the agreement do not violate any laws, they are enforceable in the courts. Since managers have to administer the contract on a daily basis, they must be very familiar with its provisions. Employees too, should not ignore the contract until there is a problem. Unions often provide employees copies of the tentative contract before it becomes final. It is a good idea to carefully read each new contract as it is being finalized to become familiar with the rules of the workplace. Once the contract is finalized, it becomes the rules by which all managers and members of the bargaining unit must abide. And, an early reading of the contract may identify unclear or ambiguous language which can be cleared up before the contract is finalized.

Finally, as an employee, before filing a grievance, you should carefully consider the effect it is likely to have. You should ask yourself whether this problem is really important enough to file a formal grievance and get other people involved. Unnecessary grievances, especially those without grounds, can severely damage human relations within the organization. Such grievances may not only drive a wedge between management and employees, but also may actually stimulate conflict among employees. Some employees who view the grievance as unnecessary may begin to disagree with other employees who support union activities without question. The result may be a relatively high degree of conflict at several levels within the organization.

aimed at improving cooperation between labor and management. These provisions include the following:

1. Blurring the distinction between labor and management. All employees, production employees and managers alike, will be paid a salary. There will be no reserved parking spaces or executive dining rooms.
2. Substantial employee autonomy and participation. Employees will be grouped in small teams (six to fifteen employees) responsible for: interviewing and hiring new employees, determining who will do specific tasks,

scheduling production, budgeting, controlling absenteeism, handling health and safety, ordering supplies, maintaining equipment, setting vacation schedules, making quality inspections, and offering suggestions for improving the way the work is performed.

3. Job security. Approximately 80 percent of the employees at the Saturn plant will be previous UAW members who have been laid off from work at other locations. These employees will be given lifetime guarantees of employment (except in the case of "severe economic conditions or a catastrophe"). Even in the case of severe economic conditions or catastrophe, union members of a joint committee can reject layoffs in favor of either a temporary plant shutdown or reduced work hours.[22]

The Saturn contract clearly places labor and management in the role of partners, not opponents. Indeed, workers are referred to as partners. Executives eat off paper plates alongside production workers in a relatively plain cafeteria.[23] Other automakers will undoubtedly push for Saturn-like agreements when their current labor agreements expire. If these cooperative agreements are successful, they are likely to begin appearing in other industries as well.

While it is too early to assess the success of such cooperative arrangements, the accompanying Human Relations in Action box describes the experience at one General Motors facility.

SUMMARY

While union membership has been declining over the past several years, it is a mistake to assume that unions are a force that no longer concerns managers. Labor unions still represent approximately 20 million workers in the United States. In addition, while unions have not been highly successful in organizing the increasing numbers of white-collar and service jobs, there are signs that union leaders are now willing to try some unusual methods to organize these types of workers.

Labor-management relations in the United States are guided by three major federal laws; the National Labor Relations Act (NLRA) of 1935, also known as the Wagner Act; the Labor-Management Relations Act (LMRA) of 1947, also known as the Taft-Hartley Act; and the Labor-Management Reporting and Disclosure Act (LMRDA) of 1959, also known as the Landrum-Griffin Act. These three federal laws guide labor relations in the private sector. Employees in the railroad and airline industries are covered by the Railway Labor Act, which is similar to the Wagner Act. In addition, employees in the public sector (e.g., employees of the federal government) are covered by Title VII of the Civil Service Reform Act of 1978. Many states have also adopted legislation covering the collective bargaining activities of state employees.

Employees become interested in joining unions because they are dissatisfied with some aspect of their employment—typically wages, working conditions, and job security. However, research has determined that dissatisfaction may not be enough to motivate employees to actually join a union. However, when dissatisfaction is coupled with the perception that employees are powerless to change their situation, interest in joining a union becomes much stronger.

The union organizing process consists of several stages: initial contact, the organizing campaign, the representation election, and certification of election results by the NLRB. In order for the NLRB to set a date for a representation election, the union must be able to show sufficient employee interest in the union. This is typically done by getting employees to sign authorization cards. The NLRB requires that at least 30 percent of the employees in the proposed bargaining unit sign authorization cards. Both management and the union are prohibited from interfering with, restraining, or coercing employees in their decision regarding union representation.

Disagreements will arise even with a clearly written labor agreement. These disagreements arise because contract negotiators could not have foreseen all possible situations and therefore a complication may arise that is not covered by the labor agreement. In addition, it is difficult to write contract language that is interpreted in exactly the same manner by everyone involved. The method for handling these disagreements over the terms of the contract is the grievance procedure. The final step of most grievance procedures is binding arbitration.

Organizations that have previously been unionized may become nonunion by a decertification process. The process is procedurally similar to the organizing process. Employees who feel that the union no longer represents the interests of a majority of employees in the bargaining unit may petition the NLRB for a decertification election. If a majority of employees vote for no representation, the union is removed as the bargaining agent for the employees.

A program to remain union-free must begin with a consideration of why employees become interested in and join unions. In other words, management practices must be aimed at preventing employee dissatisfaction and preclude their perceptions of a lack of power or control. Nonunion organizations typically provide salaries, working conditions, and fringe benefits at least comparable to, and often above that of unionized organizations. In addition, nonunion organizations may encourage employee participation and involvement in decisions that affect their jobs. In order to preclude a perceived lack of power, managers in nonunion organizations are advised to listen carefully to employee complaints and suggestions and to act on those that seem important to a number of employees.

Recent examples of labor-management cooperation, such as those at the General Motors plants in Spring Hill, Tennessee and Fremont, California include three common elements: (1) increased worker autonomy and participation, (2) decreased distinctions between labor and management, and (3) employee job security.

KEY TERMS

unions
labor agreement/contract
organizing process
initial contact
organizing campaign
representation election
NLRB
union organizers
organizing committee
no-solicitation rule
authorization cards
bargaining unit
labor law
Railway Labor Act
Wagner Act
collective bargaining
Taft-Hartley Act
featherbedding
closed shop
right-to-work laws
union shop
agency shop
maintenance of membership
open shop
Landrum-Griffin Act
Civil Service Reform Act
FLRA
grievance procedure
progressive discipline
arbitration
binding arbitration
strike
lockout
decertification election
decertification process

DISCUSSION QUESTIONS

1. Why do managers need a knowledge of labor law and labor-management practices if union membership has been declining for several years?
2. Why do employees join unions?
3. Describe the several steps that make up the organizing process from the union's perspective. From management's perspective.
4. What can management do during an organizing campaign? What is management prohibited from doing during an organizing campaign?
5. What is a bargaining unit?
6. What are the major provisions of the Wagner Act?
7. What are the major provisions of the Taft-Hartley Act?
8. What are the major provisions of the Landrum-Griffin Act?
9. What is a grievance procedure? Why is one needed, since in unionized organizations there is a labor contract to guide labor-management relations?
10. Explain progressive discipline.
11. What advice concerning human relations can you give to managers who must manage under

a labor agreement? How can managers improve human relations in their department or work group when a labor agreement covers nearly everything?
12. Describe the decertification process.
13. You have just been hired as a consultant by an organization gearing up to deal with a union organizing attempt. What advice would you give to this organization regarding how to remain union-free?
14. Describe some of the new attempts at labor-management cooperation. What effect do you think these will have?

EXERCISE 18.1

Attitudes Toward Unions

The purpose of this exercise is to provide students with an opportunity to examine their attitudes toward unions. Using the following scale, indicate your attitudes toward the listed statements.

Strongly
Disagree   Disagree   Neutral
1   2   3
                        Strongly
        Agree   Agree
         4   5

____ 1. Labor unions play an essential role in American society.
____ 2. Labor unions are corrupt.
____ 3. Labor unions are too strong.
____ 4. Labor unions are necessary, given current laws.
____ 5. Unions protect employees from arbitrary management decisions.
____ 6. Unions are successful in getting bigger wage increases for employees.
____ 7. Unions increase fairness in promotion decisions.
____ 8. Unions provide employees with job security.

Scoring

General Attitudes Toward Unions. First, reverse the score on items 2 and 3 (e.g., if you scored 1, change it to 5; if you scored 5, change it to 1 and so on). Then add items 1, 2, 3, and 4:_____. The higher you score, the more positive your attitudes toward unions in general.

Union Instrumentality (belief that unions actually lead to improved wages, working conditions, job security, etc.). Add items 5, 6, 7, and 8:_____. The higher your score, the stronger your belief that unions are instrumental in improving wages and working conditions for employees.

Now calculate average scores for various subgroups within your class (e.g., male/female, older/younger, liberal/conservative, business major/liberal arts major, former union member/no experience with unions). How do the scores on the two scales compare among these various subgroups? How do you explain these differences and similarities?

How do your personal attitudes toward unions compare with those of your classmates? What factors account for these differences in attitudes?

CASE 18.1

Memphis Software, Inc.

The labor agreement between Service Employees of the Mid-South, Local 4800 and Memphis Software, Inc., a developer and marketer of personal computer software, is about to expire. In thirty days, representatives of the union and representatives of the employer will begin negotiations on a new three-year contract. The vice-president of personnel at Memphis Software has called all department supervisors together for a meeting to begin preparations for the contract negotiations. "I want to be fully prepared when negotiations begin next month. One thing that I want to accomplish is to clean up contract language in a number of areas. We've had far too many grievances filed during the past three years, and I believe that the primary reason for this is unclear contract language. I've had copies made of several clauses which seem to account for a high percentage of previous grievances. I want each of you to take a copy and do two things before our next meeting. First, write a clear description of what you believe the current contract clause says. Write these explanations in simple language so that someone not familiar with labor agreements can understand them. Also make a note of any problems the current language may cause. Then rewrite the clause so that it more clearly reflects the intent of the contract. At our next meeting, we'll go through these until we reach agreement on exactly how each clause should read."

Selected contract clauses which have resulted in a high percentage of grievances appear here, along with a supervisor's interpretation of the intent of the clause. Rewrite each clause so that it is clearer and less likely to be misinterpreted and result in grievances.

UNCLEAR LABOR CONTRACT CLAUSES

Section 8.1: Reporting pay. When there is no work, or not enough work, and an employee is permitted to report for work on his regular shift without being notified not to report, then the employee shall receive a minimum of four hours' pay at whatever rate is applicable."

Interpretation. The intent of this passage is to provide employees with a half day's pay when they report to work in good faith, but for reasons beyond their control, no work is available. The problem with this clause, and the reason for many grievances, is that employees claim they should be paid when equipment breaks down, or electric power is out. I wouldn't be surprised if some employees filed for reporting pay even if they went out on strike! Further, there is a problem with what constitutes notification of employees and when notification has to occur to release the company from its responsibility to pay employees reporting pay. I would also like to be able to assign employees other work such as cleanup or minor repair in the event their assigned work is unavailable.

Vacation pay. After six months of full-time employment, each employee earns paid vacation time at the rate of one day for each month of full time employment. Vacations may be taken during the months of June, July, August, and September. Employees not taking earned vacation time may receive, upon request, a cash payment equal to their normal rate of pay at the time the request is made, for the unused vacation time. Vacation time may not be carried over from year to year.

Interpretation. While this was the subject of only one grievance last year, it may have been a very important one in that the arbitrator's award may have set a precedent for other employees. An employee retired on July 1 of last year after twenty-three years of service. This employee had not taken any vacation pay during the year and on December 31 showed up in the Personnel Office asking for his cash payment for the six vacation days he had earned by working the first six months of the year. The grievance went all the way to arbitration and the arbitrator ruled that the contract language did not prevent such a payment. Clearly, we want to pay only current employees for unused vacation days.

Sick pay. An hourly employee with one or more years of continuous service, absent because of personal illness for which benefits are not payable under Workers' Compensation, will receive sick pay for the absence according to the following schedule:

Continuous Service	Maximum Days of Sick Pay in Each Calendar Year
1 through 5 years	3
6 through 10 years	5
11 through 20 years	7
Over 20 years	10

The rate of pay for sick pay will be the employee's regular hourly pay rate or based upon weekly salary.

Interpretation. This clause is intended to provide uninterrupted income for employees who are ill and cannot meet their work responsibilities. It is not intended to provide for personal time off for errands, leisure activities, and so on. Unfortunately, this policy is abused as employees make sure they take all of the sick days they earn each year. Further, supervisors have a real headache administering this clause since employees won the right through the grievance/arbitration process to take partial days off, even down to a single hour.

REFERENCES

[1] Bernstein, A. & Zellner, W. Detroit vs. the UAW: At odds over teamwork. *Business Week,* August 24, 1987, 54–55; Bernstein, A. & Rothman, M. Steelmakers want to make teamwork an institution. *Business Week,* May 11, 1987, p. 84.

[2] Ropp, K. State of the unions. *Personnel Administrator,* 1987, *32*(7), 36–40.

[3] Hagburg, E.C. & Levine, M.J. *Labor relations: An integrated perspective*. St. Paul, MN: West Publishing Company, 1978.

[4] Hoerr, J., Glaberson, W.G., Moskowitz, D.B., Cahan, V., Pollock, M.A. & Tasini, J. Beyond unions: A revolution in employee rights is in the making. *Business Week,* July 8, 1985, 72–77.

[5] Sloane, A.A. & Witney, F. *Labor relations*. Fifth edition. Englewood Cliffs, NJ: Prentice-Hall, Inc., 1985.

[6] Lawler, E.E., III & Mohrman, S.A. Unions and the new management. *Academy of Management Executive,* 1987, *1,* 293–300.

[7] Hamner, W.C. & Smith, F.J. Work attitudes as predictors of unionization activity. *Journal of Applied Psychology,* 1978, *63,* 415–421; Heneman, H.G., III & Sandver, M.H. Predicting the outcome of union certification elections: A review of the literature. *Industrial and Labor Relations Review,* 1983, *36,* 537–559.

[8] Brett, J.M. Why employees want unions. *Organizational Dynamics,* 1980, *8,* 47–59.

[9] What supervisors can do about union organizing. *Supervisory Management,* 1981, *26,* 10–15.

[10] Brankey, E. & Schnake, M.E. Exceptions to compulsory union membership. *Personnel Journal,* 1988, *67*(6), 114–122.

[11] Fossum, J.A. *Labor relations: Development, structure, process*. Third edition. Plano, TX: Business Publications, Inc., 1985.

[12] Anderson, J.C., O'Reilly, C.A., & Bushman, G. Union decertifications in the U.S.: 1947–1977. *Industrial Relations,* 1980, *19,* 100–107.

[13] Kilgour, J.G. Decertifying a union: A matter of choice. *Personnel Administrator,* 1987, *32*(7), 42–51.

[14] Holley, W.H. & Jennings, K.M. *The labor relations process*. Second edition. Chicago: Dryden Press, 1984; Coleman, F.J. Once a union, not always a union. *Personnel Journal,* 1985, *64,* 42–45.

[15] Ibid.

[16] Porter, A.A. & Murman, K.F. A survey of employee union-avoidance practices. *Personnel Administrator,* 1983, *28,* 66–71, 102.

[17] Wentz, C.A. Preserving a union-free workplace. *Personnel,* 1987, *64*(10), 68–72.

[18] Rand, J.F. Preventive maintenance techniques for staying union-free. *Personnel Journal,* 1980, *59,* 497–499.

[19] Falahee, J.W. Concession bargaining: The time is now! *Personnel Administrator,* 1983, *28,* 27–28; The Bureau of National Affairs Editorial Staff. Givebacks highlight three major bargaining agreements. *Personnel Administrator,* 1983, *28,* 33–35, 70.

[20] Nicholson, T. & Manning, R. Saturn gets a launching pad. *Newsweek,* August 5, 1986, p. 42.

[21] Feldman, D. Helping displaced workers: The UAW-GM Human Resource Center. *Personnel,* 1988, *65*(3), 34–36.

[22] Edid, M. A new labor era may dawn at GM's Saturn. *Business Week,* July 22, 1985, 65–66; Edid, M. How power will be balanced on Saturn's shop floor. *Business Week,* August 5, 1985, 65–66.

[23] Taylor, A. Back to the future at Saturn. *Fortune,* August 1, 1988, 63–72.

WHAT DO YOU THINK? NOTE

There is no correct or incorrect answer to this question. One's position often depends on one's background. Students whose relatives or friends have benefited from union membership tend to be supportive. Students whose friends and relatives hold management or professional positions tend to see few advantages from union membership. Try to step beyond your emotions and values. Analyze this issue objectively. Exactly what can union members expect to gain from their membership today? Does the answer to this question differ by type of occupation or job? For example, do factory workers and professional football players get the same things from their union membership? What about actors and writers in Hollywood? College professors?

CHAPTER NINETEEN

Human Relations in International Organizations

PROLOGUE

Because of the dominance of U.S. media, universities, business, and influence in the world, people in other countries know a great deal about us. In comparison, many U.S. citizens are still relatively uninformed about life in other developed and developing nations. This may put the United States at a distinct disadvantage as the world continues to "become smaller" due to advances in communications technology and the continued internationalization of business. How many of the following common customs and business practices did you know?

- In Bulgaria, the gestures for *yes* and *no* are the opposite of those in the United States.
- In Turkey, it is considered rude to cross your arms while facing someone.
- In East Germany, France, the Netherlands, and Turkey it is a sign of disrespect to put your hands in your pockets when speaking with someone.
- In Finland, it is considered to be too casual and rude to cross your legs so that one ankle rests on the other knee.
- In Greece, it is an insult to wave American-style showing your palm with your fingers extended.
- In Ireland, the phrase "get a ride" is obscene.
- In Spain, the common American "OK" sign with thumb and index finger forming a circle is a vulgar gesture.
- It is important to be punctual to business meetings in Sweden, Switzerland, Bulgaria, Denmark, Finland, France, West Germany, Greece, Italy, Norway, Austria, and Romania; however punctuality is not as important in Ireland, Portugal, and Spain.
- In Belgium, Italy, Spain, and Turkey, do not try to discuss business during your first meeting with someone. First meetings are used to get acquainted. However, in Switzerland, it is acceptable to get right to the point.[1]

LEARNING OBJECTIVES

After successful completion of this chapter, you should be able to:

- Understand the importance of international business,
- Define "culture" and describe its effects on employee and managerial behavior,
- Recognize why understanding cultural differences is important to good human relations,
- Describe some important ways in which employees from other cultures may differ,
- Explain how U.S. management practices may not be effective in foreign countries or with employees from other cultures,
- Describe important differences between Japanese and American management practices, and
- Explain whether Japanese management practices can be applied in American organizations.

THE INTERNATIONALIZATION OF BUSINESS

In his acceptance speech at the annual meeting of the Academy of International Business on October 28, 1982, after becoming the first recipient of the International Business Leader of the Year award, Jacques Maisonrouge, senior vice president of IBM Corporation, described the changes occurring in the business world.

> "Business has become international. As a result, it has grown extremely competitive; it is subject to very rapid change; and it is affected by a number of relatively new social forces.. . .Common information made instantly available to the peoples of the developed countries, for example, has generated similar economic appetites around the world. Barriers to international trade have also been shrinking rapidly. . ."[2]

Later in his speech, he described the two essential characteristics of successful managers of today's modern organizations: a true global perspective and the ability to manage human resources. Managers must exhibit sensitivity in relations with others, help employees develop and feel they are part of an important team, and learn to perform unpleasant tasks simply because the tasks must be performed. Just as important, managers must rid themselves of whatever prejudices they have formed concerning people who are somehow different from themselves.[3] Finally, a global perspective requires that managers begin looking beyond the borders of their own country. Many decisions in today's modern organizations have international implications. There are few businesses today, for example, that can afford to ignore the threat of both present and potential foreign competition.

There is little question that business has become "internationalized." Today, very few organizations are not somehow affected by international trade. Rapid worldwide communication and information transmission has moved us toward the "global village."[4] Several years ago, markets may have stopped at international boundaries; today these national boundaries have little to do with product and service markets.

The typical exterior of McDonald's restaurants in Japan.

U.S. Multinational Corporations

Many organizations that we think of as being "American" actually receive a substantial portion of their profits from operations in foreign countries. In fact, several firms which are very well known in the United States are actually owned by firms in other countries: Lever Brothers (Netherlands), Shell Oil (Netherlands), Miles Laboratories (West Germany), Great A & P Tea Co. (West Germany), American Motors (France), and Amdahl (Japan).[5] In 1984, twelve of the twenty largest **multinational corporations** were U.S. firms.[6] In addition, firms from other countries are increasingly locating operations in the United States. Thus, both the number and importance of multinational corporations are growing.

There are no signs to suggest anything but a continuation of this trend. Therefore, it is becoming increasingly common for employees of virtually any type of organization, regardless of where that organization is headquartered, to be involved in, or at least be affected by, international business. In fact, with the increasing numbers of foreign-owned corporations such as Honda, Sony, and Mitsubishi locating operations in the United States, there is an increasing probability that you may become an employee of a foreign corporation while working right here in the "good old U.S.A." It is also highly probable that you may find yourself managing or working alongside at least one employee from another culture, even if you remain in the United States and work for an American corporation with no foreign operations. It is therefore important that you have some understanding of how culture affects behavior, accepted business practices, and human relations. Human relations between managers and indi-

Understand the importance of international business.

viduals or groups from other cultures can be easily damaged because of the managers' lack of knowledge concerning the customs or accepted behaviors of those cultures.

BUSINESS PROBLEMS DUE TO LACK OF CULTURAL UNDERSTANDING

There are some interesting stories about problems caused by a failure to carefully consider cultural differences. One major airline operating in Brazil began advertising plush "rendezvous lounges" on its jets. The airline discovered later that this phrase translated in Portuguese as a "room for making love."[7] The advertisement obviously did not have the effect the airline had hoped. Other problems in translating advertising messages to a foreign language have been identified. The well-known phrase used by General Motors, "Body by Fisher" translates in Flemish as "corpse by Fisher."[8] In Germany, Pepsi's jingle "Come alive with Pepsi" translates into "Come alive out of the grave with Pepsi."[9] General Motors' Chevrolet Nova, a very popular model in the United States, didn't do as well in Puerto Rico. It may have been because Nova sounds very much like the Spanish phrase "no va" which means "doesn't go"—not a particularly good name for an automobile.[10] And, unfortunately, "Coca Cola" translates in Chinese as "bite the head of a dead tadpole."[11] Would you drink from a bottle which had this phrase on its label?

Not all problems experienced by multinational organizations have been the result of translation difficulties. Most problems can be attributed to a lack of familiarity with the culture and customs of the countries in which the firm

Knowledge of a country's culture, customs, and business practices are necessary for business meetings with foreign business persons.

was operating. For example, in Southeast Asia Pepsodent toothpaste ran its well-known advertisement which included the phrase "You'll wonder where the yellow went when you brush your teeth with Pepsodent." However, Southeast Asian people commonly chew betel nut, which discolors teeth; black teeth are a symbol of prestige.[12] In England, Campbell soup wasn't selling as well as the company had hoped. After investigating, they found that the British were used to ready-to-eat canned soup. Campbell's soup was concentrated and required the addition of water. To the British, it appeared that the smaller cans of Campbell soup, which were being sold at approximately the same price as the larger cans of British ready-to-eat soups, were not a good buy. Actually, when water was added to the Campbell soups, consumers got the same amount of soup as they did from the British soups. Campbell then added water and increased the size of the cans and sales began to improve.[13]

Knowledge of a country's culture and customs are necessary for business meetings with individuals and groups. Your company may never get the opportunity to operate in a particular country if, during the first meeting with representatives of that country, you make serious errors that exhibit a lack of familiarity with their business practices. For example, in the United States it is common to have an attorney present during business meetings and negotiations. However, to do so in France might be interpreted as a lack of trust. Further, decision making in France is likely to be much slower than in the United States because all aspects of the decision are carefully considered and many people within the organization are consulted for their inputs. The French might not react favorably to an aggressive, impatient American pushing them for a decision.[14] In Ireland, Portugal, and Spain, being punctual for meetings is not considered to be extremely important. In other words, arriving thirty or forty-five minutes late for a meeting may be interpreted as being "on time" in these countries. However, while you should expect this and not be bothered by the tardiness of your foreign business associates, it is probably a good idea for you to be on time to such meetings.[15]

Thus, there are differences in behavior in general, and business and management practices in particular, across various countries and cultures. As organizations continue to internationalize, managers must become aware of these differences to manage effectively. In this chapter, culture will be examined, with a discussion of its possible effects on the practice of management. The question of whether or not management theories and practices developed in the United States might be effective in different cultures will be specifically addressed. Finally, given the great popularity of Japanese management techniques, a comparison of Japanese and American management practices will be made. Additional Japanese business practices are presented in the accompanying Human Relations in Action box.

CULTURE

Culture is defined as "patterns of thought and manners which are widely shared."[16] Another author describes culture as "the collective mental programming of the people in an environment. Culture is not a characteristic of indi-

Define "culture" and describe its effects on employee and managerial behavior.

RETURN TO THE PROLOGUE

The customs and business practices presented in the Prologue suggest a number of cultural differences that might have an impact on your effectiveness as a manager of foreign employees in a U.S. organization, as an employee of a foreign manager in a U.S. subsidiary of a foreign firm, or as a manager working abroad in either a U.S.-owned or foreign-owned organization. A large number of American employees working for foreign managers have had great, sometimes career-ending, difficulty adjusting to cultural differences. Given the increasing numbers of Japanese-owned and operated organizations in the United States, many examples can be found of American employees and Japanese managers.

American employees sometimes become uncomfortable since Japanese managers rarely give advice or feedback. In addition, they tend to never say "no." Instead of explicitly saying "no" to an employee, Japanese managers usually do not respond, or say something like "the matter needs further study."

The workday for Japanese executives never ends before 11:00 P.M. However, this schedule often includes a nightly trip to a restaurant or bar with co-workers at about the time an American manager would head for home. An American manager who might leave for home at 6:00 P.M. or 7:00 P.M.—perfectly acceptable in the United States—is likely to be viewed as a failure by his Japanese counterparts. Japanese managers also keep their work lives and private lives completely separate. Displaying pictures of one's family in the office, common in the United States, is frowned on by Japanese executives.[17]

A lack of knowledge of any of these business practices could damage your career in a Japanese-owned organization. Similar differences exist between American business practices and those in other countries. Thus, the manager or employee who goes to work for a foreign organization not only has the two traditional tasks of doing the technical portion of one's job and getting along with co-workers, but also a third—learning the business practices and customs of a new culture.

---

viduals; it encompasses a number of people who were conditioned by the same education and life experience."[18] Culture leads to particular beliefs and preferred ways of behaving. Thus, cultural differences might be expected to result in different ways of managing across various countries. Stated differently, a particular management technique or style may not be effective in all cultures. A recent study provides evidence that managers in different countries do have different ideas about the process of management.[19] Exhibit 19.1 shows some of the results from this study, illustrating the substantial diversity in the degree to which managers from various countries agreed with the statements regarding the practice of management. Over half of the managers from Switzerland, France, and Italy agreed that "most managers seem to be more motivated by obtaining power than by achieving objectives." Less than one-third of the managers from Denmark, the Netherlands, and Germany agreed with this statement. One of the more interesting results, and one in which there is a substantial difference of opinion among the managers from these various countries is the statement, "It is important for a manager to have at hand pre-

CHAPTER NINETEEN: Human Relations in International Organizations

HUMAN RELATIONS IN ACTION

Japanese Business Practices

Bowing. When a Japanese business person meets a fellow Japanese, he bows by bending his body forward. Japanese do not typically bow (*ojigi*) when they meet someone from another country. Thus you should probably not bow when meeting a Japanese business associate, but rather shake hands as is the custom in the United States.

Gifts. Japanese business persons generally give a small gift when meeting a potential business associate for the first time. If you receive a gift from a Japanese business associate, you should simply accept it with thanks. You may open the gift at that time in front of that person. You should feel no obligation to reciprocate. In addition, if you do present a gift to a Japanese business associate, do not expect it to be opened in front of you.

Decision making. Japanese typically take much longer than Americans to make decisions. This is due to the Japanese management practice of involving many people, from high ranking managers to nonmanagerial employees.

Business meetings. Japanese managers spend a substantial portion of each day in meetings (three hours and fifty-eight minutes or 39 percent of each workday).

Business cards. It is a Japanese custom to exchange business cards when introduced to someone. When meeting, you should always present your business card and accept the other person's card with thanks.

Guest room. When visiting a Japanese organization, you are not usually taken to the office of the person with whom you have an appointment. Instead, you are likely to be taken to a guest room. The Japanese manager you are meeting will probably bring a number of associates along, to familiarize them with the topic under discussion. This numerical imbalance is not intended to facilitate a stress interview conducted by the group, or to gain an advantage in negotiations. It is a common practice, prescribed by the Japanese practice of involving many people in decision making and the general emphasis on the group or work team.

Source: Otsubo, M. A guide to Japanese business practices. *California Management Review,* 1986, *28,* 28–42.

---

cise answers to most of the questions that subordinates may raise about their work." Over half of the managers from France and Italy agreed with this statement, while less than 20 percent of the managers from Sweden, the United States, and the Netherlands did so.

As an employee, how would you respond to this statement, in relation to your expectations of your manager? How do your expectations compare with others in your class? What does this suggest about American employees?

Now change your perspective to that of a manager. As a manager, how would you respond to this same statement? How do you interpret the finding that less than 20 percent of managers from the United States responded that they thought it was important for a manager to have at hand precise answers to most of the questions that subordinates may raise about their work? Develop your own interpretation before looking at the note at the end of the chapter.

WHAT DO YOU THINK?

Exhibit 19.1
Beliefs about managers from nine countries*

Statement	DENMARK	GREAT BRITAIN	NETHERLANDS	GERMANY	SWEDEN	USA	SWITZERLAND	FRANCE	ITALY	BELGIUM
1. Most managers seem to be more motivated by obtaining power than by achieving objectives.	25	32	26	29	42	36	51	56	63	—
2. The manager of tomorrow will be, in the main, a negotiator.	63	61	71	52	66	50	41	86	66	84
3. Most organizations would be better off if conflict could be eliminated forever.	19	13	17	16	4	6	18	24	41	27
4. It is important for a manager to have at hand precise answers to most of the questions that subordinates may raise about their work.	23	27	17	46	10	18	38	53	66	44

*Numbers represent percent of managers from each country who agreed with the statement.
Source: Compiled from: Laurent, A. The cultural diversity of Western conceptions of management. *International Studies of Management and Organization*, 1983, 13, 75–96.

While this study does not provide a model for systematically studying cultural differences, it does provide evidence that culture may affect management practices. Therefore, not only are managers from different cultures liable to exhibit different management styles, but also employees from different cultures may *expect* certain management styles and techniques. Thus, management techniques developed in the United States may not work well in other cultures. One author summed up the results of this and other related research as follows.[20]

"A comparative analysis across national cultures brings the startling evidence that there is no such thing as Management with a capital M. The art of managing and organizing has no homeland. Every culture has developed through its own history some specific and unique insight into the managing of organizations and of their human resources.

Comparative research shows that managers from different national cultures hold different assumptions as to the nature of management and organization. These different sets of assumptions shape different value systems and get translated into different management and organizational practices. . . ."

Recognize why understanding cultural differences is important to good human relations.

Dimensions of Culture

A more systematic model for examining cultural differences was developed by Geert Hofstede.[21] Cultures can be compared on the basis of four dimensions:

"(1) **Power distance**, that is the extent to which the members of a society accept that power in institutions and organizations is distributed unequally.
(2) **Uncertainty avoidance**, that is the degree to which the members of a society feel uncomfortable with uncertainty and ambiguity, which leads them to support beliefs promising certainty and to maintain institutions protecting conformity.
(3) **Individualism**, which stands for a preference for a loosely knit social framework in society in which individuals are supposed to take care of themselves and their immediate families only; as opposed to **Collectivism**, which stands for a preference for a tightly knit social framework in which individuals can expect their relatives, clan, or other in-group to look after them, in exchange for unquestioning loyalty.
(4) **Masculinity**, which stands for a preference for achievement, heroism, assertiveness, and material success; as opposed to **Femininity**, which stands for a preference for relationships, modesty, caring for the weak, and the quality of life. In a masculine society even the women prefer assertiveness (at least in men); in a feminine society, even the men prefer modesty."[22]

Managers and employees from countries whose general population scores high on each of these four cultural dimensions can be expected to have much different ideas about management and work in general than individuals from countries whose general population scores low on these dimensions. Some specific differences which might be expected are presented in Exhibit 19.2.

Describe some important ways in which employees from other cultures may differ.

These differences in **dimensions of culture** may be translated into some specific differences in management and individual behavior in organizations. For example, Hofstede reports on the experience of six U.S. automobile workers who spent three weeks in the Saab-Scania plant in Soedertaelje, Sweden. This plant had implemented a "humanized" system where teams of workers assembled automobiles from start to finish, in contrast to one individual performing a single task over and over as cars move by on an assembly line. The American workers disliked the Swedish work methods requiring collaboration with other members of the team. In American plants, workers were left much more on their own. This attitude is consistent with the very low *individualism* score for Sweden and the high *individualism* score for the United States.[23]

> **Exhibit 19.2**
> Implications of cultural differences
>
> ### Power Distance Dimension
>
> **Low Power Distance**
> - inequality should be minimized.
> - subordinates and superiors are people who are very similar to me.
> - everyone should have equal rights.
> - emphasis should be upon reward, legitimate, and expert power.
>
> **High Power Distance**
> - inequality is a fact of life in organizations.
> - subordinates see superiors as being different from themselves.
> - superiors see subordinates as being different from themselves.
> - people who have power are entitled to privileges.
> - emphasis placed upon coercive and referent power.
>
> ### Uncertainty Avoidance Dimension
>
> **Low Uncertainty Avoidance**
> - no great concern for time.
> - aggressive behavior is undesirable.
> - differences of opinion or deviance is not threatening.
> - willingness to take risks.
> - belief that there should be as few rules as possible.
>
> **High Uncertainty Avoidance**
> - frequently experience anxiety and stress.
> - time is not to be wasted.
> - urge to work hard.
> - aggressive behavior is acceptable.
> - different ideas and opinions are dangerous.
> - unwillingness to take risks.
> - need for written rules and regulations.

Exhibit 19.3 presents a map showing how fifty different countries and three regions of the world cluster on the four cultural dimensions. For ease of presentation and interpretation, only two dimensions were plotted at a time. The United States ranks below average on *power distance,* well below average on *uncertainty avoidance,* extremely high (the highest of all countries) on *individualism,* and well above average on *masculinity*.[24] Since most of the current management theories have been developed in the United States, the question arises, "To what extent do American management theories reflect the unique culture of the United States?" Another way of stating this question is, "To what extent can American management theories be applied in other countries or with people from other cultures?"[25]

Exhibit 19.2 *(continued)*

Individualism Dimension

Low Individualism
- oriented toward groups, "we" consciousness.
- identity of individual is based in the social system.
- emphasis on belonging to organizations, need to belong.
- preference for group decisions.

High Individualism
- self-orientation, "I" consciousness.
- identity is not tied to group membership.
- emphasis on individual initiative and accomplishment.
- need for autonomy.
- preference for individual decisions.

Masculine Dimension

Low Masculinity
- concern for people.
- concern for quality of life and environment.
- sympathy for less fortunate.
- belief that individuals should not try to be better than others.
- intuition.

High Masculinity
- concern for material possessions.
- concern for performance and growth.
- need to achieve.
- try to excel and be the best.
- decisiveness.

Source: Compiled from Hofstede, G. National cultures in four dimensions: A research-based theory of cultural differences among nations. *International Studies of Management and Organizations*, 1983, *13*, 46–74.

Can U.S. Management Theories Be Applied in Other Cultures?

Using Exhibit 19.3 as a reference, questions can be raised regarding several leading American management and behavioral science theories. For example, Maslow's Hierarchy of Needs (discussed in Chapter 5) is a well-known theory of motivation.[26] This theory places achievement-type (self-actualization and growth) needs near the top of the hierarchy, reflecting the great importance placed on individual achievement and accomplishment in the United States. A high need for achievement is consistent with the cultural dimensions of *individualism* and *masculinity* (see Exhibit 19.2). From Exhibit 19.3, it can be seen that the United States is higher than most other countries on a plot of these

Exhibit 19.3
Maps of how countries cluster on four cultural dimensions

488

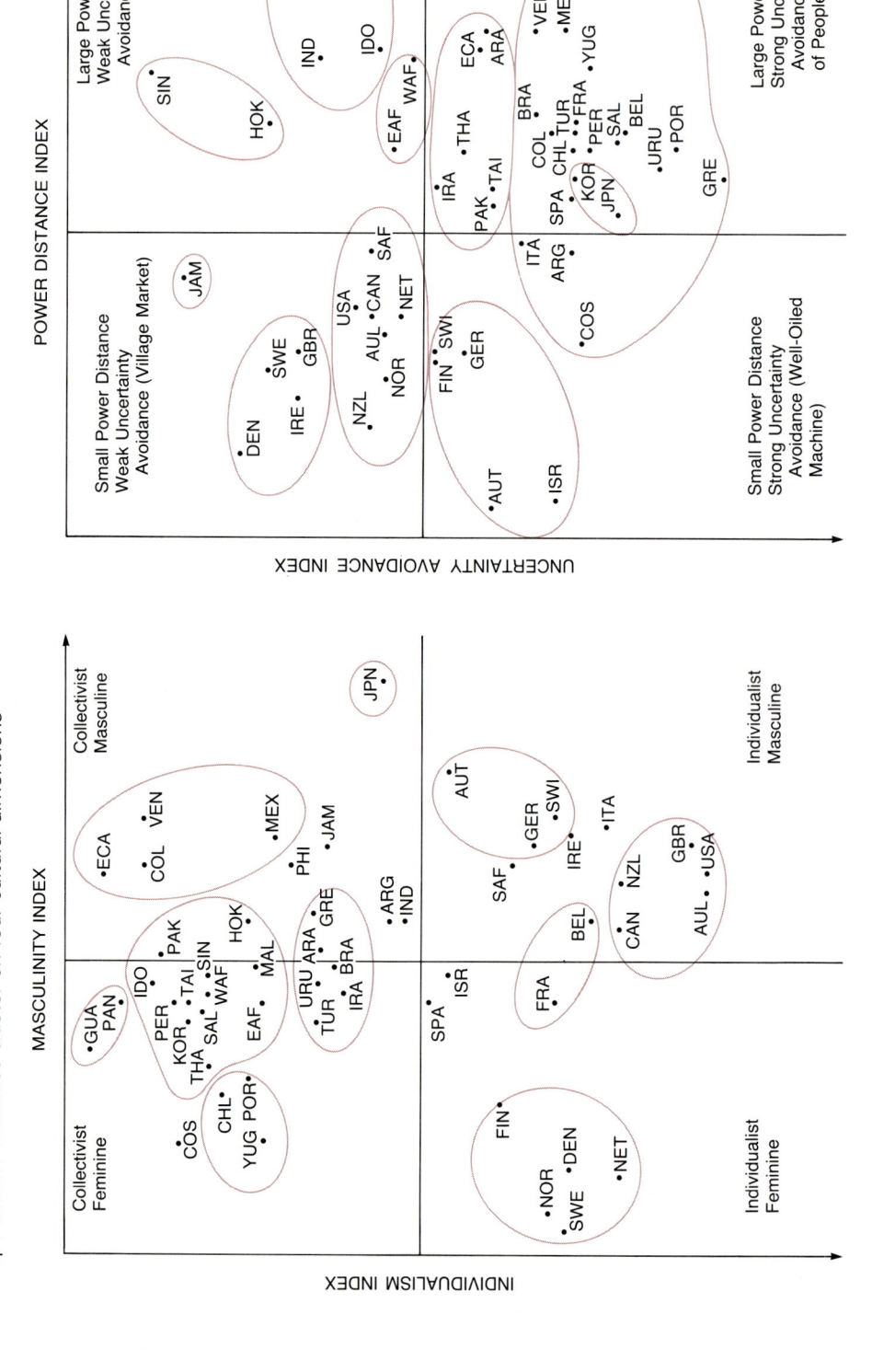

COUNTRY ABBREVIATIONS

ARA	Arab Countries (Egypt, Lebanon, Lybia, Kuwait, Iraq, Saudi-Arabia, U.A.E.)	JAM	Jamaica
ARG	Argentina	JPN	Japan
AUL	Australia	KOR	South Korea
AUT	Austria	MAL	Malaysia
BEL	Belgium	MEX	Mexico
BRA	Brazil	NET	Netherlands
CAN	Canada	NOR	Norway
CHL	Chile	NZL	New Zealand
COL	Colombia	PAK	Pakistan
COS	Costa Rica	PAN	Panama
DEN	Denmark	PER	Peru
EAF	East Africa (Kenya, Ethiopia, Zambia)	PHI	Philippines
ECA	Ecuador	POR	Portugal
FIN	Finland	SAF	South Africa
FRA	France	SAL	Salvador
GBR	Great Britain	SIN	Singapore
GER	Germany	SPA	Spain
GRE	Greece	SWE	Sweden
GUA	Guatemala	SWI	Switzerland
HOK	Hong Kong	TAI	Taiwan
IDO	Indonesia	THA	Thailand
IND	India	TUR	Turkey
IRA	Iran	URU	Uruguay
IRE	Ireland	USA	United States
ISR	Israel	VEN	Venezuela
ITA	Italy	WAF	West Africa (Nigeria, Ghana, Sierra Leone)
		YUG	Yugoslavia

Source: Hofstede, G. The interaction between national and organizational value systems. *Journal of Management Studies*, 1980, *22*, 347–357.

two dimensions. However, for countries in the *collectivist/feminine* quadrant of Exhibit 19.3, these motivation theories may be inappropriate. Achievement and accomplishment may not be so highly valued in these countries. Instead, individuals in countries scoring high on *femininity* may place more emphasis on quality of life than on achievement and accomplishment. Individuals in countries high on *uncertainty avoidance* may place more emphasis on safety and security needs. Individuals in countries scoring high on *collectivism* may place more emphasis on social needs than on individual accomplishment.[27] Thus, hierarchies of needs may be culture-specific. Maslow's Theory may require some modification in the form of rearranging the order of needs to make them more directly applicable to other countries and cultures.

Another well-known theory discussed in Chapter 5 is Herzberg's Two-Factor Theory.[28] This theory was the impetus for a great deal of research and practice concerning the enrichment of individual jobs. As Hofstede points out, job enrichment in the U.S. focused on making individual jobs more meaningful, while in other countries which scored higher on *femininity*, (e.g., Sweden), job enrichment efforts were aimed at groups or teams of employees.[29]

Explain how U.S. management practices may not be effective in foreign countries or with employees from other cultures.

In Chapters 13 and 15, several bases of power were discussed as a background to leadership theory and organizational politics, respectively. The specific base of power used by any manager will be affected by culture. For example, individuals from countries high on *collectivism* might rely more on referent and legitimate power than on reward power. Individuals from countries high on *femininity* are likely to rely most heavily on referent power. Individuals from countries high on *power distance* could be expected to rely on legitimate, coercive, and reward power. Individuals from countries high on *individualism* might rely on reward and expert power.

These differences might well be reflected in a manager's leadership style. Chapter 13 identified four primary leadership styles. Directive leadership styles are likely to be used by managers from countries high in *power distance* and *uncertainty avoidance*. Supportive leadership styles would be displayed by managers from cultures high on *femininity*. Participative leadership styles might be used by managers from cultures scoring low on *individualism* (i.e., high *collectivism*). Achievement-oriented leadership styles are to be expected with managers from cultures high on *masculinity*.

Of course, countries may exhibit varying degrees of all four cultural dimensions. Therefore, it may be inappropriate to simply analyze various management theories on the basis of one isolated cultural dimension (e.g., achievement-oriented leadership may be most appropriate in countries reflecting high *masculinity*). Rather, all cultural dimensions must be considered simultaneously when analyzing a particular country or culture. Recently, a "cultural map" was proposed which groups similar countries together in a single diagram that facilitates comparison and analysis.[30] This cultural map is presented in Exhibit 19.4. Comparing this clustering of countries with the diagrams based upon Hofstede's work reveals substantial similarity. For example, using Hofstede's diagram of *masculinity* and *individualism* from Exhibit 19.3, Austria, Germany, and Switzerland are shown grouped together. In the cultural

Exhibit 19.4
Cultural map of countries

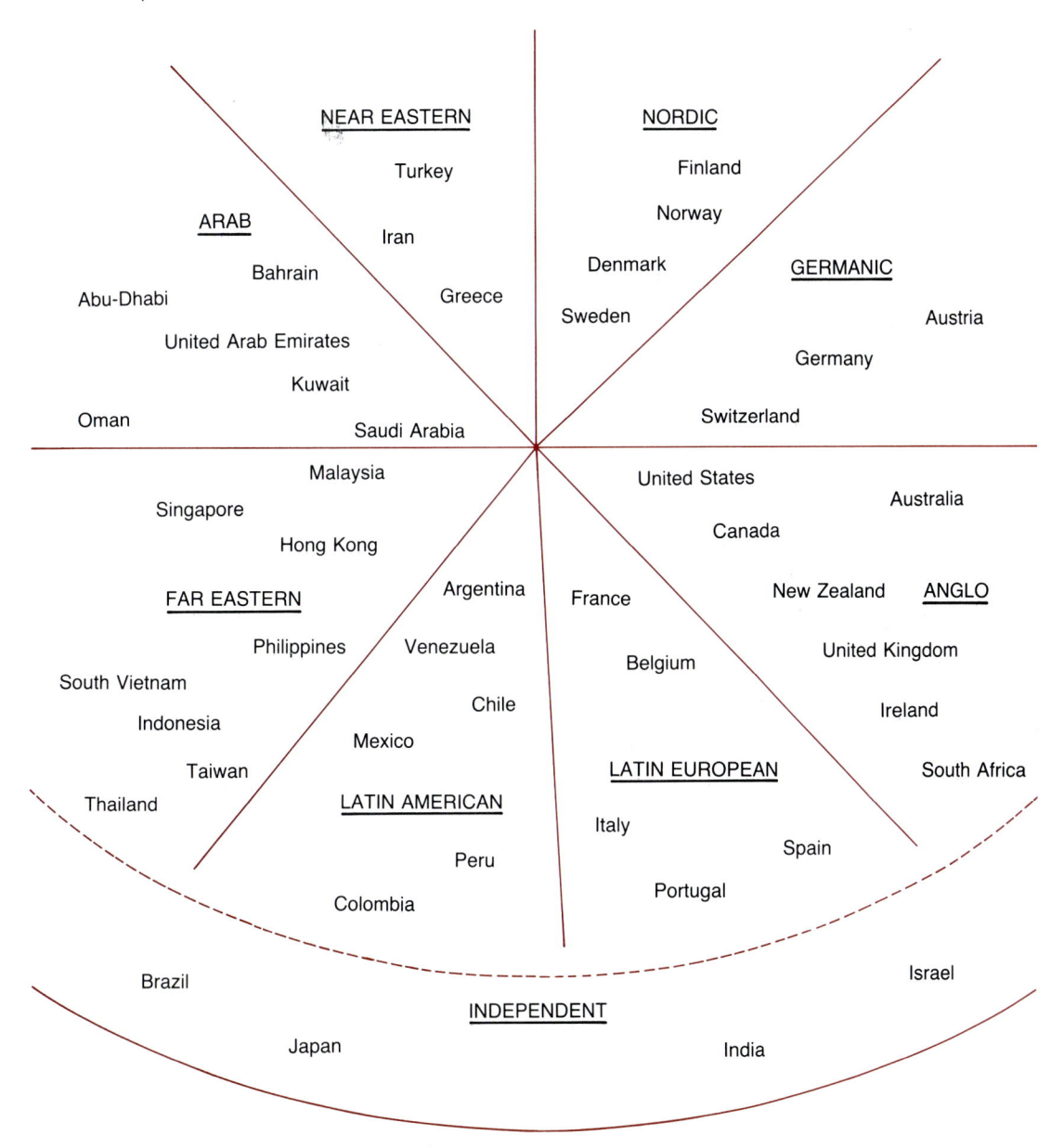

NEAR EASTERN
Turkey
Iran
Greece

ARAB
Bahrain
Abu-Dhabi
United Arab Emirates
Kuwait
Oman
Saudi Arabia

NORDIC
Finland
Norway
Denmark
Sweden

GERMANIC
Austria
Germany
Switzerland

United States
Canada
Australia
New Zealand

ANGLO
United Kingdom
Ireland
South Africa

FAR EASTERN
Malaysia
Singapore
Hong Kong
Philippines
South Vietnam
Indonesia
Taiwan
Thailand

LATIN AMERICAN
Argentina
Venezuela
Chile
Mexico
Peru
Colombia

LATIN EUROPEAN
France
Belgium
Italy
Spain
Portugal

INDEPENDENT
Brazil
Japan
India
Israel

Source: Ronen, S. & Shenkar, O. Clustering countries on attitudinal dimensions: A review and synthesis. *Academy of Management Review,* 1985, 10, 435–454.

map in Exhibit 19.4, these countries are also grouped into the Germanic cluster.

Using Hofstede's four cultural dimensions, each of these clusters can be described. Exhibit 19.5 provides these descriptions.

> **Exhibit 19.5**
> Descriptions of culture clusters
>
> **Anglo Cluster**
> low to medium power distance
> low to medium uncertainty avoidance
> high individualism
> high masculinity
> **Latin European Cluster**
> high power distance
> high uncertainty avoidance
> high masculinity
> medium to high individualism
> **Near Eastern Cluster**
> high power distance
> high uncertainty avoidance
> low individualism
> medium masculinity
> **Arab Cluster**
> high power distance
> medium uncertainty avoidance
> low individualism
> medium masculinity
> **Germanic/Nordic Cluster**
> low to medium power distance
> low to medium uncertainty avoidance
> high individualism
> low masculinity (high femininity)
> **Latin American cluster**
> high power distance
> high uncertainty avoidance
> high masculinity
> low individualism
> **Far Eastern Cluster**
> high power distance
> low to medium uncertainty avoidance
> low individualism
> medium masculinity

Source: Compiled from Ronen, S. & Shenkar, O. Clustering countries on attitudinal dimensions: A review and synthesis. *Academy of Management Journal,* 1985, *10,* 435–454; Hofstede, G. Motivation, leadership and organization: Do American theories apply abroad? *Organizational Dynamics,* 1980, *9,* 42–63; Hofstede, G. The interaction between national and organizational value systems. *Journal of Management Studies,* 1985, *22,* 347–357.

Recognizing cultural differences may provide managers with some important information on how to manage in the short term. However, the definitions of culture presented earlier suggest that culture is *learned*. Anything that has been learned can be "unlearned." Therefore, it is important to recognize that culture may change, but, it will probably change slowly. On the other hand, individuals who accept employment in a foreign country may adapt to the culture of that country relatively quickly. As a result, you cannot assume that simply because one of your employees is from Asia, that he will always exhibit all of the characteristics of that culture. For example, after some period of time in the United States he may respond better to American management practices than to management practices adapted to the Asian culture. The accompanying Human Relations in Action box provides a description of business practices in a culture that many people from Western cultures have predicted would never change.

HUMAN RELATIONS IN ACTION

Capitalism in China

During the Cultural Revolution in China around ten years ago, leaders condemned private enterprise and personal wealth as "tails of capitalism" that should be cut off. Recently, Chinese leaders have implemented important changes that may start these tails wagging. These relatively substantial changes include: encouraging privately owned businesses, allowing individuals to make profits and accumulate wealth, and allowing prices to be determined by market forces rather than by the state bureaucracy. These changes are already beginning to have an impact. Average income in China has increased by approximately 66 percent between 1980 and 1985. Products such as bicycles, radios, and watches which were once very scarce, are now commonplace. Families now have their sights set on refrigerators, television sets, washing machines and motorcycles. A recent *Business Week* article describes one factory setting where these changes have had a positive impact.

> All of China wants TVs, and at the Beijing Television Factory monthly output has soared 30 percent since Deputy Manager Jin Ahaogui began offering piece-rate bonuses for each set produced above target. Jin, a plant hero who discovered bonuses after attending a course on Western-style management, is elated about the resulting $81,000 increase in his profits. (p. 53)

Source: Jones, D.E., Elliott, D., Terry, E., Robbins, C.A., Gaffney, C. & Nussbaum, B. Capitalism in China. *Business Week,* January 14, 1985, 52–59.

JAPANESE VERSUS AMERICAN MANAGEMENT

The similarities and differences between Japanese and American management practices have received a great deal of attention in recent years. As Japanese organizations became a major competitor in world markets and the productivity of Japan surpassed that of the United States, American managers began to examine Japanese management practices for ways to solve productivity problems in America. More recently, a number of Japanese corporations have located manufacturing operations in the United States. In 1987, it was estimated that there were approximately 250,000 Americans working for Japanese-owned firms in the United States. Projections for the year 2000 are that this number will increase to approximately 1 million.[31]

Describe important differences between Japanese and American management practices.

While interest in Japanese management techniques continues, there is still some disagreement on whether Japanese management practices can be applied in America, or whether they are culturally-bound. Before examining this issue, a comparison of Japanese and American culture will provide the necessary background. Some general cultural differences between the United States and East Asian countries appears in Exhibit 19.6.

The information in Exhibits 19.2, 19.4, and 19.5 provides some insight into cultural differences between America and Japan. One of the major characteristics of U.S. culture is the emphasis placed on individualism. In Japan, the group is more important than the individual, reflected by Japan's relatively low score on the *individualism* dimension. "Japanese regard human beings as members of groups that are inevitably interrelated and dependent on one an-

Exhibit 19.6
Cultural differences between United States and East Asian countries

United States	East Asian Countries
Wealth is more important than equity.	Equity is more important than wealth.
Consumption is highly valued.	Saving and conserving resources are highly valued.
Individual is the most important part of society.	Group is the most important part of society.
Little respect is shown for age and traditional values.	Great respect is shown for age and traditional values.
Emphasis on individual motivation.	Emphasis on group motivation.
Nuclear families.	Cohesive and strong extended families—family ties are important.
Protestant work ethic has declined.	Highly disciplined and motivated work force and societies.
Distrust of government.	Public service is a moral responsibility.
Personal conflicts common—many lawyers.	Avoidance of personal conflicts—few lawyers.
Fluid society; no close social ties.	Network of intricate social ties.
Informality is important.	Strong sense of protocol and rank.
Education is an investment in individual success.	Education is an investment in the prestige of the family.

Source: Schnitzer, M.C., Liebrenz, M.L. & Kubin, K.W. *International business.* Cincinnati: South-Western Publishing Company, 1985, 150.

other—not as single, independent individuals."[32] The rankings (out of 50 countries and 3 regions) of these two countries on the four cultural dimensions are as follows (the higher the number the higher the score or ranking on that dimension): *power distance*—Japan 21, U.S. 40; *uncertainty avoidance*—Japan 44, U.S. 11; *individualism*—Japan 28/29 (tie with Argentina), U.S. 50; and *masculinity*—Japan 50, U.S. 36. Thus, the United States scores somewhat higher than Japan on *power distance,* and much higher on *individualism.* Japan scores much higher on *uncertainty avoidance* and somewhat higher on *masculinity.* These cultural differences may be reflected in the predominant management practices of each country.

One of the best-known descriptions of **Japanese management** is described in *Theory Z* by William Ouchi.[33] After studying the characteristics of **Theory Z,** which are summarized in Exhibit 19.7, compare it to Theory X and Theory Y discussed in Chapter 1. However, it should be pointed out that these management practices are representative of only the largest Japanese companies (300

> ## HUMAN RELATIONS IN ACTION
>
> ### Working for a Japanese Manager
>
> As pointed out in the Chapter, Japanese organizations are increasing investments in the United States. Plants such as the NUMMI plant in California and the Chrysler-Mitsubishi joint venture in Normal, Illinois are well-known examples. The result is that by the year 2000, nearly one million Americans could be working for Japanese organizations in the United States. While many Americans may also be hired as managers, there is a good chance that managers in these firms, particularly at higher levels of management, will be Japanese. Here are some good ideas on how to work for a Japanese manager.
>
> 1. Don't push for raises and promotions. Because of lifetime employment or long-term job security, the Japanese are in no hurry to promote employees. Raises are often tied closely to seniority or length of service in Japanese organizations. In addition, asking for a raise might be interpreted as a lack of loyalty to the company. Japanese expect loyalty in return for job security.
> 2. Learn to be patient. Decision making tends to be much slower in Japanese-run organizations. This is because the Japanese involve many people in the process, soliciting inputs from a variety of sources. Meetings may be much longer than Americans are used to (or even comfortable with) due to the higher degree of participation in Japanese organizations.
> 3. Avoid conflict and confrontation. The Japanese are not comfortable with these disruptions. The emphasis is on teamwork and cooperation.
> 4. Forget about normal work hours. Japanese tend to work long hours. You shouldn't leave work before the president. This action might be interpreted as a lack of loyalty to the company.
> 5. Forget about your job description. Get used to doing what needs to be done, whether it is in your job description or not. Accept responsibility and use your initiative. One of the biggest complaints the Japanese have of American workers is that they tend to do only what they're told and nothing more.
>
> ---
>
> Source: Copeland, J.B., Shapiro, D., Williams, E. & Matsumoto, N. How to win over a Japanese boss. *Newsweek*, February 2, 1987, 46–48.

or more employees). And, these techniques typically are not used with temporary or female employees. Smaller companies, temporary employees, and female employees are commonly used in Japan as buffers to protect workers in larger corporations from business fluctuations.[34]

These specific management techniques are used to accomplish three general strategies, which in turn are aimed at the overall goal of developing human resources. These three general strategies are discussed here.[35]

1. **Develop an internal labor market**. Employees (primarily male) hired after graduating from high school or university are typically provided with "lifetime employment." This commitment translates into employment security until the age of fifty-five, at which time many Japanese workers retire. However, it should be pointed out that there is some movement toward extending the retirement age in Japan to sixty. With the promise of lifetime employment, it becomes possible to adopt a policy of infrequent performance evaluation and slow promotion.

> **Exhibit 19.7**
> Japanese management practices
>
> - Lifetime employment
> - Intensive training
> - Frequent transfer of employees
> - Slow evaluation and promotion
> - Nonspecialized career paths
> - Implicit control mechanisms
> - Support for and promotion of cooperation at all levels
> - Collective decision making
> - Collective responsibility
> - Holistic concern
> - Bottom-up decision making
> - Quality circles

Source: Compiled from Ouchi, W.G. *Theory Z: How American business can meet the Japanese challenge.* New York: Avon Books, 1981; Marsland, S. & Beer, M. The evolution of Japanese management: Lessons for U.S. managers. *Organizational Dynamics,* 1983, *11,* 49–67.

2. **Articulate a unique company philosophy.** The most common component of company philosophies in Japanese organizations is *Wa*—the quality of relationships and teamwork. Thus, many Japanese company philosophies emphasize cooperation, teamwork, and harmony.
3. **Engage in intensive socialization.** Japanese organizations promote extensive training and orientation of new employees as well as employees who transfer to new jobs within the organization. This training is often a form of socialization of the employee to the company's philosophy. Much of the program involves familiarizing the new employees with the organization; it actually has little to do with job skills. Employees are provided an opportunity to learn new job skills through job transfers.

These three strategies as well as several specific management techniques are presented in a model of Japanese management (Exhibit 19.8). This model serves as a background for an analysis of whether these Japanese management techniques are culturally bound, or whether they can be applied effectively in organizations in other cultures. Of primary interest is whether Japanese management techniques will work in U.S. organizations.

JAPANESE MANAGEMENT TECHNIQUES IN U.S. ORGANIZATIONS

Explain whether Japanese management practices can be applied in American organizations.

One way to assess the applicability of Japanese management techniques in the United States is to examine the extent to which U.S. subsidiaries of Japanese corporations have successfully implemented these practices. Two recent studies address this issue.

Exhibit 19.8
A model of Japanese management

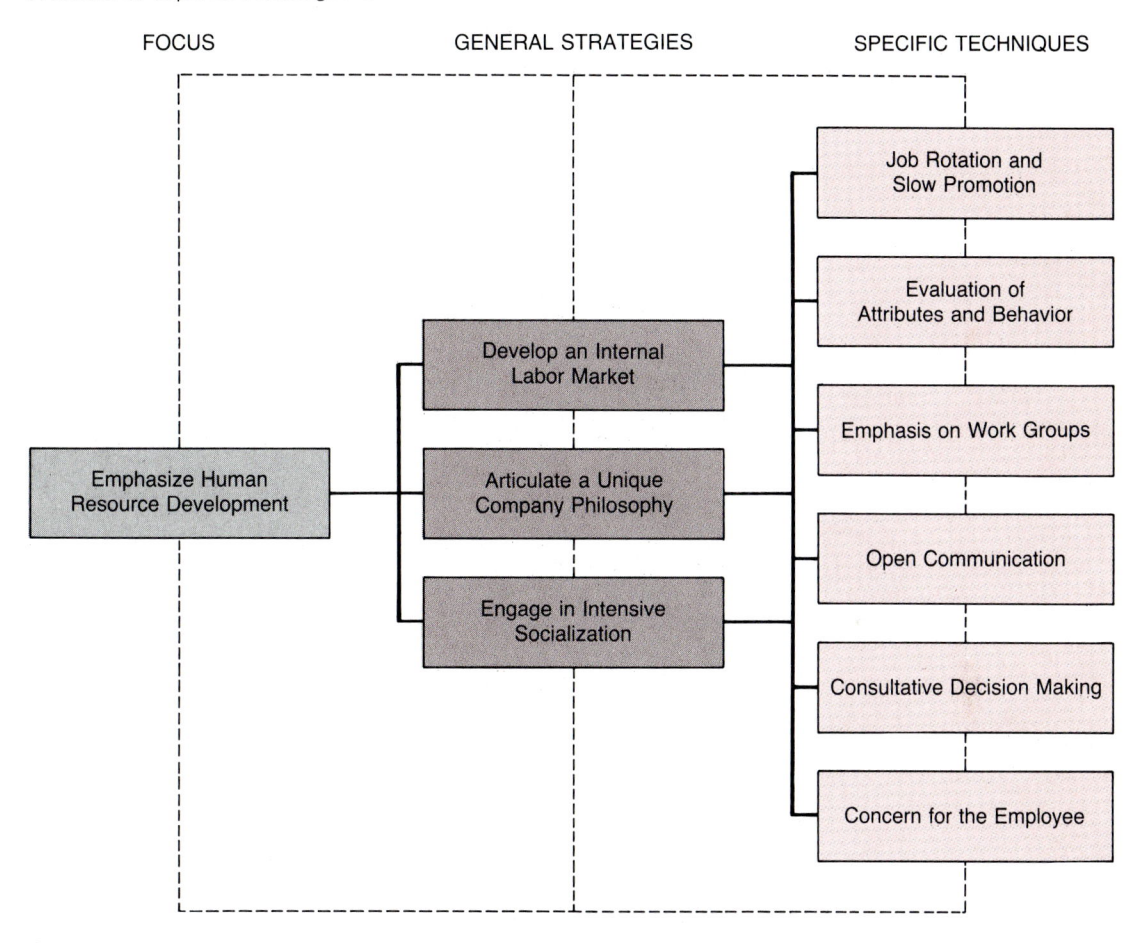

```
        FOCUS                GENERAL STRATEGIES           SPECIFIC TECHNIQUES

                                                          ┌──────────────────────┐
                                                          │ Job Rotation and     │
                                                          │ Slow Promotion       │
                                                          └──────────────────────┘

                                                          ┌──────────────────────┐
                                                          │ Evaluation of        │
                                                          │ Attributes and Behavior│
                              ┌──────────────────┐        └──────────────────────┘
                              │ Develop an Internal│
                              │ Labor Market     │        ┌──────────────────────┐
                              └──────────────────┘        │ Emphasis on Work Groups│
  ┌────────────────────┐      ┌──────────────────┐        └──────────────────────┘
  │ Emphasize Human    │──────│ Articulate a Unique│
  │ Resource Development│     │ Company Philosophy│       ┌──────────────────────┐
  └────────────────────┘      └──────────────────┘        │ Open Communication   │
                              ┌──────────────────┐        └──────────────────────┘
                              │ Engage in Intensive│
                              │ Socialization    │        ┌──────────────────────┐
                              └──────────────────┘        │ Consultative Decision Making│
                                                          └──────────────────────┘

                                                          ┌──────────────────────┐
                                                          │ Concern for the Employee│
                                                          └──────────────────────┘
```

Source: Hatvany, N. & Pucik, V. An integrated management system: Lessons from the Japanese experience. *Academy of Management Review,* 1981, 6, 469–480.

In a study of executives of sixty-three Japanese subsidiaries operating in the United States, Bowman found that many of the well-known Japanese management techniques were being applied. However, they were being modified slightly, to better fit American employees and managers.[36] While only 3.3 percent of the subsidiaries surveyed reported offering lifetime employment to employees, they did go to great lengths to avoid having to lay off employees (e.g., company-wide pay cuts, job transfers, work hour reductions, hiring freezes, and early retirement incentives). As already pointed out, the Japanese place great emphasis on groups and teamwork, while Americans tend to be individualistic. In Japan, work tends to be assigned to groups or work teams rather than to individuals. In these Japanese subsidiaries, almost 62 percent reported they did not assign work to teams. However, their job descriptions

DEVELOPING YOUR HUMAN RELATIONS SKILLS

The implications of the information presented in this chapter are relatively clear for you, both as a manager and as an employee.

1. Get to know the culture and business practices of the country in which you are working, or in which your employer is based. Your foreign employer will undoubtedly be quite pleased to see you make an effort to learn more about his country's culture.
2. Language is often a problem for many American managers and employees. While many foreign business persons have learned to speak English, not as many Americans have learned a foreign language. In addition to showing your interest in the culture of your employer, learning to speak the language which the top executives speak will help you understand their practices and values. The head of the U.S. branch of Rodior, a Paris fashion house, regularly practices his French. "I can see from the reaction of my French colleagues that they are pleased I am making the effort." An American manager for an Italian company echoes this sentiment. "I knew I made a major breakthrough when I gave a twenty-minute speech in Italian to a group of engineers and received thundering applause." Another American manager working abroad at Toyota believes that knowing how to speak the language of your host country or employer helps you most at the social level, where most of the important business contacts are made.[37]
3. If your career involves a long-term assignment in a foreign-owned organization, the old slogan "When in Rome, do as the Romans do" may be good advice. Don't try to Americanize your employing organization. Don't cling to American customs and practices which offend or make foreign employees uncomfortable. You must not only learn the culture of your employer's country, but also you must accept it and behave in a manner consistent with that culture.

tend to be less specific than in typical American firms, encouraging workers to be more willing to go beyond their job description to help fellow employees. Similarly, quality circles (QCs) are relatively widespread in Japan, but not in the Japanese subsidiaries. However, again these subsidiaries seem to have modified the basic Japanese management practice to better fit American culture. Many reporting they did not use QCs also reported that they held informal department meetings at the beginning and end of each shift. The activities during these meetings are very similar to those in quality circles.[38] Thus, Japanese subsidiaries in the United States seem to be implementing many of the traditional Japanese management techniques. However, they also seem to be modifying them to reflect the culture of the United States. The practices of these Japanese subsidiaries were summarized by the author of this study, "Many of these subsidiaries seem to be creating a corporate culture of mutual

Exhibit 19.9
Executive attitudes toward employees and Japanese management (percent)
Total n = 65

Statement	Strongly Agree	Agree	Undecided	Disagree	Strongly Disagree
American workers in our company generally have responded in a negative way to Japanese-style management techniques.	5.2 (3)	15.5 (9)	8.6 (5)	60.3 (35)	10.3 (6)
Employees regard company growth and achievement as being linked to improvements in their own careers.	8.2 (5)	62.3 (36)	13.1 (8)	13.1 (8)	3.3 (2)
Management officials in this company are interested not just in the achievements and capabilities of employees but also in their feelings and personal lives.	18.0 (11)	62.3 (36)	8.2 (5)	9.8 (6)	1.6 (1)
The core of Japanese personnel management is deliberate attention to the humanistic aspects of work.	12.3 (7)	45.6 (20)	15.8 (9)	24.6 (14)	1.8 (1)
The most important part of Japanese management is its emphasis on the scientific aspects of manufacturing techniques.	1.7 (1)	30.8 (18)	21.7 (13)	38.3 (23)	8.3 (5)
American companies can become competitive with Japanese firms primarily through new investment and automation.	13.6 (8)	35.6 (21)	18.6 (11)	28.8 (17)	3.4 (2)
American firms must adopt a more people-oriented management approach if they expect to compete successfully with their Japanese counterparts.	15.0 (9)	50.0 (30)	15.0 (9)	18.3 (11)	1.7 (1)

involvement, holistic concern, and employee security that integrates the social and economic desires of employee and employer alike."[39]

Employees of Japanese subsidiaries tend to react favorably to these modified Japanese management techniques. Reactions of executives (who are primarily Americans) of the Japanese subsidiaries in the U.S. are reported in Exhibit 19.9. Further, most of these executives believe that American organizations could become more competitive by adopting many of these people-oriented Japanese management techniques.[40]

SUMMARY

The "internationalization" of the world economy has made it increasingly important for managers to become aware of differences in culture and business practices in a number of foreign countries. There are volumes of well-known humorous stories describing business mistakes arising from a lack of understanding of the culture in which the firm was operating. However, these cases were not humorous at the time, since many resulted in substantial financial losses for the company involved.

Culture is defined as patterns of thought and manners which are widely shared. National culture is similar to the concept of organizational culture discussed in Chapter 16. Important dimensions of culture include: *power distance, uncertainty avoidance, individualism,* and *masculinity/femininity*. Cultural differences raise the question of whether U.S. management theories and practices can be applied in other countries by managers of multinational corporations. With increasing Japanese investment in the United States, the converse of this question is also appropriate. Can Japanese management techniques be applied in the United States? Three specific management techniques characteristic of Japanese management are: (1) develop an internal labor market, (2) articulate a unique company philosophy, and (3) engage in intensive socialization.

KEY TERMS

multinational corporations
culture
power distance
uncertainty avoidance
individualism/collectivism
masculinity/femininity
dimensions of culture
Japanese management
Theory Z

DISCUSSION QUESTIONS

1. Why is an understanding of cultural differences important for managers interested in promoting good human relations in their organizations?
2. What is culture? How does it affect behavior in organizations?
3. What are the four dimensions of culture identified in the chapter? How does the United States rate on these dimensions?
4. Develop a hierarchy of needs, using Maslow's need categories for the following countries: Thailand, Colombia, Austria, and Greece. (Refer to Exhibit 19.4 and Exhibit 19.5).
5. What are some of the most well-known Japanese management techniques?
6. How do the Japanese management techniques mentioned in the chapter fit with what you know about Japanese culture?
7. How have traditional Japanese management techniques been modified by Japanese subsidiaries in the United States to better fit American culture?
8. Take a position on the following statement and be prepared to defend it: "Japanese management techniques cannot be applied in American organizations."

EXERCISE 19.1

Modifying Theory to Fit Cultures

Pick any theory or management technique described in other chapters of this book (other than Maslow and Herzberg). Using Exhibits 19.2, 19.4, and 19.5 as guides, modify this theory to fit another cultural cluster (other than the Anglo cluster). In other words, restate this theory so that it is applicable to employees in the cultural cluster you choose. Be prepared to present your findings to the class.

CASE 19.1

Japanese Management in Arkansas

Japanese investment in the United States has increased dramatically over the past few years as Japanese companies have opened automobile manufacturing plants, purchased ailing U.S. businesses, and entered into partnerships with U.S. firms such as the Diamond Star Motors joint venture between Mitsubishi and Chrysler. Yoshitaka Sajima, vice-president of Misui & Company, says that economic distinctions between the United States and Japan are blurring. "The United States and Japan are not just trading with each other anymore—they've become part of each other." There are now approximately 500 Japanese firms that have manufacturing or assembling operations in the United States.

These firms typically employ a distinctive Japanese management style, which in many cases has been highly successful. Case in point: when Toyota took over the General Motors plant in Fremont, California, the absenteeism rate was 20 percent and there were generally around 5,000 grievances outstanding. At the end of eighteen months of Toyota management of the plant, the plant was producing the same number of cars per year (approximately 240,000) with half as many workers. Further, there were only two grievances outstanding and the absenteeism rate was less than 2 percent. Some of the major differences in management that the Japanese bring to their U.S. operations include flexible work teams, emphasis on quality, expectations of employee loyalty, increased responsibility for employees, and minimization of differences between managers and employees. Executive dining rooms and reserved parking spaces are rare. Executives often wear the same uniforms as assembly-line workers.

However, Japanese management isn't working everywhere. Sanyo Manufacturing Corporation's large microwave and television manufacturing plant in Forrest City, Arkansas has faced two violent strikes and two years of operating losses since Sanyo took over the plant from Whirlpool's Warwick Electronics division. After assuming control of the plant, Sanyo attempted to implement Japanese management techniques such as quality circles. Employees would not support these changes, and according to them, managers then began taking a harder line. When contract talks opened with the union, Sanyo asked for greater flexibility in work rules and reduced medical benefits. The result was a three-week strike, during which pickets carried signs that said "Japs go home" and "Remember Pearl Harbor." Cars were overturned, windows were broken, and guns were fired into the air. After the strike, management removed chairs and benches from employee restrooms and eliminated perfect-attendance awards for employees.

Sanyo's Japanese executives, who emphasize cooperation and teamwork as important elements of increased productivity and quality, are frustrated by the union's stance. One Sanyo vice-president described his perception of employees at the Arkansas plant, "They come here for eight hours' work and eight hours' pay. As long as they get that, they don't care what happens to our production. Here, there's no sacrifice." The president of the local union countered with, "Trust really isn't there. Seniority isn't going to cause them to go broke. Bad management will."

QUESTIONS

1. What reasons can account for the failure of Japanese management to work at this particular plant when it seems to have worked so well at similar plants in comparable locations?
2. What mistakes were made by Sanyo Corporation as they assumed control of the plant?

Source: Bernstein, A., Cook, D., Engardio, P. & Miles, G.L. The difference Japanese management makes. *Business Week,* July 14, 1986, 47–50; Byrne, J.A. At Sanyo's Arkansas plant the magic isn't working. *Business Week,* July 14, 1986, 51–52; Holstein, W.J., Engardio, P. & Cook, D. Will Sake and sour mash go together? *Business Week,* July 14, 1986, 53–55; Holstein, W.J. Japan U.S.A. *Business Week,* July 14, 1986, 44–46.

3. Is there anything that can be done now to reduce tensions between management and labor and make the Arkansas plant another Japanese management success story?
4. Assume that you are an American manager hired by a Japanese firm such as Sanyo. What steps would you take to implement typical Japanese management practices such as teamwork, quality circles, flexible work rules, slow evaluation and promotion, collective decision making, and frequent transfer of employees?
5. Are there any characteristics of Japanese management that you believe cannot be used with U.S. workers?

REFERENCES

[1]Braganti, N.L. & Devine, E. *The traveler's guide to European customs and manners*. Deephaven, MN: Meadowbrook Books, 1984.

[2]Maisonrouge, J.G. The education of a modern international manager. *Journal of International Business Studies,* 1983, *14,* p. 143.

[3]Ibid, 141–146.

[4]McLuhan, M. *Understanding media: The extensions of man*. New York: McGraw-Hill Paperbooks, 1965.

[5]*Forbes,* July 5, 1982, 115–126.

[6]*Forbes,* July 2, 1984, 129–132,134.

[7]Ricks, D.A., Fu, M.Y.C. & Arpan, J.S. *International business blunders*. Columbus, Ohio: Grid, Inc., 1974.

[8]Mazze, E.M. How to push a body abroad without making it a corpse. *Business Abroad,* August 10, 1964.

[9]Ricks, et al, 1974, Ibid.

[10]Ricks, D.A., Mahojon, V. & Lay, H.W. Blunders in international marketing: Fact or fiction? *Long Range Planning,* 1984, *17,* 78–82.

[11]Ricks, D.A. *Big business blunders: Mistakes in multinational marketing*. Homewood, Illinois: Dow Jones-Irwin, 1983.

[12]Ricks, et al., 1974, Ibid.

[13]Ricks, et al., 1983, Ibid.

[14]Nees, D. Doing business in France. *TWA Ambassador,* February 1987, 23–24.

[15]Braganti, N.L. & Devine, E. *The traveler's guide to European customs and manners*. Deephaven, MN: Meadowbrook Books, 1984.

[16]Child, J. & Kieser, A. Contrast in British and West German management practice: Are recipes for success culture-bound? Paper presented at the conference on cross-cultural studies of organizational functioning. Hawaii, 1977.

[17]Rice, F. Should you work for a foreigner? *Fortune,* August 1, 1988, 123–134.

[18]Hofstede, G. Motivation, leadership, and organization: Do American theories apply abroad? *Organizational Dynamics,* 1980, *9,* 42–63.

[19]Laurent, A. The cross-cultural puzzle of international human resource management. *Human Resource Management,* 1986, *25,* 91–102.

[20]Hofstede, G. The interaction between national and organizational value systems. *Journal of Management Studies,* 1985, *22,* 347–357.

[21]Hofstede, 1980, Ibid; Hofstede, G. National culture in four dimensions. *International Studies of Management and Organization,* 1983, *13,* 46–74.

[22]Hofstede, G., 1983, Ibid.

[23]Hofstede, G., 1983, Ibid.

[24]Hofstede, G., 1983, Ibid.

[25]Hunt, J.W. Applying American behavioral science: Some cross-cultural problems. *Organizational Dynamics,* 1981, *10,* 55–62.

[26]Maslow, A.H. A theory of human motivation. *Psychological Review,* 1943, *50,* 370–396.

[27]Hofstede, G., 1980, Ibid.

[28]Herzberg, F., Mausner, B. & Snyderman, B. *The motivation to work*. New York: John Wiley, 1959.

[29]Hofstede, 1980, Ibid.

[30]Ronen, S. & Shenkar, O. Clustering countries on attitudinal dimensions: A review and synthesis. *Academy of Management Review,* 1985, *10,* 435–454.

[31]Powell, B., Martin, B., Lewis, D., Turque, B., Raine, G. & Cohn, B. Where the jobs are. *Newsweek,* February 2, 1987, 42–46.

[32]Marsland, S. & Beer, M. The evolution of Japanese management: Lessons for U.S. managers. *Organizational Dynamics,* 1983, *11,* 54.

[33]Ouchi, W.G. *Theory Z: How American business can meet the Japanese challenge*. New York: Avon Books, 1981.

[34]Marsland & Beer, 1983, Ibid, 49–67.

[35] Hatvany, N. & Pucik, V. An integrated management system: Lessons from the Japanese experience. *Academy of Management Review*, 1981, *6*, 469–480.

[36] Bowman, J.S. The rising sun in America: Part one. *Personnel Administrator*, 1986, *31*, 63–67, 114–119.

[37] Rice, F. Should you work for a foreigner? *Fortune*, August 1, 1988, 123–134.

[38] Bowman, 1986, Ibid, 63–67, 114–119.

[39] Bowman, J.S. The rising sun in America: Part two. *Personnel Administrator*, 1986, *31*, 81–91.

[40] Ibid.

This finding may be interpreted in a variety of ways, however, it may be suggesting that managers in France and Italy feel a stronger need to be in control of their subordinates' activities; they are reluctant to allow subordinates to find answers for themselves. On the other hand, managers from Sweden, the United States, and the Netherlands may be more willing to allow subordinates to find answers to their own problems and have more control over their work.

WHAT DO YOU THINK? NOTE

Glossary

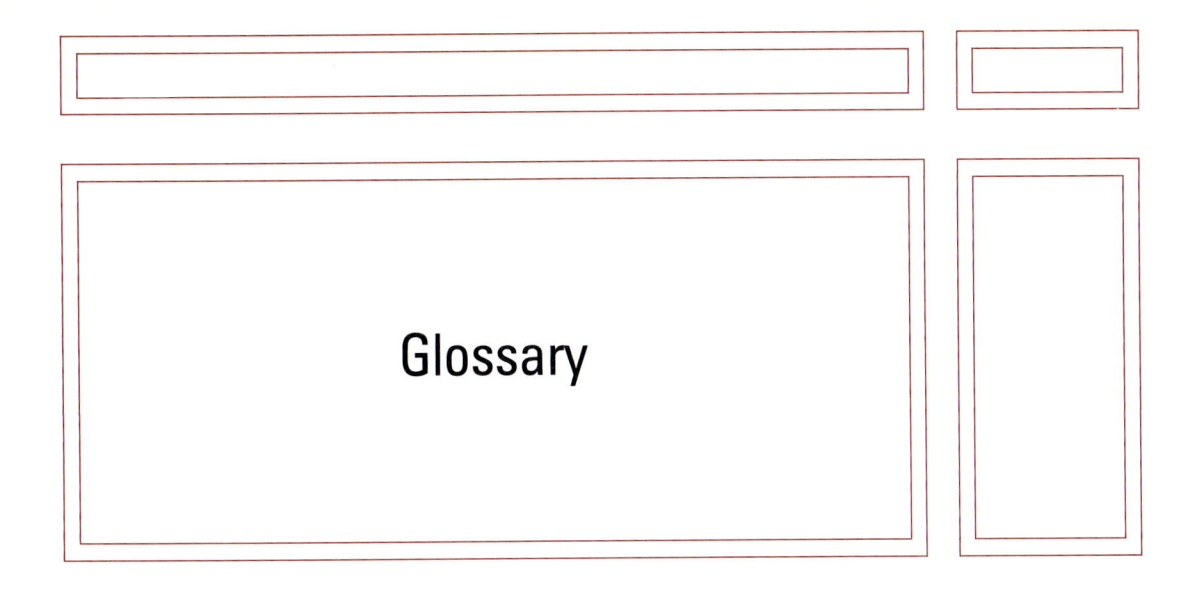

ability The degree to which an employee is capable of performing.

absenteeism Defined in terms of the frequency and severity with which employees miss scheduled work hours. Also includes lateness or tardiness.

accommodating Type of reaction to a conflict in which individuals are unassertive and cooperative.

achievement orientation A need to continually try to improve, do things better, and accomplish important goals.

achievement-oriented leadership style Leader sets challenging goals and high performance standards, encourages employees to continually improve their performance, and maintains high expectations of employees.

active listening Assuming responsibility for receiving intended messages, and becoming actively involved in the communication.

agency shop Employees who choose to not join the union must contribute to the union in an amount approximately equal to union dues.

aggressive strategy Strategy for dealing with change in which plans and means of implementing plans are developed in advance of any change actually taking place. Based on forecasts of environmental events.

ambiguity of terms Refers to traits or characteristics on a performance appraisal rating scale which may be interepreted differently by different raters.

antecedent conditions of conflict Sources of conflict, such as misunderstanding, scarce resources, stress.

appointed leaders Individuals who are placed in positions of authority by organizations.

arbitrator Neutral third party who is brought in to hear the positions of both labor and management and to reach a decision regarding the grievance.

assertiveness The degree to which an individual or group focuses on satisfying their own needs and accomplishing their own goals.

attitude Opinions about people, objects, places, or events, which reflect an individual's likes and dislikes.

attribution A process where we attempt to determine the causes of another individual's behavior.

authoritarianism The extent to which an individual believes there should be power and status differences within organizations.

authorization cards Cards employees sign indicating their interest in having the National Labor Relations Board hold a representation election.

autonomy The degree to which a task permits employees to use their own discretion and judgment in deciding how the work is to be performed.

505

avoidable turnover Turnover due to causes that could have been prevented by the organization.

avoidance Short-term or temporary conflict resolution technique in which the conflict is ignored.

avoidance culture Culture in which employees develop the belief that what they do really doesn't make any difference. Employees do only enough to get by.

avoiding A type of reaction to a conflict in which individuals are both unassertive and uncooperative.

bargaining unit Group of employees with similar interests and performing similar activities who will be represented by a particular union.

base of power Source of power on which managers may rely in order to influence employees.

behavioral sciences Fields which study human behavior, such as psychology, sociology, organizational behavior, and management.

behavior-based appraisals Performance appraisal formats which place the emphasis of the rating on specific behaviors instead of traits or characteristics. Examples are behaviorally anchored rating scales (BARS) and behavioral observation scales (BOS).

bet-your-company culture Culture characterized by high risk and slow feedback. Slow, tedious, and deliberate decision-making process.

binding arbitration Agreement between labor and management that both will abide by the arbitrator's decision.

biofeedback techniques Attaching individuals to equipment which measures physical and chemical changes within the body so the individuals can learn to evoke the relaxation response.

bizarre employee behavior Employee conduct of an unusual nature, usually not covered in the employee handbook or labor agreement.

brainstorming Technique for increasing creativity where the focus is on idea generation, not idea evaluation. Cricitism of ideas is prohibited. Members are encouraged to come up with wild ideas.

building alliances/coalitions A type of political activity that involves establishing friendships and networks of relationships in order to get assistance, support, and information.

bureaucratic culture Culture where top managers are preoccupied with exerting control over employees. Organization develops many rules and policies and becomes inflexible and depersonalized.

cafeteria style benefits Program where employees are free to choose at least some of their fringe benefits.

capacity to perform Includes ability, health, age, job knowledge, skills, education, and endurance.

career The sequence of work-related experiences over the life of an individual. A series of jobs.

career development Responsibility of both the individual and the organization. Involves activities designed to help the individual grow, develop new skills, and continue to progress within a chosen profession or occupation.

career management Consists of two related sets of activities, career planning and career development.

career paths A series of jobs or positions through which an individual is likely to progress within the organization.

career planning The responsibility of individuals. Involves self-assessment, exploration of career opportunities, goal setting, and monitoring.

career stages Changes most individuals go through as they progress through their work careers.

cause Condition that created the problem.

centralization Important decisions are made by a small group of top executives.

central tendency A type of rater error where all employees are rated toward the center of the scale.

character assassination A type of political behavior aimed at damaging the image or credibility of another person.

charismatic culture A culture which develops around a particularly strong, charismatic leader. Employees become highly dependent on this leader and follow his or her directions without question.

Civil Service Reform Act Labor law that covers employees in the public sector. Modeled after the Wagner Act, it created the Federal Labor Relations Authority (FLRA).

closed shop Employees are required to join the union before being hired.

closure Perceptual problem where we fill in gaps in messages with what we expect or want to be there.

GLOSSARY

coercive power The authority or ability to punish employees or withhold rewards.

cognitive dissonance Psychological discomfort that results from an inconsistency between attitudes and behavior.

cohesiveness The strength of group members' desire to remain members of the group.

collaborating A type of reaction to a conflict in which individuals are both assertive and cooperative.

collectivism Dimension of national culture that stands for a preference for a tightly knit social framework in which individuals can expect their family and relatives to look out for them.

command groups Relatively permanent groups that are typically represented on the organizational chart. Each group consists of a manager and employees.

commitment When individuals agree with the goals of the person trying to influence their behavior. Individuals are willing to exert maximum effort to accomplish these goals.

common law A body of law based upon decisions made by judges in actual court cases, and not based upon legislation.

common sense theories Theories based only on observation and not scientific research.

competing Type of reaction to a conflict in which individuals are assertive and uncooperative.

competition Occurs when individuals or groups are trying to accomplish goals that are incompatible with those of another, or are trying to acquire limited resources. Different from conflict in that there is no intentional blocking of opponents' efforts to accomplish goals or acquire resources.

compliance Members go along with the group because of overt pressure. Individuals allow themselves to be influenced but they are not enthusiastic and exert only minimal amounts of effort.

compromising A type of reaction to a conflict in which individuals exhibit moderate assertiveness and moderate cooperation.

conceptualization of conflict Process in which parties to a conflict try to understand it and determine why it exists.

concessions Givebacks—union agreements to lower wages or benefits to prevent employee layoffs.

conflict The process which begins when one party perceives that the other has frustrated or is about to frustrate some concern of his or hers.

conflict aftermath The result of a conflict episode.

conflict episode The complete five-stage conflict process.

conflict stimulation A conflict management technique that increases the amount of conflict present in an organization.

conformity When members voluntarily go along with the group.

confrontation Confronting problem employees with documented evidence that a problem exists.

consensus An aspect of the attribution process that refers to how others respond in the same situation.

consistency An aspect of the attribution process that refers to the extent to which the same individual engages in the same behavior over time.

constructive feedback Feedback that is intended to be helpful and corrective.

contingent workers Part-time and temporary employees, also referred to as "disposable" employees.

continuous reinforcement schedule Rewards are administered every time an employee engages in a correct behavior.

cooperativeness The degree to which individuals or groups consider the needs and goals of the other party to the conflict.

counseling Openly communicating with employees about how their job performance and behavior compares with organizational expectations. Consists of four steps: confrontation, constructive feedback, active listening, and goal setting.

creativity The process of developing original, imaginative, and innovative perspectives on situations, or the reorganization of experience into new configurations. Consists of four stages: preparation, incubation, insight, and verification.

critical incident file A narrative record of specific examples of an employee's job performance.

culture Patterns of thought and manners that are widely shared within a nation or geographic region. Not to be confused with organizational culture.

decentralization Employees at lower levels in the organization are included in making important decisions.

decertification election Election held by the NLRB by which employees vote on whether they want their current union to continue as their bargaining representative.

decertification process Process by which employees remove a union as their bargaining representative.

defamation Area of common law that allows employees to bring charges against a previous employer for statements that damage their reputation or ability to find replacement employment.

denial Process by which individuals unconsciously deny that painful or extremely embarrassing information exists.

departmental orientation Covers job-specific information such as job duties, performance expectations, work rules, work hours, and introductions to coworkers.

dependent care Caretaking facilities for children and elderly family members of employees.

directive leadership style Leader provides specific instructions for performing tasks, sets performance standards, schedules work to be done, and develops rules and regulations.

distinctiveness An aspect of the attribution process that refers to how unusual the behavior is for a particular employee.

distress Stress that has negative results for an individual.

dominant culture The culture of the overall organization.

dominant leadership style The leadership style with which a manager is most comfortable.

downward communication Communication to employees, initiated by managers. The purpose is usually to provide employees with information that will help them perform their jobs.

dysfunctional turnover Turnover of top performers or employees with special skills who will be difficult to replace.

effort → performance expectancy (also called E1) Refers to the employee's confidence in his or her ability to perform the task.

electronic communications systems A network of personal computers or terminals, linked together electronically, on which employees can send messages to one another. Also called electronic message systems and electronic mail.

emergent leaders Individuals who are able to influence others by means other than formal authority, such as personality, interpersonal skills, expertise, and knowledge.

employee assistance programs (EAPs) Agreements between organizations and professional counselors to provide assistance to employees with substance abuse or emotional problems.

employee rights Rights of employees while at work. Some employee rights are protected by law, others by custom. These include the right to personal privacy, free speech, and due process.

employment-at-will doctrine Assumption that employers could fire employees at any time for a good reason, a bad reason, or no reason at all.

esteem needs Self-esteem has to do with the need for a positive self-image. Esteem of others refers to the need for recognition and attention from others.

eustress Stress that has positive results for an individual.

expert power Ability to influence others as a result of a specialized skill or knowledge.

external locus of control Belief that an individual's behavior is not a strong determinant of fate.

external recruitment Recruiting applicants from the outside to fill open positions.

extinction Ignoring a particular behavior.

extrinsic job satisfaction Satisfaction of needs external to the individual, such as pay, physical working conditions, promotions, and fringe benefits.

extroversion A tendency to be outgoing and gregarious.

feasible alternative A decision alternative that, if implemented, would result in at least a minimally acceptable solution to the problem. Also, the organization must have the ability and resources to implement the alternative.

featherbedding Practice of unions requiring employers to pay for work not actually performed, or to pay for more workers than are actually needed on a job.

felt conflict Conflict that is strong enough or important enough to cause one or both parties to experience tension or anxiety.

femininity A dimension of national culture that stands for a preference for relationships, modesty, caring for the weak, and quality of life.

fixed interval reinforcement schedule A reward is administered after the passage of a certain amount of time.

fixed ratio reinforcement schedule A reward is administered after the employee engages in a certain number of correct behaviors.

flexible time off A program that combines vacation days and sick days into one pool. Employees may take off the days they have earned for any reason.

flexible work scheduling Policy that allows employees to schedule their own work hours.

forcing A conflict resolution technique in which managers rely on their formal authority and impose a decision on the parties to the conflict.

formal groups Groups initiated by the organization to accomplish organizational goals.

forming First stage of group development, characterized by a great deal of uncertainty.

friendship groups Relatively permanent informal groups that arise because members enjoy interacting with one another.

frustration-regression process What happens when satisfaction of an important need is blocked. Individuals psychologically distort the situation and allow previously satisfied needs to again become manifest.

functional turnover Turnover of poor performers or problem employees.

functions of work Reasons people work. The five functions are economic, social, status, identity, and growth.

gainsharing A pay system that links salary increases to group or team performance.

general adaptation syndrome (GAS) Chemical reaction that takes place when individuals experience stressors in their environment. Consists of three stages: alarm, resistance, and exhaustion. Also called the "fight or flight response."

givebacks Concessions; union agreements to lower wages or benefits to prevent employee layoffs.

global economy Term used to refer to the increasing internationalization of business. Many businesses now operate beyond the borders of their native country.

"good citizen" behaviors Behaviors that are closely related to job satisfaction. Examples include keeping the work area clean and orderly, coming to work on time, and helping other employees.

grapevine Informal communication system. Arises because employees have a need for more information than they are receiving from formal communication sources.

graphic rating scale Form of performance appraisal scale which consists of a set of traits or characteristics and a very simple measurement scale. Most widely used form of performance appraisal, but highly susceptible to rater errors.

grievance procedures A specified sequence of events for handling disagreements in a unionized organization. Recently becoming more common in nonunion organizations.

group Two or more persons who are interacting with one another in such a manner that each person influences and is influenced by each other person.

groupshift A process whereby group members exaggerate their initial positions.

groupthink Group members are more concerned with reaching agreement or consensus than they are with making a high-quality decision.

halo effect The tendency to perceive all characteristics of an individual based upon one extremely favorable or unfavorable characteristic.

halo error Same as halo effect.

harshness A type of rater error where a manager rates all of her employees toward the negative end of the scale.

Hawthorne Studies Important behavioral science research often cited as the beginning of the human relations movement.

homeostasis Balance; equilibrium.

human relations The study of human behavior with the goal of understanding how to design work settings so that employees perform up to their potential, cooperate with other employees, and satisfy their own individual needs and goals.

hygiene factors Extrinsic factors, similar to Maslow's physiological, safety, and esteem needs.

idea checklists A list of idea-generating questions used to stimulate creativity.

image building Acceptable image building involves taking great care in one's grooming and reputation. Unacceptable image building involves taking credit for things that you did not do and trying to create an image of something you are not.

implied contract Verbal or written statements on which employees rely as a term or condition of their employment.

individual expectations Refers to an individual's expectations of what the employing organization will provide to each employee in terms of rewards, fringe benefits, challenge, responsibility, and participation in decision making.

individualism A dimension of national culture that stands for a preference for a loosely knit social framework in which individuals are supposed to take care of themselves and their immediate families only.

individualization Process by which employees try to change the organization so that it better meets the employees' expectations.

individual rewards Allocated to individuals or groups solely on the basis of their level of performance.

individual roles Group roles that are aimed at accomplishing individual goals with little thought to group goals. Usually dysfunctional to the group.

informal groups Groups that arise naturally in organizations. They are not purposely formed by the organization, nor do they appear on the organizational chart.

information overload Occurs when individuals receive more information than they are capable of effectively processing. Some of it is necessarily excluded.

information power Ability to influence others due to control of or access to scarce and important information.

ingratiation A type of political activity that involves using flattery and praise to influence others.

intellectual ability Cognitive ability, ability to perform mathematical calculations, use words in spoken and written communication, perceive small details rapidly, visualize objects in three dimensions, and identify relationships by pulling together pieces of seemingly unrelated information.

interest groups Relatively temporary informal groups that arise because of a common interest, activity, or problem.

intergroup conflict Conflict that occurs between two or more groups.

inter-individual conflict Conflict that occurs between two or more individuals.

internalization Members go along with the group because group goals are consistent with the beliefs and values of individual group members.

internal locus of control Belief that an individual's behavior is the primary determinant of what happens to him or her.

internal recruitment Policy of filling jobs by promoting current employees, rather than hiring from the outside.

interpersonal communication Transmission of signals or symbols from a sender to a receiver, with the intent of sharing meaning.

intimate space From physical contact to 18 inches from an individual.

intragroup conflict Conflict that occurs within a group.

intrinsic job satisfaction Satisfaction of needs internal to the individual, such as challenge and interest, freedom to plan one's own work, and participation in important decisions.

introversion A tendency to be reserved and sensitive to one's own feelings.

involuntary absenteeism Employees miss work due to factors beyond their control, such as accidents and illness.

Japanese management Techniques used effectively in Japanese organizations; emphasis is on the group, infrequent performance evaluation, slow promotion, and lifetime employment.

job analysis An objective examination of the work, specific duties, and responsibilities of a particular job.

job description A written statement that describes the job—the primary duties, responsibilities, and working conditions.

job design Structural change at the job level; job enrichment.

job enlargement Adding more of the same kinds of tasks to an employee's job.

job enrichment Adding motivating properties of tasks to jobs. The purpose is to make a job more meaningful, challenging, and interesting and to provide employees with more responsibility, autonomy, and opportunities for growth.

job maturity The ability to perform.

job posting Practice of posting descriptions of open jobs on a bulletin board so that interested employees can apply for them.

job rotation Rotating employees among similar jobs.

job satisfaction An attitude that reflects an individual's likes and dislikes regarding his or her work experience.

job sharing Two or more individuals share one full-time job.

job shock When a job does not meet an employee's expectations in important ways.

job specifications A written statement of the minimum qualifications, training, education, and experience necessary to adequately perform a particular job.

kinesics A type of nonverbal cue that includes body motions such as facial expressions, eye movements, head movements, and movements of the arms, legs, and general body.

Landrum-Griffin Act Passed in response to widespread corruption within labor unions. Requires labor leaders to report finances and internal activities to the Secretary of Labor.

latent conflict The parties are not yet aware of any blockage or potential blockage of goals.

latent need A need that is currently inactive and exerting no influence on an individual's behavior.

law of effect States that behavior that results in pleasurable consequences tends to be repeated, while behavior that results in unpleasurable consequences tends to be eliminated.

leadership The process of influencing members of an organization to engage in activities that will contribute to organizational goal accomplishment.

legitimate power Power that stems directly from one's formal position in an organization.

leniency A rater error where a manager rates all his or her employees toward the high performance end of the scale.

lockout A work stoppage initiated by management. Management locks the doors and refuses to allow employees into the work site.

locus of control The degree to which an individual believes that his or her actions can influence what happens to him or her.

lump sum salary increases Pay system where employees receive their salary increase in a lump sum which is not added to their base pay.

maintenance of membership Employees are not required to join the union, but those who do join must remain members for the length of the labor agreement.

maintenance roles Group roles that are concerned with building and maintaining the group.

management The study of all aspects of directing organizations and employees.

management by objectives (MBO) Management and performance appraisal system where employees and managers jointly agree on an employee's objectives, and the employee's job performance is measured by the degree to which these objectives are accomplished.

manifest conflict Stage of the conflict process when the conflict becomes observable.

manifest need A need that is currently activated and exerts a strong influence on an individual's behavior.

masculinity A dimension of national culture that stands for a preference for achievement, heroism, assertiveness, and material success.

maturity-immaturity continuum Theory developed by Chris Argyris which suggests that most organizations and managers treat employees in ways that encourages them to remain immature.

mental locks Narrow thinking, which blocks creativity.

mentor A higher-level manager who acts as a sponsor and counselor to a lower-level employee.

merit pay Salary increases are determined on the basis of job performance or productivity.

modeling Managers exhibit the core values of the organization's culture through their behavior; managers serve as examples for employees.

motivating properties of tasks Factors that make work intrinsically motivating, challenging, and interesting. They include autonomy, skill variety, task identity, task significance, and task feedback.

motivation A drive to reduce tension experienced as a result of an important unsatisfied need.

motivators Intrinsic factors similar to Maslow's self-esteem and self-actualization needs.

moving Term used to refer to actual implementation of a change.

GLOSSARY

multinational corporations Corporations with operations in more than one country.

negative reinforcement Occurs when an employee engages in an organizationally desired behavior to avoid an unpleasant outcome.

negligent hiring and retention Area of common law where an employee engaged in activities unrelated to normal work activities and away from the work location injures another person.

networking Making use of personal contacts such as friends, professors, family members, classmates, and parents as a source of employment information.

neuroticism An individual's emotional instability.

no-fault absenteeism control Falls in between "push" and "pull" strategies. Avoids the problem of managers having to determine whether the reasons given for an absence are legitimate. Employees typically given a decision-making leave day to decide if they can obey the rules and be at work when scheduled.

nominal group technique (NGT) A technique designed to encourage all members of a decision making group to participate.

nontraditional employees Employees who enter occupations that were previously reserved for the opposite sex (e.g., male nurses, female firefighters).

nonverbal communication Anything (other than words) that communicates.

norming Third stage of group development in which members begin developing close relationships and accepting group norms.

norms An acceptable pattern of behavior that is shared by a group's members.

no-solicitation rule Nonemployee union organizers are prevented from entering the worksite. All other forms of solicitations (e.g., charities) also must be prohibited.

obedience One person uses power over another person to demand submission to requests.

office automation Advances in computer and communications technology in the office.

opportunity to perform Environmental variables beyond the control of the individual employee, such as equipment, tools, materials, supplies, working conditions, and organizational policies and rules.

optimizer Decision maker who searches for all possible decision alternatives before making a choice to ensure that the absolute best alternative is chosen.

organizational behavior The study of the behavior of individuals and groups in organizations.

organizational culture A fairly stable set of taken-for-granted assumptions, shared beliefs, meanings, and values that form a kind of backdrop for action.

organizational expectations Refers to expectations of employees such as level of effort and performance, loyalty and commitment to the organization, and adherence to organizational rules and policies.

organizational heroes Individuals who exemplify the core values of the organization's culture and who serve as role models for others.

organizational orientation Covers information about the overall organization, its products and activities, its top managers, history, policies and rules, and personnel matters.

organizational politics Any use of power that is not sanctioned or authorized by the organization.

organizers Union employees who visit worksites to determine how much interest there is in the union and to try to generate more interest among employees in union membership.

organizing campaign Effort by the union to generate interest among employees in joining the union and signing authorization cards to hold a representation election.

organizing committee Made up of union organizers and employees who are interested in the union. Primary task is to generate interest in the union.

orientation The process of providing new employees with detailed information about the organization and the job.

outlaws Organizational heroes who bring about needed change and creativity in the organization. Their behavior may conflict with some of the values of the organization.

paranoid culture Culture characterized by distrust, suspicion, and a focus on identifying enemies.

parental leave Time off for new parents. Some organizations provide paternity leave in addition to maternity leave.

participative leadership style Leader keeps employees informed about organizational activities and plans, asks employees for suggestions, and includes employees in decision making.

part-time employees Employees who work less than full time. Some are voluntary part-time employees, while others are involuntary part-time workers.

pay-for-knowledge Also called pay for skill. A pay program under which employees earn salary increases based on what they learn, rather than on output or seniority.

pay openness A policy whereby salary and/or salary increase information is made available to employees.

pay secrecy A policy, common in many organizations, whereby salary and salary increase information is not made available to employees.

people change Change that involves changing the attitudes and/or behaviors of either individuals or groups.

perceived conflict Second stage of the conflict process, point at which one or both parties become aware of the conflict.

perception The process by which individuals receive and interpret information about their environment. Put more simply, perception is how each of us sees the world.

perceptual defense/distortion The process by which individuals unconsciously change messages and information so that it is consistent with their values and beliefs.

perceptual expectation We hear and see what we expect, rather than what is or isn't there.

perceptual filtering When individuals purposely do not receive certain messages. Similar to selective perception.

performance gap A difference between current conditions and desired conditions.

performance → outcome expectancy Also called E2, refers to an employee's perception that promised rewards will be delivered if the employee successfully performs.

performing Fourth and final stage of group development where group resources and energy are directed toward accomplishing group goals.

personality A relatively stable pattern of reacting to people, ideas, or objects.

personal problems Emotional problems stemming from family problems, divorce, death of family member or close friend, and severe illness.

personal space From eighteen inches to four feet from an individual.

physical ability Individual's capabilities with respect to strength, flexibility, and manual dexterity.

physiological needs Basic needs necessary for survival, such as food, water, and shelter.

politicized culture Culture that facilitates the development of organizational politics.

positive attendance control A "pull" strategy that rewards employees for good attendance, rather than punishing them for poor attendance.

positive discipline Future-oriented discipline intended to correct behavior. Emphasis is on impersonal and objective administration of discipline and on specific behaviors under the employee's control. Goal is to make employees responsible for their own behavior. Includes a decision-making leave for successive rule violators. Also called discipline without punishment.

positive reinforcement Administering a desired reward after an employee engages in a correct behavior.

power distance A dimension of national culture; the degree to which members of a society accept that power in institutions and organizations is distributed unequally.

preretirement counseling Programs designed to assist employees making the transition from work to retirement.

primacy A type of rater error where raters give greater weight to an employee's performance during the first part of the rating period.

proactive strategy Strategy for dealing with change in which plans are developed for a number of expected changes. These plans are then implemented after one of the predicted changes actually occurs.

problem A current or potential situation that may prevent the organization from accomplishing its goals.

problem recognition First step of the decision-making process. The awareness that a problem exists.

problem solving A conflict-resolution technique

where the parties openly exhange views and information in an attempt to uncover the cause of the conflict. The parties then search for a solution that will satisfy the goals of both parties.

process culture Culture characterized by low risk and slow feedback. Emphasis is on doing things the "right way," and on the status quo.

progressive discipline Increasingly severe punishments for successive rule violations.

projection When we perceive our own characteristics, attitudes, and beliefs in others.

proxemics Spatial relationships.

psychological employment contract The set of both individual expectations of the organization, and organizational expectations of the individual.

psychological maturity The motivation to perform.

psychology The study of individual behavior.

public space More than twelve feet from an individual.

punishment Administering an unpleasant consequence as a result of an employee engaging in an organizationally undesired behavior.

"push" absenteeism control strategies Based on the traditional system of progressive discipline. Also called negative absenteeism control.

qualitative overload Employees perceive they do not have the ability to accomplish assigned work activities.

qualitative underload Employees are assigned work activities that do not challenge and stimulate them.

quality circles (QCs) A small group of employees who voluntarily meet regularly to discuss quality problems and make recommendations to management for correcting these problems.

quality of worklife (QWL) Programs designed to improve the quality of the human experience in the work place. Most QWL programs include adequate and fair compensation, safe and healthy working conditions, opportunities to use and develop skills and abilities, opportunities for growth and development, social integration in the organization, employee rights, balance of work and nonwork, and meaningful, socially responsible work.

quantitative overload Employees perceive they have been assigned more work than they can complete on time.

quantitative underload Employees do not have enough work to keep them busy.

Railway Labor Act Covers employees in the airline and railroad industries. Basically echoes the provisions of the Wagner Act, as amended by the Taft-Hartley and Landrum-Griffin Acts.

rater errors Common perceptual problems that interject bias or inaccuracy into rater judgments.

reactive strategy Strategy for dealing with change that involves waiting for a change to occur and then developing a plan for dealing with it.

realistic job preview (RJP) Practice of providing job applicants with accurate information, both good and bad, about the job and the organization.

recency A type of rater error where raters give greater weight to an employee's performance during the most recent part of the rating period.

reciprocity A type of political activity that involves doing favors for others so they are obligated to do favors for you.

recruitment Process of ensuring that the organization has available adequate numbers of qualified job applicants.

referent power Ability to influence others because of their respect and admiration for the manager; charisma.

refreezing Making a change permanent.

relations-oriented leader behaviors Leader behaviors related to employee welfare, morale, and motivation.

relaxation response A reaction, similar to meditation, that individuals can learn to evoke to reduce stress. Basically the opposite of the general adaptation syndrome. Goal is to reverse the chemical reaction in the body that results from too much stress.

representation election Held by the National Labor Relations Board (NLRB) to determine if a majority of employees wish to be represented by a union.

resistance When individuals attempt to ignore or fight an attempt to influence their behavior.

respondeat superior Area of common law that covers situations where an employee, during normal working hours, does something that injures another person.

results-oriented performance appraisals Type of performance appraisal format where the emphasis of the rating is placed on results or degree to which an employee accomplishes objectives. MBO is the most popular form of results-oriented performance appraisal.

reward power Ability to influence employees because of the authority or ability to reward them.

right-to-work laws Laws, currently passed by twenty states, which make it illegal for collective bargaining agreements to include any clause that requires employees to join a union.

rites Dramatic activities, usually performed before an audience, that reinforce the culture of an organization.

rituals Relatively small events aimed primarily at reducing anxiety before a rite or ceremonial.

robotics The use of robots to perform repetitive or dangerous tasks.

role A set of expected behaviors associated with a particular position within a group.

role ambiguity When individuals are not sure of exactly what is expected of them.

role conflict When an individual occupies two or more roles (either within the same group or in separate groups) that place conflicting demands on the individual.

role overload When individuals perceive that the demands placed on them exceed their abilities.

role underload When individuals perceive that their abilities exceed the demands of their roles.

safety needs Need for a safe physical and emotional environment.

satisficer Decision maker who does not search for all possible alternatives before making a choice, but rather selects the first feasible alternative.

scapegoating Type of political activity that involves attacking or blaming others.

selection The process of choosing employees to fill particular positions or jobs within the organization.

selective perception Process that screens out certain messages and stimuli to which individuals are exposed.

self-actualization needs The need to grow and develop and reach one's full potential, to be "all that you can be."

self-assessment First step in the career planning process. Goal is to determine your most important values, attitudes, and interests and match these with the characteristics of successful individuals working in various occupations.

semiautonomous work groups Group members decide how tasks are to be performed and which members will perform them, interview job applicants, establish goals, train new employees, control costs, conduct quality control inspections of their own work, and develop better methods of performing tasks.

semistructured interview Interview that consists of 80 to 90 percent structured questions with the remaining time spent in unstructured questions.

sexual harassment Demands for sexual favors as a condition of employment; unwelcome sexual advances that create a hostile working environment.

situational heroes Employees who stand out or excel in a particular situation. They may influence only a few employees. An example is the "employee of the month."

skill variety The degree to which a task requires employees to use a variety of skills and abilities.

socialization The continual process of modifying the set of individual expectations based on experience with the organization.

social needs The need to interact with others and to develop friendships on the job. Need to be accepted and liked by others.

social satisfaction Satisfaction with the social aspects of the work experience including the opportunity to develop close friendships at work and to interact with others on the job.

social space From four to twelve feet from an individual.

social support The assistance received from others, or the availability of other people to turn to for help. Helps individuals manage stress. Three types of social support are emotional, esteem, and network.

sociology The study of group behavior.

staffing Process that includes the activities of recruitment, interviewing, selection, orientation, and termination.

status A measure of an individual's rank or prestige within a group.

stereotyping When someone is judged based on a perception of the group to which she belongs.

stories Anecdotes that describe some event in the organization's history and are usually a blend of truth and fiction. Stories communicate the core values on which the organization's culture is based.

storming Second stage of group development, characterized by conflict.

strength of a culture The degree to which the culture affects behavior. Determined by the homogeneity of group members, length of group membership, stability of group membership, and the intensity of group experience.

stress A chemical reaction that takes place in the body, caused by a state of tension resulting from a situation or event that places unusual or extreme physical or psychological demands on an individual.

stressors Events that bring on stress.

strike A work stoppage initiated by a union. Employees refuse to enter the work site.

structural change Change to the formal structure of an organization, the formal authority and responsibility relationships, formal communication channels, work flows, or organizational policies and procedures.

structured interview Interviewer reads questions from a prepared interview checklist.

subculture Culture that develops around subunits or departments.

substance abuse Alcohol or drug abuse.

sunk costs Investments of time, energy, effort, and experience. Reason for employee resistance to change.

supportive leadership style Leader shows concern for the personal needs of employees, and works to develop good interpersonal relations among members of the work group.

symptom An observable event or condition that indicates a problem exists.

system rewards Administered to individuals just for being a member of the organization.

Taft-Hartley Act Important federal labor law that identified unfair labor practices by unions. Outlawed featherbedding and closed shops. Gave states the right to pass right-to-work laws.

task feedback The degree to which completion of a task provides clear feedback about quality and quantity of performance.

task group Relatively temporary formal group formed to deal with a specific problem or project.

task identity The degree to which an employee's task leads to an identifiable portion of work.

task-oriented leader behaviors Leader behaviors related to completing tasks effectively and on time.

task-relevant maturity Employees' ability and motivation to perform assigned tasks.

task roles Group roles concerned with getting the job done.

task significance The degree to which an individual's task performance is important to other people, either inside or outside the organization.

technological change Change in the process used to produce an organization's basic unit of output (product or service).

temporary employees Employees who work less than 12 months per year. Often used during periods of heavy work load.

termination The end of an individual's employment with an organization. Four types of termination are layoff, resignation, retirement, and discharge.

Theory X Belief that employees dislike work and will try to avoid it, and that employees must be closely controlled to get them to perform.

Theory X-Theory Y Theory developed by Douglas McGregor that describes two ways in which managers typically view employees.

Theory Y Belief that work is as natural as play and that most employees are capable of self-control and self-motivation.

Theory Z A description of how Japanese management techniques can be modified to better fit American employees and organizations.

time management Involves identifying how you spend your time and identifying how to use your time more efficiently.

tough-guy, macho culture Culture characterized by high risk and quick feedback. Organization values short-term success over long-term prosperity.

Type A personality Unable to relax, extremely active and energetic, perfectionist, very competitive and aggressive.

Type B personality Relaxed and sociable.

Type T personality One who seeks thrills, excitement, and stimulation—a risk taker.

GLOSSARY

Type t personality One who avoids thrills, excitement and overstimulation—a risk avoider.

unavoidable turnover Turnover that is beyond the control of the organization, such as retirements, deaths, and transfers of a spouse.

uncertainty avoidance A dimension of national culture, the degree to which members of a society feel uncomfortable with uncertainty and ambiguity.

unfreezing Preparing individuals for change.

union shop Employees are required to join the union within a specified time period, usually 30 to 90 days after being hired.

union steward Union representative on the shop floor or in a department. Counterpart of the organization's representative, the first-line supervisor.

unstructured interview Interviewer pursues any line of questioning that seems appropriate.

upward communication Communication to managers that is initiated by employees. The purpose is usually to make managers aware of performance problems, constraints, or possible improvements.

valence The degree to which an employee desires a particular reward or work outcome.

value A general belief about some way of behaving or some end state that is preferable to the individual. Values include an individual's sense of what is right and wrong, or good and bad.

value system The entire set of an individual's values, prioritized in order of their importance to that individual.

variable interval reinforcement schedule Rewards are administered after the passage of a certain time interval, on average. The specific time interval between rewards varies.

variable ratio reinforcement schedule Rewards are administered after a certain number of correct behaviors, on average. The specific number of correct behaviors required between rewards varies.

vicarious learning Learning that occurs as a result of employees observing the direct reinforcement of others. Also called indirect learning.

visionary heroes Leaders who serve as models for all employees. They transmit the organization's culture to employees by their words and actions.

vocalics A type of nonverbal cue that has to do with characteristics of the voice such as pitch, rate of speech, and volume.

voluntary absenteeism A conscious choice of an employee to be absent from work.

Wagner Act Important federal labor law that ensures employees' rights to form and join unions. Identified a number of unfair labor practices by management.

white-collar workers Employees whose primary product/service is information rather than cars, steel, paper or chemicals. Term is used to refer to employees in the service sector of the economy and to differentiate these employees from traditional blue-collar factory workers.

willingness to perform Includes motivation, job satisfaction, job involvement, clarity of work assignments, and perceptions of equity.

work hard/play hard culture Culture characterized by low risk and fast feedback, fast pace, continuous activity, and persistence.

wrongful discharge Area of common law based on the idea that employees should be discharged only for a good, job-related reason.

Index

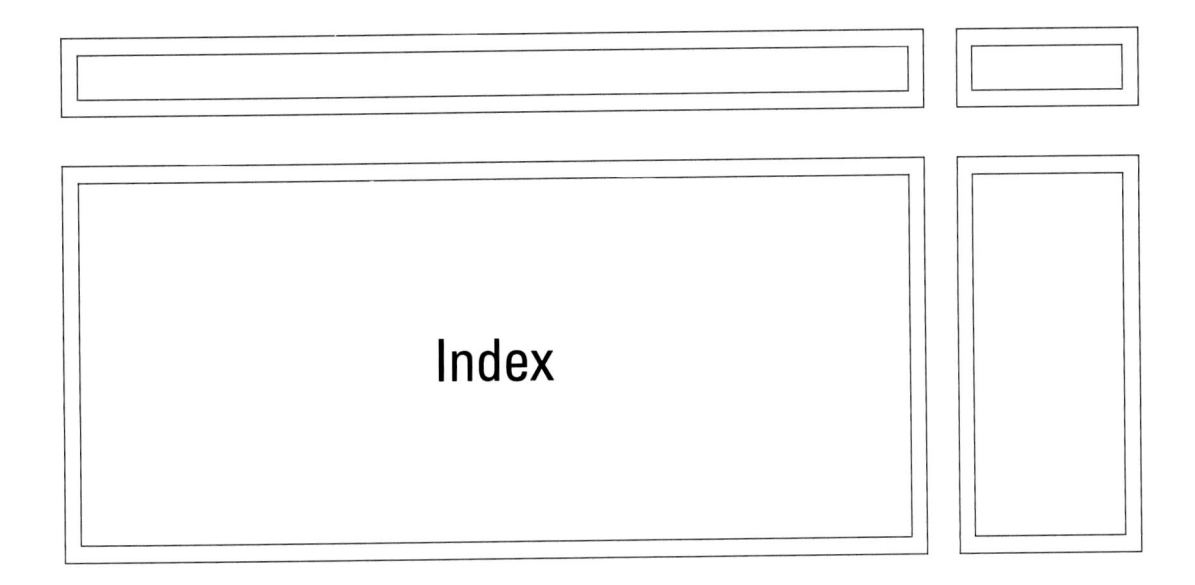

ability, 110
absenteeism, 209
accommodating, 365
achievement orientation, 109
achievement-oriented leadership style, 344
active listening, 157, 220
Admiral Hyman Rickover, 155
affiliation, 309
affirmative action, 54
Age Discrimination in Employment Act of 1967, 54
agency shop, 459
aggressive strategy, 432
aging U.S. population, 17
AIDS, 54
AIDS policy, 56
alcohol abuse, 202
ambiguity of terms, 180
Amdahl, 479
American Lung Association, 310
American Motors, 479
antecedent conditions, 359
Apple Computer, 255
application blanks, 69
appointed leaders, 334
arbitration, 462
arbitrator, 462
Argyris, Chris, 12
Ash, Mary Kay, 409
assertiveness, 364

AT&T, 254
attitudes, 19, 99, 102
attitudes and behavior, 102
attribution, 97, 360
authoritarianism, 108
authorization cards, 456
autonomy, 28, 122
avoidable turnover, 213
avoidance, 365, 371
avoidance culture, 418
avoider, 318
avoiding, 365, 371
Avon, 419

background checks, 69
bargaining unit, 457
bases of power, 335, 388, 490
behavior-based appraisals, 172
behavior modification, 135
behavioral observation scales (BOS), 172
behavioral sciences, 5
behaviorally anchored rating scales (BARS), 172
beliefs, 363
bet-your-company culture, 419
binding arbitration, 462
biofeedback, 243
bizarre employee behavior, 207
blocker, 318
blue collar jobs, 454

519

Boeing, 419
bona fide occupational qualification (BFOQ), 54
brainstorming, 291
Bryant, Paul "Bear," 335
building alliances/coalitions, 397
bureaucratic culture, 418

cafeteria style benefits, 190
Campbell's Soup, 481
Cancer Society, 310
capacity to perform, 200
career, 254
    development, 255
    management, 255
    opportunities, 256
    paths, 68, 268, 269
    planning, 245, 255
    stages, 261
Carey, Frank T., 431
categories of needs, 122
Caterpillar, Inc., 331, 346
cause, 281
CBS, 254
central tendency, 178
Century 21, 419
ceremonials, 413
change, 252, 430, 432
character assassination, 394
charisma, 335
charismatic culture, 418
charismatic leader, 335
Chevrolet Nova, 480
Chrysler Corporation, 411
Civil Rights Act of 1964, Title VII, 52
Civil Service Reform Act of 1978, 459
closed shop, 458
closure, 151
Coca Cola, 480
coercive power, 335, 388
cognitive dissonance, 103
Coldwell Banker, 419
collaborating, 366
collectivism, 485
command groups, 306
commitment, 389
common law, 57
common sense theory, 6
communication process, 148
communications, 364, 376, 414, 423
competing, 364
competition, 376, 381

compliance, 314, 389
compromising, 365
conceptualization of conflict, 360
concessions, 468
conducting the interview, 71
conflict, 358
    aftermath, 360
    episode, 360
    process, 359
    resolution, 371
    stimulation, 373
conformity, 314
confrontation, 217
conservative shift, 286
constructive feedback, 156, 218
continuous raises, 190
continuous reinforcement schedules, 137
consensus, 98
consistency, 98
contrast, 96
control group, 7
coordinator/summarizer, 317
cooperativeness, 364
core time, 267
cost of living increases, 189
counseling, 217
creating obligations, 396
creative organizations, 292
creative process, 289
creativity, 288
criteria for reward allocation, 185
critical incident file, 184
cultural map, 491
culture, 481
culture management techniques, 397, 421

decertification election, 466
decertification process, 466
decision making, 278
decision making leave, 217
decision making process, 278
defamation, 59
Dallas Cowboys, 132
denial, 95
departmental orientation, 73
dependent care, 267
devil's advocate, 286
dimensions of culture, 485
direct learning, 138
directive leadership style, 344
discharge, 74

discipline, 210, 214
discipline without punishment, 217
distinctiveness, 98
distress, 230
dominant culture, 415
dominant leadership style, 337
dominator, 317
Domino's Pizza, 419, 420
Dorsett, Tony, 132
downward communications, 158
drug abuse, 202
Du Pont, 254
dysfunctional outcomes of conflict, 368
dysfunctional turnover, 213

Eastman Kodak, 254, 288
economic function, 26
educational levels, 19
effective groups, 324
effort, 186
effort ⟶ performance expectancy, 134
electronic
   communication, 162
   communications systems, 162
   mail, 162
   messages, 162
   office, 237
emergent leaders, 335
emotional support, 233
employee
   assistance programs (EAPs), 204, 205
   expectations, 133
   of the month, 411
   participation, 245
   problems, 200
   related situational variables, 340
   rights, 39
   theft, 206
employer liability for employee misconduct, 57
employment at will doctrine, 58
employment references, 69
employment related law, 52
encourager, 317
environmental factors, 155, 390, 432
Equal Employment Act of 1972, 53
equal employment legislation, 52
Equal Employment Opportunity Commission (EEOC), 53
Equal Pay Act of 1963, 54
equality, 186
equity theory, 130

esteem needs, 124
esteem support, 233
ethical behavior, 100
eustress, 231
evaluator, 317
expectancy theory, 133
expectations, 93
experimental group, 7
expert power, 335, 388
external recruitment, 68
externals, 110
extinction, 136
extrinsic job satisfacation, 36
extrinsic needs, 129
extroversion, 108
extroverts, 108
Exxon, 419

feasible alternative, 282
featherbedding, 458
federal employment-related law, 52
Federal Labor Relations Authority (FLRA), 459
feedback, 156
felt conflict, 359
femininity, 485
fixed interval reinforcement schedule, 138
fixed ratio reinforcement schedule, 138
flexible time off, 266
flexible work schedule, 267
flight or fight response, 230
follower, 317
forcing, 371
formal groups, 306
forming, 312
founder, 409
friendship groups, 307
frustration-regression process, 126
functional outcomes of conflict, 369
functional turnover, 213

gainsharing, 191
gatekeeper, 317
general adaptation syndrome (GAS), 230
General Electric, 254, 452
General Foods, 124, 352
General Motors, 350, 433, 469, 480
givebacks, 468
global economy, 15
global village, 478
goal setting, 221, 257
"good citizen" behaviors, 37

INDEX

Goodyear, 288, 452
Gorbachev, Mikael, 357
grapevine, 159, 394
graphic rating scales, 172
Great A & P Tea Company, 479
grievance procedure, 461
group, 305
   cohesiveness, 321, 368, 376
   decision making, 283
   decision making techniques, 287
   development, 312
   leader, 318
   norms, 313
   roles, 315
   size, 319
   structure, 313
groupshift, 286
groupthink, 284
growth, 27
guidance, 309

halo effect (error), 93, 178
handicapped person, 54
harmonizer, 317
harshness, 180
Hawthorne Studies, 8
Heart Fund, 310
Hercules, Inc., 437
Hershey Foods Corporation, 407, 409
Hershey, Milton Snavely, 408, 414
Herzberg's Two Factor Theory, 128, 490
homeostasis, 442
Honda, 479
human relations, 4, 368, 417, 462
human resource planning, 269
hygiene factors, 128

Iacocca, Lee, 335, 411
IBM Corporation, 199, 423, 431, 478
idea checklists, 292
identity, 27, 311
image building, 395
Immigration Reform and Control Act of 1986, 57
implementation, 282
implied contract, 58
incompatible goals, 363
incubation, 289
indicators of stress, 244
indirect learning, 139
individual
   expectations, 32
   rewards, 134, 185
   roles, 317
   stress management techniques, 241
individualism, 485
individualization, 35
Industrial Revolution, 8
infeasible solution, 281
informal groups, 10, 307, 438
informal organization, 10,
information, 72
   giver, 316
   overload, 92, 370
   power, 389
   seeker, 316
ingratiation, 396
initial contact, 455
insight, 289
instrumental learning, 135
intellectual ability, 111
intensity, 96
interest groups, 308
inter-group conflict, 362, 366
inter-individual conflict, 361
intra-group conflict, 362
internal recruitment, 66
internals, 110
international business, 478
internationalization of business, 15, 478
interpersonal attraction, 311
interpersonal communication, 148
interviewing, 259
interviews, 70
intrinsic job satisfaction, 36
intrinsic needs, 129
introversion, 108
introverts, 108
involuntary absenteeism, 209
isolation, 240

Japanese business practices, 483
Japanese management, 493
Japanese management practices, 498
jargon, 414
job, 254
   design, 435
   enlargement, 130
   enrichment, 129, 435
   insecurity, 239
   maturity, 338
   posting, 68, 270
   rotation, 130

INDEX

job, *continued*
   satisfaction, 36, 103
      of American workers, 37
      and job performance, 37
   security, 454
   sharing, 268
   shock, 263

Kennedy, John F., 335
Kierkegaard, Soren, 423
kinesics, 153
Kodak, 10–5, 254, 288

labor
   agreement, 460
   contract, 460, 465
   law, 457
   -management cooperation, 468
   shortages, 15
Landrum-Griffin Act, 459
latent conflict, 359
latent need, 123
law of effect, 135
layoff, 74
leaders, 332
leadership, 332, 334, 336, 344
   behaviors, 336
   style, 344, 490
legitimate power, 335, 388
leniency, 180
levels of people change, 437
Lever Brothers, 479
Life Cycle Theory of Leadership, 338
lifetime employment, 496
listening, 157
lockout, 464
locus of control, 110
lump-sum salary increases, 191

maintenance of membership, 459
maintenance roles, 317
management, 4
management by objectives (MBO), 172
manager-employee communications, 158
manager-related situational variables, 342
managerial malpractice, 58
managing
   conflict, 371
   organizational politics, 397
   stress, 240
manifest conflict, 360

manifest need, 122
March of Dimes, 310
marketing yourself, 258
Mary Kay Cosmetics, 409
masculinity, 485
Maslow's Hierarchy of Needs, 124, 487
maternity leave, 267
Maturity-Immaturity Continuum, 13
McDonald's Restaurants, 161, 419
McDonnel-Douglas, 419
McGregor, Douglas, 10
mentor, 265
merit pay, 188
mid-life crisis, 265
Miles Laboratories, 479
Mitsubishi, 479
Mobile Oil, 419
modeling, 422
monitoring, 261
Mothers Against Drunk Driving (MADD), 310
motivating properties of tasks, 27, 130
motivation, 120
motivators, 128
moving, 440
multinational corporations, 479
Murray's Manifest Needs Theory, 122
Muscular Dystrophy Association, 310

National Labor Relations Board (NLRB), 455, 456, 457, 458
nature of jobs, 16
need for independence, 340
need satisfaction, 121, 308
negative (push) absenteeism control strategies, 210
negative reinforcement, 136
negligent hiring and retention, 57
networking, 257
network support, 233
neuroticism, 109
no-fault absenteeism control, 210
nominal group technique (NGT), 287
nonverbal communication, 153
norming, 312
norms, 313
no solicitation rule, 455
novelty, 96
numerical ability, 113

obedience, 314
Occupational Safety and Health Act of 1970, 56

Occupational Safety and Health Administration (OSHA), 56
office automation, 436
open shop, 459
operant conditioning, 135
opportunity to perform, 200
optimizers, 281
organizational
　behavior, 6
　career development, 268
　culture, 408, 439
　environments, 430
　expectations, 33
　heroes, 411
　orientation, 73
　politics, 386, 387
　stress management, 244
　stress management techniques, 244
organizers, 455
organizing
　campaign, 455
　committee, 455
　process, 455
orientation, 73
orientation programs, 35, 73
Oscar Mayer, 350
ostracism, 314
Ouichi, William, 494
outcomes of conflict, 368
outcomes of stress, 230
outlaws, 412
overtime, 239

paranoid culture, 417
parental leave, 267
participation, 444
participative leadership style, 344
part-time workers, 16
paternity leave, 267
pay
　for knowledge, 192
　for skill, 192
　openness, 188
　secrecy, 188
Pennsylvania Light and Power Company, 236
people change, 437
Pepsi, 480
Pepsodent, 481
perceived conflict, 359
perception, 90, 149, 364
perception and communication, 149, 364
perceptions of inequity, 130

perceptual
　defense/distortion, 93, 151
　expectation, 151
　filtering, 150
performance
　appraisal, 170, 271, 422
　appraisal feedback interview, 180
　evaluation, 239
　gap, 278
　problems, 200
　performance ⟶ outcome expectancy, 134
performing, 313
personality, 105
　and behavior, 105
　development, 105
　traits, 108
physical
　ability, 113
　proximity, 311
　work setting, 236
physiological needs, 124
planned change, 439
political behaviors, 394
politicized cultures, 418
positive (pull) absenteeism control strategies, 210, 211
positive attendance control, 211
positive discipline, 217
power, 309, 335, 388
power distance, 485
Pregnancy Discrimination Act of 1978, 53
pre-retirement counseling, 271
pressure, 229
primacy, 179
proactive strategy, 431
problem, 278
　definition, 280
　recognition, 278
　solving, 372
process culture, 419
Proctor and Gamble, 452
progressive discipline, 76, 206, 210, 215, 462
projection, 94
promote-from-within policy, 66
protege, 265
providing information to applicants, 72
proxemics, 153
psychological employment contract, 33
psychological maturity, 338
psychology, 5
public policy, 58
public sector labor law, 459

punishment, 136
purpose of reward systems, 185
purposes of performance appraisals, 170

Quad/Graphics, Inc., 125
qualitative overload, 237
qualitative underload, 238
quality circles (QCs), 42, 347, 498
quality of work life (QWL), 38, 43
quantitative overload, 236
quantitative underload, 237

rater errors, 178
reactions to conflict, 364
reactive strategy, 431
Reagan, Ronald, 333, 357
realistic job preview, 34, 72
recency, 179
reciprocity, 396
recognition seeker, 318
recruitment, 66
referent power, 335, 388
refreezing, 440
reinforcement theory, 135
relations-oriented leader behaviors, 337
relaxation, 243
relaxation response, 243
repetition, 96
representation, 456
resignation, 74
resistance, 389
resistance to change, 456
respondeat superior, 57
results-oriented appraisals, 172
resumes, 69, 258
retirement, 74, 265
reward administration, 186, 422
reward power, 335, 388
right-to-work laws, 458
risky shift, 286
rites, 412
rituals, 413
robotics, 437
role, 306, 315
   ambiguity, 318, 363
   conflict, 318
   overload, 318
   related problems, 318
   underload, 318
rule violations, 205, 215

Saab-Scania, 485
safety needs, 124

salary increase, 189
satisfaction of needs, 121, 308
satisfaction and productivity, 37
satisficers, 281
satisficing, 281
Saturn Plant, 192, 350, 468
scapegoating, 394
scarce resources, 362
schedules of reinforcement, 137
Schein, Edgar H., 415
scientific research, 7
security, 308
selective perception, 92
self-actualization needs, 125
self-assessment, 256
self-esteem, 124, 308
semi-autonomous work groups, 348, 435
semi-structured interview, 71
seniority, 186
service industry, 15
sexual harrassment, 53
Shell Oil, 479
shift work, 239
situational
   heroes, 411
   leadership theories, 340
   variables, 340
skill variety, 28, 130
Skinner, B.F., 135
social
   function, 27
   needs, 9, 124
   pressure, 284
   satisfaction, 36
   support, 232
socialization, 35, 425
sociology, 6
Sony, 479
sources of conflict, 362
sources of information, 279
Squibb, 161, 336, 343
staffing process, 52, 66
Stanley Home Products, 409
state and municipal laws, 60
status, 27, 153, 308, 319
status symbols, 319
stereotyping, 94
stewards, 466
stories, 413, 423
storming, 312
stress, 229
stressors, 234

strike, 464
structural change, 433
structured interview, 71
Students Against Drunk Driving (SADD), 310
subcultures, 415
substance abuse policy, 203
sunk costs, 443
support, 309
supportive leadership style, 344
symptoms of alcohol and substance abuse, 203
system rewards, 134, 185

Taft-Hartley Act, 458
task
    feedback, 30
    groups, 306
    identity, 29
    -oriented leader behaviors, 337
    relevant maturity, 338
    roles, 315
    significance, 29
team building, 245, 347
teamwork, 346, 348
technological change, 435
technology, 435
telecommuting, 40
teleconference, 16
temporary employees, 16
termination, 74
termination for good reason doctrine, 58
theory, 6
Theory X and Theory Y, 10
Theory Z, 494
Thompson, John, 357
3M Company, 277, 288
time, 156
time management, 241
time pressure, 343
tolerance for ambiguity, 340
tough-guy, macho culture, 418
Toyota, 452, 469
traditional merit pay plans, 188
training and development, 269
trait-based appraisals, 172
trends in society, 228
Tsubouchi, Hisao, 333
turnover, 207, 212
Two-Factor Theory, 128, 490
Type A/Type B, 110, 231, 232, 238
Type T, 111

Type T personality, 89, 111
types
    of change, 432
    of conflict, 361
    of culture, 417
    of groups, 306
    of interviews, 71
    of performance appraisals, 172
    of reinforcement, 136
    of values, 100
typical group decision making process, 287

unavoidable turnover, 213
uncertainty, 390
uncertainty avoidance, 485
unfreezing, 439
union
    membership, 453
    organizers, 455
    shop, 459
    stewards, 466
Union Carbide, 254
Union National Bank, 141
unions, 452
United Auto Workers, 469
United Way, 310
unmet expectations, 33
unstructured interview, 71
upward communications, 158
U.S. economy, 15

valence, 133
valid reasons for discharge, 76
value differences across occupations, 100
values, 99, 363
variable interval reinforcement schedule, 138
variable ratio reinforcement schedule, 138
variable reinforcement schedule, 138
verbal ability, 111
vicarious learning 35, 138
Vietnam Veteran's Readjustment Act of 1974, 56
visionary heroes, 411
vocalics, 154
voluntary absences, 209
voluntary absenteeism, 210
Volvo, 192

Wa, 496
Wagner Act, 457
Walker, Herschel, 132

Watson, Thomas J., 423
white collar jobs, 454
willingness to perform, 200
withholding or distorting information, 394
Wright, Orville, 432
women, 17

work hard/play hard culture, 419
work-related stress, 288
work-related stressors, 234
workstoppages, 464
working conditions, 187
wrongful discharge, 58

WE VALUE YOUR OPINION—PLEASE SHARE IT WITH US

Merrill Publishing and our authors are most interested in your reactions to this textbook. Did it serve you well in the course? If it did, what aspects of the text were most helpful? If not, what didn't you like about it? Your comments will help us to write and develop better textbooks. We value your opinions and thank you for your help.

Text Title _____ Edition _____

Author(s) _____

Your Name (optional) _____

Address _____

City _____ State _____ Zip _____

School _____

Course Title _____

Instructor's Name _____

Your Major _____

Your Class Rank _____ Freshman _____ Sophomore _____ Junior _____ Senior

_____ Graduate Student

Were you required to take this course? _____ Required _____ Elective

Length of Course? _____ Quarter _____ Semester

1. Overall, how does this text compare to other texts you've used?

    _____ Superior _____ Better Than Most _____ Average _____ Poor

2. Please rate the text in the following areas:

	Superior	Better Than Most	Average	Poor
Author's Writing Style	_____	_____	_____	_____
Readability	_____	_____	_____	_____
Organization	_____	_____	_____	_____
Accuracy	_____	_____	_____	_____
Layout and Design	_____	_____	_____	_____
Illustrations/Photos/Tables	_____	_____	_____	_____
Examples	_____	_____	_____	_____
Problems/Exercises	_____	_____	_____	_____
Topic Selection	_____	_____	_____	_____
Currentness of Coverage	_____	_____	_____	_____
Explanation of Difficult Concepts	_____	_____	_____	_____
Match-up with Course Coverage	_____	_____	_____	_____
Applications to Real Life	_____	_____	_____	_____

3. Circle those chapters you especially liked:
   1 2 3 4 5 6 7 8 9 10 11 12 13 14 15 16 17 18 19 20
   What was your favorite chapter? _____
   Comments:

4. Circle those chapters you liked least:
   1 2 3 4 5 6 7 8 9 10 11 12 13 14 15 16 17 18 19 20
   What was your least favorite chapter? _____
   Comments:

5. List any chapters your instructor did not assign. _____

6. What topics did your instructor discuss that were not covered in the text? _____
   _____

7. Were you required to buy this book? _____ Yes _____ No

   Did you buy this book new or used? _____ New _____ Used

   If used, how much did you pay? _____

   Do you plan to keep or sell this book? _____ Keep _____ Sell

   If you plan to sell the book, how much do you expect to receive? _____

   Should the instructor continue to assign this book? _____ Yes _____ No

8. Please list any other learning materials you purchased to help you in this course (e.g., study guide, lab manual).
   _____

9. What did you like most about this text? _____
   _____

10. What did you like least about this text? _____
    _____

11. General comments:

    May we quote you in our advertising? _____ Yes _____ No

    Please mail to: Boyd Lane
                      College Division Research Department
                      P. O. Box 508
                      Columbus, Ohio 43216-0508

    Thank you!